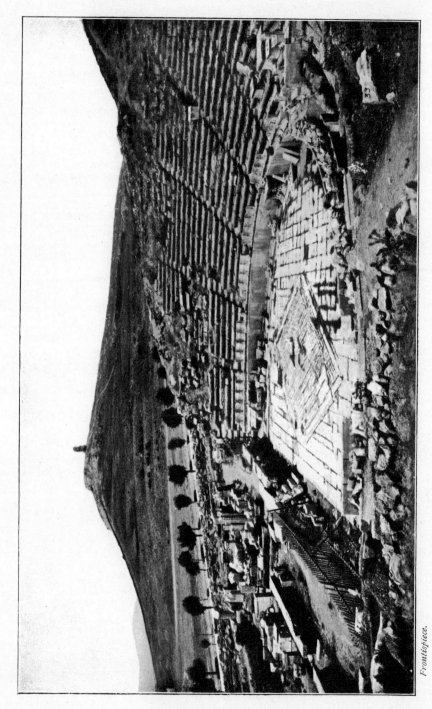

Fig. I. Theatre at Athens, from the East.

THE
ATTIC THEATRE

A DESCRIPTION OF THE STAGE AND THEATRE OF THE ATHENIANS, AND OF THE DRAMATIC PERFORMANCES AT ATHENS

BY

A. E. HAIGH

LATE FELLOW OF CORPUS CHRISTI COLLEGE, OXFORD

THIRD EDITION
REVISED AND IN PART RE-WRITTEN

BY

A. W. PICKARD-CAMBRIDGE, M.A.
FELLOW OF BALLIOL COLLEGE

WITH ILLUSTRATIONS

OXFORD
AT THE CLARENDON PRESS
MCMVII

KRAUS REPRINT CO.
New York
1969

HENRY FROWDE, M.A.
PUBLISHER TO THE UNIVERSITY OF OXFORD
LONDON, EDINBURGH
NEW YORK AND TORONTO

LC 73-94544

KRAUS REPRINT CO.
A U.S. Division of Kraus-Thomson Organization Limited

Printed in U.S.A.

PREFACE TO THE FIRST EDITION

My purpose in this book has been to collect and piece together all the available information concerning the outward features and surroundings of the old Athenian dramatic performances ; in other words, to write a history of the Attic drama from the theatrical, as opposed to the literary, point of view. The subject is one which has been practically revolutionized during the last half-century, partly through the labours of various scholars in interpreting the notices of the old grammarians, but more especially owing to the rich discoveries of inscriptions relating to theatrical affairs, and the information supplied by excavations in the old Greek theatres. But in spite of the copious accession of fresh materials, it is now more than fifty years since any work has appeared in English, in which this particular department of Greek dramatic history has been treated in a comprehensive manner. The neglect is all the more remarkable, as the subject is undeniably of great interest and importance, and this for two reasons. In the first place it is difficult to understand and appreciate the peculiar qualities of the existing Greek plays, without acquiring some knowledge of the circumstances under which they were produced, and the limitations within which the ancient dramatic poets had to work. In the second place, as the Attic drama was essentially a public institution, and formed one of the most conspicuous elements in the national life, the various details connected with its management are incidentally most instructive, because of the light which they throw upon the habits, feelings, and tastes of the old Athenians. It is owing to these several considerations that the present work has been undertaken.

Unfortunately, with the exception of a list of names and definitions in Pollux, and a few observations upon the theatre in Vitruvius, none of the ancient treatises, which dealt with the various portions of the subject, have been preserved. The materials have in consequence to be collected from the most multifarious sources—from casual remarks in ancient authors, from incidental references in the Greek dramas, from obscure and often contradictory notices in the scholiasts and grammarians, from old inscriptions, and the ruins of Greek theatres, from vases, statuettes, wall-paintings, and other works of art. In the treatment of questions which depend upon evidence of this intricate and complex character, it is inevitable that there should be much diversity of opinion, and that numberless opportunities should be afforded for ingenious conjectures and fanciful combinations. As a matter of fact the whole history of the Attic drama has been to a certain extent obscured by the mass of controversy and hypothesis to which it has given rise. My purpose throughout the following pages has been to keep close to the original sources of information, to restrict myself to such facts as seem to be fairly well established by the evidence, and to clear the subject of all those fine-drawn theories and conjectures which have no definite foundation to depend upon. For every statement concerning the Attic drama I have been careful to quote the ultimate authority, and the plan which I have adopted, in the citation of evidence, has been as follows. Where a passage is appealed to in support of some mere matter of fact, about which there could be no particular difference of opinion, I have been content to simply give the reference. But in cases where the inference is more dubious, I have quoted the original authorities in full, so as to enable the reader to judge for himself as to the validity of the views adopted in the text. It would have been impossible, within the limits of a single volume, to discuss in detail all the points concerning which controversies have been raised. The more important questions I have treated at considerable length ; but as regards matters of minute detail and trivial interest, I have merely given my own opinion in the text, and appended a statement of the evidence in the notes.

The various books, articles, monographs, and dissertations, which have been written on the subject of the Attic theatre and dramatic performances, are numerous enough in themselves to constitute a considerable literature. It will be sufficient in the present place to mention those to which I have been principally indebted. Of writings in which the subject is treated as a whole the most important is Albert Müller's *Lehrbuch der*

Griechischen Bühnenalterthümer (Freiburg, 1886)—a work which is conspicuous for the industry, learning, and sound judgement displayed in its compilation, and for the lucid manner in which an immense amount of information is compressed into a comparatively limited space. The exhaustive account which it contains of the bibliography of the subject is especially valuable. Another book which I have found of the greatest help is Schneider's *Das Attische Theaterwesen* (Weimar, 1835). It consists mainly of a citation in full of all the ancient passages which refer to performances in the theatre ; and although Schneider's own views and inferences are now mostly antiquated, and his collection of 'Quellen' requires to be supplemented, the work will always be most interesting and serviceable to students of the Attic drama. The description of the Greek dramatic performances in the third volume of Bergk's *Griechische Literaturgeschichte* (Berlin, 1884) has been exceedingly useful and suggestive ; and considerable assistance has been derived from the similar account in vol. ii. pt. 2 of Bernhardy's *Grundriss der Griechischen Litteratur* (Halle, 1880).

As regards the separate portions of the subject, the following is a list of the treatises which I have found of most assistance. For the Dionysiac festivals : Böckh's dissertation, *Vom Unterschiede der Lenäen, Anthesterien, und ländlichen Dionysien,* Berlin, 1816 ; A. Mommsen's *Heortologie,* Leipzig, 1864. For the arrangements connected with the dramatic contests and the production of a play : Rohde's article on the Proagon in *Rhein. Museum,* xxxviii. p. 251 ff. ; Sauppe's paper, *Ueber die Wahl der Richter,* &c., in *Sächs. Gesellschaft der Wissensch. zu Leipzig,* 1855 ; Petersen's *Preisrichter der grossen Dionysien,* Progr. Dorpat, 1878 ; Lipsius, *Ueber die dramatische Choregie,* in *Sächs. Gesell. der Wissensch.,* 1885. For the structure and arrangement of the theatre : Kawerau's article *Theatergebäude,* in vol. iii. of Baumeister's *Denkmäler des klassischen Alterthums,* 1888 ; Vischer's *Die Entdeckungen im Dionysostheater (Neues Schweizerisches Museum,* 1863) ; Julius's article, *Das Theater des Dionysos (Zeitschrift für bild. Kunst,* 1878) ; J. R. Wheeler's *Theatre of Dionysus (Papers of the American School of Classical Studies at Athens,* vol. i) ; Kabbadias, on the theatre at Epidaurus, in Πρακτικὰ τῆς ἐν Ἀθήναις ἀρχαιολογικῆς ἑταιρίας, 1881 and 1883 ; the account of the Greek theatre by Wieseler in vol. 83

of Ersch and Gruber's *Allgemeine Encyklopädie*, 1866 ; Wieseler's *Theatergebäude und Denkmäler des Bühnenwesens bei Griechen
und Römern*, 1851 ; and Strack's *Das altgriechische Theatergebäude*, Potsdam, 1843. On the question of the scenery:
Niejahr's *Quaestiones Aristophaneae Scaenicae* (Greifswald, 1877) ;
Sommerbrodt's *De Aeschyli re scenica* (in *Scenica*, Berlin,
1876). On the actors in the Greek drama, their costume, style,
and mode of delivery: Grysar, *De Graecorum tragoedia*, &c.
(Cöln, 1830) ; K. F. Hermann, *De distributione personarum
inter histriones in tragoediis graecis* (Marburg, 1840) ; Beer,
Ueber die Zahl der Schauspieler bei Aristophanes (Leipzig, 1844) ;
Sommerbrodt's two articles *De Histrionibus* and *De Arte
Histrionum*, in his *Scenica* ; Wieseler's *Das Satyrspiel* (Göt-
tingen, 1848) ; Dierk's two dissertations, *De tragicorum histrio-
num habitu scaenico apud Graecos* (Göttingen, 1883), *Ueber das
Costüm der griechischen Schauspieler in der alten Komödie*
(*Archaeol. Zeitung*, xliii) ; Christ's *Metrik der Griechen und
Römer* (Leipzig, 1879). On the subject of the chorus: K. O.
Müller's *Dissertations on the Eumenides* (Engl. transl., London,
1853) ; G. Hermann's *De choro Eumenidum* (Opusc. ii. p. 129 ff.) ;
Schultze's *De chori Graecorum tragici habitu externo* (Berlin,
1857) ; Sommerbrodt's *De chori tragici principibus*, in *Scenica* ;
and Arnoldt's *Die Chorpartieen bei Aristophanes* (Leipzig, 1873).

In conclusion I wish to express my obligations to Professor
Gardner for his assistance in various questions connected with
archaeology, and to Mr. Evelyn Abbott for many valuable
suggestions and criticisms. I have to thank the Council of the
Hellenic Society for their permission to reproduce the illustration of a chorus of birds from the *Hellenic Journal*. I desire
at the same time to acknowledge the great courtesy with
which Dr. Dörpfeld, of the German Archaeological Institute,
has supplied me with the latest information concerning his
excavations in the theatre of Dionysus, and his views on Greek
theatres in general.

OXFORD, *June*, 1889.

PREFACE TO THE SECOND EDITION

Since the first edition of this book was published many important additions have been made to our knowledge of the Greek stage. Various theatres have been excavated for the first time; fresh inscriptions have been discovered; and the evidence of the ancient authorities has been examined and sifted with the minutest care. The effect has been to throw a new light on many points which were previously obscure. In order to incorporate these results in the present edition, it was found necessary to make considerable alterations in the book. The third and fourth chapters—those dealing with the Theatre and the Scenery—have been entirely re-written. The first chapter, on the Dramatic Contests at Athens, has been re-written in parts. The other chapters have been carefully revised throughout, and numerous corrections and additions have been inserted, especially on such subjects as the choregia, the theoric fund, the theatre-tickets, and the costume of the actors and the chorus. Eleven new illustrations have been added. The old ones have been mostly retained, with the exception of the ground-plan and the two views of the theatre at Athens, which have been replaced by more accurate representations.

The number of books, treatises, and articles which have been written on the subject during the last few years is so great that it would be impossible to mention them all. I propose in the following list to specify only those which I have found most useful, and to which I am chiefly indebted. Many others will be referred to in the notes. The most important work of recent years on the Greek theatre is Dörpfeld and Reisch's *Das griechische Theater* (Athens, 1896). The admirable and exhaustive account of the Theatre of Dionysus at Athens, which is given in this book, has superseded all previous descriptions. Dörpfeld appears to have now proved conclusively that the stone theatre at Athens was not earlier than the fourth century B.C., and his views on the subject have been followed in the present edition. The book also contains a valuable summary of the chief points of interest in other theatres recently excavated, and a complete exposition of Dörpfeld's theory about the Greek stage. Some further developments and modifications of this theory will be found in two articles lately published by Dörpfeld in the *Bulletin de Correspondance Hellénique*, 1896, p. 563 ff., and in *Athenische Mittheilungen*, 1897, p. 439 ff. After reading through Dörpfeld's arguments, and those of other scholars who support his views, I am still of opinion that the old theory is the right one, and that the Greek actors performed on a stage from the first; though no doubt the stage of the fifth century was much lower than that of later times. Among other writings which deal with the subject of the Greek theatre as a whole I may mention the following : — Oehmichen, *Das Bühnenwesen der Griechen und Römer*, München, 1890 ; Navarre, *Dionysos*, Paris, 1895 (a lucid and well-written summary); the valuable articles by Prof. Jebb in Smith's *Dictionary of Antiquities* (v. *Theatrum*), and by Prof. P. Gardner in Jevons and Gardner's *Manual of Greek and Roman Antiquities*; and Bethe's *Prolegomena zur Geschichte des Theaters im Alterthum*, Leipzig, 1896. This last book, though often rather fanciful in its conclusions, is full of useful information and interesting suggestions.

To turn to the treatises on special portions of the subject. The point which has been most discussed in recent years is the question of the stage. The following are among the more important articles which have been written in favour of Dörpfeld's views : — White, *The Stage in Aristophanes* (*Harvard Studies*, ii. pp. 159-205) ; Bodensteiner, *Scenische Fragen im griechischen Drama* (Leipzig, 1893) ; Capps, *The Chorus in the later Greek Drama* (*American Journal of Archaeology*, x. 3. pp. 287–325), *The Stage in the Greek Theatre* (New Haven, 1891), *Vitruvius and the Greek Stage* (*Studies in Classical Philology*, Chicago, 1893, p. 3 ff.). The opposite side of the question has been defended by Todt, *Noch einmal die Bühne des Aeschylos* (*Philologus*, 1889, p. 505 ff.) ; Curtius, *Orchestra und Bühne* (*Berliner Philolog. Wochenschrift*, 1893, p. 97 ff.) ; Prof. E. Gardner, *A Plea for Vitruvius* (*Supplementary Papers of the Hellenic Journal*, 1892, p. 92 ff.) ; Lechat, *Épidaure* (Paris, 1895, p. 215 ff.) ; Zacher, *Die erhöhte Bühne bei Aristophanes* (*Philologus*, 1896, p. 181 ff.) ; Chamonard, *Bulletin de Corr. Hellénique*, 1896, p. 294 ff. (an admirable criticism) ; and also in various reviews of Dörpfeld's book, and especially by Bethe (*Göttingische gelehrte Anzeigen*, 1897, pp. 701-28), and by A. Müller (*Berl. Philolog. Wochenschrift*, 1897, pp. 1121-31). Special views, which may be regarded as a sort of compromise between the ordinary theory and that of Dörpfeld, are advocated by Weismann in *Die scenische Aufführung der griechischen Dramen* (München, 1893), *Zur Thymele-frage* (*Jahrb. für classische Philologie*, 1895, pp. 673-9), *Scenische Anweisungen, &c.* (Bamberg, 1896); and by Christ in *Jahrb. für classische Philologie*, 1894, p. 27 ff., p. 157 ff., and *Sitzungsberichte der bayer. Akad. der Wissenschaften*, 1894, pp. 1-52. All these articles, together with others which might be mentioned, have been of great service in the preparation of the present edition. Opinions may differ as to the soundness of the views which they respectively advocate. But there can be no doubt that this exhaustive discussion of the subject has brought to light many new facts, and cleared up many difficulties.

As regards the theatres which have been recently explored and excavated, I have consulted (in addition to Dörpfeld's book) the following sources :—Hermann, Bohn, and Fränkel, *Ausgrabungen zu Pergamon*, Berlin, 1888, p. 40 ff. (theatre at Pergamon); *Athen. Mittheilungen*, 1894, p. 65 ff. (theatre at Magnesia); *Papers of the American School of Archaeological Studies at Athens*, 1888, pp. 1-34 (Thoricus); *American Journal of Archaeology*, 1891, p. 253 ff., 1895, p. 331 ff. (Eretria); *Ibid.* 1889, p. 267 ff., 1893, p. 388 ff. (Sicyon); Defrasse and Lechat, *Épidaure*, Paris, 1895 (Epidaurus); Schultz, Gardner, and Loring in *Excavations at Megalopolis, Supplement to Hellenic Journal*, 1892 (Megalopolis); Chamonard, *Bulletin de Corr. Hellénique*, 1896, p. 256 ff. (Delos); *Athen. Mittheilungen*, 1893, p. 404 ff. (Tralles); Lanckoronski, *Städte Pamphyliens und Pisidiens*, Wien, 1892 (contains a very valuable account, with excellent plans and illustrations, of certain Asia Minor theatres hitherto but little known); Schrader, *Berl. Philolog. Wochenschrift*, April 16, 1898, pp. 508, 509 (a brief preliminary notice of the interesting theatre at Priene, lately excavated).

The subject of the choregic arrangements has been ably treated by Capps in his *Dramatic Synchoregia at Athens* (*American Journal of Philology*, xvii. 3. pp. 319-28), which I have followed in most points. For certain questions connected with the Dionysiac festivals I have consulted with advantage Körte's article *Zu Dionysos-Festen* (*Rhein. Museum*, 1897, pp. 168-74), and Wachsmuth, *Das Thukydideische Urathen* (*Abhandl. der Sächs. Gesellschaft der Wissenschaften*, xviii. pp. 1-56). As for the costume of actors and chorus, the most valuable and instructive of recent treatises are Körte's *Studien zur alten Komödie* (*Jahrb. des archaeol. Instituts*, 1893, pp. 61–93), and his articles in *Athen. Mittheilungen*, 1894, p. 346 ff., and in Bethe's *Prolegomena*, p. 339 ff. ; Crusius, in *Philologus*, xlviii. p. 696 ff. ; Poppelreuter, *De Comoediae Atticae Primordiis*, Berlin, 1893 ; Loeschcke, *Athen. Mittheilungen*, 1894, p. 519 ff. ; and Bethe's *Prolegomena*, p. 35 ff. Other articles on special points from which I have taken various suggestions are—Neckel, *Das Ekkyklema* (Friedland, 1890) ; Cook, *The Thymele in Greek Theatres* (*Classical Review*, Oct. 1895) ; Reisch, *Griechische Weihgeschenke* (Wien, 1890) ; and Svoronos, Περὶ τῶν Εἰσιτηρίων (*Journal International d'Archéologie Numismatique*, 1898, i. pp. 37–120). I should also mention Albert Müller's *Die neueren Arbeiten auf dem Gebiete des griech. Bühnenwesens* (*Philologus*, Suppl. vi. 1891)—an interesting and judicious criticism of the various writings about the Greek stage which had appeared shortly before the publication of the article.

It will be seen that many of the authorities mentioned in the preface to the first edition have been superseded, at any rate in part, by these more recent investigations. But I have thought it best to reprint the earlier list, since there are few of the old authorities which are not still worth consulting on some point or another.

I gladly take this opportunity of expressing my obligations to various friends for the corrections and suggestions which they have sent to me. I have derived many valuable hints from the reviews and notices of the first edition, and especially from the very friendly and useful criticism by Mr. L. C. Purser in *Hermathena*, and from that by Mr. H. Richards in the *Academy*. I am greatly indebted to Professor E. Gardner for the photograph of the Epidaurian theatre which is reproduced in Fig. 7 ; and to the Council of the Hellenic Society for their permission to copy from the *Hellenic Journal* the illustration of a satyric chorus. I have to thank the Provost of Oriel, Professor P. Gardner, Mr. F. Madan, Rev. G. C. Richards, and other friends for their help and advice in various matters ; and Dr. Albert Müller, Professor White, and Mr. Capps for their kindness in sending me writings of theirs on the subject of the Greek stage which have proved of very great service.

OXFORD, *July*, 1898.

PREFACE TO THE THIRD EDITION

AFTER the lamented death of Mr. Haigh, the Delegates of the Clarendon Press entrusted me with the revision of his book for a third edition, and his relatives kindly supplied me with the materials which he had collected for a revision. I have tried to follow as far as possible such indications as I could find of his own intentions in regard to the new edition. He had re-written parts of Chapters I and II, and his review of Puchstein's *Die griechische Bühne* showed sufficiently what view he took of that work. He also left careful analyses of many papers which had appeared in periodicals since the second edition, with occasional criticisms. It is clear from the manner in which the portions of the book referred to were re-written that he intended to cut out many of the repetitions, both of matter and expression, which had been allowed to remain in the second edition. I have therefore felt at liberty to follow him in this respect; but the space gained has been almost all filled by the new matter which it has been necessary to insert, either at the suggestion of his own notes, or in consequence of important writings on the subject since the last edition.

Since 1898 the inscriptions bearing upon the Greek drama have been the subject of thorough investigation at the hands of Prof. Edward Capps, Dr. Adolph Wilhelm, and others. The complete treatment of all the inscriptional evidence in the latter's *Urkunden dramatischer Aufführungen in Athen*, just published, is an invaluable contribution to the history of the Greek theatre and drama, and I have made as much use of it as the time of its publication allowed, the revision of the present volume having been almost completed by that date. It was beyond the scope of the present work to embark on a full discussion of the points of detail on which the chief authorities on the inscriptions differ; but I have re-written many of the notes on these points, and have tried to give sufficient indications of the character of the evidence. Further, in re-writing Appendix B, as it was necessary to do in the light of recent work on the subject, I have thought it best to give the reader access to considerably more of the inscriptional material, though still omitting many fragments whose readings, date, or meaning were too uncertain to allow them to be of value to the ordinary student.

Puchstein's book, *Die griechische Bühne*, above referred to, is the other work of first-rate importance in connexion with the Greek theatre which has appeared since 1898. There has been much controversy in regard to the theories contained in it, and Dr. Dörpfeld has published a reply to most of Puchstein's contentions (*Athenische Mittheilungen*, 1903, 383 ff.). But though in several points of detail Puchstein's position seems to be open to criticism, it is very difficult to believe that Dr. Dörpfeld has improved his case for his own theory; and I have followed both Mr. Haigh's view and my own conviction, in not modifying in any essential point the opinions expressed in the last edition. I have, however, altered the expressions 'Lycurgean' and 'Hellenistic' in most cases where they were applied in the last edition to the stage-buildings of different periods, since Puchstein's work makes it at least an open question whether some of the 'Lycurgean' work is not to be ascribed to an earlier period, and some of the 'Hellenistic' work to Lycurgus. Mr. Haigh's manuscript notes show, I think, that he would have approved of this. The new section on Puchstein's theory follows in most points the lines of Mr. Haigh's article on the subject in the *Classical Review*. I have inserted a number of references to the writings of Puchstein, Dörpfeld, and others who have taken part in the controversy as to the stage-buildings; and I have in many cases written fresh notes upon these and other points which have come into dispute since 1898, or upon which fresh light has been thrown. In cases where I could find no warrant in Mr. Haigh's own notes or writings for the views expressed, I have included these notes in square brackets, and I have, so far as I could, avoided inserting in the text anything with which I had reason to think he would have disagreed.

On one point on which there has recently been much controversy, the site of the Lenaeum, I have thought it best to relegate the discussion to a new Appendix; partly owing to its complicated character, and partly because I am not sure that Mr. Haigh would have entirely agreed with my views. He had not of course seen Miss Harrison's *Primitive Athens*, and I do not think he had read some other recent writings on the subject, when he began to re-write Chapter I; in particular, he seems not to have been acquainted with Nilsson's *Studia de Dionysiis*

Atticis—the most valuable contribution of recent years to discussions on the festivals. I have therefore allowed myself
a fairly free hand in dealing with this topic. I am much indebted to Mr. W. H. Forbes of Balliol College for his kind
criticisms on this part of my work.

The following are the principal writings which have been
published since the last edition, and which I have been able to
consult, besides those already named : E. Capps, papers in the
*American Journal of Philology, American Journal of Archaeo-
logy,* and *Chicago Decennial Publications,* vol. vi ; Miss Harrison,
Prolegomena to the Study of Greek Religion ; E. A. Gardner,
Ancient Athens ; Roberts and Gardner, *Greek Epigraphy,* vol. ii ;
Mazon, *Sur le Proagon* (Rev. de Philologie, 1903) ; A. Müller,
Untersuchungen zu den Bühnenalterthümern, and papers in *Philo-
logus* and *Berlin. Philolog. Wochenschrift;* Noack, *Das Pro-
skenion in der Theaterfrage* (Philologus, lviii); Exon, *A New
Theory of the Eccyclema* (Hermathena, xxvi); Dörpfeld, papers
in *Hermes* and *Athenische Mittheilungen;* Frei, *De certamini-
bus Thymelicis;* Hampel, *Was lehrt Aischylos' Orestie für die
Theaterfrage?;* Flickinger, *The meaning of* ἐπὶ τῆς σκηνῆς *in the
Fourth Century* B.C. ; Engelmann, *Archäologische Studien zu den
Tragikern;* P. Gardner, *The Scenery of the Greek Stage* (J. Hell.
Stud., 1899) ; Devrient, *Das Kind auf der antiken Bühne* ;
Dignan, *The Idle Actor in Aeschylus* ; Völker, *Berühmte Schau-
spieler im griechischen Alterthum* ; J. W. White, *An Unrecognized
Actor in Greek Comedy* (Harvard Stud. Class. Phil., 1906);
Hense, *Die Modificirung der Maske in der griechischen Tragödie* ;
Körte, *Das Fortleben des Chors im griechischen Drama* (Neue
Jahrb. für Philol., 1900); Navarre, *Utrum Mulieres Athenienses
scenicos ludos spectaverint;* Römer, *Über den litterarisch-aesthe-
tischen Bildungsstand des attischen Theaterpublikums* ; Foucart,
Le Culte de Dionysos en Attique ; besides the reviews of many
of these works, and the introductions and notes to Starkie's,
Rogers's, Sharpley's, and van Leeuwen's editions of a number
of plays of Aristophanes, and various articles in Pauly-
Wissowa, *Real-Encyclopädie.*

A. W. PICKARD-CAMBRIDGE.

BALLIOL COLLEGE, *January,* 1907.

CONTENTS

LIST OF ILLUSTRATIONS

THE ATTIC THEATRE

CHAPTER I

DRAMATIC CONTESTS AT ATHENS

§ 1. *General Character of the Contests.*

THE Attic drama, like most ancient forms of art and poetry, was originally the offspring of religious enthusiasm. It was developed out of the songs and dances in honour of Dionysus, the god of wine and vegetation. In course of time, as it assumed a regular dramatic shape, its range of subject was extended far beyond the limits of the Bacchic mythology. Its religious significance was also gradually diminished, and it began to be written more and more from the purely human point of view. But in spite of these changes, its outward connexion with the Bacchic worship was preserved unimpaired throughout the whole period of its history. Dramatic representations at Athens were confined, from first to last, to the great festivals of Dionysus. They were regarded as a religious ceremonial, as an act of homage to the god. They never became, as with us, an ordinary amusement of everyday life. During the greater part of the year the Athenians had to be content with other forms of entertainment. It was only when the annual festivals of Dionysus came round that they were able to gratify their passion for the stage. On such occasions their eagerness and enthusiasm were proportionately great. The whole city kept holiday, and gave itself up to pleasure, and to the worship of the wine-god. Business was abandoned; the law-courts were closed; distraints for debt were forbidden during the continuance of the festival; even prisoners were released from gaol, to enable them to share in the common festivities.[1] The theatre, the chief centre of attraction, was thronged with spectators; and the number of plays provided

---

[1] Dem. Androt. § 68, and schol. ad loc.; Meid. § 10, &c.

B

was large enough to compensate for their scarcity at other periods. Several days in succession were devoted to the drama. Tragedies and comedies followed one another without intermission from morning till evening. In the midst of these pleasures the religious aspect of the performance, as a ceremony in honour of Dionysus, established in obedience to the direct commands of the oracle,[1] was not forgotten. The audience came with garlands on their heads, as to a sacred gathering. The statue of Dionysus was brought to the theatre, and placed in front of the stage, so that the god might enjoy the spectacle along with his worshippers.[2] The chief seats in the theatre were mostly occupied by priests, and the central seat of all was reserved for the priest of Dionysus.[3] The performance of plays was preceded by the sacrifice of a victim to the god of the festival. The poets who wrote the plays, the choregi who paid for them, and the actors and singers who performed them, were all looked upon as ministers of religion, and their persons were sacred and inviolable. The theatre itself possessed all the sanctity attaching to a divine temple. Any form of outrage committed there was treated, not merely as an offence against the ordinary laws, but as a sacrilegious act, and was punished with corresponding severity. The ordinary course of law was not considered sufficient, and they were dealt with under an exceptional process at a special meeting of the Assembly.[4] It is recorded that on one occasion a certain Ctesicles was put to death for merely striking a personal enemy during the procession.[5] Merely to eject a man from a seat which he had taken wrongfully was a piece of sacrilege punishable with death.[6] These various characteristics of the Attic drama—its limitation to certain annual festivals, and its religious associations—have no parallel on the modern stage, apart from isolated survivals like the performance at Ober-Ammergau. The modern theatre has long since been divorced from ecclesiastical influence, and is unrestricted as to season. But its original surroundings were not dissimilar. The Mysteries and Miracle Plays from which it is descended, and which were

[1] Dem. Meid. §§ 51-3.
[2] See below, p. 9.
[3] C. I. A. iii. 240-384. Hesych. s.v. νεμήσεις θέας.

[4] Dem. Meid. §§ 8-10.
[5] Ibid. § 180.
[6] Ibid. § 178.

performed year by year for the instruction of the people on the great Feast-days of the Church, suggest many points of comparison with the exhibitions at the Attic Dionysia.

Another remarkable feature of the ancient theatre is the fact that almost all the dramatic representations were arranged in the form of a contest. Prizes were offered by the managers of the festival, and poets and actors exhibited their plays in competition with one another. The victory was awarded by the decision of a carefully selected jury. It is curious to notice how strongly implanted in the Greek nature was this passion for anything in the shape of a contest. It was not peculiar to the drama, or to the Athenian festivals, but prevailed throughout Greece in all festal gatherings where music and poetry were performed. Every Greek city of any importance had its annual meetings, with a long list of competitions. There were contests in choral singing of various kinds; contests in original poetry, and in the recitation of ancient epics; contests between harp-players, flute-players, trumpeters, and heralds. In this respect a Greek festival was not unlike a Welsh Eisteddfod, with its rival bards and choruses. In the case of the drama the element of competition must have added largely to the interest of the entertainment, and must have acted as a powerful stimulus upon the minds of poets and performers alike. The fertility of the old Attic dramatists, and the energy which enabled them to produce, in extreme old age, such masterpieces as the Agamemnon of Aeschylus, the Oedipus Coloneus of Sophocles, and the Bacchae of Euripides, may have been partly due to the invigorating influence of the contests, and the rivalry which they engendered.

The management of the dramatic performances was in the hands of the State, and was entrusted to the same official who had the general control of the festival. The superintendence which he exercised was not merely a formal one. His duties were important and carefully defined. He had to select the poets who took part in the competitions, and the plays which they exhibited. He had to choose the actors, and distribute them among the different poets. He was also responsible for seeing that the work of preparation was carefully carried out. The expense of the performance was one of the regular public burdens, and was imposed in turn upon the richer citizens.

In modern times there is no example of a theatre so entirely dependent upon the State. In England the drama is left solely to private enterprise. In countries like France and Germany, though certain theatres receive subventions from the State, and are subject to a code of rules, the government takes little part in the direction of their affairs. But the Athenian drama stood on a different footing. As a sacred ceremonial, closely connected with the religious worship of the State, it was naturally placed under public control. Even from the secular point of view it was considered a fitting object for the attention of statesmen. To provide for the amusement and instruction of the people was, according to the Greeks, one of the regular duties of a government; and they would have thought it unwise to abandon to private venturers an institution which possessed the educational value and wide popularity of the drama. For the audience to which the Athenian poet addressed himself was in reality a gathering of the whole body of his fellow countrymen. The theatre of Dionysus was capable of containing nearly twenty thousand people. Books were not plentiful, and their use was confined to a limited class. The ordinary Athenian depended for his literary pleasures upon the various public performances and recitations of poetical compositions. The drama was, therefore, much more to him than to a modern playgoer. At the present day, when continual supplies of fresh literature are accessible to every one, it is hard to realize the excitement and expectancy with which an Athenian looked forward to the annual exhibition of dramas at the Dionysia. It was here that his taste for novelty in literature was gratified. It was here that he found an equivalent for the books, magazines, and newspapers of modern civilization. Hence he was able to sit day after day, from morning to evening, listening to tragedy and comedy, without any feeling of satiety. The enthusiasm with which the drama was regarded, and the direct manner in which the author was brought into contact with the whole body of his countrymen, contributed to make the vocation of the dramatic writer one of the very greatest importance. The leading tragic poets especially exercised a most profound influence upon the national mind and character. They were the teachers of the people. Their writings were invested with an almost Homeric sanctity, and appealed to as authorities on questions of science and morality. Maxims and quotations from their plays were upon every one's lips. Many passages in Aristophanes and Plato prove the enormous influence for good and evil which was exercised by the Greek tragic poets, and there is probably no other instance in history of a drama which was so thoroughly popular, and formed so essential a part of the national life.[1]

§ 2. *Earliest history of Dramatic Competitions.*

The establishment of these dramatic contests under State management dates, not from the earliest period of the drama, but from the time when it had begun to assume a fixed and definite shape. Originally there were no public competitions. The various innovations upon the old hymns to Dionysus, out of which the drama was evolved, were carried out at first by voluntary effort. Thespis is said to have introduced tragedy into Athens. But his earliest exhibitions were given on his own responsibility, and as a private speculation.[2] The development of comedy was also the result of individual enterprise. The performance was for a long time left to amateurs, and regarded as of no importance. It was only when the drama had attained a certain pitch of excellence, and become widely popular, that it was taken in hand by the State, and annual contests introduced.[3] The date of their institution cannot always be determined exactly. It differed in the case of different festivals, and in the case of tragedy as compared with comedy. But there is sufficient evidence to show that no contest was earlier in date than the latter half of the sixth century.

All these competitions, as we have seen, were confined to the festivals of Dionysus.[4] In Attica these were of four kinds. There were the Rural Dionysia, celebrated in the various Attic demes; and there were the feasts held in Athens itself, the Anthesteria, the City Dionysia, and the Lenaea.[5] The importance

---

[1] See esp. Aristoph. Ran. 1008 ff., 1054 ff. ; Plat. Rep. 598 D, E.

[2] Plut. Solon. p. 95 B. ἀρχομένων δὲ τῶν περὶ Θέσπιν ἤδη τὴν τραγῳδίαν κινεῖν, καὶ διὰ τὴν καινότητα τοὺς πολλοὺς ἄγοντος τοῦ πράγματος, οὔπω δὲ εἰς ἅμιλλαν ἐναγώνιον ἐξηγμένου κτλ.

[3] Aristot. Poet. c. v.

[4] For dramatic exhibitions in other parts of Greece, see The Tragic Drama of the Greeks, p. 436.

[5] Gilbert (Die Festzeiten der attischen Dionysien, 1872) and more recently Dörpfeld (Das griechische Theater, p. 9) have attempted to show that the Lenaea was only a part of the

of these gatherings from the theatrical point of view varied
considerably. The Anthesteria seems at no time to have had
much connexion with the drama. The Rural Dionysia were
merely provincial celebrations, and depended almost entirely
for their supply of plays upon the Athenian theatre. The City
Dionysia and the Lenaea were the really significant festivals
in the history of the ancient stage. It was here that the great
Attic poets exhibited their works, and it was here that the drama
was first brought to perfection. Each festival had its peculiar
character. At the City Dionysia tragedy held the chief place;
at the Lenaea comedy was of most importance. Various
indications show that this was the case. In the list of proceedings at the City Dionysia tragedy is placed last of all,
as being the chief attraction; while in the list referring to the
Lenaea the same place is assigned to comedy, and for the same
reason.[1] Again, the dithyramb, the original source of tragedy,
was from the first a prominent feature at the City Dionysia,
though unknown at the Lenaea till a late period.[2] On the other
hand the comic actors' contest was introduced into the Lenaea
long before it was extended to the City Dionysia. This difference
between the two festivals, as regards the type of drama preferred
by each, was probably due to some original difference in the cult
of the two deities, Dionysus Eleuthereus and Dionysus Lenaeus,
to whom they were respectively consecrated.[3]

§ 3. *The City Dionysia.*

The City Dionysia, the feast of Dionysus Eleuthereus,[4] was
the most famous and magnificent of all the Bacchic festivals, and

Anthesteria, and that the Anthesteria
was only the Athenian counterpart of
the Rural Dionysia. Gilbert was refuted
by Schömann, Alterth. ii. 579-99.
Wachsmuth, Abhandl. der Sächs. Gesell.
der Wissensch. xviii. p. 33 ff., and Körte,
Rhein. Mus., 1897, p. 168 ff., show that
an inscription C. I. A. ii. 834 b proves
that there must have been a considerable interval between the Lenaea and
Anthesteria. It is an account of the
sums expended by the ἐπιστάται Ἐλευσινόθεν in B.C. 329-328. In col. ii. 46
we read ἐπιστάταις ἐπιλήναια εἰς Διονύσια
θῦσαι ΔΔ; in ii. 68, twenty-two lines
later, εἰς Χοὰς δημοσίοις ἱερεῖον κτλ.
(The adjective ἐπιλήναιος is also found

in the papyrus of Ath. Pol. c. 57, and
the inscription confirms the reading
ἐπιληναίων, which editors alter to ἐπὶ
Ληναίῳ). [The whole subject of the
Dionysiac festivals has been investi-
gated afresh by Nilsson (Studia de
Dionysiis Atticis, 1900), who proves
at length the separateness of the four
festivals.]

[1] Dem. Meid. § 10.
[2] See below, p. 9.
[3] [See articles on Dionysus in Pauly-
Wissowa, Real-Encycl., and Preller-
Robert, Griech. Mythologie.]
[4] Paus. i. 29; Philostrat. Vit. Soph.
p. 549.

was therefore also called the Great Dionysia, or simply the
Dionysia, without any further epithet.[1] It was held from the
first inside the city, at the sacred enclosure of Eleuthereus[2]
on the south of the Acropolis. Hence the name City Dionysia,
to distinguish it from the Anthesteria and the Lenaea, which, at
any rate in early times, were celebrated outside the walls.
A poet who brought out his plays at this festival was said
to exhibit them 'in the city'; if successful, he was said to
have won 'a city victory'.[3] The feast lasted for at least five
days, and possibly for six. It took place in the month
Elaphebolion, at a date corresponding to the end of March.[4]
The spring was then just beginning, and the sea had again
become navigable.[5] Consequently the city was crowded with
visitors from all parts of Greece. It was at this season that the
allies came to Athens to pay the annual tribute. Ambassadors
from foreign states often chose this time for the transaction
of diplomatic business. Large numbers of strangers were
attracted by mere pleasure, and the celebrity of the festival.
Aeschines, in his rhetorical language, describes the audience
in the theatre at the City Dionysia as consisting of the 'whole
Greek nation'.[6] The presence of so many strangers gave
a lively appearance to the streets, in marked contrast to the
quietness which prevailed at the winter festival of the Lenaea.[7]
The Athenians gladly seized this opportunity of displaying
before foreign Greeks the glories of their city. The various
spectacles provided, the religious ceremonial, the trains of

[1] Διονύσια τὰ ἐν ἄστει C. I. A. ii. 341, 402, 404; Διονύσια τὰ ἀστικά Thuc. v. 20; Διονύσια τὰ μεγάλα Athen. Pol. c. 56, C. I. A. ii. 312, 331; Διονύσια Athen. Pol. c. 56.
[2] This is proved by the inscription on the chief seat at the theatre, Ἱερέως Διονίσου Ἐλευθερέας (C. I. A. iii. 240).
[3] νίκη ἀστική Diog. Laert. viii. 90. To produce plays at the City Dionysia was ἐν ἄστει διδάσκειν Schol. Aristoph. Ran. 67, or εἰς ἄστυ καθιέναι Arg. ii. Aristoph. Aves: cf. διδασκαλία ἀστική Plut. X Orat. 839 D.
[4] The feast of Asclepius and the Proagon were on the 8th of Elaphebolion, Aeschin. Ctesiph. § 67; the Proagon took place 'a few days' before the City Dionysia, Schol. ibid.: the

City Dionysia cannot therefore have begun before the 10th. The festival must have terminated on the 15th, since after it came the Pandia, the next day the ἐκκλησία ἐν Διονύσου, and the next day, when the first assembly mentioned by Aeschines and Demosthenes took place, was the 18th. See Aeschin. Ctes. § 68; Fals. Leg. § 61; Dem. Meid. § 8.
[5] Stormy weather sometimes interfered with the proceedings. In the time of Demetrius a snowfall prevented the procession. Theophr. Char. 3; Plut. Demetr. p. 894 B.
[6] Aeschin. Ctes. § 43; cf. Dem. Meid. § 74.
[7] Aristoph. Ach. 505, 506; Thuc. v. 23.

sacrificial victims, the choral songs and dances, the tragedies and comedies exhibited before countless multitudes in the vast open-air theatre, were all calculated to impress strangers with the wealth, public spirit, and artistic supremacy of Athens.

The first day of the festival was devoted to a grand religious procession, in which the ancient image of Dionysus Eleuthereus, preserved in one of his temples at the foot of the Acropolis, played a prominent part.[1] There was a tradition that this statue, together with the cult of the deity, had been originally brought to Athens from Eleutherae, a border town between Attica and Boeotia. The procession was instituted to commemorate this sacred event. The statue was taken out of its shrine, and carried along the road to Eleutherae as far as a certain temple near the Academy. It was then brought back again, following on its return the actual route traversed on its first entrance into Athens.[2] As a spectacle, this procession was the most magnificent part of the whole festival. Athenians of every class, men, women, and even girls, came out to witness or take part in it. The casual encounters which took place on these occasions might serve as a foundation for the plots of the New Comedy.[3] The members of the procession were dressed in brilliantly coloured garments. Some of them wore ornaments of gold, and had masks upon their faces. The rich drove in chariots; the poorer classes walked on foot.[4] In front came the archon, the manager of the festival, attended by various magistrates and priests. The ephebi, equipped with shields and spears, acted as escort to the sacred image.[5] A long train of victims followed, partly provided by the State, partly offered by individuals, or by different classes of the population.[6] The canephori, young virgins bearing upon their heads the baskets containing the sacrificial implements, formed one of the most picturesque features in the show. The choregi were also there, attended by their respective choruses, all dressed in striking costume. When Demosthenes served as choregus to his tribe, he had a gold crown and embroidered mantle made

---

[1] The procession must have been on the first day, for (1) in Dem. Meid. § 10 it comes first in the list of proceedings, (2) it was not till after the procession was over that the statue was placed in the theatre to witness the dramatic and dithyrambic contests.

[2] Paus. i. 29. 2, 38. 8; Philostrat. Vit. Soph. p. 549.
[3] Menand. Fragm. 558 (Kock).
[4] Plut. Cupid. Divit. 527 E.
[5] C. I. A. ii. 420, 470, 471.
[6] C. I. A. ii. 471, 741.

specially for use at the procession. Alcibiades on a similar
occasion was dressed in purple, and excited much admiration by
his beauty.[1] From these few details, which happen to have been
recorded, we may form some notion of the general splendour of
the spectacle. The route followed by the procession was as
follows. On leaving the Temple of Dionysus it came first to the
market-place, where a halt was made, and a chorus danced and
sang before the statues of the twelve gods.[2] It then marched
out through the city gates along the road to Eleutherae. When
it reached the Academy the statue of the god was placed on
a pedestal, and the different victims were sacrificed. The rest
of the day was spent in feasting and merriment.[3] At nightfall
they returned to Athens by torchlight. But the sacred image,
instead of being restored to its shrine, was carried to the theatre
by the ephebi, and set up in the orchestra, so as to be present at
the entertainments given on the following days.[4]

These entertainments were of two kinds. There were the
dramatic contests, in tragedy, comedy, and satyric drama; and
there were the lyrical contests, at which dithyrambs were performed.[5] The dithyramb was a hymn in honour of Dionysus,
sung to the accompaniment of the flute by a chorus of fifty
members. The chorus stood in a circular form round the
altar, and was therefore called a 'cyclic' chorus. At the City
Dionysia there were two of these lyrical contests, one between
five choruses of boys, and the other between five choruses of
men.[6] The first contest of men took place in B.C. 509–508, in

[1] Dem. Meid. § 22; Athen. p. 534 C.
[2] Xen. Hipparch. iii. 2.
[3] Philostrat. Vit. Soph. p. 549.
[4] C. I. A. ii. 470, 471. Hence Aristophanes in the Frogs selects Dionysus
as the most experienced of dramatic
critics. Cf. also Aristoph. Eq. 536
θεᾶσθαι λιπαρὸν παρὰ τῷ Διονύσῳ. Late
writers (Philostrat. Vit. Apoll. p. 161;
Dio Chrys., orat. 31, p. 631 R) pro-
test against shedding human blood in
gladiatorial combats in the very orchestra visited by the god Dionysus.
[5] In the lists of victors at the City
Dionysia (C. I. A. ii. 971 a–e, iv. 971
f–h) the contests enumerated are
always the same, viz. παίδων, ἀνδρῶν,
κωμῳδῶν, τραγῳδῶν. Cp. Athen. Pol.
c. 56 χορηγοὺς τραγῳδοῖς καθίστησι τρεῖς

. . . ἔπειτα παραλαβὼν τοὺς χορηγοὺς τοὺς
ἐνηνεγμένους ὑπὸ τῶν φυλῶν εἰς Διονύσια
ἀνδράσιν καὶ παισὶν καὶ κωμῳδοῖς κτλ.
Dem. Meid. § 10 καὶ τοῖς ἐν ἄστει
Διονυσίοις ἡ πομπὴ καὶ οἱ παῖδες ⟨καὶ οἱ
ἄνδρες⟩ καὶ ὁ κῶμος καὶ οἱ κωμῳδοὶ καὶ οἱ
τραγῳδοί. (The words καὶ οἱ ἄνδρες
have obviously fallen out.) Cp. also
C. I. A. ii. 553 (list of victors παισὶν ἢ
ἀνδράσιν).
[6] Dem. Meid. § 156 loosely calls the
choruses of men αὐληταὶ ἄνδρες, and
the author of the first Argument to the
speech, misled by this, states that
there were αὐλητῶν χοροί at the City
Dionysia. But other passages in the
speech, e. g. §§ 15, 17, show that the
expression means not that the men
were flute-players, but that they sang

the Archonship of Lysagoras, though the system of choregia
was probably not introduced till a few years later.[1] Each chorus
was provided by one of the ten Attic tribes. Hence all ten tribes
took part in one or other of the two competitions.[2] The contest
was essentially a tribal one. The members of each chorus,
together with the choregus, were selected exclusively from the
tribe which they represented.[3] The victory of the chorus was
a victory for the tribe. The prize of victory, the tripod, though
given to the choregus, and erected in some public place at his
expense, was regarded as equally the property of the tribe.[4] In
the records of dithyrambic competitions the name of the victorious tribe was always placed in the most prominent position.
The dramatic contests, on the other hand, had no connexion
with the tribes. Actors, choruses, and choregi were chosen
indiscriminately from the whole population.[5] The performers
competed in their own interest solely, and not as representatives
of any other body. The records of dramatic victories give merely
the names of the choregus, the poet, and the principal actor.[6]
It is important to keep this difference between the two kinds of
contest clearly in view, since many mistakes have been caused
by attributing to the dramatic kind features which belong
exclusively to the dithyrambic.

§ 4. *Tragedy at the City Dionysia.*

Of the dramatic performances at the City Dionysia, which
we have next to consider, the tragic were the most important.

dithyrambs accompanied by the flute.
See Wieseler, Das Satyrspiel, pp. 46-8.

[1] [Marmor Par. ep. 46. For the archon v. Munro, Class. Rev. xv. p. 357. For choregia v. Capps, Introduction of Comedy to the City Dionysia, p. 27 ff.]

[2] Schol. Aeschin. Timarch. § 11 ἐξ ἔθους Ἀθηναῖοι [κατέστησαν] κατὰ φυλὴν πεντήκοντα παίδων χορὸν ἢ ἀνδρῶν, ὥστε γενέσθαι δέκα χορούς, ἐπειδὴ καὶ δέκα φυλαί. λέγονται δὲ οἱ διθύραμβοι χοροὶ κύκλιοι, καὶ χορὸς κύκλιος.

[3] Dem. Meid. § 13; Antiphon orat. vi. §§ 12, 13.

[4] Lysias xxi. § 2; Dem. Meid. § 5 τῆς φυλῆς ἀδίκως ἀφαιρεθείσης τὸν τρίποδα. The choregus of a dithyrambic chorus

was said χορηγεῖν τῇ φυλῇ. Plut. X orat. 835 B ἐχορήγησε κυκλίῳ χορῷ τῇ αὑτοῦ φυλῇ ἀγωνιζομένη διθυράμβῳ : Isaeus v. § 36 οὗτος γὰρ τῇ μὲν φυλῇ εἰς Διονύσια χορηγήσας τέταρτος ἐγένετο, τραγῳδοῖς δὲ καὶ πυρριχισταῖς ὕστατος. (Bentley's emendation, τέταρτος ἐγένετο τραγῳδοῖς,καὶ πυρριχισταῖς ὕστατος makes Dicaeogenes fourth in the tragic contest, in which there were never more than three competitors.)

[5] In the time of Aristotle the choregi in comedy were appointed by the tribes. But this was a late innovation, and produced no change in the character of the contest. See chap. ii. § 2.

[6] C. I. A. ii. 971 (printed in Appendix B). Ibid. ii. 1234 ff.

The City Dionysia was specially connected with the growth of the tragic drama, and it was here that the earliest public contests in tragedy were established. The first competition was held in B. C. 535, and was rendered doubly memorable by the fact that Thespis, now an old man, took part in the performance, and won the prize of victory.[1] Shortly before this time Pisistratus, who was a great patron of art and literature, had returned from exile, and begun his last tyranny. It must have been under his auspices, therefore, that tragedy was first officially recognized by the State, and made an annual institution. As to the character of these early contests, and the arrangements concerning the number of poets and plays, nothing has been recorded.[2] It is uncertain whether the regulations were the same as those which afterwards prevailed during the fifth century. But we are told that the tragic poet Choerilus, who began to exhibit in 523, composed no less than a hundred and sixty plays.[3] The largeness of the number would seem to show that even in the sixth century it was the custom for each competing poet to bring out several plays at each festival.

When we turn to the fifth century, the information is fairly complete. Several records have been preserved, referring chiefly to the three great tragic poets, and giving a more or less detailed account of the results of the competitions. It may be interesting to mention some of these records. The earliest refers to the year 499, and tells us that three poets— Aeschylus, Choerilus, and Pratinas—took part in the tragic contest.[4] From the next we learn that in 472 Aeschylus won the first prize, and that the plays he exhibited were the Phineus, Persae, Glaucus, and the satyric drama Prometheus.[5] In 467, Aeschylus was first with the Laius, Oedipus, Septem

---

[1] Marm. Par. ep. 43 ἀφ' οὗ Θέσπις ὁ ποιητὴς [ἐφάνη], πρῶτος ὃς ἐδίδαξε [δρ]ᾶ[μα ἐν ἀ]στ[ει, καὶ ἐ]τέθη ὁ [τ]ράγος [ἆθλον], ἔτη . . . The date is mutilated, but must have fallen between 542 and 520, the preceding and subsequent epochs. Suidas s. v. Θέσπις (ἐδίδαξε δὲ ἐπὶ τῆς πρώτης καὶ ξ' ὀλυμπιάδος) doubtless refers to the same contest, which may therefore be assigned to B. C. 536-5

[2] [Capps (The Introduction of Comedy into the City Dionysia) renders it highly probable that choregia was

not introduced until about B. C. 502.]

[3] Suidas s. v. Χοιρίλος. The same lexicon, s. v. Πρατίνας, says that Pratinas composed fifty plays, of which thirty-two were satyric : but it is unsafe to draw inferences from this as to relative proportion of satyric plays and tragedies in these early days, since the numbers may refer merely to the plays which happened to be preserved in the time of the grammarians.

[4] Suidas s. v. Πρατίνας.

[5] Arg. Aesch. Persae.

contra Thebas, and the satyric play Sphinx; Aristias was
second with the Perseus, Tantalus, and the satyric play Palaestae,
written by his father Pratinas; Polyphradmon was third with
the Lycurgean tetralogy.[1] The name of one of the plays of
Aristias has doubtless dropped out accidentally, as there is no
other instance of poets competing at the same festival with a
different number of plays. A very interesting record is that
for the year 458, when Aeschylus was again victorious, this
time with the Orestean group of plays, the Agamemnon,
Choephori, Eumenides, and satyric Proteus.[2] In 438 Sophocles
was first; Euripides was second with the Cressae, Alcmaeon in
Psophis, Telephus, and Alcestis. In 431 Euphorion was first,
Sophocles second, and Euripides third with the Medea,
Philoctetes, Dictys, and satyric play Theristae. In 428 Euripides
was first (the Hippolytus being one of his plays), Iophon second,
Ion third.[3] Among the last of the notices is that for the year
415, when Euripides, who produced the Alexander, Palamedes,
Troades, and satyric drama Sisyphus, was defeated for the first
prize by an obscure poet called Xenocles, who produced the
Oedipus, Lycaon, Bacchae and satyric play Athamas. After
Euripides' death, in B.C. 406, his Iphigenia in Aulis, Alcmaeon,
and Bacchae were produced by his son at the City Dionysia.[4]
The evidence of these various records, when compared with one
another, proves conclusively that during the whole, or almost
the whole, of the fifth century there was no variation in the
arrangement of the tragic contests at the City Dionysia. The
rule as to the number of poets and plays was as follows. At
each festival three poets appeared as competitors,[5] and each
poet was required to exhibit four plays, consisting of three
tragedies and a satyric drama.[6] If the number seems surprising,

[1] Arg. Aesch. Sept. c. Theb.
[2] Arg. Aesch. Agam.
[3] Args. Eur. Alcest., Med., Hippol.
[4] Aelian Var. Hist. ii. 8; Schol. Aristoph. Ran. 67.
[5] Athen. Pol. c. 56; C. I. A. ii. 972, 973, 975.
[6] Cp. Diog. Laërt. iii. 56. Θρασύλλος
δέ φησι καὶ κατὰ τὴν τραγικὴν τετραλογίαν ἐκδοῦναι αὐτὸν (sc. τὸν Πλάτωνα)
τοὺς διαλόγους, οἷον ἐκεῖνοι τέτρασι
δράμασιν ἠγωνίζοντο, Διονυσίοις, Ληναίοις,
Παναθηναίοις, Χύτροις, ὧν τὸ τέταρτον ἦν

σατυρικόν· τὰ δὲ τέτταρα δράματα ἐκαλεῖτο τετραλογία. Thrasyllus was a
philosopher of the time of Tiberius.
The passage οἷον . . . τετραλογία is
probably an explanatory interpolation
by Diogenes himself. The statement
that the four plays of a tetralogy
were performed at four different festivals is absurd in itself, and abun-
dantly disproved by inscriptions and
other evidence (e. g. Schol. Aristoph.
Ran. 67).

we should remember that an ancient drama was only about half
the length of a modern one, and that four plays of this type
could easily have been got through in a single day. On one
occasion the rule just mentioned appears to have been partially
relaxed. In 438 Euripides was allowed to substitute the
Alcestis, a tragedy with a slightly comic tinge, for the usual
satyric drama. Whether this practice ever became common in
the fifth century is uncertain. The records give no further
instance. In all other cases where they mention the names
of the four plays produced, the last is a satyric play. It was
this custom of concluding the three tragedies with the licentious merriment of the satyrs which suggested to Ion of Chios
his well-known remark, that virtue, like a tragic poet's group of
plays, should always contain a satyric element.[1]

The four plays exhibited by each poet might be composed on
two different systems. They might form independent works of
art, and have no inner connexion with one another; or they
might deal with successive phases of the same legend, and be
fused into a single artistic whole. The general name for the
group of plays was 'didascalia', or a 'teaching'[2], because
in ancient times the author had to teach them to the actors.
But when they were connected together by unity of subject,
they were denoted by a special term. The four plays were
called a 'tetralogy';[3] the three tragedies, regarded apart
from the satyric drama, were called a 'trilogy'. As applied to
the drama, however, both words first occur at a comparatively
late date:[4] and as, to judge from their etymology, they seem

[1] Plut. Pericl. p. 154 E.
[2] Plut. l. c.; Id. X orat. 839 D
διδασκαλίας ἀστικὰς καθῆκεν ἐξ . . . καὶ
ἑτέρας δύο Ληναϊκάς; Anthol. Pal. vii. 37
ἡ δ' ἐνὶ χερσὶν | κούριμος, ἐκ ποίης ἥδε
διδασκαλίης ;
[3] That the word τετραλογία was
applied only to a group of four plays
connected in subject is proved by the
statement of Suidas (s.v. Σοφοκλῆς)
that Sophocles abandoned the practice
of exhibiting 'tetralogies', though
we know that he exhibited four plays
at a time ; and also by the application
of the word by Greek writers to the
Oresteia of Aeschylus (Schol. Aristoph.
Ran. 1155), the Pandionis of Philocles
(Schol. Aristoph. Av. 282), the Lycurgeia of Aeschylus (Schol. Aristoph.

Thesm. 135), and the Lycurgeia of
Polyphradmon (Arg. Aesch. Sept. c.
Theb.).   All these were groups of
plays on a single subject.
[4] Schol. Aristoph. Ran. 1155
τετραλογίαν φέρουσι τὴν Ὀρεστείαν αἱ
Διδασκαλίαι (i.e. the Διδασκαλίαι of
Aristotle). The other passages where
τετραλογία occurs in a dramatic sense
are Diog. Laërt. iii. 56, ix. 45 ; Schol.
Plat. Apol. p. 330 ; Schol. Aristoph.
Ran. 1155, where it is said that the
grammarians Aristarchus and Apol-
lonius disregarded the satyric plays
and spoke only of trilogies ; Schol.
Av. 282, Thesm. 142 ; Arg. Aesch.
Sept. c. Theb. τριλογία is found only
in Schol. Aristoph. Ran. 1155 ; Diog.
Laërt. iii. 61 ; Suidas s.v. Νικόμαχος.

properly to denote groups of speeches rather than groups of plays, it is possible that their dramatic application is a secondary one, and that the grammarians applied to the drama the word 'tetralogy' which properly denoted such groups of four speeches about fictitious cases as those of Antiphon, and afterwards formed the word 'trilogy' by analogy to denote three plays connected in subject with each other but not with the satyric play. In earlier times such collective titles as Lycurgeia, Oresteia, and the like were used.[1] The practice of writing plays in trilogies and tetralogies is chiefly associated with the name of Aeschylus. Whether it was invented by him, or inherited from his predecessors, is uncertain. We have no information as to the manner in which the poets of the sixth century were accustomed to combine their plays together. But whatever the origin of the system may have been, it was undoubtedly Aeschylus who first perceived the various developments of which it was capable, and brought it to perfection. In his hands it became a mighty instrument for the inculcation of religious truths. The central idea in the moral system of Aeschylus was the disastrous effect of sin, not only upon the sinner himself, but also upon his remote descendants. The curse entailed in the sinful act clung to a family from one generation to another. In the trilogy, with its wide range of time and subject, he was able to trace the whole course of this hereditary evil, and to follow the crime from its original commission down to the period of its final expiation. The Orestean trilogy, which has fortunately been preserved, is a magnificent example of his method. The Agamemnon depicts the murder of the returning chieftain by his adulterous wife. In the Choephori vengeance is taken on the murderess, after years of waiting, by her own son. In the Eumenides the matricide, a prey to remorse, is hunted from place to place by the Furies of his mother, until their rage is at length appeased by divine intervention. These successive pictures of crime and vengeance form a series of unapproachable grandeur. The general effect of the whole may be appreciated even by a modern reader. But in the ancient theatre the impression produced must have been far more vivid, as one play followed another upon the stage, and

---

[1] Aristoph. Thesm. 135, Ran. 1124. See, on these titles, The Tragic Drama of the Greeks, p. 114.

the dark scenes of guilt were unfolded in due sequence before the very eyes of the audience.

Apart from the Oresteia, very little is recorded about the tetralogies written by Aeschylus. He is known to have composed a Lycurgeia, on the fate of Lycurgus, the Thracian king and opponent of Bacchus; and an Oedipodeia, on the fortunes of the house of Oedipus. It is also fairly certain that he treated the legends about Hector, Ajax, Prometheus, and the daughters of Danaus in trilogic form. But these are the only instances for which there is clear evidence. No doubt most of his plays were written as tetralogies. Still, he does not seem to have adhered to the system on every occasion. The plays which he exhibited in 472—the Phineus, Persae, Glaucus, and satyric drama Prometheus—had apparently no connexion with one another.[1] There are also, among the titles of his lost dramas, several, such as the Sisyphus and the Atalanta, which seem to stand in an isolated position, and to be hardly capable of combination. In some cases, again, he may have adopted the tetralogic form only in part. The three tragedies may have formed a trilogy, while the concluding satyric drama was on a different subject. Thus the satyric Prometheus was produced, not with the Promethean trilogy, as we should have expected, but in a different combination altogether. There is no less uncertainty as to the structure of the lost tetralogies. It would be a mistake to assume that they were all as perfect in arrangement as the Oresteia. Even from the few remains and notices preserved we can see that the tetralogy was a flexible form of art, and could be treated in various ways. The connexion between the parts might be tightened or relaxed at will. In the Theban trilogy—the Laius, Oedipus, and Septem contra Thebas—there was a long lapse of years between the separate plays. In the Oresteia the intervals of time are much shorter. In the Lycurgeia, which described the invasion of Thrace by Dionysus, his defeat, capture, and final victory, the three plays followed so closely in point of time, that they must have been like successive acts in a single drama. Again, the trilogies might differ in respect of artistic completeness. The Oresteia forms a perfect whole. The legend is traced to its

---

[1] [Donaldson, Theatre of the Greeks, p. 118, suggests possible connexions; but they are highly conjectural.]

conclusion, and ends satisfactorily with the purification of Orestes. But the Theban trilogy was treated more in the chronicle fashion. It closed abruptly at a point where the course of events was still unfinished. The final scene of the Septem is full of forebodings of impending calamity. So marked is this feature, that before the discovery in recent years of the record which proves that the Septem was the last play of the three, all critics were agreed that it must have been followed by another tragedy.[1] This example shows us the necessity of caution in dealing with the whole subject of tetralogies. Since there is so much uncertainty as to the number of them written by Aeschylus, and the manner in which he wrote them, it is dangerous to go beyond the limits of direct evidence. Various schemes have been propounded by scholars, in which the titles of the lost plays are all arranged in tetralogic groups. But these systems must be regarded as entirely conjectural.

The satyric drama, by which the three tragedies were followed, was a survival from the primitive period of the Bacchic worship. With its strange medley of incongruous elements, of valour and cowardice, passion and merriment, heroic dignity and coarse indecency, it reproduced the various qualities of the ancient dithyramb. The chorus was always composed of satyrs. The leading characters consisted partly of heroes from the tragic stage, partly of semi-ludicrous personages, such as Silenus, Autolycus, and Polyphemus. The presence of the tragic kings and heroes in the midst of these disreputable associates and undignified surroundings was one of the most curious features in the performance. It had to be managed with great tact by the poet. The dignity of the heroes was not to be unduly lowered, and yet they must not seem too exalted for their company.[2] In the case of a tetralogy the awkwardness of the situation would be greatly intensified. Here the satyric drama dealt with the same legend as the preceding tragedies, but from a humorous point of view. It often happened that the very same hero whose disastrous fate had just been exhibited in the

[1] [Other critics, however, suppose that the final scene was added in some later revision of the play, after Sophocles' Antigone had been written, or when it became customary to present single plays of Aeschylus (see below, p. 74), which would often be shorter than those of other poets, and might therefore be lengthened by the addition of a scene.]

[2] Cp. Hor. Ars Poet. 225 ff.

trilogy was reintroduced under a sportive aspect. In the satyric play Lycurgus, which concluded the Lycurgean tetralogy, the chief part must have been taken by Lycurgus himself. In the Sphinx, the last play of the Oedipodeia, Oedipus must have appeared in person. This practice of concluding the tragic spectacle with a burlesque representation of the same or similar characters and incidents seems a questionable proceeding to modern taste. It would be difficult to defend it on artistic grounds. It originated not so much in the desire to provide a comic relief after the tragedies as in religious conservatism. The dramatic performances were part of a Bacchic festival. But the Bacchic element had long been discarded by tragedy. The satyric play, which still remained true to the primitive type, was therefore retained in the programme, in order to appease the god and to keep up the religious associations of the drama.

During the earlier part of the fifth century the practice of writing plays in tetralogies seems to have been generally adopted, not only by Aeschylus, but by all other tragic poets. One such tetralogy, the Lycurgeia of Polyphradmon, happens to have been recorded. It was Sophocles who first gave up the system, and regularly composed his four plays on independent subjects.[1] The example set by Sophocles was followed by the younger generation. Even as early as 467, when Aeschylus brought out his Oedipodeia, and Polyphradmon his Lycurgeia, the third poet, Aristias, competed with a group of disconnected plays. After the death of Aeschylus the tetralogy speedily went out of fashion. It was never attempted by Euripides. In fact during the latter half of the fifth century only three tetralogies are mentioned. A Pandionis was written by Philocles, the nephew of Aeschylus, who naturally followed

---

[1] Suidas s.v. Σοφοκλῆς· καὶ αὐτὸς ἦρξε τοῦ δρᾶμα πρὸς δρᾶμα ἀγωνίζεσθαι, ἀλλὰ μὴ τετραλογίαν. The words seem to imply that he exhibited only one play at each festival : but the didascalic records show that this cannot have been the case. Probably, therefore, Suidas has misunderstood and misquoted his authority, who meant to say that Sophocles exhibited not single plays but groups of plays unconnected in subject. The suggestion of Oehmichen (Philol. Wochenschr., 1887, p. 1058) that after the reform of Sophocles each poet exhibited one of his plays on each successive day of the competition, and that this is what Suidas means, is rendered most improbable by the fact that tetralogies were still occasionally written ; and that Sophocles would have no power, as poet, to make such a change in the arrangement of the festival.

in his uncle's footsteps. An Oedipodeia was composed by
Meletus, the prosecutor of Socrates. Plato is also said to have
written a tetralogy before he abandoned poetry for philosophy.[1]
After the end of the fifth century all traces of the tetralogy
disappear. One reason for its decline in popularity and rapid
discontinuance may have been the increased length of plays.
A tragedy of the later poets was considerably longer, and
contained much more incident, than a tragedy of Aeschylus.
A trilogy composed of dramas of this bulk would have been
a vast and laborious undertaking. Another reason may have
been the gradual change in religious sentiment. The doctrine
of the hereditary curse in families, which the trilogy was
admirably adapted to exemplify, no longer held a prominent
place in the moral ideas of post-Aeschylean poets. The chief
motive of their tragedy was human passion rather than religious
truth. In such circumstances the trilogy, as a form of art,
had no advantages sufficient to compensate for the unwieldiness
of its size.

It has been worth while to discuss in some detail the arrangement of the tragic contests at the City Dionysia during the fifth
century, because this was the great period of Attic tragedy.
The fourth century is of less importance. For the first half of
the century there is a complete blank in our information on the
subject. But when we come to the latter half, we have the
evidence of an interesting inscription, which contains a full
record of the tragic performances at the City Dionysia for the
years 341 and 340.[2] From this record it appears that considerable
changes had now been made in the annual programme. The
old system, by which each of the three poets was required to
exhibit a satyric play, had been abandoned. A single specimen
of this type of drama was now considered sufficient, and was
produced at the commencement of the proceedings. The satyric
drama, with its primitive coarseness, had little attraction for
the more refined taste of the fourth century; and it was only
religious scruples which caused it to be retained at all. The
satyric play was followed by an old tragedy, written by one of
the three great tragic poets. In 341 the play chosen was the
Iphigeneia of Euripides, in 340 it was the Orestes. This

---

[1] Schol. Aristoph. Av. 282 ; Schol.   Var. Hist. ii. 30.
Plat. Apol. p. 330 (Bekk.) ; Aelian   [2] C.I.A. ii. 973 (quoted in Appendix B).

practice was also a new departure.[1] In the fifth century the
exhibition of old tragedies was, with rare exceptions, unknown
at the City Dionysia. After these two preliminary performances
came the contest with original plays. The number of poets was
still there, as in former times. But the number of plays was
diminished, and seems to have varied from year to year. In
341 each poet exhibited three tragedies; in 340 each poet
exhibited two. Theodectes, who flourished in the middle of
the fourth century, wrote fifty tragedies and engaged in thirteen contests.[2] Aphareus wrote thirty-five admittedly genuine
tragedies, and engaged in eight contests, between 368 and 341.[3]
This seems to imply that in most of the contests they produced
four plays; but the conclusion is not certain, for they may have
written plays which were never intended for the stage, as their
contemporary Chaeremon did.[4] The reduction in the number
of original plays points to a gradual decline in the vitality of the
tragic drama at Athens. These various changes must have
been made in the course of the sixty years preceding the period
of the inscription. But the exact date of their introduction
cannot be determined.

With the close of the fourth century the famous period of
Athenian tragedy came to an end. After this date the only
tragic poets of any celebrity were those who flourished at
Alexandria. But though the genius of the Attic poets was
exhausted, there was no immediate cessation in the production
of new plays. The contests were still maintained. A long
series of inscriptions shows that, down even to the Christian
era, 'original tragedies' continued to be the chief ornament of
the City Dionysia. The names of several Athenian tragic
poets belonging to this period have been preserved in theatrical
records. One of them was a descendant of Sophocles. As
to the character of the contests, and the proportion of old
tragedies to new ones, nothing is known. After the first

---

[1] [If the inscription C.I.A.ii. 971 c recorded by Pittakis, L'ancienne Athènes,
p. 168, is reliable, an old tragedy was
performed in B.C. 387-386. The
phrase used is παλαιὸν δρᾶμα παρεδίδαξαν οἱ τραγῳδοί: but the interpretation of this fragment is full of difficulties, see Wilhelm, Urkunden dramat.
Aufführungen in Athen, p. 22 ff. The
use of the expression παρεδίδαξαν (cf.

παραχορήγημα) seems to show that at
this date the performance of an old
tragedy was exceptional; while in the
inscription recording the years 341,
&c., it would seem to be treated as a
regular part of the festival.]
[2] Suidas s.v. Θεοδέκτης; Steph.
Byz. s.v. Φάσηλις.
[3] Plut. X Orat. 839 D.
[4] Aristot. Rhet. iii. 11.

century A. D. the composition of original tragic dramas for
the stage was finally discontinued in all parts of Greece, and
must therefore have been abandoned at the City Dionysia.
But the festival itself still continued to flourish; and the
reproduction of old plays may have lasted, there as elsewhere,
for one or two centuries later.[1]

§ 5.   *Comedy at the City Dionysia.*

Very little is known about the early history of the comic
contests at the City Dionysia. The date of their first institution
can only be fixed approximately. Aristotle tells us that they
were of later origin than those in tragedy.[2] This being so,
they cannot have reached back further than about 500 B. C.
On the other hand, there is an inscription which proves that
they were already in existence in 463.[3] Their establishment
must therefore be assigned to some period within the first four
decades of the century. The number of poets who were allowed
to compete differed at different epochs. In the fifth century
it was always three, as in tragedy.[4] But early in the fourth

[1] See The Tragic Drama of the
Greeks, p. 444 ff. : and (for the City
Dionysia in the second century A. D.)
cp. C. I. A. iii. 78; Philostr. Vit. Soph.
p. 549; Paus. i. 29, ii. 38, 8.

[2] Aristot. Poet. ch. v. καὶ γὰρ
χορὸν κωμῳδῶν ὀψέ ποτε ὁ ἄρχων ἔδωκεν,
ἀλλ᾽ ἐθελονταὶ ἦσαν.

[3] C. I. A. ii. 971 a (quoted, Appendix B) [B. C. 463 is the latest
possible date of the events referred
to in this part of this inscription.
Capps (Introduction of Comedy into
City Dionysia) with great probability dates them 473-472 ; he fixes
the date of the granting of a comic
chorus (whether at the Lenaea or City
Dionysia is uncertain) by the archon
at 487, when, according to Suidas s. v.
Χιωνίδης, Chionides began to exhibit;
and the date of the first choregia in
tragedy at about 502. This would
justify sufficiently Aristotle's ὀψέ ποτε.
Suidas' date for Chionides' first exhibition is not really inconsistent with
the Dorian tradition recorded by Aristotle that Epicharmus was πολλῷ
πρότερος Χιωνίδου καὶ Μάγνητος, since
the generally recorded date of the

former, B. C. 488 onwards, is most
probably a 'floruit' date, based on
the time of his first performances at
Syracuse, not the date of the beginning
of his career at Megara Hyblaea,
which may have been a good deal
earlier. Capps shows ground for
believing that Aristotle and Suidas—
the former directly, the latter perhaps
indirectly—obtained their knowledge
from the official records, and are
therefore quite reliable. At the head
of the inscription, C. I. A. ii. 971 a, are
the words πρῶ]τον κῶμοι ἦσαν τ[ῶν . . .,
which must originally have formed
part of the general heading of the
whole inscription, whose earlier
columns are lost. Capps conjectures
(with some reason) that it originally
ran ἀπὸ (name of archon) ἐφ᾽ οὗ πρῶτον
κῶμοι ἦσαν τῶν ἐν ἄστει Διονυσίων οἵδε
ἐνίκων. But κῶμοι cannot mean
'comedies', as Köhler and Wilamowitz
assumed when they dated the beginning of choregia in comedy by this
inscription. Cf. Wilhelm, Urkunden
dramatischer Aufführungen in Athen,
pp. 11 ff, 241 ff.]

[4] Args. Aristoph. Nubes, Pax, Aves.

century it was raised to five, both at the City Dionysia and
at the Lenaea, and this continued ever afterwards to be the
regulation number.[1] The increase was probably due, partly
to the growing popularity of the comic drama, partly also to the
fact that, owing to the curtailment of the chorus, comedies were
now less expensive to produce, and took less time to perform.
Each poet competed with a single play. This was the invariable
practice on the comic stage, both at the City Dionysia and at
the Lenaea. The exhibition of groups of plays, after the
manner of the tragic poets, was unknown in the history of
comedy. Still, in spite of this rule, an author was sometimes
enabled to bring out two plays at the same festival. But in
order to do so he had to take the place of two poets, and to
compete as it were against himself. The number of comedies
remained the same. Thus in 422 Aristophanes made a double
appearance, and was first with the Prelude, and second with
the Wasps. Leucon, his sole antagonist, was third with the
Ambassadors.[2] In 288 Diodorus was second with the Corpse,
and third with the Madman.[3] Such cases, however, were
apparently very rare, and must have been due either to some
exceptional dearth in the supply of dramatists, or to the marked
inferiority of the other poets who had applied for permission to
compete.

We have seen that comedy was much later than tragedy in
obtaining official recognition from the State. It also continued

[1] Arg. Aristoph. Plutus (festival uncertain); Ath. Pol. c. 56 (City Dionysia); C. I. A. ii. 972 (Lenaea), 975 (City Dionysia). [If C. I. G. xiv. 1097 is rightly restored and interpreted by Wilhelm, l. c., p. 195 ff., it would seem as if there were five competitors as early as B.C. 434 at the Dionysia; this is very difficult to reconcile with the consistent mention by the Arguments of three only.]

[2] Arg. Aristoph. Vespae. [The passage, however, is almost certainly corrupt, and most editors are now agreed that in its existing form, according to which Philonides brought out both the Προάγων and the Σφῆκες, it cannot stand; and that even if both plays can have been the work of Aristophanes, they cannot both have been produced by Philonides. For

the various emendations, vide Kanngiesser, Über die alte komische Bühne, p. 270; Petersen, Fleck. Jahrb. lxxxv. p. 662; Leo, Rhein. Mus. xxxiii. p. 404; the introductions to Rogers and van Leeuwen's editions of the Wasps; and a brief summary in Excursus I of Starkie's edition. It is very doubtful whether there is good evidence for the practice alluded to, as regards the fifth century B.C.]

[3] C. I. A. ii. 972. [The inscription leaves no room for doubt here, except for the remote possibility that there may have been two poets of the name Diodorus. Capps, Amer. Journ. Archaeol., 1900, argues almost conclusively that the inscription is to be dated 290-288, and not 353. the date given by Mr. Haigh, and generally accepted until recently.]

to grow and develop much longer.   A sure symptom of decline, both in tragedy and comedy, was the tendency to fall back upon the past, and to reproduce old plays, instead of striking out new developments.   In the case of tragedy this custom had already begun to prevail as early as the middle of the fourth century.   But comedy was still at that time in the height of its career.   A fresh direction was being given to the art, under the leadership of Menander and Philemon, by the evolution of the New Comedy, a comedy of manners and everyday life. There was no desire as yet to have recourse to the ancient poets.   In a record of comic contests for the year 288,[1] the plays exhibited are all new ones.   But when we reach the second century the custom of performing old comedies is found to have been fully established.   Numerous records of the comic performances during that period have been preserved, and in every case the five new comedies are preceded by an old one.[2] There had been occasional revivals before this, for instance in the year 340, but these seem to have been exceptional.[3] Among the plays reproduced are Menander's Ghost and Misogynist, Philemon's Phocians, and Posidippus' Outcast. It is noticeable that all these revivals were limited to the New Comedy.   There is no trace of a reproduction of plays from the Middle and the Old.   Nor is this surprising.   The comedy of early times was so local and personal in its allusions, and depended so much for its interest upon contemporary events, that it could not be expected to attract the ordinary public of a later generation.

From the records just referred to it is evident that during the second century B.C. comedy still flourished as vigorously as ever at the City Dionysia.   The festival had sometimes

---

[1] C. I. A. ii. 972. [Mr. Haigh wrote 353, but see note on previous page.]

[2] C. I. A. ii. 975 (quoted, Appendix B).   [If Capps is right in dating the fragment 975 f between B.C. 308 and 290, the practice must have been begun by that date ; see Amer. Journ. Arch., 1900, p. 89 ff., but Wilhelm, Urkunden dramat. Aufführungen in Athen, p. 68, disputes the date, and with some reason.   See also Wilhelm, ibid.; p. 149.   The practice is proved for the early part of the

second century by fragment a.]

[3] [The evidence for this is a fragment of an inscription published by Wilhelm, loc. cit., p. 27 ff., and connecting with C. I. A. ii. 971 h.   See Appendix B.   The expression used παλαιὸν δρᾶμα παρεδίδαξαν οἱ κωμῳδοί (cp. παραχορήγημα), when compared with the expressions used in 975 a, &c., shows that the performance was exceptional, and the play is not mentioned ; cp. the parallel expressions in the case of tragedy, p. 19, supra, n. 1].

to be abandoned, owing to the pressure of war and other calamities. But whenever there was a contest, five new plays were exhibited. After the second century the notices about this festival come to an end. But it is well known that in other parts of Greece original comedies continued to form a part of the programme at various festal gatherings down to the first century of the Christian era.[1] We may therefore conclude without much doubt that they were retained at the City Dionysia for an equally long period.

§ 6. *Order of Contests at the City Dionysia.*

Before leaving the subject of the City Dionysia, it may be interesting to say a few words about the performances as a whole, and the order in which they took place. The programme to be gone through was a long one. In the fifth century it consisted of five choruses of boys, five choruses of men, three comedies, and three groups of tragedies, each containing four plays. As to the arrangement of these various items there is not much information.[2] But one thing seems certain, that the three groups of tragedies must have been exhibited on three successive days. It is difficult to see what other system was possible. Two groups, consisting of eight dramas, would have been far too much for a single day.[3] Nor can we suppose that plays belonging to the same group were performed on different days. If this had been the case, the value of the tetralogic form of composition would have been almost entirely destroyed. Further than this, there is a passage in Aristophanes which seems to prove that tragedies and comedies were produced on the same day. In the Birds,[4]

[1] C. I. G. 1585, 1587, 2759; Athen. Mitth.,1894, pp.96,97; Ἐφημ.Ἀρχαιολ., 88₄, pp. 120, 124, 126; Rangabé, Antiq. Hellén., vol. ii. no. 965.

[2] The fact that inscriptions (C. I. A. 971 a–e, iv. 971 f–h) and the law of Evegorus, quoted Dem. Meid. § 10, all mention first chorus of boys, then choruses of men, then comedy, then tragedy, proves nothing, as there is nothing to show that the contests are being spoken of in order of performance, rather than in order of relative importance.

[3] Arist. Poet. ch. xxiv. suggests that an epic poem should be shorter than the old epics, and about equal to that of the tragedies offered at one hearing (τὸ πλῆθος τῶν τραγῳδιῶν τῶν εἰς μίαν ἀκρόασιν τιθεμένων). A performance of four tragedies a day would give about 6,000 lines of tragedy (including satyric drama), while the Iliad contains about 15,000 lines, and the Odyssey about 12,000.

[4] Aristoph. Av. 785 ff. οὐδέν ἐστ' ἄμεινον οὐδ' ἥδιον ἢ φῦσαι πτερά. | αὐτίχ' ὑμῶν τῶν θεατῶν εἴ τις ἦν ὑπόπτερος, |

which was brought out at the City Dionysia, the chorus remark
that it would be a delightful thing to have wings. They say
that if one of the spectators was tired with the tragic choruses,
he might fly away home, have his dinner, and fly back again
in time for the comic choruses. It appears to follow from this
that the comedies were performed after the tragedies. As there
were three comedies during the fifth century, and three groups
of tragedies, the arrangement must have been that each tragic
group was performed in the morning of three successive days,
and was followed in the afternoon by a comedy. The festival
as a whole lasted for five or six days. The first day was taken
up by the procession. Three more were taken up by the
tragedies and comedies. The remaining one or two days would
be devoted to the dithyrambs. Such was the system during
the life-time of Aeschylus and Sophocles. In the fourth century,
when the number of comedies had been raised to five, the
number of tragedies diminished, and a satyric drama and an
old tragedy placed at the head of the tragic contests, various
rearrangements would be necessary. But there is nothing
to show how they were carried out.[1]

§ 7. *The Lenaea.*

The Lenaea was a festival in honour of Dionysus Lenaeus.[2]
It was celebrated, at any rate, during the earliest times, in
a sacred enclosure called the Lenaeum.[3] Hence the feast was
also termed the 'Contest at the Lenaeum', or the 'Epilenaean
Dionysia'; and the poet who won a prize there was said to
have been 'victorious at the Lenaeum'.[4] The site of the

εἶτα πεινῶν τοῖς χοροῖσι τῶν τραγῳδῶν
ἤχθετο, | ἐκπτόμενος ἂν οὗτος ἠρίστησεν
ἐλθὼν οἴκαδε, | κᾆτ' ἂν ἐμπλησθεὶς ἐφ'
ἡμᾶς αὖθις αὖ κατέπτετο. Müller (Griech.
Bühn., p. 322) and others take ἐφ' ἡμᾶς
to mean generally 'to us in the theatre'.
But in that case there would be no
point in the sentence. There is obviously a contrast between ὑμεῖς, the
spectators, and ἡμεῖς the comic chorus.
The same contrast is emphasized in
the previous group of trochaics, vv.
753-68. Lipsius accepts the change
of τραγῳδῶν to τρυγῳδῶν ('the other
comic choruses' as opposed to ἡμεῖς,
the Birds), and infers that all the

comedies were performed in one day
by themselves (Ber. der K. S. Ges.
der Wiss. zu Leipzig, philol.-histor.
Classe, 1885, p. 417). But the change
is quite gratuitous and makes the whole
passage feeble and obscure.

[1] [See p. 69.]
[2] [Either connected with ληνός 'wine-
press' or λῆναι = βάκχαι, vid. Appendix C.]
[3] [See Appendix C for authorities
and for a discussion of the site of the
Lenaeum and its relation to the temple
of Dionysus ἐν Λίμναις.]
[4] [See Appendix C.]

Lenaeum is unfortunately a matter in much dispute, and no certain conclusion has been arrived at. Except that it was in or close to the market-place, the site of which is itself uncertain, nothing definite can be said about it.

The Lenaea was a winter gathering. It was held in the month of Gamelion, at a time corresponding to the end of January.[1] The weather was still often stormy, and the sea was not yet considered safe for voyagers.[2] Consequently there were few visitors in Athens. The festival was a domestic sort of holiday, confined to the Athenians themselves. The proceedings were simple and unpretentious, as compared with the splendid ceremonial and vast audiences at the City Dionysia. Aristophanes, in the Acharnians, which was produced at the Lenaea, says he can now abuse Athens as much as he likes, without being accused of degrading her in the eyes of foreign Greeks.[3] The entertainments at the Lenaea consisted of a procession, and of contests in tragedy and comedy.[4] The procession was not an impressive spectacle, like that at the City Dionysia, but was conducted in primitive fashion by men who drove about in wagons, and assailed the bystanders with abuse and ridicule.[5] The festival as a whole was much shorter than the City Dionysia.

The early history of tragedy at the Lenaea is veiled in obscurity. The first piece of information on the subject which we possess belongs to the latter part of the fifth century. It consists of a record of the tragic performances at the Lenaea for the years 419 and 418.[6] In both these years the number of poets who competed was two, and each of them exhibited three tragedies.[7] There is no mention of a satyric play. Again,

---

[1] Bekk. Anecd. p. 235, 6; C. I. A. ii. 834 b, col. 2, where the expenditure on the Lenaea is placed about the middle of the sixth prytany, i. e. in Gamelion. [Nilsson, Studia de Dionysiis Atticis, pp. 1-37, confirms the date here given, after a very full discussion.]

[2] Plat. Symp. 223 c; Theophrast. Char. 3.

[3] Aristoph. Ach. 501 ff.

[4] Dem. Meid. § 10 καὶ ἡ ἐπὶ Ληναίῳ πομπὴ καὶ οἱ τραγῳδοὶ καὶ οἱ κωμῳδοί. That there were no dithyrambs at the Lenaea is proved by this passage, and by C. I. A. ii. 553, which enumerates

the festivals at which dithyrambic choruses competed, viz. City Dionysia, Thargelia, Prometheia, Hephaesteia. C. I. A. ii. 1367, recording a dithyrambic victory at the Lenaea, is of comparatively late date.

[5] Suidas s.v. τὰ ἐκ τῶν ἁμαξῶν σκώμματα.

[6] C. I. A. ii. 972 (see Appendix B).

[7] Hence in Diod. Sic. xv. 74 δεδιδαχύτος Ληναίοις τραγῳδίαν (of Dionysius' victory in 367), the expression διδάσκειν τραγῳδίαν probably means 'to compete in the tragic contests', and implies nothing as to the number of plays

we are told that in 416 Agathon won a tragic victory at the
Lenaea.[1] These two notices comprise all that is known about
tragedy at this festival during the fifth century. They appear
to prove that towards the close of the century the tragic contests
had become a regular institution, though the number of poets
and plays was much smaller than at the City Dionysia. Whether
the contests were of recent origin, or reached back for many
years, cannot be ascertained. During the fourth century new
tragedies continued to be produced at the Lenaea without any
cessation. In 367 Dionysius, the tyrant of Syracuse, won the
tragic prize there. Aphareus, who flourished about 350,
exhibited there on two occasions. Theodectes, the pupil of
Aristotle, obtained one victory at the Lenaea; Astydamas, his
contemporary, obtained seven.[2] As to the arrangement of the
contest during this period, and the number of plays produced,
there is no information. But it is probable that the new
tragedies were preceded by an old one, as at the City Dionysia.
After the fourth century nothing further is known about the
connexion of the Lenaea with the tragic drama.[3] The
festival continued to be celebrated down to the second
century A.D., and possibly later.[4] But whether tragedies,
either old or new, were still included in the programme, is
quite uncertain.

Comedy was the special product of the Lenaea, and was
regarded as of more importance than tragedy. It was doubtless
at this festival that comic contests were first regularly organized.
The date is not recorded. But they must have been in existence at any rate as early as 463,[5] since at that time they were
already included in the City Dionysia. There is also another
piece of evidence. Chionides, one of the early comic poets, is
said to have begun to exhibit plays in 487. It is unlikely that
the exact year of his first appearance would have been remembered, unless it had referred to a regular public contest.
Hence we may probably assume that comic contests had been

presented. Cf. Plat. Symp. 173 A ὅτε
τῇ πρώτῃ τραγῳδίᾳ ἐνίκησεν Ἀγάθων,
' won his first tragic victory'.

[1] Athen. p. 217 A.
[2] Diod. Sic. xv. 74; Plut. X Orat.
839 D; C. I. A. ii. 977 b, c (see Appendix B).

[3] [C.I.A. ii. 1289 shows that tragedy
was still performed in B.C. 307-306.
This is the last mention of it. (Capps,
Amer. Journ. Arch., iv. p. 76.)]
[4] C. I. A. iii. 1160.
[5] See above, p. 20, note 2.

established as early as 487; and if so, they may have been
established at the Lenaea.[1] But they cannot go back beyond
about 500, since comedy in general was a later institution than
tragedy. The first definite and dated record of a comic contest
at the Lenaea is for the year 425, when Aristophanes produced
his Acharnians.[2] From this time forward the history of comedy
at the Lenaea is much the same as its history at the City
Dionysia. During the fifth century there were three competing
poets, and each brought out a single play.[3] In the fourth
century the number of poets was varied to five.[4] The practice
of exhibiting an old comedy as a prelude to the new ones was
introduced in the course of the next hundred years.[5] In the
second century original comedy was still flourishing as vigour-
ously as ever at Athens, though none of the records so far dated
with certainty refer to the Lenaea.[6] There is no evidence as to
its later course.

A few remarks may be made here on the relative importance
of the Lenaea and the City Dionysia from the theatrical point
of view. The City Dionysia was much the most splendid and
imposing gathering of the two. It was attended by larger
crowds of people, and was subjected to stricter regulations.
Aliens were not allowed to take part in the choruses; metics
were forbidden to serve as choregi.[7] No such prohibitions

---

[1] [Capps (Introduction of Comedy
into the City Dionysia, p. 25) shows
that whether the victory of Chionides
recorded by Suidas was won at the
Dionysia or Lenaea, there is no reason
for doubting the existence of contests
in 487 B. C., on the evidence of inscriptions. C. I. A. ii. 977 d as it stands
must have been preceded by another
column of names of victors, which
would almost certainly take us back
as far; and there was room for the
name of Chionides above that of
Magnes in 977 i (Dionysian victors) in
a position which would imply an early
date for his first victory; cp. also
Amer. Journ. Philol. xx. pp. 396, 397.]

[2] Arg. to Acharn.

[3] Args. to Acharn.,Equit.,Vesp.,Ran.

[4] See p. 21, note.

[5] [If Capps is right, C. I. A. ii. 975 f
proves that old comedies were acted
at the City Dionysia at a date between
308 and 290, but this date is very un-

certain; see p. 22, note. C. I. A. ii.
972, col. 1, which Capps, followed by
Wilhelm, dates soon after B. C. 290,
does not show any sign of the practice; it may have begun at the City
Dionysia, and have been afterwards
extended to the Lenaea; but it is not
easy to believe this without confirma-
tory evidence; and the difficulty is
avoided if Capps' date for 975 f is not
accepted.]

[6] [C. I. A. ii. 977 gives lists of tragic
and comic poets and actors. In the
case of the comic poets and actors,
some names (those of Agathocles and
Biottus) are known from 975 d to
belong to the middle of the second
century; but it is not certain to what
festival the part of this inscription in
which their names occur (fragm. m)
belongs.]

[7] Schol. Aristoph. Plut. 954; Plut.
Phoc. c. 30.

existed at the Lenaea. It must obviously have been a much
greater honour for a poet to produce his plays at the City
Dionysia, before the vast concourse of citizens and strangers,
than in the comparative privacy of the Lenaea. In tragedy this
was more particularly the case. The great tragic poets, after
their fame had been once established, seem to have mostly
confined themselves to the City Dionysia. Sophocles, for
instance, won eighteen victories there, and only two or six
at the Lenaea.[1] The Lenaea would be generally reserved for
inferior poets, or for youthful authors who had still their
reputation to make. Thus in 418 one of the competitors was
an obscure poet called Callistratus.[2] In 416 the victor was
Agathon, who had never yet obtained a tragic prize.[3] Foreign
poets may also have been generally confined to this festival.
It was here that Dionysius, the tyrant of Syracuse, won his
solitary success.[4] The circumstances were rather different in
regard to comedy. The leading comic poets seem to have
made little distinction between the two festivals. Aristophanes
produced his plays indifferently at both.[5] Cratinus won six
Lenaean victories as opposed to three in the City, Teleclides
five as opposed to three.[6] In explanation of this fact we should
remember that comedy was the chief feature at the Lenaea,
tragedy an appendage. Also, as the competitors in comedy
only produced one play at a time, a poet of a fertile mind would
need two contests in the year in order to exhibit what he had
written. Still, in spite of the more equal distribution of the
comic poets between the two festivals, there can be little doubt
that even in comedy a 'City victory' was always the highest
distinction.[7]

[1] See The Tragic Drama of the Greeks, p. 128, note 4.
[2] C. I. A. ii. 972, col. II.
[3] Athen. p. 217 A ; Plat. Symp. 173 A.
[4] Diod. Sic. xv. 74.
[5] The Acharnians, Equites, Vespae, and Ranae at the Lenaea ; the Nubes, Pax, and Aves, at the City Dionysia.
[6] C. I. A. ii. 977 d, i.
[7] [See Capps, Amer. Journ. Philol. xx. p. 396, who remarks that Aristophanes (Equit. 517 ff.) referring to the great poets of the past, omits Teleclides and Hermippus, who had been very successful at the Lenaea, and was especially disappointed at failing to obtain a 'City victory' with the Nubes in 423, after his two Lenaean victories. The reason suggested, however, for the omission of these two poets can hardly be correct, as Cratinus, who is mentioned, was also especially successful at the Lenaea.]

§ 8. *Rural Dionysia and Anthesteria.*

The Rural Dionysia were provincial festivals, held about the end of December[1] in the country districts of Attica. Originally they were very simple in character.[2] The villagers, holding aloft the phallus, marched in procession to the altar of Dionysus, where a goat was sacrificed, and songs and dances performed in honour of the god. Then came various country sports; and the day ended in drinking and merriment. Later on, as the people advanced in wealth and refinement, the dignity of many of these festivals was much increased. Dramatic contests began to be introduced, in imitation of those already established in Athens. Eventually, by the end of the fifth century, all the larger Attic towns appear to have provided themselves with theatres and annual theatrical exhibitions. The most important of these local gatherings was that in the Peiraeeus, which was supported by contributions of money from the state treasury, and attended by large crowds from Athens and the neighbouring districts. The procession, with which the proceedings commenced, must have been a striking spectacle. The whole body of the ephebi took part in it. Then there were contests in tragedy and comedy. The fame of these contests is shown by the fact that even distinguished poets, such as Euripides, occasionally appeared as competitors; and that foreign ambassadors, if present in Athens at the time, were invited to attend as a matter of course.[3] Among other festivals which seem to have acquired more than a local celebrity, we may mention those of Collytus where Aeschines acted the part of Oenomaus in the play of Sophocles,[4] Eleusis,[5] Salamis,[6] and Icaria, and at these proclamation was made of crowns which had

---

[1] [Nilsson (Studia de Dionysiis Atticis, p. 108) shows that the festival was probably not celebrated in all the demes at precisely the same time, though it always took place after the autumn sowing, being in fact in origin a ceremony designed to secure the fertility of the new-sown seed. Cf. Plat. Rep. v. p. 475 D ὥσπερ δὲ ἀπομεμισθωκότες τὰ ὦτα ἐπακοῦσαι πάντων χορῶν περιθέουσι τοῖς Διονυσίοις οὔτε τῶν κατὰ πόλεις οὔτε τῶν κατὰ κώμας ἀπολειπόμενοι. There must also have

been time for the troupes of actors to move from one place to another.]
[2] See Aristoph. Ach. 69, 241 ff. Also Plut. de Cup. div. p. 527 D; id. Non suav. viv. sec. Epic. p. 1098 B; Heraclitus fr. 127 Byw.
[3] Dem. Meid. § 10; C. I. A. ii. 164, 467, 468, 589, 741; iv. 2, 834 b; Aelian Var. Hist. ii. 13.
[4] Dem. de Cor. § 180; Aeschin. Timarch. § 157.
[5] C. I. A. iv. 574 b, c, g.
[6] Ibid. ii. 469, 470, 594.

been bestowed on deserving citizens.[1] At Aixone there were performances of comedies, but tragedies are not mentioned.[2] At Phlya there were dramatic performances, probably of both kinds.[3] The remains of a theatre have been found at Thoricus.[4]

The plays produced at these rustic Dionysia were mostly old ones, which had already been successful on the Athenian stage. The exhibition of new and original dramas was exceptional, and confined to a few important towns.[5] Usually the proceedings took the form of a contest between troupes of actors, who competed with plays of established reputation. Prizes were offered by the different demes, and companies were formed in Athens for the purpose of touring the country, and contending against one another. Aeschines in his youth served as tritagonist in a troupe of this kind, having been hired for a provincial tour by 'the ranters', Simylus and Socrates.[6] These constant revivals of old plays at the Rural Dionysia are a fact of some importance in the history of the Attic drama. It was in this way that the Athenian audience was familiarized with the masterpieces of the past, which might otherwise have been forgotten. In Athens itself there were not many opportunities of seeing them acted. There were only two dramatic festivals in the year, and these were mostly given up to original compositions. Yet the audience was obviously well acquainted with the older dramas. The frequent parodies and allusions in Aristophanes prove that this was the case.[7] It was at the Rural Dionysia that they acquired their knowledge. The spectators in the Athenian theatre consisted partly of natives of Athens, partly of citizens from the country districts. For the natives there were the festivals of the adjoining demes, such as Collytus and the Peiraeeus; for the provincials there were

---

[1] C. I. A. iv. 1282 b, 1285 b.

[2] Ibid. ii. 585.

[3] Isaeus viii. § 15. We also hear of such celebrations at Brauron (Ar. Pax 874, with Schol. ; Schol. in Dem. Conon. § 35 ; Suidas s. v. Βραύρων); and at Myrrhinus (C. I. A. ii. 575, 578).

[4] Dörpfeld u. Reisch, Griech. Theat. p. 109 ff.

[5] In addition to the instance at the Peiraeeus recorded above, the only known example is at Salamis, C. I. A. ii. 470 Διονυσίων τῶν ἐν Σαλαμῖνι τραγῳδῶν τ[ῷ καινῷ ἀγ]ῶνι, if the restoration be correct.

[6] Dem. de Cor. § 262.

[7] [It must be admitted that it is not easy to reconcile this with Aristot. Poet. ix, where it is said that even the well-known plays or legends are well known only to few, ἐπεὶ καὶ τὰ γνώριμα ὀλίγοις γνώριμά ἐστιν, ἀλλ' ὅμως εὐφραίνει πάντας. Aristotle may be speaking particularly of his own day, when probably few poets or plays had the celebrity enjoyed by the plays of the three great tragedians of the previous century.]

their own local gatherings. Both classes therefore would have many chances of witnessing the reproduction of celebrated plays.

The Anthesteria had so little connexion with the drama that it is unnecessary to describe the manner in which it was celebrated.[1] Regular performances of plays were apparently unknown there during the classical period. The only trace of anything theatrical is a certain contest between comic actors, which took place on the Chytri, the last day of the festival. The victor at this contest was allowed the undisputed right of acting at the forthcoming City Dionysia a month later.[2] Probably the performance consisted in the recitation of selected portions of a comedy by the different competitors. The contest had fallen into disuse during the latter part of the fourth century, but was restored by the orator Lycurgus. In much later times, during the first century A. D., we hear of 'tragic monodies' and 'comic parabases' being performed at the Anthesteria.[3] But the notice is too slight and vague to enable us to judge as to the general character of the exhibition.

§ 9. *The Judges.*

The institution of the dramatic contests at the different Attic festivals has now been described in detail. As regards the management of the competition many points still remain to be considered, viz. the selection of the judges, the mode of giving the verdict, the prizes for poets and actors, and the public records of the results. First as to the judges. The number of the judges in the comic contests was five.[4] The number in the tragic contests was probably the same, but there is no direct evidence upon the subject. The process of selection seems to have been as follows.[5] Several days before the actual

---

[1] [Vid. J. E. Harrison, Proleg. to the Study of Greek Religion, c. i.]

[2] This seems to be the meaning of Plut. x orat. 841 F εἰσήνεγκε δὲ καὶ νόμους (sc. Lycurgus), τὸν περὶ τῶν κωμῳδῶν ἀγῶνα τοῖς Χύτροις ἐπιτελεῖν ἐφάμιλλον ἐν τῷ θεάτρῳ, καὶ τὸν νικήσαντα εἰς ἄστυ καταλέγεσθαι, πρότερον οὐκ ἐξόν, ἀναλαμβάνων τὸν ἀγῶνα ἐκλελοιπότα. The contest must be the same as the ἀγῶνες Χύτρινοι quoted

from Philochorus by Schol. ad Aristoph. Ran. 220. [See Nilsson, Studia de Dionysiis Atticis, p. 57.]

[3] Philostrat. Vit. Apoll. p. 158.

[4] Schol. Aristoph. Aves, 445; Suidas s.v. ἐν πέντε κριτῶν γόνασι.

[5] There is no consecutive account in any ancient writer of the mode of selecting the judges and of voting. Our knowledge of the subject has to be pieced together from the three follow-

commencement of the festival the Council, assisted by the
choregi, elected by vote a preliminary list of judges. A certain
number of names were selected from each of the ten tribes
of Attica. The different choregi, as was natural, endeavoured
to get their own partisans upon the list. The names of the
persons chosen were then inscribed upon tablets, and the tablets
were placed in ten urns, each urn containing the names
belonging to a single tribe. The urns were then carefully

ing passages : (1) Plut. Cim. p. 483 E
ἔθεντο δ᾽ εἰς μνήμην αὐτοῦ καὶ τὴν τῶν
τραγῳδῶν κρίσιν ὀνομαστὴν γενομένην.
πρώτην γὰρ διδασκαλίαν τοῦ Σοφοκλέους
ἔτι νέου καθέντος, ᾿Αψεφίων ὁ ἄρχων,
φιλονεικίας οὔσης καὶ παρατάξεως τῶν
θεατῶν, κριτὰς μὲν οὐκ ἐκλήρωσε τοῦ
ἀγῶνος, ὡς δὲ Κίμων μετὰ τῶν συστρατή-
γων προελθὼν εἰς τὸ θέατρον ἐποιήσατο
τῷ θεῷ τὰς νενομισμένας σπονδάς), οὐκ
ἀφῆκεν αὐτοὺς ἀπελθεῖν, ἀλλ᾽ ὁρκώσας
ἠνάγκασε καθίσαι καὶ κρίναι δέκα ὄντας,
ἀπὸ φυλῆς μιᾶς ἕκαστον. (2) Isocrat.
xvii. § 43 Πυθόδωρον γὰρ τὸν σκηνίτην
καλούμενον, ὃς ὑπὲρ Πασίωνος ἅπαντα
καὶ λέγει καὶ πράττει, τίς οὐκ οἶδεν ὑμῶν
πέρυσιν ἀνοίξαντα τὰς ὑδρίας καὶ τοὺς κριτὰς
ἐξελόντα τοὺς ὑπὸ τῆς βουλῆς εἰσβλη-
θέντας ; καίτοι ὅστις μικρῶν ἕνεκα καὶ
περὶ τοῦ σώματος κινδυνεύων ταύτας
ὑπανοίγειν ἐτόλμησεν, αἳ σεσημασμέναι
μὲν ἦσαν ὑπὸ τῶν πρυτάνεων, κατεσφρα-
γισμέναι δ᾽ ὑπὸ τῶν χορηγῶν, ἐφυλάτ-
τοντο δ᾽ ὑπὸ τῶν ταμιῶν, ἔκειντο δ᾽
ἐν ἀκροπόλει, τί δεῖ θαυμάζειν εἰ κτλ.
(3) Lysias iv. § 3 ἐβουλόμην δ᾽ ἂν μὴ
ἀπολαχεῖν αὐτὸν κριτὴν Διονυσίοις, ἵν᾽
ὑμῖν φανερὸς ἐγένετο ἐμοὶ διηλλαγμένος,
κρίνας τὴν ἐμὴν φυλὴν νικᾶν. νῦν δὲ
ἔγραψε μὲν ταῦτα εἰς τὸ γραμματεῖον,
ἀπέλαχε δέ. καὶ ὅτι ἀληθῆ ταῦτα λέγω
Φιλῖνος καὶ Διοκλῆς ἴσασιν. ἀλλ᾽ οὐκ
ἔστ᾽ αὐτοῖς μαρτυρῆσαι μὴ διομοσαμένοις
περὶ τῆς αἰτίας ἧς ἐγὼ φεύγω, ἐπεὶ
σαφῶς ἔγνωτ᾽ ἂν ὅτι ἡμεῖς ἦμεν αὐτὸν οἱ
κριτὴν ἐμβαλόντες, καὶ ἡμῶν εἵνεκα
ἐκαθέζετο. The first of these passages
refers to a dramatic contest, the third to
a dithyrambic one. It is uncertain to
which the second refers. But there is
no reason to suppose (with Oehmichen,
Bühnenwesen, p. 206) that the mode of
selecting the judges was different in
the dramatic and the dithyrambic contests. That there were ten urns for
the names on the preliminary list of
judges is inferred from the plural ὑδρίαι

in Isocrates. That a second list of
judges was appointed by lot from the
larger list before the commencement of
each contest, and that this second list
consisted of ten persons, one from each
of the ten tribes, seems to be proved
by the words of Plutarch, κριτὰς μὲν
οὐκ ἐκλήρωσε τοῦ ἀγῶνος ... ἀπὸ φυλῆς
μιᾶς ἕκαστον. That there was another
selection of judges by lot after the
contest, and that the number of judges
who actually decided the result was
smaller than the number of those who
sat through the performance and voted,
is proved by two expressions in the
above passages : (1) ἔγραψε μὲν ταῦτα
εἰς τὸ γραμματεῖον, ἀπέλαχε δέ, i. e. he
voted in my favour, but his vote was
not drawn ; (2) ἡμῶν εἵνεκα ἐκαθέζετο.
Καθίζειν and καθέζεσθαι were the regular
words used of a judge at a contest. It
is clear therefore that the person here
referred to sat through the performance
as a judge, but that after the performance was over his vote was not
drawn by lot.

The above conclusions are those of
Petersen (Preisrichter der grossen Dionysien). Mommsen (Bursian's Jahres-
bericht, lii. pp. 354–8) raises some
objections. He suggests (1) that the
plural ὑδρίαι is merely rhetorical, and
that there was only one urn for all the
names, (2) that the selection of a second
list of judges before the contest is not
mentioned by Lysias, and was probably
a fiction of Plutarch's. It may be
replied that Lysias had no occasion to
refer to this preliminary ballot. He
was not giving an account of the entire
system of judging, and therefore only
mentioned the points which enforced
his argument. Still, it must be con-
fessed that the evidence about the
judges is very fragmentary, and that
Petersen's scheme depends largely on
conjecture.

locked up and sealed in the presence of the prytanes and
choregi, handed over to the custody of the treasurers, and
deposited in the Acropolis. The preliminary list of judges
was kept a secret from every one except the Council and the
choregi, in order that no improper influence might be brought
to bear upon them. The penalty for tampering with the urns
was death. It is not known from what class the nominees
were selected, or whether any property qualification was necessary. Obviously the judges in the dramatic and dithyrambic
contests had a very delicate office to perform. If their verdict
was to be of value, it was necessary that they should be men
of culture and discernment. It is most likely therefore that
there was some limitation upon the number of persons qualified
to act in this capacity.

Until the time of the festival the preliminary list of citizens
remained sealed up in urns in the Acropolis. On the first day
of the competitions the ten urns were produced in the theatre,
and placed in some prominent position. The persons whose
names were contained in the urns were all present in the
theatre. Probably they received a special summons from
the archon shortly before the festival. At the commencement
of the contest the archon proceeded to draw a single name
from all the urns in succession. The ten persons whose names
were drawn constituted the second list of judges, and each
of them represented one of the ten tribes of Attica. After
being selected by lot in the manner described, they were called
forward by the archon, and took a solemn oath that they would
give an impartial verdict.[1] They were then conducted to seats
specially appointed for them, and the contest began.[2] At the
end of the performances each of them gave his vote, writing
upon a tablet the names of the competitors in order of merit.[3]
These tablets, ten in number, were then placed in an urn, and
the archon proceeded to draw forth five of them at random.
The result of the competition was decided in accordance with

---

[1] Dem. Meid. § 17 ὀμνύουσι παρεστη-
κὼς τοῖς κριταῖς. Aristoph. Eccles. 1163
μὴ 'πιορκεῖν, ἀλλὰ κρίνειν τοὺς χοροὺς
ὀρθῶς ἀεί.

[2] Special seats were assigned to the
judges at Alexandria, and no doubt
the Attic custom was followed there :

cp. Vitruv. vii. praef. § 5 cum secretae
sedes iudicibus essent distributae.

[3] Aelian Var. Hist. ii. 13 καὶ προσ-
έταττον τοῖς κριταῖς ἄνωθεν Ἀριστοφάνην
ἀλλὰ μὴ ἄλλον γράφειν. Lysias iv. § 3
ἔγραψε μὲν ταῦτα ἐς τὸ γραμματεῖον.

these five lists, and the persons whose tablets were drawn from the urn constituted the ultimate body of five judges. It thus appears that up to the very last the judges who recorded their votes were not sure whether the votes would eventually have effect, or turn out to be so much waste paper. This uncertainty was of course a great obstacle to intimidation and bribery. After the competition was over, and the verdict announced, the names of the five judges, whose votes had decided the day, were not kept secret. It was known how each of them had voted. But the other votes, which had been recorded but not drawn from the urn, were destroyed without being made public.[1] It was naturally considered a much greater honour to win a victory by the unanimous vote of all five judges than by a mere majority of one.[2] But it is very doubtful whether any public record was kept of the number of votes by which a victory was gained.

Whether the decision of the judges was generally given with discernment, and how far it corresponded with the ultimate verdict of posterity, is a question of some interest. Both Aeschylus and Sophocles were usually successful, and this speaks highly for the taste of the judges. Aeschylus won thirteen victories; and as he produced four plays on each occasion, it follows that no less than fifty-two of his plays obtained the first prize. Whether the total number of his plays was seventy or ninety, the proportion of victories was very large.[3] Sophocles was equally fortunate. He won eighteen victories at the City Dionysia, and at least two at the Lenaea.[4] The number of his plays, as given by different authorities, varies from a hundred-and-four to a hundred-and-thirty.[5] Thus on the lowest estimate considerably more than half his plays gained the first position. Euripides was not so successful. He only won five victories, though he wrote between ninety and a hundred plays.[6] His failure was partly due to

[1] This follows from Lysias iv. § 3 ἐβουλόμην δ' ἂν μὴ ἀπολαχεῖν αὐτὸν κριτὴν Διονυσίοις, ἵν' ὑμῖν φανερὸς ἐγένετο ἐμοὶ διηλλαγμένος, κρίνας τὴν ἐμὴν φυλὴν νικᾶν. νῦν δὲ ἔγραψε μὲν ταῦτα εἰς τὸ γραμματεῖον, ἀπέλαχε δέ.

[2] Aristoph. Aves 445–7 XO. ὄμνυμ' ἐπὶ τούτοις, πᾶσι νικᾶν τοῖς κριταῖς | καὶ τοῖς θεαταῖς πᾶσιν. ΠΕ. ἔσται ταυταγί.

| XO. εἰ δὲ παραβαίην, ἐνὶ κριτῇ νικᾶν μόνον.

[3] Vita Aeschyli; Suidas s.v. Αἰσχύλος.
[4] See above, p. 28.
[5] The number of his plays is given as 123 by Suidas, and as 104 or 130 in the Life.
[6] Vita Eur.

the fact that he often had the misfortune to contend against
Sophocles. He was beaten by Sophocles in 438 and 431, and
probably on many other occasions of which no record has been
preserved.[1] But at other times he was defeated by very inferior
poets. In 415 he was beaten by Xenocles, and on another
occasion by the obscure poet Nicomachus.[2] But the most
surprising verdict of which there is any record is the defeat of
the Oedipus Tyrannus of Sophocles by Philocles, the nephew
of Aeschylus.[3] Of course the other three plays, along with
which the Oedipus Tyrannus was produced, may not have been
of equal merit. Still it must always seem an extraordinary fact,
and a proof of the fallibility of Athenian judges, that a play
which is generally allowed to be one of the greatest dramas
of antiquity should have been defeated by a third-rate poet
such as Philocles.

Verdicts of this indefensible character might be due to various
causes. The judges might be corrupt, or might be intimidated.
The spirit of emulation ran very high at these contests, and
men were often not very particular as to the means by which
they obtained the victory. There is an instance in one of the
speeches of Lysias. The defendant is showing that the prosecutor had been on very friendly terms with him a short time
before. The proof he brings forward is that when he was
choregus at the City Dionysia he got the prosecutor appointed
on the preliminary list of judges for the express purpose of
voting for his own chorus. The prosecutor was pledged to
vote for the chorus of the defendant, whether it was good or
bad. He appears to have actually done so; but unfortunately,
at the final drawing, his name was not selected, and his vote
was therefore of no value.[4] Another example of the use of
corruption is afforded by the case of Meidias, who is said to
have won the victory with his chorus of men at the City
Dionysia by bribing or intimidating the judges.[5] Similarly at
a contest of boys' choruses, Alcibiades, in spite of his outrageous
conduct in assaulting a rival choregus, won the first prize, because
some of the judges were afraid to vote against him, and others

---

[1] Args. to Eur. Alcestis and Medea.　　[3] Arg. to Soph. Oed. Tyr.
[2] Aelian Var. Hist. ii. 8 ; Suidas s.v.　　[4] Lysias iv. § 3.
Νικόμαχος.　　　　　　　　　　　　　　　　[5] Dem. Meid. §§ 5, 17, 65.

had been bought over to his side.[1] The verdict of each individual judge was made public. Hence it is easy to see that judges might often be afraid to incur the hostility of rich and unscrupulous citizens by voting against them. The above instances all refer to dithyrambic contests. No doubt in these cases, as the whole tribe was concerned with the result, party feeling ran exceptionally high. In the dramatic competitions only individuals were engaged, and there was less general excitement about the result. Yet even here corrupt influences were sometimes employed. Menander, the greatest comic poet of his time, was often defeated by Philemon owing to jobbery and intrigue similar to that described above.[2]

One not unfrequent cause then of unfair verdicts must have been corruption and intimidation. There is also another point to be kept in view in estimating the value of the decisions of the ancient judges. The plays of Sophocles and Euripides were no doubt immeasurably superior, as literary works, to the plays of Philocles, Xenocles, and Nicomachus, by which they were defeated. And yet in these and similar instances the verdicts of the judges may perhaps have had some justification. One is apt to forget the importance of the manner in which the play was presented upon the stage. Even in modern times an inferior play, if well mounted and acted, is more impressive than a good play badly performed. This must have been still more the case in the ancient drama, where the singing and dancing of the chorus formed such an important element in the success of the performance. It can easily be seen that, however well a play was written, if it was ill-mounted, and if the chorus was badly trained, this would greatly diminish the chances of success. Now the ancient poet was dependent upon his choregus for the mounting of the piece and for the selection of the chorus. If the choregus was rich and generous the play was put upon the stage in the very best manner, with all the advantages of fine dresses and a well-trained chorus. An ambitious choregus spared no pains to do his part of the work thoroughly. But if the choregus was a miserly man he tried to do the thing as cheaply as possible. He hired inferior singers, and cut down the prices of the dresses and other

---

[1] Andocid. Alcibiad. § 20 ἀλλὰ τῶν κριτῶν οἱ μὲν φοβούμενοι οἱ δὲ χαριζόμενοι νικᾶν ἔκριναν αὐτόν. [2] Aul. Gell. N. A. 17. 4.

accessories. Hence the success of a play depended nearly as much upon the choregus as upon the poet. Several examples illustrate this fact. Demosthenes, shortly before his death, is said to have dreamt that he was acting in a tragedy in a contest with Archias; but although he was highly successful, and produced a great impression upon the audience, he was defeated in the contest because of the wretched manner in which the play was mounted upon the stage.[1] Then there is the case of Nicias. He was a man of great wealth, but not of commanding talents. Accordingly he tried to win popularity by the magnificence with which he performed his duties as choregus. The result was that he obtained the victory in every competition in which he engaged.[2] Antisthenes is another instance of a rich choregus who, although he knew nothing about music and poetry, was always successful in his contests, because he spared no expense in the preparations.[3] There is an example of a different kind of choregus in one of the speeches of Isaeus. A certain Dicaeogenes regarded his office of choregus merely as a burden, and tried to perform it in the most economical manner. The consequence was that he was always unsuccessful. He engaged in a dithyrambic and tragic contest, and in a contest of pyrrhic dancers. On the first occasion he was last but one, on the other two occasions he was last.[4] Obviously the tragic poet who had the misfortune to be associated with Dicaeogenes would have a very small chance of success. The above examples show very clearly that the money of the choregus was almost as important towards securing victory as the genius of the poet.

The best critics would attend mainly to the merits of the piece in itself, apart from the splendour of the accompaniments. But the mass of the spectators would be dazzled by gorgeous dresses and effective singing and dancing. And the mass of the spectators had a great deal to do with the verdict. If they were strongly in favour of a particular poet, it was difficult for the judges to act in opposition to their wishes. The judges were liable to prosecution and imprisonment if their verdict was supposed to be unjust; and the case would be tried before

[1] Plut. Demosth. 859 D εὐημερῶν δὲ καὶ κατέχων τὸ θέατρον ἐνδείᾳ παρασκευῆς καὶ χορηγίας κρατεῖσθαι.

[2] Id. Nicias, 524 D.
[3] Xen. Memor. iii. 4. 3.
[4] Isaeus v. § 36.

a jury chosen from the very audience which they had thwarted.[1]
That the multitude on occasions made their wishes known most
emphatically, and brought great pressure to bear upon the
judges, is shown by Aelian's account of the first performance
of the Clouds. The story is a fable, but is interesting as an
illustration of the occasional behaviour of an Athenian audience.
It is said that the people were so delighted with the Clouds, that
they applauded the poet more than they had ever done before,
and insisted on the judges placing the name of Aristophanes
first upon the list.[2]   Plato laments on several occasions the
despotism exercised by the audience in the theatre. In former
times, he says, the verdict was not decided by 'hisses and
unmusical shouts, as at the present day, nor by applause
and clapping of hands', but the rabble were compelled by
the attendants to keep quiet. In another place he says that
the judge should be the instructor, not the pupil, of the
audience, and should refuse to be intimidated by their shouts
into giving a false verdict. But at the present day, he adds,
the decision rests with the multitude, and is practically decided
by public vote, and the result is the degeneracy of poets and
spectators alike.[3] These passages of Plato prove how much
the judges were under the dominion of the audience ; and
a general audience would be especially likely to be carried
away by the splendour of the choregic part of the exhibition,
by the music, dancing, and scenery. But on the whole, in
spite of occasional cases of corruption, and in spite of the
despotism of the multitude, one would be inclined to say,
arguing from results, that the judges performed their duties
well. The best proof of their fairness lies in the continued
success of Aeschylus and Sophocles.[4]

§ 10. *The Prizes.*

When the contest was ended, and the decision of the judges
had been announced, the names of the victorious poet and of
his choregus were publicly proclaimed by the herald, and they
were crowned with garlands of ivy in the presence of the

[1] Aeschin. Ctesiph. § 232.   A–C.
[2] Aelian Var. Hist. ii. 13.   [4] [Cp. Butcher, Harvard Lectures,
[3] Plato, Legg. 700 C–701 A. 659   p. 173 ff.]

spectators. The crowning probably took place upon the stage, and was performed by the archon.[1] There is no mention of any special prize for the choregus, in addition to the honour of the crown and the public proclamation of his victory. It is often stated that the successful choregus received a tripod from the State, which he was expected to erect upon a monument in some public place, with an inscription recording his victory. But this was only the case in the dithyrambic contests. In these contests each choregus appeared as the representative of one of the ten tribes of Attica; the tripod which he received belonged really to the tribe, and was intended to serve as a tribal monument.[2] The dramatic choregi had no such representative character, nor were they provided with any memorial of victory by the State.

As to the rewards for the poets, the tradition was that in the earliest times the prize for tragedy was a goat, the prize for comedy a basket of figs and a jar of wine.[3] After the dramatic contests had been regularly organized, each of the competing poets received a payment of money from the State, differing no doubt in amount, according to the place he gained in the competition.[4] Nothing is known as to the value of these prizes. But as the ancient dramatist had not only to write his plays, but also to superintend their production, the demands upon his time and energy must have been very great, and the rewards would be correspondingly large. Some idea of the scale on which the amounts were graduated, according to the place of each poet in the competition, may be gathered from the analogy of the dithyrambic contests instituted by Lycurgus in the Peiraeeus. In these contests not less than three choruses were to take part, and the prizes were to be

[1] Alciphron ii. 3; Plut. An seni &c. p. 785 B; Athen. p. 217 A στεφανοῦται Ληναίοις; Aristid. vol. ii. p. 2 (Dindf.) τοῦτον στεφανοῦν καὶ πρῶτον ἀναγορεύειν.

[2] Dem. Meid. § 5; Lysias xxi. § 2; Schol. Aeschin. Timarch. § 11; Isaeus vii. § 40; 2nd Arg. to Dem. Meid. p. 510. The monuments of Lysicrates and Thrasyllus, which were surmounted with tripods (Stuart and Revett, Antiquities of Athens, vol. i. chap. iv. pt. 3, vol. ii. p. 31), were in honour of victories with dithyrambic choruses; cp. C. I. A. ii. 1242, 1247.

[3] Marmor Par. epp. 39, 43.

[4] Schol. Aristoph. Ran. 367 τὸν μισθὸν τῶν κωμῳδῶν ἐμείωσαν; Eccles. 102 τὸν μισθὸν τῶν ποιητῶν συνέτεμε; Hesych. s.v. μισθός· τὸ ἔπαθλον τῶν κωμικῶν ... ἔμμισθοι δὲ πέντε ἦσαν. As the competitors in comedy were five, this last passage proves that *all* the competing poets received a reward of money.

ten minae for the first chorus, eight for the second, and six for the third.[1] The payment of the dramatic poets was probably arranged in a somewhat similar proportion. Towards the end of the fifth century the prizes were reduced in amount by certain commissioners of the Treasury, named Archinus and Agyrrhius. Accordingly in the Frogs of Aristophanes these two statesmen are placed in the list of bad men who are not allowed to join the chorus of the initiated.[2] The fact that all of the competing poets received a reward of money need cause no astonishment. They were the poets chosen, after selection, to provide the entertainment at the annual festivals. They were not selected until their plays had been carefully examined by the archon and found to be of the requisite merit. To be allowed to exhibit at all was a considerable distinction. There was nothing dishonourable for an ordinary poet in being placed last in the competition. No doubt for one of the great dramatic writers such a position was regarded as a disgrace. When Aristophanes was third it is spoken of as a distinct rebuff.[3] But to obtain the second place was always creditable. It is mentioned as a proof of the greatness of Sophocles that he 'obtained twenty victories and was often second'. When he was defeated for the first place by Philocles, the disgrace consisted, not in his being second, but in his being beaten by such an inferior poet.[4] At the same time to be second was never regarded as a 'victory'. The title of victor was reserved for the first poet. This is proved by the passage about Sophocles just quoted, and also by the fact that in the list of victors at the City Dionysia only the names of the first poets in the tragic and comic contests are enumerated.[5] It is clearly owing to an error that the second poet is sometimes spoken of as a victor.[6]

§ 11. Contests between actors.

In addition to the rewards just mentioned, prizes for acting were instituted in later times. At first the principal competitors

---

[1] Plut. X orat. 842 A.
[2] Aristoph. Ran. 367, and Schol. ad loc.
[3] Arg. Aristoph. Nub.
[4] Vit. Soph.; Aristid. vol. ii. p. 344 (Dindf.).

[5] C. I. A. ii. 971 a-e, iv. 971 f-h.
[6] Arg. Aristoph. Vesp. ἐνίκα πρῶτος Φιλωνίδης. Arg. Nub. ὅτε Κρατῖνος μὲν ἐνίκα Πυτίνῃ, Ἀμειψίας δὲ Κόννῳ. Arg. Pax ἐνίκησε δὲ τῷ δράματι ὁ ποιητὴς ... δεύτερος Ἀριστοφάνης Εἰρήνῃ.

in the dramatic contests were the choregus and the poet. Upon their efforts the success of a play mainly depended. It was to them that the rewards of victory were assigned, and it was their names which were recorded in the public monuments. But as time went on the profession of the actor gradually increased in importance. Eventually the success of a play came to depend principally upon the actors. The competition was extended to them. A prize was offered for the most successful actor as well as for the most successful poet. The name of the victorious actors began to be recorded in the official lists. As regards the date of these innovations the following facts may be gathered from existing monuments. At the City Dionysia contests between tragic actors were established for the first time about the year 446 B.C.[1] Contests between comic actors at this festival are not mentioned in the inscriptional records of performances during the fifth and fourth centuries.[2] In the second century they seem to have become a regular institution, but nothing certain can be ascertained concerning the intervening period.[3] At the Lenaea, contests between tragic actors can be traced back as far as 420 B.C.,[4] and contests between comic actors as far as about 289 with certainty,[5] and considerably earlier with fair probability.[6]

[1] C. I. A. iv. 971 f.

[2] C. I. A. ii. 971 a-e, iv. 971 f-h. Hence Rose's ingenious emendation of the conclusion to the first Arg. to the Pax—τὸ δὲ δρᾶμα ὑπεκρίνατο Ἀπολλόδωρος, ἡνίκα ἑρμῆν λοιοκρότης [ἐνίκα Ἕρμων ὁ ὑποκριτὴς Rose]—must be regarded as very doubtful, as the Pax was produced at the City Dionysia.

[3] C. I. A. ii. 975 a-e : see also note 6 below.

[4] C. I. A. ii. 972, col. ii. The mention of the victorious actor's name shows that the comic list in this inscription, like the tragic, must refer to the Lenaea.

[5] [C. I. A. ii. 972, col. i, as dated by Capps (Amer. Journ. Arch. xx. p. 74 ff.), who shows almost conclusive grounds for substituting this date for the date 354 hitherto generally accepted, and is followed by Wilhelm.]

[6] [Circ. B.C. 330, according to Capps, l. c. p. 84. The date depends upon the conjectural restoration of some fragments of C. I. A. ii. 977, especially fragment u. If Wilhelm's restoration of C. I. A. ii. 1289 is correct (Urkunden dramat. Aufführungen in Athen, pp. 149, 209 ff.) there is evidence of contests of comic actors in B. c. 307-6 ; and the inscription 974 c, elucidated by Wilhelm, l. c., p. 43, shows that there were contests in 313-312 ; but it is not certain to which festival this inscription belongs. Wilhelm, l. c., p. 253, even infers, from a restoration of C. I. A. ii. 977 l (i' according to his numbering), that these contests existed as early as the beginning of the fourth or end of the fifth century : the restoration is highly probable, and if it is correct, contests of comic actors can be traced back nearly as far as contests of tragic actors ; but again it is uncertain to which festival the inscription refers, and it is going too far to use the combined evidence of this inscription, and the Arg. to the Pax,

These contests were limited to the principal actors or protagonists in each play. The subordinate actors, the deuteragonist and tritagonist, had nothing to do with them. The
principal actor in a Greek play was a much more important
personage than even the 'star' in a modern company. The
actors in a Greek play were limited to three in number, and
each of them had to play several parts in succession, by means
of changes in dress and mask. Hence the protagonist had to
perform not only the principal part, but also several of the
subordinate ones. Besides this, the composition of most Greek
tragedies was designed with the express purpose of bringing
out into strong relief the character of the principal personage.
The incidents were intended to draw forth his different emotions: the subordinate characters were so many foils to him.
As a consequence, the success of a Greek play depended almost
wholly upon the protagonist. In the ordinary language of the
times he was said to 'act the play', as if the other performers
were of no importance. To take an example from existing
inscriptions, it is recorded that in 340 'Astydamas was victorious
with the Parthenopaeus, acted by Thessalus, and the Lycaon,
acted by Neoptolemus'.[1] This is the regular form of the old
records both in tragedy and comedy. Demosthenes uses
similar language. Referring to the Phoenix of Euripides, he
says that 'Theodorus and Aristodemus never acted this play'.
The form of the language is proof of the overwhelming importance of the protagonist.[2] The only other point to be noticed is
that the success of the actor was quite independent of the
success of the play in which he was performing. Thus in
one of the comic contests of the second century the prize for
acting was won by Onesimus. But the play in which he acted,
the Shipwrecked Mariner, only won the second place. The
successful comedy, the Ephesians, was acted by Sophilus.
Similarly in the tragic contests of the year 418 the prize for
acting was won by Callippides; but the poet Callistratus, whose
three tragedies he performed, was only second. The tragedies
of the successful poet were acted by Lysicrates.[3]

The actors' contests which we have hitherto been describing

as emended, to prove the existence of
contests at the City Dionysia in
421 B.C.]

[1] C. I. A. ii. 973.
[2] Dem. Fals. Leg. § 246.
[3] C. I. A. ii. 975 b, 972.

took place at the performance of new tragedies and comedies, and existed side by side with contests between poets and choregi. But there were other occasions in which actors met in competition. The reproduction of old plays generally took the form of contests between actors. These contests were of two kinds. In the first kind each actor performed a different play. At the same time the victory was decided, not by the merits of the play, but by the skill of the actor. There are several references to competitions of this sort. For instance, before the battle of Arginusae, Thrasyllus is said to have dreamt that he was engaged in a contest in the theatre at Athens, and that he and his fellow generals were acting the Phoenissae of Euripides, while their opponents were acting the Supplices.[1] The most frequent occasion for reproductions of old plays in this manner must have been afforded by the Rúral Dionysia in the different townships of Attica. The dramatic performances at these festivals were mostly confined, as we have already seen, to the exhibition of old tragedies and comedies. The town offered a prize for acting, and the leading Athenian actors came down with their companies and took part in the contest, each performing a different play. But at the great Athenian festivals, the Lenaea and the City Dionysia, there are no traces of such competitions to be found in the records. They may have been introduced in late times; but during the more flourishing period of the drama, when the older poets were reproduced at these festivals, one play seems to have been considered sufficient.[2]

The second kind of competition with old plays differed from the first in this respect, that each actor performed the same play. For instance, Licymnius, the tragic actor, is said to have defeated Critias and Hippasus in the Propompi of Aeschylus. Andronicus, another tragic actor, was successful in the Epigoni on one occasion; and it is implied that his opponents acted the same play.[3] In contests of this description it is not probable

---

[1] Diod. Sic. xiii. 97.
[2] For the City Dionysia see above, pp. 18 and 24. For the Lenaea there is no evidence, but the practice was probably much the same. See p. 26.
[3] Alciphron iii. 48 κακὸς κακῶς ἀπόλοιτο καὶ ἄφωνος εἴη Λικύμνιος ὁ τῆς

τραγῳδίας ὑποκριτής. ὡς γὰρ ἐνίκα τοὺς ἀντιτέχνους Κριτίαν τὸν Κλεωναῖον καὶ Ἵππασον τὸν Ἀμβρακιώτην τοὺς Αἰσχύλου Προπομποὺς κ.τ.λ. Athen. p. 584 D Ἀνδρονίκου δὲ τοῦ τραγῳδοῦ ἀπ' ἀγῶνός τινος, ἐν ᾧ τοὺς Ἐπιγόνους εὐημερήκει, πίνειν μέλλοντος παρ' αὐτῇ κτλ.

that the whole play was acted by each of the competitors, but only special portions of it. The contest would be useful for purposes of selection. When the custom arose of prefacing the performances of new tragedies and new comedies by the reproduction of an ancient drama, it would be necessary for the state to choose the actor who was to manage the reproduction. Very probably the selection was made by a competition of the kind we are describing, in which a portion of an old play was performed by each of the candidates. The contests between comic actors at the Chytri have already been referred to.[1] Most likely they were of the same description.

§ 12. *Records of dramatic contests.*

It is difficult in modern times to realize fully the keenness of the interest with which the various dramatic contests were regarded by the old Athenians, and the value which was attached to victories obtained in them. The greatest statesman was proud to be successful with a chorus in tragedy or comedy. It was a proof both of his taste and of his munificence. The tragic poet held as high a place in the popular estimation as the orator or the general. Victorious competitors were not content with the mere temporary glory they obtained. Every care was taken to perpetuate the memory of their success in a permanent form. Elaborate records were also erected by the state. A description of the various kinds of memorials, of which fragments have been preserved, will be a convincing proof of the enthusiasm with which the drama was regarded in ancient times.

First, as to the private monuments. These were erected by the victorious choregi, and appear to have differed widely in style and costliness, according to the wealth and taste of the individuals. Thus the mean man in Theophrastus, when he had been successful with a tragic chorus, was content to erect a mere wooden scroll in commemoration of his victory.[2] Another cheap device was to dedicate some article of theatrical costume, such as an actor's mask.[3] But the ordinary form of

---

[1] See above, p. 31.
[2] Theophrast. Char. 22 ταινία ξυλίνη.
[3] Lysias xxi. § 4 κωμῳδοῖς χορηγῶν

Κηφισοδώρῳ ἐνίκων, καὶ ἀνήλωσα σὺν τῇ τῆς σκευῆς ἀναθέσει ἐκκαίδεκα μνᾶς.

memorial, in the case of the dramatic contests, consisted of a marble tablet, containing a painting or sculptured relief.[1] At first, no doubt, these tablets were of small size and simple workmanship; but in course of time, with the growth of luxurious habits, they began to assume a more elaborate form. For instance, the monument set up by Xenocles in 306 was about fourteen feet high, the tablet being enclosed in a magnificent architectural structure, with columns and entablature.[2] The paintings and reliefs upon the tablets were no less variable. Some of them depicted masks, or crowns of victory, or similar emblems; others contained representations of Dionysus or Silenus. Sometimes groups of figures were portrayed, such as a chorus of singers with the choregus in the centre. Sometimes a scene was inserted from the tragedy or comedy in which the victory had been obtained.[3] But though the tablets differed in magnificence, the inscriptions upon them were generally simple and concise, and consisted merely of the names of the poet and choregus, and of the archon for the year, with the addition in later times of the name of the actor. The record inscribed by Themistocles in honour of his tragic victory in 476 ran as follows:[4]—

> Choregus, Themistocles of Phrearria:
> Poet, Phrynichus:
> Archon, Adeimantus.

As regards public memorials, we can hardly doubt that from the earliest period records of the different contests were preserved in the official archives. But in addition to these documentary registers, elaborate monuments of stone were erected by the state in or near to the theatre of Dionysus. Considerable fragments of these monuments have been discovered by recent excavations. They may be divided into three classes. The first class consisted of records of all the contests at some one particular festival. Such records were of the most general description, and contained merely a list of victors' names. Fragments have been discovered of the records of the contests

---

[1] Plut. Themist. 114 C πίνακα τῆς νίκης ἀνέθηκε. Aristot. Pol. viii. 6 ἐκ τοῦ πίνακος ὃν ἀνέθηκε Θράσιππος.
[2] C. I. A. ii. 1289; Bull. Corr. Hell. iii. pl. 5.

[3] Reisch, Griechische Weihgeschenke, p. 118 ff.
[4] Plut. Themist. 114 C. Cp. C. I. A. ii. 1280, 1285 (a metrical inscription), 1289, iv. 1280 b, 1282 b, 1285 b, &c.

at the City Dionysia during the fifth and fourth centuries.[1] The style is the same throughout. The boys' choruses are mentioned first, then the choruses of men, then comedy, and tragedy last of all. In the dithyrambic contests the names of the victorious tribe and choregus are given; in the dramatic contests the names of the victorious choregus and poet. The only difference between the earlier and later portions of the record is that towards the middle of the fifth century the name of the tragic actor begins to be appended.

The second class of public monuments was devoted to the record of one particular kind of contest at a particular festival. Records are extant of tragedy at the Lenaea in the fifth century, and at the City Dionysia in the fourth; also of comedy at the Lenaea in the third century, and at the City Dionysia in the second.[2] The names of all the competing poets are given, together with the titles of the plays they produced, and the names of the actors who performed them. At the end comes the name of the actor who won the prize for acting. If there was any reproduction of an old tragedy or comedy, the name of the play is given, together with the name of the actor.

The third class of monument consisted of lists of tragic and comic actors, and tragic and comic poets, with numerals after each of them, denoting the number of victories they had won in the course of their career. There were separate lists for the City Dionysia and the Lenaea. There were consequently eight lists in all, four for each festival. Numerous fragments have been discovered, but unfortunately the most interesting parts are not always the best preserved.[3] Still, they throw light upon several small points in connexion with the drama. One fragment confirms the statement of Diodorus, that the number of Sophocles' victories was eighteen. At any rate that is proved to have been the number of his victories at the City Dionysia. Cratinus is represented as having won three victories at the City Dionysia and six at the Lenaea. This tallies exactly with the account of Suidas, who gives the total number of his victories as nine.[4]

---

[1] C. I. A. ii. 971 a-e, iv. 971 f-h. See Appendix B.

[2] C. I. A. ii. 972, 973, 975. See Appendix B.

[3] C. I. A. ii. 977, iv. 977.

[4] Diod. Sic. xiii. 103; Suidas s.v. Κρατῖνος.

None of the public monuments, of which fragments have been recovered, appear to have been erected before the third century, or, at the earliest, the latter part of the fourth century B.C. But there can be no doubt that similar monuments existed at a much earlier period. These earlier records, together with the choregic inscriptions and the documents in the public archives, must have been the source from which Aristotle derived the information contained in his two books about the contests at the Dionysia. Of these two books the first was called ' Dionysiac Victories', and though it is never quoted by ancient writers, it probably contained the same sort of information as the first and third classes of public monuments. The other book was called the ' Didascaliae', and is very frequently referred to and quoted from.[1] It contained lists of the poets who competed at each festival, together with the names of the plays they produced. It was therefore similar to the second class of monuments. 'Didascalia,' in its dramatic sense, meant originally the teaching and training of a chorus. It then came to denote the play or group of plays produced by a poet at a single festival.[2] Lastly, it was used to denote a record concerning the production of a play or group of plays. It is in this sense that Aristotle used it as the title of his book. The work would not be a mere compilation from existing records and monuments. It must have required some care and research. For instance, when a poet had his plays brought out vicariously, we cannot doubt that the name of the nominal author was entered in the public records, and not that of the real poet. Aristophanes usually brought out his plays in this manner. Then again a poet's plays were sometimes brought out after his death in the name of his son. In these and similar cases it would be the duty of the compiler of a work like Aristotle's to correct the mistakes of the public records, and to substitute where necessary the name of the real author of the play. Corrections of this kind were no doubt made by Aristotle and his successors. The Didascaliae of Aristotle is the ultimate source of our information as to the production and the success of the plays of the great Athenian dramatists. Callimachus,

---

[1] Diog. Laërt. v. 1. 26. A complete list of the quotations from Aristotle's Διδασκαλίαι is given in Bekker's Aristotle, vol. v, p. 1572.
[2] See pp. 13 (note 2), 61.

the grammarian of Alexandria, wrote a book of a similar kind, based upon Aristotle's work.[1] It was from Callimachus that Aristophanes, the grammarian, derived the information which he incorporated in his Arguments to the Greek plays.[2] The existing Arguments are mainly fragments of the work of Aristophanes.[3] Thus the process of derivation from Aristotle can be traced step by step. The list of victors at the City Dionysia for the year 458, which was dug up at Athens a few years ago, tallies in every particular with the facts recorded in the Argument to the Agamemnon of Aeschylus.[4]

[1] Suidas s.v. Καλλίμαχος ; Schol. Aristoph. Nub. 552.

[2] Etym. Mag. s.v. πίναξ.

[3] Trendelenburg, Gramm. Graec. de Arte Tragica Iudiciorum Reliquiae, p. 3 foll.

[4] C. I. A. iv. 971 f. See above, p. 20, note 3. [It is not at all improbable that the extant inscriptions which have been described in this section were to a great extent based on the work of Aristotle himself, this work being itself based on earlier records now lost. It would only be natural that the theatre officials would take advantage of so important a compilation as the Διδασκαλίαι and Νίκαι Διονυσιακαί of Aristotle, and might well have extracts from it engraved on stone in the theatre. The fact that the last record in C. I. A. ii. 971 belongs to the year 328 B.C. has also led some writers to conjecture that this whole inscription represents the work of Aristotle. This view is confirmed by the fact that Aristotle, with Callisthenes, prepared a record of Pythian victors for the temple of Delphi, which was engraved on stone at the public cost, B.C. 331. (Homolle, Bull. de Corr. Hell. xxii. 261, 631 ; Bourguet, ibid. xxiv. 504 ; Dittenberger, Sylloge Inscr. Gr. 915.) Cp. Reisch in Pauly-Wissowa, Real-Encycl., Art. Didaskaliai ; Wilhelm, Urkunden dramatischer Aufführungen in Athen, pp. 13–15. The latter work gives a very complete account of the extant inscriptions.]

CHAPTER II

THE PREPARATION FOR THE CONTESTS

§ 1. *The Poets.*

DRAMATIC performances at Athens, as was pointed out, were entirely in the hands of the state. They were sacred institutions in honour of Dionysus, and their regulation was as much the duty of the government as the management of any other religious ceremonial. Of the two festivals to which they were confined, the City Dionysia was superintended by the archon eponymus, the Lenaea by the archon basileus. These two archons were therefore responsible for the dramatic exhibitions at their respective festivals.[1] They had not much to do with the details of preparation. Their function was rather one of general supervision. They had to select the proper persons, set them to work, and see that they performed their work efficiently. At Athens this was a complex matter, and required a good deal of arrangement. The requisite number of poets had to be chosen and their plays approved. Choregi had to be appointed to pay the expenses of the different choruses. Actors had then to be engaged and distributed among the poets. It was the duty of the archon to make all these selections, and to bring poets, actors, and choregi together. In the present chapter we shall explain in detail the manner in which these various arrangements were carried out.

When a poet wished to compete at one of the festivals, he

---

[1] Ath. Pol. cc. 56, 57. The archons superintended the various contests themselves, but were assisted by curators in the organization of the processions. These ἐπιμεληταὶ τῆς πομπῆς were ten in number at the City Dionysia. Until 352 they were elected by the people from the general mass of the citizens, and paid the expenses of the procession themselves. After 352 they were chosen by lot, one from each tribe, and received 100 minae from the state to cover expenses. In the third century the system of election was reintroduced. The curators at the Lenaea were also curators of the Eleusinian mysteries (ἐπιμεληταὶ τῶν μυστηρίων), four in number, and elected by the state, two from the people generally, one each from the Κήρυκες and Εὐμολπίδαι. See Sandys' notes ad loc.

sent in his application to the archon, together with copies of the
plays he proposed to exhibit. As it was a great honour to be
allowed to take part in the competitions, there was usually no
lack of applicants. The archon then read through the plays
submitted to him, and proceeded to select, from among the
various candidates, the number of poets required by the particular festival. If it was tragedy at the City Dionysia which he
was providing for, he would choose three poets ; if it was tragedy
at the Lenaea, he would choose two. In comedy the number of
poets was originally three, and in later times five. When the
archon accepted a poet's application, and placed him on the
official list of competitors, he was said to 'grant him a chorus ',
because the next step was to provide him with a choregus, who
paid the expenses of his chorus. In the same way, when a poet
applied for permission to exhibit, he was said to 'ask for
a chorus'.[1] The task imposed upon the archon of deciding
between the rival claims of the dramatic poets must have been
a very difficult and a very invidious one. Even if he acted with
the best intentions, he could hardly avoid giving offence. Sometimes there were manifest cases of jobbery and favouritism. One
archon refused a chorus to the great comic poet Cratinus ;
another gave a chorus to a certain Cleomachus in preference to
Sophocles.[2] But it is unlikely that instances of this kind were
very common. Probably in most years the poets of the highest
reputation were chosen. In a city like Athens, where the
magistrates were entirely at the mercy of the people, it would
be impossible for them to disregard popular opinion in a very
flagrant manner.

Some of the old scholiasts say that a poet was not allowed to
exhibit till he had reached the age of thirty or forty.[3] But this
is clearly a mistake. The only limit of age in any of these
Bacchic contests was that which prohibited a man under forty
from serving as choregus to a chorus of boys. As for the
dramatic poets, they were free to compete as soon as they had
reached twenty, passed their dokimasia, and been enrolled as
full citizens. Most of the great poets seem to have begun their
career at a very early age. Aeschylus was only twenty-five

[1] Suidas s. v. χορὸν δίδωμι ; Athen.
p. 638 F ; Cratinus fr. 15 (Kock); cf.
Aristot. Poet. c. v, Ath. Pol. l. c.

[2] Cratinus l. c.
[3] Schol. Aristoph. Nub. 510, 530.

when he made his first appearance. Sophocles began to exhibit at twenty-eight, Euripides at twenty-six,[1] while Aristophanes must have been even younger when he brought out the Knights.[2]

It was not uncommon at Athens for a poet to have his plays produced by a friend, instead of coming forward in his own person. Various motives might lead him to do so. A young poet, feeling diffident about his powers, might wish to make his first experiments anonymously. This was apparently the reason why the first three plays of Aristophanes—the Banqueters, Babylonians, and Acharnians—were brought out by Callistratus.[3] It was not till 424, when the Knights was exhibited, that Aristophanes applied for a chorus in his own name. In the parabasis to this play he explains that the reasons which made him keep in the background at first were caution and timidity, and a feeling that one ought to proceed warily in the business of comic writing, and advance by slow degrees, just as a steersman begins by serving as a rower.[4] Sometimes, again, a poet wrote a play for his son, and allowed him to bring it out and get the credit of the authorship, so as to give him a successful start in his dramatic career. Aristophanes for this reason entrusted his two last comedies to his son Araros; and Sophocles is said to have entrusted his son Iophon with tragedies.[5] It occasionally happened also that a wealthy citizen, with literary ambitions, bought a play from a clever but needy author and exhibited it as his own. Plato, the poet of the Old Comedy, is said to have made an income by sales of this kind.[6] Probably, however, the commonest reason for vicarious production was the mere desire to escape trouble and responsibility. The older poets had superintended in person everything connected with the bringing out of a play. In later times, as play-writing became more and more a purely literary pursuit, it was natural

---

[1] Suidas s. v. Αἰσχύλος; Marm. Par. ep. 56; Vita I Eurip.

[2] Schol. Aristoph. Ran. 504; Arg. Aristoph. Equit.; cf. Suidas s. v. Εὔπολις. [The remarkable didascalic inscription (974 c) printed by Wilhelm, Urkunden dramat. Aufführungen in Athen, p. 45, and reproduced in Appendix B, notices of a certain Ameinias (probably), who won the third place with his play, that ἔφηβος ὢν ἐνεμήθη. Wilhelm shows that this

use of νέμειν and its cognates, to signify permission to compete, was a technical one, and quotes conclusive parallels.]

[3] Schol. Aristoph. Nub. 531; Anon. de Com. (Kaibel Com. Fr. p.8); Suidas s. v. Σαμίων ὁ δῆμος; Arg. Aristoph. Acharn.

[4] Aristoph. Equit. 512-44; cf. Nub. 528-31.

[5] Arg. Aristoph. Plutus; Schol. Aristoph. Ran. 73.

[6] Suidas s. v. Ἀρκάδας μιμούμενοι.

for authors occasionally to transfer the theatrical part of the business to other shoulders. They hired stage-managers to look after the rehearsals, and they got theatrical friends to make the necessary arrangements with the archon. Aristophanes, in the middle of his career, entrusted many of his comedies to Philonides and Callistratus.[1] The Autolycus of Eupolis was brought out by Demostratus; Philippus, son of Aristophanes, is said to have competed frequently with plays of Eubulus.[2] Aphareus, the rhetorician and tragic poet of the fourth century, though he exhibited in eight contests, never brought out a play in his own name.[3] In these and similar cases it is difficult to suggest any other motive than love of ease.

As regards the relationship between the poet and the friend who produced his plays for him, there are one or two points which deserve notice. It was the nominal poet who applied to the archon, received the chorus, and undertook the whole responsibility. At the same time the name of the real poet was often quite well known. Of course, if secrecy was an object, this would not be so. When a father wrote plays for his son, or a needy author sold plays to a literary aspirant, the real authorship must have been concealed, at any rate for a time. But in other cases it seems to have been an open secret from the first. Aristophanes, in the Knights, says that many people had been asking him why he gave his plays to Callistratus instead of applying for a chorus in person.[4] In the Wasps, which is generally supposed not to have been brought out by himself, he refers to the author of the play in terms only applicable to himself.[5] Here, then, there was no attempt at concealment. At the same time the nominal author must have been the one officially recognized by the state. It must have been he who received the rewards of victory, and whose name was stated as victor in the public records. It is true that in the records which have been preserved the practice is to give the name of the real author, and to add as a note that the play was actually brought out by such and such a person. But this can hardly have been the original form of the entry. It must be due to the corrections of the grammarians who collected and edited the notices.

[1] Args. Aristoph. Av., Lysist., Vesp., Ran.
[2] Athen. p. 216 D; Vit. Aristoph.
[3] Plut. X orat. 839 D.
[4] Aristoph. Equit. 512, 513.
[5] Id. Vesp. 1016-22.

§ 2. *The Choregi.*

The next point to consider is the nomination of the choregi, who provided the choruses. In the case of the dithyrambic contests, which were tribal in character, the choregi were appointed by the separate tribes, the appointment taking place one month after the last festival.[1] But as the drama had no connexion with the tribal system, the dramatic choregi were taken indiscriminately from the general mass of citizens. They were nominated by the archon in charge of each festival immediately after his accession to office in July.[2] This, at any rate, was the original system. But about the middle of the fourth century a change was made in the case of the comic choregi. Their appointment was transferred from the archon to the tribes.[3] Ten choregi were required every year, and each tribe had to supply one. By this innovation the election of the comic choregi was assimilated to that of the dithyrambic. But the change was a mere piece of administrative detail, and had no further significance. The comic contests remained, as before, independent of the tribal arrangement, and the name of the tribe never appears in the records of the contests.[4]

The choregia was one of the public burdens which had to be undertaken in turn by the richer citizens. Any man of sufficient wealth might be called upon after he had reached the age of twenty, though no one under the age of forty could be choregus to a boys' chorus.[5] The order was fixed by law. But a citizen of unusual generosity and ambition might volunteer for the office out of his proper turn. The defendant in one of the speeches of Lysias tries to favourably impress the jury by explaining to them that he has supplied eight choruses in nine years, in addition to such burdens as the war-tax and the trierarchy.[6] Sometimes, however, there was a difficulty in finding, even among those who were liable, a sufficient number of rich men to fill the office. This was especially the case towards the end of the Peloponnesian War, when there had been long and heavy drains

[1] Arg. ii to Dem. Meid.
[2] Athen. Pol. c. 56.
[3] Ibid.
[4] C. I. A. ii. 971 d, iv. 971 h.

[5] Lysias xxi. §§ 1–5 ; Aeschin. Timarch. §§ 11, 12 ; Harpocrat. s. v. ὅτι νόμος.
[6] Lysias l. c.

upon the resources of the state.[1]   Accordingly in 406 it was found necessary to lighten the burden.   A law was passed that each dramatic chorus at the City Dionysia should be provided by two choregi instead of one, thus diminishing the cost to individuals by half.   This law was only intended as a temporary expedient.   It was not applied to the Lenaea[2]; and even at the City Dionysia it was repealed in the course of the next fifty years.[3]

The institution of the choregia lasted till nearly the end of the fourth century.[4]   But about the year 318 it was abolished, and a new system adopted in its place.[5]   The providing of the choruses was now undertaken by the state, and an officer called the Agonothetes was elected annually to carry out the arrangements.   This official had the general management of the musical and dramatic contests, and had to perform all the duties which had previously fallen to the choregi, and even to erect the tripods and other memorials of victory.[6]   Though assisted by contributions from the state, he had to bear the greater part of the expenses himself, and was always chosen on account of his

[1] In the time of Demosthenes the tribe Pandionis was for three years unable to supply a dithyrambic choregus.   Dem. Meid. § 13.

[2] Schol. Aristoph. Ran. 406, who suggests that the system was also extended to the Lenaea.   But this is disproved by Lysias xxi. § 4, where the defendant says he was choregus (not synchoregus) to a comic chorus in B.C. 402.   The synchoregia cannot, therefore, have been applied to both festivals.

[3] C. I. A. ii. 971 c (tragic choregus at City Dionysia for 387) [but the interpretation of this fragment is very difficult].   Tragic synchoregi occur twice in inscriptions at the beginning of the fourth century (C. I. A. ii. 1280, iv. 1280 b); and are mentioned by Isaeus v. § 36 (B.C. 389) and Lysias xix. § 29 (B.C. 394–389); but as the festival is not mentioned by either author, it may have been the Lenaea, and so no inference can be drawn as to the discontinuance of the synchoregia. In C. I. A. iv. 971 h we find a comic choregus in 329; in C. I. A. iv. 1280 b (beginning of fourth century) and ii.

1280 b (middle of fourth century) we find comic synchoregi, but as the latter inscription was found at a distance from Athens, it may refer to the Rural Dionysia, at which joint choregi were sometimes appointed; e. g. C. I. A. iv. 1282 b mentions three tragic choregi in partnership at Icaria.

[4] The statement of Schol. Aristoph. Ran. 406, that soon after the institution of synchoregi the choregia as a whole was abolished by Cinesias is disproved by Ath. Pol. c. 56, which shows that choregi were a regular institution in the latter half of the fourth century.   Capps (Am. J. Arch. 1895, p. 316) conjectures that the scholiast's error arose from his misunderstanding of the epithet χοροκτόνος, applied to Cinesias as a bad poet, not as a legislator against choruses.

[5] There were still choregi in 319 (C. I. A. ii. 1246, 1247).   But Nicanor was appointed Agonothetes immediately after the death of Antipater (Plut. Phoc. 31), who died in 319.

[6] C. I. A. ii. 302, 307, 314, 331, 379.

wealth.[1] At this time the cost of the tragic and comic choruses would not be very great, as the choral part of the drama had begun to disappear. But there were other expenses connected with the dramatic choregia, all of which he would have to meet. The change of system was no doubt rendered necessary by the circumstances of the time and the dearth of rich citizens. But it must have robbed the festivals of much of their interest. In former days the keenness of the rivalry between the individual choregi had contributed largely to the vitality of the contests. All this source of excitement was now lost by the substitution of a single all-powerful official. The name of the Agonothetes occurs frequently in inscriptions during the third century. After this date there is no mention of any further changes till about the first century A. D., when there seems to have been a sort of antiquarian revival, and an attempt was made to reintroduce the old choregi.[2] But the Agonothetes was still retained as general manager of the competitions.

When the archon had selected the poets who were to exhibit, and had made up his list of the choregi who were to supply the choruses, the next thing necessary was to arrange choregi and poets together in pairs. Each choregus had one poet assigned to him, for whose chorus (or choruses) he was responsible. The process of pairing was a matter of great importance to the competitors. A choregus who obtained an inferior poet would be severely handicapped in the contest; and a poet who was joined to a mean and parsimonious choregus would be equally unfortunate. If the arrangement had been left to the magistrate, it would have given numerous opportunities for corruption and favouritism. The Athenians, as usual, evaded this difficulty by the use of the lot.

There is, indeed, no definite information as to the manner in which the assignment was carried out in the case of tragic and comic choruses. But in the case of the dithyrambic choruses there are full accounts of the manner in which similar arrangements were made; and it will not be difficult, from the analogy

---

[1] C. I. A. ii. 314, καὶ εἰς ταῦτα πάντα ἐκ τῶν ἰδίων ἀναλώσας πολλὰ χρήματα. This phrase, however, does not imply that he paid the whole of the expenses; and the formula ὁ δῆμος ἐχορήγει, constantly found in agonothetic inscriptions, seems to show that the people bore a part [e.g. C. I. A. ii. 1289, quoted App. B].

[2] C. I. A. iii. 78 (Agonothetes and choregus together); ibid. 79, 83, 84 (choregi alone); ibid. 1, 10, 121, 457, 613, 721, 810, 1091 (Agonothetes alone).

of these proceedings, to form a fairly clear conception of the proceedings in regard to tragedy and comedy. Some time before the festival a meeting of the ecclesia was held, at which the distribution took place under the superintendence of the archon. The proceedings were quite public, and any Athenian citizen who wished could be present. The choregi first drew lots for order of choice, and then each chose his own flute-player. The choregus who had obtained the privilege of choosing first selected the flute-player whom he considered to be the best of the ten. So they went on till all the flute-players were chosen. The scene was a lively one. The success of the choregus, and in consequence the success of his tribe, depended to a certain extent upon his luck in getting a good or bad flute-player. Hence the whole process was followed with the greatest interest by the crowds of spectators present. As each lot was drawn, the result was greeted with expressions of triumph or disappointment by the partisans of the different choregi.[1] The above information is derived from the account given by Demosthenes, in the speech against Meidias, of the preliminary arrangements for the dithyrambic contests. Nothing is there said about the choice or assignation of the poets. Probably in this contest only old dithyrambs were reproduced, and there were no poets to be assigned. That such was often the case is proved by inscriptions.[2] But when the contest was with original dithyrambs, and poets were required, they seem to have been allotted to the choregi in much the same manner as the flute-players. The defendant in one of the speeches of Antiphon says that, when he was choregus to a chorus of boys at the Thargelia, the poet Pantacles was assigned to him by lot[3].

[1] Demosth. Meid. §§ 13, 14; 2nd Arg. to Meidias, p. 510.

[2] C. I. A. ii. 1246 Νικίας Νικοδήμου Ξυπεταίων ἀνέθηκε νικήσας χορηγῶν Κεκροπίδι παίδων· Πανταλέων Σικυώνιος ηὔλει· ᾆσμα Ἐλπήνωρ Τιμοθέου· Νέαιχμος ἦρχεν. In this case the dithyramb performed was the Elpenor of the celebrated poet Timotheus. When old dithyrambs were performed, and no poet was necessary, a professional trainer was hired to look after the chorus. Such was the διδάσκαλος mentioned by Demosthenes (Meid. § 17).

[3] Antiphon, orat. vi. § 11 ἐπειδὴ χορηγὸς κατεστάθην εἰς Θαργήλια καὶ ἔλαχον Παντακλέα διδάσκαλον κτλ. Pantacles was a poet, and not a mere trainer of choruses, like the διδάσκαλος hired by Demosthenes. This is proved by a passage in Etym. Mag. v. διδάσκαλος· ἰδίως διδασκάλους λέγουσιν οἱ Ἀττικοὶ τοὺς ποιητὰς τῶν διθυράμβων ἢ τῶν κωμῳδιῶν ἢ τῶν τραγῳδιῶν. Ἀντίφων ἐν τῷ περὶ τοῦ χορευτοῦ· ἔλαχόν, φησι, Παντακλέα διδάσκαλον· ὅτι γὰρ ὁ Παντακλῆς ποιητής, δεδήλωκεν Ἀριστοτέλης ἐν ταῖς Διδασκαλίαις. When there was a poet, a professional trainer was not usually required. The poet undertook the training of the chorus.

§ 3. *Selection of the Actors.*

Poets and choregi having been associated together in pairs, there still remained the selection and appointment of the actors. The manner in which they were appointed differed very considerably at different periods. To take the case of tragic actors first. Before the time of Aeschylus, when tragedy was more a lyrical than a dramatic performance, consisting of long choral odes interspersed with recitatives, actors did not exist as a separate class. Only one actor was required in each play, and his part was taken by the poet.[1] But when Aeschylus increased the number of actors to two, and converted tragedy from a lyrical into a dramatic form of art, the poets ceased to perform in their own plays, and the actor's profession came into existence. For the next fifty years or so it does not appear that the state took any part in the selection of the actors. It left the matter in the hands of the poets. Particular actors are found to have been permanently connected with particular poets. Aeschylus is said to have first employed Cleander as his actor, and to have afterwards associated a second actor with him in the person of Mynniscus.[2] Tlepolemus acted continuously for Sophocles.[3] It is stated, on the authority of Ister, that Sophocles was accustomed to write his plays with a view to the capacities of his actors.[4] This story, whether true or not, shows that he chose his actors himself, at any rate during the earlier part of his career. But as the actors grew in importance, their selection was no longer left to the choice of individual poets, but was undertaken by the state. Henceforth we cease to hear of particular poets and actors being permanently associated together. The statement of Thomas Magister, that Cephisophon was the actor of Euripides, appears to be a mere conjecture, as Cephisophon is nowhere else described in that way.[5] The change in the method of selection was probably introduced about the middle of the fifth century, when the contests in acting were established, and the position of the actors received its first official recognition. Under the new arrangement, three protagonists were first of all selected by

[1] Aristot. Rhet. iii. 1.
[2] Vita Aesch.
[3] Schol. Aristoph. Nub. 1267.
[4] Vita Soph.   [5] Vita Eur.

the archon. There is no information as to the way in which
they were selected. They may have been chosen by means of
a small competition, similar to that between comic actors at the
Chytri. The subordinate actors were apparently not chosen
by the state, but each protagonist was allowed to provide his
own deuteragonist and tritagonist.[1] When the three leading
actors had been chosen they were assigned to the three competing tragic poets by lot. Probably the system was the same
as in the assignation of the flute-players to the dithyrambic
choruses. The poets would first draw lots for order of choice,
and then each poet would choose his actor. The actor performed all the tragedies of the poet to whom he was allotted.
Thus in 418 the three tragedies of Callistratus were acted by
Callippides; the three tragedies of his rival were acted by
Lysicrates.[2] The actor who won the prize for acting was
permitted to compete as a matter of course at the next festival
without having to submit to the process of selection by the
archon. Such was the system adopted during the latter half
of the fifth century.[3] How long it lasted cannot be determined;
but when we come to the middle of the fourth century, a further
alteration is found to have been introduced. By this time the
importance of the actors had increased to a still greater extent.
In fact, Aristotle says that in his day the success of a play
depended much more upon the actor than the poet.[4] It was
probably felt that under the old arrangement the poet who
obtained by lot the greatest actor had an unfair advantage over
his rivals. A new system was therefore introduced, by which
the talents of the actors were divided with perfect equality
among the poets. Each tragedy was performed by a separate
actor. All the actors appeared in turn in the service of each of
the poets. Thus in 341 Astydamas exhibited three tragedies.

[1] Dem. Fals. Leg. §§ 10, 246; de Cor. § 262.
[2] C. I. A. ii. 972.
[3] Suidas s. v. νεμήσεις ὑποκριτῶν· οἱ ποιηταὶ ἐλάμβανον τρεῖς ὑποκριτὰς κλήρῳ νεμηθέντας, ὑποκρινομένους (? ὑποκρινου-μένους) τὰ δράματα· ὧν ὁ νικήσας εἰς τοὐπιὸν ἄκριτος παραλαμβάνεται. Ob-viously ὁ νικήσας denotes, not the vic-torious poet, nor yet the actor who acted for him, but the actor who won the prize for acting. Τοὐπιόν ap-parently means 'the next festival'.

The victorious actor was allowed to act at the next festival as a matter of course. The 'three actors' are the three protagonists required at each tragic contest, and not the three actors required by each poet. This is proved by the words ὧν ὁ νικήσας, which imply that the three actors mentioned all took part in the actors' contest. But the actors' contest was limited to the protagonists; the subordinate actors had nothing to do with it. See above, p. 42.
[4] Aristot. Rhet. iii. 1.

His Achilles was acted by Thessalus, his Athamas by Neoptolemus, his Antigone by Athenodorus. The three tragedies of
each of his competitors were performed by the same three
actors.[1] By this arrangement no poet had any advantage over
his rivals, but as far as the excellence of the actors was concerned all were on exactly the same level. The system just
described appears to have been retained without alteration
during the remaining period of Attic tragedy.

The mode of distributing the actors in comedy was much the
same as that in tragedy. During the earlier part of the fifth
century the poets were left to choose their own actors. Thus
the comic poet Crates is said to have begun his career as actor
to Cratinus. But in later times no instances are to be found
of comic actors being permanently connected with particular
poets. The story that Philonides and Callistratus were actors
of Aristophanes is a mere fiction of one of the old commentators,
based upon a misunderstanding.[2] It is evident, therefore, that
the state began to undertake the selection and appointment of
the comic actors about the same time that a corresponding
change was made in regard to tragedy. No doubt the mode of
distribution was identical. The actors were first appointed by
the state, and the poets then drew lots for them. As the comic
poets competed with single plays, only one method of distribution was possible, and there was no need of the further alteration which was afterwards made in tragedy. The number of
poets in the comic contests was originally three, and in later
times five. A corresponding number of actors would be required.
Sometimes, however, a smaller number was selected, and one
actor appeared in two comedies. In 288 Aristomachus was the
actor assigned both to Simylus and Diodorus. About B.C. 160
Damon is found occasionally acting in two comedies at the same
competition.[3] It is not likely that such a course was adopted
except on occasions when it was impossible to obtain five comic
actors of fairly equal merit.

---

[1] C. I. A. ii. 973.

[2] Schol. Aristoph. Equit. 534 ; Vita
Aristoph.(Dindf. Prolegom. de Comoed.
p. 36). The commentator, misunderstanding the expression that certain
plays of Aristophanes were brought
out by Philonides and Callistratus
(ἐδιδάχθη διὰ Φιλωνίδου κτλ.), concluded that these persons were actors.

[3] C. I. A. ii. 972, 975 c and d.

§ 4. *The Training of the Chorus.*

The archon had now for the present finished his part of the business. He had seen that the proper number of poets, actors, and choregi had been chosen. He had seen that each choregus was provided with his own poet and actor. It was now the duty of choregus and poet to attend to the subsequent preparations. The choregus was responsible for the selection and payment of the chorus. He had also to provide a room for them to rehearse in.¹ Very little is known concerning the relations between the choregus and his chorus. Such few details as have been recorded refer rather to the dithyramb than to the drama. The dithyrambic choruses were selected exclusively from the tribes which they represented in the competition. Each tribe had a specially appointed agent, who was employed by the choregus to collect his chorus for him.² But the drama having nothing to do with the tribes, there was no limitation upon the selection of the dramatic choruses. Aristotle happens in one place to remark that a tragic and a comic chorus often consisted of much the same individual members.³ It is quite clear, therefore, that the dramatic choruses were chosen from the general body of citizens, and that a man might serve in two of them at the same time. There was probably a class of professional singers who made their livelihood by serving in these choruses. A rich choregus would have a great advantage over his rivals by offering higher pay, and so securing better singers. The stories about the boarding and lodging of the choreutae also refer mainly to the dithyrambic choruses. The choregus in Antiphon's speech lodged his chorus in his own house, and gave special directions that every delicacy which was ordered by the trainer should be provided for them.⁴ But this was a chorus of boys. The professionals who served in the dramatic choruses are not likely to have been lodged in the house of the choregus, especially as they were often in the service of two choregi at

---

¹ Xen. Hiero ix. 4, Resp. Athen. i. 13. The training-room was called διδασκαλεῖον (Antiphon orat. vi. § 11), or χορηγεῖον (Bekk. Anecd. p. 72, 17; Pollux iv. 106, ix. 42).

² Antiphon orat. vi. §§ 11–13; Pollux iv. 106. The agent was called χορολέκτης.
³ Aristot. Pol. iii. 3.
⁴ Antiphon l. c.

the same time.   However, it seems that the diet of the choruses
was well attended to, so that the members should appear in
the best possible condition on the day of the contests.   Plutarch
mentions eels, lettuce, garlic, and cheese as delicacies provided
for this purpose.   The appetite of the Attic choreutae passed
into a proverb.[1]

During the earlier period of the Athenian drama the principal
part in the training and instruction of the chorus was undertaken by the poet himself.   In fact, the regular name at Athens
for a dramatic or dithyrambic poet was didaskalos, or 'the
teacher', owing to the part he took in teaching his play or
poem to the chorus.   In the same way, when a poet brought
out a tragedy or a comedy, the technical expression was that
he 'taught' such and such a play.   The play, or group of
plays, exhibited by a single poet was called a 'teaching'[2].   In
addition to the evidence supplied by these expressions, there
is also no lack of direct testimony as to the important part taken
by the older poets in the production of their plays.   In fact,
they were quite as much stage-managers as poets.   The older
dramatic writers, such as Thespis, Pratinas, Cratinus, and
Phrynichus, were called 'dancers', not only because of the
prominent part which the chorus and the dancing filled in
their plays, but also because they gave instruction in choric
dancing.[3]   Aeschylus is said to have superintended personally
the whole of the training of his choruses, and to have invented
many new dances and movements for them.   His innovations
in regard to the scenery and the dresses of the actors entirely
transformed the outward appearance of the drama.[4]   This
intimate connexion between the poet and the stage, between
the literary and the theatrical part of dramatic production,
continued to exist during the great period of Athenian drama.
Sophocles appeared personally in some of his plays.   In the
Thamyris he played the harp.   In the Nausicaa he won great
applause by the skill with which he played ball in the scene

[1] Plutarch Glor. Athen. 349 A;
Suidas s. v. φαρυγγίνδην· ὡς ἀριστίνδην·
σκώπτοντες γὰρ τὴν γαστριμαργίαν τῶν
χορευτῶν Ἀττικοὶ οὕτω λέγουσι.
[2] Suidas s. v. διδάσκαλος; Aristoph.
Ran. 1026 εἶτα διδάξας Πέρσας κτλ.;
Anthol. Pal. vii. 37 (of a mask of Antigone or Electra) ἐκ ποίης ἥδε διδασκαλίης; Plut. Pericles 154 E ἀλλ' Ἴωνα
μὲν ὥσπερ τραγικὴν διδασκαλίαν ἀξιοῦντα
τὴν ἀρετὴν ἔχειν τι πάντως καὶ σατυρικὸν
μέρος ἐῶμεν.
[3] Athen. p. 22 A.
[4] Athen. p. 21 C; Vit. Aeschyli;
Philostrat. Vit. Apoll. p. 244.

where Nausicaa is sporting with her maidens.[1] Euripides also seems to have superintended the training of his choruses in person, as there is a story in Plutarch which represents him as singing over one of his odes to the choreutae.[2]

The poet was assisted in his task by a subordinate, who looked after the routine part of the work, and was called a hypodidaskalos, or 'assistant teacher'. This was the proper term to denote the professional trainer, as opposed to the didaskalos, or poet.[3] But towards the end of the fifth and the beginning of the fourth century the practice in these matters underwent a change. Poetry and stage-management began to be sharply discriminated from one another. A class of literary dramatic writers arose, such as Theodectes and Aphareus, who were quite as much rhetoricians as poets. They knew nothing about the details of training a chorus, or preparing a play for representation. In these circumstances the greater part of the management was undertaken by the professional instructor. The term didaskalos, which had originally been confined to the poet, was now applied to these hired trainers.[4] A class of men came into existence who made choral instruction their regular business. One of these, named Sannio, is mentioned by Demosthenes, and was celebrated for his skill in training tragic choruses.[5] These professional teachers were hired and paid by the choregus. A rich choregus had a great advantage in being able to secure the best assistance. Xenophon mentions the case of a certain choregus called Antisthenes, who knew little or nothing about music and choruses himself, but was always successful in his competitions, because he took care to provide himself with the most skilful trainers procurable.[6] It is obvious that in these later times, when the poets ceased to attend to the details of stage-management, the importance of the professional trainers must have been very much increased. The hiring of a good trainer would be one of the first conditions of success.

[1] Eustath. Odyss. p. 1553.
[2] Plut. De Audiendo, 46 B.
[3] Photius v. ὑποδιδάσκαλος; Plat. Ion p. 536 A.
[4] Thus the trainer hired by Demo-sthenes for his chorus is called διδά-σκαλος, Dem. Meid. § 17.
[5] Dem. Meid. §§ 58, 59.
[6] Xen. Mem. iii. 4. 3.

§ 5. *The Expenses of the Choregia.*

It will now be possible to form some conception of the expenses which the choregus had to meet. The principal item was the hire of the chorus during the whole period of training. This part of the expenditure was borne entirely by the choregus without any assistance from the state.[1] Then again, he had to provide an instructor for his chorus. As the competition between rich choregi was of the keenest character, the services of a really good instructor must have been expensive. In the third place, a flute-player was required. In the dithyrambic choruses the flute-players were selected by the state, and assigned by lot to the choregi. But in the dramatic choruses they appear to have been chosen by the choregus himself, who would therefore have to pay their salary.[2] Fourthly, the various mute characters that appeared upon the stage, such as the attendants upon kings and queens, were supplied by the choregus. This is proved by the story in Plutarch of a tragedian at Athens who was going to act the part of a queen, and who refused to perform unless the choregus would provide him with a train of female attendants dressed in expensive fashion.[3] The number and splendour of the mute characters would add greatly to the magnificence of the spectacle, and form a considerable item in the expenses of a wealthy choregus. It is also probable that in early times, when the actors were chosen by the poets, their salary was

---

[1] Xen. Resp. Athen. i. 13 χορηγοῦσι μὲν οἱ πλούσιοι, χορηγεῖται δὲ ὁ δῆμος ... ἀξιοῖ οὖν ἀργύριον λαμβάνειν ὁ δῆμος καὶ ᾄδων καὶ τρέχων καὶ ὀρχούμενος ... ἵνα αὐτός τε ἔχῃ καὶ οἱ πλούσιοι πενέστεροι γίγνωνται. First Arg. to Dem. Meid., p. 509 χορηγὸς ... ὁ τὰ ἀναλώματα παρέχων τὰ περὶ τὸν χορόν. Plut. Glor. Athen. 349 B. The statement of the Scholiast on Dionysius Thrax (Bekk. Anecd. p. 746), that every comic and tragic poet was supplied with a chorus 'supported by the state', appears to be merely a loose way of saying that the dramatic choruses were provided by choregi appointed by the state. The author of the 2nd Arg. to the Meidias says that the choregus

'received sums of money for the support of the chorus'. But his authority is of the weakest description. He is quite mistaken as to the Dionysiac festivals, imagining that the Great Dionysia was a triennial affair, as opposed to the Small or annual celebration. Hence his testimony is of no value in the face of other authorities.

[2] The name of the flute-player is inserted in all dithyrambic records except the earliest, but never in the dramatic records. This seems to show that their status was different, and that the dramatic flute-player was not appointed officially.

[3] Plut. Phocion p. 750 C.

paid by the choregus. But later the selection and payment of the actors were undertaken entirely by the state.[1] The principal part then of the expenditure of the choregus consisted in paying the salaries of the various persons just mentioned. In addition to this, he had to provide the dresses of the chorus, which were often very magnificent. For example, the comic poet Antiphanes mentions the case of a choregus who ruined himself by dressing his chorus in gold. Demosthenes supplied his chorus of men with golden crowns.[2] Sometimes the love of splendour degenerated into mere vulgar ostentation. Unnecessary magnificence in the appointments of a comic chorus is mentioned by Aristotle as a proof of vulgarity. On the other hand, economical choregi saved expense by hiring second-hand dresses from the dealers in theatrical costumes.[3] Another item in the expenses of the choregia was the supply of dresses for the various mute characters and subordinate personages. With the dresses of the actors themselves the choregus had probably nothing to do. As for the ordinary kinds of scenery, they were part of the permanent fixtures of the theatre, and would be provided by the lessee. But when anything very special in the way of scenery was required by the necessities of a particular play, it is most probable that the expenses were borne by the choregus. As far, then, as can be gathered from ancient notices, the expenses of the choregia consisted in the hire of the chorus, the instructor, the flute-player, and the mute characters; in providing dresses for the chorus and the mute characters; and in supplying such exceptional scenery as the theatre did not possess.

A choregus who was anxious for victory, and who was ready to spend money over the production of the play, would easily be put to very considerable expense. The defendant in one of the speeches of Lysias tells us that a tragic chorus cost him thirty minae, a comic chorus sixteen, a chorus of boys fifteen. It follows that a comic chorus was only about half as expensive as a tragic one, and cost about the same as a chorus

---

[1] The actors were assigned by the state to the poets, and not to the choregi : hence it is quite clear that in later times the choregi did not pay for them. See Suidas s. v. νεμήσεις ὑποκρι-τῶν.

[2] Antiphanes apud Athen. p. 103 E; Dem. Meid. § 16.
[3] Aristot. Eth. Nic. iv. 6. Pollux vii. 78 τοὺς δὲ τὰς ἐσθῆτας ἀπομισθοῦντας τοῖς χορηγοῖς οἱ μὲν νέοι ἱματιομίσθας ἐκάλουν, οἱ δὲ παλαιοὶ ἱματιομισθωτάς.

of boys. On the other hand, a chorus of men at the City Dionysia cost fifty minae. These figures bear out the statement of Demosthenes, that a chorus of men was much more expensive than a tragic chorus. The chorus of men consisted of fifty members; and the payment of so large a number, together with the dresses and crowns which the choregi used to provide them with, would easily account for the expense. A tragic chorus consisted of only fifteen members, and yet it cost about twice as much as a comic chorus, which consisted of twenty-four. But we must remember that the tragic chorus had to perform in several plays, the comic chorus in only one. Also it does not appear to have been customary to spend very much money upon a comedy. In another speech of Lysias, a certain Aristophanes is said to have expended fifty minae over two tragic choruses. He was therefore rather more economical than the person mentioned above, who spent thirty minae over one.[1] It would be very interesting to be able to form some conception of the amount which these sums would represent at the present day. It appears that in the time of Aristophanes the daily wages for common and unskilled labour were three obols.[2] If we take as a modern equivalent the case of the agricultural labourer who gets ten shillings a week, or one shilling and eightpence per day, it follows that three obols in ancient Attica were equivalent to about one shilling and eightpence at the present time. If this calculation is anywhere near the mark, then a choregus who spent thirty minae on a tragic chorus would be spending a sum equivalent to about £500 of our money. The sixteen minae paid for a comic chorus would represent about £266. Comparisons of this kind are very conjectural; but they enable one to form some idea of the immense sums of money which must have been spent at Athens in the course of a single year upon dramatic and choral performances. There were eight dramatic and ten dithyrambic choruses at the City Dionysia. There were seven or eight dramatic choruses at the Lenaea. Besides this there were dithyrambic choruses at the Thargelia, Prometheia, and Hephaesteia; and dithyrambic and pyrrhic choruses at the

[1] Lysias xxi. §§ 1-5, xix. §§ 29, 42; Dem. Meid. § 156.
[2] Aristoph. Eccles. 307; Böckh, Public Economy of Athens, i. p. 157 (Engl. transl.).

Panathenaea. The expenses of all these choruses were drawn
from a single small state, about the size of an English county,
in which wealth was by no means abundant. It is easy therefore to see that there was not much exaggeration in the
complaint of Demosthenes, that the Athenians spent more upon
their festivals than they ever spent upon a naval expedition.[1]

If the choregi neglected their duties, and were careless about
the efficiency of their choruses, it was the duty of the archon to
bring pressure to bear upon them.[2] But such interference was
not often necessary. On the contrary the rivalry between the
choregi was so keen, and their desire for victory so great, that
it often led them into expenses which they could not afford.
Demosthenes says that men frequently spent all their property
upon these competitions.[3] The choregus in Antiphanes has
already been referred to, who reduced himself to beggary by
his extravagance in providing golden dresses for his chorus.
Besides the mere spirit of emulation there was another induce-
ment to lavish vast sums upon these choregic displays. For
a wealthy politician it was an easy means of gaining popularity,
and increasing his influence in the state. Nicias is said to
have owed a great deal of his power to the splendour of his
choruses, upon which he spent more money than any of his
contemporaries or predecessors.[4] With the double motives of
ambition and emulation at work, it was natural that considerable
jealousy should be excited between the rival choregi, the 'anti-
choregi', as they were called. Sometimes this hostility ended
in blows. When Taureas and Alcibiades were competitors with
choruses of boys, a dispute having arisen as to the parentage
of one of the boys in Alcibiades' chorus, the matter ended in
a personal conflict in the orchestra.[5] Demosthenes, in his
speech against Meidias, cites many examples of the bitterness
and animosity with which choregi regarded one another. He
adds that there would have been some excuse for the assault
of Meidias upon himself if it had been caused by the jealousy of
a rival choregus.[6]

---

[1] Demosth. Philipp. i. § 35.
[2] Xen. Hiero ix. 4 καὶ γὰρ ὅταν
χοροὺς ἡμῖν βουλώμεθα ἀγωνίζεσθαι, ἆθλα
μὲν ὁ ἄρχων προτίθησιν, ἀθροίζειν δὲ
αὐτοὺς προστέτακται χορηγοῖς καὶ ἄλλοις
διδάσκειν, καὶ ἀνάγκην προστιθέναι τοῖς

ἐνδεῶς τι ποιοῦσιν.
[3] Dem. Meid. § 61.
[4] Plutarch Nicias, p. 524 D.
[5] Andocid. Alcibiad. § 20.
[6] Dem. Meid. §§ 58-66.

§ 6. The Performances in the Theatre.

When the preparations were all completed, a few days before the actual festival there was a preliminary ceremony called the Proagon. It took place in the Odeum, a sort of smaller theatre to the south of the Acropolis, not far from the theatre of Dionysus. The Proagon was a kind of show or spectacle, and served as an introduction to the actual performances at the festival. Each of the tragic poets who were about to compete in the approaching contest appeared upon the stage in the presence of the people, accompanied by his choregus, his actors, and the members of the chorus. All of them wore crowns upon their heads; but the actors were without their masks and their stage dresses. As they paraded upon the stage some announcement was made to the people, of which the exact nature is not known. But it is very likely that this occasion was taken for making known to the people the names of the poet and his actors, together with the titles of the tragedies shortly to be performed, and other information of a similar character. At the same time the people would have an opportunity of becoming acquainted with poets and actors who were making their first appearance. The splendour of the dresses of choruses and choregi, upon which great sums of money were spent, would make a spectacle of some magnificence, and appeal to the popular taste. At the Proagon which followed shortly after the death of Euripides, it is said that Sophocles appeared upon the stage in a dark-coloured dress, and introduced his actors and chorus without the usual crowns. It is nowhere definitely stated that the comic and dithyrambic poets and choruses took part in the Proagon. But the whole of our information about the ceremony is derived from one or two brief and casual notices, in which very few details are given. It is hardly probable that only tragedy was represented. The magnificence of the spectacle would be very much increased by the large and gorgeously-dressed choruses of boys and men.[1]

---

[1] Our knowledge of the Proagon is derived from the following passages:— Aeschin. Ctesiph. §§ 66, 67 ὁ γὰρ μισαλέξανδρος νυνὶ φάσκων εἶναι . . . γράφει ψήφισμα . . . ἐκκλησίαν ποιεῖν τοὺς πρυτάνεις τῇ ὀγδόῃ ἱπταμένου τοῦ ἐλαφηβολιῶνος μηνός, . ἣν τῷ Ἀσκληπιῷ ἡ θυσία καὶ ὁ προάγων. Schol. Aeschin.

Ctesiph. § 67 ἐγίγνοντο πρὸ τῶν μεγάλων Διονυσίων ἡμέραις ὀλίγαις ἔμπροσθεν ἐν τῷ ᾠδείῳ καλουμένῳ τῶν τραγῳδῶν ἀγὼν καὶ ἐπίδειξις ὧν μέλλουσι δραμάτων ἀγωνίζεσθαι ἐν τῷ θεάτρῳ· δι' ὃ ἐτύμως προάγων καλεῖται. εἰσίασι δὲ δίχα προσώπων οἱ ὑποκριταὶ γυμνοί. Vita Euripid. λέγουσι δὲ καὶ Σοφοκλέα, ἀκούσαντα ὅτι

During the period of the actual contests the audience met in
the theatre every morning soon after daybreak. Considering
the number of plays which had to be produced, it was necessary
that the proceedings should begin at an early hour.[1] The vast
gathering of spectators, like all public meetings at Athens, was
first of all purified by the offer of a small sacrifice. Then libations were poured in front of the statue of the god Dionysus.[2]
If the festival was the City Dionysia, before the tragedies began
the opportunity was taken to proclaim the names of citizens
upon whom crowns had been bestowed, together with the
services for which they had been granted. The proclamation
before such a vast multitude of citizens was naturally considered
a very great honour.[3] During the period of Athenian supremacy
another striking ceremony preceded the tragedies at the City
Dionysia. The tribute collected from the dependent states was
divided into talents, and solemnly deposited in the orchestra.[4]
Then the orphans whose fathers had been killed in battle, and
who had been educated by the state, and had now reached the
age of manhood, were brought forward upon the stage equipped
in complete armour. The herald made a proclamation, recount-
ing what the state had done for them, and they were then
publicly discharged from state control to take their place as

---

ἐτελεύτησε, αὐτὸν μὲν ἱματίῳ φαιῷ ἤτοι
πορφυρῷ προελθεῖν, τὸν δὲ χορὸν καὶ τοὺς
ὑποκριτὰς ἀστεφανώτους εἰσαγαγεῖν ἐν
τῷ προάγωνι, καὶ δακρῦσαι τὸν δῆμον.
Schol. Aristoph. Wasps 1104 οἱ δ' ἐν
ᾠδείῳ· ἔστι τόπος θεατροειδής, ἐν ᾧ
εἰώθασι τὰ ποιήματα ἀπαγγέλλειν πρὶν
τῆς εἰς τὸ θέατρον ἀπαγγελίας. That
the Proagon was a contest is out
of the question. The contest was to
follow some days later. Nor can it
have been a dress rehearsal, as part of
one day would not have sufficed for
the rehearsal of twelve tragedies and
five comedies. Προάγων denotes ' the
ceremony before the contest ', just as
πρόγαμος means ' the ceremony before
the marriage '. The expression of the
Schol. on Aeschines τῶν τραγῳδῶν
ἀγών is probably due to a misunderstanding of the word προάγων. The
passage in Plato's Symposium 194 A
(ἐπιλήσμων μεντἂν εἴην, ὦ Ἀγάθων, . . .
εἰ ἰδὼν τὴν σὴν ἀνδρείαν καὶ μεγαλοφρο-
σύνην ἀναβαίνοντος ἐπὶ τὸν ὀκρίβαντα
μετὰ τῶν ὑποκριτῶν καὶ βλέψαντος ἐναντία

τοσούτῳ θεάτρῳ, μέλλοντος ἐπιδείξεσθαι
σαυτοῦ λόγους, καὶ οὐδ' ὁπωστιοῦν ἐκπλα-
γέντος κτλ.) probably refers to the
Proagon. If so ἀπαγγέλλειν in the
Schol. and ἐπιδείξεσθαι λόγους both
probably refer to an announcement of
the plots or subjects of the plays
(λόγος is so used, Aristoph. Vesp. 54,
Pax 50, and Hesych. λόγος· ἡ τοῦ δράματος ὑπόθεσις). See Mazon, Revue de
Philologie, 1903, pp. 263 ff. That there
was a Proagon before the Lenaea as
well as the City Dionysia seems
natural in itself, and is implied by the
use of the plural in such inscriptions
as C. I. A. ii. 307 ἐπετέλεσε δὲ καὶ τοὺς
προάγωνας τοὺς ἐν τοῖς ἱεροῖς κτλ.

[1] Aeschin. Ctesiph. § 76 ἅμα τῇ
ἡμέρᾳ ἡγεῖτο τοῖς πρέσβεσιν εἰς τὸ θέατρον. Demosth. Meid. § 74.

[2] Suidas s. v. καθάρσιον; Pollux viii.
104 ; Plut. Cimon p. 482 E ; Philostrat. vit. Apoll. p. 161.

[3] Aeschin. Ctesiph. §§ 48, 230.

[4] Isocrat. viii. § 82.

ordinary citizens.[1] After these preliminaries had been gone through the dramatic performances commenced. The order in which the different plays were to be performed was determined by lot.[2] Each poet, as his turn came, was summoned by name by the public herald and ordered to produce his play.[3] The summons to each poet was accompanied in later times by the blowing of a trumpet, a custom which originated as follows. On one occasion an actor called Hermon had left the building, expecting that his comedy would come on late. But as it was called for sooner than he expected, there was a hitch in the proceedings owing to his absence. The blowing of the trumpet was therefore instituted to mark the commencement of each new performance, and let people in the neighbourhood of the theatre know at what rate the contest was progressing.[4] The order in which the poets competed was determined by lot, as stated above. It was considered an advantage to be drawn last, as the latest performance left the most vivid impression upon the minds of the judges. This would be especially the case in such competitions as lasted over three days. The Ecclesiazusae of Aristophanes was drawn first for performance. The poet therefore, in the course of this play, implores the judges not to let the ballot damage his chances, but to judge the choruses on their merits, unlike the courtesans, who forget all except their latest lovers.[5]

At the end of each competition the judges wrote their verdicts upon tablets. Five of these tablets were drawn by lot, and decided the result. The names of the victorious poet and choregus were then proclaimed by the herald, and they were crowned with a chaplet of ivy in the presence of the spectators. At the conclusion of the festival the successful

---

[1] Aeschin. Ctesiph. §§ 153, 154.

[2] Aristid. περὶ ῥητορικῆς, vol. ii. p. 2 (Dindf.).

[3] The passage from Philochorus (Athen. p. 464 E καὶ τοῖς χοροῖς εἰσιοῦσιν ἐνέχεον πίνειν καὶ διηγωνισμένοις ὅτ᾽ ἐξεπορεύοντο ἐνέχεον πάλιν) affords no warrant for assuming, with Müller (Griech. Bühnen, p. 373), that before the commencement of each play the poet and his chorus entered the orchestra and offered a libation to Dionysus. [Aristoph. Ach. 11 ἀλλ᾽ ὠδυνήθην ἕτερον αὖ τραγῳδικόν, | ὅτε δὴ

᾽κεχήνη προσδοκῶν τὸν Αἰσχύλον, | ὁ δ᾽ ἀνεῖπεν, εἴσαγ᾽, ὦ Θέογνι, τὸν χορόν, is generally taken to refer to this point in the proceedings. But it is not likely that the names, &c., of the poets would be unknown to the spectators, when the Proagon had taken place only a few days before; see p. 66; and Mazon is probably right (Rev. de Philologie, 1903, p. 264) in making the lines refer to the Proagon itself.]

[4] Pollux iv. 88.

[5] Aristoph. Eccles. 1154 ff.

poet celebrated his victory by a solemn sacrifice, followed by
a grand banquet, at which most of his friends were present.
The members of the chorus were also there, and probably
the choregus and the actors. The scene of Plato's Symposium
is laid in Agathon's house the day after the banquet in honour
of his first tragic victory. Socrates had avoided the banquet
itself, because of the crush of people, but came next day to
a more private gathering.[1] A victory, especially at the City
Dionysia, was regarded as a splendid distinction. On one
occasion Ion of Chios, after winning the first prize in both
the tragic and the dithyrambic contests at the same festival,
showed the extent of his joy by making a present of a jar of
Chian wine to every Athenian citizen.[2]

The next day but one after the conclusion of the City
Dionysia a special assembly of the people was convened in
the theatre of Dionysus to discuss matters connected with
the festival. No doubt a similar assembly was held after the
Lenaea, though the fact is nowhere actually stated. At this
assembly the conduct of the archon, who had had the management of the festival which was just over, was taken into consideration. Any neglect of his duties, or any unfairness in the
choice of poets and actors, would be punished. At the same
time crowns and other distinctions were voted in honour of
officials who had performed their duties in connexion with the
festival satisfactorily. It has been pointed out that the judges
in the dramatic and dithyrambic contests were liable to prosecution and punishment if they were suspected of dishonesty in
their verdicts. Probably such charges were brought forward
and decided at this assembly in the theatre. Then came the
hearing of complaints as to any violation of the sanctity of the
festival.[3] The aggrieved person stated his charges before the
assembled people: the defendant made his reply: the people
then proceeded to vote. If they acquitted the defendant there
was an end of the matter. But if they voted against him the
prosecutor then carried the case before the ordinary law-courts,
where, of course, the previous verdict of the people weighed
very much in his favour.[4]

[1] Plat. Symp. 173 A, 174 A.
[2] Athen. p. 3 F; Schol. Aristoph.
Pax 835.
[3] Cf. ch. i. § 1.
[4] Dem. Meid. §§ 8–10; C. I. A. ii.
114, 307, 420.

§ 7. *Reproduction of Old Plays.*

At Athens, during the fifth century, when the drama was in its most flourishing state, plays were usually exhibited once, and once only. There were only two festivals in the whole year at which regular theatrical performances could be held. Consequently, as long as the creative period of the drama lasted, the few days given up to them barely sufficed even for a single performance of the various new compositions. Nor were repetitions necessary. The theatre at Athens was of enormous size, so that every man had a chance of seeing a play when it was first brought out. If it was successful, and he wished to see it again, he had numerous opportunities of doing so at the Rural Dionysia, where reproductions were the rule. For these reasons the Athenian stage of the fifth century was confined almost exclusively to original works. When a play had once been performed, it was never seen again, as far as Athens was concerned, unless it happened to be of extraordinary merit. It is stated on the authority of Dicaearchus that the Frogs of Aristophanes 'was so much admired on account of its parabasis that it was actually repeated'.[1] The language here used implies that such a repetition was a very unusual circumstance. It is true that when the Capture of Miletus, the historical play of Phrynichus, caused so much commotion in the theatre the Athenians are said to have passed a law that 'for the future no one should exhibit this drama'.[2] But the law must have referred to its reproduction at the Rural Dionysia.

At Athens then during the fifth century even successful plays were only exhibited once. But if a play was unsuccessful, the poet was allowed to revise and rewrite it, and to compete with it again in its improved shape.[3] The revision of unsuccessful plays seems to have been a common practice with the Athenian dramatic writers. It is mentioned as rather a peculiarity in the comic poet Anaxandrides, that when one of his comedies was unsuccessful, he used to destroy it at once, without taking the trouble to emend it and try his fortunes with it a second time.[4] Many plays were revised and re-exhibited in this manner, and

---

[1] Arg. Aristoph. Ran. οὕτω δὲ ἐθαυμάσθη τὸ δρᾶμα διὰ τὴν ἐν αὐτῷ παράβασιν ὥστε καὶ ἀνεδιδάχθη, ὥς φησι Δικαίαρχος.
[2] Herod. vi. 21.

[3] A revised edition of a play was called διασκευή, Athen. p. 110 C.
[4] Athen. p. 374 A.

in consequence many plays existed in ancient times in a double form. Such was the case with the Lemnian Women of Sophocles, and the Autolycus and Phrixus of Euripides.[1] The Hippolytus of Euripides which we at present possess is a revised edition pruned of its original defects.[2] The Clouds of Aristophanes on its first appearance was very unsuccessful, and was altered in many important particulars before it reached the form in which it has come down to us.[3] Among the other plays of Aristophanes, the Peace, the Plutus, and the Thesmophoria-zusae were brought out a second time in a corrected form. Instances of the revision of plays are not uncommon among the writers of the Middle and New Comedy. Sometimes the original title was retained in the revised version, as for instance in the Heiress of Menander. Sometimes a new title was adopted. Thus the Braggart Captain of Diphilus appeared subsequently as the Eunuch.[5]

One remarkable exception to the general practice demands notice. In the Life of Aeschylus it is said that the Athenians felt such an admiration for him, that they passed a decree after his death that any one who offered to exhibit his plays should receive a chorus from the archon. This does not mean that his plays were to be performed as a mere isolated exhibition, apart from the regular contests, but that any person might be allowed to compete at the ordinary tragic contests with plays of Aeschylus instead of new plays of his own. If any one offered to do so, the archon was bound to give him a chorus. He would then take his place as one of the three competing poets; but while his rivals exhibited new and original tragedies, he would confine himself to reproducing tragedies of Aeschylus. Probably the men who undertook these revivals were in most cases celebrated actors. In this way the plays of Aeschylus were often brought into competition with the plays of later writers, and appear to have been generally successful. Philostratus refers to the custom.[6] He says that the Athenians invited Aeschylus after

[1] Nauck, Frag. Trag. Graec. pp. 215, 441, 627.
[2] Arg. Eur. Hipp.
[3] Arg. Aristoph. Nub.
[4] Arg. Aristoph. Pax ; Meineke, Frag. Com. Graec. i. pp. 1074, 1130.
[5] Meineke, iv. 116, 377. Additional instances of revision of plays are to be found in the Autolycus of Eupolis, the Synoris of Diphilus, and the Phryx of Alexis. The Demetrius of Alexis appeared subsequently as the Philetae-rus, the Ἀγροικοι of Antiphanes as the Butalion. See Meineke, ii. 440; iii. 36, 403. 500 ; iv. 412.
[6] Philostrat. vit. Apoll. p. 245.

his death to the festivals of Dionysus, and that his plays were acted over again, and were victorious a second time. This passage makes it quite clear that the tragedies of Aeschylus were exhibited in the ordinary contests, and not as a separate performance by themselves. There is a reference in the beginning of the Acharnians to a competition of this kind. Dicaeopolis had come to the theatre to see the tragic contests.[1] He was expecting that the performance would commence with plays of Aeschylus; but to his disgust the frigid Theognis was the first to be called upon.[2] Here then is a picture of a contest in which the tragic poet Theognis was opposed by a competitor who exhibited, not plays of his own, but plays of Aeschylus. It is to the practice of reproducing his plays after his death that Aeschylus alludes in the Frogs, when he remarks that his poetry has not died with him, like that of Euripides.[3] Quintilian refers to the same custom, though his language is not quite accurate. He says that the tragedies of Aeschylus were sublime, but rough and unfinished; and therefore the Athenians permitted subsequent poets to polish and revise them, and exhibit them at the competitions in their amended form; and in this way many of them won the prize.[4] This story, however, of the revision of the plays of Aeschylus by subsequent poets (as distinct from their corruption by actors) is not otherwise supported.[5]

From this reproduction of old plays of Aeschylus must be carefully distinguished those instances where plays, which Aeschylus had left unpublished at his death, were produced for the first time by his son Euphorion. It is said that Euphorion won four victories with his father's unpublished tragedies. In a similar manner the Oedipus Coloneus of Sophocles was produced for the first time by his grandson four years after the poet's death. And after the death of Euripides, his Iphigeneia in Aulis, Alcmaeon, and Bacchae were brought out by his son at the City Dionysia.[6] On such occasions as these, although no doubt the real authorship of the plays was perfectly well known at the time, the relative appeared

---

[1] [Or more probably to the Odeum to see the Proagon; see p. 69, n. 3.]
[2] Aristóph. Acharn. 9-12.
[3] Id. Ran. 868.
[4] Quint. Inst. x. 1. 66.

[5] [See, however, note on p. 16, on the Septem of Aeschylus.]
[6] Suidas s. v. Εὐφορίων; Arg. Soph. Oed. Col.; Schol. Aristoph. Ran. 67.

as the nominal author. He asked for a chorus from the archon in his own name. The plays he produced were new ones. There is therefore no similarity between instances of this kind and those occasions when a man asked for a chorus, not in his own name, but in order to produce old plays of Aeschylus.

It was not till the fourth century that the reproduction of old plays developed into a regular custom. The practice was at first confined to tragedy. This branch of the drama had passed beyond the period of healthy growth, and already showed symptoms of decay. The three great tragic poets of the fifth century had in their several lines exhausted the capabilities of Attic tragedy. Their successors were mostly feeble imitators of Euripides. Under such circumstances the tendency to fall back upon the early drama naturally became more prevalent. In the records of the City Dionysia during the latter half of the fourth century it is found that the series of new tragedies was invariably preceded by the performance of an old one.[1] The same practice was also no doubt adopted at the Lenaea. The actors who had the privilege of conducting these revivals would be selected by the archon, probably after a small preliminary competition of the kind described in the previous chapter.[2] It appears that these actors, in preparing the old plays for reproduction, were sometimes inclined to tamper with the text, and to introduce what they considered improvements, just as the plays of Shakespeare were adapted for the stage by Garrick in the last century. A law was passed by the orator Lycurgus to put a stop to this practice. It was enacted that a public copy should be made of the works of Aeschylus, Sophocles, and Euripides, and deposited in the state archives; and that the actors, in their performances, should not be allowed to deviate from the text of the copy.[3] It is very probable that this authorized version eventually found its way to Alexandria. Ptolemy the Third was a great collector of manuscripts. He borrowed from

[1] See above, pp. 18 and 26.
[2] See above, p. 31.
[3] Plut. X orat. 841 F εἰσήνεγκε δὲ καὶ νόμους . . . τὸν δέ, ὡς χαλκᾶς εἰκόνας ἀναθεῖναι τῶν ποιητῶν, Αἰσχύλου, Σοφοκλέους, Εὐριπίδου, καὶ τὰς τραγῳδίας αὐτῶν ἐν κοινῷ γραψαμένους φυλάττειν, καὶ τὸν τῆς πόλεως γραμματέα παραναγιγνώσκειν τοῖς ὑποκρινομένοις· οὐκ ἐξεῖναι γὰρ αὐτὰς ὑποκρίνεσθαι. The general meaning of the passage is clear, though the text is corrupt. Various emendations have been proposed, e. g. παρ' αὐτὰς ὑποκρίνεσθαι, Wyttenbach; αὐτὰς ἄλλως ὑποκρίνεσθαι, Grysar: ἄλλως ὑποκρίνεσθαι, Dübner.

the Athenians an old copy of the works of Aeschylus, Sophocles, and Euripides, promising to return it after he had made a transcript, and depositing fifteen talents as security. The transcript was made in the best possible style. Ptolemy then proceeded to keep the original manuscript for himself, and sent back merely the transcript to Athens. The Athenians had to console themselves with the fifteen talents which were forfeited. This old copy of the tragic writers was most probably that made in accordance with the law of Lycurgus.[1]

Athenian comedy, as was previously pointed out, continued to grow and develop long after tragedy had been reduced to a state of stagnation. The need for the reproduction of old comedies was therefore not felt until a much later epoch. The first recorded instances of revivals of this kind belong to the second century B.C. The system which was then introduced appears to have been identical with that adopted in the case of tragedy. A single old comedy was exhibited at each festival as a prelude to the new ones. As far as our information goes the specimen selected was tàken in every case from the works of Menander and his contemporaries.[2]

To turn once more to tragedy. The fourth century was an age of great actors, just as the fifth century had been an age of great poets. The principal actors of the fourth century filled a more important place in the history of tragedy than the dramatic poets themselves. Their fame was chiefly derived from their impersonations of characters out of the great tragedies of the past. A novel interpretation of a celebrated rôle, such as that of Antigone or Medea, was a much greater event in dramatic circles, and excited far more discussion, than the production of a new play. In exactly the same way the great English actors of the last hundred years or so are remembered, not so much for the new dramas which they brought out, as for their impersonation of parts like Hamlet and Othello. From the numerous references to Athenian actors of the fourth century, and to the old tragedies which they exhibited, it is possible to glean some interesting facts in regard to these revivals. We are able to trace the course of the popular taste, and to discover who were the favourite poets,

---

[1] Galen Comm. ii. on Hippocrat. Epidem. iii. (p. 607 Kühn).
[2] See above, pp. 22 and 27.

and which were the plays in most demand. The three great masters of tragedy, Aeschylus, Sophocles, and Euripides, occupied a position by themselves in popular estimation, and quite overshadowed all other poets. This is proved by the law of Lycurgus. But though the existence of the law shows that the tragedies of Aeschylus were occasionally reproduced, and were therefore liable to corruption, it does not appear that in this later age Aeschylus was very popular upon the stage. The only allusion to a particular revival of his plays is that which occurs in one of the letters of Alciphron, where the tragic actor Licymnius is said to have been victorious in the Propompi of Aeschylus.[1] On the other hand, the reproductions of plays of Sophocles and Euripides are very frequently referred to. And it is a significant fact that when the actor Satyrus was consoling Demosthenes for the ill-success of his first speech before the assembly, and wished to point out to him the defectiveness of his elocution, he asked him to repeat 'a speech out of Sophocles or Euripides', implying that these were the two poets whom every one knew.[2] In the Poetics of Aristotle the laws of the drama are based upon the plays of Sophocles and Euripides, while Aeschylus is comparatively disregarded. The simplicity of his plots and the elevation and occasional obscurity of his language were distasteful to an age which looked for ingenuity in the management of the incidents, and rhetorical facility in the style. These qualities were found to perfection in Euripides, and there can be no doubt that he was the favourite poet of the fourth century. The records of the tragic performances at the City Dionysia for the years 341-339 B.C. show that in each of these years the old tragedy selected for exhibition was one by Euripides. In 341 it was the Iphigeneia, in 340 it was the Orestes. The title of the play produced in 339 is lost, but the author was Euripides.[3] Other plays of his which were favourites at this time were the Cresphontes, the Oenomaus, and the Hecuba, in all of which Aeschines is said to have played the part of tritagonist. The Oenomaus and the Hecuba are also mentioned as plays in which the great actor Theodorus was especially effective. In the dream of Thrasyllus before the battle of Arginusae the plays

[1] Alciphron. Epist. iii. 48.   [2] Plut. Demosth. p. 849 A.
[3] C. I. A. ii. 973.

which were being acted were the Phoenissae and the Supplices
of Euripides.¹ Though the story of the dream is apocryphal,
these two tragedies were doubtless popular ones during the
fourth century. As to the plays of Sophocles, it is said that
Polus, the contemporary of Demosthenes, and the greatest
actor of his time, was celebrated for his performance of the
leading parts in the Oedipus Tyrannus, the Oedipus Coloneus,
and the Electra. The Antigone of Sophocles was often acted
by Theodorus and by Aristodemus. A certain Timotheus used
to make a great impression in the part of Ajax. Lastly, the
Epigoni of Sophocles is mentioned in connexion with Andronicus, another contemporary of Demosthenes.² It is interesting
to observe that of the plays which the popular taste of the
fourth century had begun to select for revival by far the greater
number are among those which are still extant.

¹ Demosth. de Cor. §§ 180, 267;   28 (ii. p. 211 Meineke); Demosth.
Aelian Var. Hist. xiv. 40; Plut. Fort.   Fals. Leg. § 246; Schol. Soph. Ajax
Alexand. 333 F; Diod. Sic. xiii. 97.   865; Athen. p. 584 D.
² Aul. Gell. vii. 5; Stob. Flor. 97,

CHAPTER III

THE THEATRE

§ 1. *Introductory.*

THE theatre at Athens, whether regarded from the historical or the architectural point of view, is one of the most interesting buildings in the world.[1] It was apparently the first stone theatre erected in Greece, and may therefore be regarded as the prototype of all other ancient theatres, both Greek and Roman. It cannot indeed claim to have been contemporary with the most glorious period of the Attic drama. Recent investigations have shown that the greater part of it cannot be dated before the middle of the fourth century with any certainty. Still, it occupied almost exactly the same site as the old wooden theatre in which the plays of Aeschylus, Sophocles, and Euripides were first exhibited. It no doubt reproduced in a more permanent form the main features and characteristics of that ancient theatre. It was itself the scene of those great revivals of Attic tragedy in the fourth century to which we have already alluded. In connexion with a building of such importance the smallest details are not without interest. The object of the chapter will be, firstly, to give an account of the existing remains and present condition of this theatre; secondly, to determine what must have been its original form and appearance, before the primitive design had been obscured by later alterations; thirdly, from the evidence thus collected, and from other sources, to draw such inferences as seem possible concerning the older theatre of the fifth century. It

---

[1] Throughout the present chapter my account of the existing remains of the Athenian theatre has been taken almost entirely from Dörpfeld and Reisch, Das griechische Theater, 1896. Dörpfeld's minute and admirable description of the theatre has superseded all previous treatises on the subject. For the old authorities see Preface to the First Edition, p. viii.

To face p. 78.

FIG. 2.   THEATRE AT ATHENS, FROM THE NORTH.

will be necessary at the same time to make occasional references
to various other Greek theatres, both for the purpose of illustration and comparison, and also in order to fill up the gaps
in our information caused by the ruinous condition of the
Athenian theatre. Many of these other theatres have lately
been excavated in a thorough and systematic manner, at
Epidaurus, Megalopolis, Delos, Eretria, and elsewhere. The
discoveries made in the course of the excavations have added
greatly to our knowledge of the Greek stage.

The construction and general arrangement of a Greek theatre
differed widely from any form of theatre to be found at the
present day. The Greek theatre was exposed to the open air,
and had no roof or covering of any kind. It was generally
built upon the slope of a hill in or near the city. It was of
enormous magnitude, compared with a modern theatre, being
intended to contain at one and the same time the whole theatre-
going population of the city. The largest part of it consisted
of the auditorium, or tiers of seats for the spectators. These
seats rose one above the other like a flight of steps, and
were arranged in the form of a semicircle with the two ends
prolonged. The flat space at the bottom of the auditorium,
corresponding to the stalls and pit in a modern theatre, was
called the orchestra or ' dancing-place', and was used by the
chorus only, the spectators being entirely excluded from it.
At the further end of the orchestra, facing the tiers of seats,
rose the stage and the stage-buildings. The stage was a long
platform, much narrower than a modern stage, and was reserved
for the actors, as opposed to the chorus. The open-air building,
the performance in broad daylight, the vast crowds of spectators,
the chorus grouped together in the centre, the actors standing
on the narrow stage behind them—all these characteristics of
a Greek theatrical exhibition must have combined to produce
a scene to which there is no exact parallel at the present day.
This fact should be kept clearly in view, in discussing all
questions connected with the Greek stage. Many errors have
been caused, and many unnecessary difficulties have been
raised, owing to the failure to realize the essential difference
between the external features of the ancient and the modern
drama.

§ 2. *The old Wooden Theatres at Athens.*

The type of theatre described above was of course only developed very gradually by the Athenians. It came into existence side by side with the growth of their drama. At first there was no permanent theatre. Attic tragedy grew out of the dithyrambs performed by choruses in honour of Dionysus. For such exhibitions all that was required was an orchestra, or circular dancing-place. The chorus performed in the middle, the spectators ranged themselves all round the ring. The first innovation was the introduction of a dialogue between the coryphaeus and the choreutae in the intervals of the choral odes. For the purpose of carrying on this dialogue the coryphaeus used to mount upon the sacrificial table which stood beside the altar in the centre of the orchestra.[1] Such sacrificial tables are often found in ancient vase paintings by the side of the regular altars, and were used for cutting up the victims, or for receiving various bloodless offerings such as cakes and vegetables.[2] Both the table and the altar were called by the same name, Thymele.[3] This table, on which the coryphaeus took his stand, surrounded by the choristers, was the prototype of the stage in the later Greek theatre. The next step in the development of the drama and of the theatre was the introduction of a single actor by Thespis. This actor took the part in the dialogue previously played by the coryphaeus. But the part was now much expanded and developed. The actor, instead of remaining in the centre of the orchestra throughout the performance, used to come and go, and appear in many rôles in succession, using a different costume on each occasion. A booth was erected just outside the orchestra, for him to change his dress and mask in. The

[1] Pollux iv. 123 ἐλεὸς δ' ἦν τράπεζα ἀρχαία, ἐφ' ἣν πρὸ Θέσπιδος εἰς τις ἀναβὰς τοις χορευταῖς ἀπεκρίνατο. Etym. Mag. s. v. θυμέλη· τράπεζα δὲ ἦν ἐφ' ἧς ἑστῶτες ἐν τοῖς ἀγροῖς ᾖδον, μήπω τάξιν λαβούσης τραγῳδίας. Dörpfeld (Griechische Theater, pp. 34, 278) thinks the ἐλεός was the altar step, which in some cases was of great size. Cp. the specimen he gives on p. 34. He quotes Pollux iv. 123 θυμέλη, εἴτε βῆμά τι οὖσα, εἴτε βωμός. But this passage does not mean that Pollux thought the thymele was partly an altar and partly a platform. It means that he was uncertain which of the two it was. Probably he was thinking of the later sense of θυμέλη = 'the stage'.

[2] Cp. Cook on the Thymele in Greek Theatres, Classical Review, October 1895, p. 371, and below, p. 108, with notes.

[3] Suidas s. v. σκηνή; Pollux iv. 123; Etym. Mag. s. v. θυμέλη.

platform on which he stood during the delivery of the dialogue was removed from the centre of the orchestra, and placed immediately in front of the booth, to facilitate his exits and entrances. This change led inevitably to others. The chorus, which had previously stood in a circle round the coryphaeus, now drew themselves up in lines facing the actor's platform, so as to converse with him in a natural manner. The spectators, instead of being ranged all round the orchestra, were confined to two-thirds of it. The remaining portion was taken up by the stage.

Such then was the arrangement of the theatre in the latter part of the sixth century. There was a booth with a small platform for the actor. In front of it lay the orchestra, occupied by the chorus. The audience sat in rows round the orchestra, facing the platform. At this early period the seats provided for the audience were only temporary erections. They were called 'ikria', and consisted of wooden benches rising in tiers one above the other, and resting on wooden supports.[1] The booth and platform were also mere temporary constructions of wood. But in these rude erections, hastily put up each year for the annual performances, were already to be found all the essential parts of the later Greek theatres. Nothing more was required than to change the material from wood to stone, and to introduce greater elaboration into the design. In course of time the old wooden benches developed into the magnificent amphitheatres of which the remains still survive. The booth and platform were converted into imposing stage-buildings. The recollection of their origin was preserved in their name. Even in the latest times, when the stage-buildings of a Greek theatre had come to be elaborate structures of stone, they were still called by the name 'skene', which means properly a booth or tent.

In this sketch of the early history of the Greek theatre one point deserves especial notice. The most important part of the whole building, and that which formed the starting-point in the process of development, was the orchestra, or place for

[1] Hesych. s. v. παρ' αἰγείρου θέα ... τὰ ἴκρια, ἅ ἐστιν ὀρθὰ ξύλα ἔχοντα σανίδας προσδεδεμένας, οἷον βαθμούς, ἐφ' αἷς ἐκαθέζοντο πρὸ τοῦ κατασκευασθῆναι τὸ θέατρον. Cp. Bekk. Anecd. p. 354; Hesych. and Suidas s.v. ἴκρια; Eustath. Od. p. 1472.

the chorus. The auditorium and the stage-buildings were only later additions. In all theatres of purely Greek origin the orchestra continued to maintain its prominent position. All other parts were subordinated to it. The general conception of a Greek theatre was that of a building with a circular dancing-place in the centre, and with tiers of seats arranged round two-thirds of the ring, while the remaining side was occupied by the stage. The result was that all the spectators had an equally good view of the orchestra, while many of them had only a very poor view of the stage. This arrangement was no doubt quite natural at first, when the chorus was still the most conspicuous feature in the drama. But it may seem remarkable that it should have been retained in later times. We should remember, however, that ancient theatres were built, not only for the drama, but also for choral and musical competitions of the most various kinds. Among the Greeks these latter were held solely in the orchestra, and had nothing to do with the stage. As they far exceeded the dramatic performances in number, it was essential in a Greek theatre that every member of the audience should have a clear and direct view of the orchestra; the view on to the stage was a matter of secondary importance. In Roman theatres the case was different. Here all performances, choral, musical, and dramatic, were transferred to the stage; the orchestra was given up to the spectators. The arrangements were, therefore, considerably modified. The orchestra and auditorium were reduced in size to a semicircle.[1] The consequence was that the stage became a much more prominent object, and that all the spectators had a fairly good view of it.

To return to the wooden theatres of the sixth century. As regards the place in which they were erected, there is some difficulty. The remains of an old orchestra belonging to the sixth century were discovered not many years ago in the enclosure of Dionysus Eleuthereus at the foot of the Acropolis. It follows, therefore, as a matter of practical certainty that the dramatic performances at the City Dionysia must have been given from the first in this orchestra, within the enclosure of the god of the festival. No doubt in the same way the

---

[1] All theatres, in which the orchestra consists of an exact semicircle, are either Roman, or built under Roman influence. See Vitruv. v. 6.

Lenaeum was the original site of the performances at the Lenaea;[1] but the site of the Lenaeum itself is much disputed. The most probable view is that it was in or adjoining the market-place : but it is not certain where the market-place itself lay.[2] There was an old proverb in use at Athens, by which a bad seat at any spectacle was called the ' view from the poplar '. The grammarians, who apparently follow Eratosthenes, give the following explanation. They say that at the old dramatic exhibitions the wooden benches for the spectators reached as far as a certain poplar ; and that the people who could not get seats on the benches used to scramble up the poplar.[3] It is possible that the story is an attempt to account by conjecture for a current proverbial expression ; but it may represent a genuine tradition.

Till the end of the sixth century the Athenians were contented with the rough temporary erections just described. But in 499, the year in which Aeschylus made his first appearance, there was an accident at one of their dramatic performances. The wooden benches on which the spectators were sitting collapsed. In consequence of this accident, as Suidas tells us, they resolved to build a more permanent theatre.[4] It was generally supposed, until quite recent times, that the theatre here mentioned was the great stone theatre still in existence. But Dörpfeld has made it certain that at least a great part of this building is not earlier than the middle of the fourth century ; and though Puchstein is possibly right in seeing traces of a stone theatre dating from the end of the fifth century, this does not take us back to the time of Aeschylus.[5] What then was the building to which Suidas refers ? The answer to this question has been supplied by a recent discovery of a very interesting kind. On digging down into the earth foundations of the present auditorium it has been ascertained that these foundations consist of two layers. The upper one belongs to the fourth century, as is shown by the fragments of pottery

---

[1] The term θέατρον Ληναϊκόν mentioned by Pollux (iv. 121) may refer to the old wooden theatre in the Lenaeum.

[2] See Appendix C for a discussion of the site of the Lenaeum.

[3] Suidas s.v. ἀπ' αἰγείρου θέα. Hesych.

s.vv. αἰγείρου θέα, παρ' αἰγείρου θέα, θέα παρ' αἰγείρῳ. Eustath. Od. p. 1472.

[4] Suidas s.v. Πρατίνας ... συνέβη τὰ ἴκρια, ἐφ' ὧν ἐστήκεσαν οἱ θεαταί, πεπεῖν, καὶ ἐκ τούτου θέατρον ᾠκοδομήθη 'Αθηναίοις.

[5] See below, p. 130.

embedded in it; the lower one is proved by similar evidence
to be not later than the fifth.[1] It follows, therefore, that the
Athenians must have built earth embankments for the support
of the auditorium as early as the fifth century, and it is doubtless
to this work that Suidas alludes.   The innovation adopted in
499, in consequence of the accident, was not the erection of
a stone theatre, but the substitution of solid earth foundations
for the 'ikria' or wooden supports on which the seats had
previously rested.   The new theatre still resembled the old one,
in that the benches and the stage-buildings were made of wood;
but greater security and permanence were afforded by the
erection of the embankments.   The site chosen for this new
theatre was the enclosure of Eleuthereus, where the City
Dionysia, the most important of the dramatic festivals, was
held.   From this time forward all theatrical performances were
transferred to the same enclosure.   The Lenaeum was abandoned
as a place of dramatic entertainment.   The contrary opinion,
that the old wooden theatre at the Lenaeum continued to be
used for the Lenaean festival until the erection of the stone
theatre in the fourth century,[2] is most improbable.   The need
for a secure auditorium in place of the previous 'ikria' would
be felt just as much at the Lenaea as at the City Dionysia.   But
there is no trace or record of a permanent theatre at the
Lenaeum.   The recurrence of the expression 'contests at the
Lenaeum' down to the latter part of the fourth century proves
nothing.[3]   The phrase might easily have been retained, after its
local significance was gone, by a kind of survival common in all
languages.   In just the same way the performances at the City
Dionysia were still distinguished from all others as performances 'in the city', when the reason for the distinction had long
since disappeared.

A few faint traces of this theatre of the fifth century are
still to be discerned amid the remains of the later building,
and will be found indicated in the plan (Fig. 3).[4]   The orchestra
was the same as that which had already existed in the sixth
century.   Its position is determined by two fragments of

---

[1] Dörpfeld and Reisch, Griechische
Theater, p. 31.
[2] Wilamowitz, Hermes, xxi. p. 622.
Griech. Theater, p. 9.
[3] Aristoph. Acharn. 504; Plat. Prot.

327 D; Dem. Meid. § 10 (law of
Evegorus); C. I. A. ii. 741 (334-331
B.C.).
[4] Griech. Theater, pp. 26 ff.

the border, marked *q* and *r*, and by some excavations in the
rock at *i*. It lay a few yards to the south-east of the later
orchestra. One peculiarity of this orchestra of the sixth and
fifth centuries is that, when it was originally constructed, its
southern portion stood about six feet above the level of the
adjacent ground. It was, therefore, supported and enclosed on
this side by a wall of the same height, to which the fragments
q and *r* belong. Later on the inequality of level was removed by piling up earth along the border-wall. Probably
this alteration was made towards the end of the sixth century,
when stage-buildings began to be erected; though it is
possible that at first the gap between the orchestra and the
stage-buildings was merely covered over with a wooden flooring. A similar instance of an orchestra built on a slope, and
ending on one side in a raised terrace, has been found at
Thoricus.[1] But in this case, as there were no stage-buildings,
the inequality was allowed to remain. Very likely the theatre
was not used for dramatic purposes. As regards the auditorium
of the fifth century, the earth embankments for the reception
of the seats have already been described. Three pieces of
ancient masonry, marked *k*, *l*, and *m* in the plan, may perhaps
be regarded as parts of the supporting walls which terminated
these embankments on each wing. The stage-buildings, being
made of wood, have left no trace behind them of any kind.
Their probable character will be discussed later on.

It is evident, from the above description, that the theatre
of the fifth century was a far less imposing structure than
was once supposed. The result of recent excavations has
been to modify largely all our previous notions as to the
great period of the Athenian drama. In place of the majestic
stone theatre, in which it was once thought that the plays of
Sophocles and Euripides were produced, we have now to
picture to ourselves a simple wooden building, resting on
earth foundations, and devoid of all architectural ornament.
The difference is no doubt a great one. Still, it is not perhaps
so great as might appear at first sight. The impressiveness
of the old Greek drama, regarded as a spectacle, depended
on other considerations than the magnificence of the building

---

[1] Griech. Theater, p. 111.

in which it was exhibited.   When the vast roofless amphitheatre was filled from end to end with the concourse of
citizens and strangers, it would make little difference in the
significance of the scene whether the benches were of wood
or stone.   The orchestra of a Greek theatre was always much
the same in character, in the grandest as well as in the simplest
theatres; and the graceful evolutions of the chorus under the
open sky would be equally effective in both.   The long scenic
background, with its painted decorations, cannot have varied
much in appearance, whether it rested on a wall of stone or
on a wall of timber.   Although, therefore, the theatre of the
great Athenian dramatists was an unpretentious structure, as
compared with those which were erected in after times, it
is unnecessary to suppose that there was any corresponding
inferiority in the outward splendour of the performances.

§ 3.   *The Stone Theatre.*

The stone theatre, which we have now to describe, is ascribed
by Dörpfeld to about the middle of the fourth century.   His
reasons for assigning this date to it are as follows.[1]   In all the
older portions of the building, which belong to the original
plan, there is a certain similarity in the style of the workmanship, and in the nature of the materials employed, which points
to the fourth century as the date of erection.   We have seen,
too, that the upper foundations of the auditorium are proved
to be not earlier than the fourth century by the fragments of
pottery which they contain.   Further than this, various minute
pieces of evidence, leading to the same conclusion, have been
discovered in different parts of the building.   One of the stones
used in the western wing of the auditorium bears, as a mason's
mark, the Ionic letter Omega—a letter which was not introduced
into Athens before the year 403 B.C.   (It must, however, be
admitted that the argument drawn from this stone is not quite
conclusive, as it is probable that the Ionic alphabet was in
private use before the archonship of Euclides in 403.[2])   Another
stone in the same wing contains an inscription, and has been

[1] Griech. Theater, pp. 36 ff.   p. 415.   Roberts and Gardner, Greek
[2] Fürtwängler, Sitzungsber. der   Epigraphy, ii. Introd. p. xiii.
Akad. der Wiss. zu München, 1901,

built into the wall with the inscription inverted.[1] As the inscription itself is not earlier than the middle or end of the fifth century, the wall for which the stone was employed must obviously belong to a later period. Again, part of the basis of a statue has been found in the theatre, inscribed with the first half of the name 'Astydamas'. The basis is shown by its shape to have fitted on to the inside corner of the west wing of the auditorium. As it is known that a statue of Astydamas was erected in the theatre about the year 340, it follows that this portion of the auditorium must have been finished at that date.[2] These archaeological indications are supported by literary evidence. A decree of the people has been preserved, belonging to the year 330 B.C., in which a vote of thanks is passed to a certain Eudemus of Plataea for lending a thousand yoke of oxen for ' the construction of the Panathenaic race-course and the theatre '.[3] There is also the series of decrees and notices, referring to the finance administration of the orator Lycurgus, and ascribing to him, among other things, the 'completion of the theatre'.[4] Lycurgus was finance minister between 338 and 326, and died about 325. The evidence shows beyond doubt that Lycurgus did important work in connexion with the theatre, and that the theatre was considerably changed, in the third quarter of the fourth century B.C.[5] But it has been recently argued by Puchstein that there are traces of a stone theatre of earlier date, which he assigns to the last years of the fifth century. He would throw back to this date a great part of the work generally termed Lycurgean, and would ascribe to Lycurgus the construction of the stage-buildings generally termed Hellenistic and assigned to the first or second century B.C. The evidence for this must be considered later. The theory is not improbable, and would solve some difficulties;

---

[1] C. I. A. i. 499. Cp. p. 132.
[2] Tragic Drama of the Greeks, p. 430.
[3] C. I. A. ii. 176.
[4] Plut. X orat. 841 C καὶ τὸ ἐν Διονύσου θέατρον ἐπιστατῶν ἐτελεύτησε. Id. Psephism. iii. πρὸς δὲ τούτοις ἡμίεργα παραλαβὼν τούς τε νεωσοίκους καὶ τὴν σκευοθήκην καὶ τὸ θέατρον τὸ Διονυσιακὸν ἐξειργάσατο καὶ ἐπετέλεσε. Paus. i. 29. 16 οἰκοδομήματα δὲ ἐπετέλεσε μὲν τὸ θέατρον ἑτέρων ὑπαρξαμένων. Hyperid. or. dep. 118 Kenyon ταχθεὶς

δὲ ἐπὶ τῇ διοικήσει τῶν χρημάτων εὗρε πόρους, ᾠκοδόμησε δὲ τὸ θέατρον,τὸ ᾠδεῖον, τὰ νεώρια, τριήρεις ἐποιήσατο, λιμένας.
[5] [Aristoph. Thesm. 395 (B.C. 411) and Cratinus, Frag. Incert. 51 (before B.C. 422) call the spectators' seats ἴκρια, ' benches ' : but the name might survive after the material had been changed from wood to stone ; and Puchstein may be right in dating this before the end of the fifth century. See below, p. 131.]

but at the same time it is not so certain as to justify the definite rejection of the older view, and it will be more convenient to discuss it separately.[1]

In the so-called Hellenistic reconstruction of the stage-buildings which has been referred to, the essential feature was the building of a stone-columned proscenium or stage front, and it is this which Puchstein now refers to Lycurgus. In the first century A.D. the stage-buildings were again reconstructed. Part of the frieze still remains, with an inscription dedicating the work to the Emperor Nero.[2] About two centuries later a certain Phaedrus erected a new stage, and commemorated the fact by some verses on one of the steps.[3] At this point all traces of the history of the theatre are lost. During the Middle Ages it disappeared so completely from view that its very site was forgotten. For a long time modern travellers knew nothing upon the subject. The true site was first pointed out by Chandler in 1765. In 1862 excavations were commenced by the German architect Strack, and continued for three years. The theatre was again exposed to view, and large portions of it were found to have been preserved. Some further discoveries were made in 1877. Lastly, in 1886, 1889, and 1895 new excavations have been carried on under the direction of Dörpfeld, acting for the German Archaeological Institute. The result of these latest investigations has been to clear up many doubtful points in the history of the building, and the arrangement of its various parts.

The new theatre, like the old one, was erected in the enclosure of Dionysus Eleuthereus. This enclosure lay at the foot of the Acropolis, by which it was bounded on the northern side. Its southern boundary may possibly be identical with certain fragments of an old wall, marked *x* in the plan. Within the enclosure were two temples of Dionysus, of which the foundations have recently been discovered. The oldest, marked *t*, was the nearest to the Acropolis, and is assigned by Dörpfeld to the sixth century. It contained the ancient image of Dionysus Eleuthereus which was carried in the annual procession at the City Dionysia. The more recent temple (*u*)

---

[1] See below, p. 130.
[2] C. I. A. iii. 158.
[3] C. I. A. iii. 239 σοὶ τόδε καλὸν ἔτευξε

φιλόργιε βῆμα θεήτρου | Φαῖδρος Ζωίλου
βιοδώτορος Ἀτθίδος ἀρχός.

lay a few yards to the south of the old one. In it stood a gold and ivory statue of Dionysus made by Alcamenes towards the end of the fifth century. The temple itself was probably of the same date.[1] Near this temple are the remains of a square foundation (w), also of the fifth century, which possibly served as the basis for an altar.[2] The site chosen for the new theatre was almost identical with that of the old one, but lay a few yards further to the north-west. The reasons for this change were apparently twofold. By bringing the auditorium closer to the Acropolis, it was possible to make a more extensive use of the slope of the hill as a support for the tiers of seats. At the same time a larger space was left between the orchestra and the old temple of Dionysus, and so afforded more room for the stage-buildings. In one respect the position of the theatre differed from that usually adopted in later times. The auditorium faced almost directly towards the south. This arrangement was generally avoided by the Greeks, and Vitruvius expressly warns architects against the danger of adopting it, because of the terrible heat caused by the midday sun glaring into the concavity of the theatre.[3] But at Athens there were special reasons on the other side. If the theatre was to be built in the enclosure of Eleuthereus, the only natural position was along the slopes of the Acropolis, and facing towards the south. The rising ground supplied an excellent foundation for the central portion of the auditorium. The choice of any other situation would have involved the erection of costly and elaborate substructures. The Athenians, therefore, from motives of economy, preferred the southern aspect, in spite of its obvious disadvantages. The same course was also adopted in the theatres of Eretria and Syracuse.

In proceeding to describe in detail the form and construction of the theatre it will be convenient to take the different portions in succession. A Greek theatre is naturally divided into three parts, the auditorium, the orchestra, and the stage-buildings. In the following description the auditorium will be considered first, the orchestra next. The stage-buildings, as forming the most difficult part of the whole subject, will be reserved for the last.

---

[1] See E. A. Gardner, Ancient Athens, p. 435.

[2] Paus. i. 20 3; Griech. Theater, pp. 10 ff.

[3] Vitruv. v. 3. 2.

§ 4. *The Auditorium.*

The auditorium, or the portion of the theatre containing the seats for the spectators, was called the 'cavea' in Latin; but there was no technical name for it in Greek. In almost all Greek theatres it was built upon the side of a hill, so that the natural slope of the ground might serve as a foundation for the tiers of seats. At Athens, as we have seen, the rising ground at the foot of the Acropolis was utilized for this purpose, and supported the central part of the building. It was only at the two wings, on the east and west, that artificial substructures were necessary, in order to bring the back seats up to the proper height. The walls by which the auditorium was bounded on the outside have been preserved to a certain extent, and suffice to mark clearly the original shape of the building. On the western side of the theatre, from *a* to *b* in the plan (Fig. 3)[1], where a strong support was required for the embankment, a device was adopted which is still commonly employed at the present day. If a single wall had been erected, it must have been of enormous width. As a substitute two narrow walls were built in parallel lines, with cross-walls at intervals, and the intervening space was filled up with earth. Thus the same result was obtained at a less expense. Along the north-western curve of the theatre, between *b* and *c*, a single wall proved sufficient, owing to the diminishing size of the embank-ment. At the point *c* the rock of the Acropolis abutted upon the theatre, and was hollowed out into a regular curve. This is without doubt the portion of the theatre referred to by the ancients as Katatome, or 'the Cutting'.[2] In the rock at this place is a natural grotto enlarged by artificial means, and 34 ft. long by 20 ft. broad. Here Thrasyllus erected an elaborate monument to commemorate his victory with a chorus of men in 319 B.C. In front of the grotto stood three columns supporting an entablature, and surmounted by a statue of Dionysus. On the architrave was an inscription recording the

---

[1] The plan is copied from that given in Griech. Theater, Tafel I.

[2] Harp. s.v. κατατομή· Ὑπερείδης ἐν τῷ κατὰ Δημοσθένους. καὶ καθήμενος κάτω ὑπὸ τῇ κατατομῇ. Φιλόχορος δὲ ἐν ἕκτῃ οὕτως· Αἰσχραῖος Ἀναγυράσιος ἀνέθηκε τὸν ὑπὲρ θεάτρου τρίποδα καταργυρώσας, νενικηκὼς τῷ πρότερον ἔτει χορηγῶν παισί, καὶ ἐπέγραψεν ἐπὶ τὴν κατατομὴν τῆς πέτρας. Bekk Anecd. p. 270. 21 κατα-τομὴ ἡ ὀρχήστρα ἡ νῦν σίγμα, ἡ μέρος τι τοῦ θεάτρου κατετμήθη, ἐπεὶ ἐν ὄρει κατεσκεύασται.

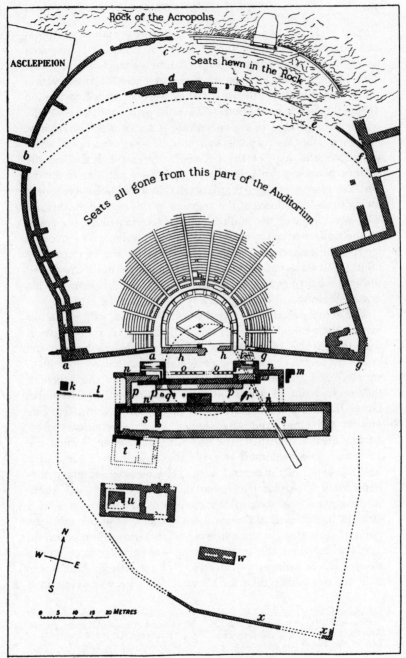

Rock of the Acropolis

ASCLEPIEION

Seats hewn in the Rock

Seats all gone from this part of the Auditorium

N
W — E
S

0   5   10   15   20 METRES

FIG. 3.   GROUND-PLAN OF THEATRE AT ATHENS.

victory of Thrasyllus. Inside the grotto were statues of Apollo and Artemis destroying the children of Niobe. In modern times the grotto has been converted into a chapel of Our Lady. The columns and entablature were in excellent preservation when Stuart visited Athens, but they were shattered by a mine during the Greek revolution. Above the grotto are two columns, which were erected to commemorate victories with dithyrambic choruses. On the capitals can still be seen the holes made to receive the legs of the tripods.[1] After the Katatome the eastern boundary wall, from f to g, is very peculiar in shape. But the reason of the irregularity has not yet been explained, owing to the scantiness of the remains in this part of the theatre. The two wings of the auditorium are terminated on the south by the walls marked a-a and g-g. These walls are of unequal length, the eastern wall being about 111 ft., the western only 88 ft. They are not in the same straight line, but if continued inwards would meet in an obtuse angle in the orchestra. This arrangement was the one generally adopted by the Greeks.

The above description, together with the plan, will give a fair idea of the general outline of the auditorium. If we compare it with the theatre of Epidaurus (Fig. 6), which was built at the end of the fourth century, and designed on one harmonious plan, we shall perceive at once the great inferiority of the Athenian theatre in point of grace and symmetry of outline. In most Greek theatres the auditorium was of the same width from one end to the other, and was shaped in a symmetrical curve. In the theatre at Athens the two wings of the auditorium are narrowed so considerably towards the south as to be less than half the depth of the central part. The outside boundary does not run in a regular curve, but is very much flattened where it encounters the rock of the Acropolis, and terminates in a straight line at each of the southern corners. But the strangest point of all is that the eastern wing, at its termination, is several yards wider than the western wing—an arrangement utterly destructive of symmetry of design. The theatre at Athens was built for use rather than for show. Its shape was determined

<hr />

[1] Paus. i. 21. 5; C. I. A. ii. 1247; Stuart and Revett's Antiquities of Athens, ii. 8. For a detailed description of the Thrasyllus monument see Harrison and Verrall, Mythology and Monuments of Ancient Athens, pp. 266 ff.; E. Gardner, Ancient Athens, p. 403.

by the conformation of the ground and by the situation of the adjoining rocks. Although, therefore, it is the most interesting of Greek theatres on account of its historical associations, in point of mere beauty it cannot take the highest rank.

We now come to the interior of the auditorium. The boundary between the auditorium and the orchestra is denoted by the dark line in the plan. It will be observed that in the theatre of Dionysus the inside boundary of the auditorium consists of a semicircle with the two ends prolonged in parallel straight lines. This was not the plan usually followed in Greek theatres. In most of the later theatres the two ends of the semicircle were prolonged in the same curve as before, so that the inside boundary of the auditorium formed about two-thirds of a regular circle. The effect of this arrangement was that the spectators sitting at the extremities of the two wings faced towards the centre of the orchestra, and away from the stage. Nor is this surprising. It was previously pointed out that in Greek theatres, where the choral and musical contests greatly outnumbered the dramatic, the orchestra was always the most important part of the whole building. But the arrangement adopted at Athens, of prolonging the two ends of the semicircle in a straight line, had the advantage of giving the spectators in the wings a much better view of the stage. The same plan was also adopted in the theatre of the Peiraeeus, and in the theatres of Assos, Acrae, and Termessos. At Epidaurus and Magnesia a third plan was pursued, differing from both the above. The two ends of the semicircle were prolonged, not in a straight line, nor yet in the same curve as before, but from a new centre, and with a longer radius, so that while they converged to a certain extent, they did not converge so much as in the ordinary Greek theatres. This arrangement, which may be regarded as a compromise between the other two, is perhaps the most beautiful of them all. It is apparently recommended by Vitruvius, though the passage in which he refers to it is extremely ambiguous and has been interpreted in various other ways.[1]

The interior of the auditorium consisted of a series of stone seats rising tier above tier in a gentle slope from the boundary of the orchestra to the outside extremities of the building.

[1] See Griech. Theater, pp. 169 ff.; Capps, Vitruvius and the Greek Stage, pp. 18 ff.

Immediately under the cliff of the Acropolis the seats were carved out of the living rock. With this exception they were made of Peiraic limestone. In some of the upper portions of the theatre they were fixed upon conglomerate foundations. But in most parts they were placed directly upon the bare earth, and were therefore easily capable of being removed. For this reason the greater number of them have disappeared, having been taken away during the Middle Ages for building purposes. All that remain are from twenty to thirty rows in the bottom of the theatre, and portions of a few rows at the top. From these, however, it is possible to obtain a clear conception of the style and arrangement of the auditorium. In order to make the following description more intelligible, an illustration is here inserted, consisting of a restoration of the extremity of the eastern wing (Fig. 4). In this illustration a is the orchestra, b the eastern entrance into the orchestra, c the southern boundary wall of the east wing of the auditorium.[1]

To proceed with the description of the seats. The lowest step of the auditorium rose about ten inches above the level of the orchestra, and then sloped gently upward towards the front row of seats, where it reached a height of fourteen inches. It was built of large slabs of stone, and formed a sort of passage between the orchestra and the seats. The curve of the seats did not coincide exactly with the curve of the orchestra, but was drawn from a centre rather more to the south, and receded slightly on the two wings. As a consequence the passage was wider at the sides than in the centre, the width at the sides being about eight feet, the width at the centre only four. The same variety of curve is found in the theatre at the Peiraeeus; and Dörpfeld supposes that it was adopted in order to give more room at the entrances of the passage, where the press of people would be the greatest.[2] The first row of seats was far superior to the others, and consisted of marble thrones with backs to them. Each throne was about 25 inches wide and 23 inches deep. In the centre was the throne of the priest of Dionysus, slightly larger than the others, and elaborately and beautifully carved. This throne, unlike the rest, was pro-

[1] The illustration is copied, with a few alterations, from Zeitschrift für bildende Kunst, xiii. p. 197.
[2] Griech. Theater, p. 51.

vided with a canopy resting on wooden posts, the holes for
which are still visible.   Many of the thrones, including that
of the chief priest, had receptacles in front of them in which
footstools might be placed.   The thrones were originally sixty-
seven in number, but only sixty of them are now preserved.
Fourteen of these were no longer standing in their proper
position at the time of the first excavations.   Some of them
had been designedly removed in Roman times, when certain
alterations were made in the front row; others had been
accidentally displaced.   Most of them have now been restored
to their original sites.   That the thrones were erected at the

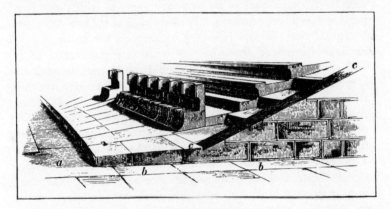

FIG. 4.

latest by the time of Lycurgus appears to be proved by the
excellence of the workmanship.   Each of them has an inscription in the front, recording the title of the priest or official for
whom the seat was reserved.   These inscriptions are all of the
Hellenistic or Roman period ; but behind them are faint traces
of older inscriptions, which may possibly go back to the fourth
century.   The practice of erecting superior seats in the first
row for people of distinction was a common one in Greek
theatres.   At Megalopolis, for example, the front bench was
provided with a back, though it was not divided into separate
seats, as at Athens.   In the theatre of Epidaurus there were
three rows of superior workmanship, one at the bottom of the
auditorium and two others half-way up the slope, one on each

side of the longitudinal passage. But the most peculiar arrangement was that adopted at Oropus and Priene. At Oropus five magnificent thrones were placed inside the ring of the orchestra itself, and well in front of the lowest tier of seats, each throne standing a few yards distant from the other. At Priene a long stone bench with a back was erected in the same position, and in this bench five thrones were inserted at regular intervals.[1]

Immediately behind the line of thrones there was a vacant space about 33 inches wide. Then came what appears to be a small step. But Dörpfeld has shown that this step is merely the back part of an ordinary seat, of which the front portion has been removed. In the original theatre there was a regular tier of seats following closely on the thrones. But in later times the front half of this tier was taken away. The object of the change, as Dörpfeld thinks, was to open out a wide space for the reception of a row of wooden thrones, which might serve as a supplement to the marble ones.[2] After the step, which we have just described, began the first of the ordinary tiers of seats, which were continued in exactly the same style from this point up to the top of the building. The shape of the seats is very much the same as in other Greek theatres. Their dimensions are as follows. Each seat was 13 inches high, and was hollowed out slightly in front, so that the person sitting on it might have more freedom for his legs. The surface of the seat was 33 inches across, and was divided into three distinct portions. The first part was for sitting upon, and was 13 inches deep. The second part was 2 inches lower, and was intended to receive the feet of the persons upon the seat above. It was 16 inches across. The third part was merely a narrow edge, of the same level as the first part, and 4 inches deep. The height of the tiers, as we have seen, was 13 inches. If we add to this the 2 inches of the depression in front, it raises the height of the actual seat to 15 inches. A seat of this kind would be rather low for a man of average size. But it was the practice of the Greek spectator to provide himself with a cushion, which

---

[1] Gardner and Loring, Excavations at Megalopolis, p. 74; Griech. Theater, pp. 101, 121; Schrader, Berl. Phil. Wochenschrift, April 16, 1898, p. 508.

[2] Griech. Theater, p. 44.

would raise the surface to a more comfortable level. The structure of the tiers in the manner described appears to have been due to a desire for economy in the use of space. In a Greek theatre, where an immense number of people had to be accommodated with seats in tolerable proximity to the orchestra and stage, it was necessary to place them as close together as possible. If the surface of each tier had been perfectly flat from front to back, the distance between the successive tiers must have been considerably increased, in order to obtain a height of 15 inches. The depression in the tiers provided the requisite height, while allowing a much smaller interval. Along the front of the rows of seats were two sets of vertical lines engraved in the stone. The lines in the first set were 13 inches apart; the lines in the second, which are rather fainter, were at intervals of 16 inches. Probably the second series of lines was intended to mark off the separate seats. In the first series the intervals are too narrow for this purpose, and can only have served as general measures of distance.

For the purpose of giving access to the different parts of the auditorium a series of passages ran in divergent lines, like the spokes of a wheel, from the orchestra up to the outside boundary. The passages were fourteen in number, and the two upon the extreme south at each side adjoined immediately upon the boundary walls. In theatres of large size, such as those of Epidaurus and Aspendos, it was usual to insert extra passages in the upper part of the auditorium. The manner in which they were arranged will be seen by looking at the plan of the Epidaurus theatre (Fig. 6). At Athens the upper portion of the building has so entirely disappeared that it is impossible to say whether it ever contained additional passages of this kind. But the great size of the theatre makes it probable that such was the case. These vertical passages were always very narrow, in order to save room. At Athens they were only about 27 inches in width, the result being that not more than one person could ascend at a time. The arrangement of the steps along the passages in the Athenian theatre was altogether exceptional, and is only paralleled at the Peiraeeus. In all other Greek theatres each tier of seats had two steps corresponding to it in the vertical passages. But at Athens, and also at the Peiraeeus, there was only one step for each tier of seats. As the seats were 13 inches high, while the steps were only 8½, it was necessary to make up the difference by building the steps with a sloping surface. The surface was furrowed over, to make the ascent more easy. The fourteen passages divided the auditorium into thirteen blocks. Such blocks were called 'cunei' or 'wedges' in Latin, because of their shape. In Greek they were called 'kerkides', from their resemblance to the 'kerkis', a tapering rod used in weaving.[1] The front row in each 'kerkis' contained five marble thrones, with the exception of the two 'kerkides' on the extreme south of each wing, which contained six thrones each; so that the total number of marble thrones was sixty-seven.

In addition to the vertical passages all Greek theatres of any size were also intersected by one or two longitudinal passages, called 'praecinctiones' in Latin. These passages divided the auditorium into sections, called 'belts' or 'girdles' in Greek technical terminology.[2] A passage of this kind may still be traced in the upper part of the theatre of Dionysus. Its course is determined by the foundations at *d*, by certain excavations in the rock at *e*, and by the two entrances at *b* and *f*. The great width of the passage—about 15 feet—is explained by the fact that it was also intended to serve as a road. From ancient times there had been a road at the foot of the Acropolis, running from east to west. Traces of this old road have been discovered during the excavations of 1889, and lie about 26 feet below the level of the present auditorium. When its course was intercepted by the erection of the theatre, this passage was constructed on a larger scale than usual, to serve as a substitute. On ordinary occasions, when the theatre was empty, it would be used as a public highway.[3] That it formed a conspicuous object in the midst of the auditorium is shown by a coin in the British Museum (Fig. 5), which contains on one side a rude representation

---

[1] Pollux iv. 123.
[2] διαζώματα, C. I. G. 4283; ζῶναι, Malal. p. 222. The longitudinal passages are called δίοδοι in the Delian inscription for 269 B C. The upper belt of seats is called ἐπιθέατρον in the inscription for 250 B.C. Sec Bull. Corr. Hell., 1894, pp. 162 ff.
[3] Griech. Theater, p. 41.

of the theatre at Athens.[1] On this coin, in spite of the rough-
ness of the design, the passage stands out very prominently.
Whether there was a second longitudinal passage in the
Athenian theatre is uncertain.   But the space to the north
of the existing passage is so small when compared with the
space to the south of it, that it seems reasonable to infer that
there was another passage lower down, dividing the under part
of the auditorium into two sections.   It was the fashion in
Roman theatres to erect a portico along the top of the
auditorium, following the line of the uppermost tier of seats.[2]
But there are no traces of such a portico in the theatre at
Athens, or in any other theatre of purely Greek origin.

FIG. 5.

The following facts and measurements will give some idea
of the size and capacity of the Athenian theatre.   The distance
between the inside corners of the auditorium was 72 feet.   The
distance between the outside corners was 288 feet.   In the
centre of the auditorium, from north to south, it is calculated
that there must have been 78 tiers of seats.   Of course on each
of the two wings the number of tiers would be considerably less
than half that amount.   The arrangements throughout were
designed with the view of bringing together the largest possible
number of people within the smallest possible compass.   The
vertical passages were little over 2 feet in width.   The seats
were constructed in such a manner that the spectators could

[1] The copy is taken from Wieseler's Denkmäler des Bühnenwesens, i. 1.
[2] Vitruv. v. 6. 4.

H 2

be packed tightly together, without any space being wasted.
As the theatre was in the open air the close crowding of the
audience was no doubt much less intolerable than it would have
been in a covered building. At the same time the situation
of the spectator cannot have been a very comfortable one.
He had to remain cramped up in one position, with no back
to lean against, and with very little opportunity of moving his
limbs. That the Athenians were willing to put up with such
inconveniences for several days in succession is a proof of
their enthusiastic devotion to music and the drama. The total
number of people who could be accommodated in the theatre
at Athens is shown by recent calculations to have been about
17,000.[1] The theatres at Epidaurus and Megalopolis held
nearly the same number.[2] Plato, referring to the wooden
theatre of his own time, speaks of 'more than thirty thousand
spectators'.[3] But this must have been an exaggeration. The
old theatre of the fifth century is not likely to have been larger
and more capacious than the theatre of Lycurgus.

The auditorium, unlike the rest of the building, was subjected
to very little alteration in later times. The parts of it which are
still preserved remain in much the same state as in the age
of Lycurgus. The various successive changes in the style of
the dramatic performances, while they led to corresponding
changes in the orchestra and the stage-buildings, had naturally
no effect upon the structure of the auditorium. A few innovations were introduced in the Roman period, mostly for the
purpose of increasing the comfort of the more distinguished
spectators. We have seen that in the old theatre the only person
provided with a canopy was the priest of Dionysus. The same
luxury was now extended to all the people in the front benches.
An awning was erected on wooden posts to protect them from

---

[1] Griech. Theater, p. 45. Dörpfeld
obtains this result by allowing for
each person a space of 16 inches—
the distance between the vertical lines
already mentioned (p. 97). If 19
inches is allowed, he calculates that the
theatre would have held about 14,000
people.

[2] Megalopolis held about 17,000
(Gardner), or 18,700 (Schultz); Epidaurus about 17,000 (Gardner). These
calculations, however, should be slightly
reduced, as they are based on an
allowance of only 13 inches for each
person (see above, p. 97), which is
certainly too small, though the experience of modern theatre managers shows
that, where the seats have no dividing
arms, 14 inches is sufficient and 16
inches ample. (See Gardner, Ancient
Athens, p. 439.) See Excavations at
Megalopolis, p. 69.

[3] Plat. Symp. 175 E.

the sun. Three lines of holes for the reception of the posts may still be traced in the stone-work, one in front of the thrones, one behind, and one in the second row of ordinary seats. It seems that about this date there was an increase in the number of people for whom seats of honour were required. The front row of the ordinary benches was removed, in the way already described, to supply the necessary space. Single marble thrones were also set up here and there in the rows further back. Another change, which involved some disfigurement of the building, was made about the same time. A large stone basis, approached by steps, was erected in front of the sixth vertical passage, thus closing the approach to that passage, and also necessitating the removal of four of the marble thrones, which were placed elsewhere. The basis was probably intended as a sort of royal box, and held a special throne reserved for people of imperial rank. A similar basis was also erected, probably for the same purpose, behind the seat of the priest of Dionysus.

§ 5. *The Orchestra.*

After the auditorium the next great division of the theatre is the orchestra. This was the name given to the flat surface enclosed between the stage-buildings and the inside boundary of the auditorium. It was called the orchestra, or 'dancing-place', because in Greek theatres it was reserved for the performances of the chorus.[1] In later times it was also called the Sigma, because its shape resembled the semicircular figure which was adopted in the fourth century as the symbol of the letter sigma.[2] In one place the word 'konistra' is employed to denote the orchestra.[3] Konistra means properly the arena of a wrestling-school. It would hardly be applicable as a term for the early Greek orchestras, which were used for music and dancing, but not for gymnastic contests. Probably therefore this meaning of the word was of late origin, and first arose in the Roman period, when Greek theatres occasionally became

---

[1] Phot. s.v. ὀρχήστρα. . . τοῦ θεάτρου τὸ κάτω ἡμικύκλιον, οὗ καὶ οἱ χοροὶ ᾖδον καὶ ὠρχοῦντο.

[2] Bekk. Anecd. p. 270. 21 ἡ ὀρχήστρα ἡ νῦν σίγμα λεγομένη Ibid. p. 286. 16.

[3] Suidas s.v. σκηνή . . . ἡ κονίστρα, τουτέστι τὸ κάτω ἔδαφος τοῦ θεάτρου. The same scholium is repeated in Schol. Gregor. Nazianz. laud. patr. 355 B.

the scene of gladiatorial contests. Among the Romans the
orchestra was given up to the spectators, and the performances
of singers and dancers took place upon the stage. Hence the
later Greek commentators and grammarians often used the word
'orchestra' improperly to denote the stage, which in Roman
theatres had now become the actual dancing-place. This later
signification of the term has given rise to much confusion.
When a Greek scholiast speaks of the orchestra, it is necessary
to look carefully to the context, to see whether he means the
stage, or the orchestra in its proper sense.[1]

The orchestra in the Athenian theatre is mostly of very late
date, and contains but few traces of the original structure.
Our knowledge of the early Greek orchestra has to be derived
from other sources. Before proceeding to discuss this part of
the subject, it will be convenient in the first place to give a brief
description of the existing remains in the theatre at Athens.
The only portion of the old orchestra of Lycurgus which has
been preserved is the gutter. This gutter, which was intended
to drain off the water from the tiers of seats, ran immediately
inside the border-line of the auditorium. It was made of
limestone, and was about a yard in width. At the western
corner it was 31 inches deep, but increased in depth all the
way round to the eastern corner, where the depth was 43
inches. Here it made a sudden drop of about a yard, and
then ran off in a south-easterly direction underneath the stage-
buildings. It had no covering, except opposite the vertical
passages, where it was bridged over with slabs of limestone.
Apart from this gutter the greater part of the present orchestra
belongs to the time of Nero. At this date considerable changes
were made. The stage was probably pushed forward as far
as the two corners of the auditorium. The orchestra, having
been thus largely reduced in size, was covered over with the
marble pavement which still remains. This pavement consists
for the most part of rectangular slabs, placed in lines parallel

[1] e. g. Schol. Aristoph. Equit. 505
(of the chorus) ἑστᾶσι μὲν γὰρ κατὰ
στοῖχον οἱ πρὸς τὴν ὀρχήστραν ἀποβλέ-
ποντες· ὅταν δὲ παραβῶσιν, ἐφεξῆς
ἑστῶτες καὶ πρὸς τοὺς θεατὰς βλέποντες
τὸν λόγον ποιοῦνται. Here ὀρχήστρα
obviously = λογεῖον. Cp. Suidas s.v.

σκηνή; Isidor. Origg. xviii. 44 'orchestra autem pulpitum erat scaenae'. [A
full history of the meanings of the word
is given in A. Müller's Untersuchungen
zu den Bühnenalterthümern, pp. 77-
88]

to the stage. But in the centre there is a large rhombus-shaped
figure, bordered with two strips, and paved with small slabs
also of a rhombus shape.   In the middle of the figure is a block
containing a small circular depression, which was probably
intended to receive an altar of Dionysus.   At the time when
the pavement was constructed, the gutter was also covered over
entirely with slabs of marble, with rosette-shaped openings at
intervals.   Some of these openings have been preserved, and
are indicated in the plan.   At the same time a marble balustrade was erected in front of the first step of the auditorium.
It is marked by the dark line in the plan.   Most of it is still
standing, and consists of marble slabs bound together by iron
clamps, and 43 inches high.   The purpose of the balustrade
must have been to serve as a protection to the spectators in
the front rows, when the orchestra was given up to gladiatorial
combats or similar exhibitions.   After these innovations of the
Neronian period the orchestra seems to have been untouched
until about the end of the third century A. D., when Phaedrus
erected his new stage.   It was then made water-tight, for the
purpose of holding mimic sea-fights in it.   The gutter was filled
up, and the rosette-shaped openings closed.   Traces of the pipes
used for letting on and letting off the water for the sea-fight
have been discovered in various parts of the building.

   In the course of recent excavations underneath the orchestra
two discoveries have been made.   It appears that at some
unknown period certain tunnels of irregular shape, and too
small to serve as passages, were bored through the rock, but
filled up again as soon as made.   Also, just in front of the
Roman stage, the rock was cut away in a straight line, and the
cutting was continued as far as the stage-buildings, the interval
being filled up with earth.   The purpose of both these works is
quite uncertain.[1]

   It will be seen, from the above description, that the remains of
the Athenian theatre throw very little light upon the character
of the ancient orchestra.   Fortunately, during the last ten or
fifteen years, a large number of other theatres have been excavated, which suffered less from reconstruction, and in which
the orchestras have been left more or less in their original
condition.   The finest and best preserved of these is the theatre

   [1] Griech. Theater, pp. 57, 58.

of Epidaurus, which was built at the end of the fourth century.[1] It is described by Pausanias as the most beautiful theatre in the world.[2] A plan of the building (Fig. 6) is here inserted, together with a view taken from the north-east (Fig. 7).[3] The evidence derived from this and other theatres will enable us to clear up many questions in connexion with the orchestra, to which the Athenian theatre supplies no answer.

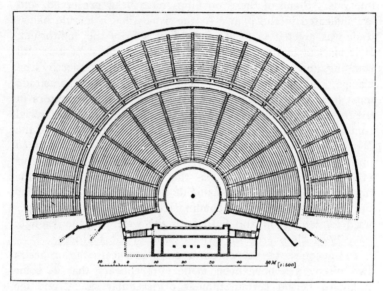

FIG. 6.

In the early Greek theatres, as already pointed out, the seats of the spectators were so arranged that every one had an excellent view of the orchestra, while the view of the stage was in many cases a very poor one. When the Romans gave up the orchestra to the spectators, and transferred all the performances to the stage, they made various alterations in the arrangement

[1] For the date see Griech. Theater, pp. 129 ff. ; Christ, Sitzungsber. bayer. Akad. der Wissen. 1894, pp. 30 ff. ; Lechat, Épidaure, p. 106.

[2] Paus. ii. 27. 5 Ἐπιδαυρίοις δέ ἐστι θέατρον ἐν τῷ ἱερῷ, μάλιστα ἐμοὶ δοκεῖν θέας ἄξιον· τὰ μὲν γὰρ Ῥωμαίων πολὺ δή τι ὑπερῆρκε τῶν πανταχοῦ τῷ κόσμῳ, μεγέθει δὲ Ἀρκάδων τὸ ἐν Μεγάλῃ πόλει· ἁρμονίας δὲ ἢ κάλλους ἕνεκα ἀρχιτέκτων

ποῖος ἐς ἅμιλλαν Πολυκλείτῳ γένοιτ' ἂν ἀξιόχρεως; Πολύκλειτος γὰρ τὸ θέατρον τοῦτο καὶ οἴκημα τὸ περιφερὲς ὁ ποιήσας ἦν.

[3] The view is copied from a photograph taken by Prof. Ernest Gardner, and kindly lent for reproduction. The plan is from Baumeister's Denkmäler, iii. p. 1735.

To face p. 104.

FIG. 7. THEATRE AT EPIDAURUS, FROM THE NORTH-EAST.

and proportions of the theatre. They largely diminished the size of the orchestra by bringing the stage several yards forward ; and at the same time they cut off considerable portions from the two ends of the auditorium. In this way they were enabled to make the stage much deeper, so as to accommodate a larger number of performers. By shortening the wings of the auditorium they abolished those seats which looked away from the stage. Vitruvius gives some interesting directions for determining the proper proportions of a Greek and Roman theatre.[1] According to his figures the orchestra in a Roman theatre constituted an exact semicircle. The front line of the stage coincided precisely with the diameter of the orchestra. In a Greek theatre the stage was placed much further back. The distance between the central point of the front line of the stage and the central point in the opposite circumference of the orchestra was six-sevenths of the diameter of the orchestra. In a Greek theatre therefore, according to this statement, if the circumference of the orchestra was prolonged so as to form a complete circle, it would be found that the front line of the stage only intersected a very small portion of that circle. None of the existing theatres coincide exactly with the rules laid down by Vitruvius. Sometimes the stage stands further back than he directs, as at the Peiraeeus. Sometimes it reaches further forward, as at Megalopolis. But in most cases the deviation is very slight, and his description, taken as a general statement, may be regarded as approximately true. The fact is instructive. The largeness of the space allotted to the orchestra by the arrangement above described enables us to realize very clearly the subordinate position of the stage in Greek theatres.

Vitruvius in the above account uses the word 'orchestra' in its ordinary sense, to denote the whole space included within the border-line of the auditorium. But we may limit the meaning of the word, and confine it to the actual dancing-place, excluding the gutter which usually ran inside the auditorium. If this is done, it will be found that in many Greek theatres the circumference of the orchestra, when prolonged, forms a complete circle, without touching the stage. The theatre of Epidaurus (Fig. 6) offers a good example.[2] The dancing-place

[1] Vitruv. v. 6 and 7.
[2] Other examples are found at Athens, the Peiraeeus, and Eretria. See Fig. 3, and the plans in Griech. Theater, pp. 98 and 112.

is here surrounded by a circular kerbstone, fifteen inches
wide, which only reaches within a yard of the stage-buildings.
It has been contended that all Greek theatres were constructed
on this principle; that the stage was pushed back sufficiently
far to allow the orchestra, in its narrower sense, to form a
complete circle. The line of the orchestra might be marked
out in stone, or it might not; but there was always room for
it.[1] This, however, is an exaggeration. There are many Greek
theatres, such as those of Delos, Assos, and Sicyon, in which
the circle of the actual dancing-place could not be completed
without encroaching upon the stage.[2] At Megalopolis (Fig. 11),
if such a circle was completed, about a third of it would be
intersected. Here the orchestra was unusually large, and the
stage was therefore brought further forward, in order to be
within a reasonable distance of the auditorium. These examples
show that the Greeks had no pedantic feeling on the subject
of the orchestra circle. No doubt in ancient times, before the
development of the drama, their orchestras formed complete
circles; and possibly they were enclosed all round with a kerbstone. The old orchestra at Athens seems to have been
so encircled. But when regular theatres with stage-buildings
began to be erected the architects appear to have discarded
the stone border, and with it the imaginary circle, and to
have contented themselves with allowing a sufficient space for
the chorus, according to the requirements of each particular
theatre. In many cases, as it happened, they left room enough
for a full circle. At Epidaurus such a circle was actually
marked out in stone. But this is the only known example; and
there are several theatres in which the stage was so placed as
to make a complete circle impossible.

At Athens, as we have seen, there was an interval of
several feet between the front row of benches and the circuit
of the orchestra. The interval was filled by a broad sloping
step, which served as a passage to the auditorium. A similar
passage is found at the Peiraeeus. But in most Greek theatres
there was no passage of this kind, and the line of seats bordered
immediately on the orchestra and the gutter by which it was
encircled. The gutter was a regular feature in Greek orchestras,

---

[1] Griech. Theater, p. 175.
[2] See the plans in Griech. Theater, pp. 117, 144, 149.

and was constructed in various styles. The Athenian type, with its broad and deep channel, and bridges at intervals, seems to have been exceptional and antique, and is not found elsewhere except at Sicyon and the Peiraeeus. In some places, such as Megalopolis, the gutter was much narrower, so as to need no bridges. At Epidaurus and Eretria, on the other hand, it was very broad and very shallow, and might be used as a passage to the auditorium in dry weather. The gutter at Epidaurus is no less than 7 feet across, and only 8 inches deep. The surface of the orchestra was in most cases, as at Athens, a few inches below the level of the front row of seats. It used often to be asserted that the surface was boarded over with planks. But this is an error, due to the fact that the Greek grammarians often used the word 'orchestra' to denote the stage.[1] The evidence of the theatres lately excavated shows that in almost every case the Greek orchestra consisted simply of earth beaten down hard and flat. It is true that the orchestra at Eretria was paved with slabs of limestone, and that at Delos, which lay on the rock, was covered with a 'coating' of some kind or another.[2] But in all other instances, as far as we know, the surface was merely of earth. Marble pavements are never found in Greek theatres, except when they had been built or reconstructed in the Roman fashion. Lines were sometimes marked on the floor of the orchestra, to assist the chorus in their evolutions.[3] Similar lines are used on the modern stage when complicated ballets are produced. Aristotle mentions cases of orchestras being strewed with chaff, and remarks that when this was done the choruses were not heard so well. But it is uncertain to what theatres or to what occasions he is referring.[4]

In every Greek orchestra there was an altar of Dionysus. The fact is proved by the express testimony of ancient writers, and also by the circumstance that the dramatic performances were preceded by a sacrifice.[5] However, there is only one

---

[1] Suidas s.v. σκηνή . . . μετὰ τὴν σκηνὴν εὐθὺς καὶ τὰ παρασκήνια ἡ ὀρχήστρα. αὕτη δέ ἐστιν ὁ τόπος ὁ ἐκ σανίδων ἔχων τὸ ἔδαφος, ἀφ' οὗ θεατρίζουσιν οἱ μῖμοι. Here the word ὀρχήστρα clearly = λογεῖον. Cp. p. 102, note.

[2] Griech. Theater, p. 116. Bulletin de Corr. Hell. 1894, p. 163 τὴν ὀρχήστραν τοῦ θεάτρου καταχρῖσαι (date 269 B.C.).

[3] Hesych. s.v. γραμμαί.

[4] Aristot. Prob. xi. 25 διὰ τί, ὅταν ἀχυρωθῶσιν αἱ ὀρχῆστραι, ἧττον οἱ χοροὶ γεγώνασιν;

[5] Suidas s.v. σκηνή . . . εἶτα μετὰ τὴν ὀρχήστραν (i. e. the stage) βωμὸς τοῦ Διονύσου. Poll. iv. 123 ἡ δὲ ὀρχήστρα τοῦ χοροῦ, ἐν ᾗ καὶ ἡ θυμέλη, εἴτε βῆμά τι οὖσα εἴτε βωμός. For the sacrifices in the theatre see p. 68.

theatre, that of Priene, in which any remains of an altar have
been discovered. In this theatre, which was excavated for the
first time in the year 1897, the altar is still found standing
in its original position. It is placed just in front of the first
row of seats, and exactly opposite the centre of the stage.[1]
Whether this was the usual position of the altar in a Greek
theatre seems doubtful. In the earliest period, when the drama
was still a purely lyrical performance, the altar stood in the
centre of the orchestra, and the chorus danced round about
it. The evidence supplied by the remains at Athens and
Epidaurus rather favours the view that in these theatres it still
occupied the same position. In the middle of the theatre at
Epidaurus there is a round stone, 28 inches in diameter,
let into the ground, so as to be on the same level with the
surrounding surface. In the middle of the stone is a circular hole.
A similar hole, as we have seen, is found in the later Athenian
orchestra. The only plausible explanation of these holes is
that they were intended for the reception of small stone altars.
It is probable, therefore, that the practice varied in regard to
the situation of the altar. In some theatres, such as those of
Athens and Epidaurus, it may have been placed in the middle
of the orchestra, after the ancient fashion. In others, such
as that of Priene, it may have been drawn further back towards
the auditorium, so as to leave a clear space for the evolutions
of the chorus. The altar of the theatre was called the Thymele,
because of the sacrifices offered upon it. It is called by this
name in a fragment of Pratinas.[2] In later times the use of the
word was extended, so as to denote, not only the altar, but
also the space round about it; and 'thymele' became a regular
name for an orchestra.[3] Later still, when the Romans substituted the stage for the orchestra, the word 'thymele', having
become identical in meaning with the word 'orchestra', was
employed in similar fashion to signify the 'stage'.[4]

[1] Schrader, Berl. Philolog. Wochenschrift, 1898, April 16, p. 509.
[2] Suidas s.v. σκηνή... μετὰ τὴν ὀρχήστραν βωμὸς τοῦ Διονύσου, ὃς καλεῖται
θυμέλη παρὰ τὸ θύειν. Etym. Mag. s.v.
θυμέλη. Pratinas apud Athen. 517 B
τίς ὕβρις ἔμολεν ἐπὶ Διονυσιάδα πολυπά-
ταγα θυμέλαν ;
[3] Phrynichus p. 163 (Lob.) θυμέλην·

τοῦτο οἱ μὲν ἀρχαῖοι ἀντὶ τοῦ θυσίαν
ἐτίθουν, οἱ δὲ νῦν ἐπὶ τοῦ τόπου ἐν τῷ
θεάτρῳ, ἐν ᾧ αὐληταὶ καὶ κιθαρῳδοὶ καὶ
ἄλλοι τινὲς ἀγωνίζονται· σὺ μέντοι ἔνθα
μὲν κωμῳδοὶ καὶ τραγῳδοὶ ἀγωνίζονται
λογεῖον ἐρεῖς, ἔνθα δὲ οἱ αὐληταὶ καὶ οἱ
χοροὶ ὀρχήστραν, μὴ λέγε δὲ θυμέλην.
[4] Bekk. Anecd. p. 292 σκηνὴ δ' ἐστὶν
ἡ νῦν λεγομένη θυμέλη. Schol. Arist.

In one or two Greek theatres subterranean passages have been discovered, leading from the stage-buildings to the middle of the orchestra. These passages are generally rather more than six feet in height, and from two to three feet wide. There is one in the theatre of Eretria, with a flight of steps leading down to it at each end.[1] Another has been found at Magnesia; but as only a small portion of it still remains, it is impossible to say where it began and where it ended, or whether it had any exit into the orchestra.[2] The passage at Sicyon is rather peculiar. A small drain runs underground from the auditorium to the centre of the orchestra, where it falls into a square tank. From the tank onwards there is a regular vaulted passage, which is continued as far as the back of the stage-buildings, and finally ends in a tunnel in the rock. Where it passes under the stage, a flight of steps leads down to it; but no traces of an entrance from the orchestra can be detected.[3] These three passages, when first discovered, were thought to have some connexion with the dramatic performances; and it was supposed that they might be used to enable ghosts to appear suddenly in the middle of the orchestra. But this theory seems to be untenable, for the following reasons. In the first place, no traces of such passages have been found at Athens, and Epidaurus, and other theatres where excavations have been carried on. But if they had been a regular contrivance in dramatic exhibitions, it is impossible to suppose that the Athenians would not have made use of them. Secondly, the passage at Sicyon not only reaches as far as the stage, but also runs right on to the back of the stage-buildings, where it would have been of no use for the purpose suggested. Thirdly, there is no decisive evidence that the passages at Sicyon and Magnesia opened out into the orchestra. Fourthly, similar passages of Roman workmanship have been discovered at

---

Equit. 149 ὡς ἐν θυμέλῃ δὲ τὸ ἀνάβαινε. [Cp. Robert, Hermes xxxii. p. 441; Bethe, ibid. xxxvi. p. 597, and Dörpfeld, ibid. xxxvii. p. 249 for more recent discussions of the meaning of θυμέλη. Dörpfeld may be right in explaining the various meanings of the word by its having originally included not only the altar, but the broad base or stone platform on which the altar stood, e.g.

in front of a temple. But Robert's connexion of the word with θεμέλιον and τιθέναι instead of with θύω is more than doubtful. See also Müller, Unters. zu den Bühnenalterth., pp. 93-108.]

[1] Griech. Theater, p. 116.
[2] Ibid. p. 156.
[3] Amer. Journ. Arch., 1891, p. 281; 1893, p. 404.

Tralles and at Magnesia, the passage in the latter place having
been substituted for the previous Greek one. But these Roman
passages had no exit into the orchestra, as the remains clearly
show. After running from the stage-buildings to the middle
of the orchestra, they branched off to right and left like the
letter T, and then stopped.[1] The fact then that the Romans
built tunnels of this kind, which had no connexion with performances in the orchestra, is a strong reason for assuming
that the Greeks might do the same. What the purpose of the
tunnels was, whether Greek or Roman, has not yet been
explained, and remains very mysterious.[2]

In all Greek theatres the front of the stage-buildings was
separated from the wings of the auditorium by a vacant space
several feet in width. Two open passages, one on the right
and one on the left, led into the orchestra. The passages
were closed on the outside by large gates, and these gates
formed the only architectural connexion between the auditorium
and the stage-buildings.[3] In some theatres, such as those
of Epidaurus and Assos, the gates which led into the orchestra
stood side by side with other gates leading into the stage-
buildings.[4] Sufficient remains of the gates at Epidaurus have
been preserved to admit of a complete restoration of them.
The present illustration represents the two gates on the
western side of the theatre (Fig. 8). The gate to the right leads
into the orchestra; that to the left leads into the stage-
buildings.[5] In the Athenian theatre, owing to the defective
character of the remains in this part, it is impossible to

[1] Athen. Mittheil., 1893, p. 407;
Griech. Theater, p. 157.
[2] [Sharpley (Aristoph. Pax Introd.,
p. 27) thinks that it is 'trifling with
words' to say that the purpose has
not been explained. He thinks it
certain that these tunnels were used
for the appearance of actors in the
orchestra, and constructs a theory of
the scenic arrangements of the Pax
on this hypothesis, assuming the
correctness of Dörpfeld's theory of
the stage. But if Dörpfeld's theory of
the stage is to be rejected, owing to
a balance of considerations against it
(see below), then these tunnels do
remain unexplained and their purpose
mysterious. The fact that at Eretria

they *could* be used as Sharpley suggests proves nothing as to the manner
in which they *were* used, unless the
theory of their use fits in with other
evidence as to theatrical performances.
We know nothing of the performances
in the theatre at Eretria ; there are no
such tunnels at Athens, and there are
other ways of explaining the Pax.]
[3] Remains of such gateways are
to be found at Sicyon, Delos, and Pergamon. See the plans in Griech.
Theater, pp. 117, 144, 151.
[4] Griech. Theater, pp. 129, 150.
[5] The illustration is taken from
Πρακτικὰ τῆς ἐν Ἀθήν. ἀρχαιολ. ἑταιρίας
for 1883.

determine whether there were two gates on each side or
only one. The passages at Athens measured nine feet across
on the outside. But they grew gradually wider, as one
approached the orchestra, because of the oblique position of
the boundary walls of the auditorium. These orchestral
passages answered a double purpose. In the first place, they

FIG. 8.

formed the principal entrance to the theatre for the general
public. In many theatres they were the only entrances. In
Athens there were two others at the upper end of the auditorium; but the main approaches in all theatres were those
between the auditorium and the stage-buildings. The spectators
came in by the orchestra, and then ascended the vertical
passages to their proper seats. In the second place, it was
by these passages that the chorus entered the orchestra at
the commencement of each play. The technical name for

the passages was 'parodoi' or 'eisodoi'.[1] In Roman theatres they were of course done away with, as the Roman stage was brought much more forward than the Greek, and the two ends coalesced with the wings of the auditorium. In place of the old open passages the Romans built vaulted entrances underneath the auditorium, and parallel with the stage. Later Greek writers, misled by the analogy of the Roman theatres, sometimes apply the terms 'vault' and 'archway' to the open side-entrances of the Greek theatre. But such language is inaccurate.[2]

§ 6. *Ruins of the Stage-buildings at Athens.*

The third and last division of the theatre consists of the stage-buildings, the 'skene', as they were called. This word has a curious history in connexion with the drama. Originally it meant the booth or tent in which the single actor of the Thespian period used to change his costume. Then as this booth gradually developed into a large and elaborate structure, the word 'skene' extended its meaning at the same time, and came to be the regular term for the stage-buildings of a theatre.[3] Later on it began to be applied not only to the whole of the buildings, but also to the more important parts of them. It was used to denote the stage or platform on which the actors performed[4]; and also the back-scene, with its painted decoration, in front of which they stood.[5] Eventually it was employed as a general term for the scene of action, or for the portions or scenes into which a play was divided.[6] These last three

[1] Πάροδοι in Schol. Arist. Equit. 149; Poll. iv. 126; εἴσοδοι in Arist. Nub. 326, Av. 296. The word πάροδος was also used to denote the entrances on to the stage, e. g. in Plut. Demetr. 905 B; Poll. iv. 128; Athen. 622 D.

[2] Vitruv. v. 6. The side-entrances are called ψαλίς in Poll. iv. 123; ἀψίς in Vit. Aristoph. (Dindf. Prolegom. de Comoed. p. 36).

[3] e. g. τῆς σκηνῆς τὸ τέγος καταλεί-ψαντι . . . εἰς τὸ λογείον τῆς σκηνῆς (Delian inscription, 279 B. C.), in Bull. Corr. Hell. 1894, pp. 162 ff.).

[4] e. g. Aristot. Poet. c. 24 τὸ ἐπὶ τῆς σκηνῆς καὶ τῶν ὑποκριτῶν μέρος. Polyb. xxx. 13 πύκται τέσσαρες ἀνέβησαν ἐπὶ

τὴν σκηνήν.

[5] Plut. Demetr. 900 D ἔλεγε νῦν πρῶτον ἑωρακέναι πόρνην προερχομένην ἐκ τραγικῆς σκηνῆς. So ἡ σκηνὴ ἡ μέση, τὰς ἐπάνω σκηνὰς καινὰς ποιῆσαι, γράψαι τὰς σκηνάς, κ.τ.λ. (Delian inscription, 274 B.C., in Bull. Corr. Hell. l.c.). Hence σκηνογραφία = scene-painting (Aristot. Poet. c. 4). [Müller, Unters. zu den Bühnenalterth., pp. 1 ff., gives fully the history of the various meanings of σκηνή.]

[6] Arg. Aesch. Pers. καὶ ἔστιν ἡ μὲν σκηνὴ τοῦ δράματος περὶ τῷ τάφῳ Δαρείου. Bekk. Anecd. iii. p. 1461 εἰς πέντε σκηνὰς διαιρεῖ τὸ δρᾶμα.

meanings of the word are still retained in its English derivative.

The question as to the structure of the stage-buildings in a Greek theatre is one of the greatest interest, because of its intimate connexion with many disputed points of dramatic history. Unfortunately, it is a subject upon which the information supplied by the existing ruins is very defective. In all the remaining theatres of purely Greek origin little has been left of the stage-buildings beyond the mere foundations, and it is impossible from such evidence to go very far in the process of conjectural reconstruction. Our knowledge of the upper part of the building has to be derived mainly from casual notices in the old grammarians. In treating this question it will be best to follow the same arrangement as in the case of the orchestra, and to begin by giving a short account of the ruins in the theatre of Dionysus at Athens. The stage-buildings at Athens were very frequently altered and reconstructed in the course of their history, and the task of distinguishing between the confused remains of the different periods has been by no means an easy one. The recent investigations of Dörpfeld have for the first time placed the matter in a fairly clear light. The results of his discoveries are indicated in the plan of the theatre already given.

The oldest stage-buildings, which Dörpfeld dates soon after the middle of the fourth century and Puchstein at the end of the fifth, are marked by cross-shading in the plan, and denoted by the letter *n*. They consisted, as will be seen, of a long and narrow rectangular structure. In the front, towards each end, were two projecting side-wings. The length of the building was 152 feet, and its depth, measured between the wings, 21 feet. The wings themselves were 25 feet wide, and projected about 17 feet on the inside. The roof of the building was originally supported by a line of columns running along the centre, of which some traces still remain. At the back of the building there was a low narrow wall, running immediately in front of the supporting wall, and fitted with square holes at regular intervals. The purpose of the wall is very obscure; but Dörpfeld conjectures that the upper story was of wood, and not of stone, and that it rested on wooden beams which were placed in these holes. Puchstein, on the other hand, believes that there was an upper story of stone. The evidence is not sufficiently clear to render a decision possible.[1] As regards the appearance of the building in the front nothing can be ascertained with certainty. The space between the side-wings evidently contained the stage, but no traces of it are to be found. It must therefore have been a temporary erection of wood. Dörpfeld supposes that the front of the two side-wings, and the front of the wall between them, were decorated with columns and entablatures about thirteen feet high.[2] But the evidence for this opinion is far from conclusive. It is founded on the fact that the stylobates used in the later side-wings were not originally designed for that position, but had obviously been used somewhere else before. Dörpfeld supposes, perhaps correctly, that they stood at first in front of the Lycurgean side-wings.[3] But this is no justification for assuming that the wall between the wings in the Lycurgean building was also decorated in the same way. The stylobate used for this part of the later building was a new one, and not an old one rearranged; and this fact seems to show that there was no such stylobate in the building of Lycurgus. Otherwise there would have been just as much reason for using it, as for using the two stylobates from the wings. On the whole then it is clear that we know very little about the old stage-building of the fourth or late fifth century beyond the shape of its ground-plan. As to its height, the material used in its upper stories, and the manner in which its front was embellished, there is no certain evidence.

The history of the stage-buildings during the next two hundred years or so is a blank. Nothing can be ascertained on this subject from the ruins. The first great alteration of which traces remain was carried out in the course of the first or second century B. C. according to Dörpfeld, the fourth century according to Puchstein. A permanent stone proscenium was then erected in the space between the wings. It is marked *o* in the plan. The front of this proscenium consisted of a row of columns supporting an entablature. Its height, as may be calculated from the traces of the columns,

---

[1] Puchstein, Die Griech. Bühne, p. 136.

[2] Griech. Theater, pp. 62 ff.

[3] Puchstein, l. c., p. 102, denies this, on the ground that these stylobates are not long enough for the foundation walls of the Lycurgean building, and cannot therefore have been originally made for them.

was about 13 feet; its depth between 9 and 10 feet. It was covered on the top with a wooden platform, resting on beams, the holes for which are still visible in fragments of the architrave. In the centre of the front part of the proscenium was a door leading out into the orchestra. This door varied in width at different periods from 4½ to 5½ feet, but there is nothing to show which was the earlier and which the later of the two widths. Traces of a smaller door, to the west of the central one, have also been discovered; but there are no traces of a door to the east. As this new stage was only about ten feet deep, smaller side-wings were required. The old wings of the earlier theatre were therefore thrown back about 5½ feet, thus adding several feet to the width of the 'parodoi'. Beyond the construction of the stone proscenium no further remains of new erections belonging to this reconstruction have been discovered; but it is probable that the upper part of the building was considerably altered at the same time.

The second great reconstruction of the stage-buildings took place in the reign of Nero, after a lapse of perhaps two hundred years. The whole of this part of the theatre was then adapted to the Roman fashion. An elaborate architectural facade, consisting of columns and entablatures, was erected at the back of the stage, the old Lycurgean wall *n* being used as a foundation. A portion of the frieze from this façade is still in existence, and contains the dedication to Nero which has already been referred to.[1] Two of the columns are also preserved in part. Behind the columns and frieze a wall was erected, according to the Roman custom; and at the same time new side-wings were built, slightly diminishing the length of the whole structure. The foundations of these erections are marked *p* in the plan. In Roman theatres, as we have seen, the stage projected much further forward than in the Greek. It was also reduced in height to five feet, so that the spectators in the orchestra might be able to see over the top. A stage of this type was doubtless erected in the Athenian theatre at the time of these reconstructions, though it has now entirely disappeared. But part of it seems to have been used for the existing stage, that of Phaedrus, by which it was replaced in the third century

---

[1] See above, p. 88.

A. D. This stage, which is four feet three inches high, is adorned in front with a bas-relief. The bas-relief has obviously been constructed out of old materials, and has been much cut about, and curtailed several inches in height, before being placed in its present situation. It seems clear that it was intended originally for the Neronian stage, which must therefore have been about five feet high. The position of the front-wall in the Neronian stage cannot be determined from the ruins, but was probably much the same as in the stage of Phaedrus (*h–h*). One peculiarity of the Neronian reconstruction is the fact that the old Greek side-wings, with their rows of columns, were allowed to remain. But how they harmonized with the new Roman wings and columns it is difficult to conjecture.[1]

The last change of which we have any trace or record was that effected by Phaedrus about two centuries later. The stage was then lowered several inches, and the front-wall erected in its present position. Half of it still remains, together with a flight of steps leading down from stage to orchestra. Such steps were common in Roman theatres, and had no doubt existed previously in the Neronian theatre. The bas-relief, which had formerly been a continuous one, was cut into sections, and arranged with recesses at intervals, the recesses being filled with stone figures. One of these—a kneeling Silenus—has been preserved. As to the purpose of this reconstruction by Phaedrus there is much uncertainty. But Dörpfeld conjectures that it may have been due, partly to the ruinous condition of the old Neronian stage, partly to a desire to make the orchestra water-tight for the purpose of holding mimic sea-fights in the manner already described.[2]

§ 7. *The Earlier Stage-buildings.*

We have now described the various traces of stage-buildings in the Athenian theatre down to the time of Phaedrus. It remains to consider the subject from a more general point of view, and to supplement and illustrate the previous narrative

---

[1] [Dörpfeld has, since the publication of his book, changed his mind, and now thinks that the Neronian stage was higher, and belonged to the Vitruvian Graeco-Roman, not to the Roman type (Ath. Mitth. 1897, p. 459; 1898, pp. 330, 347). Puchstein is inclined to agree (die griech. Bühne, p. 101). But, in fact, the evidence is insufficient to prove anything as to the height of the stage.]

[2] Griech. Theater, pp. 89-90.

by evidence derived from other sources. The first and most
interesting question concerns the structure of the stage-buildings
during the great period of the Attic drama from Aeschylus to
Aristophanes. On this point the existing remains throw very
little light. Still there are a few general conclusions which
seem to be fairly well established. It is evident, in the first
place, that the stage-buildings from the fifth down to the middle
of the fourth century, if Dörpfeld's dates are adopted—those of
the greater part of the fifth century, according to Puchstein—
must have been made of wood, and not of stone. If they had
been made of stone, it is difficult to believe that they would
have left no traces behind them. As regards their shape,
they probably resembled in general outline the earliest stone
structure, and consisted of an oblong building with projecting
side-wings. These side-wings were called 'paraskenia', because
they lay on each side of the 'skene' or stage, and are actually
mentioned by Demosthenes in his speech against Meidias as
forming a part of the theatre at that time.[1] But though the
stage-buildings of the fifth century were constructed of wood
only, they must have been firm and substantial erections, and
at least two stories in height. The use of such contrivances
as the 'mechane' and the 'theologeion', by which gods were
exhibited high up in air, would require buildings of not less
than two stories, and of considerable solidity. Hence we may
also conclude that they were permanent structures, and that
they were not put up and taken down at each festival. No
doubt, in the course of a century and a half, they were often
renewed, and often changed and modified in detail, as experience
suggested. During the first years of the fifth century, when there

[1] Harpocrat. (s.v. παρασκήνια) quotes Theophrastus for the definition of para-skenia as places on one side of the stage, used for storage purposes. The παρα-σκήνια τά τε ἐπάνω καὶ τὰ ὑποκάτω mentioned along with the σκηναί in the Delian inscription of 274 B.C. (Bull. Corr. Hell. 1894, pp. 162 ff.) were doubtless side-wings. Demosthenes (Meid. § 17) accuses Meidias of 'nailing up the paraskenia', and so preventing his dithyrambic chorus from making its appearance. Probably he nailed up the doors out of the side-wings into the parodoi. The word is also explained by the commentators as = (1) the en-trances to the orchestra (Didymus quoted by Harpocrat. l. c.), or (2) the entrances to the stage (Phot. and Etym. Mag. s. v. ; Bekk. Anecd. p. 292 ; Ulpian on Dem. Meid. § 17), or (3) the doors on each side of the main door in the back-scene (Suidas s.v. σκηνή). But these explanations are probably false inferences from the passage in Demo-sthenes, or from some other source. Cp. Müller, Unters. zu den Bühnenalt., pp. 57-62, for the history of the word παρασκήνια.

was only one actor, they must have been much smaller than
they afterwards became, when the number of the actors had
been raised to three.   But after the middle of the fifth century,
when they had reached their full size, it is unlikely that they
should have been pulled down and re-erected more often
than was rendered necessary by the mere process of decay.
Whether the stage in these early buildings was protected by
a roof or covering, running from one side-wing to the other, is
uncertain.   But a roof of this kind would have been a distinct
advantage, for the purpose of concealing the crane-like mechanism
by which the deus ex machina was exhibited.

To consider next the character of the early stage.   The stage
in Greek was called 'skene', for the reason already mentioned[1];
and 'okribas', because it consisted originally of a wooden platform.[2]   It was also called 'logeion', or the 'speaking-place',
because the actors stood there and carried on the dialogue.   It
was opposed to the orchestra, or dancing-place, in which the
chorus went through their performances.[3]   Another name for
it was the 'proskenion', from its position in front of the 'skene',
or back-wall.[4]   As regards the shape of the early stage, there
is even less archaeological evidence than in the case of the
stage-buildings.   The stage continued to be constructed of
wood long after the rest of the building had begun to be made
of stone.   As a result, all traces of it have disappeared.   But
certain inferences may be drawn from the structure of the

[1] See above, p. 112.
[2] Hesych. s.v. ὀκρίβας· τὸ λογεῖον ἐφ'
οὗ οἱ τραγῳδοὶ ἠγωνίζοντο.   Plat. Symp.
194 A ἀναβαίνοντος ἐπὶ τὸν ὀκρίβαντα
μετὰ τῶν ὑποκριτῶν.   The stage referred to in this latter passage was probably in the Odeion.   See above, p. 68,
and Mazon, Rev. de Philologie, 1903,
p. 265.
[3] Delian inscription of 279 B.C. εἰς
τὸ [λογε]ῖον τῆς σκηνῆς ; 180 B.C. τῶν
πινάκων τῶν ἐπὶ τὸ λογεῖον (Bull. Corr.
Hell. 1894, pp. 162 ff.).   Phryn. p. 163
(Lob.) σὺ μέντοι, ἔνθα μὲν κωμῳδοὶ καὶ
τραγῳδοὶ ἀγωνίζονται, λογεῖον ἐρεῖς.
Cp. Müller, l. c., pp. 49–57, for the
history of this and similar words.
[4] Delian inscription of 290 B.C. τὴν
σκηνὴν ἐργολαβήσασι καὶ τὸ προσκήνιον ;
282 B.C. εἰς τὸ προσκήνιον γράψαντι
πίνακας (Bull. Corr. Hell. l. c.).   In-

scription on architrave of proscenium at
Oropus (Griech. Theater, p. 103) ἀγωνοθετήσας τὸ προσκήνιον καὶ τοὺς πίνακας.
Polyb. xxx. 13 τούτους δὲ στήσας ἐπὶ
τὸ προσκήνιον μετὰ τοῦ χοροῦ.   The
word προσκήνιον also denoted (1) the
painted scenery at the back of the
stage.   Cp. Suidas s.v. προσκήνιον· τὸ
πρὸ τῆς σκηνῆς παραπέτασμα.   Nannio
the courtesan (fourth century B.C.)
was called 'proskenion' because of
the deceptive character of her beauty
(Athen. p. 587 B).   A representation
of Demetrius (third century B.C.) was
painted ἐπὶ τοῦ προσκηνίου.   (2) The
drop-scene (in late Greek).   Cp. Synesius (about 400 A.D.), Aegypt. 128 C
εἰ δέ τις . . . κυνοφθαλμίζοιτο διὰ τοῦ
προσκηνίου.   Cp. Müller, l.c., pp. 35 ff.,
for history of the meanings of the
word.

earliest stage-buildings represented in the ruins. If we look
at the outline of these buildings (*n–n*), we shall see that the
side-wings project about seventeen feet. But in the reconstruction which Dörpfeld assigns to the Hellenistic period, Puchstein
to the fourth century, when a stone stage (*o–o*) was erected, the
wings were drawn back about five feet on each side. It follows
almost as a matter of certainty that the wooden stage of the
earlier theatre must have been about fifteen feet deep, so as to
fill up the space between the wings.[1] This conclusion is confirmed by the remains of the original stage-buildings at Eretria,
which are the oldest hitherto found outside Athens, and which
apparently belong to the same period as the earliest ruins found
at Athens.[2] Here too we find the same outline and dimensions.
There is a long narrow building, with wings projecting about
seventeen feet on each side.[3] From this evidence we are justified
in assuming that the early Greek stage was considerably deeper
than the later one, and was not less than about fifteen feet
across. As to its height, we have no information beyond that
which is supplied by the existing dramas. These dramas however show that in the theatre of the fifth century it was easy for
the actors on the stage to converse with the chorus in the
orchestra ; and that there was nothing to prevent actors and
chorus from passing from stage to orchestra and from orchestra
to stage whenever they desired. Hence the stage of the fifth
century cannot have been raised many feet above the level of
the orchestra. The object of the stage was to place the actors
in a prominent position, and to ensure that they should not be
hidden from view by the chorus in front of them. This purpose
would easily be effected by a stage of only a few feet in height.
Some easy means of communication between stage and orchestra
must have been provided, to enable actors and chorus to pass to

[1] Dörpfeld (p. 69) denies that there
was ever a wooden stage between the
wings of the Lycurgean building. He
thinks the space was originally filled up
with a wooden proscenium, of the same
height as the later Hellenistic one of
stone ; and that both these proscenia
served as backgrounds, and not as stages.
He argues that if there had been a stage,
it must have been made of stone. But
if he is justified in assuming the existence of an early wooden proscenium,

we are surely justified in assuming
the existence of a stage of the same
material.

[2] The theatres of Epidaurus and
Megalopolis were formerly assigned to
about the middle of the fourth century.
But it now appears probable that
they were not earlier than the end of
that century. See Dörpfeld, Griech.
Theater, pp. 129 ff., 140.

[3] See the plan in Griech. Theater,
p. 112.

and fro. A long flight of steps, or a sloping ascent, may have been used for the purpose.

Such then, as far as we can tell, was the character of the stage and stage-buildings during the early period of the Greek drama. The stage-buildings consisted of a long and narrow rectangular structure, made entirely of wood, not less than two stories high, and with side-wings at each end. Between the wings was a platform about fifteen feet deep, and a few feet in height, connected with the orchestra by a flight of steps or in some similar way. This type of building lasted till the end of the fifth or middle of the fourth century. A new departure was then made. Stage-buildings began to be constructed of stone, at any rate in the lower stories. The earliest known examples are those at Athens and Eretria. But the stage itself still remained a wooden one.[1] Its depth was still about fifteen feet. As to its height we have no information.[2] The fourth century was a period of transition and development in the history of the Greek theatre; and it was probably during this century that various new experiments were made in the structure and arrangement of the stage and stage-buildings. But the first steps in the process cannot be traced in detail, owing to the lack of evidence. The final results of the various experiments, as exemplified in the theatres of a later period, will be discussed in the next section.

§ 8. *The later Stage-buildings of the pre-Roman period.*

In describing the ruins of the stage-buildings in the Athenian theatre we showed that the first great alteration made in the older structure was the erection of a stone stage. This stage was about thirteen feet high, and from nine to ten feet deep, and was enclosed between shallower side-wings. The change effected at Athens is a type of similar changes which were

---

[1] This · was probably for acoustic reasons; see below, p. 122.

[2] Dörpfeld (p. 69) argues that the original erection put up between the wings of the Lycurgean building must have been 13 ft. high, since the back-wall was adorned with columns and entablature of that height. But there is no proof of the existence of these columns and this entablature. In fact, the evidence is all the other way. See above, p. 114. Prof. E. Gardner (Excavations at Megalopolis, p. 84) thinks there is actual proof of the existence of a low wooden stage at Megalopolis in early times. The question really depends on the date of the three lower steps of the Thersilion, which he supposes to be considerably later than the stone auditorium. Dörpfeld, however (Griech. Theater, p. 140), assigns them to the same period.

carried out in most of the other Greek theatres with which we are acquainted. The recent excavations at Megalopolis, Delos, Eretria, and many other places, show that from the beginning of the second century onwards, and probably earlier, stone proscenia of the kind just described became a regular feature in ordinary Greek theatres.[1] Moreover there is evidence to prove that as early as the beginning of the third century proscenia made of wood, but resembling the later stone ones in height and depth, had begun to be erected in various cities. The theatre at Sicyon was built about this period, and the stage-buildings were to a large extent excavated out of the rock. The slopes which led up to the stage on each side, being cut out of the rock, still remain, and prove that the stage was about eleven feet above the level of the orchestra. The old wall which served as a foundation for the wooden proscenium is also partly preserved, and runs along the line of the later stone erection. In it are holes for the posts on which the wooden stage was supported.[2] At Eretria, again, the theatre was reconstructed about the beginning of the third century, and the orchestra was sunk about eleven feet into the rock, but the stage-buildings were left at their original level. Hence the wooden stage built in front of them must have been eleven feet high.[3] The theatre at Priene is somewhat exceptional. Here there are the remains of a proscenium belonging to the third century, but built of stone like those of later times. This, however, is the only instance yet discovered of a stone proscenium which can be ascribed with certainty to such an early period.[4] From these various indications it seems probable that the tall and narrow stage of the later type began to become general at the close of the fourth century, though at first it was usually made

---

[1] Griech. Theater, pp. 100, 102, 113, 120, 143, 147, 150, 156. Puchstein in many cases assigns an earlier date, e.g. at Megalopolis. (Die Griech. Bühne, p. 90.)

[2] Griech. Theater, p. 118.

[3] Ibid., p. 115. There is the foundation-wall of a wooden proscenium at Megalopolis, apparently of the third century, and running on the same line as the later stone proscenium. But whether it was of the same height is unknown. See Excavations at Megalopolis, p. 85.

[3] Schrader, Berl. Philolog. Wochenschrift, 1898, April 16, p. 508. The stone proscenium at Epidaurus has sometimes been assigned to the end of the fourth century, when the rest of the theatre was built. Dörpfeld thinks it more probable that it was a later structure (Griech. Theater, p. 232). Puchstein, however, dates the stone proscenium at Megalopolis in the third or even the fourth century.

of wood. In the course of the second and first centuries this wooden stage was replaced in most theatres by a permanent one of stone. The evidence derived from the ruins as to the size and shape of the later stage corresponds, in most cases, with the statement of Vitruvius, the Roman architect, who wrote about the end of the first century B. C. In his account of the Greek theatre of his own time he lays it down as a rule that the proscenium should be from ten to twelve feet high, and about ten feet deep.[1]

From the numerous remains of these later stone proscenia which have been excavated during the last few years it is

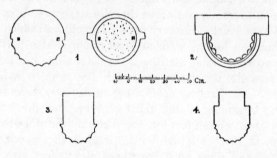

FIG. 8A.

possible to obtain a fairly accurate conception of their general character. The upper surface, or stage proper, was made of wood. The front seems to have consisted in every case of a series of stone columns supporting an entablature. The spaces between the columns were filled in with painted boards or 'pinakes', these, like the stage, being made of wood for acoustic reasons.[2] The columns themselves were adapted sometimes more and sometimes less carefully, to the purpose for which they were required.[3] In some cases, as at Athens and Sicyon, they consisted simply of entire columns. In others, the columns were provided with rims running down the centre of each side, to hold the pinakes, as at Megalopolis and Eretria. In others, the place of the columns was taken by half-columns resting

[1] Vitruv. v. 7.   [3] Ibid., pp. 17, 18. See below, p. 130
[2] Puchstein, Griech. Bühne, pp. 41 ff.

against pillars, as more convenient for holding the pinakes.
These pillars were in some cases without grooves or projections
for the pinakes, as at Epidaurus; in others, as at Priene, New
Pleuron, and Delos, they were regularly provided with them.[1]
A diagram is here given (Fig. 8 A, after Puchstein) representing
the shapes of these supports. The row of pillars would not only
serve as a support to the stage, but would serve as a background for the choral performances in the orchestra so far
as one was needed.[2] Dörpfeld, who believes that the dramatic
performances also took place entirely in the orchestra, supposes
that the pinakes were painted in scenic fashion so as to serve as
a background to the actors. There is not a particle of evidence
to support this view.[3] Not only would a back-scene interrupted
by columns be peculiar; but the accounts of the theatre of Delos
in the third century B. C. appear to demonstrate that the pinakes
were not used for this purpose. We find there that the joiner
who made a single pinax received 30 drachmae, while the painter
who painted two only received 3 drachmae 1 obol.[4] The smallness of the latter sum seems a clear proof that the painting was
not of the artistic kind we should expect in a back-scene, but
a very simple affair, suitable to the supporting wall of a stage.
It is very probable that the pinakes were painted in imitation of
folding-doors, or of wood-work divided into panels. Puchstein
conjectures that the stone structures found at Priene and Termessos, made to resemble such doors or panelled work, are
reminiscences of the earlier pinakes, and similar instances of
vacant spaces made to imitate doors are common on Lycian
grave[5] monuments and Pompeian wall-paintings. This architectural front was called the 'hyposkenion', from its position
beneath the 'skene' or stage. Pollux says it was adorned
with 'columns and small statues'.[6] Statues, however, were not

---

[1] See (besides Puchstein, l. c.)
Excavations at Megalopolis, p. 87;
Griech. Theater, p. 116. Cp. ibid.,
pp. 103, 150, for similar traces at Assos
and Oropus. The architrave of the
proscenium at Oropus bore the inscription ἀγωνοθετήσας τὸ προσκήνιον καὶ τοὺς
πίνακας (ibid., p. 102). The Delian
inscriptions of 282 B. C. and 180 B. C.
mention πίνακες εἰς τὸ προσκήνιον,
πίνακες ἐπὶ τὸ λογεῖον (Bull. Corr. Hell.
1894, p. 162).

[2] [See Bethe, Jahrb. Arch. Inst.
1900, p. 79. There is nothing absurd,
as Dörpfeld seems to think (ibid. 1901,
p. 22), in the proscenium thus serving
two purposes in the two different types
of performance. Why should it not?]
[3] See Puchstein, l. c., p. 23.
[4] Bull. Corr. Hell. 1894, p. 162.
[5] Puchstein, l. c., p. 38.
[6] Poll. iv. 124 τὸ δὲ ὑποσκήνιον κίοσι
καὶ ἀγαλματίοις κεκόσμητο πρὸς τὸ
θέατρον τετραμμένοις, ὑπὸ τὸ λογεῖον

used as a decoration during the pre-Roman period. In Roman times they appear to have been sometimes inserted in the intercolumnia, in place of the painted boards. At Epidaurus, for instance, the space between the columns in the side-wings was filled in at some late period with groups of sculpture. At Delos, statues and other votive erections were placed along the front of the proscenium.[1] Possibly Pollux may be referring to these later customs; or he may have been thinking of the Roman stage, which was sometimes decorated in front with a sculptured frieze, like that of Phaedrus in the Athenian theatre. It is evident from the ruins that there was no permanent means of communication between the orchestra and the

FIG. 9.

top of the stage. As regards the connexion with the interior of the stage the custom seems to have varied. At Priene there were three doors leading out into the orchestra.[2] At Athens the proscenium had one door in the centre, and another smaller one on the western side. But in most theatres there was only a single door, that in the centre; and this door varied in width from 3 feet 3 inches at Delos to 4 feet at Epidaurus.[3] At Megalopolis, however, and also at Thespiae, there is no door of any kind leading out from the front of the proscenium into the orchestra.[4] Probably most theatres had doors leading from

κείμενον. When Athenaeus (631 E) speaks of a flute-player waiting in the hyposkenion till his turn came to perform, it is uncertain whether the word there denotes a room under the stage, or is used generally for the whole of the stage-buildings. See Müller, Unters. zu den Bühnenalt., pp. 62-5.

[1] Griech. Theater, pp. 127, 147.
[2] Schrader, Berl. Philolog. Wochenschrift, 1898, April 16, p. 509; Puch-

stein, l. c., pp. 19, 50.
[3] Griech. Theater, pp. 99, 102, 115, 125, 147, 150, 384. Dörpfeld now thinks that there may have been three doors at Delos, but the matter is very doubtful (Bull. Corr. Hell. 1896, p. 570).
[4] Excavations at Megalopolis, p. 86. Chamonard, Bull. Corr. Hell. 1896, p. 296.

the end of the stage-buildings into the 'parodoi' or side-entrances, though they cannot always be traced, owing to the scantiness of the remains.   Their position would no doubt vary, according to the structure of the different theatres.   At Epidaurus doors of this kind were placed immediately beyond the side-wings, at each extremity of the proscenium.   The illustration which is here inserted (Fig. 9) will give a clear idea of the appearance of these proscenia.   It represents a restoration of one end of the hyposkenion at Epidaurus.   The front of the proscenium is denoted by the letter *a*, the side-wing by *b*, while *c* marks the door leading out into the parados.[1]

In size these proscenia usually conformed to the rules of Vitruvius, and were about ten feet deep, and from ten to twelve feet high.   But sometimes they were much lower than he directs.   The proscenium at Oropus was only 8 ft. 2 in. in height, that at Priene only 8 ft. 8 in.[2]   The proscenium at Delos is given variously as 8 ft. 3 in. and 9 ft. 2 in.[3]   On the other hand, the stages at Athens and at the Peiraeeus were thirteen feet above the level of the orchestra.[4]   The wings by which the stage was enclosed on each side sometimes projected a few feet beyond the front line of the proscenium, as at Athens.   Sometimes, as at Eretria, there was no projection, and the front of the wings was continuous with that of the stage.   In many theatres, again, such as those of Megalopolis and Sicyon, there were no permanent side-wings, and the stage was terminated at each end by a mere wall.[5]   In such cases it is probable that during the dramatic performances temporary side-wings of wood were erected.   The theatres of Epidaurus, Oropus, Sicyon, and the later buildings at Eretria exhibit a peculiar feature in the shape of certain ramps or sloping passages visible to the audience and leading up from the parodos and the outside of the stage-buildings to the door in the walls terminating the ends of the stage.   The position of those ramps is clearly shown in the plan of the Epidaurian

[1] The illustration is taken from Baumeister's Denkmäler, iii. plate lxv.

[2] Griech. Theater, 103.   Bull. Corr. Hell. 1896, p. 595.

[3] Chamonard (Bull. Corr. Hell. 1896, p. 296), judging from the width of the supporting columns, makes the height of the Delian proscenium 8 ft. 2 in.

Dörpfeld (ibid., p. 564), arguing that these columns must have been the same height as the pillars at the side-entrance, supposes the proscenium to have been 9 ft. 2 in.

[4] Griech. Theater, p. 99.

[5] See the plans in Griech. Theater.

theatre (Fig. 6). It is possible that they were used by the chorus for the purpose of descending from the first floor of the stage-buildings to the entrance of the parodos. But probably they served mainly for the entrance of actors who represented persons supposed to be coming from a distance. The objection of Robert and Dörpfeld[1] that the actor would have to come up the ramps and wait at the door of the side-wings in view of the audience for his cue, before he could enter—which they justly say would be a ridiculous sight—assumes what it is quite unnecessary to assume, namely, that plays were performed without practice or proper stage-management. Very little rehearsal would be required in order that the actor's arrival might be duly timed. A different device for the entrance of such actors is found at Priene and Assos. There are no side-wings, but the stage is rather longer than the back-scene or the buildings of which the back-scene formed the face, and is continued for some distance down each side of the buildings. The ends of the stage are terminated by a wall containing no door. The idea seems to have been that the persons supposed to come from a distance should make their way down one of the passages on each side of the skene, and so come round the corner of the stage. The theatres at Delos, Termessos, and Ephesus seem to have employed variations of this device.[2]

When we turn from the stage to the stage-buildings of this period, our information is very incomplete owing to the scanty nature of the ruins. But it is probable that the stage-buildings began about this period to assume a more imposing appearance than in former times. We have seen that in the case of the earlier buildings there is some doubt whether the upper stories were made of wood or of stone. After the beginning of the third century it is probable that stone began to be used for all stories alike.[3] The buildings must also have been of a considerable height, to allow of a suitable back-scene above the tall proscenium.[4] As to the decoration of the wall at the back of

[1] [Robert, Gött. Gel. Anz. 1902, p. 425; Dörpfeld, Ath. Mitth. 1903, p. 407. The latter's suggestion (l. c. 1898, p. 351) that they were used to bring stage machinery into the θεολογεῖον, which he identifies with the stage or λογεῖον, is met by the rejection of this identification ; see below, p. 164.]

[2] Puchstein, Griech. Bühne, pp. 49, 58, &c.
[3] The remains at Sicyon and Eretria show that at any rate the *first* story—that above the proscenium—was made of stone.
[4] The phrase αἱ ἐπάνω σκηναί in the Delian inscription of 274 B. C. appears

the stage nothing is known.   In the later Greek theatres, built in the Roman fashion, this wall was constructed in an elaborate architectural design.   It usually consisted of two or three rows of columns, rising one above the other, and each surmounted with appropriate entablatures and pediments. Its height was often as great at the top of the auditorium—an arrangement which was found to improve the acoustic properties of the theatre.   Back-walls of this sumptuous character are still in part preserved in the Graeco-Roman theatres of Aspendos, Tauromenium, and various other cities.   But it is uncertain how far they can be traced back into or beyond the Hellenistic period.[1]   It is still keenly disputed whether the supporting walls for the stage-buildings, found in the ruins of different theatres, are really strong enough to bear the weight of two stories.   As regards the doors which led from the back-wall on to the stage there is no positive evidence to be obtained from the existing ruins.   But Pollux and Vitruvius state that they were three in number.[2]

The most essential difference between the theatre which we

to show that the back-scene of that time must have been two stories high (Bull. Corr. Hell. 1894, p. 162), [and the large sum of 2,500 drachmae paid for painting the σκηναί and παρασκήνια, when compared with the 6 drachmae 2 obols for painting the four πίνακες ἐς τὸ προσκήνιον suggests that the former was elaborate and artistic decoration, the latter something much simpler. See above, p. 123, and Bethe, Jahrb. Arch. Inst. 1900, p. 64; P. Gardner, J. Hell. Stud. 1899, p. 259, shows reason for thinking that the painting on the σκηναί represented architectural decoration, perhaps of an elaborate kind.]

[1] [Vitruvius, vii. 5. 5, says that Apaturius of Alabanda, about the middle of the first century B.C., treated the architectural back-scene in a fantastic manner, and it is therefore probable, though the inference is not certain, that the style in a simpler form had been in vogue for some time previously.   A terra-cotta from the S. Angelo collection, belonging to the first or second century B. C., presents a back-scene of two stories (Röm. Mitth. xii. p. 140; Bethe, Jahrb. Arch.

Inst. 1900, p. 61).   There is also a vase-painting from Magna Graecia in Madrid by Assteas, representing the Mad Heracles murdering his child (Baumeister, Denkm. 732; Bethe, l.c., p. 60), with an architectural background of two stories enclosed on both sides, and with a roof.   As Assteas painted in the fourth century B. C. (Robert, art. Assteas, in Pauly-Wiss. Encycl.), Bethe, l.c., argues that the architectural back-scene was known in Magna Graecia, and probably therefore in Greece proper, at that date.   But it is uncertain whether the scene represents an actual stage performance.   The murder, so far as we know, was never presented on the stage: it took place in a room.   The scene depicted may therefore represent the scene as narrated by a messenger, and the buildings cannot be assumed to be a stage background. The inferences from the terra-cotta are equally disputed.   (Dörpfeld, Jahrb. Arch. Inst. 1901, pp. 27 ff.; Graef., Hermes 1901, pp. 81 ff.)   Cp. note on p. 172.]

[2] Vitruv. v. 6; Poll. iv. 124.

are considering and that of the fifth century lay in the substitution of a tall and narrow stage for a low and comparatively deep one. This change was far more important than a mere change of material from wood to stone. The question naturally arises, what was the reason for the alteration? The answer is to be found in the fact that the Greek drama itself passed through a no less radical transformation at the same time. In the course of the fourth century it was gradually transformed from a choral to a non-choral drama. When we come to the third century we find that the chorus, which once played the chief part both in tragedy and comedy, had sunk into insignificance. It was often discarded altogether. When retained, it had nothing to do but to sing interludes between the successive acts. Its presence no more implied that the play was a choral play than the presence of the band in a modern theatre implies that the performance is an opera. The old intercourse between actors and chorus was a thing of the past.[1] The low deep stage was no longer necessary, to enable actors and chorus to converse together, or to supply room, when required, for the presence of the chorus by the side of the actors. Under these circumstances it would obviously be an advantage to make the stage as high as possible, in order to improve the view of the upper rows of spectators. The ancient theatres were of enormous size. At Athens, for example, the topmost tier of seats was 300 feet distant from the stage, and 100 feet above the level of the orchestra. In such a theatre, the higher the stage, the better would be the view of the majority of the audience. It was doubtless for this reason that the stage was raised to about ten or twelve feet in the course of the third century. At the same time its depth was necessarily diminished, in order that the spectators in the lowest rows might be able to see down to the end of it. The loss of depth was of no importance in the acting of a play, because of the practical exclusion of the chorus from the stage.

---

[1] The point of course is not, as Dörpfeld seems to imply (Jahrb. Arch. Inst. 1901, p. 25 ; Ath. Mitth. 1903, pp. 389, 406), whether there was ever a chorus or not at this time ; but that there was no longer a chorus in close communication with the actors, as in some plays of Aeschylus, and therefore requiring a low stage. Bethe is, however, not justified in assuming that there was *no* stage in Aeschylus' time (see below, p. 172). A low one would allow sufficient intercourse between chorus and actors.

In connexion with this subject a difficulty has been raised by some scholars which deserves consideration. It is generally admitted that the Vitruvian stage was well adapted for the later kind of drama. But from the fourth century down to Roman times the theatre was used quite as much for the revival of old plays as for the representation of new ones. It is contended that the ancient plays, with their intimate connexion between actors and chorus, could not possibly have been exhibited on a stage which was raised twelve feet above the level of the orchestra. In answer to this objection it may be pointed out that the only ancient plays which were ever revived during the period with which we are now dealing were those of Sophocles and Euripides. Aeschylus and Aristophanes had gone out of fashion. The plays of Sophocles and Euripides could easily have been adapted for the Vitruvian stage by excisions and modifications in the choral part. If the chorus, as sometimes happened, took an important share in the dialogue, its part on such occasions might be given to extra characters on the stage. That the old plays were revised and adapted in this manner at a later period is proved by the express testimony of Dion Chrysostomus,[1] and there is no improbability in assuming that the same practice had begun to prevail as early as the third century B. C. It might, however, sometimes be necessary, during the revival of the ancient dramas, to provide a means of communication between stage and orchestra. In such cases temporary wooden steps were placed in front of the proscenium. There is ample evidence for the use of this contrivance. Pollux tells us that when the players entered by the orchestra they ascended the stage by means of steps.[2] Athenaeus, the writer on military engines, speaks of the steps which were placed in front of the stage for the use of the actors.[3] Steps of this kind are depicted in several vase-paintings from Magna Graecia, belonging to the third century B. C., and representing theatrical

---

[1] Tragic Drama of the Greeks, p. 452.
[2] Poll. iv. 127. See below, p. 148.
[3] Athen. de Mach., p. 29 (Wesch.) κατεσκεύασαν δέ τινες ἐν πολιορκίᾳ κλιμάκων γένη παραπλήσια τοῖς τιθεμένοις ἐν τοῖς θεάτροις πρὸς τὰ προσκήνια τοῖς ὑποκριταῖς. The meaning of this passage has been much disputed. But

Weissmann (Scenische Anweis. pp. 49 ff.) has shown conclusively, as it seems to me, from a parallel passage in Apollodorus περὶ κλιμάκων, that Athenaeus is referring, not to ladders used *on* the stage for mounting the back-scene, but to steps about 12 feet high, placed in front of the stage.

scenes.[1] There is also a wall-painting at Herculaneum, which shows us one of these flights of steps standing by itself, with an actor's mask at the top.[2] From these indications we see that, although there was no permanent means of communication between stage and orchestra in the Hellenistic theatres, a temporary connexion could always be supplied when necessary.

§ 9. *Puchstein's Theory of the Stage-buildings.*

The theory of Puchstein, already so often alluded to, ascribes to Lycurgus the construction of the proscenium consisting of stone columns and pinakes, and throws back to the end of the fifth century the Lycurgean structures usually so called. His principal ground for this change of date lies in the development which he traces in the form of the columns in question.[3] He thinks it certain that the use of full columns must have preceded that of half-columns, and that columns without special contrivances for holding pinakes must be earlier than simple ones. Thus the full columns of the proscenia of Athens, Sicyon, and the Peiraeeus, which have no such contrivances, will belong to the earliest period of stone proscenia; they will be earlier than those of Megalopolis and Eretria, which have rims for holding the pinakes, and still earlier than the plain half-columns of Epidaurus and the grooved half-columns of Priene, Assos, Delos, Pleuron, Oropus, &c. The proscenia of Priene, Pleuron, and Delos appear to belong to the third century B.C.; and Puchstein accordingly throws back the Athenian columned proscenium to the latter half of the fourth century, the time of Lycurgus. The theory is at least plausible; but it is not certain. Development is not always in a straight line or in logical order, and does not always require intervals of many years between one stage and another; different experiments may be tried simultaneously in different cases, and recurrence to old types, or preservation of them after new ones have been invented, is a common thing in the history of architecture. The form of the proscenium, therefore, cannot be used with certainty as a chronological criterion, though it may be very suggestive.

[1] See Fig. 13. Other specimens are given in Baumeister, Denkmäler, ii. pp. 819, 820; Griechische Theater, pp. 322-324.
[2] Wieseler, Denkmäl. iv. 5.
[3] Puchstein, Griech. Bühne, pp. 17 ff.

It follows, in Puchstein's view, from the earlier dating of the stone proscenium, that the so-called Lycurgean stage-building, with its deep side-wings, must have been erected some time before Lycurgus, towards the end of the fifth or beginning of the fourth century. The date which Puchstein suggests for the stone proscenium at Athens is certainly more probable on *a priori* grounds than that given by Dörpfeld. According to Dörpfeld's chronology, the earliest stage-buildings at Athens were apparently later than those at Eretria and other Greek cities. Dörpfeld has conceded that the old skene at Eretria is of the fourth or fifth century, and may be older than the Lycurgean.[1] But it is hard to believe that the city in which the drama was first developed should not have been the first also to provide itself with a permanent stage.

Professor E. A. Gardner also shows reasons of a technical character in favour of the earlier date.[2] The foundations of the chryselephantine statue of Dionysus by Alcamenes are of conglomerate and breccia. Alcamenes was at work during the latter half of the fifth century; and the later temple in the precinct below the theatre was built to contain this statue. Now, as Professor Gardner points out, it is unlikely that the Athenians would have undertaken so costly a work in the later part of the Peloponnesian war. On the other hand, there is no trace of the use of breccia in foundations in the Periclean age. The temple probably therefore dates from the time between the Peace of Nicias in 421 B.C. and the Sicilian expedition in 415 B.C. And if the temple was built then, it is not unlikely that the theatre may have been begun at the same time. The fact that the architectural technique of the theatre, particularly in the use of conglomerate blocks, is the same as that of the temple points the same way. The work may have begun about B.C. 420, and progressed gradually and continuously up to the time of Lycurgus. The exact year in which the higher stage was erected cannot, of course, be fixed.

Puchstein also doubts whether the whole of the existing auditorium was built in the time of Lycurgus.[4] There is a fragment of a wall (not marked) in front of *a—a* in the plan, which Dörpfeld does not mention in his text, though he marks

---

[1] Griech. Theater, p. 113.
[2] Ancient Athens, p. 435.
[3] Fürtwängler, Sitzungsber. der

Akad. der Wiss. zu München, 1901, pp. 411–6 : q.v. for further arguments.
[4] Puchstein, l.c., p. 138.

it in one of his plans.[1] This, Puchstein suggests, is the supporting wall of an auditorium older than the Lycurgean. Besides
this he finds evidence of stone seats in the fifth century. It has
already been mentioned that a stone built into the western wing
of the auditorium contains a fifth-century inscription.[2] This inscription consists of the words βολῆς ὑπηρετῶν, and was probably
part of a seat-step, reserved for the servants of the βουλή.
If so, there must have been a stone auditorium before the time
of Lycurgus.

A further point in Puchstein's theory concerns the height of
the stage in the building which he assigns to the fifth century.[3]
The only possible purpose of the deep side-wings was to en-
close a stage. The analogy of later theatres of the same type,
such as those of Tyndaris and Segesta, where traces of the
stage still remain, render any other conclusion indefensible.
No other hypothesis has any support from any monuments
whatever. This stage may have been of wood, proscenium
and all, and this would account for its disappearance ; or it may
have had slight stone supports, which might easily have left
no trace. The height of this old stage at Athens may be
determined approximately by a comparison with the almost
contemporary stage-buildings at Eretria, where there is evidence
to show that the stage must have been not less than nine or ten
feet from the ground. But this does not mean that still earlier
the stage was not, as previously contended,[4] a comparatively
low one, such as would be suitable for the plays of Aeschylus
and the earlier plays of Aristophanes. Nor is the existence
of a high stage about 400 B. C. inconsistent with the presence
of a chorus, as Dörpfeld thinks.[5] The decision depends not
on the presence of a chorus, but on the intimacy of the connexion between the chorus and the actors. As long as they
freely commingled together, the stage must have been moderately
low. But when the chorus ceased to take any active part in
the play, the raising of the stage would do no harm, and would
be an advantage, as giving the audience a better view of the
actors. Now it was precisely towards the end of the fifth

---

[1] Tafel iii.

[2] Cp. p. 87. Dörpfeld's objection that
the shape is not that of such seat-steps
is disposed of by a comparison with
other seat-steps elsewhere ; Puchstein,

l.c., p. 139. The inscription is C. I. A.
i. 499.

[3] l. c., p. 136.

[4] Above, p. 119, and below, § 13.

[5] See note on p. 128.

century that the chorus began to lose its old significance, and to assume the functions of mere singers of interludes.[1] Hence there would be nothing surprising if it were proved, and not merely rendered likely, as by Puchstein, that at this date the stage began to be of a greater height than formerly.

§ 10. *The Stage-buildings in Roman Times.*

We have now followed the development of the stage-buildings from the old wooden erections of the fifth century to the more solid and elaborate structures of the Hellenistic period. All that remains is to trace their history during the later ages of Roman supremacy. We have shown that at Athens the stage-buildings were practically reconstructed after the Roman fashion in the time of Nero. The same tendency had already become prevalent in other places at a much earlier period. After the middle of the first century B.C. most of the new theatres built by the Greeks were constructed in the Roman style. The majority of the old ones began about the same time to be altered and modified under Roman influence. This latter process, however, was never carried out universally. It was confined mainly to the more outlying parts of the Hellenic world, such as Sicily and Asia Minor. In Greece proper it was a comparatively rare occurrence. Athens and Argos are the only cities on the Greek mainland which are known to have Romanized their theatres. Still, looking at the Greek world as a whole, it may be said that from the time of the Christian era the great majority of Hellenic theatres were adapted to the Roman model. It was at this period that the stage-buildings began to be constructed on a more lofty scale, and their front adorned with the gorgeous architectural embellishments which we have previously described. Some idea of their magnificence may be obtained from the existing remains, and especially from those of the theatre at Aspendos, which is well preserved. A restoration of part of the interior of this theatre (Fig. 10) is here inserted.[2] The back-wall erected at Athens in the time of Nero was of the same type, though smaller in size. Façades of this imposing character may perhaps be thought too elaborate for the back-

[1] Aristot. Poet. c. 18, ad fin.
[2] The illustration is taken from Lanckoronski, Städte Pamphyliens und Pisidiens (Wien, 1892), vol. i. plate 27.

wall of a theatre. When dramas were being performed, and they were covered with painted scenery, their architectural beauty would be concealed from the eyes of the spectators. But ancient theatres were regularly used, not only for dramatic performances, but also for various other purposes, both artistic and political. On such occasions, when the stage was without scenic decoration, the architectural grandeur of the back-wall would add greatly to the beauty of the stage-buildings, and form a pleasing object to the eye. Probably, too, at many of the

FIG. 10.

dramatic exhibitions, when the action was laid before a temple or palace, painted scenery was dispensed with, and the architectural façade supplied an appropriate background.

It will be seen from the illustration that in the theatre of Aspendos there were five doors at the back of the stage. There was a large door in the centre, and two smaller ones on each side. The same arrangement was generally adopted in Graeco-Roman theatres. But Pollux and Vitruvius speak of three doors

as the regulation number.[1] Possibly, therefore, the five doors of
the later theatres were not all used during the dramatic representations. When the stage was prepared for the performance
of a play, the two doors on the outside may have been covered
up with scenery; or temporary side-wings may have been
erected in front of them. Another noticeable feature in the
theatre of Aspendos is the roof over the stage. Traces of
a similar roof are also found at Orange, and justify the conclusion that in most theatres of the Roman type the stage
was covered over.[2] Whether the same practice prevailed in
the Hellenistic theatres there is no evidence to show. But
the convenience of the arrangement is so obvious, that we can
hardly doubt that it began to be employed at a comparatively
early period.

In a large number of cases the process of Romanizing
the Greek theatres was not carried out completely. Many
theatres, whether built or reconstructed on the new model,
still retained features which were essentially Greek. This was
the case at Athens. The Greek stage was usually the same
length as one diameter of the orchestra. The Roman stage
was twice as long, and extended some distance into the wings
of the auditorium on each side. There was no open space
between the auditorium and the side-wings; the place of the old
Greek 'parodoi' was supplied by vaulted subways. But at
Athens, when the Neronian alterations were made, the stage
was not prolonged in the Roman style, but remained of the
same length as before. The entrances into the orchestra at
a and *g* were thus left open (Fig. 3). In many other places,
especially in Asia Minor, the Romanization was of a still
more partial kind. In theatres such as those of Termessos,
Perge, and Sagalassos the general outline of the building was
hardly affected by the change. The front line of the stage
was not pushed forward; the orchestra still remained nearly
a complete circle; open passages were left between the auditorium and the stage-buildings. The only important alteration
was in the size of the stage, which was lengthened at each end,
and deepened by throwing the front of the stage-buildings
farther back. The height of the stage was but slightly

---

[1] Vitruv. v. 6; Poll. iv. 124.   [2] Müller, Bühnenalt., p. 28.

diminished. In a Roman theatre it was usually five feet. But the stages at Termessos, Sagalassos, and Patara vary from eight feet to nine, and were therefore very little lower than the ordinary stage of the Vitruvian type.[1]

These examples show how trifling in many cases was the difference between the Graeco-Roman theatres and those of the purely Greek type. They also throw some light on another question of considerable interest. In Roman theatres all performances were confined to the stage; the orchestra was given up to spectators of distinguished rank. It may be asked whether the Greeks, when they built their theatres in the Roman style, adopted the same custom. The answer seems to be that they did not. It is most improbable that theatres should have been constructed in Asia Minor with the old full-sized orchestra, unless this orchestra had been intended as a place for choral performances. The fact that in many of these theatres the stage was eight or nine feet high proves the same thing. If the spectators had been placed immediately in front of it, their view would have been very much obstructed. We know, too, that in the Athenian theatre, even after the Roman stage had been introduced, the marble thrones round the orchestra continued to be the chief seats of honour. Hence it is evident that the orchestra must have been still a place for the performers, and not a place for distinguished spectators. The chief purpose of the Greeks, in Romanizing their theatres, was to provide a deep and capacious stage for spectacles of the Roman type, such as pantomimes and pyrrhic ballets. The old Greek performances were given as before in the orchestra. As far as the drama is concerned, the orchestra would seldom be required at this period, the lyrical part of tragedy and comedy having now practically disappeared. But the choral and musical competitions still flourished as vigorously as ever, and these were kept to their original place, and not transferred to the stage.

[1] See Lanckoronski, Städte Pamphyliens und Pisidiens, vol. i. pp. 51 ff., and plate 14 (Perge), vol. ii. pp. 92 ff., and plates 10-13 (Termessos), pp. 152 ff., and plate 26 (Sagalassos); Texier, Description de l'Asie Mineure, vol. iii. plates 181 and 182 (Patara), plate 215 (Myra). The stage at Termessos was 8 feet high, that at Patara 8½ feet, that at Sagalassos 9 feet. At Magnesia and at Tralles, where in other respects the theatres were more completely Romanized, the height of the stages was 7 ft. 6 in. and 9 ft. 10 in. respectively (Griech. Theater, p. 156). See also Puchstein, Griech. Bühne, on all these theatres.

§ 11. *Exceptional Stage-buildings.*

The stage-buildings which we have hitherto described have been those of the normal type. But there are several places in which peculiar and exceptional structures were erected, either for reasons connected with the nature of the ground, or for mere love of variety. Some of these may be worth mentioning. The theatre at Pergamon was apparently built about the beginning of the second century B. c.[1] But the stage-buildings, instead of being made of stone, as was usual at that period, consisted of temporary wooden erections, which were put up and taken down at each festival. Stone blocks were let into the ground, with holes for the reception of the beams by which the building was supported. When the performances were over, the whole apparatus might be removed in a short time. It was only at a later period that permanent stage-buildings were constructed. The reason for this curious arrangement, according to Dörpfeld, was to leave the way open to a temple in the neighbourhood. As the auditorium lay on a terrace, with not much room in front of it, permanent stage-buildings would have filled up the whole space, and blocked the passage to the temple.

Another remarkable instance of deviation from the ordinary practice is supplied by the theatre at Megalopolis.[2] In this theatre (Fig. 11) the place of the stage-buildings was taken by a vast council-chamber, called the Thersilion, which faced towards the auditorium. Its façade consisted of a vestibule, 26 feet high, and resting on a flight of five steps. Originally, when dramas were to be performed, a temporary wooden stage was erected in front of the Thersilion. The foundation-wall for a stage of this kind has been discovered, and lies at a distance of 24 feet from the columns of the vestibule. It is obvious therefore that the vestibule cannot itself have formed the background. A stage 24 feet across would have been far too deep for a Greek theatre. Temporary scenic decorations must have been erected some feet in front of the council-

---

[1] Griech. Theater, pp. 150 ff.
[2] See Excavations at Megalopolis, Supplementary Paper published by the Society for the Promotion of Hellenic Studies, 1892; Puchstein, Griech. Bühne, pp. 88 ff. The plan is copied from Griech. Theater, p. 134.

chamber. In later times a stone proscenium of the ordinary type was erected on the site of the old wooden one. But when this was done, it is probable that the Thersilion had fallen into ruins. Otherwise the beauty of its appearance would have been altogether marred by the stone structure in front of it.

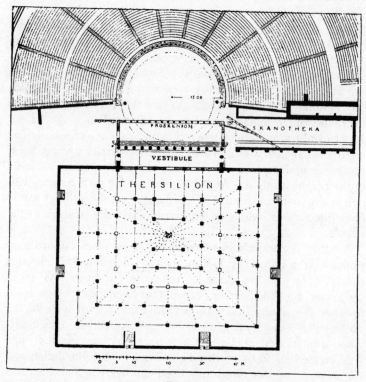

FIG. 11.

But the most peculiar of the stage-buildings which have hitherto been discovered is that at Delos. A representation of the ground-plan (Fig. 12) is inserted on the next page.[1] This

[1] From Griech. Theater, p. 144. For the description of the theatre, see ibid., pp. 144 ff. ; Chamonard, Bull. Corr. Hell., 1896, pp. 256 ff. ; Puchstein, l.c., pp. 53 ff.

building consisted of a single oblong room. In front of it was an ordinary proscenium, about ten feet deep, and eight or nine feet high, resting on half-columns. The spaces between the columns were filled, as usual, with painted boards. The curious feature is that this same proscenium was continued in a modified form round the rest of the building, so as to serve as a portico. On the sides and in the rear it rested on rectangular pillars instead of on columns. The spaces between the pillars were considerably wider than the spaces between the columns, and were left open,

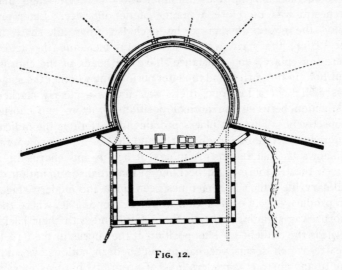

FIG. 12.

instead of being filled up with boards. Porticoes of this kind were often erected close to the stage-buildings, as a shelter from the rain; but the position of the one at Delos is altogether exceptional. Another remarkable feature in this building is the fact that the proscenium was open at each end, and was not even enclosed with a wall. When dramas were being performed, wooden side-wings must have been put up for the occasion.[1]

---

[1] Side-wings (παρασκήνια) are mentioned not infrequently in the Delian inscriptions for 274 and 269 B.C. (Bull. Corr. Hell., 1894, p. 162) as forming part of the theatre. But the present proscenium was probably erected in the second century. At that date the permanent side-wings must have been abolished.

§ 12. *Wieseler's Theory of the Greek Stage.*

In a Greek dramatic performance the relative position occupied by actors and chorus was quite unlike anything to be seen in a modern theatre. The actors appeared upon a raised platform, the chorus performed in the orchestra underneath. When the actors were present, and the dialogue was proceeding, the chorus stood with their backs towards the audience, and their faces towards the stage.[1] In the early period the stage was only of moderate height, and communication between stage and orchestra was therefore a matter of no difficulty. Later on, when the chorus began to be excluded from all share in the action, the stage was raised several feet, and the actors were thus placed some distance above the heads of the chorus. But both in the earlier and the later period, and whether the stage was a high or a low one, there was always a clearly marked distinction between the normal position of actors and chorus respectively. This fact places prominently before us the radical difference between a Greek chorus and that of a modern opera. It shows us that in the groupings of actors and chorus in a Greek theatre there could be none of that realistic imitation of ordinary life which is sometimes seen upon the modern stage. To produce effects of this kind would be impossible, where the chorus was standing beneath the actors, and with their backs towards the audience. This position of the chorus in the Greek theatre, which seems peculiar to our modern notions, was not due to any abstract considerations of propriety, but was merely the result of the peculiar circumstances under which the Greek drama was developed. Originally the performance was almost entirely lyrical, and the stage and the actors were a mere appendage. The chorus, being the principal performers, and the most prominent object of attention, occupied the central position in the orchestra. The actors were placed on a stage behind them, so as to be visible to the spectators. Eventually the dialogue between the actors completely overshadowed the songs of the chorus, and the lyrical element in the performance

---

[1] Dindorf, Prolegom. de Comoed. p. 29 καὶ ὅτε μὲν πρὸς τοὺς ὑποκριτὰς διελέγετο (ὁ χορὸς ὁ κωμικός), πρὸς τὴν σκηνὴν ἀφεώρα, ὅτε δὲ ἀπελθόντων τῶν ὑποκριτῶν τοὺς ἀναπαίστους διεξῄει, πρὸς τὸν δῆμον ἀπεστρέφετο. Ibid., p. 36 εἰσῄει (ὁ χορὸς ὁ κωμικὸς) ἐν τετραγώνῳ σχήματι, ἀφορῶν εἰς τοὺς ὑποκριτάς. Cp. ibid. p. 21 ; Dübner, Prolegom. de Comoed. p.20 ; Schol. Aristoph. Equit. 505.

was treated as a kind of interlude. But the chorus still continued to occupy that prominent position in the theatre which its original importance had assigned to it.

Since the beginning of the last century various difficulties have been raised in connexion with this subject, and various theories have been invented for the purpose of removing the supposed difficulties. All this speculation appears to have had its origin in the same source. Until quite recent years it was assumed by every scholar that the stage of the fifth century must have been of the same height and structure as the later stage described by Vitruvius. But it was felt that the dramas of the fifth century could not possibly have been written for a theatre in which the actors were raised about twelve feet above the level of the chorus. The relationship between actors and chorus in these early dramas is far too close to allow it to be supposed that they were separated by a barrier of this kind. Still, there was the testimony of Vitruvius, who said the stage was about twelve feet high, and whose measurements were supposed to apply to all theatres, early as well as late. The first attempt to meet the difficulty was made by Hermann, at the beginning of the century; and his theory was afterwards adopted and developed by Wieseler. According to this view the chorus did not stand upon the level of the orchestra, but upon a sort of subsidiary platform, erected immediately in front of the twelve-foot stage. The height of the platform, they said, was so arranged as to bring the chorus into moderate proximity to the actors, without concealing them from the view of the audience. This platform for the chorus was generally accepted by writers upon the Greek drama until about ten years ago. Its existence was defended, partly on general grounds, partly by an appeal to certain passages in ancient authors. To take the ancient authorities first. Hermann supposed that the platform was called 'orchestra' in a narrower sense. He cited a passage in Suidas, where the orchestra is described as coming next to the 'skene', and as being a wooden erection on which mimes performed. But in this passage the context clearly proves that the word 'orchestra' is used in its later sense as the 'stage'.[1] Weiseler endeavoured to

---

[1] G. Hermann, Opusc. vi. 2, pp. 152 ff. The passage occurs in Suidas and Etym. Mag., *s.v.* σκηνή; and in a more complete form in Schol. Gregor.

prove that the platform for the chorus was denoted by the word 'thymele'. Now 'thymele', as we have seen, was a word which had a great many meanings in connexion with the theatre. It denoted, first, the altar of Dionysus; secondly, the orchestra; thirdly, the stage.[1] If the passages are carefully examined in which it is asserted that 'thymele' denotes a platform for the chorus in front of the stage, it will be found that in the majority of them the word is much more naturally explained as meaning the stage itself, or the orchestra. In one or two cases the language used is apparently due to a confusion between the different meanings of the term. In no case is there a clear and definite description of a platform standing halfway up between the orchestra and the stage.[2] If such a platform had really existed, it seems incredible that there should have been no mention of it. As far, then, as ancient authorities are concerned, the theory as to the existence of a platform for the chorus finds no support.

On general grounds there are several fatal objections to the theory. In the first place, if it were correct, we should have to believe that the Greeks first of all constructed an

Nazianz. 355 B. The last version runs as follows :—μετὰ τὴν σκηνὴν εὐθὺς καὶ τὰ παρασκήνια ἡ ὀρχήστρα. αὕτη δέ ἐστιν ὁ τύπος ὁ ἐκ σανίδων ἔχων τὸ ἔδαφος, ἐφ' οὗ θεατρίζουσιν οἱ μῖμοι. εἶτα μετὰ τὴν ὀρχήστραν βωμὸς ἦν· τοῦ Διονύσου, τετράγωνον οἰκοδόμημα κενὸν ἐπὶ τοῦ μέσου, ὃ καλεῖται θυμέλη παρὰ τοῦ θύειν. μετὰ τὴν θυμέλην ἡ κονίστρα, τουτέστι τὸ κάτω ἔδαφος τοῦ θεάτρου. It is clear that ὀρχήστρα here means the stage. This appears not only from the context, but also from the fact that it is said to have been the place for the μῖμοι. Wieseler bases upon the above passage his peculiar theory that the 'thymele' was the platform for the chorus, and not an altar at all. He relies on the words τετράγωνον οἰκοδόμημα κενόν. It is true that the passage is obscure. But if it proves one thing more than another, it proves that the 'thymele' was the altar of Dionysus, and stood in the orchestra.

[1] See above, p. 108.

[2] In addition to the scholium quoted in the preceding note, the following passages are cited to prove that θυμέλη

sometimes = the special platform for the chorus, between the orchestra and the stage :—(1) Anthol. Pal. vii. 21 πολλάκις ἐν θυμέλῃσι καὶ ἐν σκηνῇσι τεθηλὼς | βλαισὸς Ἀχαρνίτης κισσὸς κ.τ.λ. (2) Corp. Ins. Gr. 6750 δόξαν φωνήεσσαν ἐνὶ σκηναῖσι λαβοῦσαν | παντοίης ἀρετῆς ἐν μείμοις, εἶτα χοροῖσι | πολλάκις ἐν θυμέλαις. (3) Schol. Aristid. iii. p. 536 (Dindf.) ὁ χορὸς ὅτε εἰσῄει ἐν τῇ ὀρχήστρᾳ ᾗ (MS. ἡ) ἐστι θυμέλη. (4) Poll. iv. 123 ἡ δὲ ὀρχήστρα τοῦ χοροῦ, ἐν ᾗ καὶ ἡ θυμέλη, εἴτε βῆμά τι οὖσα εἴτε βωμός. (5) Isidor. Origg. xviii. 47 'et dicti thymelici, quod olim in orchestra stantes cantabant super pulpitum quod thymele vocabatur.' In the first and second passages θυμέλη obviously = ὀρχήστρα. In the third passage it = ὀρχήστρα or βωμὸς Διονύσου, according as ἡ or ᾗ is read. In the fourth passage there is apparently a confusion of the two meanings of θυμέλη as 'a stage' and 'an altar'. In the fifth passage the two meanings of 'orchestra' and 'stage' are confused. [Cp. p. 108, n.]

orchestra for the chorus to perform in; then built a stage twelve feet high; then, finding they had made their stage a great deal too lofty, got out of the difficulty by erecting a platform each year, to bring the chorus within reach of the actors. To suppose that the Greeks acted in this way would be to suppose that they were altogether deficient in common sense. In the second place, it must not be forgotten that the performances at the City Dionysia consisted of dithyrambs as well as dramas. The dithyrambic chorus consisted of fifty members, and stood in a circular position. They must therefore have required a very considerable space for their performances. The oblong platform in front of the stage would not have been large enough to accommodate them, but would have been large enough to encroach very extensively upon the orchestra, and to drive the dithyrambic choruses into one end of it. That such was the case is most improbable. In the third place, in the recently excavated Greek theatres there are no traces of any appliances for the erection of the supposed platform. We should have expected to find holes in the floor of the orchestra, and sockets in the hyposkenion, for the reception of the beams by which the platform was supported. But there is no theatre in which any such traces are to be found. Fourthly, on the floor of the orchestra at Epidaurus a large circle is marked out with a stone border immediately in front of the stage (Fig. 6). It is difficult to resist the conclusion that this circle was intended for the performances of the chorus. For these reasons, combined with the silence of ancient writers, there appears to be no doubt that the platform for the chorus in front of the stage must be regarded as a fiction of modern times.

All the difficulties which this platform was invented to explain will disappear, if we assume that the stage of the fifth century was considerably lower than that of later times. It was only in the earlier period of the drama that a close communication between actors and chorus was required. In the subsequent epoch the existence of a lofty stage presents no difficulty. And the assumption of a low stage for the period of Aeschylus and his immediate successors is on general grounds the most natural one. We are told that originally, when the drama was still a lyrical performance, the coryphaeus used to mount

upon a small table, in the intervals between the odes, in order
to converse with the rest of the chorus. Later on, an actor
was substituted for the coryphaeus. Later still, in the course
of the fifth century, a second and a third actor were introduced.
Now it is absurd to suppose that, while the coryphaeus was
replaced in this tentative way by a gradually increasing number
of actors, the old table on which he performed should have
been suddenly converted into a complete Vitruvian stage,
twelve feet high, and fifty feet long. It is much more natural
to imagine that the development of the stage was also a slow
and experimental process, and that in the fifth century its
size was intermediate between the low table of the sixth
century and the tall proscenium of later times. The few traces
of archaeological evidence which we possess concerning the
early stage are distinctly in favour of this view. It is also
supported by the well-known description in Horace. Horace,
in his account of the development of Greek tragedy, tells
us that Aeschylus 'erected a stage on beams of moderate
size'.[1] Horace's information, as we know, was derived from
Greek sources. Hence it appears that the ordinary Greek
tradition favoured the belief that the early stage was a low
one, and that it contrasted in this respect with the stage of
later times.

§ 13. *Dörpfeld's Theory of the Greek Stage.*

Another theory of a far more revolutionary kind has been
propounded in recent years by Höpken[2], and amplified and
developed by Dörpfeld. Dörpfeld assumes, like Wieseler,
that the proscenium of the fifth century must have been of
the same height as that described by Vitruvius. But he
gets out of the consequent difficulty by supposing that the
proscenium was intended, not as a stage for the actors, but
as a background. He denies the existence of a stage in
purely Greek theatres either of the earlier or of the later

[1] Horace, Ars Poet. 278–80 ' post
hunc personae pallaeque repertor
honestae | Aeschylus et modicis in-
stravit pulpita tignis | et docuit ma-
gnumque loqui nitique cothurno.' [The
passage becomes still more significant
if we translate 'tignis' 'posts', i. e.

uprights. It bears this sense in Caes.
B. G. iv. 17, 3. 'Tigna bina sesqui-
pedalia paulum ab imo praeacuta . . .
in flumen defixerat.' See P. Gardner,
J. Hell. Stud. 1899, p. 257.]
[2] Höpken, De Theatro Attico,
Bonn, 1884.

period. He believes that in all Greek theatres the actors and the chorus performed together in the orchestra. The proscenium represented the palace or other building before which the action took place. The front-wall of the stage-buildings immediately behind the proscenium represented merely the sky. This theory has been the subject of much discussion and controversy during the last twenty years. As it has been accepted by several scholars, it will be necessary to consider it in detail. I propose in the present section to explain the grounds on which, as it seems to me, it must be regarded as untenable; and to discuss at length the evidence on which the belief in the existence of a Greek stage is founded. In dealing with this subject it will be convenient to divide the period covered by the Greek drama into two parts, and to consider first the later part, from about 300 B.C. onwards; and then to return to the earlier period, that of the fourth and fifth centuries. The evidence in the two cases is somewhat different, and will be more clearly understood if taken separately.

1. THE LATER STAGE.—First, then, as to the later or 'Hellenistic' period. Recent excavations, as was previously pointed out, have now given us a fairly clear idea as to the shape and structure of the stage-buildings during this period. We now know that from the beginning of the third century onwards, or, if Puchstein is right, from a considerably earlier date, the stage-buildings in an ordinary Greek theatre, though varying in detail, conformed to the same general type. They consisted of a long rectangular structure, in front of which was a narrow platform, usually about twelve feet high and ten feet deep. This platform was called the 'proskenion'. In the third century it appears to have been generally made of wood. But in the course of the second and first centuries, or in the fourth century, if Puchstein is right, a stone proscenium was substituted for the old wooden ones in almost every theatre. What then was the purpose of this proscenium, this long platform, twelve feet high and ten feet deep, which we find in all Greek theatres after the fourth century? For an answer to this question we naturally turn to Vitruvius, who wrote a book about architecture towards the end of the first century B.C.,

and in the course of it gave a detailed description of Greek
and Roman theatres. Vitruvius tells us that every Greek
theatre has a stage, and that this stage is from ten to twelve
feet high and about ten feet deep. Its narrowness is due to the
fact that it is only used by the actors in tragedy and comedy;
all other performers appear in the orchestra.[1] He adds that
the Roman stage is much lower and much deeper, and this for
two reasons. It had to be deeper, because all the performers
appeared upon it. It had to be lower, because in a Roman
theatre the spectators sat in the orchestra, and would not
therefore have been able to see over the top of a twelve-foot
stage.[2] Here then we seem to have a clear and final answer
to our question. The proscenium which we find in all Greek
theatres after about 300 B. C., and in some perhaps a century
earlier, answers exactly to the description of Vitruvius. It must
therefore have been intended to serve as a stage.

Dörpfeld, it is well known, refuses to accept this conclusion.
But his method of dealing with the testimony of Vitruvius has
changed since he wrote his book on the Greek theatre. He
then supposed that Vitruvius had been guilty of an error.
While admitting that he was correct in his measurements of
the Greek proscenium, he asserted that he had made a mistake as to its purpose; that he had confused the background
of the Hellenistic theatre with the stage of the Roman.[3]
But this explanation is one which it is impossible to accept.
It is absurd to suppose that Vitruvius was mistaken. He

---

[1] Vitruv. v. 7 'ita a tribus centris hac
descriptione ampliorem habent orche-
stram Graeci et scaenam recessiorem
minoreque latitudine pulpitum, quod
λογείον appellant, ideo quod eo tragici
et comici actores in scaena peragunt,
reliqui autem artifices suas per orche-
stram praestant actiones, itaque ex eo
scaenici et thymelici graece separatim
nominantur. Eius logei altitudo non
minus debet esse pedum decem, non
plus duodecim.' Whether under 'reliqui artifices' Vitruvius included the
dramatic chorus is very doubtful. The
dramatic chorus had almost disappeared
in his day. Moreover 'thymelici' as
opposed to 'scaenici' generally means
the competitors in musical and literary
contests, as opposed to the competitors
in dramatic contests. But the words
of Vitruvius about the position of the
actors upon the stage are free from all
ambiguity. [Cp. Frei, de Certaminibus
Thymelicis. Dörpfeld's suggestion
(Deutsche Littztg. 1901, p. 1816) that
dramatic actors were called σκηνικοί
because they were nearer the σκηνή,
and musical performers θυμελικοί as
being in the centre of the orchestra,
round the θυμέλη, forces the words to
fit his theory, but gives a far less
natural meaning to the distinction.
According to this, the members of the
chorus in the drama also ought to be
called θυμελικοί.]
[2] Ibid. v. 6.
[3] Griech. Theater, p. 364.

was a professional architect, writing about his own special subject, and writing at the very time when many of these Greek proscenia were being erected. His remark about the Greek stage is not introduced as an *obiter dictum*, but is made the basis of the distinction which he draws between Greek and Roman theatres. He had evidently therefore thought about the subject. But even if we suppose that he could make a mistake of this kind, even if we suppose that he had never been in Greece, and never seen a Greek play acted there, still it is incredible that such an absurd error should have remained uncorrected in his book. The connexion between Greece and Rome was so intimate, that there must have been thousands of people in Rome who had seen Greek plays performed in a Greek theatre, and knew how it was done. If Vitruvius had made this absurd blunder, some one would have been sure to point it out to him, and he would have had it corrected.

Since the publication of his book Dörpfeld has shifted his ground on this question.[1] He now suggests a new method of explaining away the testimony of Vitruvius. He supposes that Vitruvius, when speaking of the stage in the Greek theatre, was referring, not to the ordinary Greek theatre, but to the peculiar type of Graeco-Roman theatre found in various cities of Asia Minor, such as Termessos and Sagalassos. These theatres, as we have shown, exhibited a sort of transition between the Greek and the Roman model. While their general design was Greek, their stages were partially lowered and deepened, so as to come nearer to the Roman practice.[2] In theatres of this kind Dörpfeld admits that the actors performed upon the stage; and he contends that it is to them that Vitruvius refers, and not to the regular Greek theatres, in which the actors always appeared in the orchestra. But in the first place it is difficult to believe that Vitruvius, when he speaks of the 'Greek' theatre, should mean something quite different. Why should he describe as 'Greek' a type of building which was not found in Greece proper, and which was essentially a combination of Greek and Roman attributes? In the second place, the evidence of the existing remains is

---

[1] Bull. Corr. Hell. 1896, pp. 577 ff. ; Athen. Mittheil. 1897, pp. 444 ff. ; 1903, p. 386, &c. [2] See above, p. 135.

inconsistent with the new hypothesis. Vitruvius says that the
proscenium in the Greek theatre should be from ten to twelve
feet high, and in ordinary cases about ten feet deep. Now what
do we find in the remains of the regular Greek theatres? We
find that in the great majority of cases the height and depth
answer exactly to this description. But when we turn to the
Asia Minor theatres what do we find? The average height is
from eight to nine feet, the average depth from twelve to eighteen.
In the face of these measurements it is useless to contend that
Vitruvius is alluding to the Asia Minor theatres. The type
which he describes is the ordinary Hellenistic type.[1]

The two facts already mentioned—first, the fact that Vitruvius
tells us that every Greek theatre should possess a stage of
a certain height, and secondly, the fact that all Greek theatres
after about 300 B. c. are found to possess a stage corresponding
to his description—these two facts appear sufficient in themselves to decide the whole question. But there is no lack
of further evidence. Various ancient writers may be cited as
witnesses. Pollux, in his description of the Greek theatre,
says that 'the stage is appropriated to the actors, the orchestra
to the chorus'.[2] Later on he says that the actors, when they
'enter by the orchestra, ascend the stage by means of steps'.[3]

[1] [The discussion is continued by
Bethe, Hermes, 1898, pp. 313 ff., and
Dörpfeld, Ath. Mitth. 1898, pp. 326 ff. ;
1903, pp. 424 ff. The latter admits that
the Hellenistic stage corresponds
better in depth with Vitruvius' rule,
and his further arguments in support
of his theory are very unconvincing.
(As regards some of them, see pp. 158 ff.)
In various other details the Hellenistic
and Asiatic theatres nearly all deviate
from the exact figures given by Vitruvius, though the approximations are
in most cases close. One theatre
corresponds in one point with the
figures given, one in another, as one
would expect : and in most points,
other than those above mentioned,
neither the Hellenistic nor the Asiatic
type has much advantage over the
other in respect of precise correspon-
dence. (See Noack, Philologus, lviii,
pp. 9 ff.) The clearest result of Dörpfeld's controversy with Bethe, and
later with Puchstein, is that theatres
of both types varied much more than

most writers have allowed. Why
should they not have done so? At
the same time, Vitruvius' rules are as
nearly in accordance with the general
features of the Hellenistic type as
general rules can be reasonably expected to be.]

[2] Poll. iv. 123 καὶ σκηνὴ μὲν ὑποκριτῶν
ἴδιον, ἡ δὲ ὀρχήστρα τοῦ χοροῦ. Dörpfeld (p. 347, and Ath. Mitth. 1903,
p. 419) says that σκηνή here = ' the
stage-buildings '. But the mention
of the λογεῖον in the previous line of
Pollux, and the description of the
ὑποσκήνιον, almost immediately afterwards, as ὑπὸ τὸ λογεῖον κείμενον,
clearly show that the type of theatre
described by Pollux was one which
possessed a stage. If so, this stage
must have been used by the actors.

[3] Poll. iv. 127 εἰσελθόντες δὲ κατὰ
τὴν ὀρχήστραν ἐπὶ τὴν σκηνὴν ἀνα-
βαίνουσι διὰ κλιμάκων. Here too Dörpfeld (p. 347, and Ath. Mitth. 1903,
p. 406) thinks σκηνή = the i.ouse in
the background, and that the sentence

The scholiasts to the extant dramas often speak of the performance in a Greek theatre as being partly in the orchestra and
partly on the stage. The commentator on the Frogs asserts
that the scene with Charon and the ferry-boat must be 'either
upon the logeion, or in the orchestra'. Later on he says that
Dionysus here appears 'not on the logeion, but in the orchestra'. The scholiast on the Knights discusses the question
why the sausage-seller should 'ascend from the parodos on
to the logeion'. There are other scholia to the same effect,
which it would be tedious to quote.[1] In these passages from
the scholiasts and from Pollux the point to notice is the
following. They do not merely say that there was a stage
in Greek theatres, but they describe the performance as one
partly on the stage, and partly in the orchestra. Dörpfeld
says they are all mistaken; that they lived after the Christian
era, and were confusing the Greek theatre with the Roman.
But this would not account for their mistake, if mistake there
were. In Roman theatres all performances were confined
to the stage; the orchestra was occupied by senators and
other distinguished persons. How then can Pollux and the
scholiasts have got this notion of a performance in which stage
and orchestra were used at the same time? There was nothing
in the Roman practice to suggest it. It can only have been
derived from the Greek theatre. But apart from this, the
suggestion that Pollux and the scholiasts were misled by their
recollection of Roman customs is not a fortunate one. It
implies that their writings were the result of personal observa-
tion. But no one can read a page of them without perceiving
that they were merely compilations from Alexandrian sources.

refers to cases like Aristoph. Nub. 1486,
where Strepsiades climbs on to the
roof. But why should the actors have
used steps to mount the house only
when they entered the theatre by the
orchestra? They would need them
just as much if they entered by the
doors in the back-scene.

[1] Schol. Ran. 183 ἠλλοιῶσθαι χρὴ
τὴν σκηνὴν καὶ εἶναι κατὰ τὴν Ἀχερουσίαν
λίμνην τὸν τόπον ἐπὶ τοῦ λογείου ἢ ἐπὶ
τῆς ὀρχήστρας. Ibid. 299 ἀποροῦσι δέ
τινες πῶς ἀπὸ τοῦ λογείου περιελθὼν καὶ
κρυφθεὶς ὄπισθεν τοῦ ἱερέως τοῦτο λέγει.
φαίνονται δὲ οὐκ εἶναι ἐπὶ τοῦ λογείου

ἀλλ' ἐπὶ τῆς ὀρχήστρας. Schol. Equit.
149 ἵνα, φησίν, ἐκ τῆς παρόδου ἐπὶ τὸ
λογείον ἀναβῇ. διὰ τί οὖν ἐκ τῆς
παρόδου; τοῦτο γὰρ οὐκ ἀναγκαῖον. Ibid.
506 λέγεται δὲ παράβασις . . . ἐπειδὴ
παραβαίνει ὁ χορὸς τὸν τόπον. ἑστᾶσι
μὲν γὰρ κατὰ στοῖχον οἱ πρὸς τὴν
ὀρχήστραν (i.e. the stage) ἀποβλέποντες·
ὅταν δὲ παραβῶσιν, ἐφεξῆς ἑστῶτες καὶ
πρὸς τοὺς θεατὰς βλέποντες τὸν λόγον
ποιοῦνται. Vit. Aesch. p. 8 (Dindf.)
τὰ γὰρ δράματα συμπληροῦσιν οἱ πρεσ-
βύτατοι τῶν θεῶν, καὶ ἐστι τὰ ἀπὸ τῆς
σκηνῆς καὶ τῆς ὀρχήστρας θεῖα πάντα
πρόσωπα.

The scholiasts in many cases mention their authorities, and these authorities often go back as far as Aristophanes and Aristarchus, and even beyond. They do indeed confuse the evidence a good deal, when they try to reconcile different statements, or when they misapply statements of earlier authorities to particular passages, and explain the passages wrongly; but the statements themselves are due to Alexandrian tradition, not to their own observations. When they say that Greek dramas were performed partly on the stage and partly in the orchestra, it is evident that the Alexandrians thought the same. The testimony of Pollux and the scholiasts is really testimony of the third century B.C.

Another writer whose words appear to be decisive on this question is Horace. His statement about Aeschylus, to the effect that he 'erected a stage on beams (or posts) of moderate size', has already been quoted.[1] It is true that Horace is often inaccurate in his description of the early Greek drama. It may be contended, therefore, that his account of the reforms of Aeschylus is only of doubtful authority. But one thing is certain, that Horace, in describing the development of the Greek theatre, would never have mentioned the erection of a stage, unless a stage had been a regular part of the Greek theatres of his own day. Dörpfeld, in dealing with this passage, offers two alternatives. He first suggests that 'pulpitum' means the 'stage-buildings'. But he cites no authority for such a meaning, and none is to be found. The word 'pulpitum' in Latin always means a stage or platform. Then, if the first alternative seems unsatisfactory, he suggests that Horace has made a slip, and that he was confusing the Greek stage with the Roman.[2] But Horace, as we know, was for a long time in Athens, and must have often seen Greek plays performed. It is hardly conceivable, therefore, that he should have made a mistake on such a simple matter as the presence or absence of a stage.

To turn next to the archaeological evidence. Excavations have brought to light several facts which bear closely upon this subject of the stage. The evidence derived from this source appears to be even more fatal to the new theory than

---

[1] See above, p. 144, and note 1.   [2] Griech. Theater, p. 348.

the literary testimony. One of the most convincing proofs is that afforded by the structure of the stage-buildings at Sicyon, Eretria, and Oropus.[1] We have seen that, according to Dörpfeld's view, the proscenium was the background, and the action of the drama took place in front of it, in the orchestra. Obviously, if this was so, the most important part of the stage-buildings must have been the rooms immediately behind the proscenium, or in other words, behind the back-scene. Now what do we find at Sicyon? We find that one-third of the space behind the proscenium consisted of solid rock. The Sicyonians, in order to save the expense of erecting a lofty auditorium, excavated their theatre out of the rock to a depth of about twelve feet. But they attached so little importance to the rooms behind the proscenium, that they did not take the trouble to excavate the whole of this part. They left one-third of it as it was. It was only when they came to the first floor of the stage-building, the floor on a level with the top of the proscenium, that they provided clear room from end to end of the structure. Their conduct, on Dörpfeld's theory, was very peculiar.[2] But the people of Eretria acted in a still stranger manner. They too excavated their theatre out of the rock. But they left the whole of the space behind the proscenium unexcavated. Consequently at Eretria the ground-floor of the stage-buildings was on a level, not with the floor of the orchestra, but with the top of the proscenium. There could hardly be a more decisive proof that at Eretria the actors appeared, not in front of the proscenium, but on the top of it. Then there is the case of Oropus. Here the stage-buildings were built upon the ground, and the rooms behind the proscenium were originally open from end to end. But later on the Oropians proceeded to fill up the greater part of the space with earth, and left only a narrow passage immediately behind the proscenium. Such conduct is irrecon-

---

[1] Griech. Theater, pp. 103, 113-16, 118.

[2] [Noack (Philologus, lviii. p. 6) argues that the reason was that at the north end, where the rock is not cut away, it is much higher, and the cutting and removal would be very expensive. But we know nothing of the willingness or unwillingness of the Sicyonians to spend money on public and religious objects, and the simpler theory seems to be that the space was not wanted. The same remark applies to Noack's explanation of the case of Eretria by considerations of expense.]

cilable with the supposition that the proscenium was the back-scene.[1]

Another proof is afforded by the height of the proscenium. The normal height, as already shown, was about twelve feet. But some proscenia, such as those at Athens and the Peiraeeus, were as much as thirteen feet. On the other hand others were considerably less. That of Oropus, for instance, was only about eight feet high; and the columns which supported the entablature were only six feet six inches.[2] On Dörpfeld's view these proscenia, with their architectural front, represented the palace or other building before which the action took place. What then are we to think of a palace about fifty feet long, and only eight feet in height? The background at Oropus during the performance of a tragedy must have been a most peculiar one. We should remember that the Greek tragic actor walked upon 'cothurni', which added about six inches to his stature. He also wore a mask with a lofty 'onkos', which raised his height by another six inches. Consequently the Greek tragic actor, when equipped for the stage, can hardly have stood less than about six feet six. This being so, if Dörpfeld's view is correct, it follows that the actor who took the part of the king at Oropus must have been just about the same height as the columns which supported the roof of his own palace. When he made his entrance through the central door of the palace, he would have to bend his head, in order to avoid knocking it against the cross-beams. Surely the theory is a weak one which involves such ridiculous consequences. If the Greeks had adopted a background of this absurdly diminutive height, without any reason for doing so, this fact alone would have been strange enough. But it must appear stranger still that, having once adopted it, they should proceed to add about twelve inches to the stature of their actors, in order to make the disproportion between the size of the actors and the size of the palace still more preposterous.[3]

The reason which Dörpfeld gives for the lowness of the

---

[1] [Noack, l.c., contends that the division of the skene and filling of half the space with earth is later work, and throws no light on the scheme of the Hellenistic theatre. This is very doubtful; but even if it were proved the other cases quoted would be sufficient for the argument in the text.]

[2] See above, p. 125.

[3] This point is well brought out by Chamonard, Bull. Corr. Hell. 1896, p. 296.

proscenium—the background, as he calls it—is as follows. He says that such proscenia were first erected at Athens in the fifth century, and were intended to represent an ordinary house of that period. But the ordinary Athenian house of the fifth century was, he asserts, about twelve feet high.[1] To this theory there are several answers. In the first place, as we have seen, some proscenia were only about eight or nine feet in height; which is far lower than any ordinary Greek house, either at Athens or elsewhere. In the second place there is no clear evidence to show that the Athenian house of the fifth century was twelve feet high. From the remains lately discovered at Delos it appears that in the better class of houses there even the first story was more than twelve feet.[2] But granting, for the sake of argument, that an Athenian house of the fifth century was of the size which Dörpfeld supposes, it is difficult to see what this has got to do with the height of the scenic background. The Athenian theatre, we should remember, was developed originally as a place for tragedy rather than as a place for comedy. The background therefore must have been intended to represent, in most cases, a palace or a temple. But why should this palace or temple have been made the same height as an ordinary house? Moreover, the proportions must have appeared extraordinary. A structure about fifty feet long, and twelve feet high, would be altogether unlike any palace or temple. Dörpfeld replies to this that it is impossible on the stage to represent buildings as large as they really are; that in modern scene-paintings the representations of palaces and temples are much reduced in size as compared with the originals.[3] This is quite true. But they are reduced to scale, and in a proper proportion. A modern scene-painter, in representing St. Paul's, would no doubt have to make his representation much smaller than the actual St. Paul's. But in diminishing the height he would diminish the width at the same time. No modern scene-painter would produce a temple fifty feet long and twelve feet high; nor can we suppose that the ancients would have put up with a similar disproportion.

Again, there is the question as to the doors in the proscenium. If it was the background, it ought to have had three

[1] Griech. Theater, p. 381.   [2] Chamonard, l. c., p. 294.
[3] Griech. Theater, p. 381.

doors, the usual number in a Greek back-scene, as Pollux and
Vitruvius tell us. But in most of the proscenia discovered
there is only one door. In two of the proscenia, those at
Megalopolis and Thespiae, there is no door of any kind.
Even the single door, when it is found, is very narrow for
the central door of the back-scene. At Epidaurus it is only
four feet wide, at Oropus only 3 feet 8 inches, at Delos only
3 feet 3 inches.[1] A door so narrow as this would be altogether
unsuitable as the central door of the palace, and quite inconsistent with the use of the ekkyklema. When we come to
the Graeco-Roman theatres, where the wall at the back of
the stage has in many cases been preserved, there we find
everything corresponding closely with the descriptions of the
grammarians. There is always the requisite number of doors,
and the central door is of considerable width. At Termessos
it is about seven feet.[2] As regards the absence of the three
doors in the proscenium Dörpfeld gives the following explanation. These Hellenistic proscenia, as we see from the remains,
consisted of an entablature resting on columns. The spaces
between the columns were filled in with wooden boards.
Dörpfeld suggests that when doors were required they might
be provided *ad libitum* by removing the intervening boards.[3]
But if three doors were regularly required in the dramatic
performances, it is most improbable that they should not have
been provided as a permanent fixture in the proscenium. It
is most improbable that the Greeks should have put themselves to the trouble of opening out these temporary doors
at each festival. In any case we can hardly doubt that, if
the proscenium had been the back-scene, the Greeks would
always have provided at least one permanent door, and
would not, as at Megalopolis and Thespiae, have erected
proscenia in which there was no door of any kind. The
absence of a door in these two places seems to prove
conclusively that communication between the orchestra and

---

[1] See above, p. 124.
[2] Lanckoronski, Städte Pamphyliens,
&c., vol. ii. plate 10.
[3] Griech. Theater, p. 380. [Also
Noack, Philologus, lviii. pp. 2 ff. ; to
whom Puchstein, Griech. Bühne, pp. 30
ff., replies sufficiently. The evidence
of the vases (see below), where actors
are shown acting *on* a stage with
columns in front, is conclusive against
his contention that the *only* proper
support for a stage is a wall, and that
therefore the columns of the proscenium
can only represent a back-scene.]

the space behind the proscenium was a matter of no importance.

Another piece of archaeological evidence is supplied by the vase-paintings found in the Greek cities of South Italy.[1] Two specimens are here inserted.[2] These paintings, which have already been briefly referred to, belong to the third century B.C. They represent comic scenes acted by the Phlyakes. The Phlyakes were a sort of farcical comedians, whose performances were not unlike those of the oldest Attic comedy. In many

ΔΑΙΦΑΛΟΣ   ΗΡΑ   ΕΝΕΥΑΛΙΟΣ

FIG. 13

of these paintings they are represented as acting on a stage.[3] The stage, in most cases, is obviously made of wood, and varies in character from a rude and simple platform to an erection of some solidity. In one or two instances, however, it is a tall and elaborate structure, apparently built of stone, and adorned with columns in front, just like the proscenia

---

[1] On the subject of these vase-paintings see especially Heydemann, Die Phlyakendarstellungen auf bemalten Vasen, Jahrb. Kais. Deutsch. Archäol. Inst. 1886, pp. 260 ff. Bethe, Prolegomena zur Geschichte des Theaters, pp. 278 ff. Reisch, in Griech. Theater, pp. 311 ff.

[2] They are taken from Wieseler's Denkmäler, ix. 14 and 15 (= Baumeister. figs. 1828 and 1830).

[3] Fig. 13. Cp. the specimens in Wieseler's Denkmäl. ix. 8 ; Griech, Theater, pp. 315, 322, and 323 ; Baumeister's Denkmäl., figs. 902, 903, 1826, 1827, 1829.

we have been discussing.[1] Often there is a flight of steps
leading down to the orchestra.[2] In one case the action is
taking place partly on the stage and partly in the orchestra.
One of the actors is represented as actually ascending the
steps to the stage.[3] This evidence seems to prove beyond
a doubt that in the Greek cities of South Italy, during the
third century B. C., performances were sometimes given in
theatres with a tall stage, and that both stage and orchestra
were employed for the purpose, and were connected by steps.

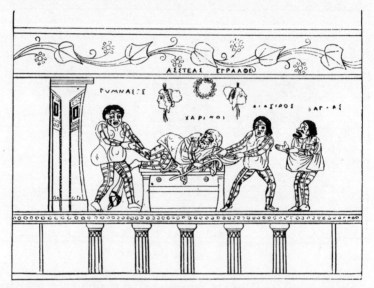

FIG. 14.

Dörpfeld now admits that this was the case. But he contends
that the arrangement was an exceptional one, intended only
for the farces of the Phlyakes. For these performances, he
allows, wooden stages were erected, and the exhibition took
place partly on the stage and partly in the orchestra. But
the regular dramas—the tragedies, and the comedies—were
performed solely in the orchestra.[4] All this, however, is the

---

[1] Fig. 14. Cp. also the specimen in
Griech. Theater, p. 318.
[2] Fig. 13. Cp. also Griech. Theater,
pp. 322-4 ; Baumeister, figs. 902, 903.

[3] Baumeister, fig. 903.   Griech.
Theater, p. 322.
[4] Griech. Theater, p. 327.

purest assumption.[1] There is not a particle of evidence to support it. It is altogether improbable that a different arrangement should have been adopted in the case of these farces, and in the case of the regular drama. Besides this, as we have already pointed out, in one or two of the paintings the stage on which the Phlyakes are performing is apparently a permanent stone erection, and not a mere temporary platform of wood. It seems certain, therefore, that the Greeks of South Italy during the third century B.C. provided a stage for their actors in all dramatic performances; and, this being so, we can hardly doubt that the same was the case in Greece generally.

One or two further objections to the new theory may be briefly mentioned. If we look at the plan of the theatre at Epidaurus (Figs. 6 and 7), it will be found that the stone border of the circular orchestra reaches to within two or three feet of the proscenium. If the actors had performed in front of the proscenium, they would have been sometimes inside the stone border, and sometimes outside of it; and the whole arrangement strikes one as awkward and unsymmetrical. Again, in the theatre at Delos (Fig. 12), statues and other votive offerings were erected immediately in front of the columns of the proscenium. The bases on which they rested still remain.[2] But, if the proscenium had been the background, it is difficult to suppose that this place would have been chosen for such erections. When the proscenium was uncovered by scenery, and represented an ancient palace, these votive offerings and statues would have been altogether inappropriate as a part of the back-scene. When painted decorations were to be set up, they would have formed an inconvenient obstacle in the way of the mechanical arrangements. And if they were required to serve as scenery, why were they only employed at Delos? The probability therefore is that they were a mere architectural decoration of the stage-front.[3]

We have now gone through the principal arguments, literary and archaeological, which demonstrate the existence of a stage

[1] [The same must be said of his later suggestion (Jahrb. Arch. Inst. 1901, p. 36) that the columns on the Phlyakes vases are not really curtailed, and do not therefore point to a taller stage, but are complete and imply a stage between three and four feet high.]

[2] Griech. Theater, p. 147.

[3] Puchstein, Griech. Bühne, p. 24.

during the Hellenistic period. It remains to consider the reasons which induce Dörpfeld, in spite of this apparently overwhelming evidence, to deny the existence of such a stage. And in judging this question we must remember the fact already mentioned, that the chorus, at this time, had ceased to take an active share in the play, and that its functions were hardly more important than those of a band of musicians in a modern theatre. To turn now to Dörpfeld's reasons. He says, in the first place, that these proscenia of the Vitruvian type would have been too narrow for the performance of a play.[1] But their narrowness has often been exaggerated, owing to inaccurate calculations. None of them, as it now appears, were less than from nine to ten feet in depth.[2] But a stage about ten feet deep, and from fifty to sixty feet long, would be amply sufficient for the performance of a Greek play, when the chorus was confined to the orchestra. The fact has been proved by actual experiment. Most English scholars have probably seen the Greek plays produced in the open-air theatre at Bradfield. The stage there is only ten feet deep and thirty feet long. Yet every one who has been present at one of these performances must admit that there was plenty of room upon the stage. I am informed that on one occasion, in the funeral procession in the Alcestis, as many as sixty people were brought upon the stage at the same time, and without any inconvenient crowding.[3] It is clear then that the Vitruvian stage, which was just as deep and twice as long as that at Bradfield, would have been large enough to accommodate the chorus as well as the actors in an ancient Greek drama, and would have been more than large enough for the performance of a play in which the chorus was practically confined to the orchestra.

Dörpfeld further objects that these Hellenistic proscenia were too high to have served as a stage, since the spectators in the front rows would have been too far below the actors to see the

[1] Griech. Theater, p. 361.

[2] The stage at Athens was about 9 ft. 3 in.; at Epidaurus about 10½ ft. (Griech. Theater, pp. 78, 128). That at Delos was about 10 ft. (Chamonard, Bull. Corr. Hell. 1896, p. 306). As Lechat (Épidaure, p. 208) points out, it is necessary, in calculating the depth, not to measure from wall to wall, but to take into account the projecting cornice. In some cases, as he also remarks, the wall of the back-scene may have been narrower than the wall beneath, on which it rested; and this would add slightly to the depth of the stage.

[3] These facts and measurements have been kindly supplied to me by Dr. Gray.

latter properly.[1]   It is only in the Asiatic theatres, where the front
seats of the auditorium were raised so as to give a good view of
the actors, that he will allow that the actors appeared on the high
stage ; in such cases the height of the seats would make a ten-foot
stage virtually equivalent to a five-foot one, such as the Romans
employed.   But in the first place, we find that at Mantinea also
the lowest seats were raised four feet above the orchestra, so that
this is not a peculiarity of Asiatic theatres.[2]   In the second place,
if these proscenia were too high for a stage, they would have been
much too low for a background.   Their height varied from eight
to thirteen feet; and a stage of thirteen feet would be far less of
an anomaly than a back-scene of eight feet.   Further, it has been
shown by Maass[3] that the height of the proscenium varies very
regularly with the distance of the proscenium from the central
point of the circle of the auditorium.   The nearer this point,
the lower the stage.   The object of this can only have been to
accommodate the height of the stage to the view of the audience.
It would be inexplicable unless the actors were on the top of the
proscenium.   It seems also to be proved that in most cases the
greater part of the actor's person would easily be visible from
the greater number of seats,[4] including the lowest or front rows.
When it was necessary, as it was through the greater part of
the fifth century, for chorus and actors to communicate more or
less intimately with one another, the stage was lower, and the view

---

[1] Griech. Theater, p. 342 ; Ath.
Mitth. 1898, pp. 337, 345, &c.

[2] Fougères, Mantinée et l'Arcadie,
pp. 165 ff.   According to Dörpfeld's
theory that the proscenium was the
back-scene, these lowest seats would
be on a level with the roof of the
back-scene, which is absurd.   His
argument that in cases where a removal
of the lower rows or steps of seats is
certain (as at Assos, Pergamon, and
Delphi), we may assume that the
theatre was converted from the supposed stageless Hellenistic type to the
Asiatic, is most unconvincing.   Why
were the rows not similarly removed
at Priene and Magnesia, though the
high stage was erected there ?   If he
can suppose that in these cases seats
were allowed to remain which were
bad for dramatic performances, why
not in other cases ?

[3] Wochenschr. für Klass. Phil. 1899,
p. 260.

[4] [For controversy on this point,
cf. A. Müller, Unters. zu den Bühnenalt., pp. 108 ff. ; Dörpfeld, Ath.
Mitth. 1899, p. 310 ; Müller, Philologus, lix. p. 330. Müller accepts Maass'
conclusions, though he corrects some
of his figures.   Both Müller and Dörpfeld calculate how much of the orchestra or of the actor on the stage
could be seen by the spectators in
different parts of different theatres.
But any conclusions drawn from such
calculations are precarious ; we have
no reason to suppose that there was
a larger proportion of good seats in
ancient theatres than in modern ; still
less that the front seats were all
necessarily better for seeing the actors,
any more than front seats or other
seats of honour are in many cases in
modern theatres.]

from some seats therefore less good ; but when the chorus ceased
to take a share in the dialogue, it became both possible and
natural to raise the height of the stage and so improve the view.

Another objection of Dörpfeld's is that in the existing proscenia there is no trace of any means of communication between
the stage and the orchestra.[1] But we have shown that such
communication was seldom required at this time, owing to the
insignificance of the chorus ; and that, when it was wanted, it
was supplied by temporary wooden steps. Dörpfeld replies
that, if the stage was thirteen feet high, the steps must have
been so large as to project a long way into the orchestra, and
produce an unsightly appearance. But this result could have
been avoided without difficulty. Where the stage was exceptionally lofty, the steps might have been placed in a parallel
line to it. At Tralles, where there is a proscenium of the
Graeco-Roman type, and nearly ten feet high, such steps are
actually found, lying parallel to the stage, and on each side
of the door which leads out from the front wall of the stage
into the orchestra.[2] A similar arrangement might easily have
been adopted, when necessary, in the Hellenistic theatres.

In support of his theory Dörpfeld brings forward an argument based on the theatre at Megalopolis (Fig. 11). We have
already described the peculiar construction of this theatre, in
which the Thersilion took the place of the ordinary stage-
buildings. In front of the Thersilion, and twenty-four feet
distant from it, is the foundation-wall of a wooden proscenium.
This proscenium, however, appears to have been of later date
than the original theatre. Dörpfeld supposes that, before its
erection, the actors performed their parts immediately in front
of the Thersilion, and on the level of the orchestra. He bases
his belief on the following grounds. The façade of the Thersilion rested on a flight of five steps, each about thirteen inches
high. To one side of the Thersilion was a building, apparently
called the Skanotheka, and probably used for storing the scenic
decorations. In this building are the remains of a low wall,
running in the same straight line as the bottom of the flight of
steps, and about the same length as the stage must have been.
Dörpfeld supposes that this wall was used, in the original state

---

[1] Griech. Theater, p. 342.   [2] Athen. Mittheil. 1893, p. 410.

of the theatre, for working a 'scaena ductilis'. He supposes that, when dramas were to be performed, a wooden scene-painting was pushed out along this wall immediately in front of the lowest step of the Thersilion, and served as a background. The actors in front of it must have been on the floor of the orchestra.[1] But this arrangement appears to be impossible. If the back-scene had been placed in the position he supposes, immediately in front of the steep flight of steps, the representation of dramas would have been little short of ridiculous. The actor entering from the back-scene would have had to come down these steps to reach the threshold of the door. At first little more than his legs would have been seen, at any rate by the spectators in the upper part of the theatre. His whole person would hardly have become visible until he reached the lowest step. For a tragic actor to make his entrance in this way would have been far from dignified. Also, in plays like the Hippolytus and the Alcestis, when a sick woman on a couch had to be carried out, it would have been extremely awkward to have to carry her down a flight of steps as steep as those at Megalopolis. The ekkyklema would, of course, have been quite impossible to work. Again, it seems certain that the supposed 'scaena ductilis' would itself be quite unworkable. Is it likely that a huge painted board, more than a hundred feet long and more than twenty-five feet high, was pulled out in front of the Thersilion to serve as a back-scene? The 'scaena ductilis' (cf. Serv. ad Verg. Georg. iii. 24), which Dörpfeld thinks was such as has been described, was not a contrivance of this sort, but was a small affair, a variety of the 'scaena versilis' or periaktos; it was drawn *apart*, to disclose a new scene behind, and was not drawn across the stage. Moreover, the construction of ancient theatres, even of those with side-wings, shows that there was no room and no opportunity for the hauling to and fro of huge boards such as Dörpfeld imagines. It is true that much remains obscure in regard to the theatre at Megalopolis; but this solution at least is out of the question.[2] Although, therefore, the Skanotheka at Megalopolis may very likely have been used for the storage of scenery, it is clear that this scenery, when used, cannot have been put up in the place which Dörpfeld suggests.

[1] Griech. Theater, pp. 138, 139.
[2] See Puchstein, Griech. Bühne.
p. 88; and P. Gardner, J. Hell. Stud. 1899, p. 258.

Another argument against the ordinary theory is based by Dörpfeld on the remains of the theatre at Delos (Fig. 12). We have shown that at Delos the proscenium was continued, though in a different form, round the sides and back of the stage-buildings.[1] Dörpfeld argues that it cannot have been a stage, as it would be absurd to erect a stage all round the stage-buildings.[2] If this is so, we might reply that it cannot have been a background either, since it would be equally absurd to construct a background in the same position. But as a matter of fact there is nothing in the arrangement at Delos which conflicts in any way with the ordinary opinion about the Greek stage. The erection at the sides and the back of the stage-buildings, though of the same height as the erection in front, was different in structure, and formed an open portico. The erection in front was like the usual Hellenistic proscenium, and must have been designed for the same purpose. If the proscenium in other theatres was intended for a stage, it must have been intended for a stage at Delos.

Dörpfeld has a theory about the origin of the Roman stage, which he brings forward as a strong argument in favour of his other views. According to Vitruvius the Roman stage was developed out of the Greek. The difference in size was due to the following reasons. The Romans preferred to give up the orchestra to the spectators and to transfer all performances to the stage. It was necessary, therefore, to deepen the stage, in order to find room for the additional performers. It was also necessary to lower it, in order to allow the spectators in the orchestra to have a clear view.[3] Dörpfeld says that this account of the matter is erroneous. According to his theory the Roman stage was discovered by accident rather than by design. The Romans, when they first began to adapt the Greek theatre to their own purposes, found the orchestra too large, and consequently divided it in two. The half nearest the auditorium they dug out to a depth of five feet, and placed spectators there. The other half they used for theatrical and other performances, just as it had been used by the Greeks. In this way they found that they had got what was practically a stage five feet high; and for the future, instead of digging out the nearer half of the

---

[1] See above, p. 138.   [2] Griech. Theater, p. 146.   [3] Vitruv. v. 6.

orchestra, they started on the level, and built a raised stage.
The Roman stage therefore represents, not the Greek proscenium, but the further half of the Greek orchestra; and
this fact proves that it was in the orchestra that the Greek
actors performed.[1] This theory is no doubt extremely ingenious.
But unfortunately it appears to be inconsistent with the facts
of the case. If it was true, we should expect to find the
stage in all Roman theatres occupying the site of one half
of the Greek orchestra, and the back of the Roman stage
corresponding to the front of the Greek proscenium. Now
in the normal Roman theatre this is more or less the case.
The Romans eventually reduced their orchestra to a semicircle,
and brought their stage forward to the position described by
Dörpfeld. But the Graeco-Roman theatres of Asia Minor, to
which we have already referred, fail entirely to correspond to
his hypothesis. These theatres were among the earliest to be
built in the Roman fashion, and might therefore be expected,
more than any others, to exemplify the process of transition
which he describes. But what do we find? We find that the
stage, so far from occupying one half of the orchestra, stands
in exactly the same position as the old Greek proscenium.
The orchestra in these theatres still forms nearly a complete
circle. The stage is deepened by pushing the back-scene more
into the rear. Further than this, the height of the stage is
not five feet, as it ought to be, but from eight to nine feet.[2]
These examples seem to prove that Vitruvius is more correct
than Dörpfeld in his view of the matter; and that the Roman
stage was really a modification of the Greek. When we find
in these Asia Minor theatres a Roman stage standing in exactly
the same position as the proscenium in the Greek theatres, and
differing only in being longer and deeper, and two or three
feet lower, we can hardly resist the conclusion that the Greek
proscenium was the prototype of the Roman, and that it was
intended for the same purpose.

The proscenium in a Greek theatre was called, among other
names, the 'logeion' or 'speaking-place'. It is so called by
Vitruvius, and the word 'logeion' occurs in Delian inscriptions
as early as the third century B. C.[3] This being so, we are

---

[1] Griech. Theater, pp. 385 ff.   [2] See above, p. 135.

[3] See above, p. 118.

naturally led to ask how this fact is to be reconciled with Dörpfeld's theory. If the proscenium was the background, and not the stage, why should it have been called 'logeion' or the speaking-place? Dörpfeld gives the following answer. He says that in Greek tragedies the gods, when exhibited in a super-natural manner, used to make their appearance on the palace roof, or, in other words, on the proscenium; and that it was therefore called the 'theologeion', or for shortness the 'logeion'.[1] But this statement will not bear examination. The usual device for revealing gods in supernatural splendour was the mechane, and not the theologeion. Even when the theologeion was employed, there is no evidence to show that it was identical with the palace roof.[2] The contrivance for enabling actors to stand on the roof of a palace or other building was called the 'distegia'. Instances of its employment are rare. In the extant dramas there are only eight or nine certain examples.[3] If, therefore, the proscenium really represented the building in the background, the top of it cannot have been called the 'speaking-place' because the actors spoke from it. Eight or nine instances out of forty-four dramas are insufficient to justify us in regarding it as a regular speaking-place. The plain statement of Vitruvius, that the 'pulpitum' of the actors was in Greek called 'logeion', Dörpfeld attempts to get round by supposing that the place which had been the 'theologeion', or, more shortly, 'logeion'—the speaking-place of gods—retained its name by a natural conservatism when employed by actors. This is ingenious; but it is surely far more natural to suppose that it was called 'logeion' all along because it was the regular speaking-place for all actors, and not only for occasional gods.[4]

<hr/>

[1] Griech. Theater, p. 365. Ath. Mitth. 1903, p. 395.

[2] On these points see below, pp. 209–15. Even if we suppose that the theologeion was used in the cases mentioned on p. 213 to exhibit the deus ex machina, the text of the plays shows that the god appeared *above* the roof, and not upon it. Cp. Ion. 1549 ὑπερτελὴς οἴκων, Orest. 1631 ἐν αἰθέρος πτυχαῖς.

[3] See below, p. 186.

[4] [It is also argued (Noack, Philologus, 1899, 1; Robert, Gött. Gel. Anz. 1902, 418; Dörpfeld, Ath. Mitth. 1903, p. 403) that, because in all the Roman and Graeco-Roman theatres, where the actors stood on the logeion, the back-scene which formed their background was decorated with columns, while the proscenium was not so decorated, it follows that when the proscenium *was* so decorated, i.e. in the earlier periods, it and not the wall above and behind the logeion must have been the actors' background, and the actors must have played in front of the proscenium. But this is no proof at all, unless it is assumed that decorations were *only* employed

We have now considered the principal arguments which can be brought forward on either side concerning this stage question, as far as it relates to the later period. Some minor points have been omitted; but they would not affect the question very much either way. The result appears to show that, at any rate as far as the later period is concerned, the evidence in favour of a stage altogether outweighs any considerations which can be adduced on the other side.

2. THE EARLIER STAGE. We now come to the earlier and more important period, the period of the fifth century, when the drama was still in reality a choral drama, and the fourth century, during which the chorus was rapidly declining in importance, but was still commonly employed.

For the fourth century we have the testimony of Aristotle. Aristotle in many places speaks of the songs of the actors as τὰ ἀπὸ τῆς σκηνῆς, in opposition to the songs of the chorus, τὰ τοῦ χοροῦ.[1] Further he speaks of the actor's part as being played ἐπὶ τῆς σκηνῆς.[2] According to the usual interpretation of these passages, he means that the actors played their part 'upon the stage', and sang their songs 'from the stage'. Dörpfeld, however, proposes in these cases to translate the word σκηνή as the 'background', and not as the 'stage'. He supposes Aristotle to mean that the actors performed 'at the background', and sang their songs 'from the background'. He denies that the two expressions imply the existence of a stage.[3] Now the translations which he suggests may be possible, as far as

to make backgrounds for actors, and *only* disused because not wanted for this purpose. This is neither likely in itself, nor is it confirmed by anything in the evidence.

Dörpfeld also argues Ath. Mitth. 1903, p. 396) that the grooves for wheels, of which traces are found leading out of the door in the back-scene on to the logeion at Eretria. prove that the logeion was used by gods only, as ordinary personages in chariots came only through the side entrances into the orchestra. But all that can be argued from these grooves is that the logeion was used for something on wheels, whether chariots or the ekkyklema, which Dörpfeld rejects. There is nothing to show

who used the vehicle, whatever it may have been. If an actor could do so when representing a god, he could do so when representing a mortal. Cp. Fossum, Amer. J. **Arch**. 1898. p. 187; cp. P. Gardner, J. Hell. Stud. 1899, p. 252.]

[1] Aristot. Probl. xix. 15 τὰ μὲν ἀπὸ σκηνῆς οὐκ ἀντίστροφα, τὰ δὲ τοῦ χοροῦ ἀντίστροφα· ὁ μὲν γὰρ ὑποκριτὴς ἀγωνιστής, ὁ δὲ χορὸς ἧττον μιμεῖται. Poet. c. 12 ἴδια δὲ τὰ ἀπὸ τῆς σκηνῆς καὶ κομμοί... κομμὸς δὲ θρῆνος κοινὸς χοροῦ καὶ ἀπὸ σκηνῆς.

[2] Poet. c. 24 διὰ τὸ ἐν μὲν τῇ τραγῳδίᾳ μὴ ἐνδέχεσθαι ἅμα πραττόμενα πολλὰ μέρη μιμεῖσθαι, ἀλλὰ τὸ ἐπὶ τῆς σκηνῆς καὶ τῶν ὑποκριτῶν μέρος μόνον. Cp. cc. 13. 17.

[3] Griech. Theater, pp. 284. 346.

the Greek is concerned.   But it is very difficult to believe
that they are the right translations in these particular passages
of Aristotle.   Aristotle's words seem to clearly imply that there
was some essential and conspicuous difference between the
position of the actors and that of the chorus.[1]   But if, as
Dörpfeld thinks, they all performed together in the orchestra,
there would be no such distinguishing mark.   It is true that
the actors might, for the most part, be rather nearer to the
stage-buildings; and the chorus might, for the most part, be
rather more distant from them.   But practically they would
be standing in the same place; there would be no pronounced
difference.   Aristotle's words appear to be explicable only on
the supposition that the actors appeared upon a stage, the
chorus in the orchestra.

For the fifth century we have the evidence supplied by the
use of certain words in Aristophanes.   In three places, where
an actor is approaching the back-scene, he is said to 'mount
up' (ἀναβαίνειν).[2]   In two other places, where he is leaving the
back-scene, he is said to 'go down' (καταβαίνειν).[3]   In all these
passages there is nothing in the circumstances of the drama to
suggest that the action was taking place on raised ground.
The expressions can only refer, as the scholiast says, to the
stage.   It has been proposed to translate the two words as
'come on' and 'depart' respectively.[4]   But such a usage of

[1] [Flickinger (The Meaning of ἐπὶ
τῆς σκηνῆς in Writers of the Fourth
Century, Chicago, 1902) tries to show
that ἐπὶ τῆς σκηνῆς in Aristotle and
Demosthenes does not mean 'on the
stage' in any sense which would imply
an elevated stage, but simply 'at the
performance', 'as part of a play', &c.,
like ἐπὶ θέατρον later.   He succeeds in
interpreting the passages consistently
with this, and in showing that in later
writers the words often bore this
meaning.   But the changed application
of many technical terms, e.g. ὀρχήστρα,
θυμέλη, &c., in later writers shows
that no reliance is to be placed on the
supposed analogy; and the other
meaning still seems by far the most
natural in Aristotle. Dörpfeld (Deutsch.
Littztg. 1901, p. 1817) thinks that the
absence of the expression ἀπὸ τῆς
ὀρχήστρας to balance ἀπὸ τῆς σκηνῆς is
very significant as proving that all
performers alike were in the orchestra.
It needs only the most elementary
logic to dispose of this argument. Cp.
Müller, Unters. zu den Bühnenalt., for
the full history of the words σκηνή, &c.

[2] Equit. 148 δεῦρο δεῦρ', ὦ φίλτατε.
ἀνάβαινε σωτὴρ τῇ πόλει καὶ νῷν φανείς.
Acharn. 732 ἄμβατε ποττὰν μάδδαν.
Vesp. 1342 ἀνάβαινε δεῦρο χρυσομηλο-
λύνθιον.

[3] Eccles. 1151 τί δῆτα ἐιατρίβεις ἔχων,
ἀλλ' οὐκ ἄγεις | τασδὶ λαβών; ἐν ὅσῳ δὲ
καταβαίνεις, ἐγὼ | ἐπάσομαι κ.τ.λ. Vesp.
1514 ἀτὰρ καταβατέον γ' ἐπ' αὐτούς.
In the last passage καταβατέον might
perhaps mean 'I must contend with
them'.   But it is more probable that
the meaning here is the same as in the
other passage.

[4] Bodensteiner, Scenische Fragen,
pp. 699, 700. Capps, The Stage in
the Greek Theatre, pp. 67, 68.

the terms is otherwise unknown in Greek. Moreover, in one place—the scene in the Knights—this translation is proved to be impossible. Here Demosthenes calls out to the sausage-seller, 'mount up here' (ἀνάβαινε δεῦρο). He then shows him the people, the markets, and the harbours; and tells him that he will be lord of all. But this is not enough. He says, 'you have not seen all yet', and bids him 'mount up on to this table also'; and then proceeds to show him the islands round about.[1] These words show conclusively that ἀναβαίνειν must mean 'mount up' in the previous passage, and likewise determine the meaning of this word, and of καταβαίνειν, in the parallel passages.

The extant dramas have been carefully ransacked during the last few years,[2] and it is not likely that many new points will now be discovered. Much of the evidence that has been brought forward on both sides of the question is really of little value. It depends upon a too scrupulous and literal interpretation of the text, or upon a forgetfulness of the fact that there is much that is conventional in all dramatic performances. For instance, when old men are approaching the palace, and complain of the steepness of the way, this fact is supposed to be a proof of the existence of a stage.[3] It is suggested that they enter by the orchestra, and that the ascent of which they complain is the ascent on to the stage. But, if this was so, these old men must have timed their entrance very exactly, so as to reach the foot of the stage just when they came to the verses in which they began to grumble about the ascent. And this, combined with the obvious inadequacy of the ascent on to the stage to represent a really fatiguing road, would make the whole proceeding rather ludicrous. It seems more natural to assume that their remarks had no reference to the stage, and that the steepness of which they complain was left to the imagination of the spectators.

---

[1] Equit. 169 ἀλλ' ἐπανάβηθι κἀπὶ τοὐλεὸν τοδί. The significance of this line, as regards the present question, was first pointed out by Zacher. Philologus, 1896, p. 181. Cp. Müller, l. c., pp. 1 ff.

[2] Harzmann, Quaestiones Scenicae, 1889. White, The Stage in Aristophanes, 1891. Capps, The Stage in the Greek Theatre, 1891. Bodensteiner, Scenische Fragen, 1893. Weissmann, Die scenische Aufführung der griechi-schen Dramen, 1893. Hampel, Was lehrt Aeschylos' Orestie für die Theaterfrage? 1899. Engelmann, Archäologische Studien zu den Tragikern, 1900. Krause, Quaestiones Aristophaneae Scenicae, 1903.

[3] Eur. El. 489, Ion 727, Herc. Fur. 119. In the last passage it is the chorus which makes the complaint; so that in this case, if there was any visible ascent, it cannot have been the ascent on to the stage.

Then again, the appearances of ghosts and spectres are cited
as evidence in favour of a stage. It is said that they could not
be made to appear from underground, unless there was a raised
platform out of which they ascended. Now there is no doubt
that in the later theatre ghosts were made to arise from beneath
the earth. Pollux gives a description of the mechanism by
which it was done. But there is no certain proof that they
made their appearance in this way during the fifth century.
It would be unsafe, therefore, to infer anything from these
spectral apparitions concerning the structure of the early theatre.
Again, there are those scenes in which the chorus might be
expected to enter the palace, but fail to do so. For instance,
when Medea's children are being murdered, and call out for
help, the chorus, after proposing to rush to their assistance,
eventually remain where they are and sing an ode.[1] But it is
unnecessary, in this and in similar cases, to explain their inaction
by supposing that there was any difficulty in passing from the
orchestra to the palace because of the stage which lay between.
A sufficient reason is to be found in the fact that, if they had
gone into the palace, the scene of action would have been left
empty.

It will be best to disregard all evidence of this inconclusive
kind, and to confine our attention to those points which really
throw light upon the question as to the relative position of
actors and chorus during the fifth century. The following
facts seem to be established. It is evident that the chorus
sometimes entered and sometimes departed through the back-
scene. Instances are not very common; there are only about
six in the extant dramas.[2] Still, they undoubtedly occur. It is
evident, too, that the actors sometimes entered by the orchestra.
They must have done so when they entered along with the
chorus, and they probably did so when they entered in chariots
or wagons.[3] This gives us about seven instances where the
actors came in by the orchestra. They may have done so much
more frequently. This is a point which will be considered later

---

[1] Eur. Med. 1275. Cp. Agam. 1344,
Cyclops 630, Hipp. 780, Hec. 1042,
&c.
[2] Aesch. Choeph. 22, 1063 ; Eum.
140. Eur. Troad. 176; Hel. 385, 517.
In Aristoph. Av. 667 Procne (the flute-
player of the chorus enters from the
back-scene, and then descends into the
orchestra. Several other instances are
given by Capps, pp. 9, 10 ; but they
are all very doubtful.
[3] See below, pp. 191, 201.

on. But these seven cases are the only ones for which there is any convincing evidence. On the other hand, it was a common thing for actors and chorus to depart together through the orchestra. Many plays end in this way, such as the Eumenides and the Septem. In Aristophanes it is a favourite form of conclusion for actors and chorus to go off through the orchestra in a joyful procession.[1] The general result then is this, that it was plainly permissible in the fifth century for the chorus to enter or leave by the back-scene, and for the actors to enter or leave by the orchestra; though the last of these practices is the only one of which there are many certain examples. But when we pass on from these entrances and exits, and look at the rest of the play, we find that it is very unusual, during the course of the action, for the chorus to come on the stage, or for the actors to go into the orchestra. The instances in which, apart from entrances and exits, the actors and the chorus can be shown to have come into close physical contact with one another, are remarkably few. We may mention, as examples, the scene in which the chorus tries to prevent Creon from seizing Antigone, and the scene where the farmers mount the stage to draw the statue of Peace out of the well. Opinions may differ as to individual cases, but the total number of instances of this kind does not amount, at the outside, to more than about fifteen.[2] The conclusion we may draw from this evidence is as follows. There was nothing in the fifth century theatre to prevent the actors from moving into the place occupied by the chorus, and there was nothing to prevent the chorus moving into the place occupied by the actors. But, except when they were entering or leaving the scene of action, they do not appear to have done so usually, but to have kept apart from one another.

What then does all this prove as regards the stage? On the one hand, it proves conclusively that the stage of the fifth century cannot have been as high as the ordinary later or Hellenistic stage. If the fifth-century stage had been twelve feet above the level of the orchestra, there would have been the greatest awkwardness in actors and chorus passing from

---

[1] See below, p. 191.

[2] The following instances appear to be certain—Aesch. Suppl. 208, 832; Choeph. 22 ff. Soph. Oed. Col. 826 ff. Eur. Suppl. 1, 815: Hel. 1627 ff.: Rhesus 681; Iph. Aul. 599. Aristoph. Pax 246 ff. Many other examples will be found in the treatises already mentioned; but the evidence for most of them appears to be very slight.

one place to the other.   But, on the other hand, it does not in
any way exclude the possibility of there having been a stage
of some kind or another.   If we suppose that the fifth-century
stage was lower and deeper than that of later times, and that it
was connected with the orchestra by a long flight of steps, or
by a sloping ascent, all difficulties about the performance of the
extant dramas disappear.   Actors and chorus could easily pass
from stage to orchestra, or vice versa.   The fact that they so
seldom came into contact with one another, except when entering
or leaving the theatre, is a strong confirmation of the view that
there was a stage of some kind, and that it was reserved in most
cases for the actors, while the usual place for the chorus was in
the orchestra.

   The main reason for the employment of a stage must have
been to make the actors clearly visible to the audience, and
to prevent the view of them being impeded by the chorus in
the orchestra.   A few feet of elevation would be sufficient to
produce this result.   Dörpfeld, it is true, denies that any such
precaution was necessary.   He denies that the actors, even
without a stage, would have been hidden from view by the
chorus.[1]   But if we look at the plan of a Greek theatre, it
is clear that if the actors were in the orchestra, and the chorus
stood in front of them, the chorus must have obstructed the
view of a great many of the spectators.   In fact we have
ancient testimony to that effect.   The tragic chorus stood in
three rows.   We are told that the worst and most ungainly
choristers (the 'laurostatae', as they were called) were placed
in the middle row, because they were not clearly seen by the
spectators.[2]   But, however the chorus stood, there could only
have been *one* row between these 'laurostatae' and the audience.
If, then, the actors had been in the orchestra, with *three* rows
of choristers in front of them, the obstruction to the view would
obviously have been very much greater.   And it is important
to remember that the spectators who would have suffered most
by this arrangement would have been the occupants of the
lowest tiers of seats.   Now these seats were reserved as seats
of honour, and were confined to high officials and distinguished
citizens.   Hence, if Dörpfeld's theory is correct, the distinction

---

[1] Griech. Theater, pp. 353 ff.   [2] Phot. and Hesych. s.v. λαυροστάται.

which the Athenians bestowed upon their leading citizens cannot
have been one of very much value. The benches which they
assigned to them must have been the worst seats for view in the
whole theatre.[1]

Dörpfeld further objects that, if we suppose a low stage at
Athens in the fifth century, the history of the Greek stage
becomes a very fantastic and peculiar affair. We have first
a stage of five or six feet, then in the next period it rises to
about twelve feet, then later on in the Roman period it suddenly
drops to five again. His own theory, he says, is much simpler.
There was no stage at all till the Roman period, and then a
stage of five feet was erected.[2] But the figures given by Dörpfeld
are quite fallacious. There was no sudden rise and fall of the
kind he describes. We have no means of determining the
exact height of the stage during the fifth century. But when
we come to the later period we find that it was not fixed at
twelve feet, but varied from eight to thirteen. There was no
settled rule. Architects naturally tried new experiments.
Different heights were adopted in different places. Probably
there was just the same variety and love of experiment in the
early period. Again, when we come to the Roman period, we
do not find that the height of the stage was suddenly fixed
at five feet. In many places it was as much as eight or nine.
Wherever we look in the history of the Greek theatre, we
perceive a gradual transition from one type of stage to another;
and the reasons for the successive changes are generally to
be explained by the varying circumstances of the contemporary
drama.

The archaeological evidence on the subject of the early stage
has already been discussed.[3] Unfortunately it amounts to very
little. The oldest stage-buildings, being made of wood, have
disappeared without leaving any trace behind them. However,
such evidence as can be obtained tends to confirm the testimony
of the dramas themselves, and to show that the stage of the
fifth century was lower and deeper than that of subsequent
times. There is also this point to be taken into consideration.
The existence of a lofty stage during the Hellenistic period and

[1] [Seats of honour are not of course necessarily the best for seeing or hearing (see p. 159, note), but they are not likely to be the worst.]

[2] Griech. Theater, p. 363.

[3] See above, p. 118.

perhaps from the fourth century onwards appears to be now
proved by irresistible testimony. This being so, it is altogether
improbable on general grounds that there should have been no
stage at all during the preceding period. To suppose that the
Greeks began without any stage of any kind, and then after so
long a time suddenly erected a stage about twelve feet high, is
a most unlikely hypothesis. But if we imagine that a stage
existed from the first, and that it was a low one in the fifth
century, and was then gradually raised in consequence of the
changed character of the drama, the process becomes much more
intelligible. The presence of a stage during the later period is
strong presumptive evidence in favour of an earlier one.[1]

The last few years have been prolific in new theories on
the subject of the stage. Most of them may be regarded as
developments or modifications of Dörpfeld's views. Before
leaving this subject it may be well to give a brief account of
the more important of them. Bethe considers that there can
no longer be any doubt as to the existence of the Hellenistic
stage. He also agrees that the passages in Aristophanes prove
the use of a low stage at the time when Aristophanes wrote.
But for the greater part of the fifth century he denies its
existence. He considers that the first Greek stage was erected
in 427 or in 426, and that this date was an important epoch in
the development of the theatre. He founds his belief on the
fact that after this date there is no further instance of the use
of the ekkyklema, while before this date there is no example of
the use of the mechane, the theologeion, and the drop-scene.[2]
But, in the first place, it is by no means clear why the presence
or absence of these contrivances should involve the existence
or non-existence of a stage. In the second place, his dates are

---

[1] [Frei, De certaminibus thymelicis,
traces back to the second half of the
fourth century the distinction of
θυμελικοί and σκηνικοὶ ἀγῶνες, and so
proves the existence of a stage at that
time. Engelmann, Archäol. Stud. zu
den Tragikern, supports Dörpfeld's
view by reference to vase paintings,
which he thinks were suggested by
theatrical scenes, and represent actions
taking place in the orchestra, with the
columnar προσκήνιον as background.
But the background could in most cases
be equally well the back of the stage;
and it is not certain that the vases in
question present dramatic scenes at
all. Columns, &c., are common on all
vases to indicate a house or a temple,
where there is no reference to a stage;
and in black-figured vases, where all
such reference is out of the question,
we find Prometheus and Odysseus tied
to columns instead of to a rock or a
mast. See E. A. Gardner, Class.
Rev. 1901, p. 432.]

[2] Bethe, Prolegomena zur Geschichte
des Theaters. pp. 205 ff.

open to question. There is no proof, as we shall see later on, that the machinery which he mentions was introduced or discontinued at the time specified. Another theory has been put forward by Weissmann. He, too, accepts the Hellenistic stage, but agrees with Dörpfeld that in the fifth century actors and chorus performed on the same level. However, he thinks that the passages in which old men complain of the steepness of the road prove that there must have been a raised platform which they had to ascend. As one of these passages— that in the Hercules Furens—is spoken by the chorus, he comes to the conclusion that there was a large platform for actors and chorus combined. This platform extended from the back-scene over a considerable part of the orchestra, and on it stood the actors and chorus, both on the same level.[1] To this it may be answered, that the evidence on which he relies is far too slight a justification for such a sweeping hypothesis. Also on general grounds it is inconceivable that the Greeks, when they already possessed an orchestra which was admirably adapted for choral performances, should have taken the trouble to erect a huge platform on the top of it. Christ agrees in the main with Weissmann. He accepts the Hellenistic stage for the later period, and also the platform for the chorus in the orchestra during the fifth century. But he thinks the passages in Aristophanes prove that the actors even then stood higher than the chorus. He therefore supposes two stages: one immediately before the back-scene, for the actors; and another larger and lower one in the orchestra, for the use of the chorus.[2] He thus eventually comes round to the same conclusion as Wieseler, though by a very different process. His theory, however, is open to the same objections as that of Weissmann. This orchestral platform is utterly improbable in itself, and is unsupported by any sufficient evidence. Lastly, there is Robert's hypothesis. Robert denies the existence of a stage during the fifth century; but supposes that one was erected in the course of the fourth century for the performance of new plays, in which there was practically no chorus. Henceforth new plays were acted on the stage, old plays in front of

[1] Scenische Aufführung, p. 37. Jahrb. für classische Philologie, 1895, pp. 673 ff. See above, p. 167.

[2] Jahrb. für class. Philologie, 1894, pp. 161 ff.

it, in the orchestra.[1] But it is impossible to suppose that in the same theatre, and at the same festival, the proscenium should have served at one time as a stage, and at another time as a background. Nor is there anything in the ancient authorities to support such a view.

§ 14. *Various Details.*

To return to the subject of the construction of the theatre in general. It is obvious that, considering the enormous size of the building, and the immense numbers of spectators which it was intended to accommodate, the greatest attention must have been bestowed upon its acoustic properties. Vitruvius is most emphatic upon the necessity of keeping this object in view, when choosing a site for a theatre. The situation against the side of a hill, and the gentle and symmetrical upward slope of the tiers of seats, are mentioned as qualities by which acoustic excellence was ensured. The height of the stage-buildings was also of great importance. It was found that the best results were obtained by making them exactly the same height as the uppermost parts of the auditorium.[2] That this was the ordinary practice during the Roman period is proved by the remains of various theatres, such as those of Aspendos and Orange. But whether, at any time during the Greek period, stage-buildings were constructed on this enormous scale is very doubtful. Another matter on which the ancient architects insisted was the wooden flooring of the stage, which tended to make the voices of the actors more audible. When Alexander the Great wished to have a stage built entirely of bronze, it was pointed out to him that this material would be fatal from the acoustic point of view.[3] Vitruvius mentions a peculiar practice which was adopted for the purpose of adding resonance to the voices of the actors. Hollow vessels of bronze, of different tones, were suspended in niches in various parts of the auditorium. When a sound was uttered of the same tone as that of any of the vessels, its resonance was increased. He states that this custom, though not adopted in Rome, existed in many Greek and

[1] Hermes, 1897, pp. 450 ff.
[2] Vitruv. v. 6.

[3] Plut., Non posse suaviter, &c. 1096 B.

Italian theatres; and that Mummius, after his capture of
Corinth, brought back several of these vessels from the theatre
there.[1] In the remains of the existing theatres no traces are
to be found of the niches he describes. It is probable that
the whole plan was merely an experiment adopted in a few
special cases. As far as Athens was concerned, no such extra-
neous assistance to the voice was necessary. Experiments at
the present day have shown that the acoustic properties of the
theatre of Dionysus are excellent; and this must have been
still more the case when the stage-buildings were standing.
Probably therefore, in spite of the vast numbers of the audience,
the persons in the back rows could hear the words spoken in
the orchestra and upon the stage much more clearly than might
at first have been supposed.

Another point mentioned by Vitruvius in connexion with
the theatre is the advantage of erecting porticoes in the rear
of the stage-buildings, to serve as a shelter for the people
in case of a sudden shower of rain, and also for the convenience of the choregi. He adds that at Athens there were
three buildings close to the theatre, which served admirably
for this purpose. These were the Odeion, the temple of
Dionysus, and the Portico of Eumenes.[2] The Odeion here
referred to was that built by Pericles, which probably stood
on the eastern side of the theatre, though its exact site has
not yet been determined with certainty.[3] The temple of
Dionysus mentioned by Vitruvius is apparently the older of
the two temples, marked *t* in the plan, and lying to the
south-west of the stage-buildings. The Portico of Eumenes
is supposed to have been built by Eumenes II, in the beginning
of the second century, and it is thought that traces of it are
to be found stretching westwards from the theatre.[4] Immediately to the south of the stage-buildings are the foundations
of a long rectangular erection, belonging to the same date
as the stage-buildings themselves, and marked *s* in the plan.
This erection was no doubt a portico, built in the fourth
century for the purpose described by Vitruvius. In the theatre
itself there was no protection for the general mass of the
people either from the sun or from the rain. The huge canvas

---

[1] Vitruv. v. 5.

[2] Id. v. 9.

[3] Plut. Pericles, 160 A.   Pausan. i.

14. I.   See Gardner, Ancient Athens;
Harrison, Primitive Athens.

[4] Same references,

awnings, suspended upon masts, which the Latin writers refer to, were an invention of the Italians, and were only adopted in Greek theatres at a very late period.[1]

The interior of the theatre at Athens was decorated with the statues of various public persons, some distinguished, others not. In the time of Lycurgus bronze statues were erected in honour of Aeschylus, Sophocles, and Euripides.[2] Pausanias mentions that in his time there were several statues of dramatic poets in the theatre, but, with the exception of Sophocles, Euripides, and Menander, they were all very obscure individuals.[3] The base of Menander's statue, with an inscription recording his name and the name of the sculptor, has been discovered near the western parodos. Its original site, however, is unknown.[4] Astydamas, the tragic poet, was voted a statue in the theatre on account of the excellence of his tragedy called Parthenopaeus. He wrote an epigram to be inscribed upon the base, regretting that he had not been born in the time of the great tragic writers, so as to be able to compete with worthy antagonists. The Athenians were so disgusted with his conceit, that they refused to allow the epigram to be inscribed, and the expression, 'to praise one's self like Astydamas,' passed into a proverb.[5] The statue of Astydamas originally stood at the inside corner of the auditorium on the western side, and there was probably a corresponding statue on the eastern side.[6] One of the grammarians says that there were also statues of Themistocles and Miltiades in the theatre, each with a captured Persian standing beside him. But his statement is probably a fiction, invented to explain the passage on which he was commenting, and which he misunderstood.[7] In later times, it is stated, a statue of Eurycleides the conjuror was erected in the theatre.[8] It is probable that during the reign of Hadrian thirteen statues of him were placed in the thirteen different blocks of the auditorium. The inscriptions on the bases of four of these statues have been

---

[1] Val. Max. ii. 4. 6. C. I. G. 4283.
[2] Plut. X. orat. 841 F.
[3] Pausan. i. 21. I.
[4] Griech. Theater, p. 71.
[5] Suidas s.v. σαυτὴν ἐπαινεῖς.
[6] See above, p. 87.
[7] Schol. Aristid. iii. p. 535, Dindf. So Wilamowitz. Aristoteles und Athen,

i. p. 263. Christ, however (Sitzungs. bayer. Akad. der Wissen. 1894, p. 3), thinks the statement about the statues is true, though the scholiast was mistaken in applying it to the passage in Aristides.
[8] Athen., p. 19 E.

found in the existing remains of the theatre.[1] In addition to the statues, various votive offerings were erected in the two side-entrances. Many of the bases were still in their original position when the theatre was first excavated, but they have now mostly disappeared. Four of them, however, still remain. One of them supported the memorial erected by Xenocles in 306, to commemorate his services as Agonothetes. The other three belong to the Roman period.[2] There were also various inscriptions and tablets connected with theatrical affairs. A copy of the decree of the Amphictyonic Council, conferring certain privileges upon the Athenian actors, was inscribed on stone and put up in the theatre.[3] Numerous records of dramatic and dithyrambic contests were erected either in the theatre or in the immediate neighbourhood. There were lists of the victors in all the competitions at the Lenaea and the City Dionysia. There were lists of all the tragedies and comedies ever produced in the theatre at Athens. There were lists of all the poets and actors who had competed there, with the number of their victories appended to each name. An account of these various records has already been given at the end of the first chapter.

Before concluding this description of the theatre of Dionysus it may be interesting to give some account of the various other purposes for which it was used at different times, in addition to its primary object as a place for dramatic representations and contests of dithyrambic choruses. The recitations of the rhapsodists, and the competitions between the harp-players, were also transferred to the same place from the Odeion, in which they had been held previously.[4] Besides this, various ceremonies unconnected with art took place in the theatre during the festivals of Dionysus. Those which took place at the commencement of the City Dionysia have already been mentioned.[5] The annual cock-fight in commemoration of the Persian invasion was also held in the theatre.[6] But the most

[1] C. I. A. iii. 469.
[2] Griech. Theater, p. 70. For the inscription on the Xenocles monument see C. I. A. ii. 1289.
[3] C. I. A. ii. 551.
[4] Hesych. s. v. ᾠδεῖον.
[5] See ch. ii.
[6] Aelian. Var. Hist. ii. 28. On the outside of the arms, in the throne of the priest of Dionysus, there are two bas-reliefs, in which kneeling Cupids are depicted in the act of setting cocks to fight. The significance of the reliefs is explained by the fact that the annual cock-fight was held in the theatre.

important of the non-dramatic purposes for which the theatre
came to be used was that of a meeting-place for the assemblies
of the people. In the fifth and fourth centuries the regular
place of assembly was the Pnyx. But already at a very early
period special assemblies used to be held in the theatre after
each festival of Dionysus, to discuss matters connected with
the festival.[1] These semi-religious meetings probably paved
the way for the later practice of holding ordinary meetings
there. As early as the year 411, on the occasion of the over-
throw of the Four Hundred, Thucydides mentions that an
assembly of the people was held in the theatre.[2] It was in
the theatre that the meeting was convened which condemned
Phocion and his friends to death in 317 B.C.[3] In 295 Demetrius,
after capturing the city, summoned a gathering of the people
in the theatre.[4] These meetings were all of a special character,
and were not regular assemblies of the people ; but they served
as precedents for the use of the theatre for political, as opposed
to religious and artistic, purposes. Similarly, we are told on
the authority of Aristotle that the Ephebi received their shields
and spears from the state at assemblies of the people in the
theatre.[5] After the middle of the third century the theatre
became the regular meeting-place. The Pnyx henceforward
was only used for assemblies for the election of magistrates.[6]
In this later period the theatre was also used for various exhibitions which seemed unworthy of its character as a temple
of Dionysus. Sword-swallowers, conjurors, and exhibitors of
puppet-shows are mentioned among the entertainers who occupied the stage which had formerly been dignified by Euripides.[7]
But the greatest degradation which the theatre at Athens ever
suffered was when, under the influence of Roman custom, it
was given up to gladiatorial combats. This was a pollution
which called forth indignant protests from writers such as
Philostratus and Dion Chrysostom.[8]

[1] Dem. Meid. § 9.
[2] Thuc. viii. 93, 94.
[3] Plut. Phoc. 757 D.
[4] Id. Demetr. 905 A. Müller (Bühnenalt. p. 74) is mistaken in stating, on
the authority of Diod. xvi. 84, that on
the news of the capture of Elatea in
339 the Athenians hastily assembled
in the theatre. That they met in the
Pnyx is proved by the passage in Dem.

de Cor. § 169. Diodorus is merely
using the language of his own time,
when the theatre was the regular
meeting-place.
[5] Harpocrat. s. v. περίπολος.
[6] Poll. viii. 132.
[7] Plut. Lycurg. 51 E. Athen. 19 E.
Alciphron iii. 20.
[8] Dion Chrysost. or. xxxi. p. 386
(Dindf.). Philostrat. vit. Apoll. iv. 22.

CHAPTER IV

THE SCENERY

§ 1. *General Character of the Scenery.*

In the production of a play the chief objects on which care and money were bestowed were the training of the chorus, the payment of the actors, and the supply of suitable dresses. The scenery was never made a prominent feature of the exhibition. All that was required was an appropriate background to show off to advantage the figures of the performers. The simplicity in the character of the ancient scenery was a necessary result of the peculiar construction of the stage. The Attic stage, though from sixty to seventy feet long, was apparently never more than about fifteen feet in depth, and was still further contracted in after times. On a long and narrow platform of this kind, any representation of the interior of a building would be out of the question. All those elaborate spectacular illusions, which are rendered practicable by the great depth of the modern stage, were impossible. Nothing more was required than to cover over the wall at the back with a suitable view. Again, not only were the mechanical arrangements simple, but the number of scenes in use upon the Attic stage was very limited. Not only was a change of scene in the course of the same play practically unknown, but there was often very little difference between one play and another as regards the character of the scenery required. Each of the three great branches of the drama had a background of a conventional type, specially appropriated to itself, and this typical background was the one usually adopted. When therefore a series of tragedies was being exhibited, or a series of comedies, it must often have happened that the same scenery would do duty for several plays in succession.

The use of painted scenery, natural as it appears to us, was only invented very gradually by the Athenians. For a long time the erection at the back of the stage continued to retain its

N 2

original character. It was regarded, not as a back-scene, but merely as a retiring-place for the actors. The notion of covering it over with painted scenery, in such a way as to make it represent the supposed scene of action in the play, was a development of comparatively late times. The old drama had no scenic background. The action was supposed to take place in some open region; the decorations were confined to such properties as could be put up on the stage; the wooden hoarding in the rear was nothing more than the front of the actors' room. Things were still in this primitive condition when Aeschylus wrote his four earlier plays. The progress of the art of scenic decoration can be traced very distinctly by comparing these plays with his later tragedies. In the first four there is no mention of any scenery, no clear definition of the exact spot where the action is taking place. The scenic appliances are limited to properties erected in front of the hoarding. In the Supplices the scene is laid in an open district at some distance from the city. In the centre is an altar of the gods, at which the suppliants take refuge.[1] Otherwise there is a total absence of local colouring. In the Persae, the next in order of his plays, the action is also laid at a distance from the palace. The only object mentioned as actually in sight is the tomb of Darius.[2] In the Septem the performers are gathered together within the walls of Thebes beside an altar on some rising ground, from which the towers of the city are visible.[3] But there is no clear definition of the scene, and no mention of any palace or other building from which the actors make their entrance. In the Prometheus the action takes place in a rocky region of Scythia. But in all probability the cliff to which Prometheus is chained was merely built up upon the stage. There is nothing in the play to suggest an elaborate representation of the view. In these four plays the background was still a bare wall with doors for the actors. It had no scenic significance. But when we come to the Oresteia, the last dramatic production of Aeschylus, a great change is noticeable. The scene is

[1] Aesch. Suppl. 189.
[2] Pers. 659. The palace is often referred to (159, 230, 524, 849, 1038); but this does not show that it was supposed to be visible. And the fact that Atossa made her first entrance on a chariot (159, 607), though coming from the palace, seems to prove that it was out of sight.
[3] Septem 95, 240, 265, 549, 823.

now laid in front of a building which is clearly defined and
frequently referred to. In the first two tragedies it is the
palace of Agamemnon at Argos; in the third it is the temple
of Apollo at Delphi, and later on the temple of Athene at
Athens.[1] The contrast between these plays and the earlier
ones, as regards local colour and allusions to the scene of
action, is very marked and conspicuous, and denotes a considerable advance in the art of mounting a play. The old
actors' booth had now become a regular scenic background.[2]
The bare hoarding was covered with painting, to represent
a palace, or a temple, or whatever else might be required.
This conclusion, which may be deduced from the extant dramas
themselves, is confirmed by the ancient traditions as to the
introduction of scene-painting. Aristotle says it was invented
by Sophocles; Vitruvius apparently ascribes it to Aeschylus.[3]
Whichever statement be correct, it is clear, from the fact
of its being attributed to both poets, that it must have been
introduced at that particular period when both were exhibiting
upon the stage. It cannot be placed earlier than the first
appearance of Sophocles in 468, or later than the last appearance of Aeschylus in 458. Moreover Sophocles, if he really
invented it, is not likely to have done so immediately on
his first appearance. The most probable date, therefore, is
some period not very long before the production of the
Oresteia, and subsequent to the production of the four early
plays of Aeschylus.

---

[1] Agam. 3, Choeph. 22, Eum. 35,
242.
[2] Reisch (Griech. Theater, pp. 194,
200) thinks the actors' booth was
originally in the side-entrance to the
orchestra. He thinks the first stage-
buildings were erected about 465, when
scenery was introduced; and that these
buildings were henceforth used for
actors' rooms. But it is much simpler
to suppose that the actors' booth stood
fronting the spectators from the first,
and that it was gradually converted
into a stage-building.
[3] Aristot. Poet. c. 4 τρεῖς δὲ καὶ
σκηνογραφίαν Σοφοκλῆς. Vitruv. vii.
praef. § 11 primum Agatharchus Athenis
Aeschylo docente tragoediam scaenam
fecit et de ea commentarium reliquit.

Prof. Jebb (Dict. Antiq. ii. p. 816)
thinks the two statements may be reconciled by supposing that the words
'Aeschylo docente tragoediam' merely
fix the date, without implying that
Aeschylus had anything to do with the
innovation. [Prof. P. Gardner (J. Hell.
Stud. 1899, p. 253) points out that,
according to Vitruvius, Agatharchus,
like Democritus and Anaxagoras, seems
to have studied perspective theoreti-
cally; and the story that he was en-
ticed by Alcibiades into his house, and
not released till he had painted its
interior, combined with Vitruvius'
notice, suggests that he was precisely
the kind of painter for a stage; while
the date suggested has nothing chrono-
logically against it.]

By the middle of the fifth century, then, we may regard the use of painted scenery as fully established. Taking this date as our starting-point, it will be interesting to consider the question as to the number and character of the scenes most in use upon the Attic stage. Our principal authority will be the Greek plays still in existence. Vitruvius divides scenery into three classes—tragic, comic, and satyric. According to his description, the salient features in a tragic scene were columns, pediments, statues, and other signs of regal magnificence. In comedy the scene represented a private house, with projecting balconies, and windows looking out upon the stage. The scenery in the satyric drama consisted of a rustic region, with trees, caverns, mountains, and other objects of the same kind.[1] The above list is not intended to be an exhaustive one. It merely describes in general outline the type of scene which was most characteristic of each of the three great branches of the drama. At the same time, it is more exhaustive than might at first sight be supposed. If the extant Greek dramas are examined, it will be found that in the great majority of cases the scenery conforms to the general type described by Vitruvius. To take the tragic poets first. Twenty-five tragedies by Sophocles and Euripides have been preserved. In no less than seventeen out of the twenty-five the scene is laid in front of a palace or temple.[2] In all these cases the general character of the scenery would be exactly such as Vitruvius describes. The prominent feature would be a magnificent building, with columns, pediments, and statues. Of the remaining eight tragedies, there are four in which the scene consists of an encampment, with tents in the background.[3] The other four all require special scenery. In the Philoctetes the scene is laid in front of a cavern in a desert island. In the Ajax it is laid partly before the tent of Ajax, partly in a solitary quarter by the sea-shore. The background in the Oedipus Coloneus consists of a country region, with the sacred enclosure of the Eumenides in the centre. Finally, the Electra of Euripides is altogether exceptional in having its scene laid

[1] Vitruv. v. 6.
[2] Viz. Soph. O. R., Antig., Electr., Trach. ; Eur. Alc., Med., Hipp., Herc. Fur., Phoen., Hel., Orest., Bacch., Ion,

Iph. Taur., Andr., Suppl., Heraclid.
[3] Viz. Eur. Hec., Troad., Iph. Aul., Rhesus.

before a humble country cottage. On the whole, the evidence
of the extant tragedies tends to confirm the statement of
Vitruvius, and exemplifies the conventional character of Greek
tragic scenery. In the great majority of instances the background would be an imposing pile of buildings, adorned with
various architectural embellishments. As to the satyric drama,
the Cyclops of Euripides is the only specimen of this class
of composition which has been preserved. The scene there
corresponds exactly to the descriptions of Vitruvius, and consists of a country region, with the cave of Polyphemus in
the centre. There can be little doubt that in most satyric
dramas the background was of much the same character. As
the chorus always consisted of satyrs, whose dwelling was in
the forest, the scene of the play would naturally be laid in
some deserted country district. The scene in the New Comedy
was almost invariably laid in front of an ordinary private house,
as is proved by the adaptations of Plautus and Terence. As to
the Old Comedy, in six out of the eleven comedies of Aristophanes, the background consists merely of a house, or of houses
standing side by side.[1] In four others the principal part of the
action takes place before a house. In the Thesmophoriazusae
the scene consists of a house and a temple standing side by
side. In the Lysistrata there is a private house, and near it
the entrance to the Acropolis. In the Acharnians the opening
scene takes place in the Pnyx ; the rest of the action is carried
on before the houses of Dicaeopolis, Euripides, and Lamachus.
The scene in the Knights is laid partly before the house of
Demos, and partly in the Pnyx. The only comedy in which
the scenery is of an altogether exceptional character is the
Birds, in which the background consists of a wild country
region, filled with rocks, and trees, and bushes. It appears,
therefore, that even in the Old Comedy there was not much
variety in the scenery.

As regards the style of the ancient scene-painting, and the
degree of perfection to which it was eventually brought, it is
difficult to speak with any certainty. But in the fifth century,
at any rate, there can be little doubt that the scenery was of
the simplest description. Landscape-painting was still in its

---

[1] Viz. the Wasps, Peace, Clouds, Frogs, Ecclesiazusae, Plutus.

infancy, and altogether subordinated to the painting of the human
figure. When landscapes were introduced into a picture, they
were suggested rather than worked out in detail.[1] A city was
represented by a few houses, a forest by a few trees, and so on.
The paintings for the stage were probably of the same general
type. The scenes most in use were front views of temples,
palaces, and dwelling-houses. In such cases a rough indication
of the different buildings would be considered sufficient. That
they were depicted with any completeness and realism is far
from likely, though the newly discovered art of perspective
was undoubtedly applied to architecture and the painting of
architectural scenes much earlier than to landscape.[2] It is true
that the personages in the extant dramas often use words which
seem to imply an elaborate architectural background. They
speak of columns, triglyphs, cornices, and pediments.[3] In the
Ion they even admire in detail the bas-reliefs with which the
temple front was decorated.[4] But it is not certain that the
objects mentioned were all of them actually represented upon
the stage. Many of them may have been left to the imagination. As for natural scenery, there was probably very little of
this in the early theatre. If the action was laid in a country
region, as in the Philoctetes and the Oedipus Coloneus, and in
the generality of satyric plays, the necessary effect might be
produced by a few rocks, and trees, and other similar objects.
In later times it was customary, when the background represented a palace or temple, to insert a landscape on either side.[5]
Even in the plays of the fifth century there are occasional references to such landscapes. Helen, standing before the palace
of the Egyptian king, points to the 'streams of the Nile' as
flowing close by. The old man in the Electra, when he reaches
the palace of the Atreidae, shows Orestes the country round
about, with Argos and Mycenae in the distance. The Trojan

[1] [This was so not only in vase paintings, but in such elaborate works as
those of Polygnotus at Delphi : cp. P.
Gardner, J. Hell. Stud. 1899, p. 254.]
[2] [See P. Gardner, J. Hell. Stud.
1899, pp. 255 ff.]
[3] Bacch. 590, 1211 ; Orest. 1569;
Iph. Taur. 113, 130.
[4] Ion 190 ff. [It is noticeable that
the occurrence of the technical terms
of architecture and other arts is particularly common in Euripides, who
shows special acquaintance with the
arts and their processes. This may
perhaps confirm the otherwise uncertain tradition (Vit. Eur.) that he was
once a painter : cp. Huddilston, The
Attitude of the Greek Tragedians towards Art.]
[5] Such scenes were depicted on the
periaktoi, Poll. iv. 126, 131. See below, p. 197.

captives descry, from the Greek encampment, the smoke and flames of burning Troy.[1] But here again we may doubt whether, on the contemporary stage, these places were really visible to the spectators. At any rate, if they were delineated at all, it was probably in a slight and symbolical fashion. As time went on the art of scenic decoration was much improved and elaborated. In the Hellenistic period it seems to have reached a fairly high degree of development. Natural phenomena were now depicted with more **realism**. Seas and rivers, earth and sky, are mentioned among **the objects** delineated. Even regions in Hades and Tartarus were represented upon the stage.[2] The progress of landscape-painting in general among the later Greeks naturally produced its effect upon the work of the scenic artists. But it would be an anachronism to attribute efforts of this ambitious kind to the contemporaries of Sophocles and Euripides.

The introduction of magnificent decorations appears to be always a later development in the history of the drama. On the Elizabethan stage the back-scene consisted of a bare wall, and anything in the way of spectacular effect was provided by the movements and groupings of the actors. To produce an impression by scenic means would have been alien to the taste of the Athenians of the fifth century. In the dramatic performances of that period the conspicuous feature was the chorus in the foreground, with its graceful arrangement and picturesque dresses. Above the chorus, on the narrow stage, stood the actors and mute figures, arranged in line, and dressed in brilliant colours. The long scene in the rear was so far decorated as to form a pleasing background, and show off the persons of the actors to advantage. But no attempt was made to produce a realistic landscape, or to convey the ideas of depth and distance. In its general effect the scene upon the stage resembled a long frieze or bas-relief, with the figures painted in brilliant colours, rather than a picture with a distant perspective.

---

[1] Eur. Hel. 1, Troad. 1256 ; Soph. El. 4 ff.

[2] Poll. iv. 131 καταβλήματα . . . κατεβάλλετο ἐπὶ τὰς περιάκτους ὅρος δεικνύντα ἢ θάλατταν ἢ ποταμὸν ἢ ἄλλο τι τοιοῦτον. Anon. de comoed. (xx. 28

Dübner) πολυτελέσι δαπάναις κατεσκευά- ζετο ἡ σκηνὴ . . . πεποικιλμένη παρα- πετάσμασι καὶ ὀθόναις λευκαῖς καὶ μελαί- ναις . . . εἰς τύπον θαλάσσης ταρτάρου ᾅδου . . . γῆς καὶ οὐρανοῦ κ.τ.λ.

§ 2. *Mechanical Arrangements for the Scenery.*

The scenery consisted of painted curtains or boards, attached
to the wall at the back of the stage.[1] As the mechanical
arrangements for fixing them up have not been described by
any of the ancient writers, a detailed account of the matter
is impossible. But some facts can be deduced from the
testimony of the existing dramas. In every Greek play
the action was supposed to take place in the open air. The
scene was generally laid before some building or tent, or in
a country district with a rock or cavern in the background.
The upper portion of the painted scene represented merely
the sky, and was probably the same in all dramas. The lower
portion delineated the building or landscape which the particular
play required. It used to be commonly supposed that this
lower portion projected two or three feet in front of the upper;
that the back-scene was not a flat surface from top to bottom,
but that a narrow ledge or platform ran across from wing
to wing about half-way up.[2] The object of this hypothesis was
to provide room for the 'distegia'. The distegia was a contrivance which enabled actors to take their stand upon the roof
of a palace or private house.[3] Eight or nine instances of
its use are to be found in the existing Greek plays. Thus
the Agamemnon of Aeschylus opens with the watchman sitting
upon the roof of the palace at Argos, and waiting for the
beacon's signal. In the Phoenissae of Euripides Antigone
and the attendant mount upon the roof to get a view of the
army encamped outside the city. In the concluding scene of
the Orestes Hermione, Orestes, and Pylades are seen standing
upon the roof of the palace. Examples also occur in comedy.
In the Acharnians the wife of Dicaeopolis views the procession from the roof of the house. At the commencement of the
Wasps Bdelycleon is seen sleeping upon the roof, and later

---

[1] Poll. iv. 131 καταβλήματα δὲ ὑφάσματα ἢ πίνακες ἦσαν ἔχοντες γραφὰς τῇ
χρείᾳ τῶν δραμάτων προσφόρους· κατεβάλλετο δὲ ἐπὶ τὰς περιάκτους. Ibid. 125
κλίσιον . . . παραπετάσμασιν δηλούμενον.
Suid. s. v. προσκήνιον τὸ πρὸ τῆς σκηνῆς
παραπέτασμα. Anon. de comoed. (xx.
28 Dübner) σκηνὴ πεποικιλμένη παραπετάσμασι καὶ ὀθόναις.

[2] So Müller, Bühnenalt. pp. 118,
142.
[3] Poll. iv. 129 ἡ δὲ διστεγία ποτὲ μὲν
ἐν οἴκῳ βασιλείῳ διῆρες δωμάτιον, οἷον
ἀφ' οὗ ἐν Φοινίσσαις ἡ 'Αντιγόνη βλέπει
τὸν στρατόν, ποτὲ δὲ καὶ κέραμος, ἀφ' οὗ
βάλλουσι τῷ κεράμῳ· ἐν δὲ κωμῳδίᾳ
ἀπὸ τῆς διστεγίας πορνοβοσκοί τι κατ-
οπτεύουσιν ἢ γρᾴδια ἢ γύναια καταβλέπει.

on his father Philocleon tries to escape through the chimney. At the end of the Clouds Strepsiades climbs up a ladder to the roof of the phrontisterion, in order to set it on fire. In the Lysistrata Myrrhina and Lysistrata are seen upon the battlements of the Acropolis. The distegia may also have been used in that scene of the Supplices where Evadne appears upon the summit of a cliff, and then flings herself down.[1] In all these cases it used to be imagined that the standing-room for the actor was provided in the way described; that the lower part of the scene projected two or three feet, and so furnished a permanent platform in the background. But this theory is improbable on several grounds. We have seen that the distegia was only employed in comparatively few instances. It seems unlikely, therefore, that an elaborate structure of this kind should have been erected merely to meet these occasional requirements. Further than this, if the scene had been divided in half by a horizontal line, and the lower half had protruded several feet, this arrangement, though suitable enough when the background was a palace, would have been absurdly inappropriate when a country district was to be represented. It is also questionable whether the ancient stage was wide enough to permit the arrangement. It may have been possible in early times; but the Vitruvian stage, which was only ten feet across, can hardly have been encroached upon to the extent of two or three feet. It is far more probable that the back-scene was flat from top to bottom. This supposition is more in harmony with the simple style of the ancient scenery. As for the distegia, it was provided most likely by a projecting balcony or upper story, which might be introduced when required, without encroaching upon the narrow stage. Such balconies were not uncommon in Greek and Roman houses.[2] And that they were used in the theatre is expressly stated by Vitruvius, who tells us that the houses in comedy were of the type called 'Maeniana', or houses with projecting galleries.[3] In ordinary cases the distegia would resemble a structure of this kind. But where the surroundings were exceptional, as in the Lysistrata, it might easily be

---

[1] Agam. 3, Phoen. 89, Orest. 1567–75, Acharn. 262, Vesp. 68 and 144, Nub. 1485–1503, Lysist. 864, 874, and 883, Eur. Suppl. 990.
[2] Dict. Antiq. i. pp. 663, 666.
[3] Vitruv. v. 6.

decorated in such a way as to conform to the rest of the scenery.

If the scene represented a dwelling-house, there were windows in the upper story, out of which the characters could peer upon the stage. Such windows are mentioned by Vitruvius, and instances of their use occur in the extant comedies. For example, Philocleon, in the Wasps, tries to escape out of an upper window, and in the Ecclesiazusae the old woman and the young girl are seen looking out of one.[1] It need hardly be remarked that the doors of the building represented by the painted scenery would correspond more or less closely with the permanent doors in the back-wall, so as to admit of easy ingress and egress to the actors. In the same way, if the scene was a cavern in a country region, the entrance to the cavern would be made to correspond with the central door in the wall at the back. Concerning the manner in which the scenery was finished off at the top nothing can be laid down for certain. It is not even known whether the stage was covered with a roof or not. But the analogy of Roman theatres, and the general convenience of the arrangement, are in favour of such a covering.[2]

§ 3. *The Entrances to the Stage.*

The question as to the number and the character of the entrances leading upon the stage is of some importance in connexion with the Greek drama. In order to avoid confusion in dealing with this subject, it is necessary to distinguish carefully between the permanent doors in the walls surrounding the stage, and the temporary doors or entrances which were left when the scenery had been put up. First, as to the permanent doors. We have shown already that the remains of the purely Greek theatres are so defective, that it is impossible, from the evidence which they supply, to come to any conclusion as to the number of these doors. But it is evident, from the statements of Pollux, that the Hellenistic type of theatre, which is the one he describes, must have possessed

---

[1] Vitruv. v. 6.   Vesp. 379, Eccles. 924, 930, 961-3.
[2] See above, p. 135.

at least five such doors. It must have had three doors in the wall at the back of the stage, and two doors at the sides, one leading from each of the wings. Probably the same plan was adopted in the older buildings of the fourth and fifth centuries, whether of stone or wood. In later times, when the Graeco-Roman theatres were erected, the stage was considerably lengthened, and in consequence the number of the doors in the wall at the back was raised to five. But it has been pointed out in the last chapter that in all probability only three of these doors were used in the course of the actual performances, and that the two outer ones were either covered over by the scenery, or concealed by temporary side-wings of wood.[1]

The next point to be considered is the number of the entrances which had to be provided when the scenery was erected, and the stage was made ready for a dramatic performance. Pollux and Vitruvius, in speaking of the scenery and stage decorations, agree in saying that there were three doors at the back of the stage.[2] But this statement is much too universal. In the majority of cases, no doubt, there were three such doors. When the scene represented a palace, or temple, or dwelling-house, three doors appear to have been always used. But when the scene was of an exceptional character, the number of the entrances from the back of the stage would vary according to the requirements of the play. For instance, in the Philoctetes there would only be a single entrance, that from the cavern. In the first part of the Ajax the only entrance would be that leading out of the tent; in the second part there would be no entrance at all, the background consisting merely of a solitary region by the sea-shore. In the Cyclops, the only opening at the back of the stage was the mouth of Polyphemus' cave. In such plays as the Prometheus of Aeschylus, and the Andromeda of Euripides, the background consisted of rocks and cliffs, and there was no entrance from that quarter. It is clear, therefore, that the statement that a Greek scene was provided with three doors or entrances at the back is not universally true, but only applies to the majority of cases.

[1] See above, p. 135.   [2] Poll. iv. 124, 126 ; Vitruv. v. 6.

Some details concerning the character of the three doors
may be gathered from the statements in Pollux and Vitruvius.[1]
When the scene was a palace, the central door was decorated
with regal grandeur. The side-doors were supposed to lead
to the guest-chambers. Occasionally one of the side-doors
led to a guest-chamber, the other to a slaves' prison. In
comedy, the character and arrangement of the doors would
vary considerably, according as the scene was laid in front
of one, or two, or three dwelling-houses. In the last case,
of which an example is supplied by the Acharnians, there
would be one door for each of the three houses. Sometimes
one of the side-doors represented the way into an outhouse,
or workshop, or stable. Sometimes it led into a temple, as
in the Thesmophoriazusae. In comedy, no doubt, there was
much greater diversity as to scenic details than in tragedy.

A curious regulation concerning the usage of these three
doors is mentioned by Pollux.[2] He says that the central
door was reserved for the principal character, the door to
the right for the secondary characters, the door to the left
for those of least significance. It is plain that this statement
must be taken with very considerable deductions. In the first
place, it only applies to tragedy, and only to those plays in
which the background represented a palace or similar building.
Even then it cannot have been by any means universal. In
fact it only applies to dramas of the type of the Oedipus
Tyrannus, in which the principal character is at the same time
a person of the highest rank. In such cases it is very likely
that his rule about the doors was observed. It would be in
harmony with the statuesque and conventional character of
Greek tragedy. But there are many plays in which it would
be absurd to suppose that any such regulation was adopted.
For instance, in the Antigone it can hardly be imagined that

<hr/>

[1] Vitruv. v. 6 'ipsae autem scaenae
suas habent rationes explicatas ita uti
mediae valvae ornatus habeant aulae
regiae, dextra ac sinistra hospitalia.'
Poll. iv. 124 τριῶν δὲ τῶν κατὰ τὴν
σκηνὴν θυρῶν ἡ μέση μὲν βασίλειον ἡ
σπήλαιον ἡ οἶκος ἔνδοξος ἡ πᾶν τοῦ
πρωταγωνιστοῦ τοῦ δράματος, ἡ δὲ δεξιὰ
τοῦ δευτεραγωνιστοῦντος καταγώγιον· ἡ
δὲ ἀριστερὰ τὸ εὐτελέστατον ἔχει πρόσωπον ἡ ἱερὸν ἐξηρημωμένον, ἡ ἄοικός ἐστιν.

ἐν δὲ τραγῳδίᾳ ἡ μὲν δεξιὰ θύρα ξενών
ἐστιν, εἱρκτὴ δὲ ἡ λαιά. τὸ δὲ κλίσιον
ἐν κωμῳδίᾳ παράκειται παρὰ τὴν οἰκίαν,
παραπετάσμασι δηλούμενον, καὶ ἔστι μὲν
σταθμὸς ὑποζυγίων . . . ἐν δὲ 'Αντιφάνους
'Ακεστρίᾳ καὶ ἐργαστήριον γέγονεν.
Throughout this passage Pollux is
guilty of his usual fault of converting
particular cases into general rules.

[2] See the previous note.

the tyrant Creon entered only by a side-door, while the central door, with its regal splendour, was reserved for the oppressed heroine Antigone. Similarly, in the Electra, it is ridiculous to suppose that Clytaemnestra entered from the inferior part of the palace, Electra from the more magnificent. There can be no doubt that Pollux, in his statement about the doors, has been following his favourite practice, and has made a general rule out of a few special instances.

The openings at the back of the stage always led out of some building, tent, cavern, or other dwelling-place. They could only therefore be used by persons who were supposed to be inside the dwelling-place. People coming from the neighbourhood, or from a distance, had to enter the stage in a different way. For this purpose doors in the side-wings were provided.[1] The subject of these side-entrances on to the stage has been much discussed in recent years.[2] Many scholars have endeavoured to prove that they were a late invention, confined to the Hellenistic theatre, and that they never existed in the fifth century. They suppose that in the old Athenian theatre the only side-entrances were those in the orchestra, and that the actors who entered or departed otherwise than through the back-scene always used the orchestra for this purpose. Now it is no doubt true, as we have already shown, that they used it sometimes. There are about twenty cases in which actors and chorus leave together in a sort of procession, chiefly at the end of a play[3]; and there are two cases in which they enter together.[4] There are also those scenes—about five in number—when the actors enter in

---

[1] Poll. iv. 126 παρ' ἑκάτερα δὲ τῶν δύο θυρῶν τῶν περὶ τὴν μέσην ἄλλαι δύο εἶεν ἄν, μία ἑκατέρωθεν, πρὸς ἃς αἱ περίακτοι συμπεπήγασιν. Vitruv. v. 6 'secundum ea loca versurae sunt procurrentes, quae efficiunt una a foro, altera a peregre, aditus in scaenam'. Phot. s. v. παρασκήνια· αἱ εἴσοδοι αἱ εἰς τὴν σκηνήν. Schol. Aristoph. Lysist. 321 νῦν ἐστιν ἡμιχόριον τὸ λέγον ἐκ γυναι-κῶν εἰσερχομένων ἄνωθεν . . . τὸ δὲ ἄλλο ἡμιχόριον ἐξ ἀνδρῶν κάτωθεν ἐπερ-χομένων.

[2] See Harzmann, Quaestiones Sceni-cae, pp. 43 ff.; Bodensteiner, Sce-nische Fragen, pp. 703 ff.; Capps, The Stage in the Greek Theatre, pp. 12 ff.; Weissmann, Scenische Aufführung, pp. 25 ff., 76.

[3] Cf. Aesch. Suppl. 1018; Pers. 1076. Eur. Suppl. 1231; Alc. 741. Aristoph. Acharn. 1231; Vesp. 1535; Pax 1357; Ran. 1524. For other in-stances see Bodensteiner, p. 690. Only one of these cases—the funeral proces-sion in the Alcestis—occurs in the middle of a play.

[4] Alcestis 861; Plutus 253. Capps (pp. 20 ff.) gives some additional in-stances; but for these there is no clear evidence.

chariots.[1] On all these occasions it can hardly be doubted that the actors entered and departed through the orchestra. But the other examples which have been brought forward are entirely conjectural. It is said that, when the actors and the chorus were supposed to come from the same place, they must always have used the same entrance. In the Philoctetes, for example, Odysseus, Neoptolemus, and the chorus all come from the ship. If, therefore, the sailors entered by the orchestra, the two heroes must have done the same. But there is no necessity for such an assumption. It would be absurd to demand this minute accuracy in the representation of a play. Then there are cases where an actor on the stage sees another from a distance ; but about ten lines intervene before the second actor comes near enough to enter into conversation with the first.[2] It is argued that he must have had a long way to go, and must therefore have come round by the parodos. But in all these places there is nothing to show that the person approaching was seen by the audience as soon as he was descried from the stage. He may have received his 'cue' some time after his advent was announced. It is common enough on the modern stage, when the scene is in the open air, for an actor's approach to be announced some time before he actually appears. Also, there are several cases in the ancient dramas when an actor begins to converse with the people on the stage only two or three lines after he is first seen.[3] These passages might be cited to prove that he had only a short way to go, and must therefore have come in by the stage. But in reality all inferences of this kind are far too subtle to be of any value. We can hardly imagine the ancient dramatists counting the number of yards to be walked before they settled the number of verses to be spoken. Another set of instances are those in which a character, after coming into sight, takes a long time to reach the point he is aiming at. Euelpides and Peisthetaerus stumble about during the delivery of fifty-three lines before they reach the hoopoe's dwelling-place. Dionysus and Xanthias converse for thirty-five lines before coming to the house of Hercules.[4] They too, it is said, must have entered by the

---

[1] See below, p. 201.
[2] E.g. Oed. Tyr. 1110-21 ; Agam. 498-503 ; Ion 392-401 ; Oed. Col. 310-24. See Harzmann, pp. 43 ff.
[3] E.g. Trach. 178-80, 731-4 ; Phil. 539-42.
[4] Av. 1-53, Ran. 1-35.

orchestra, otherwise they would have reached their destination much sooner. But there is no need to suppose, in these and similar cases, that the characters were moving straight forward all the time. Any actors of ordinary experience would know how to arrange their progress in such a way as to come to the right place at the right moment. Lastly, there are scenes in which an actor, on making his entrance, fails to perceive at once another actor on the stage ; or addresses the chorus before the actor; or is seen by the chorus before he is seen by the actor.[1] All this is said to prove that he must have come in by the parodos, and that the other actor was at first concealed from view by the intervening side-wings. But in the first place the ancient stage was so low and narrow that, as soon as an actor had fairly entered the orchestra, he could not fail to see the persons on the stage just as well as those in the orchestra. In the second place these arguments all depend on the same fallacy. They assume that in a dramatic performance, when an actor comes in, the question as to whom he shall see first, and which person he shall address first, is decided, not by the convenience of the poet, but by the science of optics. The experience of the modern stage is sufficient to prove that this is not the case.

It would be unsafe then to lay any stress on the instances just cited. The cases in which there are adequate grounds for supposing that the actors entered or departed by the orchestra amount to no more than about thirty. The question is whether these cases are sufficient to justify a wider inference. Are we to assume that, because the actors sometimes used the parodoi, they did so always? On the one hand it may be said that in the early theatre, with its low stage and easy communication between stage and orchestra, there was nothing to stand in the way of such a practice. On the other hand there is the fact that in the later Greek theatre the actors, when coming from a distance, usually entered by the side-wings.[2] Of course in this later theatre, with its twelve-foot stage, there were obvious reasons for doing so. Still, the existence of the practice in late times is a presumption in favour of its existence previously.

[1] E. g. Bacch. 1216 ff. ; Hec. 484 ff. ; Aj. 1040 ff. See, for other instances, Harzmann, pp. 45 ff.; Bodensteiner.

pp. 716 ff.
[2] See above, pp. 125, 126, for the various devices for such entrances.

Moreover, when side-wings had once been introduced, nothing could be more natural than to use them as entrances. The convenience to the actors would be very great. It is difficult to see why they should have been compelled to go all round by the parodoi when there was an easier mode of entrance close at hand. On the whole, therefore, it seems most probable that the side-entrances were generally used by the actors even as early as the fifth century, and that the orchestra was only employed in special cases, such as processions with the chorus.

As regards the use of these side-entrances the Athenians had a special regulation which was due entirely to local causes. The theatre at Athens was situated in such a position that the western side looked towards the city and the harbour, the eastern side towards the open country. In consequence of this fact the side-entrances upon the Athenian stage came to acquire a peculiar significance. If a man entered by the western side, it was understood that he was coming from the city where the scene of the action was laid, or from the immediate neighbourhood; or else that he had arrived from distant parts by sea, and was coming from the harbour. The eastern entrance was reserved for people who had journeyed from a distance by land. The same regulation was applied to the entrances to the orchestra. If a chorus came from the city, or the harbour, or the suburbs, it used the western parodos; if it came by land from a distance, it used the eastern.[1] It is obvious that at Athens, where play-bills were unknown, a conventional arrangement of this kind would be of great assistance to the audience,

---

[1] Vitruv. v. 6 'secundum ea loca versurae sunt procurrentes, quae efficiunt una a foro, altera a peregre, aditus in scaenam'. Vit. Aristoph. (Dindf. Prolegom. de Comoed. p. 36) ὁ κωμικὸς χορὸς συνέστηκεν ἐξ ἀνδρῶν κδ'. καὶ εἰ μὲν ὡς ἀπὸ τῆς πόλεως ἤρχετο ἐπὶ τὸ θέατρον, διὰ τῆς ἀριστερᾶς ἁψῖδος εἰσῄει, εἰ δὲ ὡς ἀπὸ ἀγροῦ, διὰ τῆς δεξιᾶς. Poll. iv. 126 τῶν μέντοι παρόδων ἡ μὲν δεξιὰ ἀγρόθεν ἢ ἐκ λιμένος ἢ ἐκ πόλεως ἄγει· οἱ δὲ ἀλλαχόθεν πεζοὶ ἀφικνούμενοι κατὰ τὴν ἑτέραν εἰσίασιν. In the Life the words ἀπὸ ἀγροῦ denote 'from a distance'. In Pollux ἀγρόθεν apparently means 'from the country in the suburbs'; but the word is obscure, and possibly corrupt. As applied to the *stage* the words 'right' and 'left' were always used from the point of view of the actors: cp. the account of the periaktoi in Poll. iv. 126. But as applied to the orchestra they were sometimes used from the point of view of the actors, sometimes from that of the audience. Hence the eastern parodos might be called the right or the left parodos, according to the point of view from which it was regarded. This is the reason of the apparent discrepancy between the statements in the Life and in Pollux. The author of the Life is looking at the orchestra from the point of view of the actors, Pollux from the point of view of the audience.

and would enable them to follow the action of the piece with greater ease and intelligence than they could otherwise have done. The custom originated in the topographical situation of the Athenian theatre, but was afterwards adopted in all other Greek theatres, and became a conventional rule of the Greek stage. The entrances to the right of the audience were used by persons from the neighbourhood; the entrances to the left by persons from a distance.

§ 4. *Changes of Scene.*

A change of scene during the actual progress of a play was a practice almost unknown upon the Greek stage during the classical period. In the extant tragedies only two instances are to be found, one in the Eumenides of Aeschylus, the other in the Ajax of Sophocles. It does not appear that in either case very much alteration in the scenery was required. In the Eumenides the earlier part of the action takes place in front of the temple of Apollo at Delphi, the latter part before the temple of Athene at Athens.[1] All that was here necessary was to change the statue in front of the temple. The background doubtless remained the same during both portions of the play. There is no reason to suppose that any attempt was made to depict the actual scenery of Delphi or of Athens. Such a supposition would be inconsistent with the rude and un-developed state of scenic decoration during the Aeschylean period, and moreover minute accuracy of that kind was foreign to the Athenian taste. In the Ajax the play begins in front of the tent of Ajax, but ends in a solitary region by the sea-shore. Here again a very slight alteration in the scenery would have been sufficient. Probably in the opening scene the tent of Ajax was represented in the centre, and there may have been some slight suggestion of a coast view on either side. During the latter part of the play the tent would be made to disappear, leaving only the coast view behind. A change of this kind

---

[1] At line 566 the scene of action is transferred in reality to the Areopagus (cf. 685 πάγον δ᾽ Ἄρειον τόνδε). But this change must have been imagined, and not represented. After Orestes and the Furies arrive in front of the temple of Athene, they remain continuously on the stage till the end of the trial.

might have been easily carried out, without much mechanical elaboration. It is to be noticed that in each of the above cases, while the scenery was being changed, both orchestra and stage were deserted by the performers. In the Eumenides it was not until Apollo had retired into the temple, and the Furies had set out in pursuit of Orestes, that the change from Delphi to Athens took place. Similarly in the Ajax both Tecmessa and the chorus had disappeared in search of Ajax before the scene was transferred to the sea-shore.

The Old Comedy was a creation of the wildest fancy, utterly unfettered by any limitations of fact or probability. The scene of the action in the plays shifts about from one place to another in the most irregular fashion. All considerations of time and space are disregarded. But it may be taken for certain that on the actual stage no attempt was made to represent these changes of scene in a realistic manner. The scenery was no doubt of the simplest and most unpretending character, corresponding to the economical manner in which comedies were put upon the stage. In all the extant plays of Aristophanes a single background would have been sufficient. For instance, in the Frogs the action takes place partly before the house of Hercules, partly in Hades before the house of Pluto. The background probably represented the houses standing side by side, or a single house may have done duty for that of Hercules and that of Pluto in turn. The opening scene of the Acharnians takes place in the Pnyx; the rest of the play is carried on before the houses of Dicaeopolis, Euripides, and Lamachus. Most likely the three houses stood in a row, the Pnyx being sufficiently represented by a few benches upon the stage. The fact that the house of Dicaeopolis was supposed to be sometimes in the town, and sometimes in the country, would be of very little moment in a performance like the Old Comedy, where the realities of existence were totally disregarded. In the Lysistrata the action is rapidly transferred from the front of a house to the front of the Acropolis. In the Thesmophoriazusae it takes place partly before a house, partly before the temple of Demeter. It is not necessary, in either of these plays, to suppose any change in the scenery. The house and the Acropolis in the one case, and the house and temple in the other, would be depicted as standing side by side. In the Knights the background throughout the play consisted of the house of Demos; and the Pnyx, as in the Acharnians, was represented by a few benches. As far then as the Old Comedy is concerned it is probable that changes of scenery in the course of a play were seldom or never resorted to. In the New Comedy, to judge from the adaptations of Plautus and Terence, they appear to have been equally infrequent.

The only appliances for changing scenery that are mentioned by the ancient Greek writers are the 'periaktoi'.[1] These were huge triangular prisms, revolving on a socket at the base. Each of the three sides of the prism consisted of a large flat surface, shaped like an upright parallelogram. One of these prisms was placed at each end of the stage, in such a manner as to fit in exactly with the scene at the back, and continue it in the direction of the side-wings. Each of the three sides was painted to represent a different view, but care was taken that in every case the painting should coincide exactly with the painting in the back-scene.[2] As the periaktos was turned round, it presented a different surface to the spectators. Accordingly it was possible, by revolving both the periaktoi, to make a change in the character of the scenery at each end of the stage, while the scene in the background remained the same as before. The

---

[1] Poll. iv. 126 παρ' ἑκάτερα δὲ τῶν δύο θυρῶν τῶν περὶ τὴν μέσην ἄλλαι δύο εἶεν ἄν, μία ἑκατέρωθεν, πρὸς ἃς αἱ περίακτοι συμπεπήγασιν, ἡ μὲν δεξιὰ τὰ ἔξω πόλεως δηλοῦσα, ἡ δ' ἑτέρα τὰ ἐκ πόλεως, μάλιστα τὰ ἐκ λιμένος· καὶ θεούς τε θαλαττίους ἐπάγει, καὶ πάνθ' ὅσα ἐπαχθέστερα ὄντα ἡ μηχανὴ φέρειν ἀδυνατεῖ. εἰ δ' ἐπιστρα-φεῖεν αἱ περίακτοι, ἡ δεξιὰ μὲν ἀμείβει τόπον (a. l. τὸ πᾶν) ἀμφότεραι δὲ χώραν ὑπαλλάττουσιν. Vitruv. v. 6 'secundum autem spatia ad ornatus comparata, quae loca Graeci περιάκτους dicunt, ab eo quod machinae sunt in his locis versatiles trigonoe habentes singulae tres species ornationis, quae, cum aut fabularum mutationes sunt futurae, seu deorum adventus cum tonitribus re-pentinis, versentur mutentque speciem ornationis in fronte , &c. Serv. on Verg. Georg. iii. 24 'scaena quae fiebat aut versilis erat aut ductilis erat. Versilis tum erat cum subito tota machinis quibusdam convertebatur, et aliam picturae faciem ostendebat'. Λ

change of τόπος means a change from one part of the same district to another; a change of χώρα means an entire change of district. Niejahr (Comment. Scaen. pp. 1 ff., Oehmichen (Bühnen-wesen, p. 241), and P. Gardner, J. Hell. Stud. 1899, p. 262, think the passage ἡ μὲν δεξιὰ . . . ἀδυνατεῖ refers, not to the periaktoi, but to the side-doors. But (1) the run of the passage is against this view, (2) δηλοῦσα could hardly be used of a door, (3) Vitruvius says the periaktoi were used for intro-ducing gods, and thus proves that θεοὺς ἐπάγει in Pollux also refers to the periaktoi.

[2] [P. Gardner, J. Hell. Stud. 1899, p. 260, disputes the view that the periaktoi stood in line with a painted background and altered a small part of it. He thinks that before the existence of a painted background the periaktoi stood alone and indicated a change of scene in a merely symbolical way.]

periaktos to the right of the audience depicted views in the immediate neighbourhood of the city where the action was taking place. The periaktos to the left represented a more remote country. This fact corresponds exactly with the regulation already referred to, that the entrances to the right of the audience were reserved for people from the immediate neighbourhood, while people from a distance came in by the left.

The principal use of the periaktoi must have been to produce a change of scene in cases where the prominent feature of the background remained the same. For instance, if the action had been taking place in front of a temple or palace, and was to be transferred to a temple or palace in a different country, the requisite alteration might easily be carried out by means of the periaktoi. The building in the background would remain the same, but the scenery on each side would be altered. Occasions for using the periaktoi might sometimes occur during the course of a single play. But such cases, as we have seen, were extremely rare. It must have been chiefly in the intervals between successive plays that the periaktoi were employed. Most Greek tragedies and comedies took place before a temple, a palace, or a private house. If therefore a series of plays was being exhibited, it might be convenient to retain the same scene in the background, and produce the necessary distinction between the different plays by altering the scenery at each side. The usage of the periaktoi was regulated by a curious conventional custom. If only one periaktos was turned round, the alteration in the scenery was, of course, confined to one end of the stage. This was done when the change of scene was supposed to be a slight one, and was merely from one part of the same district to another. But when the action was transferred to an entirely new district, then both the periaktoi were turned round, and the scenery was changed at each end. The representation of scenery on the periaktoi was probably of the simple and symbolical character which marked Greek stage scenery in general ; a rock would stand for a mountainous district, a waved blue line and a dolphin for the sea, a river god perhaps, holding a vessel of water, for a river.[1] Besides their

---

[1] [Cp. P. Gardner, J. Hell. Stud. 1899, p. 261. He interprets in this sense Pollux iv. 131 καταβλήματα δὲ ὑφάσματα ἢ πίνακες ἦσαν ἔχοντες γραφὰς τῇ χρείᾳ τῶν δραμάτων προσφόρους· κατεβάλλετο δ' ἐπὶ τὰς περιάκτους ὅρος δεικνύντα ἢ θάλατταν ἢ ποταμὸν ἢ ἄλλο τι τοιοῦτον.]

use in effecting a change of scene, the periaktoi were also employed to introduce sea-gods and objects too heavy for the mechane. It is not said how this was managed. But it is possible that, of the two sides of the periaktos which were out of sight of the audience, one contained a small ledge or balcony, on which the sea-god took his stand. As the machine rolled round, he would come suddenly into view.[1]

It is difficult to say when the periaktoi were first introduced, and whether they were used at all during the classical period of the Greek drama. They are mentioned by one grammarian among a list of stage appliances which might be ascribed to Aeschylus,[2] and it is true that they might have been used in producing the change of scene in the Eumenides from the temple at Delphi to the temple at Athens. But they could have been easily dispensed with. In fact, as far as the extant Greek dramas are concerned, there are no occasions on which it is necessary to suppose that they were used, and there are no passages in which they are referred to.[3]

The periaktoi, as stated above, are the only appliances for changing scenery that are mentioned in Greek writings. Servius describes another kind of contrivance, by means of which the scene was parted asunder in the middle, and then drawn aside in both directions, so as to disclose a new scene behind.[4] But it is probable that this invention dated from comparatively late times. There is nothing in the existing Greek dramas to suggest that such a contrivance was in use during the classical period.

§ 5. *Stage Properties, &c.*

In addition to the scenery in the background, the stage was of course decorated with such objects and properties as were required by the particular play. Aeschylus is said to have

---

[1] The suggestion is due to Navarre, Dionysos, p. 137. [Cf. Holwerda, Ath. Mitth. 1898, p. 386.] Possibly Plutarch may be referring to this contrivance when he says (de Esu Carn. 996 B) μηχανὴν αἱρεῖ ποιητικὸς ἀνὴρ σκηνῆς περιφερομένης.

[2] Cramer, Anecd. Par. i. 19.

[3] [P. Gardner, l. c. p. 260, thinks that so simple, conventional, and yet effective an arrangement is quite in the manner of the fifth century, and belongs to the same class as the ekkyklema and the mask, which were certainly Aeschylean.]

[4] Serv. on Verg. Georg. iii. 24 'scaena quae fiebat aut versilis erat aut ductilis erat . . . ductilis tum cum tractis tabulatis huc atque illuc species picturae nudabatur interior '.

been the first to adorn the stage in this manner.[1] If the
scene was a palace or temple, statues of the gods were
generally placed in front of it, and are frequently referred
to in the course of the drama. For instance, there was the
statue of Athene in front of her temple in the Eumenides,
and the statues of the tutelary deities before the palace of
the Atreidae in the Electra of Sophocles. In the Hippolytus
there were two statues in front of the palace of Theseus, one
of Artemis the huntress, and the other of Cypris, the goddess
of love. When Hippolytus returns from the hunt, he offers
a garland of flowers to the statue of Artemis, but refuses to
pay any homage to the statue of Cypris, in spite of the remon-
strances of his attendant. Again, in the country region depicted
in the Oedipus Coloneus the statue of the hero Colonus stood
in a conspicuous position.[2] Other examples of the practice
of decorating the stage with statues are often to be met
with both in tragedy and in comedy. Altars, again, were very
common objects upon the Greek stage. In the Supplices of
Aeschylus the fugitive maidens take refuge round an altar.
The Oedipus Tyrannus opens with the spectacle of a group
of Thebans kneeling in supplication before the altar of Apollo.[3]
Another constant feature in the stage decoration was the stone
obelisk in honour of Apollo of the Highways. It was an
ordinary practice among the Greeks to place such obelisks
in front of their houses. Their presence upon the stage is
often referred to by the dramatic poets.[4] Various other objects
were occasionally required by particular plays. There was the
tomb of Darius in the Persae, and the tomb of Agamemnon
in the Choephori. In the Oedipus Coloneus a rocky ledge was
needed for Oedipus to rest himself upon. In the Acharnians
and the Knights a few benches must have been erected upon
the stage to serve as a rude imitation of the Pnyx. Walls,
watch-towers, and beacon-towers are mentioned by Pollux;
and the presence of other similar decorations and erections can
be inferred from the extant tragedies and comedies.[5]

[1] Vit. Aesch. p. 6 Dindf. καὶ τὴν
ὄψιν τῶν θεωμένων κατέπληξε τῇ λαμ-
πρότητι, γραφαῖς καὶ μηχαναῖς, βωμοῖς τε
καὶ τάφοις, σάλπιγξιν, εἰδώλοις, Ἐρινύσι
κ.τ.λ.
[2] Aesch. Eum. 242; Soph. Electr.
1373, Oed. Col. 59; Eur. Hipp. 70–106.

[3] Aesch. Suppl. 188–200; Soph. Oed.
Tyr. 1–3, 142.
[4] Poll. iv. 123; Aesch. Agam. 1080
ff. ; Schol. Eur. Phoen. 631 ; Arist.
Vesp. 875.
[5] Aesch. Pers. 684, Choeph. 4; Soph.
Oed. Col. 19; Poll. iv. 127.

There was one piece of realism which the Greeks were not averse to, and that was the presence of horses and chariots in the theatre. We have already referred to the instances in tragedy where persons from a distance arrive in chariots drawn by horses or mules. The vast size of the Greek theatre made it peculiarly suitable for displays of this character. In the Agamemnon of Aeschylus, Agamemnon and Cassandra approach the palace in a chariot; Agamemnon remains seated there for a considerable time, while he converses with Clytaemnestra; he then dismounts and enters the palace, leaving Cassandra still in the chariot. In the Electra of Euripides, when Clytaemnestra comes to visit her daughter at the country cottage, she arrives in a chariot, accompanied by Trojan maidens, who assist her to dismount.[1] Animals for riding were also occasionally introduced. In the Prometheus there is the winged steed upon which Oceanus makes his entrance; and in the Frogs of Aristophanes Xanthias rides in upon a donkey.[2]

§ 6. The Ekkyklema.

Several mechanical contrivances are mentioned in connexion with the Greek stage. The most peculiar of these, and the one most alien to all our modern notions of stage illusion, is the ekkyklema.[3] We have seen that in a Greek theatre the action

[1] Aesch. Agam. 782 ff. Eur. El. 988 ff. Other instances occur in Pers. 159 (cp. 607), Troad. 569, Iph. Aul. 600. But there is no reason to infer from Aesch. Suppl. 181 and Pers. 1000 that chariots were actually introduced in these two places.

[2] Prom. 286, 395; Ran. 27. As for the horse on which Ismene is riding (Oed. Col. 312), or the captured horses of Rhesus (Rhes. 671), or the flocks of Polyphemus (Cycl. 82), it is most improbable that these were brought into the theatre.

[3] The ekkyklema is described in the following passages:—Poll. iv. 128 καὶ τὸ μὲν ἐκκύκλημα ἐπὶ ξύλων ὑψηλὸν βάθρον, ᾧ ἐπίκειται θρόνος· δείκνυσι δὲ τὰ ὑπὸ σκηνὴν ἐν ταῖς οἰκίαις ἀπόρρητα πραχθέντα, καὶ τὸ ῥῆμα τοῦ ἔργου καλεῖται ἐκκυκλεῖν. ἐφ' οὗ δὲ εἰσάγεται τὸ ἐκκύ-

κλημα, εἰσκύκλημα ὀνομάζεται, καὶ χρὴ τοῦτο νοεῖσθαι καθ' ἑκάστην θύραν, οἱονεὶ καθ' ἑκάστην οἰκίαν. (The θρόνος mentioned by Pollux must be derived from some particular instance of the use of the ekkyklema. The epithet ὑψηλόν is not strictly correct: cf. p. 232.) Eustath. Il. 976. 15 τὸ ἐγκύκλημα, ὃ καὶ ἐγκύκληθρον λέγεται, μηχάνημα ἦν ὑπότροχον, ὑφ' οὗ ἐδείκνυτο τὰ ἐν τῇ σκευῇ ἢ σκηνῇ. Schol. Aesch. Choeph. 973 ἀνοίγεται ἡ σκηνὴ καὶ ἐπὶ ἐκκυκλήματος ὁρᾶται τὰ σώματα. Schol. Arist. Thesm. 96 ἐπὶ ἐκκυκλή-ματος γὰρ φαίνεται. Schol. Arist. Acharn. 408 ἐκκύκλημα δὲ λέγεται μηχάνημα ξύλινον τροχοὺς ἔχον, ὅπερ περι-στρεφόμενον τὰ δοκοῦντα ἔνδον ὡς ἐν οἰκίᾳ πράττεσθαι καὶ τοῖς ἔξω ἐδείκνυε, λέγω δὴ τοῖς θεαταῖς. Schol. Aesch. Eum. 64 καὶ δευτέρα δὲ γίγνεται φαντασία· στρα-

always took place in the open air, before some temple or dwelling-place. It was impossible to transfer the scene to the inside of the building because of the continual presence of the chorus in the orchestra. Still, it might sometimes happen that a powerful dramatic effect could be produced, if a deed accomplished indoors was exposed to view. The most natural way of doing this would have been to draw aside the back-scene, and reveal a portion of the interior. But in the Greek theatre, owing to the narrowness of the stage-buildings, such a device was hardly practicable. Even if the stage-buildings had been made deeper, there were obvious objections in the way. The relative position of the auditorium and the stage was such that, if a room had been opened out behind the back-scene, a large part of the audience would not have been able to see into it. In any case, the back part of the room would have been almost in the dark. Further than this, the whole arrangement was far too elaborate for the simple notions of the ancient stage-managers. For these reasons a more primi-tive device was adopted. Scenes inside the house or palace were revealed by means of the ekkyklema. This was a small wooden platform, rolling upon wheels, which was kept inside the stage-buildings. When it was required to be used, one of the doors in the background was thrown open, and it was pushed forward on to the stage. Upon it was arranged a group of figures, representing in a sort of tableau the deed or occur-rence which had just taken place inside the building. It was mostly used in cases where a murder had been committed. The ekkyklema was rolled out upon the stage, and on it were seen the corpses of the murdered persons, the murderers standing beside them with the bloody weapons in their hands. It might be rolled through any of the three doors at the back of the stage. The contrivance was of course a purely con-ventional one, due to the necessities of the Greek theatre.

φέντα γὰρ μηχανήματα ἔνδηλα ποιεῖ τὰ κατὰ τὸ μαντεῖον ὡς ἔχει. Schol. Arist. Nub. 184 ὁρᾷ δὲ ὡς φιλοσόφους κομῶντας, στραφέντος τοῦ ἐγκυκλήματος. Schol. Clem. Alex. iv. 97 σκεῦός τι ὑπότροχον ἐκτὸς τῆς σκηνῆς, οὗ στρεφομένου ἐδόκει τὰ ἔσω τοῖς ἔξω φανερὰ γίνεσθαι. Reisch (Griech. Theater, p. 236) thinks the last four passages, in which the word στρέφειν is used, refer to a different kind of machine, by which the back-scene was rolled apart, and disclosed the interior. But this is to lay too much stress on the exact words of the grammarians. They are all obviously referring to the same device. See below, p. 206.

All pretence of realism and illusion was abandoned. But this was a point on which the Greeks did not lay very much stress. In such matters custom is everything. To a modern spectator, used to elaborate stage effects, the device would appear intolerable. But the Greeks, living at a time when stage decoration was in its infancy, were less exacting in their demands. And when they had once accepted the ekky-klema as a conventional contrivance for exhibiting interiors their plastic genius would enable them to use it to the best advantage. The sudden spectacle of the murderer standing beside his victim's body, with the instrument of death in his hands, might easily be formed into a most impressive tableau.

The ekkyklema was probably invented towards the middle of the fifth century, about the time when the actor's booth was first converted into a regular back-scene. It is used twice in the Oresteia. In the Agamemnon, after the murder has been committed, the platform rolls out, and reveals the person of Clytaemnestra, standing over the dead bodies of Agamemnon and Cassandra. In the Choephori there is a parallel scene. Orestes is brought into view standing beside the bodies of Aegisthus and Clytaemnestra, and pointing to the net in which his father had been entangled and slaughtered many years ago. He is seized with frenzy, descends from the ekkyklema, and hastens away to the temple of Apollo at Delphi. The platform is then withdrawn into the palace.[1] During the rest of the century there are many instances of the use of the ekkyklema in tragedy. In the Ajax the interior of the tent is exposed to view by this contrivance ; and at the end of the Antigone the body of Eurydice is exhibited, lying beside the altar at which she has stabbed herself. In the Hippolytus, after the suicide of Phaedra, her dead body is displayed upon the ekkyklema, and Theseus takes from it the letter in which she makes her charge against Hippolytus. In the Electra of Sophocles the door is thrown open at the command of Aegisthus, and the platform rolls out and exhibits Orestes and Pylades standing beside the corpse of Clytaemnestra, which is covered with a cloth. Aegisthus him-self removes the cloth, and then Orestes and Pylades descend

---

[1] Agam. 1379, 1404, 1440. Choeph. 973, 981.

to the stage, and the platform is drawn back again. In the Hecuba the sons of Polymestor, who have been slaughtered inside the tent, are made visible to the spectators by means of the ekkyklema.   In the Hercules Furens Hercules is exhibited lying prostrate between the bodies of his wife and children, with his face covered up, and his limbs chained to the broken column which he had thrown down in his frenzy.   Amphitryon then comes out of the palace, and loosens his chains.   Later on Theseus arrives, and uncovers his face and helps him to rise. He then descends to the stage, and the ekkyklema is rolled back into the palace.   Lastly, in the Electra of Euripides, the bodies of Aegisthus and Clytaemnestra are shown to the audience by means of this device.[1]

The ekkyklema is also occasionally used in Comedy. Aristophanes, on two occasions, employs it in a burlesque sort of way, when he is introducing tragic poets on the stage.   In the Thesmophoriazusae, Euripides and Mnesilochus call at the house of Agathon to borrow some female clothing. Agathon is rolled out on the ekkyklema, lends them some articles which are brought to him from inside the house, and then, when he is tired of their importunity, orders himself to be 'rolled in again as fast as possible'.   In the Acharnians Dicaeopolis goes to the house of Euripides to borrow a tragic dress.   Euripides is upstairs in his study writing tragedies, and cannot come down, but allows himself to be rolled out, and supplies the necessary dresses.[2]   These two passages in Aristophanes, where the mechanism of the apparatus is carefully emphasized in order to add to the ridicule, are very valuable as evidence concerning the structure of the ekkyklema.   The device is also used in the Clouds to show the inside of the phrontisterion.   The disciples of Socrates are seen hard at work on their studies, with globes, diagrams, black-boards, and other scholastic materials round

---

[1] Ajax 346; Antig. 1293, 1301; Hipp. 808, 857; Soph. El. 1458–75; Hec. 1051, 1118; Herc. Fur. 1029–1402; Eur. El. 1177, 1243, 1276.
[2] Thesm. 95, 96 ΕΥ. σίγα. ΜΝ. τί δ' ἐστιν; ΕΥ. Ἀγάθων ἐξέρχεται. | ΜΝ. καὶ ποῖός ἐστιν; ΕΥ. οὗτος οὑκκυκλούμενος, 238 ἐνεγκάτω τις ἔνδοθεν δᾷδ' ἢ λύχνον, 265 εἴσω τις ὡς τάχιστά μ' εἰσκυκλησάτω. Id. Acharn. 399 αὐτὸς δ' ἔνδον ἀναβάδην

ποιεῖ, 408, 409 ΔΙ. ἀλλ' ἐκκυκλήθητ'. ΕΥ. ἀλλ' ἀδύνατον. ΔΙ. ἀλλ' ὅμως. | ΕΥ. ἀλλ' ἐκκυκλήσομαι· καταβαίνειν δ' οὐ σχολή.   The word ἀναβάδην usually means 'with one's feet up', and is so taken by many scholars in the present passage.   But καταβαίνειν in l. 409 seems to prove that here at least it must mean 'upstairs'.

about them.   In the Knights, when the Propylaea is thrown
open, and reveals a vision of ancient Athens, with Demos
dressed up in the antique style, the spectacle may possibly have
been produced by means of the ekkyklema.[1]

From the examples of the use of the ekkyklema which
have just been cited we may gather some further particulars
as to its character and construction.   It appears that persons
upon the ekkyklema could easily descend to the stage, and
that persons on the stage could easily touch those on the
ekkyklema.   It follows that it must have been a low platform,
not much above the level of the stage.   As regards its length
and breadth, it was evidently large enough to support several
persons.   At the same time it cannot have been of any very
great size.   Its width must have been less than the width of
the doors in the background, to permit of its being rolled
through them.   Its depth cannot have been very great, because
of the narrowness of the Greek stage.   In the Acharnians,
when Euripides is rolled out, he is represented as still sitting
in his room upstairs.   But it is unlikely, as some suppose, that
in this case the platform was made taller than usual, to produce
the effect of an upper story.   As Euripides has to hand various
articles to Dicaeopolis, who is standing on the stage, there
cannot have been much difference of level between the two.
The exact mechanism of the ekkyklema, however, remains
uncertain.   It is practically undisputed that the grooves or rails
found at Eretria, running on to the later stage straight from its
back-scene were intended for some such contrivance to run on.[2]
On the other hand it has been argued from the use of certain
words in the scholiast's descriptions that the ekkyklema must
have revolved on a pivot,[3] and it has been suggested that the
mechanism was like that of which a diagram is given in the

---

[1] Nub. 181 ff., Equit. 1327.
[2] [Fossum, Am. J. Arch. 1898, p.
188; Dörpfeld, Ath. Mitth. 1903, p. 396.
See above, p. 165 n.]
[3] [Exon, Hermathena, 1900, pp. 132 ff.;
Navarre, Revue des Études Anciennes,
1901, p. 102.   The words are περι-
στρεφόμενον, στραφέντα, and the variant
ἐγκύκλημα (compared with ἐγκύκλιος,
&c., of rotatory movement): see above,
p. 201.   Exon also doubts if ἀνοίγεται

ἡ σκηνή could be used of opening a door
for the ἐκκύκλημα to pass, and thinks
that the portion of the back-scene
which formed part of the ἐκκύκλημα on
his theory was by the side of the door,
and that there was a similar apparatus
by each door.   But this is pressing the
meaning of ἀνοίγεται ἡ σκηνή too closely.
The words of Pollux, however, do
suggest that the ἐκκύκλημα could be
adapted to any of the three doors.]

accompanying figure, where *ss* is the stage, *ww* the back-scene,
a shows the ekkyklema at rest and not in use, *b* shows it in
process of being rolled round for use, *c* shows it after being
rolled out. This, however, finds no confirmation in anything in
the ruins; the straight rails at Eretria are against it, and the
words referred to may be explained by the use of a windlass or
similar mechanism used in rolling out the ekkyklema. Judging
from the width of the rails at Eretria, the width of the ekkyklema may have been about ten feet, and the doors must
therefore have been rather larger. The suggested revolving
ekkyklema might afford more standing room, but there is not
sufficient evidence of its existence.

In addition to the passages already mentioned, there are two
other places in the extant dramas where the scholiasts say

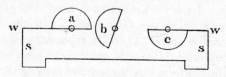

FIG. 14 A.

that the ekkyklema was employed. But they appear to have
been mistaken in both cases. The first instance is in the
Thesmophoriazusae. The action of this play begins before
Agathon's house, but after about three hundred lines is
transferred to the front of Demeter's temple, where the
women hold their assembly. At this point there is a stage-
direction to say that 'the Thesmophorion is rolled out'.[1] If
these words mean that the scene was laid in the interior of
the temple, and that the ekkyklema was rolled out in order
to represent it, the suggestion is undoubtedly wrong. It would
be absurd to imagine that the rest of the play was transacted
on a small platform like the ekkyklema. But possibly the
author of the note was referring, not to the ekkyklema, but
to some mechanism by which he believed that the necessary
change of scene was brought about. The second place is the

---

[1] Schol. Thesm. 284 παρεπιγραφή. ἐκκυκλεῖται ἐπὶ τὸ ἔξω τὸ θεσμοφόριον. The words ὠθεῖται τὸ ἱερόν are inserted in the text. These παρεπιγραφαί were stage-directions appended to the text of the plays; but when and by whom they were written is unknown.

well-known scene at the beginning of the Eumenides.[1] The play opens with the speech of the priestess, delivered in front of the temple. Then, when she departs, the interior of the temple is suddenly brought into view, and shows us Orestes kneeling before the altar, with the sleeping Furies round about him, and Apollo and Hermes standing close by. To suppose, as the scholiast suggests, that this effect was produced by the ekkyklema, is hardly possible. The platform would have been far too small to accommodate a whole tragic chorus, together with three actors. At the same time, though the explanation of the scholiast appears impracticable, it is difficult to suggest any other way in which the scene might have been acted. We cannot assume that the back-scene was drawn apart, and disclosed the inside of the temple in a set-piece, after the modern fashion. This mode of revealing interiors was apparently never used on the Greek stage. If it had been possible, there would have been no need to invent the ekkyklema. It has been suggested that the spectacle was not really exhibited to the audience; that Apollo, Hermes, and Orestes appeared alone in front of the temple; that the ghost of Clytaemnestra called to the Furies through the temple door; and that it was not until then that the Furies came into sight, rushing out in obedience to her summons. But the general character of the scene, and the expressions used in the course of the dialogue, appear to be fatal to this supposition.[2] In fact, the difficulty is one for which no satisfactory solution has yet been found.

The ekkyklema seems to our notions such a rude device, that many critics have been led to deny its existence, at any rate during the classical period. They allow that it must have been used in later times, as it is described in detail by Pollux: but they refuse to believe that it could have been tolerated by the Athenians of the fifth century.[3] The evidence, however,

[1] Schol. Eum. 64.

[2] When Apollo (l. 67) says καὶ νῦν ἀλούσας τάσδε τὰς μάργους ὁρᾶς, it is hardly conceivable that the Furies should not have been visible to the audience. Also l. 179 ἔξω, κελεύω, τῶνδε δωμάτων τάχος | χωρεῖτε implies that they were still inside the temple: but according to the theory in the text they had come out of the temple at l. 140.

[3] Reisch, Griech. Theater, pp. 234 ff.; Capps, The Stage in the Greek Theatre, pp. 237 ff. Neckel (Das Ekkyklema, pp. 7 ff.) thinks the ekkyklema was too rude a device for the taste of Aeschylus and Sophocles, and that it was first introduced in the time

in its favour is too strong to be set aside in this way. The
passages in which it is parodied by Aristophanes correspond
so closely with the descriptions of Pollux that they must
obviously refer to the same mechanical device.[1] There are
also the numerous other scenes in which an interior is revealed.
It is difficult to see how the Greeks, with their peculiar stage
arrangements, could have acted these scenes, except by some
such contrivance as the ekkyklema. Those who deny its
existence explain away these passages in various ways. They
say that in many cases the bodies might have been carried
out on to the stage, or arranged just outside the door, so as
to be visible to the spectators. On other occasions they
suppose that the back-scene was drawn aside, and showed
the interior of the building. But there are several scenes to
which none of these explanations would apply. In the Hercules
Furens Hercules is shown chained to the broken column, and
we cannot suppose that the column was carried out on to the
stage. Nor can the spectacle have been exhibited inside the
palace front. It must have been outside ; since Amphitryon,
as soon as Hercules begins to rouse himself, proposes to fly
within the palace for refuge.[2] In the same way the scholars
of Socrates cannot have been carried out, along with their
globes and diagrams. Yet they too must have appeared upon
the stage, and not inside the building; for it is explained to
Strepsiades that they cannot remain long 'in the open air
outside'.[3] It is impossible, therefore, to account for these and
other scenes in the way suggested.[4] They must have been
effected by the ekkyklema. As for the objection that the
ekkyklema was a device too clumsy for the refined taste of
the fifth century, though admissible in later times, this is
a kind of argument which is not supported by experience.

of Euripides. Bethe (Prolegomena,
pp. 104 ff.) thinks it was used by
Aeschylus and Sophocles, but gradually dropped by Euripides.
   [1] Reisch (pp. 237 ff.) explains the
two scenes in the Thesmophoriazusae
and the Acharnians by supposing that
Agathon and Euripides were rolled out
on couches. But this theory destroys
all the point and humour of the scenes.
   [2] Herc. Fur. 1008, 1070.
   [3] Nub. 184, 198.
   [4] Additional proofs that the bodies

were not *carried* out are (1) Agam.
1379, where Clytaemnestra says she is
standing on ' the very spot where she
struck the blow', (2) Antig. 1301,
where Eurydice is seen lying beside
the altar at which she had stabbed
herself. That the ekkyklema-scenes
were *outside* the building, and on the
stage, is also proved by Eur. El. 1245,
1276, where the Dioscuri, though
standing above the palace roof, can
see the bodies of Clytaemnestra and
Aegisthus.

The history of the drama in many countries shows that the greatest literary and dramatic excellence may coexist with the utmost simplicity and clumsiness in the stage arrangements. It was so in England and it was so in France. The drama of these two countries reached its highest point at a period when the art of stage decoration was in a most primitive condition. On general grounds it would be more reasonable to assume that the ekkyklema was impossible to the Hellenistic Greeks, than that it was impossible to the Greeks of the time of Sophocles. If the former could tolerate it, the latter are not likely to have made any difficulty.

A contrivance called the exostra is occasionally referred to by the grammarians, and is mentioned in a Delian inscription of the third century B.C. The name implies that it was something which was 'pushed out' upon the stage. The metaphorical use of the word in Polybius and Cicero proves it to have been a platform on which objects were exhibited in a conspicuous manner. It is probable, therefore, that the statement of the ancient writers is correct, and that the exostra was merely the ekkyklema under another name.[1]

§ 7.   The Mechane and Theologeion.

Another appliance of even greater importance than the ekkyklema, and one very frequently employed upon the Greek stage, was the 'mechane' or Machine.[2]   It consisted of a sort

[1] Poll. iv. 129 τὴν δὲ ἐξώστραν ταὐτὸν τῷ ἐκκυκλήματι νομίζουσιν. Hesych. s.v. ἐξώστρα· ἐπὶ τῆς σκηνῆς τὸ ἐκκύκλημα. Delian incription of 274 B.C. (Bull. Corr. Hell. 1894, p. 162) τὰς ἐξώστρας . . . ἐπισκευάσαι. Polyb. xi. 6. 8 τῆς τύχης ὥσπερ ἐπίτηδες ἐπὶ τὴν ἐξώστραν ἀναβιβαζούσης τὴν ὑμετέραν ἄγνοιαν. Cic. de Prov. Cons. § 14 iam in exostra helluatur, antea post siparium solebat.

[2] Poll. iv. 128 ἡ μηχανὴ δὲ θεοὺς δείκνυσι καὶ ἥρως τοὺς ἐν ἀέρι, Βελλεροφόντας ἢ Περσέας, καὶ κεῖται κατὰ τὴν ἀριστερὰν πάροδον, ὑπὲρ τὴν σκηνὴν τὸ ὕψος. Schol. Luc. Philops. vii. p. 375 (Lehmann) ἄνωθεν ὑπὲρ τὰς παρ' ἑκάτερα τῆς μέσης τοῦ θεάτρου θύρας . . . μηχανῶν δύο μετεωριζομένων ἢ ἐξ ἀριστερῶν θεοὺς καὶ ἥρωας ἐνεφάνιζε παρευθύ, ὥσπερ λύσιν

φέροντας τῶν ἀμηχάνων.   Aristoph. Daedal. fr. 9 (Meineke) ὁ μηχανοποιός, ὁπότε βούλει τὸν τροχὸν | ἐλᾶν ἀνεκάς, λέγε, χαῖρε φέγγος ἡλίου. The μηχανή was also called ἐώρημα, Suidas. s. v. [This should probably be αἰώρημα.] The ropes to which the actor was suspended were called αἰῶραι ; Poll. iv. 131 αἰώρας δ' ἂν εἴποις τοὺς κάλως οἷ κατήρτηνται ἐξ ὕψους ἀνέχειν τοὺς ἐπὶ τοῦ ἀέρος φέρεσθαι δοκοῦντας ἥρως ἢ θεούς. The hook by which he was fastened was ἅρπαξ or ἀγκυρίς ; Bekk. Anecd. i. 232 (of the Crane) ἅρπαξ . . . ἐξ οὗ ὁ ἐσκευασμένος ὑποκριτὴς τραγῳδεῖ. Plut. Prov. 116 (of the Fig-Branch) ἀγκυρίς, ἀφ' ἧς οἱ ὑποκριταὶ . . . ἐξαρτῶνται . . . ζωστῆρσι καὶ ταινίαις κατειλημμένοι.

of crane with a pulley attached, by which weights could be raised or lowered. It was placed in the left or western corner of the stage, at the very top of the back-scene. It was used when the characters of a play had to appear or disappear in a supernatural manner. By its means a god or hero could be lowered from heaven down to earth, or raised up from earth to heaven, or exhibited motionless in mid-air. Sometimes the god was represented as sitting in a chariot, or on a winged steed ; but in most cases he was simply suspended from the rope by means of a hook and bands fastened round his body. The strength of the mechane must have been considerable, since it was powerful enough to support two or three people at the same time. As to the way in which it was worked, and the manner in which the actors were made to disappear from view at the top of the stage, there is no information. Unfortunately the construction of the upper part of the stage-buildings is a subject about which we are entirely ignorant. It is useless therefore to hazard conjectures concerning the exact nature of the arrangements adopted. The grammarians also speak of two other contrivances, the Crane and the Fig-branch, as used for moving people through the air. But whether they were really distinct from the mechane is far from certain. The Fig-branch is said to have been designed specially for comedy. It appears, however, from the description to have been much the same as the mechane, and was probably only a comic name for it.[1] The Crane is described as an instrument for conveying the bodies of dead heroes up into the sky. Possibly the Crane also was merely another name for the mechane ; or it may have been a separate contrivance, placed at the other end of the back-scene, and used exclusively for the removal of dead bodies. In any case it cannot have differed very much from the mechane in structure.[2] There are one or two passages in the ancient writers

---

[1] Plut. Prov. 116 κράδης ῥαγείσης· νῦν οὐχ ὁ σύκινος κλάδος, ἀλλ᾽ ἡ ἀγκυρίς, ἀφ᾽ ἧς οἱ ὑποκριταὶ ἐν ταῖς τραγικαῖς σκηναῖς ἐξαρτῶνται θεοῦ μιμούμενοι ἐπιφάνειαν. So Hesych. s.v. κράδη. Pollux (iv. 128) makes the κράδη the comic counterpart of the μηχανή, which is utterly improbable. Crusius (Philologus, 1889, p. 698) suggests very plausibly that κράδης ῥαγείσης was the beginning of a line in some comic poet, who applied the name ' fig-branch ' contemptuously to the hook of the μηχανή.

[2] Poll. iv. 130 ἡ δέ γέρανος μηχάνημά ἐστιν ἐκ μετεώρου καταφερόμενον ἐφ᾽ ἁρπαγῇ σώματος, ᾧ κέχρηται Ἡὼς ἁρπάζουσα τὸ σῶμα τὸ Μέμνονος. The scho-

where the mechane is described as a 'kind of ekkyklema', and persons are said to have been rolled out by means of it.[1] It is uncertain in these cases whether the grammarians are confusing the two machines; or whether they are thinking of the theologeion, which, as we shall see later on, may have been worked by mechanism similar to that of the ekkyklema.

Examples of the use of the mechane are fairly common both in the extant dramas and in the records of the grammarians. At the same time there is often a doubt, when a personage makes his appearance on high, whether he was exhibited by means of this device or in some other way. For the present, therefore, we will confine ourselves to those cases where the person is described as moving through the air, and where it seems clear that, if any machinery was employed, it must have been the mechane. The earliest instance is probably that in the Prometheus. Oceanus descends on a 'winged quadruped', converses some time with Prometheus, and then rides away again, saying as he goes that his steed yearns to 'skim with its wings the smooth paths of air'. We are told also that in the Psychostasia, the lost play of Aeschylus, the body of Memnon was carried by Dawn into the sky.[2] Both these instances have been doubted, but merely on general grounds, and without adequate reason. But there are two other supposed examples in Aeschylus which are far more open to question. There is the scene in the Eumenides where Athene arrives from Troas, and where it is thought that she descends from the sky. The language, however, in which she describes her journey is ambiguous and full of difficulty. In three successive lines she appears to say that she has walked, flown, and driven in a chariot.[3] It would be unsafe in a case like this to draw any inference as to the exact manner in which she made her entrance on to the stage. There is also the scene in the Prometheus where the Oceanides enter in a

liast on Lucian (quoted on p. 209) speaks of *two* μηχαναί, one at each end of the back-scene; and then proceeds to describe the ordinary μηχανή, but says nothing about the other one. Hence Oehmichen (Bühnenwesen, p. 247) conjectures that this other μηχανή was the γέρανος.

[1] Bekk. Anecd. i. 208 μηχανή ἐστι

παρὰ τοῖς κωμικοῖς ἐκκυκλήματός τι εἶδος . . . δείξεως χάριν θεοῦ ἢ ἄλλου τινὸς ἥρωος. Lucian, Philops. 29 θεὸν ἀπὸ μηχανῆς ἐπεισκυκληθῆναί μοι τοῦτον ᾤμην. Philostrat. vit. Apoll. vi. 11 ἐφ' ὑψηλῆς καὶ θείας μηχανῆς ἐκκυκλοῦσιν.

[2] Prom. 284, 394. Pollux, iv. 130.
[3] Eum. 403-5.

'winged car', halt in front of Prometheus for about a hundred
and fifty lines, and then, at his bidding, dismount from their
'swift-rushing seat' and descend into the orchestra.[1] Here, too,
the mechane has been suggested. But it is scarcely credible
that a whole tragic chorus should have been suspended in front
of Prometheus during the delivery of a hundred and fifty lines.
Even if the machinery had been strong enough to support
twelve or fifteen choristers, the spectacle would have been
ludicrous.[2] It is much better to suppose that the car was
rolled in along the stage, its previous flight being left to the
imagination of the spectators. After the time of Aeschylus
there are many instances of the use of the mechane. Euripides
often employs it to wind up his plays. At the end of the
Andromache Thetis comes into view 'voyaging through the
bright air'. At the end of the Electra the Dioscuri arrive by
a 'path impossible to mortals', and depart later on 'through
the regions of the sky'. Medea's appearance with her children
in the aerial car may be safely regarded as a further example,
though there is no mention in this case of any ascent or descent.[3]
The device is also introduced in other parts of a play. In
the Hercules Furens Iris and Lyssa come down from heaven
in a chariot; then Iris re-ascends, while Lyssa goes on into
the palace. In the Bellerophon the hero rode up to heaven on
the winged steed Pegasus; and in the Andromeda Perseus
flew down through the air to the foot of the cliff where the
heroine was chained.[4] The mechane is also parodied in many
places by Aristophanes. In the Clouds, Socrates is seen
hanging in a basket in mid-air, and studying astronomy. Iris,
in the Birds, comes floating down from the sky in such an
irregular and eccentric fashion that Peisthetaerus has the
greatest difficulty in bringing her to a standstill. In a fragment
of the Daedalus the actor who is going to ascend entreats the
man in charge of the machinery to give him warning, before he
begins to haul up the rope, by exclaiming 'hail, light of the
sun'. The ascent of Trygaeus upon a beetle in the Peace was
intended as a parody upon the Bellerophon of Euripides. The

[1] Prom. 135, 280.
[2] That the capacities of the μηχανή were not unlimited is proved by Pollux, iv. 126 θεοὺς θαλαττίους ἐπάγει, καὶ πάνθ' ὅσα ἐπαχθέστερα ὄντα ἡ μηχανὴ φέρειν ἀδυνατεῖ.
[3] Androm. 1229, Eur. El. 1235, 1349, Med. 1317 ff.
[4] Herc. Fur. 817, 872, 880. Eur. frags. 124, 306, 307. Poll. iv. 128.

speech of Trygaeus, in the course of his aerial journey, consists of a ludicrous mixture of phrases from the Bellerophon, shouts to the beetle to keep his head straight, and terrified appeals to the stage-manager to look after the security of the pulley.[1]

In addition to the mechane there was also another appliance in use upon the Greek stage for the purpose of exhibiting gods in a supernatural manner. It was called the theologeion, and represented the gods as stationary in heaven, and not as moving through the air. It consisted, apparently, of a narrow platform in the upper part of the back-scene.[2] Probably it was similar in construction to the ekkyklema, and was usually invisible, but was pushed forward through an opening at the back when required. It has been suggested that the theologeion was in reality nothing more than the palace roof. But this theory is hardly a plausible one. When the gods were to be exhibited in celestial splendour in the sky, it would have been undignified and incongruous to place them on the roof of a human habitation. Also the position of the theologeion is expressly described as being high up above the stage.[3] As regards its usage, the only recorded instance is that in the Psychostasia of Aeschylus. Zeus was there represented as sitting in heaven, holding scales in his hands, in which were placed the destinies of Achilles and Memnon respectively. On each side of him stood Thetis and Dawn, supplicating for the lives of their sons. The scene was in imitation of that in the Iliad, where Zeus weighs the fates of Achilles and Hector.[4] It is probable that the theologeion was also used in the Peace, in the scene where Trygaeus ascends to heaven, and converses with Hermes in front of the palace of Zeus.[5]

The relationship between the theologeion and the mechane has been much discussed during the last few years, and various

---

[1] Nub. 218, Av. 1199, Daedal. frag. 9, Pax 154 ff.

[2] A supposed representation of a theologeion on a medallion of the Roman period, found at Orange, is given in Baumeister, fig. 1832, and Griech. Theater, p. 335. Jupiter, Minerva, and Victoria are depicted as sitting on a tall and narrow stage, while Mars and Hercules confront one another underneath. But there is nothing to show that the scene represents a theatrical performance.

[3] See next note. See also p. 164.

[4] Poll. iv. 130 ἀπὸ δὲ τοῦ θεολογείου ὄντος ὑπὲρ τὴν σκηνὴν ἐν ὕψει ἐπιφαίνονται θεοί, ὡς Ζεὺς καὶ οἱ περὶ αὐτὸν ἐν Ψυχοστασίᾳ. Plut. Aud. Poet. 17 A.

[5] Niejahr, however (Quaest. Scaen. pp. 20 ff.), suggests that Trygaeus only rose a short distance upon the beetle, then descended to earth again, and that his own house then did duty as the house of Zeus. [Cp. Sharpley's edition of the Peace, Introduction.]

theories have been brought forward on the subject. Some of the critics think the mechane was the older and more primitive device, and that the theologeion was invented towards the end of the fifth century, to serve as a substitute, and avoid the awkwardness of the previous arrangement.[1]   Others take exactly the opposite view, and regard the theologeion as the simple contrivance of the early drama, and the mechane as a later and more picturesque piece of machinery.[2]   Neither of these views can be maintained except by a somewhat arbitrary treatment of the evidence.   We have clear testimony as to the existence both of the mechane and of the theologeion in the time of Aeschylus ; and it seems uncritical to reject this testimony in the one case, and accept it in the other.   As regards the question of priority, it is impossible to come to any decision, owing to the paucity of the early dramas which have been preserved. But there is one point which deserves consideration.   We have seen that there are several cases at the close of a play in which the mechane was unquestionably used to introduce the god who solved the difficulties of the plot.   The god's arrival is described in language which leaves no doubt upon the subject.   But there are many other cases in which he appears for a similar purpose, and in which he is simply described as standing in some elevated position, and nothing is said about any flight through the air.[3] There are also several plays at the end of which the god appears abruptly, without any notice as to his standing-place, or the manner in which he **arrived** ; but in which it is evident, from the analogy of the other dramas, that he appeared above the heads of the ordinary actors.[4]   In both these latter classes of play there is some uncertainty as to the nature of the machinery employed.   The question may be raised whether, when there is no mention of any movement through the air, the god was introduced by the mechane or by the theologeion. Was he floated down from the sky, or pushed out through the back-scene ?   Some scholars maintain that the theologeion was the device used in these particular cases ; and the sup-

[1] Wilamowitz, Herakles, i. p. 148.
[2] Reisch, Griech. Theater, pp. 227 ff. Bodensteiner, Scenische Fragen, pp. 665 ff.   Bethe (Prolegomena, p. 133) thinks neither the mechane nor the theologeion were used before about 427, when he supposes there was a great reorganization of the scenic arrangements (see above, p. 172).

[3] Ion 1549, Rhesus 886, Orest. 1631.
[4] Hipp. 1282, Iph. Taur. 1435, Eur. Suppl. 1183, Hel. 1642, Phil. 1409, Bacch. 1331.

position is no doubt possible. But, on the other hand, the
fact that there is no allusion to the mechane in the course of
the dialogue proves nothing as to its presence or its absence.
There are many places in which, though the ekkyklema was
obviously employed, the text contains no reference to it. Also
it is clear that from the beginning of the fourth century the
mechane became the regular contrivance for introducing gods
at the close of a drama. Plato remarks that the tragedians,
when in a difficulty, 'have recourse to the mechane, and sus-
pend their gods in mid-air.' Antiphanes, the comic poet,
ridicules the practice of hanging out the mechane at the end
of a tragedy. Aristotle speaks of the mechane as the invariable device on such occasions. The phrase ' deus ex machina '
appears already in the fourth century as a proverbial expression
for an unexpected benefactor.¹ It seems more probable, therefore, that the mechane was regularly used, even in the fifth century, for the same purpose. We have several cases in which it
must have been so employed, and none in which it is necessary
to introduce the theologeion. The only known example of the use
of the theologeion is that in the Psychostasia. Any further cases
in which its presence is assumed must be purely conjectural.

Before leaving this subject a few remarks may be made on
the general question of the appearances of the gods in tragedy.
In the early drama the gods often played an important part
in the action of the piece. They came down to earth and
mixed with mankind after the old Homeric fashion. Their
arrivals and departures might be conducted in a supernatural
manner, but when they were once on the stage they moved
about like ordinary human beings. Such is still the case in
plays like the Eumenides of Aeschylus. But later on, as the
tone of the drama became more entirely human, the gods
began to be excluded more and more from any real share in
the plot. Their occasional presence at the scene of action
was managed with more dignity and splendour. It is rare
to find them appearing side by side with human beings, as

¹ Plat. Cratyl. 425 D οἱ τραγῳδοί, ἐπειδάν τι ἀπορῶσιν, ἐπὶ τὰς μηχανὰς καταφεύγουσι θεοὺς αἴροντες. Antiphanes (Meineke, iii. p. 106) ἔπειθ' ὅταν μηδὲν δύνωντ' εἰπεῖν ἔτι | . . . αἴρουσιν ὥσπερ δάκτυλον τὴν μηχανήν, | καὶ τοῖς θεω-μένοισιν ἀποχρώντως ἔχει. Aristot. Poet. c. 15. Demosth. p. 1025 ὥσπερ ἀπὸ μηχανῆς. Schol. Plat. Bekk. p. 381 ἀπὸ μηχανῆς θεὸς ἐπεφάνη· Μένανδρος Θεοφορουμένη.

Athene apparently does in the Rhesus and in the opening
scene of the Ajax.[1] The Bacchae is an exceptional case, since
Dionysus is there disguised as a young man. But usually,
in the later drama, the intervention of the gods was restricted
to the beginning and the end of the play, when they came
forward to speak the prologue and the epilogue. In such
cases they no longer join with mortal men in the free and
easy intercourse of the Homeric period. Their movements
are more dignified and celestial. It is true that in the prologues, when they are alone, and no human beings have
yet intruded on the stage, they make their entrance on foot,
and walk the earth like ordinary men.[2] But at the end of
the play, when the stage is occupied by mortals, they disdain
to tread the same ground with them, and are exhibited in the
sky by means of the mechane. Even in the prologues it
appears that the same practice was introduced in the course
of the fourth century, and that henceforth all apparitions of
the gods, both at the beginning and the end of a play, were
made equally supernatural.[3] This formal introduction of deities
at the beginning and the close, which was now practically the
sole survivor of the old divine participation in the drama, is
the subject of a well-known criticism by Aristotle. He allows
that it is perfectly legitimate, when the gods are carefully
excluded from the action, and are brought in merely to give
information about the past, or to predict the future. But he
strongly censures the later practice of employing them at the
end of a tragedy to solve the difficulties of the plot. He says
that in a well-constructed play the conclusions should be the
natural result of the preceding incidents, and there should be
no need of any supernatural agency.[4] Euripides has generally
been regarded as the chief offender against his rule, and as

---

[1] Rhesus 596 (cp. 627) ; Ajax 1–133.
[2] Cp. Hipp. 53 ἔξω τῶνδε βήσομαι
τόπων. Ion 76 ἐς δαφνώδη γύαλα βήσομαι
τάδε. In the Troades, though Hecuba
is on the stage during the speech of
Poseidon and his colloquy with Athene,
she is lying prostrate on the ground,
overcome with grief, and is unconscious
of their presence.
[3] Aristot. Poet. c. 15 ἀλλὰ μηχανῇ
χρηστέον ἐπὶ τὰ ἔξω τοῦ δράματος, ἢ ὅσα
πρὸ τοῦ γέγονεν ἃ οὐχ οἷόν τε ἄνθρωπον

εἰδέναι, ἢ ὅσα ὕστερον ἃ δεῖται προ-
αγορεύσεως καὶ ἀγγελίας. Here ὅσα πρὸ
τοῦ γέγονεν apparently refers to the
prologue. For the practice of later
times cp. Evanthius de Commedia, p. 6
Reif. (quoted by Bethe, Prolegom.
p. 133) 'deinde θεοὺς ἀπὸ μηχανῆς, id
est, deos narrandis argumentis machi-
natos, ceteri Latini ad instar Graecorum habent'.
[4] Aristot. Poet. c. 15.

the author of the custom which he condemns. But it will be found, on examining his plays, that there are very few of them in which the god is really used as a last resort. There are only two instances in which he can be said to solve the problems of the situation. In the other cases he is introduced, not so much to set matters right, as to inform the characters of the destiny which awaits them. His function is confined to announcing the future course of events.[1] These, therefore, are what Aristotle would call permissible uses of the 'deus ex machina'.

§ 8. *Other Mechanical Contrivances.*

Several other devices in use upon the Attic stage are briefly mentioned by Pollux, but his descriptions are so meagre and obscure that little can be inferred as to their exact character. Charon's Steps was a contrivance for bringing ghosts and spectres up from the other world. It can hardly have been anything else than a flight of steps leading out upon the stage from underneath. The 'anapiesma' was used by river-gods, Furies, and other subterranean beings for the purpose of appearing above ground. The word 'anapiesma' seems to mean something which was pushed back. It is probable, therefore, that the contrivance was merely the ordinary trap-door of the modern theatre, through which the spectral being was raised on to the stage.[2] Whether these two devices were used as early as the fifth century is somewhat doubtful. There are few occasions in the extant plays and fragments where they would have been serviceable, and none where they are absolutely necessary. The ghost of Darius in the Persae arises out of his tomb, and the ghost of Achilles in the lost Polyxena of Sophocles apparently revealed himself in the same way.[3] In these two cases it is needless to suppose any special apparatus beyond the tomb itself. The ghost of Clytaemnestra in the Eumenides, and that of Polydorus in the Hecuba, may possibly

---

[1] See the Tragic Drama of the Greeks, p. 245.

[2] Poll. iv. 132 αἱ δὲ Χαρώνιοι κλίμακες, κατὰ τὰς ἐκ τῶν ἐδωλίων καθόδους κείμεναι, τὰ εἴδωλα ἀπ' αὐτῶν ἀναπέμπουσιν. τὰ δὲ ἀναπιέσματα, τὸ μέν ἐστιν ἐν τῇ σκηνῇ ὡς ποταμὸν ἀνελθεῖν ἢ τοιοῦτόν τι πρόσωπον, τὸ δὲ περὶ τοὺς ἀναβαθμούς, ἀφ' ὧν ἀνέβαινον Ἐρινύες.

[3] Pers. 659, Nauck, Trag. Graec. Frag. p. 246 προφαινομένου ὑπὲρ τοῦ τάφου.

have risen from underground.   But there is nothing in the text
of the plays to show that this was the case, and an entrance
in the ordinary manner would have satisfied all requirements.
Some critics suppose that in the Prometheus the punishment
which had been threatened by Hermes was actually carried out
before the eyes of the spectators, and that the tragedy ended
with the disappearance of Prometheus beneath the stage.   But
a melodramatic conclusion of this kind seems far from probable,
and out of keeping with the character of the ancient drama.
It is more likely that when the play was over the actor simply
walked off the stage, or was concealed from view by a curtain.
Or he may have remained in position until the beginning of
the next piece, the Prometheus Unbound, in which he was again
represented as chained to a cliff.   The 'bronteion' was a device
for imitating the noise of thunder behind the scenes, and was
of a very simple character.   Pebbles were poured out of a jar
into a large brazen vessel; bags were filled with stones and
flung against a metal surface; or leaden balls were dropped
upon a sheet of leather stretched tight.[1]   The 'keraunoskopeion'
was obviously intended to imitate lightning, though the description in Pollux is unintelligible.   But Heron, the mathematician,
speaks of a device used in automaton theatres, by which a plank,
with a flash of lightning painted on a dark background, was
shot out of a box into a receptacle below.   Possibly Pollux may
be alluding to an arrangement of this kind.[2]   The 'stropheion'
was some sort of revolving machinery, by which heroes were
exhibited in heaven, or deaths at sea or in battle were represented.   The 'hemikyklion' was semicircular in shape, and
gave a distant view of a city, or of a person swimming in the
sea.   The 'hemistrophion' is merely mentioned by name, and
no description of it is appended.[3]

The question whether a drop-scene was used in the Athenian
theatre during the great period of the drama is one which has
not yet been satisfactorily settled.   In Roman theatres a drop-

[1] Schol. Nub. 292; Poll. iv. 130;
Heron (in Thevenot, Mathematici
Veteres, p. 263). See Weismann, Scen.
Anweis. pp. 45 ff.
[2] Poll. iv. 130 κεραυνοσκοπείον . . .
περίακτος ὑψηλή.   Heron, l. c. p. 265.
Weismann (l. c. p. 48), who was the
first to draw attention to the passage in

Heron, supposes that there was a periaktos high up in the back-scene, and
that an apparatus like that of Heron's
was fastened to all three sides of it, so
that by revolving the periaktos three
successive flashes might be exhibited.
[3] Poll. iv. 127, 131, 132.

scene was invariably used between the different plays, the
mechanism being exactly the reverse of that employed in modern
times. When a play was going to begin, the curtain was let
down into a narrow crevice in front of the stage, and at the end
of the performance was drawn up again.[1] There can be no doubt
that similar curtains were used in Greek theatres at a later
period; but the question is whether they were used at Athens
during the fifth and fourth centuries. There are no references
to anything of the kind in the extant Greek dramas, and there
are no passages in ancient writers which can be held to prove
the existence of a drop-scene in the early Athenian theatre.[2]
The question must therefore be discussed on general grounds.
To our modern notions a drop-scene appears to be almost a
necessity in the case of plays which commence with the actors
already in position upon the stage. In the Greek drama such
plays are not infrequent. For instance, in the opening scene of
the Oedipus Tyrannus the Thebans are discovered kneeling at
the altar before the palace of the king. In the Troades, when
Poseidon comes forward to speak the prologue, he sees Hecuba
stretched upon the ground in an attitude of despair. The Orestes
of Euripides opens with Orestes stretched upon a bed in front of
the palace, and his sister Electra watching beside him. Many
other examples might be cited of plays which begin with the
actors already in a fixed position. Unless, therefore, a drop-scene

---

[1] Ovid, Met. iii. 111; Hor. Ep. ii. 1.
189.

[2] The following passages are cited in
proof of the existence of a drop-scene:
—(1) Athen. 536 A γενομένων δὲ τῶν
Δημητρίων Ἀθήνησιν ἐγράφετο ἐπὶ τοῦ
προσκηνίου (ὁ Δημήτριος) ἐπὶ τῆς οἰκου-
μένης ὀχούμενος. Here προσκήνιον more
probably denotes the scene at the
back of the stage. (2) Suid. s.v. προ-
σκήνιον· τὸ πρὸ τῆς σκηνῆς παραπέτασμα·
ἡ δὲ τύχη παρελκομένη τὴν πρόφασιν
καθάπερ ἐπὶ προσκήνιον παρεγύμνωσε τὰς
ἀληθεῖς ἐπινοίας. Suidas has here mistaken the meaning of the passage he
quotes, in which προσκήνιον = 'the
stage'. (3) Synesius (flor. about 400
A.D.) Aegypt. p. 128 C εἰ δέ τις . . .
κυνοφθαλμίζοιτο διὰ τοῦ προσκηνίου.
Even if προσκήνιον means the drop-
scene in this passage, it would be no
proof of the existence of a drop-scene

in classical times. (4) Poll. iv. 122
(speaking of the theatre) ἔξεστι δὲ καὶ
τὸ παραπέτασμα αὐλαίαν καλεῖν, Ὑπερεί-
δου εἰπόντος ἐν τῷ κατὰ Πατροκλέους· οἱ
δὲ ἐννέα ἄρχοντες εἰστιῶντο ἐν τῇ στοᾷ,
περιφραξάμενοί τι μέρος αὐτῆς αὐλαίᾳ.
Suidas s.v. αὐλαία, and Bekk. Anecd. p.
463 αὐλαία τὸ τῆς σκηνῆς παραπέτασμα·
κέχρηται δὲ αὐτῷ Ὑπερείδης ἐν τῷ κατὰ
Πατροκλέους. Hesych. s.v. αὐλαία . . .
τὸ τῆς σκηνῆς παραπέτασμα. Et. Mag.
p. 170 λέγονται δὲ αὐλαίαι καὶ τὰ
παραπετάσματα τῆς σκηνῆς, ὡς παρὰ
τῷ θεολόγῳ. It is obvious that the
grammarians here cited were thinking
of a drop-scene. But the passage they
refer to in Hypereides has nothing to
do with a drop-scene. It is doubtful,
therefore, whether this testimony is of
any value except for the practice of
later times. It can hardly be considered
decisive for the classical period.

was used between the plays, it would have to be supposed that the actors came on the stage in full view of the people, took up the required position, and then began the dialogue. There would be a great sacrifice of illusion in such a mode of commencement. Besides this, the drop-scene would of course be a natural and obvious mode of concealing the stage from view while the scenery was being altered between the different plays. For these reasons it has been inferred that the Athenians cannot have done without one. But, on the other hand, it has already been pointed out that it is a great mistake to apply our modern notions of propriety to an ancient dramatic performance. The Greeks did not lay very much stress upon realism and illusion in their scenic arrangements. They were satisfied with simple and conventional methods of representing events upon the stage. Such devices as the ekkyklema and the periaktoi would never have been tolerated by them, if their aim had been to produce an illusion by the accurate imitation of real objects. Hence it is possible that in the dramas just referred to they were quite content for the actors to come forward and take up their position in full view of the audience, before the play actually commenced. That such a supposition is not inadmissible is proved by the custom of the early English drama. On the Elizabethan stage we know for a fact that there was no drop-scene, and that in many cases a tableau had to be arranged before the eyes of the spectators before the action could begin. Yet the audience of those days was not dissatisfied. The Athenians may have been equally indifferent in the matter of the drop-scene. At the same time there is no evidence to prove that such was the case. And the drop-scene is a very convenient device, and one that would naturally suggest itself. On the whole therefore it seems safest, until further evidence is forthcoming, to regard the question as an open one.[1]

[1] Bethe (Prolegomena, pp. 198 ff.) thinks the drop-scene was introduced into the Greek theatre about 427 B.C., at the same time as the raised stage. His reason is that none of the plays which begin with a tableau are previous to 427 in date. But the Agamemnon commences with the watchman reclining on the palace roof. The Heracleidae (probably anterior to 427) opens with a group of suppliants at an altar. The Oedipus Rex, which also begins with a tableau, is of unknown date, and there is nothing to show that it was later than 427.

CHAPTER V

THE ACTORS

§ 1. *Rise of the Actor's Profession.*

BEFORE proceeding to give an account of the actors in the ancient Greek drama, there are one or two points which ought to be made clear, in order to avoid possible misconceptions. In the first place the actors and the chorus were entirely distinct from one another. The chorus was chosen and paid by the choregus, and performed in the orchestra. The actors were hired by the state, and their proper place was upon the stage. The term 'hypokrites', or 'actor', was never applied to the members of the chorus. It was not even applied to all the performers upon the stage, but only to such of them as took a prominent part in the dialogue. The various mute characters, such as the soldiers and attendants, and also the subordinate characters who had only a few words to say, were not dignified with the title of 'actor'. In the second place it should be remembered that the Greek actors invariably wore masks, and were consequently able to appear in several parts in the course of the same performance. When, therefore, it is said that in the early history of Greek tragedy only a single actor was employed in each play, this does not imply that the number of characters was limited to one. All it implies is that only one character could appear at a time. The number of actors in a Greek play never exceeded three, even in the latest period. But the effect of this regulation upon the capacities of the Greek drama was less cramping and restrictive than might have been supposed. There was no limitation to the number of mute and subordinate characters which might be introduced at any time upon the stage. There was no restriction upon the number of the more prominent characters, provided they were not brought upon the stage simultaneously. The only limitation was this—that not more than three of the more prominent characters could take part in the dialogue in the course of the same scene.

The principal function of the actors was to carry on the dialogue and work out the action of the play. The principal function of the chorus was to sing the odes which filled up the pauses in the action. Of course very frequently the chorus took part in the dialogue ; but, speaking in general terms, the dialogue was the business of the actors. Such was the condition of things during the best period of the Attic drama. But in former times the case had been very different. At first the whole performance was a choral one, and consisted simply of the songs and hymns chanted at the festivals of Dionysus. There were no actors and there was no dialogue. The history of the early development of the drama is in other words the history of the gradual introduction of actors and dialogue into a choral entertainment, and the gradual increase in the importance of the dialogue, until eventually it overshadowed the choral part altogether. The first step in the process by which a lyrical performance was converted into a dramatic one was as follows. The custom arose of filling up the intervals between the different portions of the choral songs with recitations by the leader of the chorus, and dialogues between him and the other members. For this purpose the leader of the chorus used to mount upon a small table. The subject of the recitations and the dialogues would be the same as the subject of the ode, and would in most cases refer to the adventures of the god Dionysus. In these interludes by the leader of the chorus lay the germ of the drama. The performance as a whole was still essentially lyrical, but the practice of inserting dialogue had been established.[1] In the case of tragedy the next step forward was taken by Thespis. He introduced a single actor, who took the part which had previously been taken by the leader of the chorus, and filled up the pauses in the choral odes either with monologues or with dialogues between himself and the leader.[2] Not much is known about the drama of Thespis except that it

---

[1] Poll. iv. 123 ἐλεὸς δ' ἦν τράπεζα ἀρχαία, ἐφ' ἣν πρὸ Θέσπιδος εἶς τις ἀναβὰς τοῖς χορευταῖς ἀπεκρίνατο. Arist. Poet. c. 4 καὶ ἡ μὲν (τραγῳδία ἐγένετο) ἀπὸ τῶν ἐξαρχόντων τὸν διθύραμβον, ἡ δὲ (κωμῳδία) ἀπὸ τῶν τὰ φαλλικά.

[2] Diog. Laert. iii. 56 ὥσπερ δὲ τὸ παλαιὸν ἐν τῇ τραγῳδίᾳ πρότερον μὲν μόνος ὁ χορὸς διεδραμάτιζεν, ὕστερον δὲ Θέσπις ἕνα ὑποκριτὴν ἐξεῦρεν ὑπὲρ τοῦ διαναπαύεσθαι τὸν χορόν.

was still essentially lyrical. But as he is said to have employed masks, it is clear that the single actor might appear in different characters in successive scenes, and in this way some approach might be made to a dramatic representation of a story.[1] The decisive innovation was due to Aeschylus. He introduced a second actor, and effected a total change in the character of the performance. Henceforward the intervals between the choral odes were filled with dialogues between the two actors upon the stage, instead of dialogues between the single actor and the leader of the chorus. At the same time Aeschylus cut down the length of the choral odes, and made the dialogue the essential and prominent feature of the performance.[2] The result was a radical change in the nature of tragedy: it became a dramatic instead of a lyrical form of art. During the greater part of his career Aeschylus was contented with two actors. Three at least out of his seven extant plays are written for performance by two actors only.[3] This limitation upon the number of the performers necessitated great simplicity in the construction of the play, since it was impossible for more than two personages to take part in the dialogue at the same time. Hence the earlier plays of Aeschylus, though essentially dramatic in comparison with anything which preceded them, are simple in plot and lyrical in tone when compared with the tragedies of his successors. The different scenes rather serve to unfold a series of pictures than to develop a complicated plot. Descriptive speeches take the place of animated dialogue. Sophocles added greatly to the capacities of the drama by introducing a third actor.[4] He was thus enabled to give much

---

[1] Suidas s.v. Θέσπις.

[2] Aristot. Poet. c. 4 καὶ τό τε τῶν ὑποκριτῶν πλῆθος ἐξ ἑνὸς εἰς δύο πρῶτος Αἰσχύλος ἤγαγε καὶ τὰ τοῦ χοροῦ ἠλάττωσε καὶ τὸν λόγον πρωταγωνιστὴν παρεσκεύασεν.

[3] Viz. the Supplices, Persae, and Seven against Thebes. In the concluding scene of the Seven the part of Ismene would not be taken by a regular actor. Apparently the opening scene of the Prometheus requires three actors, unless we are to adopt the very improbable supposition that the person of Prometheus was represented by a wooden figure, which was nailed to the rock, and from behind which the

protagonist spoke the part. [In favour of the lay figure, see Wecklein's Edition of the Prometheus, Introd. p.54; Navarre, Annales de la Faculté des Lettres de Bordeaux, Rev. des Études Anciennes, 1901; against it, Bodensteiner, Jahrb. für class. Philol., Suppl.-bd. xix. p. 674; Bethe, Proleg. p. 180, &c.]

[4] Aristot. Poet. c. 4; Diog. Laert. iii. 56; vit. Soph.; Suidas s.v. Σοφοκλῆς. The Life of Aeschylus assigns the introduction of the third actor to Aeschylus, but adds that Dicaearchus ascribed it to Sophocles. The passage in Themistius (xxvi. p. 316 D) καὶ οὐ προσέχομεν Ἀριστοτέλει ὅτι τὸ μὲν πρῶτον ὁ

greater variety and spirit to the dialogue. In his hands for the first time tragedy became completely dramatic, and the lyrical element was thrust still further into the background. The innovation of Sophocles was adopted by Aeschylus in his later years, and the Orestean trilogy—the last and most elaborate of his works—requires three actors. Under Sophocles tragedy received its full development. The number of actors in tragedy was henceforward limited to three.

The satyric drama was intimately connected with tragedy, and the number of actors was apparently the same. Thus the Cyclops of Euripides, the only extant satyric play, requires three actors. In the Naples vase-painting, which represents the performers in a satyric play, three actors are depicted.[1] It is true that the Alcestis of Euripides, which was performed in place of the usual satyric drama, only requires two actors. But the number in this case was probably due to the choice of the poet, and not to any official regulation. In regard to comedy, very little is known as to the steps by which it was developed. The source of comedy lay in the phallic songs performed at the festivals of Dionysus. The dramatic element originated in the interludes by the leader of the chorus. The process of development must have been much the same as in tragedy; but the names of the persons who introduced actors and dialogue into comedy were forgotten even in Aristotle's time. The only piece of information upon the subject is to the effect that Cratinus was the first to limit the number of actors to three, and that before his time there was no regulation as to the number of persons introduced upon the stage. After the time of Cratinus there were no further innovations, and the number of the actors in comedy was permanently fixed at three.[2]

This number was never exceeded either in comedy or in tragedy. All the extant Greek plays could be performed by three actors. It is sometimes said that the Oedipus Coloneus

χορὸς εἰσιὼν ᾖδεν εἰς τοὺς θεούς, Θέσπις δὲ πρόλογόν τε καὶ ῥῆσιν ἐξεῦρεν, Αἰσχύλος δὲ τρίτον ὑποκριτήν (a. l. τρίτον ὑποκριτάς) is doubtful, and cannot weigh against Aristotle's definite statement in the Poetics. The balance of evidence is distinctly in favour of the conclusion that the third actor was first introduced by Sophocles.

[1] Baumeister, Denkmäler, No. 422; Eur. Cyclops 197 ff.

[2] Arist. Poet. cc. 4, 5; Anon. de Comoed. (Dindf. Prolegom. de Comoed. p. 27); Diomedes, p. 490 K.

of Sophocles requires four actors; but this is not the case. Although there are several occasions on which Ismene appears upon the stage simultaneously with three other personages, still on each of these occasions she does not say a word, but is merely a mute figure. It is evident therefore that during this portion of the play her part was taken by a 'super', while at the beginning and end of the play, where she had speeches to make, the part was acted by the tritagonist.[1] It might at first sight appear that the comedies of Aristophanes require more than three actors; but investigations have shown that there is not one of his plays which could not be performed by this number, assisted by a supply of 'supers'.[2]

The smallness of the number of the actors necessarily limited the capacities of the Greek drama. The realistic effect produced by a promiscuous conversation between a large group of persons was impossible upon the Greek stage. Sometimes a certain awkwardness was caused by the limitation in the number of the performers. For instance, at the end of the Orestes of Euripides, Orestes is seen upon the roof of the palace threatening to kill Hermione, and Pylades is standing beside him. Menelaus from below makes a piteous appeal to Pylades, but Pylades says not a single word in reply, but leaves Orestes to answer for him. His silence is very unnatural, and is only to be accounted for by the fact that there was no actor to spare, and therefore the poet could not put any words in his mouth. Two of the actors were already employed in playing the parts of Orestes and Menelaus, and the third was required for Apollo, who comes on the scene immediately afterwards. Consequently the part of Pylades had to be taken by a mute personage. Again there is the scene at the end of the Electra of Euripides. Orestes has heard his fate, and as he leaves the stage he bids farewell to Pylades, and urges him to marry his sister Electra. Pylades maintains a stolid silence, and the Dioscuri reply on his behalf. Here again his silence is due to the necessities of the case. The three actors with whom the poet was supplied were all employed, and Pylades was merely a dumb figure. Similar instances of awkward and almost ludicrous silence on the part of certain characters will occur to

[1] Soph. O. C. 1117 ff., 1249 ff., 1500 ff.
[2] Cp. Beer, Über die Zahl der Schauspieler bei Aristophanes, Leipz. 1844.

all readers of the Greek drama.   But they are not so numerous
as might have been expected, and it is astonishing to find how
successfully the Greek drama, keeping within its own peculiar
limits, was able to accomplish its ends with three actors
only.

There were several advantages in the smallness of the
number.   In the first place the dialogue gained in clearness
and simplicity, owing to the fewness of the persons taking
part in it.   This simplicity was especially well suited to the
severe and statuesque character of Greek tragedy, in which
the rapid movement of a dialogue between a large number of
persons would have been altogether inappropriate.   In the
extant Greek tragedies even the three actors permitted by
custom are used with considerable reserve.   In most cases one
of them stands by in silence, while the other two carry on the
dialogue.   The two change from time to time, but it is only on
rare occasions and for brief periods that all three converse
promiscuously together.   There was another obvious advantage
in the restriction.   As only three actors were needed, it was
easy to ensure that they should all be performers of first-rate
excellence.   In modern times the large number of actors required
constitutes a great difficulty.   It is rare to see the subordinate
characters in a play of Shakespeare even tolerably performed.
The effect of the piece is spoiled by the feebleness of the princes,
dukes, lords, and ladies who crowd the stage.   In the Greek
drama, owing to the limitation upon the number of the performers, this difficulty was avoided, and a high standard of
excellence maintained throughout the play.   It was all the more
necessary, among the Greeks, to take some precaution of this
kind, since the size of the theatre demanded unusual powers in
the actor.   In a modern theatre an actor, however poor, can at
any rate usually be heard.   But in the vast open-air theatre at
Athens it required a man with an exceptionally clear and powerful voice to make himself audible to the vast multitude of
spectators.   It cannot have been an easy task to find actors who
combined histrionic talent with voices of sufficient power, and
if a large number had been required, there would have been
great difficulty in meeting the demand.

The original Greek word for an actor was 'hypokrites'.
Etymologically the word seems to have meant 'one who

answers '.[1]   In the times before Aeschylus, when there was only
one actor, all the dialogue was necessarily carried on between
the actor and the chorus.   It is therefore not improbable that
the duty of replying to the questions and remarks of the chorus
may have been regarded as the salient feature in the performance
of the actor, and have given rise to his name, as the old grammarians assert.   In the course of the fourth century the old
Attic word for an actor went out of use, and a new one was
substituted.   Henceforward actors were generally called 'artists ',
or ' artists of Dionysus '.[2]

As far as tragedy is concerned, the art of acting may be said
to have commenced in the time of Thespis.   But actors did not
come into existence as a separate class until many years afterwards.   Before the period of Aeschylus, when only a single
actor was required, his part was taken by the poet.   It is
expressly said that Thespis was 'himself acting, according to
ancient custom ', at that performance which excited the disapproval of Solon.[3]   But when a second actor was introduced
by Aeschylus, then the actor's profession became of necessity
distinct from that of the poet.   For some time afterwards the
poets continued to act occasionally in their own tragedies, side
by side with the professional actors.   But the practice went
gradually out of fashion in the course of the earlier part of the
fifth century.   Aeschylus appears, from the statement in his
Life, to have abandoned the stage even before the introduction
of a second actor.[4]   Sophocles was prevented from appearing
as an actor by the weakness of his voice.   It is true that he

sometimes performed in public. In the Thamyris he played the harp, and in the Nausicaa he delighted the spectators by his skill with the ball. But it is not likely that on either of these occasions he took a regular actor's part. He probably appeared upon the scene merely as a mute character, in order to show his skill with the harp and the ball.[1] After the time of Sophocles there are no further instances of tragic poets performing in their own plays.[2] As to the early history of comic acting very little is known. Cratinus is mentioned as one of the old poets who were called 'dancers', and it is therefore probable that he acted in his own comedies. Crates is said to have begun his career as an actor of Cratinus.[3] But after his time there is no certain instance of a comic poet appearing upon the stage. The professional actor was universally employed. The statement that Aristophanes acted the part of Cleon in the Knights is due to a misconception on the part of the scholiast.[4]

It appears then that it was in the beginning of the fifth century that the profession of the actor came into existence as a distinct occupation. It grew very rapidly in importance. At first the actors who took part in the competitions were regarded as mere subordinates, and had no share in the honours and rewards. But towards the middle of the century a change was made, and prizes began to be instituted for the best actors, as well as for the best poets. The names of the actors began to be recorded in the official lists of victors, side by side with those

[1] Vit. Soph. πρῶτον μὲν καταλύσας τὴν ὑπόκρισιν τοῦ ποιητοῦ διὰ τὴν ἰδίαν μικροφωνίαν ; Athen. p. 20 F ; Eustath. Od. p. 1533.

[2] Müller (Griech. Bühnenalt. p. 184) states, on the authority of Zenob. Prov. v. 100, that Astydamas the Elder acted in his own tragedy, the Parthenopaeus. The words in Zenobius are εὐημερήσας ἐν τῇ ὑποκρίσει Παρθενοπαίου. But this is merely a carelessness of expression, on which no stress can be laid. In the account given by Suidas (s. v. σαυτὴν ἐπαινεῖς) of the same occurrence the expression is εὐημερήσαντι ἐπὶ τραγῳδίας διδασκαλίᾳ Παρθενοπαίου. The Parthenopaeus was really written by Astydamas the Younger. See the Tragic Drama of the Greeks, p. 430.

[3] Athen. p. 22 A ; Schol. Aristoph. Equit. 534.

[4] Vit. Aristoph. p. 34 Dindf.; Arg. ii. Equit. The story arose from a misunderstanding of the phrase καθιέναι τὸ δρᾶμα δι' ἑαυτοῦ. The Knights was the first play Aristophanes produced in his own name. See Meineke, Frag. Com. Gr. ii. 928 ff. Antiphanes is said (Müller, Die griech. Bühnen, p. 184) to have acted one of his own comedies, the evidence being the inscription in Corp. Ins. Att. ii. 972 ['Αντιφάνη]ς πέμ(πτος) 'Ανασῳζο(μένοις)· [ὑπεκρίνετο Ἀντ]ιφάνης. But it is by no means certain that the name of the poet is rightly filled in as Antiphanes. Even if it is, it does not follow that the actor Antiphanes was the same person.

of the poets and choregi.[1] In the fourth century the actors
sprang into still greater prominence. The art of acting tended
to outshine the art of dramatic writing. An age of great actors
succeeded to an age of great poets. The same phenomenon is
not uncommon in the theatrical history of other nations. In
England, for instance, a period of dramatic productiveness
was followed by a period of sterility and insignificance, and
from the time of Garrick downwards the names of the great
actors, who have made themselves famous by interpreting the
masterpieces of Shakespeare, are more conspicuous than the
names of dramatic authors. In Athens the fourth century was
the period when acting was brought to the greatest perfection.
To such an extent had the importance of the actor's profession
increased, that in Aristotle's time a play depended more for
its success upon the skill of the actor than upon the genius of
the poet. The effect upon dramatic writing was most pernicious.
The poets began to write their plays with a view to exhibiting
the capacities of the actors. Scenes which had no connexion
with the plot were introduced for the sole purpose of enabling
an actor to make a display of his talents.[2] Sophocles is said
by one of the old grammarians to have been guilty of the same
sort of practice. But if there is any truth in the statement,
the evil effects are not very apparent in the extant tragedies.[3]
The charge might be brought with more plausibility against the
monodies of Euripides, which are often feeble from a literary
point of view, but would enable an actor with a fine voice to
make a great impression. However, it was not until the fourth
century that the influence of the actors became so universal
as to inflict distinct injury upon the art of dramatic writing.

The selection of the necessary number of actors for each
dramatic performance was, except in very early times, undertaken by the state. The details in connexion with this arrangement have already been discussed in a previous chapter.[4]
The main points may be recapitulated here. During the early
part of the fifth century the poets chose their own actors.
Certain poets and certain actors were permanently associated

[1] See chap. i. p. 44
[2] Aristot. Poet. c. 9 λέγω δ' ἐπεισοδι-
ώδη μῦθον ἐν ᾧ τὰ ἐπεισόδια μετ'
ἄλληλα οὔτ' εἰκὸς οὔτ' ἀνάγκη εἶναι.
τοιαῦται δὲ ποιοῦνται ὑπὸ μὲν τῶν φαύλων
ποιητῶν δι' αὐτούς, ὑπὸ δὲ τῶν ἀγαθῶν
διὰ τοὺς ὑποκριτάς : Rhet. iii. 1 μεῖζον
δύνανται νῦν τῶν ποιητῶν οἱ ὑποκριταί.
[3] Vit. Soph. p. 3 Dindf.
[4] See chap. ii. pp. 57 ff.

together. But as the actors increased in importance, they
were placed on the same footing as the poets and choregi,
and were appointed by the state. They were then distributed
among the poets by lot. In the course of the fourth century
the use of the lot was discontinued in the case of tragedy,
and a new arrangement was adopted, which was rendered
possible by the fact that each tragic poet exhibited several
tragedies at the same time. Under the new system each
tragedy was performed by a different actor, and in this way
all the competing poets enjoyed in turn the services of all
the actors. In comedy, as each poet exhibited only a single
play, the old system of distribution by lot was retained. If
an actor was engaged for one of the great Athenian festivals,
and failed to put in an appearance, he was fined by the state.
On one occasion Athenodorus, the great tragic actor, was hired
to perform at the City Dionysia. But he failed to keep his
engagement, as he preferred to be present and perform at the
festivities held by Alexander the Great in Phoenicia, after his
return from Egypt. A heavy fine was inflicted upon him in
consequence, and was paid by Alexander.[1]

§ 2. *The distribution of the Parts among the Actors.*

It has been shown that the number of the actors in a Greek
play was limited to three. The principal actor was called the
protagonist; next in importance came the deuteragonist; the
tritagonist played the inferior characters.[2] The importance
of the protagonist on the Greek stage has been pointed out
already.[3] In the ordinary theatrical language of the time a
play was said to be 'acted by' the protagonist, as if the other
actors were of no account. The protagonist was publicly appointed by the state, but was allowed to choose the second and
third actors at his own discretion. In the same way the prize
for acting at each festival was confined to the protagonists.
In tragedy more especially the protagonist was a person of the
greatest importance. The whole structure of a Greek tragedy
was designed with the object of fixing the interest upon some
grand central figure. The significance of the other characters

[1] Plut. Alex. p. 681 E.   Leg. § 10 ; Suidas s. v. Σοφοκλῆς.
[2] Plut. Rep. Ger. 817 A; Dem. Fals.   [3] See chap. i. p. 42, ch. ii. p. 57.

consisted mainly in their capacity to excite the passions and
draw forth the sentiments of the leading personage. This
being so, it was essential that the protagonist should concentrate
the interest upon himself; otherwise the harmony and balance
of the play would have been destroyed. Hence the subordinate
actors were strictly forbidden to attempt to outshine the protagonist. Even if they had finer voices than the protagonist,
they were made to moderate and restrain their powers, so as to
allow the protagonist to retain the superiority, and rivet the
attention of the spectators upon the central character.[1] The
jealousy of protagonists towards their fellow-actors is well
exemplified by the story about Theodorus, who had a theory
that the first speaker in a play always attracted the sympa-
thies of the audience, and therefore would never allow any
other actor, however inferior, to appear upon the stage before
himself.[2]

The distribution of the different parts among the actors was
undertaken by the poet if the play was a new one.[3] But if an
old play was being reproduced, the matter would be arranged
by the protagonist who had the management of the performance. The three actors between them filled all the parts in
a play, appearing in various characters successively. Such a
practice was rendered possible by the use of masks. An actor
had only to change his mask and his dress, and he could then

---

[1] Cic. Div. in Caecil. § 48 'ut in
actoribus Graecis fieri videmus, saepe
illum, qui est secundarum aut tertiarum
partium, cum possit aliquanto clarius
dicere quam ipse primarum, multum
summittere, ut ille princeps quam
maxime excellat,' &c.

[2] Aristot. Pol. vii. 17. The story
about Theodorus has caused some difficulty. Does it mean that Theodorus,
besides taking the principal character,
also played the part of the person who
made the first speech in the tragedy?
If so, he would have been debarred
from acting some of the most popular
tragedies of the time. For instance,
the actor who took the part of Electra
in the play of Sophocles could not act
the part of the paedagogus, since
Electra comes on the stage as soon as
the paedagogus leaves it. There would
be the same difficulty about the Orestes,
the Medea, and many other plays. It

has been suggested that the reference
is to some preliminary announcement of
the title of the play, which Theodorus
preferred to make himself, instead of
leaving it to a subordinate. Such
announcements were made in Greek
theatres in later times (cp. Lucian,
Pseudolog. 19; Heliod. Aethiop. viii.
17; Synesius, περὶ προνοίας, p. 128 D),
and may have been customary in Athens,
or in other parts of Greece, in the time
of Theodorus. But it is extremely improbable that the reference is to any
such practice. The audience would
hardly pay much attention to the voice
of the person who announced the name
of the coming play. The meaning is
probably that Theodorus used to take
the part of the character which spoke
first, whenever it was possible to do so.
In such plays as the Electra it would be
impossible.

[3] Alciphron, Epist. iii. 71.

reappear in a new character. Changes of this kind could be
effected in a very few moments, as is shown by the one or
two traditions on the subject which have been preserved by
the ancient scholiasts. For example, in the opening scene
of the Phoenissae Jocasta speaks the prologue, and then
leaves the stage. Thereupon Antigone and an old attendant
mount by a staircase on to the roof of the palace, in order to
view the Argive army encamped outside the walls. The scholiast tells us that the protagonist played the parts both of
Jocasta and of Antigone. It was necessary, therefore, after
Jocasta had left the stage, that there should be a slight interval
before Antigone appeared upon the palace roof, to give the
actor time to change his mask and dress. Euripides managed
this by making the attendant come out alone upon the roof
at first, and look about him to see that the coast is clear, while
he addresses a few words to Antigone, who is still inside the
palace. When he sees that all is safe, he calls on Antigone to
follow after him, and she thereupon mounts the staircase, and
appears to the spectators. The speech of the attendant, while
he is looking about upon the roof, consists of only fifteen iambic
lines. Thus the space of time required to speak fifteen lines
was enough to enable an actor to change from one character to
another.[1] There is a further instance which shows that even
less time was necessary. In the Choephori, when Aegisthus is
murdered, a servant rushes out upon the stage and calls to
Clytaemnestra. As Clytaemnestra comes out, he apparently
runs back into the palace. Clytaemnestra speaks five lines, and
then Orestes hastens out of the palace, followed by Pylades.
In the scene which ensues Pylades has three lines to
speak; and the scholiast says that his part was taken by the
servant who had just left the stage, so as to avoid the necessity
of four actors. The servant must therefore have changed his
mask in a very few moments.[2]

In the distribution of parts the protagonist took the principal
character. The parts of Oedipus, Electra, and Antigone, in
the plays of the same name by Sophocles, are specially
mentioned as having been acted by celebrated protagonists.
Orestes in the play of Euripides is also described as the part

[1] Schol. Eur. Phoen. 93.   [2] Schol. Aesch. Choeph. 900.

of the protagonist.[1] Usually, as in the above instances, the
chief personage gave the name to the piece. But this was
not always the case. In the Oenomaus of Sophocles the part
of Oenomaus was played by the tritagonist Aeschines. In the
Cresphontes of Euripides the principal character was Merope,
and was taken by Theodorus. The part of Cresphontes fell
to Aeschines as tritagonist.[2] In the Agamemnon of Aeschylus
most likely the protagonist played the part of Clytaemnestra, as
this is certainly the most impressive character in the play,
though not the one with which the spectators are in sympathy.
The protagonist had also to take his share of the subordinate
characters when he could be spared. It has already been mentioned that in the Phoenissae of Euripides the protagonist
appeared in the part of Antigone as well as in that of Jocasta.
At times he took even the smallest characters if the necessities
of the play demanded it. Plutarch states that the protagonist,
in the part of a messenger or an attendant, often gained more
applause than the actor who bore the sceptre and the crown.[3]
It was, in fact, the chief advantage of the Greek system that
even the subordinate characters were played with as much
excellence as the more important ones. The tritagonist took
what in modern times would be called the 'heavy' parts. It
was his special privilege, as Demosthenes remarks, to play the
tyrant and the sceptred monarch.[4] Aeschines, in his career as
tritagonist, often had to act gloomy tyrants of this kind, such as
Creon, Cresphontes, and Oenomaus. Such characters did not
require great powers in the actor. There was no pathos to be
excited, no play of conflicting emotions to be exhibited. All
that was necessary was a powerful voice, and a capacity for
declaiming verses. Most likely for the same reason the tritagonist usually spoke the prologues, which also did not require
much more in the actor than good powers of elocution. Thus
the ghost of Polydorus, which speaks the prologue in the
Hecuba of Euripides, was acted by Aeschines as tritagonist.[5]

[1] Aul. Gell. vii. 5; Stob. Flor. 97.
28; Dem. Fals. Leg. § 246; Strattis ap.
Kock, Frag. Com. Gr. i. p. 711.
[2] Hesych. s. v. ἀρουραῖος Οἰνόμαος;
Dem. de Cor. § 180; Aelian, Var. Hist.
xiv. 40.
[3] Plut. Lysand. p. 466 D.
[4] Dem. Fals. Leg. § 247.

[5] Dem. l. c., de Cor. §§ 180, 267.
[Devrient, Das Kind auf der antiken
Bühne, thinks that the words spoken
by children in the Alcestis, Andromache, &c., were declaimed by the
tritagonist from behind the stage,
while a real child appeared on the
stage and went through the gestures.]

The deuteragonist took the parts which, in point of interest, were intermediate between the leading characters and the heavy parts which fell to the tritagonist. There are not, however, any traditions as to particular characters having been played by the deuteragonist. Attempts have been made in modern times to assign the characters in the extant Greek dramas to the protagonist, deuteragonist, and tritagonist respectively.[1] Such speculations are interesting, in so far as they show that all the existing plays could be perfectly well performed by three actors. Otherwise they are not of very great value. There is generally no difficulty in deciding which was the leading character. But it is obvious that the subordinate parts might be distributed in various ways; and no doubt the arrangement differed at different periods. There are no traditions on the subject in addition to those already mentioned. Any attempt, therefore, to reproduce the exact arrangement adopted at a particular period must depend more or less upon conjecture.

§ 3. *Extra Performers.*

For every Greek play a chorus was provided by the choregus, and three actors were supplied by the state. But in most plays a certain number of additional performers was required. The parts which these extra performers had to fill may be divided, roughly speaking, into three classes. In the first place there were the various mute personages, who simply appeared upon the stage, and did nothing more. The second class consisted of minor characters with only a few words to say. In these cases extra performers were required, either because the regular actors were already occupied, or because the part was that of a boy or girl, which the regular actor would be unable to take. Thirdly, in many cases a small subordinate chorus was required, in addition to the ordinary one. The general name for the persons who undertook these parts was 'parachoregemata'.[2] This word obviously means something

---

[1] K. F. Hermann, De distributione personarum in trag. graec., 1842; Richter, Die Vertheilung der Rollen der griech. Tragödie, 1842 ; Croiset, Histoire de la Litt. grecq., iii. passim.

[2] As there is some doubt about the meaning of the word παραχορήγημα, it will be well to quote the passages where it occurs. They are (1) Schol. Aesch. Prom. 12 ἐν παραχορηγήματι αὐτῷ

which is supplied by the choregus in addition to his ordinary expenditure. It follows, therefore, that the cost of the extra performers was borne by the choregus. Properly he was only responsible for the chorus; but if additional men were required, he had to supply them. This conclusion is confirmed by Plutarch's story of a certain tragic actor who was going to appear as a queen, but refused to proceed with the part, unless the choregus provided him with a train of female attendants.[1] Extra performers were especially necessary in the Old Comedy, in which a great number of characters appear upon the stage.

It remains to consider more in detail the three classes of 'parachoregemata'[2]. The mute personages appeared most frequently in the shape of attendants, body-guards, crowds of people, and so on. The Oedipus Rex opens with a number of suppliants kneeling at the altar before the palace of the king. In the Choephori Orestes and Pylades are accompanied by attendants. The judgement scene in the Eumenides requires twelve performers to play the parts of the members of the Areopagus. In the Agamemnon, when the king and Cassandra arrive in the chariot, servants stand ready to spread carpets

εἰδωλοποιηθεῖσα Βία. (2) Schol. Aesch. Eum. 573 ἐν παραχορηγήματι αὐτῷ εἰσιν οἱ Ἀρεοπαγῖται μηδαμοῦ διαλεγόμενοι. (3) Schol. Aristoph. Ran. 211 ταῦτα καλεῖται παραχορηγήματα, ἐπειδὴ οὐχ ὁρῶνται ἐν τῷ θεάτρῳ οἱ βάτραχοι, οὐδὲ ὁ χορός, ἀλλ' ἔσωθεν μιμοῦνται τοὺς βατράχους; ὁ δὲ ἀληθῶς χορὸς ἐκ τῶν εὐσεβῶν νεκρῶν συνέστηκεν. (4) Schol. Aristoph. Pax 113 τὰ τοιαῦτα παραχορηγήματα καλοῦσιν, οἷα νῦν τὰ παιδία ποιεῖ καλοῦντα τὸν πατέρα· εἶτα πρὸς οὐδὲν ἔτι τούτοις χρήσεται. (5) Poll. iv. 109 ὁπότε μὴν ἀντὶ τετάρτου ὑποκριτοῦ δέοι τινὰ τῶν χορευτῶν εἰπεῖν ἐν ᾠδῇ, παρασκήνιον καλεῖται τὸ πρᾶγμα, ὡς ἐν Ἀγαμέμνονι Αἰσχύλου· εἰ δὲ τέταρτος ὑποκριτής τι παραφθέγξαιτο, τοῦτο παραχορήγημα ὀνομάζεται, καὶ πεπρᾶχθαί φασιν αὐτὸ ἐν Μέμνονι Αἰσχύλου. The first and second instances refer to mute personages, the third instance refers to an extra chorus, the fourth to extra performers who say only a few words upon the stage. It is therefore quite clear that the word παραχορήγημα included all classes of extra performers, as distinct from the actors and the chorus. There are no grounds for ex-

cluding the mute personages from the class of παραχορηγήματα, as Müller (Griech. Bühnenalt. p. 179) and others have done. Pollux appears to make the distinction between παρασκήνιον and παραχορήγημα lie in the fact that the former sang, the latter spoke. The distinction is a foolish one, and was probably due to Pollux's habit of generalizing from one particular instance. The word παρασκήνιον, in its present sense, only occurs in the passage of Pollux. To judge from the etymology of the word, it may have denoted performers behind the scenes. The words ἐν Ἀγαμέμνονι Αἰσχύλου in the passage of Pollux are corrupt, the corruption arising from the words ἐν Μέμνονι Αἰσχύλου which follow. There is no παρασκήνιον in the Agamemnon. The reference cannot be to the speech of Pylades in the Choephori (vv. 900–902), because (1) the Choephori could not be called the Agamemnon, (2) the part of Pylades was taken by one of the regular actors, as the scholiast ad loc. informs us.

[1] Plut. Phocion, p. 750 C.
[2] See note 2 on the previous page.

beneath their feet.[1] Probably in many other instances great
personages were accompanied by attendants, although there is
no special reference to them in the play. Not infrequently more
prominent characters appeared upon the stage as mute figures.
Pylades says nothing throughout the Electra of Sophocles and
the Electra of Euripides. In the latter play one of the Dioscuri
must also have been a dumb figure, since two actors were already
upon the stage when the Dioscuri make their appearance. The
person of Force in the Prometheus Vinctus is another example.
A very frequent occasion for the employment of mute characters was in pathetic scenes between parents and their
children. The children appear as silent figures, but give
occasion for touching speeches by their parents. There is
an example in the Ajax of Sophocles, where Ajax addresses
his son Eurysaces. But the instances in Euripides are much
more frequent. There is the celebrated scene in the Medea,
where Medea half relents at the sight of her children. There
is the address of Megara to her children in the Hercules
Furens. Other examples are to be found in the introduction
of Manto, the daughter of Teiresias, in the Phoenissae, and of
Polymestor's children in the Hecuba.[2] Mute figures were
also very useful in occasionally personating one of the regular
characters of the play, when the actor of the character was temporarily required for another purpose. It has already been
pointed out that in the middle of the Oedipus Coloneus the part
of Ismene is played by a dumb personage, to enable the previous
actor of the part to appear in another character. In the final
scene of Orestes, most of the prominent characters are brought
upon the stage together, after the fashion of a modern drama.
But only three of them can speak : Helen, Hermione, Electra,
and Pylades are all mute figures. The silence of Pylades is
especially unnatural. In cases of this kind an attempt is made
to produce effects which were hardly compatible with the limited
resources of Greek tragedy.

The second class of extra performers took all those minor
parts in which there was a certain amount of speaking or
singing, but which it was impossible for the regular actors to
take. In tragedy such performers were mostly required for

---

[1] Aesch. Choeph. 713, Eum. 678 ff.,   [2] Soph. Aj. 544 ; Eur. Med. 1021, Herc.
Agam. 908.   Fur. 454, Phoen. 834, Hecub. 978.

the boys' parts, which were unsuitable for grown-up actors.
Euripides was especially fond of introducing boys upon the
stage. In the Alcestis Eumelus bewails his mother's death in a
short ode. Another example is the mournful dialogue between
Andromache and her little son Molossus.[1] In the Old Comedy
these additional actors were frequently needed to perform small
parts at times when the three regular actors were already
on the stage. Examples are very numerous. There are the
daughters of Trygaeus in the Peace, and the daughters of the
Megarian in the Acharnians. The herald and Pseudartabas
are additional examples from the Acharnians.[2]

In the third place an extra chorus was sometimes required.
The Propompi in the Eumenides, and the chorus of boys in the
Wasps, both appear side by side with the regular chorus, and
must therefore have been personated by extra performers.
An additional chorus, consisting of shepherds, was also required in the Alexander of Euripides.[3] Sometimes the extra
chorus was not visible to the spectators, but sang behind the
scenes. In such cases the singing might be done by members
of the regular chorus, if they had not yet entered the orchestra.
Examples are to be found in the chorus of frogs in the Frogs
of Aristophanes, and Agathon's chorus in the Thesmophoriazusae.[4] Their part would be taken by members of the regular
chorus. In the opening scene of the Hippolytus a band of
huntsmen sing a short ode to Artemis upon the stage. Immediately after their disappearance the regular chorus, consisting
of women of Troezen, enters the orchestra. In this case the
huntsmen cannot have been personated by members of the
regular chorus; but it is possible that the singing was done by
the chorus behind the scenes, while the huntsmen were represented by mute figures.[5]

§ 4. *Costume of the Tragic Actors.*

The dress of the actors in tragedy was always entirely distinct
from that of the chorus. The chorus consisted originally of satyrs,

---

[1] Eur. Alc. 393, Androm. 504.
[2] Aristoph. Pax 114, Acharn. 43,
94, 729.
[3] Aesch. Eum. 1032; Aristoph. Vesp.
248; Schol. Eur. Hipp. 58.
[4] Aristoph. Ran. 209, Thesm. 104.
[5] Eur. Hipp. 61.

the half-human followers of Dionysus. Later on it came to be composed in most cases of ordinary citizens, and was dressed accordingly. But the actors represented from the first the gods and heroes of the old mythology. For them a different costume was required. The practice of the Greeks in regard to this costume was totally opposed to all modern notions upon the subject. Historical accuracy and archaeological minuteness in the mounting of a play were matters of complete indifference to the Greeks. Accordingly, when bringing these heroic characters upon the stage, they never made any attempt to produce an accurate imitation of the costume of the Homeric period. At the same time they were not content that the heroes and gods of their tragedy should appear upon the scene in the garments of ordinary life. Such an arrangement would have been inconsistent with the ideal character of Greek tragedy. A special dress was therefore employed, similar to that of common life, but more flowing and dignified. The garments were dyed with every variety of brilliant colour. The bulk of the actor was increased by padding his chest and limbs, and placing huge wooden soles under his feet. Masks were employed in which every feature was exaggerated, to give superhuman dignity and terror to the expression. In this way a conventional costume was elaborated, which continued for centuries to be the regular dress of the tragic actors. All the leading characters in a Greek tragedy were dressed in this fashion, with only such slight variations and additions as the particular case required.

The origin of this tragic costume is a subject about which very little is known. According to the later Greek tradition it was invented almost entirely by Aeschylus.[1] But this is probably an exaggeration. Aeschylus was no doubt mainly instrumental in developing and improving the costume, and giving it a definite shape. But that the whole idea of it was his own creation is hardly credible. Most likely it had existed, though in a less elaborate form, long before his time. As for its origin, the most plausible view seems to be that it was derived from the old traditional garb of the Bacchic cultus, worn by Dionysus

---

[1] Athen. p. 21 E; Hor. A. P. 278; Philostrat. vit. Apoll. vi. 11; Cramer, Anecd. Par. i. p. 19; Evanth. de trag. et com. (Gronov. Thesaur. viii. p. 1683); Suidas s. v. Αἰσχύλος.

himself and by his chief attendants.[1] Several indications point
in this direction. In early works of art Dionysus and his
followers often appear in a long flowing robe, not unlike that
of the tragic stage. They also wear a tall hunting boot, which
was sometimes called the cothurnus, and which may have been
the prototype from which the tragic cothurnus was developed.
The custom of disguising the features with a mask or some
similar device was always a regular institution in the mum-
meries connected with the Bacchic worship. The old comic
actors, before the invention of the theatrical mask, used to smear
their faces with wine, or cover them with fig-leaves. Masks
were regularly worn in the processions of Dionysus down to the
latest times. The Latin peasantry, at their Bacchic festivals,
used to cover their faces with masks made out of the bark of
trees.[2] All these facts are in favour of the conclusion that the
tragic dress, with its mask, its cothurnus, and its flowing robe,
was not so much the invention of the fifth century as a development from the old festal costume.[3] This theory has also the
advantage of ascribing a parallel origin to the dresses of the
chorus and those of the actors. While the chorus, in the older
drama, appeared in the guise of satyrs or rustic votaries of
Dionysus, the actors, whose part was more dignified, assumed
the garb of Dionysus himself and of his chief attendants. One
ancient tradition asserts that the tragic dress was copied in
later times by the hierophants and torch-bearers at the
Eleusinian mysteries.[4] Some scholars have twisted this

[1] See Crusius, Philologus, 1889,
p. 703.

[2] Schol. Aristoph. Nub. 296 ; Suidas
s.v. θρίαμβος; Plut. Cupid. Divit. 527 D;
Verg. Georg. ii. 387.

[3] Bethe (Prolegomena, pp. 35-46)
finds an additional proof of this theory
in the Bologna vase (cp. Dümmler,
Rhein. Museum, 1888, p. 355). In this
vase Dionysus is represented sitting in
a boat-shaped car, with a satyr playing
a flute on each side of him. The car
is drawn by two satyrs, and two others
are leading an ox. A boy and four
women follow behind. Bethe thinks
this scene was part of an old tragic
performance ; that the single actor of
the period always played the part of
Dionysus, and therefore naturally wore

his costume. He also thinks the car
was the prototype of the later stage,
and is identical with the wagons in
which Thespis is said to have carried
about his tragedies (Hor. A. P. 276).
Unfortunately for these theories there
is nothing to show that the procession
depicted on the vase had any connexion
with a dramatic performance. Such
processions with Dionysus in a boat-
shaped car are known to have existed
in other parts of Greece (Philostrat. vit.
Soph. i. 25 ; cp. Crusius, Philologus,
1889, p. 209); and though interesting
as illustrations of the Bacchic mythology, they throw no light on the early
history of the drama.

[4] Athen. p. 21 E.

tradition round, and suggested that it was from the hierophants and torch-bearers that the first notion of the tragic dress was borrowed. But neither view can be regarded as probable. That the two costumes were not dissimilar seems to be proved by the existence of the tradition referred to. But it is unlikely that the garb used at the performances in honour of one deity should have been borrowed from the cultus of another. The resemblance may be better explained by the supposition that both costumes were ancient religious dresses, used in the worship of Dionysus and Demeter respectively.

Whatever may have been the origin of the tragic costume, there is no doubt that the form of it which eventually prevailed upon the Greek stage dates from the time of Aeschylus. His creative genius revolutionized every department of Greek tragedy. It was he who transformed it into an essentially dramatic species of art, and gave it the characteristics of grandeur and terror. It was necessary to make a corresponding improvement in the dresses of the actors, and this reform also was effected by Aeschylus. The type of costume which he gradually developed was so well adapted to its purpose, that it continued unchanged in its principal characteristics throughout the remaining history of Greek tragedy. Subsequent generations, while making various small additions and alterations, never altogether abandoned the original design. Our knowledge of the subject is derived partly from the descriptions of Pollux and others, partly from works of art. Few of these works, unfortunately, are of early date. There is the Naples vase, belonging to the end of the fifth century, and depicting the performers in a satyric play. The two actors who take the heroic parts in this performance (Fig. 22) are dressed more or less closely in the tragic style. There is also a votive relief (Fig. 15) from the Peiraeeus, of the early fourth century, in which three tragic actors are depicted in stage costume, two of them with their masks in their hands.[1] But the work in this relief is so bare and devoid of detail, that it adds little to our knowledge. The Andromeda vase, of the same date, exhibits Andromeda chained to a rock, with Perseus and other figures on each side of her, and dressed in a costume which was evidently suggested

[1] See, on the subject of this relief, Robert, Athen. Mittheil. 1882, pp. 389 ff.

by that of tragedy, though it is not a complete theatrical dress.[1]
Numerous vases from Magna Graecia, belonging mostly to the
fourth century, represent scenes out of tragedies.[2] But these
too are not portrayed as theatrical scenes; and the costumes
of the characters, though often resembling those of the tragic
stage, cannot be regarded as regular actors' costumes. Still,
all these paintings are valuable, as exhibiting in a general way
some of the main features of the tragic dress. Apart from
examples of the above kind, the works of art on which we have
to depend are all of late date, and mostly of Italian origin.[3]
But Greek tragedies were commonly performed in Italy even in
imperial times; and Roman tragedy was in all respects a mere
reproduction of the Greek. Hence delineations of tragic scenes

FIG. 15.

and figures, though Italian in origin, present the characteristics
of the Greek stage. It would be unsafe to depend upon them
for points of minute detail. But they correspond in the main
with the descriptions of Pollux, and it is possible to obtain from
them a fairly trustworthy picture of the general appearance of
the Greek actors. The accompanying figure of a tragic actor

[1] See Bethe, Jahrb. des Archaeol.
Instituts, 1896, pp. 292 ff., and pl. 2.
[2] See especially the Medea vase
(Baumeister, Denkmäler, no. 980).
Copies of many of these vases are
given by Huddilston, in Greek Tragedy
in the Light of Vase-Paintings, 1898.
[3] A list of them will be found in
Müller, Griech. Bühnenalt. p. 226.

(Fig. 16) is copied from an ivory statuette found in the ruins
of a villa near Rieti.[1] On comparing together these various
representations, which range in date over a period of five or six
hundred years, it is interesting to find that they all bear a strong
family resemblance to one another. The pictures of the tragic
actor, whether found on Greek vases, Etruscan mosaics, or
wall-paintings of Cyrene and Pompeii, obviously belong to one
common type. In spite of considerable differences in point of
detail they portray the same general conception. This fact
confirms the ancient tradition, that the costume of the tragic
stage, in all its more important features, was definitely settled
by Aeschylus in the course of the fifth century.

The contrast between the ancient and the modern actor is
marked by nothing so conspicuously as by the use of masks.
These masks, or similar devices, were a regular feature in the
old Dionysiac worship, and were probably inherited as such
by the tragic stage, and not invented of set purpose. With the
growth of tragedy they soon acquired a new character. Thespis,
the earliest of tragic actors, is said at the commencement of
his career to have merely painted his face with white lead
or purslane. Later on he employed masks; but these were
of a very simple character, consisting merely of linen, without
paint or colouring. Choerilus introduced certain improvements
which are not specified. Phrynichus set the example of using
female masks.[2] Aeschylus was the first to employ painted
masks, and to portray features of a dreadful and awe-inspiring
character. Though not the inventor of the tragic mask, as
some ancient writers assert, he was the first to give it that
distinctive character from which in later times it never varied
except in detail.[3] After the time of Aeschylus there is no
further mention of any radical alterations or improvements in
the manufacture of masks.

The use of masks is indissolubly connected with the style
and character of Greek tragedy. It is said to have added
resonance to the actor's voice; and this was a point of great
importance in the vast theatres of the ancients.[4] Also without

[1] From Monumenti Inediti, xi. 13.
[2] Suidas s. vv. Θέσπις, Χοιρίλος, Φρύνιχος.
[3] Suidas s. v. Αἰσχύλος; Hor. A. P.
278; Evanth. de trag. et com. (Gronov. Thesaur. viii. p. 1683).
[4] Aul. Gell. v. 7.

Fig. 16.

R 2

masks it would have been impossible for one actor to play
several parts, or for men to play the parts of women. At the
same time the practice had its inconvenient side. The Greek
actor was deprived of any opportunity for displaying those
powers of facial expression which are one of the chief excel-
lences in modern acting. It was only by his gestures that he
could emphasize the meaning of what he had to say: his
features remained immovable. But niceties of facial expression would have been scarcely visible in the huge expanse of
a Greek theatre. The tragic mask, on which were depicted in
bold and striking lines the main traits in the character represented, was really much more effective, and could be seen by
the most distant spectator. Then again it must have been
difficult, if not impossible, for a Greek actor to delineate finely
drawn shades of individual character. The masks necessarily
ran in general types, such as that of the brutal tyrant, the
crafty statesman, the suffering maiden, and so on. The acting
would have to correspond. It would be difficult to imagine the
part of Hamlet acted in a mask. But the characters of Greek
tragedy were mostly types rather than individuals. The heroes
and heroines were drawn in broad general outlines, and there
was little attempt at delicate strokes of character-painting. The
use of masks no doubt helped to give this particular bent to
Greek tragedy.

Masks were generally made of linen. Cork and wood were
occasionally used.[1] The mask covered the whole of the head,
both in front and behind.[2] Caps were often worn underneath,
to serve as a protection.[3] The white of the eye was painted on
the mask, but the place for the pupil was left hollow, to enable
the actor to see.[4] The expression of the tragic mask was
gloomy and often fierce; the mouth was opened wide, to give a
clear outlet to the actor's voice. One of the most characteristic
features of the tragic mask was the onkos,[5] a cone-shaped
prolongation of the upper part of the mask above the forehead,
intended to give size and impressiveness to the face, and used
where dignity was to be imparted. It varied in size according

---

[1] Poll. x. 167; Isidor. Orig. x. 119;
Suidas s. v. Θέσπις; Verg. Georg. ii.
387; Prudent. c. Symmach. ii. 646.
[2] Aul. Gell. v. 7.

[3] Schol. Dem. Fals. Leg. § 256.
See fig. 23.
[4] Wieseler, Denkmäler, p. 42.
[5] Poll. iv. 133–5, 139.

to the character of the personage.   The onkos of the tyrant was especially large; that of women was less than that of men. A character was not necessarily represented by the same mask throughout the piece.   The effects of misfortune or of accident had often to be depicted by a fresh mask.   For instance, in the Helen of Euripides Helen returns upon the stage with her hair shorn off, and her cheeks pale with weeping.   Oedipus, at the end of the Oedipus Tyrannus of Sophocles, is seen with blinded eyes and blood-stained face.   In such cases a change of mask must have been necessary.   There are a few occasions in the extant tragedies where a change of facial expression seems to be demanded by the circumstances, but was rendered impossible by the mask.   Thus in the Electra of Sophocles, the heroine is unable to show her joy at her brother's return, and the poet has to get over this as best he can.   He makes Orestes bid her show no signs of joy for fear of arousing suspicion, while she declares that there is no risk of this, for hatred of her mother has become too engrained in her for her expression to change suddenly, and her joy itself will bring tears and not laughter.[1]

The number and variety of the masks used in tragedy may be seen from the accounts in Pollux.   For the ordinary tragic personages there were regular masks of a stereotyped character.   Pollux enumerates twenty-eight kinds.[2]   His information was derived from Alexandrian sources, and his list represents the number of masks which were employed on the later Greek stage for the ordinary characters of tragedy. It is not likely that in the time of Sophocles or Euripides the use of masks was reduced so completely to a system as in the later period; but the descriptions in Pollux will give an adequate idea of the style of the masks used in earlier times. Of the twenty-eight masks described by Pollux six are for old men, eight for young men, three for attendants, and eleven for women.   The principal features by which the different masks are discriminated from one another are the style of the hair, the colour of the complexion, the height of the onkos, and the expression of the eyes.   To take a few examples.   The strong

---

[1] [Soph. El. 1296 ff. Other cases are Aesch. Eum. 968 990) and Eur. Orest. 1317. Cf. Hense, Die Modificirung der Maske in der griech. Tragödie, ed. ii (1905), where the various cases in which a change of mask is certain or suspected are discussed.]

[2] Poll. iv. 133-41.

and powerful man, such as the tyrant, has thick black hair and
beard, a tall onkos, and a frown upon his brow. The man
wasted by disease has fair hair, a pale complexion, and a smaller
onkos. The handsome youth has fair ringlets, a light complexion, and bright eyes. The lover is distinguished by black
hair and a pale complexion. The maiden in misfortune has her
hair cut short in token of sorrow. The aged lady has white
hair and a small onkos, and her complexion is rather pale.
Attendants and messengers are marked by special characteristics. One of them wears a cap, another has a peaked beard,
a third has a snub nose and hair drawn back. One sees from
these examples how completely Greek tragedy was dominated

Fig. 17.

by conventional rules, in this as in all other respects. As soon
as a personage entered the stage, his mask alone was enough
to give the spectators a very fair conception of his character
and position.

The twenty-eight tragic masks enumerated by Pollux were
used for the ordinary characters of tragedy, and formed a
regular part of the stock of the Greek stage-manager. But
special masks were required when any unusual character was
introduced. Pollux gives a long list of such masks.[1] In the
first place there were numbers of mythological beings with
strange attributes. Actaeon had to be represented with horns,
Argo with a multitude of eyes. Evippe in the play of Euripides

[1] Poll. iv. 141, 142. Special masks were called ἔκσκενα πρόσωπα.

had the head of a mare. A special mask of this kind must have
been required to depict Io with the ox-horns in the Prometheus
Vinctus of Aeschylus.   A second class of special masks was
needed to represent allegorical figures such as Justice, Per-
suasion, Deceit, Jealousy. Of this kind are the figures of
Death in the Alcestis of Euripides, and Frenzy in the Hercules
Furens.   Lastly, there were personifications of cities, rivers,
and mountains. Five specimens of ancient tragic masks are
given in figs. 17, 18. The first is the mask of a youth,
the fifth that of a man; the second and third are probably

FIG. 18.

masks of women. The fourth is an example of one of the
special masks, and depicts Perseus with the cap of darkness
upon his head.[1]

We come now to the dress of the tragic actors. Nothing
is known as to the appearance of this dress in the time of
Thespis and his immediate successors. Our information refers
solely to the tragic costume as modified and developed by

[1] The masks in fig. 17 are copied from
Wieseler, Denkmäler, v. 20, 24, 26.
The first is a marble, the second and
third are from wall-paintings at Herculaneum. The masks in fig. 18 are
copied from the Archaeol. Zeitung for
1878. They are from wall-paintings at
Pompeii. For a list of the various works
of art illustrating the subject see Müller,
Griech. Bühnenalt. p. 273.

Aeschylus in the course of the fifth century. The object of
Aeschylus in these innovations was to add fresh splendour
to the costume, and make it worthy of the colossal beings
by which his stage was peopled. For this purpose he
employed various devices. Among these was the cothurnus, or
tragic boot, which was intended to increase the stature of the
actors, and to give them an appearance of superhuman grandeur.
It was a boot with a wooden sole of enormous thickness attached
to it. The wooden sole was painted in various colours.[1] According to some grammarians Aeschylus invented the boot
altogether;[2] others say his innovation consisted merely in
giving increased thickness to the sole, and so raising the height
of the actors.[3] This latter view is probably the correct one.
The original of the cothurnus, as already remarked, may very
likely have been the hunting boot of the same name worn by
Dionysius, which was a boot reaching high up the calf, but with
soles of ordinary size. After the time of Aeschylus the tragic
cothurnus continued to be a regular feature in theatrical costume
down to the latest period of Greek and Roman tragedy.[4] It
varied in height according to the dignity and position of the
wearers, a king, for instance, being provided with a larger
cothurnus than a mere attendant. In this way the physical
stature of the persons upon the stage was made to correspond
to their social position. In the accompanying illustration
(Fig. 19), representing a tragic scene, the difference between
the cothurnus of the servant and that of the hero is very
conspicuous.[5] Whether the cothurnus was worn by all the
characters in a tragedy, or only by the more important ones, is
uncertain. There was another tragic boot called the 'krepis',
of a white colour, which was introduced by Sophocles, and used

---

[1] The name for the tragic boot in
Greek was ἐμβάτης (Suid. s.v. Αἰσχύλος),
ὀκρίβας (Lucian, Nero c. 9), or κόθορνος
(vit. Aesch.). Cothurnus was the
regular name in Latin. Pollux (iv.
115) appears to be mistaken in calling
ἐμβάτης the comic boot, in opposition
to the notices in other grammarians.
The sole of the cothurnus was of wood,
as appears from Schol. Lucian, Epist.
Saturn. 19. Works of art show that
it was painted : see Wieseler, Denkmäler, vii, viii ; and cp. Ovid. Am. ii.

18. 15 'risit Amor pallamque meam
pictosque cothurnos'.
[2] Suidas s.v. Αἰσχύλος; Aristot. apud
Themist. or. xxvi. p. 316; Philostrat.,
vit. Apoll. vi. 11 ; Porphyr. on Hor.
A. P. 278.
[3] Vit. Aesch. p. 7 Dindf.
[4] Lucian, Nero c. 9, Necyom. c. 16,
Iupp. Trag. c. 41, de Salt. c. 27 ; Mar-
tial, viii. 3, 13, &c.
[5] The illustration is from Wieseler,
Denkmäler, ix. 1. The original is a
wall-painting from Pompeii.

by the chorus as well as by the actors.   Possibly this may have
been a boot more like those of ordinary life than the cothurnus,
and may have been worn by the subordinate characters.[1]   The
illustrations show that the cothurnus was rather a clumsy
contrivance, and that it must have been somewhat inconvenient
to walk with.   The tragic actor had to be very careful to
avoid stumbling upon the stage.   Lucian says that accidents
were not infrequent.   Aeschines met with a misfortune of this
kind as he was acting the part of Oenomaus at Collytus.   In
the scene where Oenomaus pursues Pelops he tripped up and

Fig. 19.

fell, and had to be lifted up again by the chorus-trainer Sannio.[2]
The use of the cothurnus, combined with the onkos, or prolongation of the crown of the mask, added greatly to the stature
of the tragic actor.   To prevent his seeming thin in comparison
with his height, it was found necessary to increase his bulk
by padding.   His figure was thus made to appear of uniformly
large proportions.[3]

[1] Vit. Soph. p. 2 Dindf.
[2] Lucian, Somnium vel Gallus 26;
vit. Aeschin.

[3] Phot. s. v. σωμάτια ; Lucian, de
Salt. 27.

The garments of the tragic actor were the same as the ordinary Greek dress, but their style and colour were more magnificent. They consisted of an under-garment or tunic, and an over-garment or mantle. The tunic was brilliantly variegated in colour. Sometimes it was adorned with stripes, at other times with the figures of animals and flowers, or similar ornamentation. A special tunic of purple was worn by queens. The ordinary tragic tunic reached down to the feet. But the tunics worn by females upon the stage were sometimes longer than those worn by men, and trailed upon the ground, as the name 'syrtos' implies. On the other hand, it appears from various illustrations that shorter ones were occasionally provided for attendants and other minor characters. The tunic of the tragic actor was fastened with a broad girdle high up under the breast, and flowed down in long and graceful folds, giving an appearance of height and dignity. It was also supplied with long sleeves reaching to the waist. In ordinary life sleeves of this kind were considered effeminate by the European Greeks, and were mostly confined to the Greeks of Asia. The general character and appearance of the tragic tunic is well exemplified in the illustrations already given.[1]

The over-garments were the same in shape as those worn off the stage, and consisted of two varieties. The 'himation' was a long mantle passing round the right shoulder, and covering the greater part of the body. The 'chlamys' was a short cloak flung across the left shoulder. As far as shape was concerned all the tragic mantles belonged to one or the other of these two classes, but they differed in colour and material. Pollux gives a list of several of them, but does not append any description.[2] The mere names prove that they were very gorgeous in colour. There were mantles of saffron, of frog-green, of gold, and of purple. Queens wore a white mantle with purple borders. These were the colours worn by tragic personages under ordinary circumstances. But if they were in misfortune or in exile, the fact was signified

[1] For the general account of the χιτών or tunic see Pollux iv. 115-18. The epithet ποικίλον shows that it was brilliantly coloured. As to the length of the tunic see Lucian, Iupp. Trag. c. 41, Eustath. Il. p. 954. 47, and the works of art referred to on pp. 240, 241. For the ornamentation and the girdle see the same works of art. The sleeves were called χειρίδες (vit. Aesch. p. 6 Dindf.; Lucian, Iupp. Trag. c. 41).
[2] Poll. iv. 116-18.

to the spectators from the very first by dressing them in the garb of mourning. In such cases the colours used were black, dun, grey, yellow, or dirty white.

Coverings for the head were not usually worn by the Greeks except when they were on a journey. The same practice was observed upon the stage. Thus in the Oedipus Coloneus, Ismene arrives from Thebes wearing a 'Thessalian hat'. Ladies also wore a 'mitra', or band for binding the hair. In the scene in the Bacchae, where Pentheus is dressed up as a female, one of the articles mentioned is the hair-band.[1]

Such was the tragic costume as settled by Aeschylus, and universally adopted upon the Greek stage. No stress was laid upon historical accuracy; no attempt was made to discriminate one rank from another by marked variety in the dress. The same garb in its main features was worn by nearly all the characters of a Greek tragedy. In some instances special costumes were invented for particular classes of men. Sooth-sayers such as Teiresias always wore a woollen garment of network, which covered the whole of the body. Shepherds were provided with a short leathern tunic. Occasionally also heroes in great misfortune, such as Telephus and Philoctetes, were dressed in rags.[2] But the majority of the characters wore the regular tragic costume, with slight additions and variations; and the only means by which the spectators were enabled to identify the well-known personages of mythology, and to discriminate between the different ranks of the characters, was by the presence of small conventional emblems. For instance, the gods and goddesses always appeared with the particular weapon or article of dress with which their names were associated. Apollo carried his bow, and Hermes his magic wand. Athene wore the aegis.[3] In the same way the well-known heroes of antiquity had generally some speciality in their costume which enabled the spectators to recognize them as soon as they came upon the stage. Hercules was always conspicuous by means of his club and lion's skin; Perseus wore the cap of darkness, as depicted in the illustration

---

[1] Poll. iv. 116; Soph. O. C. 314;   Rust. ii. 11.
Eur. Bacch. 833.   [3] Aesch. Eum. 181, 404; Poll. iv.
[2] Poll. iv. 116, 117; Varro, Res   117.

252   *THE ACTORS*   [CH.

already given.[1] Kings in a similar manner were distinguished
by the crown upon their head, and the sceptre in their hand.
They also had a special article of dress, consisting of a short
tunic with a swelling bosom, worn over the ordinary tunic.[2]
Foreigners were discriminated by some one particular attribute,
rather than by a complete variety in their costume.   For
example, Darius wore the Persian turban ; otherwise he was
probably dressed in the ordinary tragic style.[3] Warriors were
equipped with complete armour, and occasionally had a short
cloak of scarlet or purple wrapped round the hand and elbow
for protection.[4] Old men usually carried a staff in their hands.
The staff with a curved handle, which occurs not infrequently in
ancient works of art, was said to be an invention of Sophocles.[5]
Crowns of olive or laurel were worn by messengers who brought
good tidings ; crowns of myrtle were a sign of festivity.[6] The
above examples illustrate the mode in which the different
characters and classes were discriminated upon the Greek stage
by small varieties in their equipment.   But in its main features
the dress of the majority of the characters was the same, and
consisted of the elaborate Aeschylean costume.

The tragic costume, after having been once elaborated, was
retained for centuries without any important innovation.   The
tragic actor must have been an impressive, though rather unnatural, figure, upon the stage.   His large stature and bulky
limbs, his harsh and strongly-marked features, his tunic with its
long folds and brilliantly variegated pattern, his mantle with its
gorgeous colours, must have combined to produce a spectacle
of some magnificence.   We must remember that he was intended
to be seen in theatres of vast dimensions, in which even the
front rows of spectators were a considerable distance from the
stage, while the more distant part of the audience could only
discern general effects.   For such theatres the tragic costume
of the Greeks was admirably adapted, however unwieldy and
unnatural it may have appeared on a closer inspection.   Its
magnificence and dignity were especially appropriate to the ideal

---

[1] Poll. iv. 117.   See fig. 18.
[2] Lucian, Somn. vel Gall. 26 ; Poll.
iv. 116.   The special tunic was called
κόλπωμα.
[3] Aesch. Pers. 661.
[4] Poll. iv. 116, 117.   The cloak was

called ἐφαπτίς.
[5] Eur. Ion 743 ; Vit. Soph. p. 2
Dindf.
[6] Aesch. Agam. 493 ; Soph. O. R.
83 ; Eur. Alc. 759.

figures which move in the dramas of Aeschylus and Sophocles.

FIG. 20.

FIG. 21.

In the Frogs of Aristophanes Aeschylus is humorously made
to declare that it was only right that the demigods of tragedy

should wear finer clothes, and use longer words, than ordinary mortals. The tragedy of Euripides was altogether more human in tone, and a more ordinary costume would have been better suited to it. But the Greeks, with their strong feeling of conservatism in matters of art, clung to the form of dress already established. The result was not altogether satisfactory. The attempt to exhibit human nature pure and simple upon the Greek stage was bound to appear somewhat incongruous. It often happened that the speeches and actions of the heroes in Euripides were highly inconsistent with the superhuman grandeur of their personal appearance. In any case the step from the sublime to the ridiculous was a very short one in the case of the Greek tragic actor. The play had to be elevated in tone, and the performance of a high standard, to carry off the magnificence of the actor's appearance. Otherwise his unwieldy bulk and gloomy features excited laughter rather than tears. Lucian is especially fond of ridiculing the tragic actors of the time. He laughs at their ' chest-paddings and stomach-paddings ', 'their cavernous mouths that look as if they were going to swallow up the spectators ', and the 'huge boots on which they are mounted '. He wonders how they can walk across the stage in safety.[1] In Philostratus there is an amusing story of the extraordinary effect produced upon a country audience in Spain by the appearance of a tragic actor before them for the first time. It is said that as soon as he came upon the stage they began to be rather alarmed at his wide mouth, his long strides, his huge figure, and his unearthly dress. But when he lifted up his voice and commenced his speech in the loud and sonorous clang of the tragic stage, there was a general panic, and they all fled out of the theatre as if he had been a demon.[2] In order to give an idea of the style and character of Greek tragic acting, two representations of tragic scenes (Figs. 20 and 21) are inserted, the first of which obviously represents Medea hesitating about the murder of her children.[3]

---

[1] Lucian, de Salt. 27, Anachar. 23.
[2] Philostrat. vit. Apoll. v. 9.
[3] The illustrations are taken from

Monumenti Inediti, xi. 31, 32. The originals are wall-paintings at Pompeii.

§ 5. *Costume of Satyric Actors.*

Tragedy and the satyric drama were sister forms of art, descended from the same original.   But while tragedy advanced in dignity and magnificence, the satyric drama retained all the wild licence and merriment which in early times had characterized the dithyrambic performances in honour of Dionysus.   Its chorus invariably consisted of satyrs.   Of the characters upon the stage, with which we are at present concerned, one was always Silenus, the drunken old follower of Dionysus; the rest were mainly heroes out of mythology, or other legendary beings.

Fig. 22.

In the Cyclops of Euripides, the only extant specimen of a satyric play, the characters consist of Silenus, Odysseus, and the Cyclops.   Concerning the costume of the actors the notices of Pollux are exceedingly brief.   But it is possible to obtain fairly clear conceptions on the subject from several works of art, and more especially from the well-known vase-painting at Naples.[1]   From this painting we see that the characters in a satyric drama, with the exception of Silenus, were dressed in

[1] Baumeister, Denkmäler, nos. 422 (the Naples vase), 424, 1631; Wiese- ler, Denkmäler, vi. 1, 2 (the Naples vase), 3-10. See above, p. 240.

much the same way as in tragedy. Their masks exhibit the
same features, and their garments are of the same general description. The tunic appears to have been rather shorter, to
facilitate ease of movement, as the acting in a satyric play was
no doubt less dignified and statuesque than in tragedy. For the
same reason the tall cothurnus of tragedy does not appear to
have been worn. It is not depicted in the works of art; and
although this fact in itself is perhaps hardly decisive, since even
in representations of tragic scenes the cothurnus is occasionally
left out, still on general grounds it appears to be most improbable that the cothurnus should have been worn in the satyric
drama. But, on the whole, the heroic characters in satyric plays
were dressed in much the same fashion as in tragedy. As to
Silenus, his mask always represents a drunken old man, with
a half-bestial expression. His under-garments, as depicted in
works or art, are of two kinds. Sometimes he wears a tight-
fitting dress, encasing the whole of his body with the exception
of his head, hands, and feet. At other times he wears close-
fitting trousers, and a tunic reaching to the knees. All these
garments are made of shaggy materials, to resemble the hide of
animals.[1] Certain over-garments are also mentioned by Pollux
as having been worn by Silenus, such as fawn-skins, goat-skins,
imitation panther-skins, mantles of purple, and mantles inwoven
with flowers or animals.[2] The figures in the illustration
(Fig. 22), which is taken from the vase-painting already referred
to, represent the three actors in a satyric drama. The first is
playing the part of some unknown hero of mythology. His
tunic is rather short, and he has no cothurnus; otherwise he
exhibits the usual features of the tragic actor. The second
figure represents Hercules. His tunic is still shorter, and
barely reaches to the knees. The third figure is that of Silenus.
His body is covered with a single close-fitting garment, and he
carries a panther-skin over his shoulders. All these figures are
holding their masks in their hands.

[1] Specimens of the first kind of dress
are to be found in Wieseler, vi. 2
(= Baumeister, 422), 6, 7, 10; specimens of the second kind in vi. 8
(= Baum. 1631), 9. The tunic was
called χιτὼν χορταῖος, μαλλωτός, ἀμ-
φίμαλλος, and was apparently made of
wool: cp. Poll. iv. 118; Hesych. and

Suid. s. v. χορταῖος; Dion. Hal. A. R.
vii. 72; Ael. Var. Hist. iii. 40.
[2] Poll. iv. 118. These articles are
part of the dress of Silenus. The other
actors were dressed quite differently.
The dress of the chorus is described in
the next chapter.

§ 6. Costume of Comic Actors.

The Old Comedy was essentially the product of a particular time and place.   With its local allusions and personal satire it was unsuited for reproduction or imitation among later generations.   Consequently very few traditions were preserved concerning the style of the masks and dresses used in it.   The literary evidence is extremely scanty, and we have to depend almost entirely on works of art for our knowledge of the subject.   We have already referred to the vase-paintings from Magna Graecia (Figs. 13 and 14), depicting comic scenes acted by the Phlyakes.   These Phlyakes represented one branch of the old Doric comedy, and their performances evidently

Fig. 23.

originated in the same phallic exhibitions out of which Attic comedy was developed.   There are many points in common between the two.   In both the phallus was regularly worn.   In both a frequent source of ridicule was found in parodies of tragic dramas, or of legendary fables.[1]   On these grounds it was long since suspected that the costume of the Phlyakes might resemble that of the old Attic comedy, and might be used to illustrate it.   This opinion has been confirmed by recent investigations.[2]   An Attic vase (Fig. 23) of the early fourth century, previously overlooked, throws much light upon the subject. It gives us a picture of three comic actors dressed in their

[1] There does not appear, however, to be any instance of an old Attic comedy being acted by the Phlyakes. The scene in Baumeister no. 904, where Hercules is knocking against a door, and a slave on a donkey follows behind, was formerly supposed to be the opening scene of the Frogs. But this is very doubtful. The character in the vase-painting is the real Hercules, and not Dionysus disguised.

[2] Körte, Studien zur Alten Komödie, Jahrbuch des archaeol. Instituts, 1893, pp. 61-93.

stage costume, and holding their masks in their hands.[1]
There are also a number of terra cotta statuettes, of Attic workmanship, and belonging to the end of the fifth and the beginning
of the fourth centuries, which apparently represent figures from
the comic stage. Copies of two of these statuettes (Fig. 24) are
here inserted.[2] The costume found on the vase and in the
statuettes is much the same as that depicted in the Phlyakes
paintings. It seems certain, therefore, that the dress of the
Phlyakes was akin to that used in the old Athenian comedy;
and it is now possible, from the sources just enumerated, to
determine the general character of this latter costume.

The Old Comedy was the direct descendant of the boisterous

FIG. 24.

phallic performances at the festivals of Dionysus. Coarseness
and indecency were an essential part of it. The actors therefore regularly wore the phallus.[3] This fact, which is expressly

[1] The illustration is taken from
Compte Rendu de la Commission
Impériale Archéologique, 1870–1, plate
iv. 1. The vase was found in the
Crimea, but is now at St. Petersburg.
In the original there are two other
figures (not actors), one on each side
of the group. These have been omitted
from the copy.

[2] The two figures are from Körte,
l. c. pp. 78 and 80. Both were found
at Athens. For a complete list of
these statuettes see Körte, pp. 77–86.

[3] Schol. Aristoph. Nub. 538.

stated by the grammarians, is confirmed by the evidence of the paintings and statuettes. It is true that Aristophanes in the Clouds takes credit to himself for having discarded this piece of indecency, and for having introduced a more refined style of wit into his comedy. But whatever he may have done in the Clouds—and it is doubtful how far his words are to be taken in the literal sense—there are numerous passages to show that in most of his other plays he followed the ordinary custom.[1] Another constant feature in the old comic dress was the grotesque padding of the body in front and behind. The figures of the actors, women as well as men, were stuffed out into an extravagant and ludicrous shape. The padding, as we see from the works of art, was enclosed in a tight-fitting under-garment, which covered the whole of the actor's person except his head, hands, and feet.[2] This under-garment was made of some elastic knitted material, so as to fit close to the figure. In most cases it was dyed a flesh colour and represented the skin. But in some of the Phlyakes vases (e. g. Fig. 14) the arms and legs of the actors were ornamented with stripes, and a tight jersey was worn over the body, and painted in imitation of the naked figure. Apart from the under-garment the clothes worn by the actors were the tunic and mantle of ordinary life. References to various kinds of mantles and tunics are common in the plays of Aristophanes.[3] But it appears from the paintings and statuettes that in most cases these garments were cut shorter than those of real life, so as to display the phallus.

The masks of the Old Comedy fall into two classes, those

---

[1] Aristoph. Nub. 538 οὐδὲν ἦλθε ῥαψαμένη σκύτινον καθειμένον κ.τ.λ. Possibly Aristophanes only means that he used the φαλλὸς ἀναδεδεμένος instead of the more indecent καθειμένος. Nub. 734 seems to show that the φαλλός was used even in the Clouds. For its employment in the other plays cp. Acharn. 156 ff., 1216 ff., Vesp. 1342, Pax 1349, Lysist. 928, 937, 987 ff., 1073 ff., Thesm. 59, 141, 239, 643, 1114. [Willems, Le Nu dans la Comédie Ancienne, tries to show that Aristophanes' use of the phallus was exceptional, but without success. He also argues that in Vesp. 1342, Pax 886, Thesm. 1181, Ach. 1198, Ran.

1308 mute parts were played by ἑταῖραι absolutely nude; but the evidence is quite insufficient, and can be otherwise explained.]

[2] The padding was called σωμάτιον. Cp. Phot. σωμάτια, τὰ ἀναπλάσματα οἶς οἱ ὑποκριταὶ διασάττουσιν αὑτούς. Luc. Iupp. Trag. 41 προγαστρίδια καὶ σωμάτια. The name of the under-garment is uncertain. Müller (Bühnenalt. p. 230) thinks it too was called σωμάτιον, or the strength of Poll. iv. 115 καὶ σκευὴ μὲν ἡ τῶν ὑποκριτῶν στολὴ (ἡ δ' αὐτὴ καὶ σωμάτιον ἐκαλεῖτο). But this is very doubtful.

[3] For the references see Müller, Bühnenalt. pp. 249 ff.

S 2

for real characters, and those for fictitious ones. When real
individuals were introduced upon the stage, such as Socrates
and Euripides, the masks were portraits of the actual persons.
Before a word was spoken the character was recognized by the
audience. When Aristophanes brought out the Knights, the
general terror inspired by Cleon was so great, that the mask-
makers refused to make a portrait-mask of him, and an ordinary
mask had to be worn. Socrates, during the performance of
the Clouds, is said to have stood up in his place in the theatre,
to enable the strangers present to identify him with the character upon the stage.[1] The fictitious masks, as we learn from
the grammarians, were grotesque and extravagant in type.[2]
They are represented as such in the works of art. The mouth
is large and wide open, and the features twisted into a grimace.
At the same time the masks in the Attic representations are
less distorted and unnatural than those of the Phlyakes vases.
The expression on the masks is mostly of a cheerful and festive
kind; but sometimes crafty, thoughtful, or angry features are
portrayed. Not infrequently in the Old Comedy figures of
a fanciful and absurd character were introduced upon the
stage. Thus Pseudartabas, the King's Eye, had a mask with
one huge eye in the centre of it. The trochilus in the Birds
created laughter by its immense beak. The epops was provided with a ridiculously long crest, but seems otherwise to
have been dressed like a human figure. Iris in the Birds came
on the stage with outspread wings, swelling tunic, and a head-
covering of enormous size, so as to cause Peisthetaerus to ask
her whether she was a ship or a hat. Prometheus, with his
umbrella, and Lamachus with his nodding crests, are further
examples of grotesque costume.[3] The covering for the feet
was not, as in the later comedy, of one conventional type,
but varied according to the sex and position of the character.
Several kinds of boot and shoe are referred to in Aristophanes.[4]

As regards the origin of the actor's costume which we have
been describing nothing is known from tradition. But Körte

---

[1] Poll. iv. 143 ; Platon. de Comoed.
(Dindf. p. 21) ; Aristoph. Equit. 230 ;
Ael. Var. Hist. ii. 13.

[2] Poll. iv. 143 ἐπὶ τὸ γελοιότερον
ἐσχημάτιστο.

[3] Schol. Aristoph. Acharn. 97 ;
Aristoph. Av. 62, 94, 104, 1203 (with
Schol. ad loc.), 1508, Acharn. 575 ff.

[4] Müller, Bühnenalt. p. 253.

has a very plausible conjecture on the subject.[1] He points
out that in the early Attic representations of Bacchic scenes
there are no traces of figures resembling those of the old comic
actors. The followers of Dionysus consist of Sileni and (later
on) of satyrs. On the other hand, in the numerous Bacchic
vases found at Corinth there are no satyrs and Sileni; their
place is taken by a group of curious beings who resemble the
old comic actors in these two respects—the phallus and the
exaggerated bulk of the lower part of the body. These figures
have no generic name; but their individual names are inserted
on one of the vases, and show that they were not human
beings, but creatures of the goblin type.[2] Similar figures are
also found in vases from the Kabeirion at Thebes, but in this
case they appear as burlesque actors taking part in Bacchic
festivities.[3] Körte suggests that these goblin followers of
Dionysus were the prototype of the actors in the Old Comedy;
that it was in the neighbourhood of Corinth that they were
first transformed into performers of farce and burlesque;
and that this species of comedy, together with the ludicrous
garb of the actors, then spread over various other parts of
Greece, such as Athens, Thebes, and Magna Graecia. That
the old Attic comedy was largely indebted to that of the
northern Peloponnese is shown by various traditions; and
the debt may very well have consisted in the introduction
of these farcical comedians, and their combination with the
old Attic choruses. If this theory is correct—and there is
much to be said in its favour—it points to a curious antithesis
between the early history of tragedy and comedy. The satyrs
and the Corinthian goblins were both of them semi-human
votaries of Dionysus, and both of them played an important
part in the development of the drama. But while the satyrs
became the chorus of tragedy, the goblins changed into the
actors of the comic stage.

The New Comedy was of much longer duration than the
Old Comedy, and was much more widely spread. It continued
to flourish at Athens itself as late as the imperial epoch, and

[1] Jahrbuch des archaeol. Inst. 1893, pp. 89 ff.
[2] The vase with the names (Εὔνους, Ὀφέλανδρος, Ὀμβρικος) is given by Körte, p. 91. For another specimen see Baumeister, no. 2099.
[3] Körte, Athen. Mittheil. 1884, pp. 346 ff. See the specimen given by Cook in the Classical Review, 1895, p. 373.

was transferred to Rome in the translations of Plautus and
Terence and the other comic writers. There is no lack of
information as to the costumes generally in use.[1] In the first
place all the actors wore masks, just as in the other branches
of the Greek drama. As far as abstract fitness goes, the masks
might well have been dispensed with. As the New Comedy
was essentially a comedy of manners and everyday life, and
its chief excellence lay in the accurate delineation of ordinary
human character, it is probable that a style of representation
after the fashion of the modern stage would have been much
more appropriate to it. In a theatre of moderate size, with
actors untrammelled by the use of masks, all the finer shades
in the character-painting might have been exhibited clearly
to the spectators. But in ancient times such a thing was
impossible. To the Greek mind the use of masks was in-
separably associated with the stage; and the Greeks were in
such matters extremely tenacious of ancient custom. It is also
very questionable whether in their enormous theatres masks
could possibly have been dispensed with. At any rate they
were invariably retained in the New Comedy. But it is a
strange thing that, although in all other respects the New
Comedy was a faithful representation of ordinary life and
manners, the masks employed should have been of the most
ludicrous and grotesque character. The fact is expressly
stated by Platonius, and is borne out by the evidence of
numerous works of art.[2] There was a total disregard for
realism and fidelity to nature. The exaggerated eyebrows
and distorted mouths gave an utterly unnatural expression
to the features. Such masks were perfectly in keeping with
the tone of the Old Comedy, in which parody and caricature
predominated. But it is strange that they should have been
adopted in the New Comedy, which otherwise was praised
for holding the mirror up to nature. The reason probably
lay in the size of the theatres. The excellence and humour of
a finely-drawn mask would have been lost upon an audience

[1] For a list of the works of art
illustrating the subject see Müller,
Bühnenalt. pp. 258, 273-6.
[2] Platon. ap. Dindf. Proll. de Com.
p. 21 ἐν δὲ τῇ μέσῃ καὶ νέᾳ κωμῳδίᾳ
ἐπίτηδες τὰ προσωπεῖα πρὸς τὸ γελοιύτε-
ρον ἐδημιούργησαν . . . ὁρῶμεν γοῦν τὰ
προσωπεῖα τῆς Μενάνδρου κωμῳδίας τὰς
ὀφρῦς ὁποίας ἔχει, καὶ ὅπως ἐξεστραμμέ-
νον τὸ στόμα καὶ οὐδὲ κατ᾽ ἀνθρώπων
φύσιν. See Wieseler, Denkmäl. v. 27-
52; Baumeister, nos. 905-8.

seated at a great distance from the stage.   Of course the statement of Platonius has to be taken with some qualification.
The masks were not invariably distorted.   Some of the young
men and women were depicted with handsome, though strongly-
marked, features, as in tragedy.   But the comic characters
always wore masks of the grotesque kind just referred to.
Copies of four comic masks (Figs. 25 and 26) are given on
the next page.[1]

Pollux supplies a long list of the masks in ordinary use in
the New Comedy, with accurate descriptions of each of them.[2]
His list comprises masks for nine old men, eleven young men,
seven slaves, three old women, and fourteen young women.
In this list are included all the stock characters of the New
Comedy, such as the harsh father, the benevolent old man, the
prodigal son, the rustic youth, the heiress, the bully, the pimp,
the procuress, and the courtesan.   For all these characters
there are regular masks with strongly characteristic features.
In the plays of the New Comedy, as each personage stepped
upon the stage, he must have been recognized at once by the
audience as an old friend.   Constant repetition must have
rendered them familiar with the typical features of each sort
of character.   Certain kinds of complexion, and certain styles
of hair and eyebrow, were appropriated to particular classes.
White or grey hair was of course the regular sign of old age.
Red hair was the mark of a roguish slave.   Thick curly hair
denoted strength and vigour.   Miserly old men wore their
hair close-cropped, while soldiers were distinguished by great
shaggy manes.   The hair of the courtesans was bound up with
golden ornaments, or brilliantly-coloured bands.   Beards were
distinctive of manhood or middle age, and were not used in
the masks of youths or old men.   The complexion was always
a prominent feature in the mask.   A dark sun-burnt complexion
was the sign of rude health, and was given to soldiers, country
youths, or young men who frequented the palaestra.   A white
complexion denoted effeminacy; pallor was the result of love

---

[1] Fig. 25 is taken from Archaeol.
Zeitung, 1878, Taf. 4, and represents
the masks of a girl and a slave.   The
original is a wall-painting at Pompeii.
Fig. 26, which is taken from Monumenti Inediti, xi. 32, contains two
copies of terra cottas found at Pompeii.
It will be seen that the mask of the
girl is not unlike a tragic mask in
general character.

[2] Poll. iv. 143–54.   Cp. Quint. Inst.
xi. 3. 74.

FIG. 25.

FIG. 26.

or ill-health.   Red cheeks, as well as red hair, were given to
rogues.   The eye-brows were strongly marked and highly characteristic.   When drawn up they denoted pride or impudence,
and were used in the masks of young men and of parasites.
The hot-tempered old father, who alternated between fits of
passion and fits of affection, had one eye-brow drawn up and
the other in its natural position, and he used to turn that side
of his face to the audience which was best in keeping with his
temper at the moment.   Noses were generally of the straight

FIG. 27.

Greek type; but old men and 'parasites' occasionally had hook
noses, and the country youth was provided with a snub nose.
Sometimes the ears showed signs of bruises, to denote that
the person had frequented the boxing-school.   The modern
equivalent would be a broken nose, but among Greek boxers
the ear was the part principally aimed at.   The above abstract
of the account in Pollux, together with the illustrations on the
previous page, will give some idea of the different styles of
mask employed in the later comedy.
    The costume of the actors in the New Comedy was copied

from that of ordinary life. The covering for the foot was the
same for all the characters, and consisted of a light sort of
shoe, which was merely drawn on, without being tied in any
way.[1] Pollux gives a short account of the dresses used in
the New Comedy, from which it appears that particular colours
were appropriated to particular classes.[2] White was worn by
old men and slaves, purple by young men, black or grey by
parasites. Pimps had a bright-coloured tunic, and a variegated
mantle. Old women were dressed in green or light blue, young
women and priestesses in white. Procuresses wore a purple
band round the head. The above statements are to a certain
extent corroborated by the testimony of the works of art, but
there are numerous exceptions. They cannot therefore be
regarded as an exhaustive account of the subject. Other
details of dress and costume are mentioned by Pollux. Old
men carried a staff with a bent handle. Rustics were dressed
in a leather tunic, and bore a wallet and staff, and occasionally
a hunting-net. Pimps had a straight staff, and carried an oil
flask and a flesh-scraper. Heiresses were distinguished by
fringes to their dress. Considered as a whole the costume
of the New Comedy seems to have been even more conventional than that of tragedy. The colour of a person's dress,
the features of his mask, and small details in his equipment,
would tell the spectators at once what sort of a character he
was intended to represent. A scene from a wall-painting
(Fig. 27) is here inserted, as a specimen of the style and
outward appearance of the New Comedy.[3]

§ 7. Speech, Song, and Recitative.

The profession of acting in ancient times required a great
variety of accomplishments. The words of a play were partly
spoken and partly sung, and it was necessary that the actor
should have a knowledge of music, and a carefully cultivated
voice. He had to combine the qualities of a modern actor with
those of an operatic singer. In fact the Greek drama was not

[1] This shoe was called ἐμβάς in Greek, and soccus in Latin : see Ammon. de diff. vocab. p. 49 ; Aristoph. Nub. 858.
[2] Poll. iv. 119-20.
[3] The illustration is from Monumenti Inediti, xi. 32.

unlike a modern comic opera in this particular respect, that it
consisted of a mixture of speaking and of singing. The question
as to the mode in which the different portions of the dialogue
were delivered, and the proportion which speech bore to song
in the parts of the actors, is a matter of very great interest.
In the first place there can be little doubt that, with few
exceptions, all that portion of the dialogue which was written
in the ordinary iambic trimeter was merely spoken or declaimed,
with no musical accompaniment whatsoever. This of course
constituted by far the larger part of the dialogue. Some
remarks of Aristotle in the Poetics may be cited in proof of
the above statement. Aristotle expressly says that in certain
portions of the drama there was no music at all. In another
place he remarks that when dialogue was introduced into
tragedy, the iambic trimeter was naturally adopted as the most
suitable metre, since it is 'better adapted for being spoken'
than any other.[1] A second argument is to be found in the
practice of the Roman stage. In two of the manuscripts of
Plautus there are marks in the margin to discriminate between
the portions of the play which were spoken, and the portions
which were sung. The result is to show that, while the rest of
the play was sung, the iambic trimeters were always spoken.[2]
As Roman comedy was a close and faithful imitation of the
Greek, it follows almost as a matter of certainty that the
iambic trimeters were spoken in the Greek drama also. It is
true that in one place Lucian contemptuously remarks about
the tragic actor, that he 'occasionally even sings the iambic
lines'.[3] But this statement, at the very most, cannot be held
to prove more than that in Lucian's time iambic passages were
sometimes sung or chanted. It is no proof that such a practice
ever existed in the classical period. It is quite possible that
in the second century A. D., when the chorus had either disappeared from tragedy, or been very much curtailed, some

---

[1] Aristot. Poet. c. 6 τὸ δὲ χωρὶς τοῖς
εἴδεσι τὸ διὰ μέτρων ἔνια μόνον περαίνε-
σθαι καὶ πάλιν ἕτερα διὰ μέλους, c. 4
λέξεως δὲ γενομένης αὐτὴ ἡ φύσις τὸ
οἰκεῖον μέτρον εὗρε, μάλιστα γὰρ λεκτικὸν
τῶν μέτρων τὸ ἰαμβεῖόν ἐστιν.
[2] The mark C (canticum) denotes the
part which was sung, D V (diverbium)
the part which was spoken. These

marks are found in cod. vetus (B), and
cod. decurtatus (C), and the plays in
which they occur are the Trinummus,
Poenulus, Pseudolus, Truculentus, and
parts of others. See Christ, Metrik,
pp. 677 ff.
[3] Lucian, de Salt. 27 ἐνίοτε καὶ περιᾴ-
δων τὰ ἰαμβεῖα.

of the more emotional portions of the iambic dialogue were sung or chanted as a sort of equivalent. But Lucian himself speaks of the practice with disapproval, as a sign of bad taste and degeneracy. In the best period of the drama there can be little doubt that the ordinary iambics were spoken. The only exception was in cases where iambic lines occurred in close connexion with lyrical metres. For instance, iambics are sometimes inserted in the midst of a lyrical passage. At other times speeches in iambics alternate with speeches in a lyrical metre, and the pairs of speeches are bound up into one metrical system. In such cases the iambics were probably given in song or recitative. But the regular iambic dialogue, and in consequence the greater part of the play, was spoken without musical accompaniment.

The lyrical portions of a Greek play were almost always sung. In an actor's part the lyrical passages consisted either of solos, or of duets and trios between the characters on the stage, or of joint performances in which actors and chorus took part alternately. These musical passages were in tragedy confined mainly to lamentations and outbursts of grief.[1] In general it may be said that, both in tragedy and comedy, song was substituted for speech in those scenes where the emotions were deeply roused, and found their fittest expression in music.

In addition to the declamation of the ordinary dialogue, and the singing of the lyrical passages, there was also a third mode of enunciation in use upon the Greek stage. It was called 'parakataloge', and came half-way between speech on the one hand, and song on the other. Its name was due to the fact that it was allied in character to 'kataloge', or ordinary declamation. It corresponded closely to what is called recitative in modern music, and consisted in delivering the words in a sort of chant, to the accompaniment of a musical instrument. On account of its intermediate character it was sometimes called 'speech', and sometimes 'song'. It was first invented by Archilochus, and employed by him in the delivery of his iambics, which were partly sung, and partly given in recitative.

[1] Songs by the actors were called τὰ ἀπὸ τῆς σκηνῆς. The solos (in tragedy) were called μονῳδίαι, the duets and trios had no special name. Musical duets between actors and chorus were in tragedy called κόμμοι. Suidas s. vv. μονῳδεῖν, μονῳδία ; Aristot. Poet. c. 12.

A special kind of harp, called the klepsiambos, was originally
employed for the purpose of the accompaniment. Recitative
was subsequently introduced into the drama, as Plutarch
expressly states.[1] It is not easy to determine, by means
of the slight and hazy notices upon the subject, what were
the particular portions of a play in which recitative was
employed. But there are certain indications which seem to
show that it was used in the delivery of iambic, trochaic, and
anapaestic tetrameters, and of regular anapaestic dimeters.
Thus it is distinctly recorded of the actor Nicostratus that he
gave trochaic tetrameters in recitative to the accompaniment
of the flute.[2] Then again, the two sets of trochaic tetrameters,
which came at the end of the parabasis, cannot have been
sung, as their very name implies. The probability therefore
is that they were given in recitative.[3] Thirdly, there is a
passage in the Peace where the metre changes abruptly from
lyrics to trochaic tetrameters without any break in the sentence.[4] It is difficult to suppose that in such a case a transition
was made suddenly from song to mere speech. But the transition from song to recitative would have been quite feasible.
Fourthly, it is asserted that on those occasions when the
speech of an actor was accompanied by dancing on the part
of the chorus, the metres employed were mostly iambic and
anapaestic tetrameters.[5] But as it is impossible, in the case
of Greek performers, to imagine dancing without a musical
accompaniment, the verses must have been given in recitative.
Fifthly, in the parabasis to the Birds the nightingale is asked
to lead off the anapaests with the flute; and the scholiast
remarks that 'the parabasis was often spoken to the accom-

---

[1] Plut. Mus. p. 1140 F ἀλλὰ μὴν καὶ
'Αρχίλοχος τὴν τῶν τριμέτρων ῥυθμο-
ποιΐαν προσεξεῦρε ... καὶ τὴν παρακατα-
λογήν, καὶ τὴν περὶ ταῦτα κροῦσιν ... ἔτι
δὲ τῶν ἰαμβείων τὸ τὰ μὲν λέγεσθαι παρὰ
τὴν κροῦσιν, τὰ δ' ᾄδεσθαι, 'Αρχίλοχόν
φασι καταδεῖξαι, εἶθ' οὕτω χρήσασθαι
τοὺς τραγικοὺς ποιητάς. Athen. p.
636 B ἐν οἷς γὰρ (φησὶ) τοὺς ἰάμβους
ᾖδον, ἰαμβύκας ἐκάλουν· ἐν οἷς δὲ παρε-
λογίζοντο τὰ ἐν τοῖς μέτροις, κλεψιάμ-
βους. Hesych. s. v. καταλογή· τὸ τὰ
ᾄσματα μὴ ὑπὸ μέλει λέγειν.
[2] Xen. Symp. vi. 3 ὥσπερ Νικόστρατος
ὁ ὑποκριτὴς τετράμετρα πρὸς τὸν αὐλὸν

κατέλεγεν.
[3] The two groups of trochaic tetrameters in the parabasis were called
ἐπίρρημα and ἀντεπίρρημα. See Platon.
in Dindf. Prolegom. de Comoed. p. 21.
[4] Aristoph. Pax 1171, 1172.
[5] Schol. Arist. Nub. 1355 οὕτως
ἔλεγον πρὸς χορὸν λέγειν, ὅτε τοῦ ὑποκριτοῦ διατιθεμένου τὴν ῥῆσιν, ὁ χορὸς
ὠρχεῖτο. διὸ καὶ ἐκλέγονται ὡς ἐπὶ τὸ πλεῖ-
στον ἐν τοῖς τοιούτοις τὰ τετράμετρα, ἢ
τὰ ἀναπαιστικά, ἢ τὰ ἰαμβικά, διὰ τὸ
ῥᾳδίως ἐμπίπτειν ἐν τούτοις τὸν τοιοῦτον
ῥυθμόν.

paniment of the flute'.[1] This statement means that the anapaestic tetrameters, which constitute the parabasis proper, were given in recitative. Lastly, there is the fact that the terms 'speech' and 'song' are both used of anapaests, implying that they occupied an intermediate position.[2] For these and other similar reasons it appears probable that recitative was employed in passages written in the metres already specified, that is to say, in iambic, trochaic, and anapaestic tetrameters and in regular anapaestic dimeters. It seems too that on certain rare occasions it was used in lyrical passages.[3]

It may be interesting to collect together in this place such information as we possess concerning the musicians and musical instruments employed in the Greek drama. The instrument generally used for the accompaniment both of the singing and of the recitative was the flute.[4] The harp had formerly been employed very frequently. But it was found that the flute, being a wind instrument, harmonized better with the human voice.[5] However, the harp was occasionally introduced. In the Frogs Aeschylus calls for the harp, when he is going to give a specimen of the lyrics of Euripides. Similarly, in the parody of the choruses of Aeschylus, the recurrence of the refrain 'phlattothrat' points to an accompaniment on the harp. A harpist is depicted on the Naples vase, side by side with the flute-player.[6] In the beginning of the Birds, when the chorus makes its entrance, the regular chorus of twenty-four birds is preceded by four others, the flamingo, cock, hoopoe, and gobbler. These were apparently musicians; and the instrument which they played must have been the harp;

---

[1] Aristoph. Av. 682-4 ἀλλ', ὦ καλλιβόαν κρέκουσ' | αὐλὸν φθέγμασιν ἠρινοῖς, | ἄρχου τῶν ἀναπαίστων, and Schol. ad loc. πολλάκις πρὸς αὐλὸν λέγουσι τὰς παραβάσεις.

[2] The exodos, mostly consisting of anapaests, is described as ἅπερ ἐπὶ τῇ ἐξόδῳ τοῦ δράματος ᾄδεται in Schol. Arist. Vesp. 270, and as ὃ ἐξιόντες ᾖδον in Poll. iv. 108. But in Dindf. Proll. de Com. p. 37 it is called τὸ ἐπὶ τέλει λεγόμενον τοῦ χοροῦ. As far as the anapaestic tetrameters are concerned, the word ᾄδοντας in Aristoph. Plut. 1209, and Hesych.'s definition of ἀνά-

παιστα as τὰ ἐν ταῖς παραβάσεσι τῶν χορῶν ᾄσματα, show that they were not merely spoken: the expression λέξοντας ἔπη in Aristoph. Equit. 508 proves that they were not sung. See Christ, Metrik, pp. 680 ff.

[3] Aristot. Probl. xix. 6 διὰ τί ἡ παρακαταλογὴ ἐν ταῖς ᾠδαῖς τραγικόν ;

[4] Schol. Aristoph. Nub. 312, Vesp. 580 ; Aristoph. Eccles. 890-2.

[5] Sext. Empir. p. 751, 21 ; Aristot. Probl. xix. 43.

[6] Aristoph. Ran. 1286, 1304. Baumeister, Denkmäler, no. 422.

since later on, when the parabasis is going to begin, Procne
has to be sent for specially to play the flute-accompaniment.[1]
As regards the number of musicians and instruments, the
ordinary provision for a tragedy or comedy was a single
flute-player. In the Delphic inscriptions of the third century,
which give the names of the performers in the various contests
at the Soteria, we find that in every dramatic exhibition only
one flute-player was provided. Works of art never depict
more than one ; and one is the number mentioned by the
grammarians.[2] But extra music might be supplied in special
cases. Harpists, as we have seen, were occasionally employed,
and as many as four of them seem to have been used in the
Birds. Probably in the same way, when a special effect was
to be produced, the number of the flute-players might be
augmented. As to the costume of the musicians very little is
known. In works of art they never appear in masks. But
in the Birds it is clear that the flute-player and the four
harpists were disguised as birds, and wore masks of an
appropriate kind. Possibly in the Old Comedy the musicians
were often arrayed in the same fashion as the chorus. But
in tragedy and satyric drama the evidence of the vase-paintings
would seem to show that they had no masks, but were dressed
either in ordinary costume or in the long and ornamental
tunic of the actors.[3] Their position during the performance
was naturally in the orchestra, close to the chorus. In the
Birds Procne has to come down from the stage to the
orchestra, in order to accompany the parabasis. We are
told also that at the end of a drama the flute-player marched
out at the head of the chorus.[4] Hence we may conclude
that he entered in front of them at the beginning of a play ;
and this supposition is confirmed by the manner in which
the four harpists make their entrance in the Birds. Very
probably the usual place for the musicians was near the altar
of Dionysus.

---

[1] Aristoph. Av. 226 ff., 659 ff.
[2] Lüders, Die dionysischen Künstler,
pp. 187 ff. Schol. Aristoph. Vesp. 582
ἔθος δὲ ἦν ἐν ταῖς ἐξόδοις τῆς τραγῳδίας
χορικῶν προσώπων προηγεῖσθαι αὐλητήν,

ὥστε αὐλοῦντα προπέμπειν.
[3] See Baumeister, Denkmäler, nos.
422, 424 ; Journal of Hellenic Studies,
xi. plate 11 (reproduced in Fig. 28).
[4] Schol. Aristoph. Vesp. 582.

§ 8. *Importance of the Voice in Greek Acting.*

In ancient acting the possession of a fine musical voice was
a matter of absolute necessity. Several considerations will
make it evident that the voice of the actor, upon the Greek
stage, must have been far more important than it is at present.
In the first place a considerable portion of the words in every
Greek play was either sung or delivered in recitative. In the
second place each actor had to play several parts in succession,
and to appear sometimes as a man, and sometimes as a woman.
It would be essential, therefore, to mark the difference between
the various personages by a corresponding variety in the tone
of voice employed; and for this purpose an organ of great
flexibility and compass must have been required. In the third
place the whole character of Greek acting was largely modified
by the costume of the performers. A modern actor adds force
and emphasis to his speeches by means of the variety of his
facial expression. A single glance, a slight movement of the
features, is often enough to produce a very great effect. But
to the Greek actor this mode of impressing the spectators was
denied, owing to the use of masks. His features bore the same
settled expression throughout the play. Even his gestures, in
the case of tragedy, must have been much more restricted
than in modern times, owing to the nature of the dress which
he had to wear. On account of these limitations he was
compelled to rely mainly upon his voice for the purpose of
expressing all the fleeting emotions of the character he represented. Great skill and variety in the modulation of his tones
were needed to counterbalance the absence of facial movement.
Lastly, the Greek actor required a voice of enormous power,
in order to make himself heard. When it is remembered
that the theatre of Dionysus was in the open air, and was
capable of holding nearly twenty thousand spectators, it will
easily be seen that, in spite of the excellence of the acoustic
arrangements, the demands upon the actor's voice must have
been excessively great.

For these various reasons the first and most essential requisite in a Greek actor was a powerful and expressive voice.
As a matter of fact, whenever an actor is mentioned by an

ancient author, he is referred to in language which at the present day would seem much more appropriate to a notice of an operatic singer. It is always the excellence of the voice which is emphasized, little regard being paid to other accomplishments. And it is not so much the quality as the strength of the voice which is commended. The highest merit, on the Greek stage, was to have a voice that could fill the whole theatre. Numberless passages from ancient authors might be quoted in proof of this assertion, but a few specimens will suffice. Of Neoptolemus, the great tragic actor, it is said that 'his powerful voice' had raised him to the head of his profession.[1] Licymnius, the actor mentioned in one of the letters of Alciphron, won the prize for acting at a tragic contest on account of 'his clear and resonant utterance'.[2] Dionysius, the tyrant of Syracuse, on a certain occasion, being covetous of distinction as a dramatic writer, dispatched a company of actors to the Olympic festival, to give a performance of one of his tragedies. As he wished to ensure that the exhibition should be of the highest excellence, he was careful to choose 'actors with the best voices'.[3] In a similar manner the emperor Nero prided himself on his talents as an actor. He instituted a tragic contest at the Isthmian festival, in order to display his powers. At this contest the actor Epeirotes 'was in splendid voice, and as his tones were more magnificent than ever, he won the greatest applause'.[4] The above passages are in reference to particular actors. Remarks about acting in general are of the same type. Demosthenes is reported to have said that 'actors should be judged by their voices, politicians by their wisdom'. According to Zeno an actor was bound to have 'a powerful voice and great strength'. Aristotle defines the science of acting as being 'concerned with the voice, and the mode of adapting it to the expression of the different passions'. Lucian remarks that the actor is 'responsible for his voice only'. Plato

[1] Diod. Sic. xvi. 92 Νεοπτόλεμος ὁ τραγῳδὸς, πρωτεύων τῇ μεγαλοφωνίᾳ καὶ τῇ δόξῃ.
[2] Alciph. iii. 48 τορῷ τινι καὶ γεγωνοτέρῳ φωνήματι χρησάμενος.
[3] Diod. Sic. xv. 7 ἐξαπέστειλε τοὺς εὐφωνοτάτους τῶν ὑποκριτῶν . . . οὗτοι

δὲ τὸ μὲν πρῶτον διὰ τὴν εὐφωνίαν ἐξέπληττον τοὺς ἀκούοντας.
[4] Lucian, Nero 9 ὁ δ' Ἠπειρώτης ἄριστα φωνῆς ἔχων, εὐδοκιμῶν δ' ἐπ' αὐτῇ καὶ θαυμαζόμενος λαμπροτέρᾳ τοῦ εἰωθότος.

would expel 'the actors with their beautiful voices' from his
ideal state.[1] Finally, there is the curious fact recorded by
Cicero, that in the performance of a Greek play, when the
actors of the second and third parts 'had louder voices'
than the protagonist, they used to moderate and restrain
their tones, in order to leave him the pre-eminence.[2] These
passages, and others of the same kind which might be quoted,
read like notices about operatic singers and musical performances, and prove conclusively the supreme importance of the
voice among the ancient Greek actors.

Such being the requirements of the Greek stage, it was
necessary that the actors should receive a musical education
as elaborate as that of a professional singer in modern times.
Cicero informs us that the Greek tragic actors spent many
years in the training of their voices, and used to test them,
before each performance, by running over all their notes from
the highest to the lowest.[3] They had to be careful and ab-
stemious in their diet, as excess in eating and drinking was
found to be inconsistent with the possession of a good voice.[4]
The importance attached to this particular quality in the actor's
art was not always beneficial in its results. Actors were sometimes inclined to violate good taste by intruding into their
performances mere exhibitions of skill in the manipulation of
the voice. They were ready to catch the applause of the
populace by startling effects, such as imitations of the rushing
of streams, the roaring of seas, and the cries of animals.[5]
Moreover, it was a common fault among the ancient actors
that, as a result of excessive training, their voices sounded
artificial and unnatural. There was a special term to denote
the forced tone of voice which was caused by too much
exercise. Aristotle remarks that one of the principal excel-
lences of the tragic actor Theodorus was the thoroughly
natural character of his delivery. Unlike other actors, he
seemed to speak with his own voice.[6]

---

[1] Plut. X orat. p. 848 B τοὺς ὑποκριτὰς ἔφη δεῖν κρίνειν ἐκ τῆς φωνῆς. Diog.
Laert. vii. 20 τὴν μὲν φωνὴν καὶ τὴν
δύναμιν μεγάλην ἔχειν. Aristot. Rhet.
iii. 1. Lucian, de Salt. 27 μόνης τῆς
φωνῆς ὑπεύθυνον παρέχων ἑαυτόν. Plat.
Legg. 817 C καλλίφωνοι ὑποκριταί.
[2] Cic. div. in Caecil. § 48 'cum

possit aliquanto clarius dicere . . .
multum summittere, ut ille princeps
quam maxime excellat'.
[3] Cic. de Orat. i. § 251.
[4] Aristot. Probl. xi. 22; Athen. p.
343 E.
[5] Plut. Aud. Poet. 18 B.
[6] Aristot. Rhet. iii. 2 διὸ δεῖ λανθά-

§ 9. Style of Greek Acting.

Both in tragic and comic acting a loud and exceedingly distinct utterance must have been a matter of necessity. But in comedy the tone of voice adopted appears, as was only natural, to have been much less sonorous than that of the tragic actors, and to have approached far more closely to the style of ordinary conversation.[1] In tragedy, on the other hand, it was the conventional practice to declaim the verses with a loud and ringing intonation, and to fill the theatre with a deep volume of sound. Ancient authors often refer to the sonorous utterances of the tragic stage.[2] With bad actors the practice would easily degenerate into mere bombast. Pollux mentions a series of epithets, such as 'booming' and 'bellowing', which were applied to actors guilty of such exaggeration. Socrates and Simylus, the tragic actors with whom Aeschines went on tour in the country districts of Attica, derived their nickname of 'the Ranters' from a fault of this kind.[3]

Another point which was required from ancient actors was great distinctness in the articulation of the separate words, and a careful observance of the rhythm and metre of the verses. In this respect the Athenians were a most exacting audience. Cicero speaks of their 'refined and scrupulous ear', their 'sound and uncorrupted taste'.[4] Ancient audiences in general had a much keener ear for the melody of verse than is to be found in a modern theatre. A slovenly recitation of poetry, and a failure to emphasize the metre, would not have been tolerated by them. Cicero remarks on the fact that, though the mass of the people knew nothing about the theory of versification, their instinctive feeling for rhythmical utter-

---

νειν ποιοῦντας, καὶ μὴ δοκεῖν λέγειν πεπλασμένως ἀλλὰ πεφυκότως . . . οἷον ἡ Θεοδώρου φωνὴ πέπονθε πρὸς τὴν τῶν ἄλλων ὑποκριτῶν· ἡ μὲν γὰρ τοῦ λέγοντος ἔοικεν εἶναι, αἱ δ' ἀλλότριαι.

[1] Lucian, Anachar. c. 23 αὐτοὶ δὲ (οἱ τραγῳδοὶ) μεγάλα τε ἐκεκράγεσαν καὶ διέβαινον οὐκ οἶδ' ὅπως ἀσφαλῶς ἐν τοῖς ὑποδήμασι . . . οἱ δὲ κωμῳδοὶ βραχύτεροι μὲν ἐκείνων καὶ πεζοὶ καὶ ἀνθρωπινώτεροι καὶ ἧττον ἐβόων.

[2] Philostrat. vit. Apoll. v. 8 (p. 171 Kayser) ἐπεὶ δὲ ἐξάρας τὴν φωνὴν γεγωνὸν ἐφθέγξατο; Lucian, l. c. See also the passages quoted on p. 273.

[3] Pollux (iv. 114), speaking of tragic acting, says εἴποις δ' ἂν βαρύστονος ὑποκριτής, βομβῶν, περιβομβῶν, ληκυθίζων, λαρυγγίζων, φαρυγγίζων. Dem. de Cor. § 262.

[4] Cic. Orat. §§ 25, 27.

ance was wonderfully keen. He says that if an actor should spoil the metre in the slightest degree, by making a mistake about a quantity, or by dropping or inserting a syllable, there would be a storm of disapproval from the audience.[1] No such sensitiveness is to be found in modern theatres. It is common enough at the present day to hear blank verse declaimed as if it were prose. But among the ancient Greeks the feeling for correctness of rhythm in poetical recitations was just as instinctive as is the feeling for correctness of tune among ordinary musical audiences at the present time. If an actor in a Greek theatre made a slip in the metre of his verses, it was regarded in much the same way as a note out of tune would be regarded in a modern concert-room. As a consequence the mode of declamation practised on the ancient stage must have been much more rhythmical than anything we are now accustomed to, and the pauses and movements of the metre must have been much more clearly emphasized.

The use of appropriate gesture, in the case of Greek acting, was especially important, since facial expression was prevented by the mask, and the actor had to depend solely on the tones of his voice, and the effectiveness of his movements. In comedy, as might be expected, the gesticulation was of a free and unconstrained character, and is exemplified in numerous works of art. In tragedy, on the other hand, a more dignified style was adopted. The nature of the tragic actor's dress was sufficient in itself to make a realistic type of acting impossible. Of course it is easy to exaggerate the cumbersomeness of the ancient costume. It would be a mistake to suppose that it hampered the actor's limbs to such an extent as to prevent him moving about like an ordinary human being. Many passages in the ancient dramas prove that this was not the case. Actors could walk rapidly off the stage, or fly for refuge to an altar, or kneel down in supplication, without any difficulty.[2] They could even fall flat on the ground. Philoctetes sinks to the earth in a fainting-fit, overcome by the pain of his wound. Iolaus is knocked down by the Argive herald, while trying to protect the children of Hercules. Ajax throws himself on his sword, and Evadne flings herself

---

[1] Cic. de Orat. iii. §§ 195, 196, Parad. § 26.

[2] Antig. 76, Hel. 543, Androm. 529, Orest. 382, Hec. 339, &c.

from a rock on to the funeral pyre beneath.   Hecuba, at
the beginning of the Troades, lies stretched upon the earth
in an agony of grief; and later on, when she hears the doom
of Cassandra, she again falls prostrate.[1] But although, as we
see from these examples, the tragic actor was not debarred
from the ordinary use of his limbs, still the character of his
dress must have made violent and impetuous movements a
matter of great difficulty.   Even if they had been easy, they
would have been inconsistent with the tone of the tragic stage.
The world of Greek tragedy was an ideal world of heroes
and demigods, whose nature was grander and nobler than
that of human beings.   The realistic portrayal of ordinary
human passions was foreign to the purpose of Greek tragedy.
Scenes of physical violence or of abject prostration, such as
those which have just been mentioned, are of rare occurrence.
To be in harmony with this elevation of tone it was necessary
that the acting should be dignified and self-restrained.   Violent
movements were usually avoided. A certain statuesque simplicity
and gracefulness of pose accompanied the gestures of the tragic
actor.   On the long and narrow stage the figures were arranged
in picturesque and striking groups, and the successive scenes
in the play presented to the eye of the spectator a series of
artistic tableaux.   The representations of tragic scenes and
personages in ancient works of art are characterized by a
dignity and a repose which call to mind the creations of
the sculptor.   This sober and restrained style of acting was
developed under the influence of Aeschylus and Sophocles
during the great period of Attic tragedy.   In later times a
tendency towards realism and exaggeration in the gestures
and the movements began to show itself.   The actors of the
fourth century were censured by many critics for having de-
graded the art of acting from its former high level, and for
having introduced a style which was unworthy of the dignity
of the tragic stage.   Callippides was called an ape by the old
actor Mynniscus because of the exaggerated vehemence of
his manner.[2] But as the tragic costume, with its burdensome

[1] Phil. 819, Heraclid. 75, Ajax 865, Eur. Suppl. 1070, Troad. 36, 462. Polymestor (Hec. 1058) and the Delphic priestess (Eum. 34) speak of themselves as crawling out on all fours. But it is unnecessary to suppose that they actually made their entrance from the back-scene in this way.

[2] Aristot. Poet. c. 26 ἡ μὲν οὖν τραγῳδία τοιαύτη ἐστίν, ὡς καὶ οἱ πρότερον

accompaniments, was retained with little alteration, it must
have prevented any great advance in the direction of realism
and violent gesticulation. The statuesque style of acting continued on the whole to be characteristic of the tragic stage, and
was indeed the only proper style for Greek tragedy.

§ 10. *The Actors' Guild.*

In the course of the fourth century the members of the
theatrical profession at Athens, together with the performers
in the various lyric and musical contests, formed themselves
into a guild, for the purpose of protecting their interests and
increasing their importance. The members of the guild were
called The Artists of Dionysus. Poets, actors, and chorus-
singers, trainers, and musicians all belonged to the guild.
When it first came into existence is not known for certain.
Sophocles is said to have formed a sort of literary club,
which may have been the prototype of the guild; but it is
possible that there was no connexion between the two. At any
rate it was fully established in the time of Aristotle, by whom
it is mentioned.[1]

The guild was of great value in maintaining and enforcing
the various privileges of the members. These were very considerable. Musical and dramatic contests among the Greeks
were confined almost entirely to the great religious festivals,
and regarded as celebrations in honour of the gods. The
professionals who took part in them were ministers engaged
in the service of the gods, and their presence was necessary
for the due performance of the various observances. To
enable them to fulfil their engagements, many of the ordinary
laws and regulations were relaxed. In the first place actors
and musicians were permitted to travel through foreign and
hostile states for the purpose of attending the festivals. Even
in time of war their persons and property were ensured from
violation. Owing to this custom the actors Aristodemus and

τοὺς ὑστέρους αὐτῶν ᾤοντο ὑποκριτάς, ὡς
λίαν γὰρ ὑπερβάλλοντα πίθηκον ὁ Μυν-
νίσκος τὸν Καλλιππίδην ἐκάλει, τοιαύτη
δὲ δόξα καὶ περὶ Πινδάρου ἦν . . . εἶτα
οὐδὲ κίνησις ἅπασα ἀποδοκιμαστέα, εἴπερ
μηδ᾽ ὄρχησις, ἀλλ᾽ ἡ φαύλων, ὅπερ καὶ

Καλλιππίδῃ ἐπετιμᾶτο καὶ νῦν ἄλλοις ὡς
οὐκ ἐλευθέρας γυναῖκας μιμουμένων.
[1] Vit. Soph. ταῖς δὲ Μούσαις θία-
σον ἐκ τῶν πεπαιδευμένων συναγαγεῖν.
Aristot. Probl. xxx. 10 οἱ Διονυσιακοὶ
τεχνῖται

Neoptolemus were able to travel frequently to and fro between Athens and Macedonia during the height of the war, and to assist materially in the negotiation of the peace.[1] In the second place actors and musicians claimed to be exempt from naval and military service, in order to pursue their professional avocations in Athens and elsewhere. In the time of Demosthenes this immunity from service was occasionally granted, but had not yet hardened into an invariable custom. Demosthenes mentions the cases of two musicians who were severely punished for avoiding military service. One of them was Sannio the chorus-trainer, and the other was Aristides the chorus-singer. Meidias also is said to have used the most strenuous exertions to prevent the chorus of Demosthenes from being exempted from service.[2] At this time, therefore, it seems that such immunity was sometimes granted and sometimes not. Later on the Guild of Artists of Dionysus succeeded in getting the Amphictyonic Council to pass a decree, by which the Athenians were bound as a religious obligation to grant exemption from military service to all members of the dramatic and musical profession. In the same decree the duty of allowing them a safe passage through their territories was enforced upon the Greek nation generally. This decree was renewed towards the beginning of the third century at the request of the Guild. A copy of the decree was engraved on stone and erected in the theatre at Athens, and has fortunately been preserved.[3] A translation of the more important passages will be of interest, as throwing light upon the position of the theatrical profession at Athens. It ran as follows: 'It was resolved by the Amphictyonic Council that security of person and property, and exemption from arrest during peace and war, be ensured to the artists of Dionysus at Athens; . . . . that they enjoy that exemption from military service and that personal security which have previously been granted to them by the whole Greek nation; that the artists of Dionysus be exempt from naval and military service, in order that they may hold the appointed celebrations in honour of the gods at the proper seasons, and be released from other business, and consecrated to the service of the gods; that it be unlawful to arrest or seize

[1] Dem. Fals. Leg. § 315.   [2] Dem. Meid. §§ 15, 58-60.
[3] C. I. A. ii. 551.

an artist of Dionysus in time of war or peace, unless for debt
due to a city or a private person; that, if an artist be arrested in
violation of these conditions, the person who arrests him, and
the city in which the violation of the law occurs, be brought to
account before the Amphictyonic Council; that the immunity
from service and personal security which are granted by the
Amphictyonic Council to the artists of Dionysus at Athens be
perpetual; that the secretaries cause a copy of this decree to
be engraved on a stone pillar and erected in the temple, and
another sealed copy of the same to be sent to Athens, in
order to show the Athenians that the Amphictyonic Council
is deeply concerned in the observance of religious duties at
Athens, and is ready to accede to the requests of the artists
of Dionysus, and to ratify their present privileges, and confer
such other benefits upon them as may be possible.' In this
decree it is very noticeable that dramatic and musical performances are treated throughout as divine observances in
honour of the gods, and the actors and other professionals are
described as ministers consecrated to the service of religion.
The maintenance of their privileges is therefore a sacred obligation in which the Amphictyonic Council is deeply interested.

Another inscription has been preserved referring to the
Athenian Guild of Artists of Dionysus.[1] It appears that the
Guild had a sacred enclosure and altar at Eleusis, where they
were accustomed to offer libations to Demeter and Kore at the
time of the Eleusinian mysteries. During the disturbances of
the Sullan campaigns the altar was dismantled, and the yearly
celebrations discontinued. The inscription is a decree of the
Guild thanking a certain Philemon for his exertions in restoring
the altar and renewing the annual ceremonies.

From the time of the fourth century onwards guilds of
actors similar to that at Athens were rapidly formed in various
places throughout the Greek-speaking world. In this way the
masterpieces of Greek tragedy were made familiar to the most
remote districts to which Greek civilization had penetrated.
But it is beyond the scope of the present work to trace the
progress of the Greek drama outside the limits of Athens and
Attica.[2]

[1] C. I. A. ii. 552.
[2] For a complete account of these
guilds see Lüders, Die dionysischen

Künstler; Foucart, Les Associations
religieuses chez les Grecs.

§ 11. *Social Position of Actors.*

In Greece the profession of the actor was an honourable one,
and there was no suspicion of degradation about it, as there
was in Rome.[1] Actors and other dramatic performers were
regarded as ministers of religion. In the dramatic exhibitions
at Athens the actors were placed on the same level as the
poets and choregi. Their names were recorded in the public
archives, and in commemorative tablets; and competitions in
acting were established side by side with the competitions
between the poets. It is true that Aeschines is very frequently
taunted by Demosthenes with his theatrical career, but the
taunts are due to the fact, not that he was an actor, but that
he was an unsuccessful one. Actors at the head of their profession occupied a very distinguished position. Aristodemus,
the tragic actor, was on two occasions sent as ambassador to
Macedon by the Athenians, and was largely instrumental in
negotiating the peace.[2] The great Athenian actors were much
sought after by the monarchs of the time. Aristodemus and
Neoptolemus were frequently at the court of Philip, and
Thessalus and Athenodorus at the court of Alexander.[3]
Thessalus was a great favourite with Alexander, and was
employed by him on delicate missions.[4] The leading actors
seem to have made large incomes. For instance, Polus told
Demosthenes that he was paid a talent for acting during two
days only.[5] It is not stated whether the performance to which
he refers took place at Athens, or elsewhere; but in all
probability it was in some foreign state. There is no evidence
to show what salaries were paid to the actors at the great
Athenian festivals.

As for the lower ranks of the profession, the tritagonists,
chorus-singers, musicians, and so on, though there was nothing

---

[1] Corn. Nep. praef. 5 'in scaenam
vero prodire et populo esse spectaculo
nemini in iisdem gentibus fuit turpitu-
dini'. Livy xxiv. 24 (of Ariston the
tragic actor) 'huic genus et fortuna
honesta erant; nec ars, quia nihil tale
apud Graecos pudori est, ea deforma-
bat'.

[2] Aesch. Fals. Leg. §§ 15-19; Dem.

de Cor. § 21.

[3] Dem. Fals. Leg. § 315, de Pace
§ 6; Diod. Sic. xvi. 92; Plut. Alex.
681 D.

[4] Plut. Alex. 669 D.

[5] Plut. X orat. p. 848 B. Gellius,
N. A. xi. 9, gives the same story about
Aristodemus.

dishonourable about their calling, their reputation does not
seem to have been very high. Their strolling and uncertain
manner of life seems to have had a bad effect upon their
character. Aristotle, in his Problems, asks the question why
it is that the artists of Dionysus are generally men of bad
character. He thinks the reason is partly due to the vicis-
situdes in their fortunes, and the rapid alternations between
luxury and poverty, partly to the fact that their professional
duties left them no time for general culture.[1] His remarks of
course apply mainly to the lower grades of the profession.

§ 12. Celebrated Athenian Actors.

Before concluding this account of Greek acting some notice
of the principal Greek actors may not be out of place. Unfortunately in most cases little more is known about them than
their names. Several tragic actors of the fifth century are
referred to by ancient writers, such as Cleander and Mynniscus,
the actors of Aeschylus, and Cleidemides and Tlepolemus, the
actors of Sophocles.[2] But no details are recorded as to their
individual characteristics and different styles. One interesting
fact is known about Mynniscus, to the effect that he considered
the acting of his successors as deficient in dignity and over-
realistic. He was especially severe upon Callippides, the
representative of the younger generation of actors.[3] This
Callippides was notorious for his conceit. On one occasion,
when he was giving himself airs in the presence of Agesilaus
the Spartan, he was considerably disconcerted by being asked
by the latter whether he was 'Callippides the pantaloon'.[4]
Another tragic actor of the same period was Nicostratus, who
was especially excellent in his delivery of the long narrative
speeches of the messengers. His style was so perfect that
to 'do a thing like Nicostratus' came to be a proverbial
expression for doing it rightly.[5]

But it was in the age of Demosthenes that the most celebrated group of tragic actors flourished. Among them was

---

[1] Aristot. Prob. xxx. 10.
[2] Vit. Aesch.; Schol. Aristoph. Ran.
803, Nub. 1267.
[3] Aristot. Poet. c. 26.
[4] Xen. Symp. iii. 11; Plut. Ages. p.

607 D ἀλλὰ οὐ σύγε ἐσσὶ Καλλιππίδας
ὁ δεικηλίκτας;
[5] Macar. Cent. iii. 46; Prov. Coisl.
124.

Polus of Aegina, who was considered to be the greatest actor of his time, and whose name is very frequently referred to by later writers. He was one of the actors who had the credit of having taught elocution to Demosthenes.[1] At the age of seventy, and shortly before his death, he performed the feat of acting eight tragedies in four days.[2] A well-known story is told about him to the following effect. Soon after the death of a favourite son, he happened to be acting the part of Electra in the play of Sophocles. In the scene in which Electra takes in her hands the urn supposed to contain the ashes of Orestes, and pours forth a lamentation over his death, Polus came upon the stage with the urn containing the ashes of his own son, and holding it in his hands proceeded to act the scene with such profound depth of feeling as to produce the greatest impression upon the audience. As Gellius remarks, the acting in this case was no fiction, but a reality.[3] Another of the great actors of this time was Theodorus, about whom a few facts are recorded. The exceedingly natural tone of his delivery, and his habit of never permitting any of the subordinate actors to appear upon the stage before himself, have already been referred to. He considered that tragedy was much more difficult to act in than comedy, and once told the comic actor Satyrus that it was easy enough to make an audience laugh, but to make them weep was the difficulty.[4] His own powers in this respect were very great. Once when acting in Thessaly he produced such an effect upon the brutal tyrant Alexander of Pherae that Alexander was compelled to leave the theatre, because, as he afterwards told Theodorus, he was ashamed to be seen weeping over the sufferings of an actor, while he was perfectly callous about those of his countrymen.[5] The tomb of Theodorus, close to the banks of the Cephisus, was still to be seen in the time of Pausanias.[6]

The other leading tragic actors of this period were Aristodemus, Neoptolemus, Thessalus, and Athenodorus. The two former were frequently at the court of Philip, and took a large part in bringing about the peace of Philocrates. They

---

[1] Rhet. Graec. vi. p. 35 (Walz).
[2] Plut. an sen. 785 C.
[3] Gell. N. A. vii. 5.
[4] Plut. de se laud. 545 F.
[5] Ael. Var. Hist. xiv. 40.
[6] Pausan. i. 37. 3.

are therefore denounced by Demosthenes as traitors to their country, and advocates of Philip's interests.[1]   Neoptolemus was the actor who, at the banquet held in Philip's palace on the day before his assassination, recited a passage out of a tragedy bearing upon the uncertainty of human fortune, and the inexorable power of death.   The fact was afterwards remembered as an ominous coincidence.[2]   Thessalus and Athenodorus were often rivals.   At Tyre, after the return of Alexander from Egypt, they were the principal competitors in the great tragic contest, in which the kings of Cyprus were the choregi, and the chief generals of the army acted as judges.   On this occasion Athenodorus won, to the great grief of Alexander, who said he would have given a part of his kingdom to have ensured the victory of Thessalus.[3]   The same two actors were also competitors at the City Dionysia in the year 341, but both of them were then beaten by Neoptolemus.[4]

Among the Greeks the distinction between the tragic and the comic actors was as complete as that between the tragic and comic poets.[5]   There are no instances during the classical period of an actor attempting both branches of the profession. Still less is recorded about the great comic actors than about the actors of tragedy.   A few names are mentioned, but there is almost a total absence of details concerning their style and mannerisms.   We are told that one of Hermon's jests was to knock the heads of his fellow-actors with a stick, and that Parmenon was celebrated for his skill in imitating the grunting of a hog.[6]   Interesting criticisms on the acting and the actors in comedy are unfortunately nowhere to be found.

---

[1] See above, p. 279.
[2] Diod. Sic. xvi. 92.
[3] Plut. Alex. 681 D.
[4] C. I. A. ii. 973.
[5] Plat. Rep. 395 B ἀλλ' οὐδέ τοι ὑποκριταὶ κωμῳδοῖς τε καὶ τραγῳδοῖς οἱ αὐτοί.

[6] Schol. Aristoph. Nub. 542; Plut. Aud. Poet. 18 B. [For an account of all that is known of the celebrated Greek actors see Völker, Berühmte Schauspieler im griech. Alterthum, 1899.]

CHAPTER VI

THE CHORUS

§ 1. *History of the Chorus.*

THE history of the chorus in the Greek drama is a history
of gradual decay. In the earliest period, when both tragedy
and comedy were mainly lyrical, the members of the chorus
were the sole performers. After the introduction of actors
and dialogue the chorus still continued for a time to play
the leading part. But from the beginning of the fifth century
it began slowly to dwindle in importance, until at length it
either disappeared altogether, or sank to the position of
the band in a modern theatre. As far as tragedy is concerned the process of decline can be traced with clearness in
the existing dramas. It takes various forms. In the first
place there is a gradual diminution in the length of the part
assigned to the chorus. In the Supplices, the oldest of existing
Greek tragedies, the choral part forms no less than three-
fifths of the whole composition. In the other plays of Aeschylus, with the exception of the Prometheus, it amounts on the
average to about a half. In the tragedies of Sophocles and
Euripides the size is very much reduced. The choral part
in Sophocles varies from about a quarter of the whole in the
Ajax and the Antigone to about a seventh in the Electra and
the Philoctetes. In Euripides it varies from about a quarter in
such plays as the Bacchae and Alcestis to about a ninth in
the Orestes. It appears therefore that in the fifth century the
part of the chorus was gradually but continuously diminished
in size. Then again there is a constant tendency throughout
the century to reduce the importance of the chorus by sever-
ing its connexion with the plot. In the lyrical tragedies of
the earliest period the chorus was no doubt on most occasions

the principal object of interest, and took the leading part in the play. This is still the case in some of the extant tragedies of Aeschylus. In the Supplices, for instance, the whole subject of the plot is the destiny of the fugitive maidens who form the chorus. It is their adventures which excite the sympathy of the audience; the other characters are of very little significance. In the Eumenides the interest centres chiefly round the conduct and feelings of the Furies. Even in the Septem and the Persae, though the chorus play a less prominent part, their connexion with the plot is still a very close one. Their destiny is involved in that of the principal characters. But in the other plays of Aeschylus the chorus begins to take much the same position as it occupies in Sophocles, and in the earlier plays of Euripides. It was at this period that Attic tragedy reached its highest perfection, and the question as to the proper place of the chorus in the plot was solved in the manner most consistent with the genius of Greek drama. The chorus is now thrown much further into the background, and appears in most plays, not as a participant in the action, but merely as a sympathetic witness. While the dialogue is proceeding, it follows the course of events with the keenest interest, but seldom actively interferes. In the pauses between the action it moralizes on the significance of the incidents which have just occurred. Such is its position during the middle of the century. It has been removed from the stress and turmoil of the action into a calmer and more remote region, though it still preserves its interest in the events upon the stage. But in the later plays of Euripides a further development is noticeable. The chorus begins to lose even its interest in the action. In the pauses between the dialogue it sings odes of a mythological character, which have only the remotest connexion with the incidents of the plot. In the course of the dialogue itself it converses less frequently with the actors than it had done hitherto. There is also a tendency to transfer much of the music from the orchestra to the stage. The old duets between actors and chorus are reduced both in size and number, and their place is taken by solos and duets sung exclusively upon the stage. This tendency to exclude the chorus from the play was carried still further by Agathon, who gave up all pretence of connexion between the plot and the songs of the chorus, and converted his odes into professed interludes. In the time of Aristotle this practice had become universal. The choral odes were now regarded in much the same light as the pieces of music performed between the acts in a modern theatre.[1] Whether the chorus still took any part in the dialogue is not stated. But we can hardly doubt that the tendency already strongly marked in Euripides had been developed to its natural results, and that the tragic chorus of the later fourth century was practically excluded from all share in the conduct of the play. After the fourth century very little is known about its history. But the evidence seems to show that it was sometimes discarded even as early as the third century; and in later times this came to be more and more the ordinary custom. Even when retained, its functions were merely those of the modern band.[2]

The history of the comic chorus is very similar. If we look at the extant plays of Aristophanes, we find that in the first nine, which were all produced in the fifth century, the chorus is an important and conspicuous element. But in the tenth, the Ecclesiazusae, which was brought out in 392, there is a great change. The parabasis has disappeared, and the functions of the chorus are mainly confined to the singing of three or four odes, of no great length. In the Plutus, produced in 388, the decline of the chorus is still more marked. It has only about forty lines assigned to it in the course of the dialogue; and in the pauses between the dialogue it sang interludes unconnected with the plot.[3] During the rest of the century the comic chorus seems to have still lingered on in a position similar to that which it holds in the Plutus. The grammarians who say that it was abolished entirely by the Middle Comedy apparently exaggerate the state of affairs.[4] There was still a comic chorus in the time of Aristotle.[5] Even

---

[1] Aristot. Poet. c. 18.
[2] For details see the Tragic Drama of the Greeks, pp. 452 ff.
[3] Vit. Aristoph. p. 36 Dindf. The places for the interludes are marked χοροῦ in the text (ll. 321, 626, 801, 958).
[4] Platon. de Comoed. p. 21 Dindf. οἱ δὲ τῆς μέσης κωμῳδίας ποιηταὶ . . .

τὰ χορικὰ μέλη παρέλιπον. Platon. p. 20 says the Aeolosicon of Aristophanes had no chorus; but frag. 8 seems to show that it had. Similarly the statement of Anon. de Comoed. p. 27 Dindf., that the Plutus χορῶν ἐστέρηται, is not entirely true.
[5] Aristot. Pol. iii. 3 ὥσπερ γε καὶ χορὸν ὁτὲ μὲν κωμικὸν ὁτὲ δὲ τραγικὸν

in the New Comedy the earlier poets, such as Menander and Philemon, appear to have retained it in some of their plays, though merely for the purpose of providing interludes.[1] After the fourth century there are few traces of its presence. It is true that it was regularly used in the comedies at the Delphic Soteria during the third century.[2] It is mentioned in the accounts of the Hieropoioi at Delos in 279 B. C.[3] It is found also in one comedy of Plautus, the Rudens. But in Terence there are no signs of it. This fact, combined with the statement of the grammarians that the New Comedy had no chorus, makes it certain that after the third century it had practically disappeared.[4]

§ 2. *Size of the Chorus.*

The tragic chorus, being a direct descendant of the old dithyrambic choruses, originally consisted of fifty members.[5] After all connexion between tragedy and the dithyramb had been severed, the number of the choreutae in a tragic chorus was reduced to twelve. It has been suggested that this number was due to the practice of each poet exhibiting four tragedies at a time. It is supposed that the original chorus of fifty was divided as equally as possible among the four tragedies, so that each chorus came to consist of twelve members. The conjecture is a plausible one, but cannot be regarded as certain, owing to the scantiness of our information concerning the early

ἕτερον εἶναί φαμεν, τῶν αὐτῶν πολλάκις ἀνθρώπων ὄντων. Eth. Nic. iv. 6 κωμῳδοῖς χορηγῶν ἐν τῇ παρόδῳ πορφύραν εἰσφέρων. Athen. Pol. c. 56, where the appointment of χορηγοὶ κωμῳδοῖς is described. This probably implies a chorus; though not necessarily, as a choregus would be required to meet the other expenses of a play. [Cp. Aeschin. in Tim. § 157 πρῴην ἐν τοῖς κατ' ἀγροὺς Διονυσίοις κωμῳδῶν ὄντων ἐν Κολλυτῷ καὶ Παρμένωνος τοῦ ὑποκριτοῦ εἰπόντος τι πρὸς τὸν χορὸν ἀνάπαιστον (345 B. C.).] The substitution of an agonothetes for the choregi at the end of the fourth century may have been connected with the decline of the chorus. See above, p. 55.

[1] Vit. Aristoph. p. 36 Dindf. τὸν Πλοῦτον γράψας, εἰς τὸ διαναπαύεσθαι τὰ σκηνικὰ πρόσωπα καὶ μετεσκευάσθαι,

ἐπιγράφει χοροῦ, φθεγγόμενος ἐν ἐκείνοις ἃ καὶ ὁρῶμεν τοὺς νέους (i. e. Menander and Philemon, cp. p. 35) ἐπιγράφοντας ζήλῳ 'Αριστοφάνους.

[2] Lüders, Die dionysischen Künstler, pp. 187 ff.

[3] Bull. Cor. Hell. xiv. p. 396 ; Körte, Neue Jahrb. 1900, pp. 83 ff.

[4] Anon. de Comoed. p. 27 Dindf.

[5] Poll. iv. 110. Pollux further states that the number continued to be fifty until the Eumenides of Aeschylus was produced ; and that the people were so alarmed at the sight of the fifty Furies that they passed a law reducing the number of the tragic chorus. The story is of course a fiction, on a par with the statement in the Life, that Aeschylus was banished to Sicily as a punishment for terrifying the people with his Eumenides.

history of tragedy. The size of the tragic chorus remained
unaltered until the time of Sophocles, and in all the earlier
plays of Aeschylus twelve choreutae are employed. Sophocles
raised the number from twelve to fifteen.[1] After his time
there was no further change during the great period of the
Attic drama. The tragic chorus was always composed of
fifteen persons. The various technical terms which refer to
the arrangement of the tragic chorus are all based on the
supposition that it is a chorus of fifteen. It is not quite certain
whether the innovation of Sophocles was adopted by Aeschylus
in his later plays. The Oresteia of Aeschylus was brought
out ten years after the first appearance of Sophocles; and it
has been contended that the chorus in this trilogy contained
fifteen members. There is hardly sufficient evidence to determine the matter with any certainty.[2] On general grounds
it seems probable that Aeschylus should have followed the
example of Sophocles. At any rate there is no doubt that
after the middle of the fifth century the number of the choreutae
was fixed at fifteen.[3] The satyric chorus was of the same size
as the tragic—a natural result of the intimate connexion between
tragedy and the satyric drama.[4] The comic chorus, as long
as it continued to be an integral part of the play, invariably
consisted of twenty-four members. All the authorities are
unanimous on the subject.[5] These were the numbers adopted

[1] Suid. s.v. Σοφοκλῆς ; Vit. Soph.
p. 2 Dindf.
[2] The decision of the question depends on the passage in the Agamemnon, s.vv. 1344–71. There is no
doubt that the twelve iambic couplets,
1348–71, were delivered by twelve
choreutae. The difficulty is to decide
whether the three trochaic tetrameters,
1344, 1346, and 1347, were delivered
by three additional choreutae, or by
the coryphaeus. Either view is
plausible, and it seems impossible to
determine the matter without further
evidence. The statement of Schol.
Arist. Equit. 586, that the chorus in
the Agamemnon was fifteen in number,
is merely an inference from the passage just referred to. The statement
of Schol. Aesch. Eum. 585, that the
chorus in the Eumenides consisted of
fifteen persons, is simply grounded on
the assumption that the number was

the same as in later times. In neither
case is the evidence of any independent
value.
[3] Fifteen is the number given in Poll.
iv. 109 ; Suid. s.v. χορός ; Schol. Arist.
Av. 298, Equit. 586 ; Schol. Aesch.
Eum. 585. The number is given as
fourteen in Vit. Aesch.; Bekk. Anecd.
p. 746; Tzetzes, Prolegom. ad Lycophr.
p. 254 M. The explanation of the discrepancy lies in the fact that when
the chorus is said to consist of fourteen members the coryphaeus is not
included.
[4] Tzetzes, l. c., τὴν δὲ τραγῳδίαν καὶ
τοὺς σατύρους ἐπίσης μὲν ἔχειν χορευτὰς
ια' (? ιδ'). Id. apud Dübner, Prolegom.
de Com. p. xxiv. ἐκκαίδεκα δὲ σατύρων,
τραγῳδίας. Though the numbers are
wrong in both passages, it is plain that
the tragic and satyric choruses were of
the same size.
[5] Poll. iv. 109; Schol. Arist. Av.

HAIGH   U

in the various kinds of drama throughout the classical period
of Greek literature. But in later times, after the dramatic
choruses had been reduced to insignificance, and merely
provided the music between the successive acts, their size,
at any rate in some theatres, appears to have been diminished.
Thus the comic chorus at the Delphic Soteria contained only
seven members ; and the tragic chorus depicted on the wall-
painting at Cyrene is also a chorus of seven.[1] Whether these
cases were exceptional, or whether seven had now come to be
the usual number of a theatrical chorus, there is no evidence
to show.

The size of the chorus in the Greek drama was regulated
by conventional rules, and no change was made to suit the
requirements of a particular play. For instance, in the Supplices of Aeschylus the number of the Danaides was fifty, but
the chorus probably consisted of twelve maidens who did duty
for the fifty. In the Supplices of Euripides the actual suppliants
were the seven wives of the slaughtered chieftains, but the
chorus was raised to its proper number by the addition of female
attendants. It has sometimes been suggested that in the
Eumenides, where the Furies are twelve or fifteen instead of
three, legendary tradition was sacrificed to theatrical requirements. But, as there is no evidence to show that the number
of the Furies had been settled at three as early as the time
of Aeschylus, it is quite possible that in this case the usual
size of the chorus was not inappropriate.

§ 3. *Costume of the Chorus.*

The costume of the chorus, as already pointed out, was
entirely distinct from that of the actors. The tragic, comic, and
satyric choruses all wore masks, in accordance with the usual
Bacchic tradition.[2] In other respects their costume had
nothing in common, but was designed in accordance with
the spirit of the respective types of drama. The tragic chorus
was usually composed of old men, or women, or maidens.
In such cases they wore the ordinary Greek dress, consisting

298, Acharn. 219 ; Bekk. Anecd.
p. 746, &c.
[1] Lüders, l. c. pp. 187 ff. Wieseler,
Denkmäler, xiii. 2.

[2] Pausan. i. 28. 6 ; Schol. Arist.
Nub. 343 ; Baumeister, Denkmäler,
no. 422.

of a tunic and a mantle. No attempt was made to give them
an impressive appearance by the use of strange and magnificent
costumes, similar to those worn by the actors. Such costumes
were perfectly appropriate to the heroes and gods upon the
stage, but would have been out of place in the chorus, which
was generally supposed to represent the ordinary public.
The masks of the tragic chorus would of course be suitable
to the age and sex of the persons represented. A special
kind of white shoe, said to be the invention of Sophocles, was
worn by the tragic chorus.[1] Old men usually carried a staff.[2]
Various little details in dress and equipment would be added
according to circumstances. Thus the chorus of bereaved
matrons in the Supplices of Euripides were dressed in black
garments, and had their hair cut short, as a sign of mourning;
and carried branches twined with wool, the symbol of supplication, in their hands. The chorus of maidens in the
Choephori, who had come to offer libations at the tomb of
Agamemnon, were also dressed in black.[3] In some cases
the tragic chorus was altogether of an exceptional character,
and required a special costume. In the Supplices of Aeschylus
the daughters of the Egyptian Danaus appear to have been
dressed as foreigners. Probably the same was the case with
the Persian Elders in the Persae. The Bacchantes in the
play of Euripides carried tambourines in their hands, and
were doubtless also provided with fawn-skins and wands of
ivy.[4] But no tragic chorus ever caused a greater sensation
than the chorus of Furies in the Eumenides of Aeschylus.
Their costume was designed by Aeschylus himself, and the
snakes in the hair, which afterwards became one of their
regular attributes, were specially invented for the occasion.
As they rushed into the orchestra, their black dresses, distorted
features, and snaky locks are said to have inspired the spectators with terror.[5] But this chorus was of a very unusual
kind. In most cases the tragic chorus was composed of
ordinary men and women, and their dress was that of everyday life.

[1] Vit. Soph.
[2] Aesch. Agam. 75; Eur. Herc. Fur. 108.
[3] Eur. Suppl. 10,97; Aesch. Choeph. 10, 11.
[4] Aesch. Suppl. 234-6 ἀνέλληνα στόλον | πέπλοισι βαρβάροισι καὶ πυκνώμασι | χλίοντα; Eur. Bacch. 58.
[5] Aesch. Eum. 52; vit. Aesch. p. 4 Dindf.; Poll. iv. 110; Pausan. i. 28. 6.

The choruses of goat-like satyrs who sang the dithyrambs in honour of Dionysus were the original source both of tragedy and of the satyric drama. These satyrs appear to have been an importation from the Peloponnesus. They are unknown to the oldest Ionic traditions. Among the primitive Ionians their place is taken by the Sileni—beings of a similar type, but resembling horses rather than goats.[1] Thus in the Homeric hymns it is the Sileni who are mentioned as companions of Dionysus, and there is no reference to the satyrs.[2] In the earliest Attic vases satyrs are never depicted, but only the horse-like Sileni. That the satyrs, with their goatish horns and tails, were a Doric conception is proved by various

FIG. 28.

indications. In a fragment of Hesiod, where they are mentioned for the first time, the account of their genealogy which is given connects them with Argos.[3] We hear of 'goat choruses' as an ancient institution at Sicyon.[4] Pratinas, the first celebrated writer of satyric drama, was a native of Phlius. As for the costume of the satyrs who formed the chorus of the primitive drama there is not very much evidence of an early date. Vases depicting Bacchic scenes are sufficiently common, but few of them can be shown to have any connexion with a dramatic performance. The earliest reliable testimony is that supplied by the Pandora vase.[5] This vase, which belongs to the middle of the fifth century, contains a scene from the Pandora myth, and also a representation of a group of masked

[1] See Furtwängler, Annali dell' In-
stituto, 1877, pp. 225 ff., 449 ff.
[2] Hymn to Aphrodite, l. 262.
[3] Strabo, x. p. 471.
[4] Herod. v. 67.

[5] Journal of Hellenic Studies, xi.
plate xi, from which the present illustration is taken by permission of the
Council of the Hellenic Society.

satyrs (Fig. 28) dancing round a flute-player. The satyrs are portrayed as half men and half goats. They have goat's horns upon their heads, and goat's hoofs instead of feet; and their tails are those of goats. Such seems to have been the appearance of a satyric chorus at the time the vase was painted. The next representation in point of date is that of the Naples vase (Fig. 29), which is about fifty years later. Here there is a considerable change in the make-up of the satyrs. The goatish element is less conspicuous. The goat's horns and hoofs have disappeared, and the tail is more like that of a

FIG. 29.

horse. In fact the type begins to approximate to that of the old Ionic Sileni, or horse-deities. The only part which resembles a goat is the shaggy skin round the loins. The style of satyr here depicted is the one which eventually prevailed in the theatre. Later representations of satyric choruses portray them in much the same way as the Naples vase, with goat's loins and horse's tails, but without hoofs or horns.[1] This evidence shows us that the satyr of the fourth and

[1] Wieseler, Denkmäler, vi. 3. Baumeister, Denkmäler, no. 424. In the latter painting the tail and phallus are not visible; but this appears to be merely owing to the position of the two satyrs. It can hardly be taken as evidence that the tail and phallus had been discarded at this time.

subsequent centuries was a modification of the original conception. The earliest stage satyrs were genuine goat-deities
of the Doric type. But in the course of the fifth century
there was a reaction in favour of the indigenous Sileni or
horse-deities. The two types were mixed together, and so
produced the conventional satyr of the later theatre.[1] Some
scholars maintain that the type was the same from the first,
and that the old dancers in the tragic and satyric drama
resembled Sileni more than satyrs.[2] But this theory is
scarcely compatible with the evidence of the Pandora vase.
The fact, too, that tragedy was called the 'goat-song' seems
to prove decisively that the oldest choruses were composed
of goat-like beings.[3] There is also a fragment of a satyric
play by Aeschylus in which one of the chorus-singers is
actually addressed as a goat.[4] With this evidence before us
we can hardly doubt that the Doric satyrs were the original
performers in Attic tragedy and satyric drama, and that the
Ionic element was introduced later on.

Some other points in connexion with the satyr's costume
have still to be mentioned. The phallus, the regular symbol
of Dionysiac worship, was invariably worn. The goat-skin
round the loins was often replaced by a conventional substitute,
consisting of drawers of some woven material, to which the
tail and phallus were attached. Drawers of this kind are worn
by all the satyrs in the Pandora vase, and by one satyr in the
Naples vase, and are also found in a later painting.[5] Apart
from the drawers and the goat-skin, the satyrs are represented
in the works of art as perfectly naked.[6] But probably in the
theatre they had flesh-coloured tights, similar to those used by
the comic actors. Slippers were no doubt also used, and may
in early times have been made in imitation of a hoof, as in the
Pandora vase. In addition to the regular satyric costume the
satyrs occasionally wore other clothes, suited to the part they
played in the particular drama. Thus the satyrs in the Cyclops

---

[1] See Körte, in Bethe's Prolegomena,
pp. 339 ff.
[2] So Loeschcke, Athen. Mittheil.
1894, p. 522; Bethe, Prolegomena,
p. 38.
[3] [Miss Harrison, Proleg. to the
Study of Greek Religion, p. 421, de-
rives τραγῳδία from τράγος in the sense

of 'spelt'; but the derivation is more
than doubtful.]
[4] Frag. 207 (Nauck) τράγος γένειον
ἆρα πενθήσεις σύ γε.
[5] Wieseler, Denkmäler, vi. 3.
[6] Cp. Hor. A. P. 221 'mox etiam
agrestes Satyros *nudavit*'.

of Euripides, being servants of Polyphemus, were dressed in
the ordinary leather jerkin of the serving-man.[1]   Silenus, the
head of the troop, was not a member of the chorus, but appeared
upon the stage with the other actors.   His dress has been
described already.   He was a sort of elderly satyr, and is to
be distinguished from the old Ionic Sileni, whose appearance
was entirely different.   His origin is rather obscure ; but he
may perhaps have been a later development, suggested by the
requirements of the satyric drama.

The chorus in the Old Comedy, unlike that of the satyric
drama, was of the most varied and fanciful character, and was
drawn from every possible source.   All classes and professions were introduced at some time or another.[2]   There were
choruses of Poets, Sophists, Athletes, Trades-women, Sorcerers,
Knights, Drummers, and so on.   Foreign nations were often
represented, such as Persians, Macedonians, and Thracian
women.   Even individuals were multiplied into a species, and
produced choruses of Hesiodi and Archilochi.   When the
members consisted of human beings, they were dressed in
the tunic and mantle of ordinary life, with such slight additions as were necessary to mark the different professions
and nationalities.   The mantle was laid aside for the purpose
of dancing, as the dances of the Old Comedy were of a wild
and energetic character, and required freedom of action.[3]
The masks were of a ludicrous type, with the features
distorted.[4]   In addition to the human choruses there were
also those composed of mythological beings, such as Furies,
Amazons, Sphinxes, and Sirens.   These would be dressed no
doubt in the traditional costume.   Many choruses consisted of
fanciful and ridiculous personifications.   There were choruses
of Towns, Islands, and Merchant ships ; of Clouds and Seasons ;
of Dramas and Epistles.   In all these cases the dress and
general make-up appear to have been of a grotesque character,
and only in a remote degree emblematic of the ideas and
objects personified.   For instance, the Clouds of Aristophanes
appeared as women dressed in gaily-coloured garments, and

---

[1] Cyclops 80 σὺν τᾷδε τράγου χλαίνᾳ.
[2] See the list of titles of comedies in
Meineke,   Hist. Crit. Com. Graec.
pp. 269 ff.

[3] Arist. Acharn. 627 ἀλλ' ἀποδύντες
τοῖς ἀναπαίστοις ἐπίωμεν ; Thesm. 656
τῶν θ' ἱματίων ἀποδύσας.
[4] Schol. Aristoph. Nub. 343.

wore masks of a ridiculous type, with long noses and other exaggerations. The only resemblance to Clouds was in the colours of the dresses.[1] Probably in other similar cases the personification was carried out in the same rough-and-ready manner. Another class of choruses was composed of various kinds of animals. We have the Birds and Wasps of Aristophanes; and we hear of other poets introducing Goats, Frogs, Vultures, Storks, Ants, Fishes, Bees, Nightingales, and so on. Choruses of this kind appear to have been a favourite institution among the Athenians, quite apart from the drama. A theory has been propounded that they were survivals of an old theriomorphic form of worship, and that they were the original source of the comic chorus.[2] As for their connexion with a primitive type of religion, this is a speculative subject with which we have no concern. But the notion that they were the prototype of the comic chorus is not sufficiently supported by evidence. This chorus consisted originally of the 'comus', or band of revellers, who led the phallic processions in honour of Dionysus; and there is no reason to suppose that these revellers were dressed otherwise than as men. The varied character of the later chorus was due to the fancy and imagination of the Attic poets, who introduced all kinds of eccentric beings upon the stage, and among them choruses of animals. These latter, however, were only a small proportion of the whole, and it seems hardly justifiable to choose them out from the rest as specially connected with the origin of comedy. As regards the costume of these animal choruses, it would be highly interesting to know how it was managed. There are five vase-paintings of the early fifth century which depict such choruses dancing to the accompaniment of a flute-player; though it is doubtful whether in any case the performance is of a dramatic kind. One of these choruses consists of men disguised as horses, with knights riding on their shoulders; and it has been suggested that the chorus of Knights in Aristophanes was represented in this way.[3] Two others depict men riding on ostriches or on dolphins.[4] In these pictures, however, the whole conception

[1] Schol. Aristoph. Nub. 289.

[2] Poppelreuter, De Comoed. Atticae Primordiis, 1893, p. 15. Loeschcke, Athen. Mittheil. 1894, p. 519. Cook, Journal of Hellenic Studies, 1894, pp. 165 ff.

[3] So Poppelreuter, l.c. pp. 9–11. A copy of the vase is given on p. 8.

[4] Bollettino Archeologico Napolitano, Nuova Serie, v. tav. 7.

is far too fanciful and unreal to throw any light on the question
of the costume actually used in the theatre.   In another vase
the dancers are tall figures, with heads like those of a cock,
and bodies enveloped in long cloaks.[1]   A dress of this kind
might have been employed upon the stage ; but unfortunately
the cloaks conceal so much of the dancer's person that the
evidence of the vase is not very instructive.   The best painting for our present purpose is one which represents a chorus
of birds, and which is here reproduced (Fig. 30).[2]   The
costume is clearly delineated.   The bodies of the choreutae
are covered with a close-fitting dress, made in rough imitation

FIG. 30.

of feathers.   Two long ends hang down from each side of
the waist, and a bunch of feathers is affixed to each knee.
The arms are provided with wings.   A row of upright feathers
is attached to the crown of the head, and the mask is made
with a long and pointed nose, suggestive of the beak of a bird.
From this painting we may obtain a fairly clear idea of the
manner in which animals were imitated in the Old Comedy.
We see that there was none of the realism one meets with in
a modern pantomime.   The imitation was only carried so far

[1] Journal of Hellenic Studies, ii.
plate xiv A.
[2] The illustration is taken, by permission of the Council of the Hellenic
Society, from the Journal of Hellenic
Studies, ii. plate xiv B.   See Mr. Cecil
Smith's interesting article on the subject.

as to be generally suggestive of the animal intended. The body and legs were left unfettered, to allow of free movement in the dance. At the same time, to judge from the specimen before us, the costumes seem to have been designed with a great deal of spirit and humour, and to have been extremely well adapted to the purpose for which they were intended.

§ 4. *Arrangement of the Chorus.*

Except on rare occasions the dramatic choruses were drawn up in formations of military regularity, both on their first entrance, and during the progress of the play. They presented a perfectly symmetrical appearance in the orchestra. In this respect they offer a contrast to the choruses in a modern opera, and to the crowds which are introduced upon the modern stage. As a rule no attempt was made to imitate the fluctuating movements and haphazard grouping of an ordinary crowd. The chorus marched into the orchestra, and took up its position before the stage, with the regularity and precision of a body of soldiers. In all dramatic choruses—tragic, comic, and satyric— the rectangular formation was invariably adopted, as opposed to the circular arrangement of the dithyrambic choruses.[1] This quadrangular formation was probably of Doric origin.[2] Every dramatic chorus, when drawn up in this way, consisted of a certain number of 'ranks', and a certain number of 'files'. For instance, the tragic chorus, with its fifteen members, contained five ranks of three men each, and three files of five men each. Similarly the comic chorus, which was composed of twenty-four persons, contained six ranks of four men each, and four files of six men each. According to the Attic phraseology a chorus was said to be drawn up 'by ranks' when the different members of the same rank stood one behind the other. It was said to be drawn up 'by files' when the members of the same file were one behind the other. Accordingly, when a tragic chorus was drawn up 'by ranks', the men stood five abreast and three deep. When it was drawn up 'by files', they stood three abreast and five deep. The same regulations applied to the

---

[1] Tzetzes, Prolegom. ad Lycophr. p. 254 M, τραγικῶν δὲ καὶ σατυρικῶν καὶ κωμικῶν ποιητῶν κοινὸν μὲν τὸ τετραγώνως ἔχειν ἱστάμενον τὸν χορόν:

Bekk. Anecd. p. 746; Et. Mag. s.v. τραγῳδία; vit. Aristoph. (Dindf. Prolegom. de Com. p. 36).

[2] Athen. p. 181 C.

comic chorus. It might be arranged 'by ranks', with the men six abreast and four deep; or 'by files', with the men four abreast and six deep.[1] The arrangements throughout were of this military character. In fact the training of a choreutes was considered by many of the ancient writers to be an excellent preparation for warlike service.[2]

In the great majority of cases the chorus was supposed to consist of persons from the neighbourhood, and therefore entered

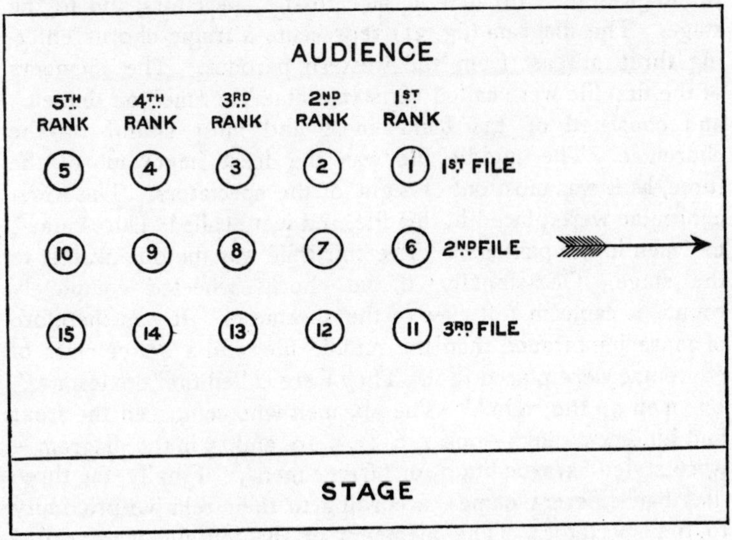

FIG. 31.

the orchestra by the western passage. Their right side was towards the stage, and their left side towards the spectators. As a consequence, the left side of the chorus was much the most conspicuous and important, and the best-trained choreutae were placed there.[3] The tragic chorus might enter five abreast

---

[1] Poll. iv. 108, 109 καὶ τραγικοῦ μὲν χοροῦ ζυγὰ πέντε ἐκ τριῶν καὶ στοῖχοι τρεῖς ἐκ πέντε· πεντεκαίδεκα γὰρ ἦσαν ὁ χορός. καὶ κατὰ τρεῖς μὲν εἰσῄεσαν, εἰ κατὰ ζυγὰ γίνοιτο ἡ πάροδος· εἰ δὲ κατὰ στοίχους, ἀνὰ πέντε εἰσῄεσαν . . . ὁ δὲ κωμικὸς χορὸς τέτταρες καὶ εἴκοσιν ἦσαν οἱ χορευταί, ζυγὰ ἕξ, ἕκαστον δὲ ζυγὸν ἐκ τεττάρων, στοῖχοι δὲ τέτταρες, ἐξ ἄνδρας ἔχων ἕκαστος στοῖχος.

[2] Athen. p. 628 F.

[3] Schol. Aristid. iii. p. 535 Dindf. ὅτε εἰσῄεσαν οἱ χοροὶ πλαγίως βαδίζοντες ἐποιοῦντο τοὺς ὕμνους καὶ εἶχον τοὺς θεατὰς ἐν ἀριστερᾷ αὐτῶν καὶ οἱ πρῶτοι τοῦ χοροῦ ἀριστερὸν στοῖχον, p. 536 τοὺς οὖν καλοὺς τῶν χορευτῶν ἔταττον εἰσιόντες ἐν τοῖς [τῶν] ἑαυτῶν ἀριστεροῖς, ἵνα εὑρεθῶσι πρὸς τὸν δῆμον ὁρῶντες.

and three deep, or three abreast and five deep, according as the formation was by ranks or by files. As a matter of fact the arrangement by files was the one almost invariably adopted. There are several technical terms in connexion with the tragic chorus, and they all refer to a chorus which is supposed to be entering from the western side, and to be drawn up three abreast and five deep. An oblong formation of this kind would evidently be more convenient in the narrow side-entrances, and would present a broader surface to the spectators and to the stage. The diagram (fig. 31) represents a tragic chorus entering three abreast from the western parodos. The members of the first file were called 'aristerostatae', or 'men on the left', and consisted of the handsomest and most skilful of the choreutae. The middle file was the least important of the three, as it was most out of sight of the spectators. The worst choreutae were placed in this file, and were called 'laurostatae', or 'men in the passage'. The third file was the one nearest to the stage. Occasionally, if the chorus wheeled completely round, it came in full view of the spectators. It was therefore of more importance than the middle file, and a better class of choreutae were placed in it. They were called the 'dexiostatae', or 'men on the right'.[1] The six men who composed the front and hindmost ranks—nos. 1, 6, 11, 5, 10, and 15 in the diagram— were styled 'kraspeditae', or 'fringe-men'.[2] Finally, the three files had different names, according to their relative proximity to the spectators. The members of the left file were called 'front-line men'; the members of the middle and right-hand files were called 'second-line men' and 'third-line men' respectively.[3]

---

[1] Poll. ii. 161 τάχα δὲ καὶ ὁ ἀριστερο-στάτης ἐν χορῷ προσήκοι ἂν τῇ ἀριστερᾷ, ὡς ὁ δεξιοστάτης τῇ δεξιᾷ. Phot. s.v. λαυροστάται· μέσον τοῦ χοροῦ· οἱονεὶ γὰρ ἐν στενωπῷ εἰσιν· φαυλότεροι δὲ οὗτοι. Hesych. λαυροστάται· οἱ ἐν τοῖς μέσοις ζυγοὶ . . . μὴ θεωρούμενοι. The ὑποκόλπιον τοῦ χοροῦ, defined by Hesych. as τῆς στάσεως χῶραι αἱ ἄτιμοι, probably included the whole file of laurostatae, though some scholars confine it to nos. 7, 8, and 9.

[2] Plut. Conv. p. 678 D ὥσπερ χοροῦ, τοῦ συμποσίου τὸν κρασπεδίτην τῷ κορυ-φαίῳ συνήκοον ἔχοντος. The κρασπε-

δῖται were also called ψιλεῖς ; cp. Suid. s.v. ψιλεύς· ἐπ' ἄκρου χοροῦ ἱστάμενος : Hesych. s.v. ψιλεῖς· οἱ ὕστατοι χορεύ-οντες.

[3] Hesych. s.v. ἀριστεροστάτης· ὁ πρωτο-στάτης τοῦ χοροῦ. Poll. iv. 106 δεξιο-στάτης, ἀριστεροστάτης, δευτεροστάτης, τριτοστάτης. [Cp. Menander fr. 165 (Kock) ὥσπερ τῶν χορῶν | οὐ πάντες ᾄδουσ', ἀλλ' ἄφωνοι δύο τινὲς | ἢ τρεῖς παρεστήκασι πάντων ἔσχατοι | εἰς τὸν ἀρι-θμόν, καὶ τοῦθ' ὁμοίως πως ἔχει. This probably means that the mute members of the chorus were placed in the third file, the δεξιοστάται or τριτοστάται,

The central position, no. 3 in the diagram, was occupied by the coryphaeus, or leader of the chorus.[1] The post of the leader was an extremely arduous one. While the dialogue was in progress, he had to carry on conversations with the actors upon the stage. During the choral odes he had to give the note to the choreutae, and superintend the dances and manœuvres. At the same time his own dancing and mimetic gestures were supposed to be a conspicuous feature in the performance. Demosthenes, speaking of dithyrambic choruses, says that the loss of the coryphaeus means the ruin of the chorus; and this must have been still more the case in a dramatic performance.[2] On the other hand the possession of a skilful leader would contribute very largely to the success of the chorus and of the drama. The choreutae on each side of the leader, nos. 2 and 4 in the diagram, were called his 'parastatae', or 'assistants', and were next in importance to the leader himself. The two choreutae on the outside, nos. 1 and 5 in the diagram, were called the 'third men'.[3] As already remarked, the coryphaeus, together with the other four members of the left file, constituted the pick of the whole chorus.

Concerning the formation in which the comic chorus entered the orchestra there is not much information. Like the tragic chorus, it might enter either by ranks or by files; that is to say, it might come in six abreast and four deep, or four abreast and six deep. There can be no doubt that the oblong formation of four abreast and six deep was the one usually adopted. It would be more suitable from every point of view. Both the tragic and the comic choruses were probably preceded into the orchestra by the flute-player.[4] On certain rare occasions the formal entrance in a rectangular body was dis-

---

whom Hesych. calls ἔσχατοι (s. v. λαυροστάται· οἱ ἐν τοῖς μέσοις ζυγοὶ ... οἱ δὲ ἐπιτεταγμένοι πρῶτοι καὶ ἔσχατοι).]
[1] Phot. s.v. τρίτος ἀριστεροῦ· ἐν τοῖς τραγικοῖς χοροῖς τριῶν ὄντων στοίχων καὶ πέντε ζυγῶν, ὁ μὲν ἀριστερὸς πρὸς τῷ θεάτρῳ ἦν, ὁ δὲ δεξιὸς πρὸς τῷ προσκηνίῳ. συνέβαινεν οὖν τὸν μέσον τοῦ ἀριστεροῦ στοίχου τὴν ἐντιμοτάτην καὶ τὴν οἷον τοῦ πρωτοστάτου χώραν ἐπέχειν καὶ στάσιν. The coryphaeus was also called χορηγός Athen. p. 633 A, χοραγός Plut.

Apophth. Lac. p. 219 E, ἡγεμών and ἡγεμὼν κορυφαῖος Dem. Meid. § 60, χοροστάτης Hesych., χορολέκτης Ael. Hist. An. xi. 1, χοροποιός Xen. Ages. ii. 17.
[2] Dem. Meid. § 60.
[3] Aristot. Met. iv. 11 ταῦτα δ' ἐστὶν ὅσα πρός τι ἐν ὡρισμένον διέστηκε κατὰ τὸν λόγον, οἷον παραστάτης τριτοστάτου πρότερον, καὶ παρανήτη νήτης· ἔνθα μὲν γὰρ ὁ κορυφαῖος, ἔνθα δὲ ἡ μέση ἀρχή.
[4] See above, p. 271.

pensed with, and an irregular mode of entrance was adopted, in order to produce a dramatic effect. The best example is in the Eumenides of Aeschylus. When the Furies made their second appearance, they came rushing into the orchestra one by one, in hot pursuit of Orestes, and created a profound sensation by their movements and appearance.[1] There is another instance in the Birds of Aristophanes. The birds begin by entering one by one. The flamingo comes first, and its appearance is criticized by the actors upon the stage. The cock follows, and is similarly criticized. Then comes the hoopoe, and after it the glutton-bird. These, as we have seen, were probably musicians. Finally, the chorus of twenty-four birds come fluttering in together, so as to block up the side-entrances.[2] In the Lysistrata the chorus is divided into two halves, one consisting of men, the other of women. The chorus of men enters first; the chorus of women follows after an interval.[3] But instances of this kind were very rare and exceptional. Usually the chorus entered in a rectangular body, with the precision of a troop of soldiers.

In most cases the entrance of the chorus took place at the conclusion of the 'prologue', or introductory scene upon the stage; and the march in was accompanied by a chant, which was called the 'parodos', or entrance-song.[4] However, in a considerable number of plays there was no parodos at all, but the chorus entered the orchestra in silence, while the first act of the drama was in progress, and then commenced a musical dialogue with the actors upon the stage. Instances of this mode of entrance are to be found in such tragedies as the Electra of Sophocles and the Orestes of Euripides.[5] A few

---

[1] Poll. iv. 109; Vit. Aesch. p. 4 Dindf.

[2] Arist. Av. 268-96.

[3] Arist. Lysist. 254, 319. In the Ecclesiazusae the chorus probably entered together at l. 285. The extra women in the first scene were not members of the chorus, but παραχορηγήματα.

[4] Arg. Aesch. Pers. τῶν δὲ χορῶν τὰ μέν ἐστι παροδικά, ὡς ὅτε λέγει δι' ἣν αἰτίαν πάρεστιν, ὡς τὸ "Τύριον οἶδμα λιποῦσα". Schol. Eur. Phoen. πάροδος δέ ἐστιν ᾠδὴ χοροῦ βαδίζοντος ᾀδομένη ἅμα τῇ εἰσόδῳ, ὡς τὸ "Σῖγα σῖγα λεπτὸν

ἴχνος ἀρβύλης τίθετε". Aristot. Poet. c. 12 defines the parodos as ἡ πρώτη λέξις ὅλου χοροῦ. He thus extends the meaning of the word so as to include, not only entrance-songs in the proper sense, but also those cases where the chorus enter in silence, and sing their odes later on. [Masqueray, Théorie des formes lyriques de la tragédie grecque, c. ii, analyses in detail the parodoi of the extant plays.]

[5] Other examples are the Prom. Vinct. of Aeschylus; the Philoctetes of Sophocles; the Medea, Heracleidae, Troades, and Electra of Euripides.

plays do not conform to either of these two conventional types.
Occasionally, for instance, there is no prologue, and the play
begins with the parodos, as in the Supplices and Persae of
Aeschylus. This was no doubt the old-fashioned mode of
commencement, derived from the times when the drama was
still entirely lyrical. Then again, in the Eumenides the
parodos is sung on the second entrance of the Furies, after
their arrival at Athens. In the Supplices of Euripides the
chorus are seen kneeling upon the stage in supplication when
the play commences. There they remain in silence during the
performance of the prologue, and then proceed to sing an ode,
in place of the usual parodos, from their position on the stage.
In the Clouds it appears that the chorus chant the first two
odes behind the scenes, and then enter the orchestra silently.
The Rhesus commences with a dialogue in anapaests between
Hector and the chorus.

The next point to be considered is the position taken up by
the chorus after entering the orchestra. On most occasions,
as already stated, the chorus came in by the western side,
drawn up in rectangular formation, with the stage on its right
hand and the spectators on its left. It advanced half-way
into the orchestra, then came to a halt, and each member of
the chorus turned round to the right, so as to face the stage.
By this manœuvre the whole chorus was made to look towards
the stage, and the arrangement by files was converted into
one by ranks. For instance, the tragic chorus, which had
entered three abreast and five deep, now stood before the stage
five abreast and three deep. The coryphaeus and principal
choreutae stood in the back line, and retained their position
nearest to the spectators, and furthest away from the stage.
This position they kept throughout the performance.[1] In a
similar manner the comic chorus, after entering the orchestra

---

[1] Müller (Die griech. Bühnenalt. p.
214), following Hermann (Opusc. vi. 2,
p. 144) supposes the whole chorus to
have wheeled completely round, so that
the left file came to be nearest to the
stage. He thinks it more natural for
the coryphaeus to have been immediately in front of the stage, where he
would be in a position to converse
with the actors. But he could do so
equally well from the centre of the

back row. And it seems most improbable that care should have been
taken, during the entrance into the
orchestra, to place the coryphaeus
and best choreutae in the line most
conspicuous to the spectators, but
that throughout the rest of the performance they should have been stationed in a position where the majority
of the spectators would hardly have
been able to see them.

four abreast and six deep, would halt in front of the stage, go
through the manœuvre just described, and convert itself into
a body standing six abreast and four deep. There is no information as to the position of the coryphaeus in the comic chorus.
But there can be no doubt that, like the tragic coryphaeus, he
stood in the back row, as near as possible to the spectators.

While the actors were upon the stage, and the dialogue was
in progress, the chorus continued to stand with their backs
towards the spectators, and their faces towards the stage,
so as to follow the course of the action.[1] This was their
normal position during the play, and, although it may seem
strange to our modern ideas, it was a necessary consequence
of the peculiar circumstances under which the Greek drama
was developed. When the stage was empty, the pauses
between the acts were filled up by the choral odes called
stasima. There is no reliable information as to the position
and movements of the chorus during the performance of
the stasima. As the singing was accompanied by dancing, the
choreutae must have been moving to and fro. But in the
absence of evidence it seems useless to venture on conjectures
as to the exact nature of the evolutions. One thing may be
regarded as certain, that during the performance of the stasima
the chorus did not continue to face towards the empty stage,
and turn their backs upon the audience. Such a position
would have been quite unnatural and unmeaning. In the
Old Comedy there was a peculiar sort of interlude called
the parabasis, which came during a pause in the action, and
consisted of a series of lyrics and addresses, delivered by
the chorus, and dealing with ordinary topics of the day.
While reciting the first part of the parabasis the chorus
wheeled completely round so as to face the spectators. Hence
the name 'parabasis', which means 'a turning aside'. The
latter part was antistrophical in form, and during its delivery
the chorus separated into two divisions, which stood facing one
another. The different portions of the parabasis were then
given by each division in turn.[2]

[1] Anon. de Com. (Dindf. Prolegom.
de Com. p. 29); Vit. Aristoph. (ibid.
p. 36); Schol. Arist. Equit. 505.
[2] Schol. Arist. Equit. 505, Pax 733.
As to the formation during the latter
part of the parabasis, it is almost certain that the chorus was then divided
into ἡμιχόρια. Two MSS. assign the
strophe and antistrophe to ἡμιχόρια in
Nubes 563, 595, Vespae 1060, 1091,

Sometimes, though not often, in the course of a play the chorus left the orchestra for a short period, and made a second entrance later on.[1] The instances of the practice which occur in the Eumenides and the Ajax were necessitated by the change of scene in those plays.[2] There is another example in the Helena of Euripides. Helen and the chorus retire into the palace, to inquire about the fate of Menelaus from Theonoe. In their absence Menelaus enters the stage, and recounts his adventures to the audience. Then Helen and the chorus return, and the recognition gradually takes place.[3] Similar temporary departures of the chorus are to be found in the Alcestis and the Ecclesiazusae; but they seem to have been of very rare occurrence.[4] At the end of the play the chorus retired by the passage from which it had entered, and was preceded by the flute-player.[5] In the Seven against Thebes the chorus leave the orchestra in two divisions, one following the body of Polyneices, the other that of Eteocles. But in most cases they probably marched out in the same rectangular formation in which they had entered.

§ 5. The Delivery of the Choral Part.

As regards the delivery of the words, the chorus, like the actors, was not confined to one manner only, but used song, speech, and recitative by turns, according to the varying character of the metre. The lyrical portions of the drama were almost invariably sung. The ordinary iambic trimeters were spoken. The systems of anapaestic dimeters, and the iambic, trochaic, and anapaestic tetrameters were delivered in recitative to the accompaniment of the flute.[6] A question now arises which is of great interest and importance in connexion with the choral part of the performance. It is obvious to any

Aves 737, 769, and the epirrhema and antepirrhema in Ranae 686, 717. See Arnoldt, Die Chorpartieen bei Aristoph. pp. 180 ff. That the half-choruses stood facing one another seems to be indicated by Hephaest. 14, p. 131, ἔστι δέ τις ἐν ταῖς κωμῳδίαις καὶ ἡ καλουμένη παράβασις, ἐπειδὰν εἰσελθόντες εἰς τὸ θέατρον καὶ ἀντιπρόσωπον ἀλλήλοις στάντες οἱ χορευταὶ παρέβαινον: Anon. de Comoed. (Dübner, Prolegom. de Com. p. xx) ἀπελθόντων δὲ τῶν ὑποκριτῶν πρὸς ἀμφό-

τερα τὰ μέρη τοῦ δήμου ὁρῶν ἐκ τετραμέτρου δεκαὲξ στίχους ἀναπαίστους ἐφθέγγετο, καὶ τοῦτο ἐκαλεῖτο στροφή.
[1] Poll. iv. 108. The temporary departure was called μετάστασις, the return ἐπιπάροδος.
[2] Aesch. Eum. 235; Soph. Ajax 815.
[3] Eur. Hel. 327 ff.
[4] Eur. Alc. 746; Arist. Eccles. 310.
[5] Schol. Arist. Vesp. 580.
[6] See chap. v. pp. 270 ff.

reader of a Greek play that many of the speeches and songs
assigned to the chorus were not intended to be delivered by
the whole of the chorus, but by individual members. This
fact is patent to every one. But when any attempt is made
to settle the exact character of the distribution the greatest
diversity of opinion prevails. Attempts have been made to
portion out the choral odes between different members and
sections of the chorus on the strength of indications supplied by the metre, or by the sense of the words.[1] But it
is plain that inferences based on evidence of this kind must
be very uncertain in character. As a matter of fact different
investigators have arrived at the most contradictory conclusions. Hence in the present state of our knowledge any
detailed account of the matter is out of the question. It will
be necessary to be content with certain general conclusions,
which are based on actual evidence, or are so plausible in
themselves as to be very widely accepted.

First, then, as to the part taken by the chorus as a whole.
In ordinary circumstances the parodos and the stasima appear
to have been sung by the whole chorus together. The parodos,
as already explained, was the song of the chorus on its first
entrance. The stasima were the long and important odes
inserted between the successive divisions of the play, in order
to fill up the pauses in the action. It is natural in itself to
suppose that these portions should have been sung by the
whole chorus, and the supposition is borne out by the statements of Aristotle.[2] Sometimes there were exceptions. For
example, the chorus in the Alcestis, on its first entrance, is
divided into two half-choruses, which sing successive passages
of the parodos alternately. In the Ion the parodos is ob-

[1] See especially Arnoldt, Die Chorpartieen bei Aristophanes (Leipzig,
1873), Die chorische Technik des Euripides (Halle, 1878), Der Chor im Agamemnon des Aeschylos (Halle, 1881) ;
Christ, Theilung des Chors im attischen
Drama (München, 1877) ; Muff, Die
chorische Technik des Sophokles(Halle,
1877), De choro Persarum (Halle,
1878), Der Chor in den Sieben des
Aeschylos (Halle, 1882) ; Hense, Der
Chor des Sophokles (Berlin, 1877),
Ueber die Vortragsweise Soph. Stasima
(Rhein. Museum, xxxii); Zielinski, Die

Gliederung der altattischen Komödie
(Leipzig, 1885).

[2] In Poet. c. 12 he defines the πάροδος
as ἡ πρώτη λέξις ὅλου χοροῦ, implying
that other odes were also sung by
the whole chorus. If so, the στάσιμα,
which were far the most important of
the other odes, must have been so sung.
Whether the expression ὅλα χορικὰ
μέλη, applied to the στάσιμα, means
' sung by the whole chorus', or merely
' unbroken ', as opposed to the κόμμοι,
is uncertain.

viously sung by subdivisions or by individuals, and not by the whole chorus. In the Frogs a long speech by the coryphaeus is inserted in the middle of the parodos. In the Lysistrata the chorus is divided throughout the play into two half-choruses, one of men, the other of women.[1] But in the majority of cases the parodos and the stasima were given by the whole body of the chorus. Not infrequently, in the middle of the dialogue, small odes were inserted which resembled stasima in their general character, but differed from them in point of brevity, and from the fact that they came in the course of the dialogue, and not during a pause in the action. They were often songs of triumph or exultation, occasioned by sudden developments in the plot ; and were accompanied by a lively dance.[2] These short odes were no doubt sung by the whole chorus, in the same manner as the stasima. It has been suggested that the strophes and antistrophes in the stasima were delivered by half-choruses in succession, and that the epode was given by the whole chorus. But there is no real evidence in support of this hypothesis, and epodes are only rarely to be met with in dramatic choruses.

In the second place some of the words assigned to the chorus were actually delivered by the coryphaeus. There is no direct testimony to this effect, but the matter hardly admits of doubt. On a great many occasions the chorus drops the tone of lyrical exaltation, and converses with the persons on the stage in an easy and familiar manner. It plays the part of an ordinary actor. In all such cases it is evident that the chorus must have been represented by the coryphaeus alone. The dialogues between the actors and the coryphaeus were a peculiar and distinctive feature of the old Greek drama. They were, in fact, a direct survival from the early period, when there was only a single actor upon the stage, and when the

---

[1] Schol. Eur. Alc. 79 ἐκ γερόντων Φεραίων ὁ χορός, διαιρεῖται δὲ εἰς δύο ἡμιχόρια. That the anapaests in Ranae 354–71, which come in the middle of the parodos, were spoken by the coryphaeus is proved by the concluding lines (ὑμεῖς δ' ἀνεγείρετε μολπὴν κ.τ.λ.), in which the rest of the chorus is commanded to begin.

[2] When these short odes were of a lively character, they were apparently called ὑπορχήματα by the grammarians, and regarded as a separate class. But even stasima might be composed in the hyporchematic style. It seems better, therefore, to regard ὑπόρχημα as a term applicable, not to short lyrics only, but to any lyrics of a lively and dance-like metre. See the Tragic Drama of the Greeks, pp. 357, 359.

dramatic element in a play was necessarily confined to conversations between the actor and the chorus. In addition to
the dialogues just mentioned, there are several other portions
of the chorus which may be assigned to the coryphaeus with
a fair amount of certainty. Such are the anapaests with which
the approach of a new personage is announced at the end of
a choral ode in tragedy. These anapaests, being delivered in
recitative, would make a gentle transition from the song of the
chorus to the speech of the actors. Then again, it is probable
that in comedy all the anapaestic tetrameters were spoken by
the coryphaeus, including the speech to the people at the commencement of the parabasis, and speeches such as that which
is inserted in the parodos of the Frogs.[1] In comedy also the
coryphaeus had frequently to address words of exhortation
and remonstrance to the rest of the chorus.[2] As regards the
anapaests at the beginning and the end of a play, the question
is far more doubtful. It was the old fashion in tragedy for
the entrance song of the chorus to commence with a series of
anapaests. The custom is retained in the Persae, Supplices,
and Agamemnon of Aeschylus, and the Ajax of Sophocles.
Most Greek plays also conclude with a few anapaests. It has
been suggested that the verses in each case were delivered by
the coryphaeus alone; but the suggestion is hardly a plausible
one. If chanted in combination by the whole body of the
chorus they would make its entrance and departure much
more impressive. It need hardly be remarked that, when the
chorus was divided into half-choruses, the part generally taken
by the coryphaeus was in this case taken by the leaders of
the two halves. For example, throughout the Lysistrata the
chorus of men and the chorus of women were represented
in the dialogue by their respective leaders. In the Seven
against Thebes the concluding anapaests would be spoken by
the leaders of the hemichoria. It is also highly probable that
the two sets of trochaic tetrameters, which come at the end
of the parabasis, were recited, not by the half-choruses, but by
their leaders.

Thirdly, certain portions of the chorus were occasionally
spoken or sung by individual choreutae. The best known

---

[1] See the previous page.
[2] e. g. Arist. Ran. 382, Vesp. 1516, Thesmoph. 655, &c.

example is in the Agamemnon, during the murder of the king, when the chorus stands outside the palace, debating helplessly as to what it ought to do, and each of the old men pronounces his opinion in turn. There is another instance in the lyrical ode at the commencement of the Eumenides. The Furies wake up, find that Orestes is gone, and reproach Apollo in a series of brief, detached sentences, each being sung by one member of the chorus.[1] The above examples admit of no doubt. Whether the practice was a common one, and whether the choral parts were frequently distributed among individual choreutae, is a matter of great uncertainty. It is manifestly unsafe to infer that it was done in all cases where the choral passage is full of mutual exhortations and addresses, and the language is broken up into disconnected sentences. For example, in the parodoi in Aristophanes the members of the chorus often address one another by name, and exhort one another to greater activity. But it does not therefore follow, as has been supposed, that these passages were delivered in portions by individuals. A chorus might be perfectly well chanted by the whole body, though written in vivid and dramatic style.[2] It is hardly safe therefore to distribute choral passages among individual choreutae except on very strong evidence. The extent to which the practice prevailed in the ancient drama must be regarded as an open question.

Fourthly, the division into half-choruses was not infrequent.[3] It might be done in two ways. In the first place the chorus throughout the whole play might be composed of two separate divisions, differing from one another in point of age, sex, or

---

[1] Aesch. Agam. 1344 ff., Eum. 140 ff., Schol. ad loc. ἀναστήσει αὐτὰς οὐκ ἀθρόως, μιμούμενος ἐμφατικῶς τὴν ἀλήθειαν, ἀλλ' ἐγείρεταί τις πρώτη, ὥστε μὴ ἀθρόως τὸν χορὸν φθέγξασθαι. Müller (Griech. Bühnenalt. p. 218) is mistaken in citing the passage in the Lysistrata, 727–80, as an example of the delivery of words by individual choreutae. The three women who take part in the dialogue are not members of the chorus, but performers upon the stage.

[2] Cp. the sensible remarks of the Schol. on Arist. Ran. 375 ἐντεῦθεν Ἀρί-σταρχος ὑπενόησε μὴ ὅλου τοῦ χοροῦ εἶναι τὰ πρῶτα· τοῦτο δὲ οὐκ ἀξιόπιστον.

πολλάκις γὰρ ἀλλήλοις οὕτω παρακελεύον-ται οἱ περὶ τὸν χορόν.

[3] Poll. iv. 107 καὶ ἡμιχόριον δὲ καὶ διχορία καὶ ἀντιχόρια. ἔοικε δὲ ταὐτὸν εἶναι ταυτὶ τὰ τρία ὀνόματα· ὁπόταν γὰρ ὁ χορὸς εἰς δύο μέρη τμηθῇ, τὸ μὲν πρᾶγμα καλεῖται διχορία, ἑκατέρα δὲ ἡ μοῖρα ἡμιχόριον, ἃ δ' ἀντᾴδουσιν, ἀντιχό-ρια. The Schol. on Arist. Equit. 589 has a curious note to the effect that, when the chorus was divided into two halves of different sex or age, the older or stronger half was always slightly more numerous. In a comic chorus there would be 13 men to 11 women, 13 women to 11 boys, and so on.

position. The chorus in the Lysistrata, consisting of one body of men, and one body of women, is an example. In the second place the chorus might be divided temporarily into half-choruses, either because of the special requirements of the play, or merely for purposes of singing and recitation. There are several certain examples in tragedy. In the Ajax of Sophocles the sailors hasten off, some to the east and some to the west, in search of Ajax. They return after a time from opposite sides of the orchestra, bringing word that they have not found him. In the Orestes, while Helen is being attacked within the palace, Electra keeps watch outside, and posts the chorus in two divisions at each end of the orchestra, to guard against surprise.[1] The examples in the Alcestis and the Seven against Thebes have already been referred to. In comedy the practice was not at all uncommon, if the testimony of certain manuscripts is to be accepted. Various choral passages in the comedies of Aristophanes are distributed between half-choruses, including the two odes at the end of the parabasis, and other lyrical pieces of an antistrophic character.[2]

A suggestion has been made that the divisions into ranks and files were utilized for musical purposes; that in tragedy, for instance, successive passages were delivered in turns by ranks of three men, or files of five men; and that the ranks and files of the comic chorus were used in the same manner. This is pure conjecture. It may or may not have been the case; but there is no evidence one way or the other. As to the musical duets it is impossible to speak with certainty. Whether they were mostly given by the whole chorus, or by halves, or smaller subdivisions, or by individual choreutae, or by the coryphaeus, is a matter concerning which there is no trustworthy information.[3] Such indications as are supplied by varieties in metre,

[1] Soph. Ajax 866 ff. ; Eur. Orest. 1258 ff.
[2] See Arnoldt, Die Chorpartieen bei Aristophanes, pp. 180 ff., where a list is given of the passages which are assigned to half-choruses by Rav. and Ven., e. g. Acharn. 1150, 1162, Nub. 563, 595, Vesp. 1060, 1091, Av. 737, 769, 1058, 1088, Eccles. 290, 301, Thesmoph. 659, Lysist. 321. [J. W. White, Harvard Stud. in Class. Phil. vol. xvii, assigns a more important part to the leader of the second semi-chorus in comedy than has usually been recognized, but the evidence is not conclusive.]
[3] Bergk's notion (Griech. Lit. iii. p. 131) that in Arist. Poet. c. 12 (κοινὰ μὲν ἁπάντων ταῦτα, ἴδια δὲ τὰ ἀπὸ τῆς σκηνῆς καὶ κόμμοι) ἴδια = 'sung by individuals or sections' is clearly wrong. ἴδια = 'not found in all plays', and the word to be supplied with ἁπάντων is δραμάτων, not χορευτῶν.

grammar, or subject, are too vague and uncertain to lead to
any definite conclusion.   Unless, therefore, further evidence of
a distinct character is discovered, this particular question will
have to be regarded as an unsettled problem.

§ 6. *The Dancing*.

In the ancient Greek drama, as in modern opera, the three
sister arts of Music, Poetry, and Dancing were all brought into
requisition.   But there was this difference—in the Greek drama
the poetry was the principal feature of the performance; the
music and the dancing were subordinate.   Moreover, dancing
was seldom introduced by itself as a mere spectacle; it was
mainly used in combination with singing, to interpret and add
vividness to the words of the song.   The music, the poetry,
and the dancing were blended together into one harmonious
whole, each part gaining an advantage by its combination with
the other two.   Most, if not all, of the choral songs were
accompanied by dances of one sort or another.   To the Greek
mind there was an inseparable connexion between song and
dance, and the notion of choral singing unaccompanied by
dancing would have appeared strange and unusual.   The
two arts had grown and developed simultaneously, as appears
from the fact that many of the technical terms in metrical
phraseology referred originally to the movements of the dance.
For instance, the smallest division of a verse was called a
'foot'.   A verse of two feet was styled a 'basis', or 'stepping'.
The words 'arsis' and 'thesis', which denoted the varying stress
of the voice in singing, originally referred to the raising up
and placing down of the foot in marching and dancing.   These
terms show how closely the two arts of dancing and singing were associated together in ancient Greece.   A choreutes
who was unable to accompany a song with expressive dance-
movements was looked down upon as an inferior performer.[1]
Dancing therefore, as might have been expected, played a
most important part in tragedy, comedy, and the satyric drama.
It was held among the Greeks in the greatest estimation, and
there was none of that feeling of degradation about it which was
common among the Romans.   A man might dance in public

---

[1] Athen. p. 628 E εἰ δέ τις . . . ταῖς ᾠδαῖς ἐπιτυγχάνων μηδὲν λέγοι κατὰ τὴν
ὄρχησιν, οὗτος δ' ἦν ἀδόκιμος.

without any loss of dignity, provided the dance was of a graceful
and becoming character. Sophocles himself, the great tragic
poet and fellow general of Pericles, was not ashamed to appear
in a dance in one of his own tragedies.[1]

At the same time it should be remembered that dancing in
ancient Greece was a very different thing from dancing in
modern times. It included a great deal more. The word
'dancing' in English necessarily implies movement with the
feet. It would be impossible in English to say that a man was
dancing, if he continued to stand in the same position. But in
Greek dancing this was not necessarily the case. The word
'orchesis', which we translate as 'dancing', had in reality a
much wider meaning. Greek dancing originated, according to
Plato, in the instinctive tendency of mankind to accompany
speech and song with explanatory movements of the body.[2]
It was essentially a mimetic performance. It included, not
only all such motions as are denoted by dancing in the
modern sense of the word, but also every kind of gesture and
posture by which various objects and events can be represented in dumb show. Its principal function was to interpret
and illustrate the words of poetry. For this purpose nothing
could be more important than appropriate gesticulation.
Hence in Greek dancing the movements of the hands and
arms played a larger part than the movements of the feet.
The same was the case in Roman dancing also. A few
quotations will illustrate this fact. Telestes, the celebrated
dancer employed by Aeschylus, was said to be able to 'depict
events with his hands in the most skilful manner '.[3] Demetrius
the Cynic, after witnessing the performance of a celebrated
dancer, exclaimed that he 'spoke with his hands '.[4] Ovid, in
his Art of Love, when advising a lover to show off his best
qualities before his mistress, tells him to sing if he has a good
voice, to dance 'if his arms are flexible '.[5] The flourishes
and gesticulations with which a professional carver cut out
a hare were called 'dancing' by the ancients.[6] Quintilian,

---

[1] Athen. p. 20 F.
[2] Plat. Legg. 816 A.
[3] Athen. p. 21 F ἄκρως ταῖς χερσὶ τὰ
λεγόμενα δεικνυούσαις.
[4] Lucian, de Salt. 63 ταῖς χερσὶ
λαλεῖν.

[5] Ovid, Ars Am. i. 595 'si vox est,
canta ; si mollia bracchia, salta '.
[6] Juv. v. 120 'structorem interea, ne
qua indignatio desit, | saltantem spectes
et chironomunta volanti | cultello'.

speaking of the gestures used in oratory, gravely says that there ought to be a considerable difference between the orator and the dancer; that the gestures of the orator should represent the general sense of the words, rather than the particular objects mentioned.[1] The bare fact of his comparing an orator with a dancer is a proof of the vital difference between ancient and modern dancing, and the importance of mere gesticulation in the former.

The purpose, then, of ancient dancing was to represent various objects and events by means of gestures, postures, and attitudes. In this kind of mimicry the nations of southern Europe are particularly skilful, as may be seen at the present day. The art was carried by the Greeks to the highest perfection, and a good dancer was able to accompany a song with such expressive pantomime as to create a visible picture of the things described. Aristotle defines dancing as an imitation of 'actions, characters, and passions by means of postures and rhythmical movements'.[2] His language indicates very clearly the unlimited capabilities of Greek dancing. Its general character will be well exemplified by the following account from Plutarch's Symposiaca. Dancing, it is there stated, might be divided into Motions, Postures, and Indications. Motions were of the greatest use in depicting actions and passions. Postures were the attitudes in which each motion terminated. For example, a dancer might halt in such a posture as to suggest Apollo, or Pan, or a Bacchante. Indications were not mimetic at all, but consisted in merely pointing out certain objects, such as the heaven, the earth, the bystanders. Dancing might be defined as poetry without words. The combination of poetry and dancing, of words and gestures, produced a perfect imitation.[3] In the above account from Plutarch we have a clear exposition of the Greek conception of dancing as the handmaid of poetry. Its function was to delineate and to emphasize the creations of the poet. This was the part which it played in the Greek drama. It is most

---

[1] Quint. Inst. xi. 3. 89 'abesse enim plurimum a saltatore debet orator, ut sit gestus ad sensus magis quam ad verba accommodatus', &c.

[2] Arist. Poet. c. 1 καὶ γὰρ οὗτοι (οἱ ὀρχησταὶ) διὰ τῶν σχηματιζομένων ῥυθ-μῶν μιμοῦνται καὶ ἤθη καὶ πάθη καὶ πράξεις.

[3] Plut. Symp. 747 B fol. The three divisions of dancing are φοραί, σχήματα, δείξεις.

important, therefore, when speaking of dancing in connexion
with the old dramatic performances, to remember the essential
difference between the ancient and modern meaning of the
words.

Some few facts have been recorded concerning the history of
dancing in connexion with the drama. In the earliest times it
consisted mainly of movements with the feet. The use of the
hands and arms in dancing, and the introduction of elaborate
gesticulation, was a development due to a later period.[1] In
the old-fashioned dramas of Thespis and his immediate successors dancing necessarily played a very important part. Both
tragedy and comedy were at that time mainly lyrical, and the
long choral odes were accompanied throughout by dances.
The early dramatists, such as Thespis, Phrynichus, Pratinas,
and Cratinus, were called ' dancers ' as well as poets, because
one of their principal duties consisted in training their choruses
in the art of dancing.[2] Phrynichus, in an epigram of which
two verses are still preserved, boasts of having discovered
more figures in dancing than there are waves in a stormy
sea.[3] The tragic dance of the sixth century, to judge from
the specimens given by Philocleon at the end of the Wasps,
was of a wild and lively character.[4] The tone of solemnity,
by which it was afterwards distinguished, was due to the innovations of Aeschylus. It was probably in the time of Aeschylus
that dancing in tragedy reached its highest pitch of excellence.
His long choruses gave ample opportunities for the display of
the dancer's skill. Moreover, the training of the chorus was
personally superintended by Aeschylus, and he is said to have
himself invented a great number of postures and attitudes to
be used in dancing.[5] Towards the end of the fifth century
the art appears to have declined in significance, along with
the general decrease in the importance of the chorus. It
began to lose something of its mimetic character. Plato, the
comic poet, who flourished at the end of the fifth century,
contrasts the mediocrity of the choral dancing in his day with
the excellence of that of a former period. In old times, he says,

---

[1] Athen. p. 630 B πρώτη δὲ εὕρηται
ἡ περὶ τοὺς πόδας κίνησις τῆς διὰ τῶν
χειρῶν. οἱ γὰρ παλαιοὶ τοὺς πόδας μᾶλλον
ἐγυμνάζοντο ἐν τοῖς ἀγῶσι.
[2] Athen. p. 22 A.

[3] Plut. Symp. 732 F σχήματα δ' ὀρχη-
σις τόσα μοι πόρεν ὅσσ' ἐνὶ πόντῳ |
κύματα ποιεῖται χείματι νὺξ ὀλοή.
[4] Arist. Vesp. 1474 ff.
[5] Athen. p. 21 E.

a good dancer was a sight worth seeing ; but the choreutae of
the present day stand in a row, like so many cripples, and bawl
out their songs, without any attempt at appropriate motions and
gestures.[1] This deterioration was a necessary consequence
of the tendency to thrust the chorus more and more into the
background.

The general character of the dancing in the Greek drama has
already been described. As far as details are concerned our
information is very defective, and only slight indications are
to be obtained from the existing plays. It is probable that,
when the parodoi commenced with a series of anapaests, the
chorus only marched in, without dancing. But all parodoi
written in lyrical metres were undoubtedly accompanied with
a dance. The iambic and trochaic tetrameters, in which many
of the parodoi in Aristophanes are written, seem to have been
generally intended for choruses which entered running, and
with an appearance of great haste.[2] The stasima, or long
choral odes between the acts, are said by many of the scholiasts
to have been unaccompanied by dancing, and to have been delivered by the chorus standing perfectly still.[3] The statement
is no doubt an error, due to false etymology. The stasima, or
'stationary songs', were so called, not because the chorus stood
still during their delivery, but because it remained all the time
in the orchestra. They were therefore opposed to the parodoi,
which were delivered while the chorus was coming in, and to
the exodoi, which were delivered while it was going out.[4] That
the stasima were accompanied by dancing is proved by several
references to dancing which they contain.[5] A tradition has been
preserved by one scholiast concerning the manœuvres of the
chorus in the stasima. It is said that during the strophe they

---

[1] Athen. p. 628 E ὥστ’ εἴ τις ὀρχοῖτ’
εὖ, θέαμ’ ἦν· νῦν δὲ δρῶσιν οὐδέν, | ἀλλ’
ὥσπερ ἀπόπληκτοι στάδην ἑστῶτες ὠρύον-
ται.

[2] Aristoph.Acharn. 204 τῇδε πᾶς ἕπου,
δίωκε, καὶ τὸν ἄνδρα πυνθάνου κ.τ.λ.,
Schol. ad loc. γέγραπται δὲ τὸ μέτρον
τροχαϊκόν, πρόσφορον τῇ τῶν διωκόντων
γερόντων σπουδῇ. ταῦτα δὲ ποιεῖν εἰώθα-
σιν οἱ τῶν δραμάτων ποιηταὶ κωμικοὶ καὶ
τραγικοί, ἐπειδὰν δρομαίως εἰσάγωσι τοὺς
χορούς, ἵνα ὁ λόγος συντρέχῃ τῷ δράματι.
Cp. Pax 301, 325, Plutus 257.

[3] Schol. Eur.Phoen. 202 ; Suidas s.v.

στάσιμον, &c.

[4] On the use of ἔξοδος in this sense
see the Tragic Drama of the Greeks,
p. 352. The word was also applied to
the whole of the concluding scene of
a tragedy.

[5] Aesch. Eum. 307 ἄγε δὴ καὶ χορὸν
ἄψωμεν. Eur. Herc. Fur. 761 πρὸς
χοροὺς τραπώμεθα. Arist. Thesmoph.
953 ὅρμα, χώρει | κοῦφα ποσίν, ἅγ’ ἐς
κύκλον, | χειρὶ σύναπτε χεῖρα. Other
passages of the same kind are not
infrequent.

moved to the right, during the antistrophe to the left; and
that during the epode they remained standing in the same
position as at first.[1] This description, however, has probably
been applied to the drama by mistake. A manœuvre of the
kind mentioned, though suitable to the circular chorus of the
dithyramb, would be out of place in the rectangular formations
of the dramatic choruses. Also it is comparatively rare to find
epodes in the stasima. As for the incidental odes, which occur
in the middle of the dialogue, many of those were written in
the lively hyporchematic style, to mark the joy of the chorus
at an unexpected turn of fortune. Some of the regular stasima
were of the same type.[2] The dances by which these odes were
accompanied were extremely brisk and energetic, in tragedy as
well as in comedy.[3] The exodoi, or concluding utterances of
the chorus, were not usually attended with dancing, but were
delivered in recitative as the chorus marched out. There is
an exception in the Wasps and the Ecclesiazusae, which are
terminated by the chorus dancing out of the orchestra. But
Aristophanes himself remarks that this was an innovation.[4]
There is no reason to suppose that in tragedy the kommoi,
or musical dialogues between actors and chorus, were unaccompanied with dancing. But naturally, if this was the case,
the dance would be of a quiet and sober kind, consisting more
of appropriate gestures and motions than of dancing in the
modern sense of the word.

During a large part of every Greek play the chorus had
nothing to say or sing, but merely stood watching the actors,
and listening to the dialogue. It would be absurd to imagine
that they remained stolid and indifferent during all this period.
Chorus and actors were supposed to form one harmonious
group, and no doubt the chorus followed the events upon the
stage with a keen appearance of interest, and expressed their
sympathy with the different characters by every kind of gesture

[1] Schol. Eur. Hec. 647 (p. 211 Dindf.).

[2] See above, p. 307, note 2.

[3] The liveliness of these dances, even in tragedy, is proved by such expressions as the following: Soph. Ajax 693 ἔφριξ᾽ ἔρωτι, περιχαρὴς δ᾽ ἀνεπτόμαν. Eur. Orest. 1353 ἰὼ ἰὼ φίλαι, κτύπον ἐγείρετε, κτύπον καὶ βοάν. El. 859 θὲς ἐς χορόν, ὦ φίλα, ἴχνος, | ὡς νεβρὸς οὐράνιον | πήδημα κουφίζουσα σὺν ἀγλαΐᾳ.

[4] Arist. Vesp. 1536 τοῦτο γὰρ οὐδείς πω πάρος δέδρακεν, | ὀρχούμενον ὅστις ἀπήλλαξεν χορὸν τρυγῳδῶν, Schol. ad loc. εἰσέρχεται γὰρ ὁ χορὸς ὀρχούμενος, οὐδαμῶς δὲ ἐξέρχεται. Eccles. 1179 αἴρεσθ᾽ ἄνω, ἰαί, εὐαί.

and by-play. Occasionally the long descriptive speeches delivered from the stage were accompanied with a mimetic dance
on the part of the chorus.[1] The events described by the actor
were represented in dumb show by the choreutae. In comedy
it was a regular practice to introduce descriptive speeches of
this sort, the metres used being iambic or anapaestic tetrameters, which were especially suitable for dancing to. There
is an example in the Clouds, where Strepsiades describes his
quarrel with Pheidippides. The various phases of the quarrel
were represented in dumb show by the chorus, keeping time
with the recitative of the actor.[2] Again, we are told that
Telestes, the dancer employed by Aeschylus, 'danced the
Seven against Thebes' so successfully as to bring the
various events before the very eyes of the spectators. The
statement no doubt refers to the dumb show with which he
accompanied the long descriptive speeches that abound in that
play.[3]

Each of the three different species of the drama had its own
special kind of dance. The tragic dance was called the 'emme-
leia'. It was grave and majestic in its motions, and was one
of the two dances approved of by Plato, and admitted into his
ideal republic.[4] Some of the postures or figures in the tragic
dance are mentioned by the ancient writers. One of them
represented a man in the act of thrusting with the sword;
another depicted a man in an attitude of menace, with clenched
fist. The rest are a mere list of names, of which the meaning
is uncertain. But it is plain from the existence of such lists
that the art of tragic dancing was reduced to a regular system,
and that the various attitudes and postures were taught in a
methodical manner.[5] We can hardly be mistaken in assuming
that as a rule the movements of the tragic dance were slow
and deliberate, and more like walking than dancing in the
modern sense. The odes called 'hyporchemata', with their

---

[1] Schol. Arist. Ran. 924 ἡ πρὸς τὰς
ῥήσεις ὑπόρχησις.

[2] Schol. Arist. Nub. 1355 οὕτως
ἔλεγον πρὸς χορὸν λέγειν, ὅτε τοῦ ὑποκριτοῦ διατιθεμένου τὴν ῥῆσιν ὁ χορὸς
ὠρχεῖτο.

[3] Athen. p. 22 A 'Αριστοκλῆς γοῦν
φησιν ὅτι Τελέστης, ὁ Αἰσχύλου ὀρ-
χηστής, οὕτως ἦν τεχνίτης, ὥστε ἐν τῷ

ὀρχεῖσθαι τοὺς Ἑπτὰ ἐπὶ Θήβας φανερὰ
ποιῆσαι τὰ πράγματα δι' ὀρχήσεως.

[4] Plat. Legg. 816 A.

[5] Suid. s.v. ξιφισμός; Hesych. s.v. ξιφί-
ζειν ; Poll. iv. 105 καὶ μὴν τραγικῆς ὀρχήσεως σχήματα σιμὴ χείρ, καλαθίσκος,
χεὶρ καταπρηνής, ξύλου παράληψις, διπλῆ,
θερμαυστρίς, κυβίστησις, παραβῆναι τέτταρα.

lively motions, were only adopted in tragedy on special occasions, to show the excessive joy of the choreutae.[1] The kommos at the conclusion of the Persae gives us a vivid picture of the general style of a tragic dance. The Persian Elders follow Xerxes on his way to the palace, bewailing the ruin of the empire in mournful strains. At each fresh exclamation of grief they fall into some new posture, first beating their breasts, then plucking their beards, then rending their garments, then tearing their hair ; and in this manner they gradually make their exit from the orchestra.[2]

The comic dance was called the 'kordax'. Its movements were coarse and lascivious, and its general style was suggestive of the phallic songs out of which comedy had been developed. It was a dance for drunken people, and no one but a man without any sense of shame would dance it when he was sober. It was considered vulgar and disgraceful by Plato, and excluded from his commonwealth.[3] Aristophanes, in the Clouds, takes credit to himself for having abandoned it in that play ; but, as the scholiast remarks, he frequently introduces it elsewhere.[4] In the comic dances the wildest movements were admissible. The chorus, at the end of the Wasps, when encouraging the sons of Carcinus to fresh exertions, bid them 'whirl round like tops, and fling their legs up into the sky'. Occasionally the circular dance of the dithyrambic chorus was adopted in comedy.[5]

The dance used in the satyric drama was called the 'sikinnis'. It was mainly a parody and caricature of noble and graceful dances, and was very violent and rapid in its movements. One of the postures used in the satyric dance was called the owl, and is variously explained by the old grammarians as having consisted in shading the eyes with the hands, or in turning the head to and fro like an owl.[6]

---

[1] See above, p. 307, note 2.

[2] Aesch. Pers. 1038 ff.

[3] Schol. Arist. Nub. 5 |2 κύρδαξ κωμική, ἥτις αἰσχρῶς κινεῖ τὴν ὀσφύν. Hesych. s.v. κόρδαξ ; Plat. Legg. p. 816 A ; Theoph. Char. 6.

[4] Arist. Nub. 540 οὐδὲ κόρδαχ' εἵλκυσεν.

[5] Arist. Vesp. 1529 στρόβει, παράβαινε κύκλῳ καὶ γάστρισον σεαυτόν, | ῥῖπτε σκέλος οὐράνιον· βέμβικες ἐγγενέσθων. Thesm. 953 ὅρμα, χώρει | κοῦφα ποσίν, ἅγ' ἐς κύκλον, | χειρὶ σύναπτε χεῖρα.

[6] Poll. iv. 99, 103 ; Athen. p. 629 F–630 A ; Dion. Hal. A. R. vii. 72 ; Phot. s.v. σκώπευμα.

§ 7. *The Music.*

The music of a Greek play was simple in its character, and
altogether subordinate to the poetry. As Plutarch remarks, it
was a sort of seasoning or relish, the words being the main
attraction.[1] Any comparison therefore between a Greek play
and a modern opera, as far as the music is concerned, must be
entirely illusive. In the first place all Greek choral singing was
in unison. The use of harmony in choral compositions was apparently unknown to the Greeks. Even in modern times Greek
Church Music has retained the practice of chanting in unison.
Consequently the general style of the music in a Greek drama
must have been exceedingly simple and severe compared with
the intricate combinations of modern music. In the second
place, the music was fitted to the words, instead of the words
being subordinated to the music. Each note of the music
corresponded, in most cases, to a separate syllable of the verse,
and the time of the music was determined entirely by the metre
of the verse. The ode was chanted in unison, syllable after
syllable, by the whole body of the choreutae. The modern
practice of adapting the words to the exigences of the music,
and making different parts of the chorus sing different words
at the same time, was altogether unknown. Hence it is probable
that the words of a Greek chorus were heard with considerable
distinctness by the whole audience. When all the singing was
in unison, and the notes of the music corresponded to the
syllables of the verse, there was no reason why this should not
be the case. In modern choral singing the poetry is so far
sacrificed to the music that even the general drift of the words
cannot usually be distinguished with much clearness. But this
could never have been the case in the ancient drama, where
the lyrical portions of the play often contained the finest poetry
and the profoundest thoughts of the whole composition. The
choreutae were doubtless made to sing with great precision and
distinctness of utterance ; and this training, combined with the
simple character of the music, would make it possible for the
words of an ancient chorus to be heard without difficulty. In
the third place, the instrumental accompaniment was limited

---

[1] Plut. Symp. 713 C τὸ δὲ μέλος καὶ τὸν ῥυθμὸν ὥσπερ ὄψον ἐπὶ τῷ λόγῳ, καὶ
μὴ καθ᾽ αὑτὰ προσφέρεσθαι.

in amount, and was never allowed to predominate. As a rule it
was given by a single flute or harp, and was the same, note for
note, as the melody. In lyrical, as opposed to dramatic, poetry
there was a tendency for the flute to overpower the voices.
Pratinas, in a lyrical fragment still preserved, complains of this
practice, saying that 'the Muse has made Poetry the mistress :
let the flute play the second part ; it is but the servant of Poetry'.[1]
These words, which only refer to a tendency in the lyrical poets
of the time, are significant as showing the Greek conception of
the relative position of instrument and voice in choral singing.
In the Greek drama, as already remarked, the instrumental
portion of the music was altogether subordinate ; and the
music as a whole was made subservient to the words and
the poetry.

Greek music was written in various Modes, as they were
called, concerning the nature of which there has been much
conflict of opinion. It is uncertain whether the Modes were
distinguished from one another, like the modern major and
minor scales, by the order of the intervals in the octave, or
whether the difference was one of pitch, like the difference
between the keys in modern music.[2] These Modes, whatever
their exact character, were each of them associated with a
particular kind of music. Every Mode had a special kind of
metre and of melody appropriated to itself, and a composition
in a given Mode was necessarily of a certain well-defined
character. The difference between the music of the several
Modes was very much the same as that between various
kinds of national music in modern times. For example, an
air in the Phrygian Mode bore the same sort of relation
to one in the Lydian as a lively Swiss song bears to a
plaintive Irish melody. Of the various Modes used in Greek
music the tragic poets selected those which were most suited
to their purpose. The Dorian and the Mixolydian Modes were
the two most commonly employed in tragedy. The Dorian
was majestic and dignified in style ; the Mixolydian was pathetic.
The one was used in the solemn and profound choral odes,

[1] Pratinas apud Athen. p. 617 B τὰν
ἀοιδὰν κατέστασε Πιερὶς βασίλειαν· ὁ δ'
αὐλὸς | ὕστερον χορευέτω· καὶ γόρ ἐσθ'
ὑπηρέτας.

[2] See, on the whole question,
Monro's Modes of Ancient Greek Music,
Oxford, 1894, Macran's Aristoxenus,
1902.

the other in cases where deep emotion had to be expressed.[1]
Besides these two principal Modes, certain others were occasionally employed. The old Ionic Mode was severe and
sober, before the degeneracy of the Ionic nation had altered
its character. It was therefore well adapted to tragedy, and
was used by Aeschylus.[2] The music of the Phrygian Mode
was passionate and enthusiastic, and was first introduced into
tragedy by Sophocles.[3] The Hypodorian and the Hypophrygian
Modes were only employed in the songs of the actors upon
the stage, and not in choral odes. The reason was that the
style of their music was better suited to realistic acting than
to choral singing.[4] Sometimes a few notes of instrumental
music were inserted by themselves, at intervals in the choral
songs, as a sort of refrain. The 'phlattothrat', which recurs
in the parody of Aeschylus's lyrics in the Frogs, is an instance
of such a refrain, the instrument used being the harp. The
flute was also employed in the same way. Such refrains were
called 'diaulia'.[5]

During the latter part of the fifth century the character of
Greek music underwent a considerable change. The severity
and simplicity of the music of the Aeschylean period were succeeded by a style in which softness, variety, and flexibility were
the prominent features. The author of the movement was
the celebrated musician Timotheus.[6] His innovations were
regarded by the philosophers and old-fashioned critics as so
many corruptions of the art of music, and as a proof of the
growing effeminacy of the age.[7] In one of the comedies of
Pherecrates the person of Music is made to complain of the
treatment she has received at the hands of various composers,
and ends her complaint by charging Timotheus with having
outraged and insulted her more than any one else had done,
and compares his florid melodies to the 'intricate movements of
ants in a nest'.[8] The new kind of music was very generally
adopted by the later tragic poets, such as Euripides and Aga-

---

[1] Plut. Mus. 1136 D-F.
[2] Heracleid. ap. Athen., p. 625 B ;
Aesch. Suppl. 69 Ἰαονίοισι νόμοισι.
[3] Vit. Soph., p. 8 Dindf.
[4] Aristot. Prob. xix. 30. 48.
[5] Arist. Ran. 1286 ff. ; Hesych. s. v.
διαύλιον· ὁπόταν ἐν τοῖς μέλεσι μεταξὺ
παραβάλλῃ μέλος τι ὁ ποιητὴς παρασιωπ-

ήσαντος τοῦ χοροῦ.
[6] Suid. s. v. Τιμόθεος. Plut. Mus.
1135 D.
[7] Suid. l. c. τὴν ἀρχαίαν μουσικὴν ἐπὶ
τὸ μαλακώτερον μετήγαγεν.
[8] Pherecrat. Cheiron. frag. 145
(Kock) ᾀδων ἐκτραπέλους μυρμηκίας.

thon, and is frequently ridiculed by Aristophanes.¹ Euripides appears to have foreseen from the first that the new style would soon become popular. On a certain occasion, when a novel composition by Timotheus was loudly hissed in the theatre, he told him not to be discouraged by his temporary want of success, as in a few years he would be sure to have every audience at his feet.² The prediction was verified by the result.

¹ Arist. Ran. 1301 ff., Thesm. 100 μύρμηκος ἀτραπούς, ἢ τί διαμινύρεται ; Schol. ad loc. ὡς λεπτὰ καὶ ἀγκύλα ἀνα-

κρουϑμένου μέλη τοῦ Ἀγάθωνος· τοιαῦται γὰρ αἱ τῶν μυρμήκων ὁδοί.
² Plut. An seni etc. 795 C.

CHAPTER VII

THE AUDIENCE

§ 1. *Composition of the Audience.*

THE theatre of Dionysus at Athens, during the period of
the Lenaea and the City Dionysia, presented a spectacle
which for interest and significance has few parallels in the
ancient or the modern world. The city kept universal holiday.
The various proceedings were in reality so many religious
celebrations. But there was nothing of an austere character
about the worship of Dionysus. To give freedom from care
was his special attribute, and the sincerest mode of paying
homage to his power was by a genial enjoyment of the
various pleasures of life. At this time of universal merriment the dramatic performances formed the principal attraction.
Each day soon after sunrise the great majority of the citizens
made their way to the southern slopes of the Acropolis,
where the theatre of Dionysus was situated. The tiers of
seats rising up the side of the hill were speedily filled with
a crowd of nearly twenty thousand persons. The sight of
such a vast multitude of people, gathered together at daybreak in the huge open amphitheatre, and dressed for the
most part in white, or in red, brown, yellow, and other rich
colours, must have been exceedingly striking and picturesque.
The performances which brought them together were not unworthy of the occasion. The plays exhibited at the festivals
of Dionysus rank among the very noblest achievements of
Greek genius. For beauty of form, depth of meaning, and
poetical inspiration they have never been surpassed. It would
be difficult to point to any similar example of the whole
population of a city meeting together each year to enjoy
works of the highest artistic beauty. It is seldom that art
and poetry have penetrated so deeply into the life of the
ordinary citizens. Our curiosity is naturally excited in regard
to the tone and composition of the audiences before which a

drama of such an exceptional character was exhibited. The object of the following chapter will be to bring together and present in one view all the available information upon this subject.

At the Lenaea, which was held in the winter, when travel-ling was difficult, the audience consisted almost exclusively of natives of Athens. The City Dionysia came about two months later, at the commencement of the spring, and attracted great crowds of strangers from various parts of Greece. Representatives from the allied states came to pay the annual tribute at this season of the year. It was also a favourite time for the arrival of ambassadors from foreign cities; and it was considered a mere matter of politeness to provide them with front seats in the theatre, if they happened to be in Athens during the celebration of the City Dionysia.[1] In addition to these visitors of a representative character, there were also great numbers of private individuals, attracted to Athens from all parts of Greece by the magnificence of the festival, and the fame of the dramatic exhibitions. Altogether the visitors formed a considerable portion of the audience at the City Dionysia. One of the great aggravations of the offence of Meidias was that his assault upon Demosthenes was com-mitted in the presence of 'large multitudes of strangers'.[2] Apparently the natives of foreign states were not allowed to purchase tickets for the theatre in their own name, but had to get them through an Athenian citizen.[3]

The composition of the purely Athenian part of the audience is a subject upon which a great deal has been written, the principal difficulty being the question as to the admittance of boys and women to the dramatic performances. In the treat-ment of this matter scholars appear to have been unduly biassed by a preconceived opinion as to what was right and proper. Undoubtedly Athenian women were kept in a state of almost Oriental seclusion. And the old Attic comedy was pervaded by a coarseness which seems to make it utterly unfit for boys and women. For these reasons some writers have gone so far as to assert that they were never present

---

[1] Dem. de Cor. § 28.
[2] Dem. Meid. § 74.
[3] Theophrast. Char. 9 καὶ ξένοις δὲ αὐτοῦ θέαν ἀγοράσας μὴ δοὺς τὸ μέρος θεωρεῖν.

at any dramatic performances whatsoever.[1] Others, while
not excluding them from tragedy, have declared that it was
an impossibility that they should have been present at the
performances of comedy.[2] But the attempt to draw a distinction between tragedy and comedy, in regard to the
admission of boys and women to the theatre, will not bear
examination. If they were present at one, they must have
been present at both. The tragic and the comic competitions
frequently took place upon the same days, and succeeded one
another without any interval; and it is difficult to suppose
that, after the tragedies were over, a large part of the audience
had to be turned out before the comedies could begin. Moreover, if women and boys had been present at the tragedies,
they would of necessity have been spectators of the satyric
dramas, which were nearly as coarse as the comedies. It is
useless therefore to endeavour to separate tragedy from
comedy in the consideration of this question.

As a matter of fact the evidence upon the subject, if considered without prejudice, makes it practically certain that there
were no restrictions of the kind suggested. The audience at
the dramatic performances, whether tragic or comic, was drawn
from every class of the population. Men, women, boys, and
slaves were all allowed to be present. The evidence from
ancient authors is too copious to be accounted for on any
other supposition. There are three passages in Plato which
in themselves are almost enough to decide the question. In
one place, speaking of poetry in general, and more especially
of tragedy, Plato says it is a kind of rhetoric addressed to
'boys, women, and men, slaves, and free citizens without
distinction'. In another place, where he is treating of the
management of his ideal republic, he says there will be no
great readiness to allow the tragic poets to 'erect their stages
in the market-place, and perform before women and children,
and the general public'. A passage of this kind would have
very little point, unless it was intended as a condemnation of
the prevailing practice. In a third place he declares that if

---

[1] E. g. Böttiger, Kleine Schriften, i.
pp. 295 ff. ; Wachsmuth, Hellen. Alter-
thumskunde, ii. p. 391 ; Bergk, Griech.
Literaturgesch. iii. p. 49.

[2] E. g. Bernhardy, Griech. Littera-
turgesch. ii. 2. p. 132 ; Böckh, Trag.
Princip. p. 37; Meineke, Menand. et
Philem. Reliq. p. 345.

there was a general exhibition of all kinds of public amusements, and the audience were called upon to state what they
were most pleased with, the little children would vote for the
conjuror, the boys for the comic poet, the young men and
the more refined sort of women for the tragic poet.[1] These
three passages of Plato are hardly consistent with the supposition that the drama was a spectacle which boys and
women were never allowed to witness.

In addition to the above evidence there are also several
places in Aristophanes where boys and women are referred
to as forming part of the audience. For instance, in the
Clouds Aristophanes prides himself on having refrained from
introducing the phallus 'to make the boys laugh'. In the
Peace he says that 'both the boys and the men' ought to
wish for his victory in the contest, because of his boldness
in attacking Cleon. In another part of the Peace, when some
barley is thrown among the male part of the spectators,
Trygaeus remarks that the women have not got any.[2] Other
passages of the same kind might be quoted. That women
were present at the New Comedy is proved conclusively
by a letter of Alciphron, in which Menander is supposed
to be writing to his mistress Glycera. In this letter he
says that nothing is dearer to him than to be crowned with
the ivy of Dionysus, as victor in the comic contest, 'while
Glycera is sitting in the theatre and looking on.'[3] Other
pieces of evidence are as follows. In Lucian's dialogue Solon

---

[1] Plat. Gorg. 502 B–E, Legg. 817
A–C, 658 A–D.
[2] Aristoph. Nub. 537-9, Pax 765,
766, 962-7. Cp. also Eupolis, Προσ-
πάλτιοι, fr. 244 (Kock) Ἡράκλεις, τοῦτ'
ἔστι σοι | τὸ σκῶμμ' ἀσελγὲς καὶ Μεγα-
ρικὸν καὶ σφόδρα | ψυχρόν. γελῶσιν, ὡς
ὁρᾷς, τὰ παιδία. Arist. Pax 50-3 ἐγὼ
δὲ τὸν λόγον γε τοῖσι παιδίοις | καὶ τοῖσιν
ἀνδρίοισι καὶ τοῖς ἀνδράσι | καὶ τοῖς ὑπερ-
τάτοισιν ἀνδράσιν φράσω | καὶ τοῖς ὑπερ-
ηνορέουσιν. [Rogers, Introd. to the
Ecclesiazusae, takes this passage, in
which women are not mentioned, to
prove that they were not present.
But the point of the jest is in the
enumeration of men in an ascending
scale of manliness, and to mention
women, even if they were present,

would have spoiled it. The other
passages which he quotes, Eccles.
165 ff., 435 ff., 1144 ff., and the situation
in the Thesmoph., are satisfied if we
suppose a large preponderance of
men; but they do not require us to
assume the exclusion of women.]
[3] Alciphron, Epist. ii. 3. [Rogers,
l. c. quotes a sentence of Glycera's
supposed reply, where she speaks of
herself as standing in the wings and
watching the performance, to prove
that ὁρώσης καὶ καθημένης ἐν τῷ θεάτρῳ
does not imply that women were in
the audience. But καθημένης ἐν τῷ
θεάτρῳ naturally and almost technically
means this; and the two passages need
not be taken to refer to the same point
in Glycera's supposed proceedings.]

tells Anacharsis that the Athenians educate their sons by taking them to tragedies and comedies, and showing them examples of virtue and vice, so as to teach them what to imitate and what to avoid.[1] In the Frogs there is the well-known passage in which Aeschylus taunts Euripides with the immorality of his plays, which have caused women of refine-ment to commit suicide from very shame. If women were never present at the performance of the tragedies of Euripides, there would be very little meaning in the reproach.[2] Then again we are told that when Alcibiades was choregus, and 'entered the theatre' dressed in a splendid purple robe, he was admired 'not only by the men, but also by the women'.[3] The shameless person in Theophrastus smuggles his sons into the theatre with a ticket which belongs to some one else. The miser never takes his sons to the theatre except when the entrance is free.[4] The regulation of Sphyromachus, pro-viding that men, women, and courtesans should sit apart from one another, can hardly have referred to any place but the theatre.[5] The cumulative effect of all these passages is difficult to resist. It is impossible to explain them all away by far-fetched interpretations. Even the story of the effect produced by the Eumenides of Aeschylus upon the audience—of the boys dying of fright and the women having miscarriages — such a story, though in itself a foolish invention, could hardly have originated unless women and boys had been regularly present at the theatre.[6] That they were admitted at a later period is proved by the direct evidence of inscriptions in the theatre of Dionysus, which show that in Hadrian's time seats were specially reserved for priestesses and other women.[7] This fact would not of course be conclusive evidence as to the custom which prevailed in the classical period of Athenian history. But, as far as it goes, it tends to confirm the conclusions based upon the evidence of ancient authors.

No doubt at first sight it appears a very startling fact that women and boys should have been spectators of the Old

---

[1] Lucian, Anachar. 22.
[2] Aristoph. Ran. 1050, 1051.
[3] Athen. p. 534 C.
[4] Theophrast. Char. 9 and 13.
[5] Schol. Aristoph. Eccles. 22.

[6] Vit. Aeschyli, p. 4 Dindf.
[7] C. I. A. iii. 282, 313, 315, 316, 321, 322, 324, 325, 333, 342, 343, 345, 350, 351, 354, 361, &c.

Comedy. But it should always be remembered that the
comedies performed at the festivals of Dionysus were a portion
of a religious celebration, which it was a pious duty to take
part in. Ribaldry and coarseness were a traditional element
in the worship of Dionysus, handed down from rude and
primitive times, and were not lightly to be dispensed with.
The Greeks in such matters were thoroughly conservative.
It was a feeling of this kind which caused the satyric drama
to be developed side by side with tragedy, in order that the
old licentious merriment of the satyrs might not be utterly
forgotten. The coarseness of the Old Comedy, being a regular
part of the celebrations in honour of Dionysus, might be
witnessed by boys and women without degradation, though
their presence at similar scenes in real life would have been
regarded in a very different manner. Where the worship of
the gods was concerned, the practice of keeping women in
strict seclusion was allowed to drop into abeyance. Women
and even girls were present at the phallic processions in
honour of Dionysus.[1] Their appearance on such occasions
was regarded as a mere matter of course. It need not therefore surprise us that women and boys should have been present
in the theatre at the performances of the Old Comedy.

Whether they were ever present in large numbers is a further
question. Even those writers who admit that their presence
was not prohibited by law, generally add that the more respect-
able women would in all probability keep away.[2] But the only
authority for such a notion is to be found in a couple of
passages in Aristophanes, which represent the husband as
present in the theatre, while the wife was at home.[3] There is
nothing so unusual in an occurrence of this kind as to warrant
any sweeping conclusions. Some people must necessarily have
remained at home, from the mere fact that the theatre would
not have been large enough to contain the whole population
of Athens, if men, women, and children had all been present.

---

[1] Aristoph. Achar. 241-6; Menand.
fr. 553 (Kock).

[2] E. g. Müller, Die griech. Bühnenalterthümer, p. 291.

[3] Aristoph. Av. 793-6 εἴ τε μοιχεύων
τις ὑμῶν ἐστιν ὅστις τυγχάνει, | κᾆθ᾽ ὁρᾷ
τὸν ἄνδρα τῆς γυναικὸς ἐν βουλευτικῷ, |

οὗτος ἂν πάλιν παρ᾽ ὑμῶν πτερυγίσας
ἀνέπτατο, | εἶτα βινήσας ἐκεῖθεν αὖθις αὖ
καθέζετο. Thesm. 395-7 ὥστ᾽ εὐθὺς
εἰσιόντες ἀπὸ τῶν ἰκρίων | ὑποβλέπουσ᾽
ἡμᾶς, σκοποῦνταί τ᾽ εὐθέως | μὴ μοιχὸς
ἔνδον ᾖ τις ἀποκεκρυμμένος.

But it is hardly probable, for the reasons already stated, that there was anything disreputable in a woman visiting the theatre. Reformers like Aristotle were in advance of ordinary public opinion in their feelings about such matters. Aristotle expresses a strong opinion that boys should be prevented from seeing or hearing any piece of coarseness or indecency.[1] Even if such ribaldry is an essential feature in the worship of any particular deity, he says that only men should be allowed to be present. The men should pay the proper homage to gods of this character on behalf of themselves, their wives, and their children; but boys should not be permitted to be witnesses of comedies and similar spectacles. This passage, in which Aristotle is combating the prevailing practice of the times, is an additional proof that boys were present at the performance of comedies, and shows clearly that when the worship of the gods was concerned ordinary public opinion did not consider such spectacles improper.[2]

Besides women and children it appears that slaves were occasionally present at the theatre. Plato in the Gorgias mentions slaves as one of the classes before which the tragic poets will not be allowed to perform in his ideal commonwealth.[3] The shameless man described by Theophrastus takes the 'paedagogus' to the theatre, along with his sons, and crowds them all into seats which did not really belong to him.[4] It is not, however, probable that the number of slaves among the audience was ever very great. Their presence would depend upon the kindness of their masters. But the two passages just quoted prove that there was no law to prevent their attendance.

§ 2. Price of Admission.

The dramatic entertainments at Athens were provided by the state for the benefit of the whole people. The entrance was

---

[1] Aristot. Pol. vii. 17 ἐπιμελὲς μὲν οὖν ἔστω τοῖς ἄρχουσι μηθὲν μήτε ἄγαλμα μήτε γραφὴν εἶναι τοιούτω· πράξεων μίμησιν, εἰ μὴ παρά τισι θεοῖς τοιούτοις οἷς καὶ τὸν τωθασμὸν ἀποδιδῶσιν ὁ νόμος· πρὸς δὲ τούτοις ἀφίησιν ὁ νόμος τοὺς ἔχοντας ἡλικίαν πλέον προσήκουσαν καὶ ὑπὲρ αὐτῶν καὶ τέκνων καὶ γυναικῶν τιμαλφεῖν τοὺς θεούς. τοὺς δὲ νεωτέρους

οὔτ' ἰάμβων οὔτε κωμῳδίας θεατὰς νομοθετητέον.

[2] [Navarre, Utrum mulieres Athenienses scenicos ludos spectaverint, 1900, discusses the evidence in detail, and comes to the same conclusions as those which are stated in the text.

[3] Plat. Gorg. 502 D.

[4] Theophrast. Char. 9.

originally free, and every man was allowed to get the best seat
he could. But, as the drama was extremely popular from the
very first, the struggle for seats caused great disturbances.
People used to come and secure places the night before the performance began; citizens complained that they were crowded
out of the theatre by foreigners; blows and fights were of frequent occurrence. It was therefore decided to charge a small
entrance fee, and to sell all the seats in advance. In this way
the crush of people was avoided, and, as each man's seat was
secured for him, he was able to go to the theatre at a more
reasonable hour.[1] The price of a seat for one day's performance was two obols. The same price appears to have been
charged for all the different parts of the theatre, with the exception of the reserved seats for priests, officials, and other distinguished persons.[2] A gradation of prices, according to the
goodness and badness of the seat, would probably not have been
tolerated by the democracy, as giving the rich too great an
advantage over the poor.

Until the close of the fifth century every man had to pay
for his place, although the charge was a small one. But the
poorer classes began to complain that the expense was too
great for them, and that the rich citizens bought up all the
seats. Accordingly, a measure was framed directing that every
citizen who cared to apply should have the price of the entrance
paid to him by the state. The sum given in this way was
called 'theoric' money. It used formerly to be supposed, on
the strength of statements in Plutarch and Ulpian, that this
theoric system was introduced by Pericles.[3] But the recently
discovered Constitution of Athens has now shown that it was
of much later date. The originator of the grant was the

---

[1] Schol. Lucian, Tim. 49 ; Suidas s. v.
θεωρικόν.

[2] Dem. de Cor. § 28 ἀλλ' ἐν τοῖν
δυοῖν ὀβολοῖν ἐθεώρουν ἄν. This passage shows that there cannot have
been any alternative between the reserved seats for distinguished persons
and the ordinary two-obol seats. Two
obols is also the sum mentioned by
Phot., Suid., and Etym. Mag. s. vv. θεωρικόν ; Etym. Mag. θεωρικά ; Liban.
Hyp. to Dem. Olynth. i ; Schol.
Aristoph. Vesp. 1184. The entrance
fee is given as one obol by Ulpian on

Dem. Olynth. i. § 1 ; and as three
obols by Schol. Dem. de Cor. § 28.
But both are no doubt mistaken. It
is given as a drachma by Schol. Lucian,
Tim. 49; Phot. and Suid. s. vv. θεωρικά ;
Philochorus apud Harp. s. v. θεωρικά.
But the drachma probably denotes the
aggregate fees for successive days at
one festival. Plat. Apol. 26 D has
most likely no reference to the theatre.
See Appendix C.

[3] Plut. Pericl. 157 A ; Ulpian on
Dem. Olynth. i. § 1.

demagogue Cleophon, who succeeded Cleon in the leadership of the democracy.   The year in which he introduced it
is not given ; but it must have been in the interval between
the death of Cleon in 422 and his own death in 404.   The
amount of the payment was two obols, the price of a single
seat.   It is said that soon afterwards Callicrates, another
demagogue, promised to raise the grant to three obols, the
object apparently being to provide an extra obol for refreshments.[1]   But this promise was probably never carried out,
as two obols is the sum usually mentioned in later times as
the theoric grant for a single day.[2]   Of course if the festival
lasted for several days, and there were performances in the
theatre on each of them, the amount given by the state would
be increased in proportion.   Thus certain authors speak of
a grant of four obols, or of six; but they are referring no
doubt to the sum given for the whole festival.[3]   The theoric
money was distributed in the different townships.   Every man
whose name was entered on the town lists as a full citizen
might claim his share.[4]   But it is probable that at first only the
poorer classes applied.   No one was allowed to obtain the
grant unless he made his application in person.   A certain
Conon, who succeeded in getting the money in the name of
his son, who was absent at the time, was fined a talent for the
offence.[5]   In its original form this theoric system may seem
not altogether indefensible.   The theatrical performances were
a sort of religious celebration, provided by the state ; and it
was unreasonable that any citizen should be debarred from
attending them by poverty.   But in the course of the fourth century the system was expanded and developed until it became a
scandalous abuse.   Grants were given, not only for the Dionysia,
but for all the other Athenian festivals, to provide the citizens
with banquets and means of enjoyment.   The rich began to
claim the money with quite as much eagerness as the poor.
The military revenues were impoverished in order to supply

[1] Ath. Pol. c. 28 (see Kenyon's and
Sandys's notes).
[2] Dem. de Contrib. § 169; Phot.,
Suid., Etym. Mag. s. vv. θεωρικόν; Etym.
Mag. s. v. θεωρικά ; Liban. and Ulpian,
ll. cc.   It was called διωβολία (Aristot.
Pol. ii. 7) or διωβελία (Ath. Pol. c. 28;
Bekk. Anecd. 237, 15).

[3] Four are mentioned in [Dem.]
Prooem. 53 ; six in Schol. Lucian, Tim.
49; Lucian, Encom. Dem. 36 ; Suid.
δραχμὴ χαλαζῶσα ; Suid., Harp., and
Phot. θεωρικά.
[4] Dem. in Leoch. § 37.
[5] Hyperid. in Dem. col. xxiv.

the Theoric Fund, which had now grown to huge proportions. A law was passed making it a capital offence even to propose to divert this theoric money to any other purpose. As a consequence the resources of the state were crippled, and the people demoralized. The theoric question became one of the chief difficulties which Demosthenes had to deal with, in his efforts to rouse the Athenian people to action against Philip.[1]

The tickets of admission in the ancient theatre appear to have generally consisted of small leaden coins stamped with some theatrical emblem.[2] Such coins could easily be renewed and stamped afresh for the different festivals. Many of them have been discovered in modern times, both in Attica and elsewhere, and date from the fifth century down to the Christian era. The specimen which is here given (Fig. 32) contains

FIG. 32.

a representation of three comic masks, with the name of the play, the Prophetess, inscribed above, and the name of the poet, Menander, underneath.[3] In addition to these leaden coins certain tickets made of ivory or bone, and apparently connected with the theatre, have also been preserved. But they are far fewer in number than the leaden coins, and only date from the Christian era. They are found solely in Graeco-Roman districts. They are too elaborate and permanent in workmanship to have served as ordinary tickets, and were probably intended for the occupants of the reserved seats in the front rows. They usually contain some figure or emblem on the one side, and a description of the emblem in Greek

[1] Harp. s. v. θεωρικά; Liban. Hyp. to Dem. Olynth. i; Ammonius, de diff. vocab., s. v. θεωρός; Dem. Olynth. i. § 19, de Cor. § 118, Philipp. iv. § 38.
[2] For a full account of these theatre-tickets see Benndorf, Zeitschrift für die österreichischen Gymnasien, 1875, pp. 579-95.
[3] The illustration is taken from Baumeister, Denkmäler, no. 1833.

on the other, together with a number in Greek and Latin.
The specimen in the text (Fig. 33) exhibits the head of Kronos
on the obverse, with the inscription 'Kronos' and the number
thirteen on the reverse.[1]   The numbers never rise higher than
fifteen, and cannot therefore refer to the individual seats in the
different rows.   Probably both the numbers and the emblems
denote particular blocks of seats.   We know that in the theatre
at Syracuse certain blocks were called after the names of gods
and princes, such as Hieron, Zeus, and Hercules; and that
in the Roman theatre Germanicus gave his name to a particular
block.[2]   It is a very plausible conjecture, therefore, that emblems like that of Kronos refer to some similar method of
designation.

Besides the two kinds of ticket just described, a large number

Fig. 33.

of bronze coins have been found in Athens and Attica, of which
the exact significance is uncertain.   But Svoronos, the latest
writer on the subject, is inclined to think that they too were
intended as marks of admission to the theatre.[3]   These coins
date from the fourth to the second century B.C.   On the obverse
they are generally stamped with an image of Athene, or
a lion's head, or a group of owls.   On the reverse there is
a letter of the alphabet, either single, or repeated more than
once (Fig. 34).   Sometimes there is no symbol on the coin,
but both the obverse and the reverse contain the same
alphabetical letter or letters.   It is possible, as Svoronos thinks,
that these coins were theatrical tickets, and that the letters,

---

[1] It is taken from Baumeister, no.
1835.
[2] C. I. G. 5369; Tac. Ann. ii. 83.
[3] Svoronos, περὶ τῶν Εἰσιτηρίων τῶν
ἀρχαίων, in Journal International

d'Archéologie Numismatique, 1898,
vol. i, pt. 1, pp. 37-120. The illustration in the text (Fig. 34) is taken
from this article.

of which there are at least fifty-two varieties, referred to various divisions of seats in the auditorium.

The receipts from the sale of places in the theatre went to the lessee. The arrangement in this matter was a peculiar one. The lessee was a person who entered into a contract with the state, by which he undertook to keep the fabric of the theatre in good repair, and in return was allowed to take all the entrance money. If he failed to keep the theatre in good condition, the state did the necessary repairs itself, and made him pay the expenses. He had to provide reserved seats in the front rows for distinguished persons, and it is uncertain whether the state paid him for these seats or not. For all the other portions of the theatre he was allowed to charge two obols and no more.[1] Occasionally, towards the end of a performance, he seems to

FIG. 34.

have allowed the people free admittance, if there was any room to spare.[2]

§ 3. *The Distribution of the Seats.*

When the theatre was full the audience numbered nearly twenty thousand persons. As to the arrangement of this enormous mass of people some few facts are known, and some

[1] The lessee was generally called ἀρχιτέκτων (Dem. de Cor. § 28), because part of his contract was to look after the buildings of the theatre. He was also called θεατροπώλης (Poll. vii. 199), from the fact of his selling seats; and θεατρώνης (Theophrast. Char. 11), from the fact of his having taken the theatre on lease. The nature of the arrangement with the lessee may be gathered from (1) C. I. A. ii. 573, in which the lessees of the theatre at the Peiraeeus engage to keep the fabric in good repair; (2) Dem. de Cor. § 28 ἢ θέαν μὴ κατανεῖμαι τὸν ἀρχιτέκτονα αὐτοῖς κελεῦσαι; (3) Ulpian on Dem. Olynth. i. § 1 ὥστε λαμβάνειν ... δύο ὀβολούς, ἵνα ... τὸν δ' ἄλλον παρέχειν ἔχωσι τῷ ἀρχιτέκτονι τοῦ θεάτρου.

[2] Theophrast. Char. 30.

inferences may be made ; but the information is not very complete. The great distinction was between the dignitaries who had reserved seats in the front, and the occupants of the ordinary two-obol seats at the back. A gradation of seats with descending prices was, as previously stated, unknown to the ancient Athenians. The privilege of having a reserved seat in the theatre was called 'proedria', and was conferred by the state.[1] From the large number of persons who enjoyed the distinction it is clear that several of the front rows must have been reserved ; and this conclusion is confirmed by the inscriptions in the theatre, which show that seats were assigned to particular individuals as far back as the twenty-fourth tier from the front.[2] The recipients of the honour, or at any rate the more prominent of them, were conducted in a solemn procession to the theatre each morning by one of the state officials.[3]

Foremost among the persons who had seats in the front rows were the priests and religious officers connected with the different divinities. That they should be distinguished in this manner was only in keeping with the essentially religious character of the ancient Greek drama. An inscription referring to the theatre at the Peiraeeus, and belonging to the third or fourth century B.C., mentions the priests specially by name as the most conspicuous members of the class who had the 'proedria'.[4] The inscriptions upon the seats in the theatre at Athens, which represent for the most part the arrangement that existed during the reign of Hadrian, place the matter in a very clear light. They enable us to determine the occupants of sixty out of sixty-seven seats in the front row ; and it is found that of these sixty persons no less than fifty were priests, or ministers connected with religion. Similarly, in the rows immediately behind the front row, a large number of places were set apart for the different priests and priestesses.[5] Such was

---

[1] Schol. Aristoph. Equit. 572. Pollux, iv. 121, states rather doubtfully that the προεδρία in the theatre might also be called πρῶτον ξύλον. If the expression was really used, it must have dated from the time when the theatre was still a wooden one.

[2] C. I. A. iii. 240-384.

[3] C. I. A. ii. 589 shows that in the Peiraeeus the demarch used to conduct the persons honoured with proedria to the theatre. A similar practice was no doubt observed at Athens.

[4] C. I. A. ii. 589 καὶ εἰσαγέτω αὐτὸν ὁ δήμαρχος εἰς τὸ θέατρον καθάπερ ἱερεῖς καὶ τοὺς ἄλλους οἷς δέδοται ἡ προεδρία παρὰ Πειραιέων. Cp. also Hesych. s. v. νεμήσεις θέας· Ἀθηναῖοι τὰς ἐν τῷ θεάτρῳ καθέδρας, ψηφίσματι νενεμημένας προεδρίας ἱερεῦσιν.

[5] C. I. A. iii. 240-384. Dörpfeld, Griech. Theater, p. 47.

the arrangement in the time of Hadrian, and t ere can be little doubt that it was much the same in its general character during the period of the Athenian democracy.

Among state officials the nine archons and the ten generals had distinguished places in the theatre. In Hadrian's time the archons occupied seats in the front row, and it is probable that this position was assigned to them from the earliest period.[1] The generals were in some prominent part of the theatre, but the exact place is not known. The snob in Theophrastus was always anxious to sit as near to them as possible.[2] Ambassadors from foreign states, as was previously pointed out, were generally provided with front seats, on the motion of some member of the Council. Demosthenes is taunted by Aeschines for the excessive politeness which he showed to Philip's ambassadors on an occasion of this kind. The lessee of the theatre at the Peiraeeus, as appears from an inscription still extant, was ordered to provide the ambassadors from Colophon with reserved places at the Dionysia. The Spartan ambassadors were sitting in 'a most distinguished part of the theatre' when they considerately gave up a place to an old man for whom no one else would make room.[3] The judges of the various contests sat together in a body, and would naturally be provided with one of the best places in the theatre.[4] The orphan sons of men who had fallen in battle received from the state, in addition to other honours, the distinction of 'proedria'. The same privilege was frequently conferred by decree upon great public benefactors, and was generally made hereditary in the family, descending by succession to the eldest male representative. An honour of this kind was bestowed upon Demosthenes.[5]

With the exception of the reserved places in the front rows, the rest of the auditorium consisted of the ordinary two-obol seats. Concerning the arrangements adopted in this part of the theatre a few details have been recorded. It appears that special portions of the auditorium were set apart for the different

[1] The thrones of seven of the archons are still preserved (C. I. A. iii. 254-60). Those of two of the Thesmothetae are missing, but no doubt stood in the front row with the others.

[2] Aristoph. Equit. 573-6 ; Theophrast. Char. 5.

[3] Aeschin. Fals. Leg. § 111, Ctesiph. § 76 ; Dem. de Cor. § 28 ; C. I. A. ii. 164 ; Cic. de Senect. § 63 ; Val. Max. iii. 5.

[4] See above p. 33.

[5] Aeschin. Ctesiph. § 154 ; Plut. X Orat., psephisms I and II, p. 851 A-F.

classes of the community.   There was a particular place for the members of the Council of Five Hundred, and another place for the Ephebi, or youths between the age of eighteen and twenty.[1] The women were separated from the men, and the courtesans sat apart from the other women.[2]   It is probable that all the women sat at the back of the theatre, at a long distance from the stage.   Foreigners also seem usually to have had a special place.[3]   The amphitheatre of seats was divided into thirteen blocks by the passages which ran upwards from the orchestra. It is very probable that in the arrangement of the audience each tribe had a special block assigned to it.   The blocks of seats were thirteen from the first.   The tribes were originally ten, though they were raised in later times to twelve and thirteen.   It is possible that the three unappropriated blocks were assigned respectively to the Council, the Ephebi, and Foreigners.[4]   But the excavations in the theatre afford grounds for inferring that there was a connexion between certain blocks and certain tribes, and the thing is not improbable in itself.[5]   The tribal divisions played a large part in the various details of Attic administration, and an arrangement by tribes would have greatly facilitated the

---

[1] Schol. Aristoph. Av. 795; Poll. iv. 122 βουλευτικὸν μέρος τοῦ θεάτρου καὶ ἐφηβικόν.

[2] Schol. Aristoph. Eccles. 22.

[3] Aristoph. Pax 962-6 TP. καὶ τοῖς θεαταῖς ῥῖπτε τῶν κριθῶν. OI. ἰδού. | TP. ἔδωκας ἤδη; OI. νὴ τὸν Ἑρμῆν, ὥστε γε | ... οὐκ ἔστιν οὐδεὶς ὅστις οὐ κριθὴν ἔχει. | TP. οὐχ αἱ γυναῖκές γ' ἔλαβον. Alexis, Γυναικοκρατία, fr. 1 (Meineke, Frag. Com. Gr. iii. p. 402) ἐνταῦθα περὶ τὴν ἐσχάτην δεῖ κερκίδα | ὑμᾶς καθιζούσας θεωρεῖν ὡς ξένας [this must mean that foreigners were in one of the extreme *side* kerkides (see p. 98), not at the *back* of the theatre].

[4] [Willems, Le Nu dans la Comédie Ancienne, 1901, places the Council in the central block, the foreigners at one side of the auditorium, the Ephebi on the other, while the tribes occupied the other ten.   A clay theatre ticket found at Megalopolis proves that blocks were assigned to special tribes in that theatre (Castrioles, Ἐφημ. Διέθνης τῆς Νομισμ. Ἀρχαιολ. 1900, p. 55).   See also Svoronos, quoted p. 333 n.]

[5] In the central block, on the third step, was a statue of Hadrian, of which the base is still preserved, erected in 112 A.D. by the Areopagus, the Council of Six Hundred, and the people of Athens (C. I. A. ii. 464). Besides this, the bases of three other statues of Hadrian, erected by different tribes, are still in existence.   They are all on the second step.   The first, erected by the tribe Erectheis, is in the first block from the eastern end; the second, erected by the tribe Acamantis, is in the sixth block from the eastern end; the third, erected by the tribe Oeneis, is in the sixth block from the western end (C. I. A. iii. 466-8). Thus the place of each statue in the series of blocks corresponded exactly with the place of the tribe in the official list of tribes.   It is therefore a highly plausible conjecture that, in addition to the statue of Hadrian in the central block, there were twelve other statues erected by the twelve tribes in the remaining blocks; and that each tribe had a special block appropriated to itself.   See Benndorf, Beiträge zur Kenntniss des att. Theaters, pp. 4 ff.

process of distributing the enormous mass of spectators among their proper seats.

Before leaving this part of the subject it may be useful to

FIG. 35.

give a complete list of the priests and officials for whom the front row was reserved in later times. It is still possible, as already stated, to determine the occupants of sixty out of the sixty-seven seats; and the arrangement, with a few exceptions,

is that of Hadrian's time.[1]   The list of names is not without
interest, as it enables us, better than any description, to form
a general conception of the sort of arrangement which was
probably adopted at an earlier period.   It also affords a curious
glimpse into the religious side of the old Athenian life, and
helps us to realize the variety and multiplicity of priests, deities,
and ceremonials.   In the very centre of the front row, in the
best place in the whole theatre, sat the priest of Dionysus
Eleuthereus, on a throne of elaborate workmanship.   A representation of the throne (Fig. 35) is inserted on the previous page.[2]
As the theatre was regarded as a temple of Dionysus, and the
drama was a celebration in his honour, it was only fitting that
his priest should occupy the most conspicuous and distinguished
position.   There is a reference to the arrangement in the Frogs
of Aristophanes, in the scene where Dionysus is terrified by
the goblins of Hades, and desperately appeals to his own priest
for protection.[3]   Of the thirty-three seats to the left of the
priest of Dionysus the occupants of twenty-six are still known,
and were as follows :—

> Priest of Zeus the Protector of the City.
> The Sacrificer.
> The Torch-bearer.
> Priest of Pythian Apollo.
> The Hieromnemon.[4]
> Priest and Chief Priest of Augustus Caesar.
> Priest of Hadrian Eleuthereus.
> King Archon.
> Chief Archon.
> Polemarch.

[1] Fourteen of the thrones were out
of place when the theatre was first
excavated (see p. 95).   The position
of some of them is rather conjectural.
In the list given in the text Dörpfeld's arrangement has been followed
(Griech. Theater, p. 47). For the inscriptions see C. I. A. iii. 240–302.
There is a very full account of the
inscriptions on the thrones in
Wheeler's article on the Theatre of
Dionysus, in Papers of the American
School of Classical Studies at Athens,
vol. i. pp. 152 ff.

[2] The illustration is taken from Zeitschrift für bildende Kunst, vol. xiii.
p. 196. On the back of the chair are
depicted two Satyrs, holding a bunch
of grapes. In the front, underneath
the seat, are two Oriental figures,
engaged in a fight with winged lions.
On the arms of the throne are figures
of Cupids, setting cocks to fight. The
appropriateness of the Satyrs, as a
decoration in the theatre of Dionysus,
is obvious. The cocks, no doubt, refer
to the annual cock-fight held in the
theatre (see above, chap. iii. p. 177).
The significance of the Oriental figures
has not yet been explained.

[3] Aristoph. Ran. 297.

[4] i. e. the representative of Athens
at the Amphictyonic Council.

The General.
The Herald.
Thesmothetes.
Thesmothetes.
Thesmothetes.
Thesmothetes.
The Sacred Herald.
. . . . and Apollo.
Diogenes the Benefactor.[1]
Priest of Attalus Eponymus.
The Iacchus-carrier.[2]
Priest of Asclepius the Healer.
Fire-bringer from the Acropolis.[3]
Priest of the People, the Graces, and Rome.
Holy Herald and Priest.
Priest of Apollo of Zoster.

All the thrones to the right hand of the priest of Dionysus have been preserved, and were occupied by the following persons :—

Interpreter appointed by the Pythian Oracle.[4]
Priest of Olympian Zeus.
Hierophant.
Priest of Delian Apollo.
Priest of Poseidon the Nourisher.
Priest of the Graces, and of Fire-bearing Artemis of the Tower.
Interpreter chosen from the Eupatridae by the people for life.
Priest of Poseidon the Earth-holder and Poseidon Erectheus.
Priest of Artemis Colaenis.
Priest of Dionysus the Singer, chosen from the Euneidae.
Bullock-keeper of Palladian Zeus.
Priest of Zeus of the Council and Athene of the Council.[5]
Priest of Zeus the Deliverer and Athene the Deliverer.
Priest of Antinous the Dancer, chosen from the Company of Actors.[6]
Priest of Apollo Patrous.
Priest of Dionysus the Singer, chosen from the Company of Actors.
Priest of Glory and Order.
Priest of Asclepius.
Priest of the Muses.

[1] A Macedonian commander of the third century, who restored Athens to freedom after the death of Demetrius.

[2] i. e. the priest who carried the Iacchus, or sacred statue of Dionysus, at the Eleusinian procession.

[3] i. e. the priest who looked after the sacrificial fire in the temple of Athene on the Acropolis.

[4] He was one of the three Exegetae, or Interpreters of sacred law, and was appointed by the Pythian oracle. A second was chosen by the people from the Eupatridae, and also had a seat in the front row.

[5] They were the guardians of the βουλή, and their altars were in the βουλευτήριον.

[6] This Antinous was a favourite of Hadrian's, and was drowned in the Nile, and afterwards deified.

Priest of Zeus the god of Friendship.
Priest of the Twelve Gods.
Statue-cleanser of Zeus at Pisa.
Priest of the Lycean Apollo.
Statue-cleanser of Olympian Zeus in the City.
Priest of the Dioscuri and the Hero Epitegius.[1]
Priest of Heavenly Nemesis.
Priest of Hephaestus.
Priest of Apollo the Laurel-wearer.
Priest of Dionysus of Aulon.
The Stone-carrier.[2]
Priest of Theseus.
Bullock-keeper of Zeus the Accomplisher.
Priest of Demeter and Persephone.

The priests enumerated here were the principal dignitaries in the Athenian hierarchy. Behind them sat a large gathering of inferior priests and priestesses. Their presence in such numbers at performances like the Old and Middle Comedy affords a curious illustration of the religious sentiment of the Athenians, and indicates clearly that the coarseness of the early comedy, and its burlesque representations of the gods and their adventures, did not constitute any offence against religion, but formed an appropriate element in the worship of Dionysus.

§ 4. *Various Arrangements in connexion with the Audience.*

The performance of plays began soon after sunrise, and continued all day long without intermission. There was no such thing as an interval for refreshments; one play followed another in rapid succession.[3] Apart from direct evidence upon the subject, it is manifest that, considering the large number of plays which had to be gone through in the time, any delay would have been out of the question. Consequently the spectators were careful to have a good meal before starting for the theatre.[4] There was also a plentiful consumption of wine and various

---

[1] Unknown.

[2] Probably an official who carried a sacred stone in some procession; but nothing is known about him.

[3] Aeschin. Ctesiph. § 76 ἅμα τῇ ἡμέρᾳ ἡγεῖτο τοῖς πρέσβεσιν εἰς τὸ θέατρον. Dem. Meid. § 74 ἐγὼ δ᾽ ὑπ᾽ ἐχθροῦ νήφοντος, ἕωθεν, κ.τ.λ. Aristoph. Av. 786–9 αὐτίχ᾽ ὑμῶν τῶν θεατῶν εἴ τις ἦν ὑπόπτερος, | εἶτα πεινῶν τοῖς χοροῖσι τῶν τραγῳδῶν ἤχθετο, | ἐκπτόμενος ἂν οὗτος ἠρίστησεν ἐλθὼν οἴκαδε, | κᾆτ᾽ ἂν ἐμπλησθεὶς ἐφ᾽ ἡμᾶς αὖθις αὖ κατέπτατο.

[4] Philochorus ap. Athen. p. 464 E Ἀθηναῖοι τοῖς Διονυσιακοῖς ἀγῶσι τὸ μὲν πρῶτον ἠριστηκότες καὶ πεπωκότες ἐβάδιζον ἐπὶ τὴν θέαν.

light refreshments in the course of the actual performances.
The time for such an indulgence was during the tedious portions
of a play, but when one of the great actors came upon the
stage the provisions were laid aside, and the audience became
all attention.[1]

The theatre must have presented a bright and festive appearance. Crowns were worn in honour of Dionysus by the express
command of the oracle.[2] The gaily-coloured dresses of the
spectators would add greatly to the brilliancy of the scene. At
the same time the comfort of the audience was not very much
consulted. The seats were of wood, or in later times of stone,
and had no backs; the people had to sit there all day long,
packed together as closely as was possible. Many men brought
cushions and carpets with them. Aeschines draws a con-
temptuous picture of Demosthenes escorting Philip's ambassadors to the theatre in person, and arranging their cushions
and spreading their carpets with his own hands. The toady
in Theophrastus, when he accompanies a wealthy man to the
theatre, is careful to take the cushion out of the slave's hands,
and to insist upon placing it ready for his patron.[3] There
was no shelter from the sun. The theatre faced towards the
south, and was entirely uncovered. But as the dramatic performances took place at the end of the winter, or early in the
spring, the heat would not usually be excessive. Probably
the sun was in many cases very welcome. If, however, any
shelter was required, hats appear to have been worn, though
the Athenians generally went bare-headed except upon a journey.[4] It has been suggested that small awnings were sometimes erected upon rods by individual spectators for their own
convenience, and that the 'purple cloths' which Demosthenes
spread out for Philip's ambassadors were awnings of this description.[5] It is true that an awning was provided for the priest
of Dionysus, as the chief dignitary of the meeting. But it is

---

[1] Philochor. ap. Athen. l. c. παρὰ δὲ
τὸν ἀγῶνα πάντα οἶνος αὐτοῖς ᾠνοχοεῖτο
καὶ τραγήματα παρεφέρετο. Aristot.
Eth. Nic. x. 5 καὶ ἐν τοῖς θεάτροις οἱ
τραγηματίζοντες, ὅταν φαῦλοι οἱ ἀγωνι-
ζόμενοι ὦσι, τότε μάλιστ' αὐτὸ δρῶσιν.
[2] Philochor. ap. Athen. l. c. καὶ
ἐστεφανωμένοι ἐθεώρουν. Dem. Meid.
§ 52.

[3] Aeschin. Ctesiph. § 76, Fals. Leg.
§ 111; Theophrast. Char. 2.
[4] Suidas s. v. Δράκων· ὑπὸ τῶν Αἰγινη-
τῶν ἐν τῷ θεάτρῳ, ἐπιρριψάντων αὐτῷ
ἐπὶ τὴν κεφαλὴν πετάσους πλείονας καὶ
χιτῶνας καὶ ἱμάτια, ἀπεπνίγη.
[5] The φοινικίδες mentioned by Aeschines (Ctesiph. § 76) were probably
coverlets or carpets.

improbable that the same convenience was extended to any
other members of the audience, at any rate in the period of
the democracy.   In Roman times awnings were erected for
the front rows of spectators ; but this was a late innovation.[1]

To keep order among a gathering of about twenty thousand
persons, crowded together in a comparatively small space, must
have been a matter of some difficulty.   Certain officers called
'staff bearers' were stationed in the theatre for the purpose.[2]
Superintendents were also appointed to maintain discipline
among the numerous chorus-singers.[3]   Disturbances were not
infrequent, and arose from various causes.   Sometimes the
rivalry between two choregi resulted in actual violence.   For
example, on one occasion, when Taureas and Alcibiades were
competitors in a dithyrambic contest, a fight broke out between
them, in the course of which Alcibiades, being the stronger
man of the two, drove Taureas out of the orchestra.[4]   That
the feeling between the choregi often ran very high has already
been pointed out in a previous chapter.   Disputes about seats
were another fertile source of disturbance.   With the exception
of the front row, the individual places were not separated from
one another, but the people sat together on the long benches.
Such an arrangement was very likely to cause confusion.
Demosthenes mentions the case of a highly distinguished
citizen, who ran great risk of being put to death, owing to
his having forcibly ejected a man from his seat.   Personal
violence in the theatre was regarded as a crime against religion,
and was strictly prohibited.   If any dispute arose, the proper
course was to appeal to the officers ; and the man who took
the law into his own hands was guilty of a capital offence.[5]

§ 5. *Character of Attic Audiences.*

The Athenians were a lively audience, and gave expression
to their feelings in the most unmistakable manner.   The noise
and uproar produced by an excited crowd of twenty thousand
persons must have been of a deafening character, and is de-

---

[1] See above, p. 100.
[2] Called ῥαβδοφόροι (Schol. Aristoph.
Pax 734), and ῥαβδοῦχοι (Pax 734):
cp. Dem. Meid. § 179.
[3] Suid. ἐπιμεληταί ἐχειροτονοῦντο

τῶν χορῶν, ὡς μὴ ἀτακτεῖν τοὺς χορευτὰς
ἐν τοῖς θεάτροις.
[4] Andocid. Alcibiad. § 20.
[5] Dem. Meid. §§ 178, 179.

scribed in the most uncomplimentary language by Plato.[1] It
was exceedingly difficult for the judges to resist such demonstra-
tions, and to vote in accordance with their own private judgement.
The ordinary modes of signifying pleasure or disgust were
much the same in ancient as in modern times, and consisted
of hisses and groans on the one hand, and shouts and clapping
of hands on the other.[2] The Athenians had also a peculiar
way of marking their disapproval of a performance by kicking
with the heels of their sandals against the front of the stone
benches on which they were sitting.[3] Stones were occasionally thrown by an irate audience. Aeschines was hissed off
the stage, and 'almost stoned to death', in the course of his
theatrical career. There is an allusion to the practice in the
story of the second-rate musician, who borrowed a supply of
stone from a friend in order to build a house, and promised
to repay him with the stones he collected from his next performance in public.[4] Country audiences in the Attic demes
used figs and olives, and similar missiles, for pelting unpopular
actors.[5] On the other hand, encores were not unknown, if
particular passages took the fancy of the audience. Socrates
is said to have encored the first three lines of the Orestes
of Euripides.[6]

If the Athenians were dissatisfied with an actor or a play,
they had no hesitation about revealing the fact, but promptly
put a stop to the performance by means of hisses and groans
and stamping with the heels. They were able to do so with
greater readiness, as several plays were always performed in
succession, and they could call for the next play, without
bringing the entertainment to a close. In this way they sometimes got through the programme very rapidly. There is an
instance of such an occurrence in the story of the comic
actor Hermon, whose play should naturally have come on late
in the day; but, as all the previous performers were promptly
hissed off the stage one after another, he was called upon

[1] Plat. Legg. 700 C.
[2] Dem. Meid. §§ 14, 226; Alciphron,
Epist. iii. 71.
[3] Poll. iv. 122 τὸ μέντοι τὰ ἐδώλια
ταῖς πτέρναις κατακρούειν πτερνοκοπεῖν
ἔλεγον· ἐποίουν δὲ τοῦτο ὁπότε τινὰ
ἐκβάλοιεν.

[4] Dem. Fals. Leg. § 337; Athen. p.
245 E.
[5] Dem. de Cor. § 262.
[6] Cic. Tusc. iv. § 63. Αὖθις seems
to have been the word used; cp. Xen.
Symp. ix. 4 ἅμα δὲ ἐβόων αὖθις.

much sooner than he expected, and in consequence was not ready to appear.[1] If the tale about the comic poet Diphilus is true, it would seem that even the authors of very unsuccessful plays were sometimes forcibly ejected from the theatre.[2]

A few scattered notices and descriptions, referring to the spectators in the Athenian theatre, show that human nature was very much the same in ancient times as at the present day. Certain types of character, which were generally to be met with among an Attic audience, will easily be recognized as familiar figures. There was the man of taste, who prided himself upon his superior discernment, and used to hiss when every one else was applauding, and clap when every one else was silent.[3] There was the person who made himself objectionable to his neighbours by whistling an accompaniment to tunes which happened to please him.[4] There were the ' young men of the town ', who took a malign pleasure in hissing a play off the stage.[5] There were the people who brought out their provisions during the less exciting parts of the entertainment.[6] There was the somnolent individual who slept peacefully through tragedies and comedies, and was not even waked up by the noise of the audience going away.[7] Certain indications show that the employment of the clâque was not unknown to Greek actors and poets. The parasite Philaporus, who had recently taken up the profession of an actor, and was anxious about the result of his first public appearance, writes to a friend to ask him to come with a large body of supporters, and drown with their applause the hisses of the critical part of the audience. Philemon, in spite of his inferior talents as a comic writer, is said to have frequently won victories from Menander by practices of this kind.[8]

The character of the Athenian audience as a whole is well exemplified by the stories of their treatment of individual poets. Although they were willing to tolerate the utmost

[1] Poll. iv. 88. The word for hissing an actor off the stage was ἐκβάλλειν; to be hissed off was ἐκπίπτειν. See Dem. de Cor. § 265, Poll. iv. 122.
[2] Athen. p. 583 F.
[3] Theophrast. Char. 11.
[4] Theophrast. Char. l. c.

[5] Alciphron, Epist. iii. 71 ἵνα, κἄν τι λάθωμεν ἀποσφαλέντες, μὴ λάβῃ χώραν τὰ ἀστικὰ μειράκια κλώζειν ἢ συρίττειν.
[6] Aristot. Eth. Nic. x. 5.
[7] Theophrast. Char. 14.
[8] Alciphron, Epist. iii. 71 ; Aul. Gell. N. A. xvii. 4.

ribaldry upon the stage, and to allow the gods and sacred legends to be burlesqued in the most ridiculous fashion, they were at the same time extremely orthodox in regard to the national religion. Any atheistical sentiments, and any violations of their religious law, were liable to provoke an outburst of the greatest violence. Aeschylus on one occasion was nearly killed in the theatre itself, because he was supposed to have revealed part of the mysteries in the course of a tragedy. He was only saved by flying for refuge to the altar of Dionysus in the orchestra.[1] Euripides also caused a great uproar by beginning his Melanippe with the line, 'Zeus, whoever Zeus be, for I know not save by report,' &c. In a subsequent production of a revised version of the play he altered the line to 'Zeus, as is reported by truth',[2] &c. In the same way sentiments which violated the moral feeling of the audience were received with intense indignation, and sometimes resulted in the stoppage of the play. The Danaë of Euripides is said to have been nearly hissed off the stage because of a passage in praise of money.[3] On the other hand, wise and noble sentiments excited great enthusiasm. Aristophanes was rewarded with a chaplet from the sacred olive because of the splendid passage in which he counsels mercy to the disfranchised citizens. Sophocles is said to have been appointed one of the generals in the Samian expedition on account of the excellent political wisdom shown in certain passages of the Antigone.[4] The partiality of the Athenians for idealism in art is shown by the reception which they gave to Phrynichus's tragedy of the Capture of Miletus, an historical drama in which the misfortunes of the Ionians were forcibly portrayed. So far from admiring the skill of the poet, they fined him a thousand drachmas for reminding them of the miseries of their kinsfolk, and passed a law forbidding the reproduction of this particular play.[5]

The enthusiasm of the Athenians for the drama was unbounded. Nowhere was the theatre more crowded. In the words of one of the old historians, they 'spent the public

---

[1] Aristot. Eth. Nic. iii. 2, and Eustath. ad loc.
[2] Plut. Amator. 756 C; Nauck, Trag. Gk. Frag. p. 511.
[3] Senec. Epist. 115; Nauck, Trag.
Gr. Frag. p. 457.
[4] Vit. Aristoph. (Dindf. Prolegom. de Com. p. 12); Arg. to Soph. Antiq.
[5] Herod. vi. 21.

revenues on their festivals, were more familiar with the stage than with the camp, and paid more regard to verse-makers than to generals'.[1] The speeches of Demosthenes are full of complaints in the same strain. The eagerness with which dramatic victories were coveted, and the elaborate monuments erected to commemorate them, have already been referred to in a previous chapter. It was not, however, till the middle of the fourth century that the devotion to this and similar amusements grew to such a height as to become a positive vice, and to sap the military energies of the people. The Athenians of the fifth century showed that enthusiasm for art and music and the drama was not inconsistent with energy of character. As a matter of fact the very greatest period of the Attic drama is also the period of the political supremacy of Athens.

As far as intelligence and discrimination are concerned, the Athenian audiences were probably superior to any audience of the same size which has ever been brought together. Their keen and rapid intellect was a subject of frequent praise among the ancients, and was ascribed to the exhilarating influence of the Attic climate.[2] They were especially distinguished for the refinement of their taste in matters of art and literature, and for the soberness of judgement with which they rejected any sort of florid exuberance. That they were keenly alive to the attractions of beauty of form and chastened simplicity of style is proved by the fact that Sophocles was by far the most successful of their tragic poets. Though Euripides became more popular among the later Greeks, Sophocles in his own lifetime obtained far more victories than any other tragic writer.[3] At the same time it is easy to form an exaggerated idea of the refinement of an Attic audience. They were drawn from all classes of the people, and a large proportion were ignorant and uncultured. Plato speaks in the most disparaging terms of them, and charges them with having corrupted the dramatic poets, and brought them down to

---

[1] Justin. 17. 9. The passage was very likely from Theopompus.

[2] Dem. Olynth. iii. § 15 καὶ γνῶναι πάντων ὑμεῖς ὀξύτατοι τὰ ῥηθέντα. Cic. de Fato § 7 'Athenis tenue caelum, ex quo acutiores etiam putantur Attici'.

[3] Cic. Orat. § 25 '(Athenienses) quorum semper fuit prudens sincerumque iudicium, nihil ut possent nisi incorruptum audire et elegans'; § 27 'ad Atticorum igitur aures teretes et religiosas qui se accommodant, ii sunt existimandi Attice dicere'.

their own level.[1] His evidence is perhaps rather prejudiced. But Aristotle, who had much greater faith in popular judgement, is not very complimentary. He divides the theatrical audience into two classes, the refined and cultured class on the one hand, and the mass of rough and ignorant artisans on the other. One of his objections to the profession of an actor or musician is that he must accommodate himself to the level of the ignorant part of his audience.[2] He mentions examples in the Poetics of the low level of popular taste, from which it appears that the average spectator in ancient times was, like his modern counterpart, fond of ' happy terminations '. He cared little for the artistic requirements of the composition ; his desire was to see virtue rewarded, and vice punished, at the end of a play. Then again, a large part of the audience, Aristotle remarks, were so ignorant as to be unacquainted with the ordinary facts of mythology, which formed the basis of most tragedies. In judging a play, they paid more regard to the actor's voice than to the poet's genius.[3] At the same time, in spite of depreciatory criticisms, it must be remembered that the true criterion of a people's taste is to be found in the character of the popular favourites. The victorious career of Sophocles, lasting over more than fifty years, is a convincing proof of the fact that, at any rate during the fifth century, the dramatic taste of the Athenians was altogether higher than that of an ordinary popular audience.[4]

---

[1] Plat. Legg. 659 B, C.
[2] Aristot. Pol. viii. 7 ἐπεὶ δ' ὁ θεατὴς διττός, ὁ μὲν ἐλεύθερος καὶ πεπαιδευμένος, ὁ δὲ φορτικὸς ἐκ βαναύσων καὶ θητῶν καὶ ἄλλων τοιούτων συγκείμενος. Ibid. 6 ὁ γὰρ θεατὴς φορτικὸς ὢν μεταβάλλειν εἴωθε τὴν μουσικήν, ὥστε καὶ τοὺς τεχνίτας τοὺς πρὸς αὐτὸν μελετῶντας αὐτούς τε ποιούς τινας ποιεῖ καὶ τὰ σώματα διὰ τὰς κινήσεις.
[3] Aristot. Poet. c. 13 δευτέρα δ' ἡ πρώτη λεγομένη ὑπὸ τινῶν ἐστι σύστασις, ἡ διπλῆν τε τὴν σύστασιν ἔχουσα καθάπερ ἡ Ὀδύσσεια καὶ τελευτῶσα ἐξ ἐναντίας τοῖς βελτίοσι καὶ χείροσιν. δοκεῖ δὲ εἶναι πρώτη διὰ τὴν τῶν θεάτρων ἀσθένειαν, ἀκολουθοῦσι γὰρ οἱ ποιηταὶ κατ' εὐχὴν ποιοῦντες τοῖς θεαταῖς. Ibid. c. 9 (of the old legends) ἐπεὶ καὶ τὰ γνώριμα ὀλίγοις γνώριμά ἐστιν, ἀλλ' ὅμως εὐφραίνει πάντας. Id. Rhet. iii. 1 ἐκεῖ μεῖζον δύνανται νῦν τῶν ποιητῶν οἱ ὑποκριταί.
[4] [Cp. Römer, Ueber den litterarisch-aesthetischen Bildungsstand des attischen Theaterpublikums, 1901.]

APPENDIX A

THE information concerning the dates at which the plays of the great Attic dramatists were produced, and the success which they met with in the competitions, is derived from various brief notices, which occur mostly in the Arguments prefixed to the different plays, and which were ultimately derived from Aristotle's Didascaliae, or from other collections of the same kind (see chap. i. p. 47). A list of these notices is here appended :—

472 B.C.

Arg. Aesch. Persae : Ἐπὶ Μένωνος τραγῳδῶν Αἰσχύλος ἐνίκα Φινεῖ, Πέρσαις, Γλαύκῳ, Προμηθεῖ.

467 B.C.

Arg. Aesch. Septem : Ἐδιδάχθη ἐπὶ Θεαγενίδου ὀλυμπιάδι οη΄. ἐνίκα Λαΐῳ, Οἰδίποδι, Ἑπτὰ ἐπὶ Θήβας, Σφιγγὶ σατυρικῇ. δεύτερος Ἀριστίας Περσεῖ, Ταντάλῳ, Παλαισταῖς σατυρικοῖς τοῖς Πρατίνου πατρός. τρίτος Πολυφράδμων Λυκουργείᾳ τετραλογίᾳ.

458 B.C.

Arg. Aesch. Agamemnon : Ἐδιδάχθη τὸ δρᾶμα ἐπὶ ἄρχοντος Φιλοκλέους, ὀλυμπιάδι ὀγδοηκοστῇ ἔτει δευτέρῳ. πρῶτος Αἰσχύλος Ἀγαμέμνονι, Χοηφόροις, Εὐμενίσι, Πρωτεῖ σατυρικῷ. ἐχορήγει Ξενοκλῆς Ἀφιδνεύς.

455 B.C.

Vit. Eurip. p. 4 Dindf. : Ἤρξατο δὲ διδάσκειν (ὁ Εὐριπίδης) ἐπὶ Καλλίου ἄρχοντος κατ᾽ ὀλυμπιάδα πα΄ ἔτει α΄, πρῶτον δ᾽ ἐδίδαξε τὰς Πελιάδας, ὅτε καὶ τρίτος ἐγένετο.

450 B.C. (?)

Arg. Eur. Rhesus : Ἐν μέντοι ταῖς διδασκαλίαις ὡς γνήσιον ἀναγέγραπται. Schol. Rhes. 529 : Κράτης ἀγνοεῖν φησι τὸν Εὐριπίδην τὴν περὶ τὰ μετέωρα θεωρίαν διὰ τὸ νέον εἶναι ὅτε τὸν Ῥῆσον ἐδίδασκε.

438 B.C.

Arg. Eur. Alcestis : Ἐδιδάχθη ἐπὶ Γλαυκίνου ἄρχοντος ὀλυμπιάδι πε΄. πρῶτος ἦν Σοφοκλῆς, δεύτερος Εὐριπίδης Κρήσσαις, Ἀλκμαίωνι τῷ διὰ Ψωφῖδος, Τηλέφῳ, Ἀλκήστιδι.

431 B.C.

Arg. Eur. Medea: Ἐδιδάχθη ἐπὶ Πυθοδώρου ἄρχοντος κατὰ τὴν ὀγδοη-κοστὴν ἑβδόμην ὀλυμπιάδα. πρῶτος Εὐφορίων, δεύτερος Σοφοκλῆς, τρίτος Εὐριπίδης Μηδείᾳ, Φιλοκτήτῃ, Δίκτυϊ, Θερισταῖς σατύροις. οὐ σώζεται.

430 B.C. (?)

Aristid. vol. ii. p. 334 Dindf. : Σοφοκλῆς Φιλοκλέους ἡττᾶτο ἐν Ἀθηναίοις τὸν Οἰδίπουν, ὦ Ζεῦ καὶ θεοί.

428 B.C.

Arg. Eur. Hippolytus : Ἐδιδάχθη ἐπὶ Ἀμείνονος ἄρχοντος ὀλυμπιάδι ὀγδοη-κοστῇ ἑβδόμῃ, ἔτει τετάρτῳ. πρῖτος Εὐριπίδης, δεύτερος Ἰοφῶν, τρίτος Ἴων.

425 B.C.

Arg. Arist. Acharnenses : Ἐδιδάχθη ἐπὶ Εὐθύνου ἄρχοντος ἐν Ληναίοις διὰ Καλλιστράτου· καὶ πρῶτος ἦν. δεύτερος Κρατῖνος Χειμαζομένοις· οὐ σώζονται. τρίτος Εὔπολις Νουμηνίαις.

424 B.C.

Arg. Arist. Equites : Ἐδιδάχθη τὸ δρᾶμα ἐπὶ Στρατοκλέους ἄρχοντος δημοσίᾳ εἰς Λήναια, δι᾽ αὐτοῦ τοῦ Ἀριστοφάνους. πρῶτος ἐνίκα· δεύτερος Κρατῖνος Σατύροις· τρίτος Ἀριστομένης Ὑλοφόροις.

423 B.C.

Arg. Arist. Nubes : Αἱ πρῶται Νεφέλαι ἐν ἄστει ἐδιδάχθησαν ἐπὶ ἄρχοντος Ἰσάρχου, ὅτε Κρατῖνος μὲν ἐνίκα Πυτίνῃ, Ἀμειψίας δὲ Κόννῳ.

422 B.C.

Arg. Arist. Nubes : Αἱ δὲ δεύτεραι Νεφέλαι ἐπὶ Ἀμεινίου ἄρχοντος.

Arg. Arist. Vespae : Ἐδιδάχθη ἐπὶ ἄρχοντος Ἀμεινίου διὰ Φιλωνίδου εἰς Λήναια· καὶ ἐνίκα πρῶτος. δεύτερος ἦν Φιλωνίδης Προάγωνι, Λεύκων Πρέσβεσι τρίτος. (See p. 21, n. 2).

421 B.C.

Arg. Arist. Pax : Ἐνίκησε δὲ τῷ δράματι ὁ ποιητὴς ἐπὶ ἄρχοντος Ἀλκαίου, ἐν ἄστει. πρῶτος Εὔπολις Κόλαξι, δεύτερος Ἀριστοφάνης Εἰρήνῃ, τρίτος Λεύκων Φράτορσι. τὸ δὲ δρᾶμα ὑπεκρίνατο Ἀπολλόδωρος *ἡνίκα ἑρμὴν λοιοκροτης*. (See p. 41, n. 2).

415 B.C.

Ael. Var. Hist. ii. 8: Κατὰ τὴν πρώτην καὶ ἐνενηκοστὴν ὀλυμπιάδα . . . . ἀντηγωνίσαντο ἀλλήλοις Ξενοκλῆς καὶ Εὐριπίδης· καὶ πρῶτός γε ἦν Ξενοκλῆς, ὅστις ποτὲ οὗτός ἐστιν, Οἰδίποδι καὶ Λυκάονι καὶ Βάκχαις καὶ Ἀθάμαντι σατυρικῷ. τούτου δεύτερος Εὐριπίδης ἦν Ἀλεξάνδρῳ καὶ Παλαμήδει καὶ Τρῳάσι καὶ Σισύφῳ σατυρικῷ.

414 B.C.

Arg. I. Arist. Aves : 'Εδιδάχθη ἐπὶ Χαβρίου διὰ Καλλιστράτου ἐν ἄστει, ὃς ἦν δεύτερος τοῖς "Ορνισι, πρῶτος 'Αμειψίας Κωμασταῖς, τρίτος Φρύνιχος Μονοτρόπῳ. Arg. II. Arist. Aves : 'Επὶ Χαβρίου .... εἰς Λήναια τὸν 'Αμφιάραον ἐδίδαξε διὰ Φιλωνίδου.

412 B.C.

Schol. Arist. Ran. 53 : Ἡ δὲ 'Ανδρομέδα ὀγδόῳ ἔτει προεισῆλθεν. Schol. Arist. Thesm. 1012 : συνδεδίδακται γὰρ τῇ 'Ελένῃ·

411 B.C.

Arg. Arist. Lysistrata : 'Εδιδάχθη ἐπὶ Καλλίου ἄρχοντος τοῦ μετὰ Κλεόκριτον ἄρξαντος. εἰσῆκται δὲ διὰ Καλλιστράτου.

409 B.C.

Arg. Soph. Philoctetes: 'Εδιδάχθη ἐπὶ Γλαυκίππου. πρῶτος ἦν Σοφοκλῆς.

408 B.C.

Schol. Eur. Orest. 371 : Πρὸ γὰρ Διοκλέους, ἐφ' οὗ τὸν 'Ορέστην ἐδίδαξε.

409–407 B.C. (?)

Arg. Eur. Phoenissae : 'Εδιδάχθη ἐπὶ Ναυσικράτους (unknown, probably ' suffectus ') ἄρχοντος ὀλυμπιάδ .... πρῶτος ...... δεύτερος Εὐριπίδης, τρίτος .... ὁ Οἰνόμαος καὶ Χρύσιππος καὶ Φοίνισσαι καὶ ... σατυρ ...... οὐ σώζεται. Schol. Arist. Ran. 53 : διὰ τί δὲ μὴ ἄλλο τι τῶν πρὸ ὀλίγου διδαχθέντων καὶ καλῶν, 'Υψιπύλης, Φοινισσῶν, 'Αντιόπης ;

405 B.C.

Arg. Arist. Ranae: 'Εδιδάχθη ἐπὶ Καλλίου τοῦ μετὰ 'Αντιγένη διὰ Φιλωνίδου εἰς Λήναια. πρῶτος ἦν· Φρύνιχ ϛ δεύτερος Μούσαις· Πλάτων τρίτος Κλεοφῶντι.

— B.C.

Schol. Arist. Ran. 67 : Οὕτω γὰρ καὶ αἱ Διδασκαλίαι φέρουσι, τελευτήσαντος Εὐριπίδου τὸν υἱὸν αὐτοῦ δεδιδαχέναι ὁμώνυμον ἐν ἄστει 'Ιφιγένειαν τὴν ἐν Αὐλίδι, 'Αλκμαίωνα, Βάκχας.

401 B.C.

Arg. Soph. O. C. : Τὸν ἐπὶ Κολωνῷ Οἰδίποδα ἐπὶ τετελευτηκότι τῷ πάππῳ Σοφοκλῆς ὁ ὑϊδοῦς ἐδίδαξεν, υἱὸς ὢν 'Αρίστωνος, ἐπὶ ἄρχοντος Μίκωνος.

388 B.C.

Arg. Arist. Plutus : 'Εδιδάχθη ἐπὶ ἄρχοντος 'Αντιπάτρου, ἀνταγωνιζομένου αὐτῷ Νικοχάρους μὲν Λάκωσιν, 'Αριστομένους δὲ 'Αδμήτῳ, Νικοφῶντος δὲ 'Αδώνιδι, 'Αλκαίου δὲ Πασιφάῃ.

APPENDIX B

The Athenian inscriptions bearing upon the drama and dramatic contests are to be found, edited by Köhler, in the Corpus Inscriptionum Atticarum, ii. 2. pp. 394 ff., iv. 2. pp. 218 ff. Since their publication in this form much work has been done in reference to them by Wilhelm, Capps, and others. The following selection gives the most important inscriptions, with the conclusions which seem to be best warranted, omitting portions the restoration of which seems too uncertain to be useful.

The conjectural dates are inserted and conjectural supplements marked off by square brackets where the evidence is reasonably good: letters enclosed in round brackets simply expand the abbreviations contained in the inscription.

I. *List of victors in the City Dionysia* (C. I. A. ii. 971, iv. 971).

The fragments have been arranged on the hypothesis that they formed part of an inscription in 15 columns of 140 or 142 lines each: Columns 1, 2, 7–12 and 16 have been lost, as well as the greater part of the remainder. Capps conjectures that the inscription began in 502–501, and that this date was that of the beginning of choregia in tragedy and dithyramb (Capps, Introd. of Comedy into the City Dionysia, p. 29). The heading, of which at present only twelve letters remain (more widely spaced than the rest of the inscription), seems to have extended over the head of the first 6 columns, and probably ran (Capps, l. c., p. 29)—

[ἀπὸ . . . . ἐφ' οὗ πρῶτ]ον κῶμοι ἦσαν τῶ[ν ἐν ἄστει Διονυσίων οἴδε ἐνίκων].

We next have fragments of Cols. III, IV, V (971 *a, f*).

Col. III.	Col. IV.	Col. V.
B. C. 473–2	B. C. 460–59	
Ξ]ενοκλείδης ἐχορήγε[ι	Πανδιονί[ς ἀνδρῶν	
Μ]άγνης ἐδίδασκεν.	Κλεαίνετ[ος ἐχορήγει	
τραγῳδῶν	κωμῳδῶν	
Περικλῆς Χολαρ(γεὺς) ἐχορή(γει)	Θαρ[. . ἐχορήγει	B. C. 447–6

5 Αἰσχύλος ἐδίδασκεν.
[ἐπὶ Χάρητος] (B.C. 472-1)
....
....
....
10 ....
....
...... ἐχ]ορήγει
... ς ἐδίδ]ασκεν.
[τραγῳδῶν]
15 ...... ἐχ]ορήγει
Πολυφράσμω]ν ἐδίδασ(κεν).
ἐπὶ Πραξιέργο]υ (B.C. 471-0)
Ἱπποθωντὶς πα]ίδων
..... ἐχο]ρήγει
20 ...... ων
... ἐχ]ορήγ[ει
[κωμῳδῶν] ...
... ἐχορήγ]ει
25

....
....
.... ἐχορή(γει)
..... ἐδίδασκεν.
ἐπὶ Φιλ]οκλέους (B.C. 459-8)
Οἰ]νηὶς παίδων,
Δημόδοκος ἐχορήγε[ι
Ἱπποθωντὶς ἀνδρῶν
Εὐκτήμων Ἐλευ(σίνιος) ἐχορή(γει)
κωμῳδῶν
Εὐρυκλείδης ἐχορήγει,
Εὐφρόνιος ἐδίδασκε.
τραγῳδῶν,
Ξενοκλῆς Ἀφιδαν(ῖος) ἐχορή(γει)
Αἰσχύλος ἐδίδασκεν.
ἐπὶ Ἄβρωνος (B.C. 458-7)
Ἐρεχθηὶς παίδων,
Χαρίας Ἀγρυλῆ(θεν) ἐχορή[γει
Λεωντὶς ἀνδρῶν
Δεινόστρατος ἐχο[ρήγει
κωμῳδῶν
.... ἐχ]ορήγ[ει.

......
......
......
Βίω[ν ἐχορήγει
κωμ[ῳδῶν
Ἀνδ[.... ἐχορήγει
Καλ[λίας ἐδίδασκε
τρα[γῳδῶν
Θα[..... ἐχορήγει
Κα[ρκίνος ἐδίδασκεν
ὑπ[οκριτὴς ....
ἐπ[ὶ Καλλιμάχου
(B.C. 446-5)

The next fragment (971 b) belongs to the years B.C. 423-1, and to Col. VII.

[κωμῳδῶν]
..... Παια[νιεὺς ἐχορήγει.
Ἕρμιππ]ος ἐδ[ίδασκε
τραγῳ]δῶν
... ω]ν Παιανιε[ὺς ἐχορή]γει,
Με]νεκράτης ἐδί[δασκεν
ὑπ]οκριτὴς Μυνν[ίσκος.
ἐ]πὶ Ἀλκαίου (B.C. 422-1)
Ἱπποθωντὶς παίδων
Ἀρίσταρχος Δεκε(λεεὺς) ἐχορή(γει)
Αἰαντὶς ἀνδρῶν,
Δημοσθένης ἐχορήγει.
κ]ωμῳδ[ῶν
..... ἐχορ]ήγ[ει

We next come to Col. XIII (fr. 971 g), B.C. 348–6.

$[\kappa\omega\mu\wp\delta\hat{\omega}\nu]$
. . . . . $[\dot{\epsilon}\chi o\rho\dot{\eta}\gamma\epsilon\iota$
$"A]\lambda\epsilon\xi\iota s\ \dot{\epsilon}\delta[\dot{\iota}\delta\alpha\sigma\kappa\epsilon\nu.$
$\tau\rho\alpha\gamma\wp\delta\hat{\omega}\nu$
$K\lambda]\epsilon\dot{o}\mu\alpha\chi os\ 'A\chi\alpha[\rho\nu(\epsilon\dot{\upsilon}s)\ \dot{\epsilon}\chi o\rho\dot{\eta}\gamma\epsilon\iota,$
$'A[\sigma]\tau\upsilon\delta\dot{\alpha}\mu[\alpha]s\ \dot{\epsilon}\delta[\dot{\iota}\delta\alpha\sigma\kappa\epsilon\nu,$
$\dot{\upsilon}[\pi o]\kappa\rho\iota\tau\dot{\eta}s\ \Theta[\epsilon\tau\tau\alpha\lambda\dot{o}s.$
$\dot{\epsilon}]\pi\dot{\iota}\ \Theta\epsilon\mu\iota\sigma\tau o\kappa\lambda\dot{\epsilon}o\upsilon s$ (B.C. 347–6)
$'E\rho\epsilon\chi\theta\eta\dot{\iota}s\ \pi\alpha\dot{\iota}\delta\omega\nu.$
$\Delta\iota o\nu\upsilon\sigma$ . . . .

The position of fr. 971 d is uncertain; Capps places it B.C. 344–3, Wilhelm, 336–5 B.C. It belongs in any case to the latter half of the fourth century.

$K\epsilon\kappa\rho o\pi[\dot{\iota}s\ \pi\alpha\dot{\iota}\delta\omega\nu$
$\Delta\iota\dot{o}\phi\alpha\nu[\tau os$ . . . $\dot{\epsilon}\chi o\rho\dot{\eta}\gamma\epsilon\iota$
$K\epsilon\kappa\rho o\pi\dot{\iota}s\ [\dot{\alpha}\nu\delta\rho\hat{\omega}\nu$
$'O\nu\dot{\eta}\tau\omega\rho\ [\dot{\epsilon}\chi o\rho\dot{\eta}\gamma\epsilon\iota$
$\kappa\omega\mu\wp\delta[\hat{\omega}\nu$
$\Delta\iota o\pi\epsilon\dot{\iota}\theta[\eta s$ . . . . $\dot{\epsilon}\chi o\rho\dot{\eta}\gamma\epsilon\iota$
$\Pi\rho o\kappa\lambda\epsilon\dot{\iota}[\delta\eta s\ \dot{\epsilon}\delta\dot{\iota}\delta\alpha\sigma\kappa\epsilon\nu$
$\tau\rho\alpha\gamma\wp\delta\hat{\omega}\nu$

We next have two passages at the bottom of Cols. XIII, XIV (971 e), the years in the former being 343–1, and in the second 331–0.

Col. XIII.

. . . .
l. 126 . . . .
. . . .
$[\tau\rho\alpha\gamma\wp\delta\hat{\omega}\nu]$
. . . . . $\dot{\epsilon}]\chi o\rho\dot{\eta}(\gamma\epsilon\iota)$
l. 130 . . . . $\dot{\epsilon}]\delta\dot{\iota}\delta[\alpha\sigma]\kappa\epsilon$
$\dot{\upsilon}\pi o\kappa\rho\iota\tau\dot{\eta}s\ 'A]\theta\eta\nu\dot{o}\delta\omega\rho os.$
$\dot{\epsilon}\pi\dot{\iota}\ \Sigma\omega\sigma\iota\gamma\dot{\epsilon}\nu o\upsilon s$ (B.C. 342–1)
$A\dot{\iota}\gamma\eta\dot{\iota}s\ \pi\alpha\dot{\iota}\delta]\omega\nu$
. . . . . $\Delta\iota]o\mu\epsilon[\dot{\upsilon}s\ \dot{\epsilon}\chi o\rho]\dot{\eta}(\gamma\epsilon\iota)$
l. 135 $'I\pi\pi o\theta\omega\nu\tau\dot{\iota}s]\ \dot{\alpha}\nu\delta\rho\hat{\omega}\nu$
. . . . $\dot{\epsilon}\kappa\ Ko\dot{\iota}]\lambda\eta s\ \dot{\epsilon}\chi o\rho\dot{\eta}(\gamma\epsilon\iota)$
$[\kappa\omega\mu\wp\delta\hat{\alpha}\nu]$

Col. XIV.

$\dot{\epsilon}]\pi\dot{\iota}\ 'A\rho\iota\sigma\tau[o]\phi\dot{\alpha}\nu o\upsilon s$ (B.C. 331–0)
$O\dot{\iota}\nu\eta\dot{\iota}s\ \pi\alpha\dot{\iota}\delta\omega[\nu$
. . . . $\tau os\ ['A\chi]\alpha\rho\nu[(\epsilon\dot{\upsilon}s)\ \dot{\epsilon}\chi o\rho\dot{\eta}(\gamma\epsilon\iota)$
$'I\pi\pi o\theta\omega\nu\tau\dot{\iota}s\ \dot{\alpha}\nu\delta\rho[\hat{\omega}\nu$
. . . . . . $os\ [\Pi]\epsilon\iota[\rho]\alpha\iota\epsilon[\dot{\upsilon}s\ \dot{\epsilon}\chi o\rho\dot{\eta}(\gamma\epsilon\iota)$
$\kappa\omega\mu]\wp\delta[\hat{\omega}\nu$
. . . .
. . . .
$\tau\rho\alpha\gamma]\wp[\delta\hat{\omega}\nu$

.... ης [ἐχορήγει

....

l. 140 [τραγῳδῶν]

.... ἐχ]ορ[ήγει

'Αστυδάμας ἐδί]δ[ασκεν

Finally, from near the top of Cols. XIV, XV (971 *h*) we have fragments from 341–0 and 330–28 respectively. Col. XIV includes a fragment first printed by Wilhelm, op. cit., p. 27.

<table>
<tr><td align="center">Col. XIV.</td><td align="center">Col. XV.</td></tr>
</table>

Col. XIV.

....

τρ]αγῳδῶν

'Αρρενείδης Παιανι(εὺς) ἐχο[ρήγει

'Αστυδάμας ἐδίδα]σκεν

ὑποκριτὴς Θεττα]λὸς

'Ε]πὶ Θεοφράστο[υ   (B. C. 340–39)

[πα]λαιὸν δρᾶμ[α . . . . .

π]αρεδίδαξα[ν οἱ] κ[ω]μ[ῳδοί

'Α]ντιοχὶς παί[δων . . . .

Col. XV.

... ς Κε[. . . .

ἐ[χορήγ]ει

Θεόφιλος ἐδίδ[ασκεν]

τραγῳδῶν

Θ]ηραμένης Κηφισι[εὺς

ἐχορ]ή[γει

. . . . κ]λης ἐδίδασ[κεν

ὑπο]κριτὴς

'Αθηνόδωρος

ἐπὶ Κηφισοφῶντος,   (B. C. 329–8)

'Ιπποθωντὶς παί[δων

II. *Record of Comic Contests at the Lenaea* (C. I. A. ii. 972, Col. I).

The inscription of which this forms a part consists of two columns, the first containing records of comic contests, the second of tragic contests, at the Lenaea. The date of the contests recorded in the first column has been generally taken to be B.C. 354–2 : but Capps (The Dating of some Didascalic Inscriptions, Amer. Journ. of Archaeology, 1900, pp. 74 ff.) has shown almost conclusively that the true date is B. C. 290–8 (it is possibly a year or two later, see Wilhelm, Urkunden dramatischer Aufführungen in Athen, p. 52, as the date of Diotimus' archonship is not absolutely certain). This column must have contained the last records of comic contests at the Lenaea which came within the plan of this inscription, as the next column begins the records of tragic contests. It would appear, therefore, that the date of the transcribing of this series of didascaliae upon stone was in all probability circ. B.C. 287. Capps conjectures (with much reason) that C. I. A. ii. 972 formed part of one great didascalic inscription arranged in the order (1) Tragedy at the Dionysia, (2) Comedy at the Dionysia, (3) Comedy at the Lenaea, (4) Tragedy at the Lenaea. The extant fragments, therefore, mark the junction of parts (3) and (4).   The original stone is now lost, and the record depends on the copies of Fourmont and Le Bas, the latter being apparently the more trustworthy.

  . . . . . τέ(ταρτος) . . . .]στίδι
  ὑπε(κρίνετο) 'Αριστόμ]αχος.
  . . . . ης πέμ(πτος) 'Ανασῳζο(μένοις),
  ὑπε(κρίνετο) 'Αντ]ιφάνης.
  ὑπο(κριτὴς) 'Ιερ]ώνυμος ἐνίκα.
  ἐπὶ Δι]οτίμου Σιμύλος   (B.C. 289–8)
  . . . σίᾳ ὑπε(κρίνετο) 'Αριστόμαχος.
  Διόδωρος δεύ(τερος) Νεκρῷ
  ὑπε(κρίνετο) 'Αριστόμαχος.
  Διόδωρος τρί(τος) Μαινομένῳ
  ὑπε(κρίνετο) Κηφίσιος.
  Φο]ινικ[ίδ]ης τέ(ταρτος) Ποητεῖ
  ὑπε(κρίνετο) . . . . .]ης

III. *Record of Tragic Contests at the Lenaea* (C. I. A. ii. 972, Col. II).

The second column of the fragment to which the last quoted list belongs; Köhler has fixed the date beyond question.

  Π]ειρ[ιθόῳ . . . . .
  ὑπε(κρίνετο) . . . . .
  ὑπο(κριτὴς) [. . . . ἐνίκα
  ἐπὶ ['Αστυφίλου . . . . (B.C. 420–19)
  'Αγα[μέμνονι . . . . . .
  ὑπ[ε(κρίνετο) . . . . . .
  'Ηρα[κ . . . . . .
  Θησ[εῖ, ...,
  ὑπ[ε(κρίνετο) . . .
  ὑπο(κριτὴς) [. . . . . ἐνίκα
  ἐπὶ 'Αρχ[ίου . . . . . .   (B.C. 419–8)
  Τυροῖ, Τ . . . .,
  ὑπε(κρίνετο) Λυσικράτ(ης).
  Καλλίστρατος . . . . . .
  'Αμφιλόχῳ, 'Ιξίονι
  ὑπε(κρίνετο) Καλλιππί[δης
  ὑπ]ο(κριτὴς) Καλλιππί[δης ἐνίκα
  ἐπ 'Α]ντ[ι]φ[ῶ]ντος Σ . . . . . (B.C. 418–7)
  . . . . . . π . . . . . .

IV. *Record of Tragic Contests at the City Dionysia* (C. I. A. ii. 973).

παλαιᾷ .] Νε[οπτόλεμος
'Ιφιγε]νείᾳ Εὐ[ριπί]δο[υ
ποη(ταί)·] 'Αστυδάμας
'Αχι]λλεῖ, ὑπε(κρίνετο) Θετταλός,
'Αθάμαντι, ὑπε(κρίνετο) Νεοπτόλ[εμος,
'Αν]τιγόνῃ, ὑπε(κρίνετο) 'Αθηνόδω[ρος.
Εὐ]άρετος [δεύ(τερος)] Τεύκρῳ,
ὑπ]ε(κρίνετο) 'Αθηνόδωρος·
'Αχι]λ[λ]εῖ, [ὑπε(κρίνετο)] Θετταλός·
. . . . . εῖ], ὑ[πε(κρίνετο) Νε]οπτόλεμος·
. . . . . . τ]ρί(τος) [Π]ελιάσιν,
ὑπε(κρίνετο) Νεοπτ]όλεμος·
'Ορέστῃ[ι, ὑπε(κρίνετο) 'Αθη]ν[όδωρος·
Αὔ[γῃ] ὑπε(κρίνετο) Θεττ[αλό]ς·
ὑπο(κριτὴς) Νεοπτόλεμος ἐνίκ[α.

ἐπὶ Νικομάχου· σατυρι(κῷ)·   (B.C. 341–0)
Τιμοκλῆς Λυκούργῳ·
παλαιᾷ· Νεοπτόλεμ[ος
'Ορέστῃ Εὐριπίδου·
π]οη(ταί)· 'Αστυδάμας
Παρθενοπαίῳ, ὑπε(κρίνετο) Θετ[ταλός·
Λυκά]ονι, ὑπε(κρίνετο) Νεοπτόλε[μος
. . . . . . οκλῆς δεύ(τερος) Φρίξῳ,
ὑπε(κρίνετο)] Θετταλός·
Οἰδί]ποδι, ὑπε(κρίνετο) Νεοπτόλ[εμος·
ὑπο(κριτὴς) Θε]ττάλος ἐνίκα.

ἐπὶ Θεο]φράστου· σατυ[ρι(κῷ)·   (B.C. 340–39)
. . . . . Φορκίσ[ι.
παλαιᾷ . . . . ό]στρ[ατος
. . . . Εὐ]ριπί[δου.

V. *Record of Comic Contests* (festival uncertain).

This inscription (which he numbers 974 *c*) was found in 1901, and is published (with restorations) by Wilhelm, op. cit., pp. 43 ff.; it is a record of the years B.C. 313–11. Col. I only is printed below ; the second column being too fragmentary.

ὑπε(κρίνετο) 'Ασκληπιόδ]ωρο[ς
Μένανδρος] πέμ(πτος) 'Ηνιόχῳ
ὑπε(κρίνετο) Κάλ]λιππος πρεσβύτ(ερος)

ὑπο(κριτὴς) Κάλλι]ππος νεώ(τερος) ἐνίκ[α
ἐπὶ Πολέμ]ωνος παλαιᾷ   (B.C. 312–11)
. . . . . . Θ]ησαυρῷ 'Αναξαν(δρίδου)
ποη(τὴς) Φιλιπ]πίδης Μύστιδι
ὑπε(κρίνετο) 'Ασκ]ληπιόδωρος
Νικόστ]ρατος δεύ(τερος)
. . . . .]οσκόπῳ
ὑπε(κρίνετο) Κ]άλλιππος νεώτε(ρος)
'Αμεινί]ας τρί(τος) 'Απολειπούσει
οὗτος ἔ]φηβος ὢν ἐνεμήθη
ὑπε(κρίνετο) 'Ασκ]ληπιόδωρος
Θεόφιλο]ς (?) τέταρτος Παγκρατιασ(τῇ)
ὑπε(κρίνετο) . . . ιπ]πος
. . . . πέμ(πτος) Π]αιδίῳ
[ὑπε(κρίνετο) . . . .]
ὑπο(κριτὴς) 'Ασκληπιόδωρο]ς ἐνίκ[α.

VI. *Record of Comic Contests at the City Dionysia* (C. I. A. ii. 975).

The inscription consists of a number of fragments. The date of
those numbered *a–e* is tolerably certain ; they range from about B.C.
190–160. The others, *f–i*, have been dated by Capps from about
B.C. 308–260 ; but these dates and the restorations suggested by
him are disputed by Wilhelm, who places the date of *f*, with a good
deal of reason, only shortly before that of *a*, and also dates *g–i*
(not included in the present selection) much later. The first part of
fragment *f* is as follows :—

. . . . . 'Ερχιεῦσιν
ὑπε(κρίνετο) . . .]μος   ('Ιερώνυμος Capps, Νικόδημος Wilhelm.)
ἐπὶ . . . . . .] οὐκ ἐγένετο
. . . . . . π]αλαιᾷ
. . . .] Φωκεῦσι Φιλή(μονος)
ποη(ταὶ) . . .] κράτης 'Απε   (Κράτης 'Απελεύθεροις Capps, 'Αριστο-
. . . . . ὑ]πε(κρίνετο) Νικόδημος   [κράτης 'Απε- Wilhelm.)
. . . . . . 'Α]νεψιοῖς.

Fragments *a–e* are arranged as forming an inscription in five
columns by Köhler (C. I. A.) as follows :—

Col. I.	Col. II.	Col. III.	Col. IV.	Col. V.
1st col. of *a*	2nd col. of *a*	—	—	—
	1st col. of *b*	2nd col. of *b*	*c*	*d*
		1st col. of *e*	2nd col. of *e*	

Wilhelm arranges them as follows, op. cit., pp. 68 ff. :—

Col. I.	Col. II.	Col. III.	Col. IV.
1st col. of *a*	2nd col. of *a*	—	—
1st col. of *b*	2nd col. of *b*	*c*	*d*
	1st col. of *e*	2nd col. of *e*	—

It is impossible at present to decide with certainty between the two arrangements. The former is here followed, but indications of Wilhelm's arrangement are also given.

Col. I is too fragmentary to be intelligible. (It includes the 1st col. of *a*.)

Col. II (the 2nd col. of *a*).

$$\Tau\iota\mu]\acute{o}\sigma[\tau\rho\alpha\tau\sigma\varsigma]\ \Lambda\upsilon\tau[\rho\sigma\upsilon\mu\acute{e}\nu\omega$$
$$\dot{\upsilon}\pi\epsilon(\kappa\rho\acute{\iota}\nu\epsilon\tau\sigma)\ \Delta\iota\sigma\gamma\epsilon\acute{\iota}\tau\omega\nu\cdot$$
$$\dot{\upsilon}\pi\sigma(\kappa\rho\iota\tau\dot{\eta}\varsigma)\ \Kappa\rho\acute{\alpha}\tau\eta\varsigma\ \acute{e}\nu\acute{\iota}\kappa\alpha$$

ἐπὶ Συμμάχου οὐκ ἐγ[ένετο	(B.C. 188-7)
ἐπὶ Θεοξένου οὐκ [ἐγένετο	(B.C. 187-6)
ἐπὶ Ζωπύρου· [παλαιᾷ·	(B.C. 186-5)

$$\text{᾽Ερ\acute{α}των Μ\epsilon[γαρικ\^{η} Σιμ\acute{υ}λου (?)}$$
$$\pi\sigma\eta(\tau\alpha\grave{\iota})\ \Lambda\alpha\acute{\iota}\nu[\eta\varsigma\ \ldots$$
$$\dot{\upsilon}\pi\epsilon(\kappa\rho\acute{\iota}\nu\epsilon\tau\sigma)\ \ldots\ldots$$

Then after an interval the 1st col. of *b* (Wilhelm makes this a continuation of Col. I of *a*, and accordingly dates it *before* the portion just given).

$$\ldots\ldots\ \text{᾽Εφ\acute{η}βοις}$$
$$\dot{\upsilon}\pi\epsilon(\kappa\rho\acute{\iota}\,\epsilon\tau\sigma)\ \ldots\ldots]$$
$$\dot{\upsilon}\pi\sigma(\kappa\rho\iota\tau\dot{\eta}\varsigma)\ \ldots\ldots\ \acute{e}]\nu\acute{\iota}\kappa\alpha$$
$$\dot{e}\pi\grave{\iota}\ \ldots\ldots\ \sigma\dot{\upsilon}]\kappa\ \acute{e}\gamma\acute{e}\nu\epsilon\tau\sigma$$
$$\dot{e}\pi\grave{\iota}\ \ldots\ldots\ \sigma]\upsilon\cdot\ \pi\alpha\lambda\alpha\iota\^{q}\cdot$$
$$\ldots\ldots\ \Mu\iota\sigma\sigma\gamma]\acute{υ}\nu\epsilon\iota\ \Mu\epsilon\nu\acute{\alpha}\nu\delta\rho\sigma\upsilon\cdot$$
$$\pi\sigma\eta(\tau\alpha\grave{\iota})\ \ldots.]\nu\eta\varsigma\ \text{᾽Αδελφα\^{ι}ς}$$
$$\dot{\upsilon}\pi\epsilon(\kappa\rho\acute{\iota}\nu\epsilon\tau\sigma)\ \ldots.]\varsigma$$
$$\ldots\ldots\ \Delta\alpha\kappa\tau\upsilon\lambda\acute{\iota}\omega$$
$$\dot{\upsilon}\pi\epsilon(\kappa\rho\acute{\iota}\nu\epsilon\tau\sigma)\ \ldots\ldots]\omega\nu$$
$$\ldots\ldots\ \Phi\iota\lambda]\alpha\theta\eta\nu[\alpha\acute{\iota}\omega.$$

Col. III (2nd col. of *b*; according to Wilhelm, a continuation of Col. II, i.e. of the 2nd col. of *a*).

$$\pi\sigma\eta(\tau\alpha\grave{\iota})\ \Kappa\rho\acute{\iota}\tau\omega\nu\ \text{᾽Εφε\varsigma\acute{\iota}οις,}$$
$$\dot{\upsilon}]\pi\epsilon(\kappa\rho\acute{\iota}\nu\epsilon\tau\sigma)\ \Sigma\acute{\omega}\phi\iota\lambda\sigma\varsigma\cdot$$

Παράμονος Ναυαγῷ,
ὑπε(κρίνετο) Ὀνήσιμος
Τιμόστρατος Φιλοικείῳ,
ὑπε(κρίνετο) Καλλίστρατος·
Σωγένης Φιλοδεσπότῳ,
ὑπε(κρίνετο) Ἑκαταῖος·
Φιλήμων νεώ(τερος) Μιλησίᾳ,
ὑπε(κρίνετο) Κράτης.
ὑπο(κριτὴς) Ὀνήσιμος ἐνίκ[α·
ἐπὶ Ἑρμογένου οὐκ [ἐγέ]νετο.   (B. C. 183-2)
ἐπὶ Τιμησιάν[ακτος· π]αλαιᾷ·   (B. C. 182-1)
Φιλόστρατο[ς Ἀποκλε]ιομένει Ποσει(δίππου)·
ποη(ταὶ) [Ἀρχικλῆς (?) Ναυ]κλήρῳ,
ὑπε(κρίνετο) . . . . . .
. . . . σ]ιν
[ὑπε(κρίνετο) . . . . .]
. . . . . . Διαδικ]αζομένοις,
[ὑπε(κρίνετο) . . . . . .]
. . . . . . μ]ένοις
[ὑπε(κρίνετο) . . . . . .]
. . . . υ]μένῳ

Then an interval in which only a few letters are legible, the 1st col.
of fragment *e.*

. . . . . . εὐ]εργετοῦντι
[ὑπε(κρίνετο) . . . . . .]
. . . . ἐξ]απατῶντι,
[ὑπε(κρίνετο) . . . . . .]
. . . ω]ν Συντ . . . .
ὑπε(κρίνετο) . . . . .]ης
. . . . . Συναγωνι . . .
ὑπε(κρίνετο) . . .]ίδης.
ὑπο(κριτὴς) . . . ξέ]νος ἐνί[κα
ἐπὶ . . . παλαι]ᾷ Προ . . .

Col. IV (according to Wilhelm, Col. III), fragment *c.*

. . . . . Μονοτ]ρόπῳ
. . . .
ποη(ταὶ) . . . . Ἀν]ασῳζομέ[νοις
[νοις, ὑπε(κρίνετο) . . .]

...... ὑμένῳ
ὑπε(κρίνετο) . . . .]ος
...... Ἀγνοοῦντι,
ὑπε(κρίνετο) Κριτόδ]ημος
...... Νε]μέσει,
ὑπε(κρίνετο) Σώ]νικος·
Παρά]μονος Χορηγοῦντι,
ὑπε(κρίνετο)] Μόνιμος
ὑπ᾽]ο(κριτὴς) Κριτόδημος ἐνίκα.
ἐ]πὶ Εὐνίκου οὐκ ἐγένε[το.   (B. C. 169-8)
ἐπὶ Ξενοκλέους· παλαι[ᾷ·   (B. C.·168-7)
Μόνιμος Φάσματι Μεν[άνδρου.
ποη(ταί)· Παράμονος τεθνηκὼς . . . . . ις
ὑπε(κρίνετο) Δάμων·
Κρίτων Αἰτωλῷ,
ὑπε(κρίνετο) Μόνιμος·
Βίοττος Ποητεῖ,
ὑπε(κρίνετο) Δάμων·
Λάμπυτος . . . .
ὑπε(κρίνετο) Κα[βείριχος (?)
Ἐπικ[ράτης . . . . .

Then after an interval 2nd col. of *e*.

ἐπὶ] Εὐερ[γ . . . . . οὐκ ἐγένετο   (B. C. 164-3)
ἐ]πὶ Ἐρίστο[υ οὐκ ἐγένετο   (B. C. 163-2)
ἐπὶ Ποσει[δωνίου οὐκ ἐγένετο.   (B. C. 162-1)
. . . .
ἐπὶ Ἀρισ[τόλα· παλαιᾷ   (B. C. 161-0)
Ἡρακ[λε . . . .
πο[η(ταί) . . . . .

Col. V (according to Wilhelm, Col. IV), fragment *d*.

ὑπε(κρίνετο) Καβεί]ριχος·
Ἐπ]ιγέ[ν]ης Λυτρουμένῳ
ὑπε(κρίνετο) Καβείριχος·
ὑπο(κριτὴς) Νικόλαος ἐνίκα·
ἐπὶ Ἀνθεστηρίου οὐκ ἐγένε[το.   (soon after B. C. 160)
ἐπὶ Καλλιστράτου οὐκ ἐγένε[το.
ἐπὶ Μνησιθέου· παλαιᾷ·
Δάμων Φιλαθηναίῳ Φιλιππ[ίδου·

πο(ηταί)· Φιλοκλῆς Τραυματίᾳ,
ὑπε(κρίνετο) Καλλικράτης·
Χαιρίων Αὑτοῦ καταψευδομέ[νῳ.
ὑπε(κρίνετο) Δάμων·
Βίοττος Ἀγνοοῦντι,
ὑπε(κρίνετο) Δάμων·
Τιμόξενος Συνκρύπτον[τι,
ὑπε(κρίνετο) Καλλικράτης·
Ἀγαθοκλῆς Ὁμονοίᾳ,
ὑπεκρίνετο Νικόλ[αος.

VII. *Lists of tragic and comic poets and actors, and the number of their victories* (C. I. A. ii. 977, iv. 977).

This inscription was no doubt based on the Νῖκαι τραγικαὶ καὶ κωμικαί of Aristotle, and afterwards carried on by additions into the second century B.C.; the order of the names is that of the first victory of each poet or actor at the contest in question, and each column of the inscription contained seventeen names. There are over thirty fragments, and it is not always possible to say whether the lists given in them refer to the Lenaea or the City Dionysia. The following selection of the fragments is based on Capps's paper on this inscription in the Amer. Journal of Philology, xx. pp. 388 ff.: and on the fuller study by Wilhelm, op. cit., pp. 89 ff.

1. Tragic poets.
    (a) At the City Dionysia.

Fragment *a*.

Αἰ]σχύλ[ος . .
Εὐ]έτης Ι
Πο]λυφράσμ[ων . . .
Νόθ]ιππος Ι
Σοφ]οκλῆς ΔΠΙΙΙ
. . . . . τος ΙΙ
Ἀριστ]ίας

Fragment *b*.

. . . . . ας . .
Καρκί]νος ΔΙ
Ἀστ]υδάμας Π[ΙΙ.]Ι
Θεο]δέκτας ΠΙΙ

'Αφαρ]εὺς ΙΙ

.... ν . Ι

.... ΙΙ

(*b*) Festival uncertain.

Fragment *c*.

...... ας Ι

.... δης Ι

..... ράτης Ι

'Αστυδ]άμας . .

.... ΙΙ

2. Comic poets.

(*a*) At the City Dionysia.

Fragments *i* and *k*, together with two fragments first published by Wilhelm, l. c., p. 106, and arranged by him in three columns as follows :—

[ἀστικαὶ ποιητῶν]	Τηλεκλεί]δης ΙΙΙ	Νικοφῶ[ν . . .
[κωμικῶν]	......] ς Ι	Θεόπομπ[ος
[Χιωνίδης . . .]	—	Κη]φισό[δοτος
—	—	. . .] ι [. . .
—	Φερ[εκράτης . .	
—]ς Ι	Ἑρμ[ιππος . .	
—	'Αρι[στομένης . .	
Μάγνη]ς ΔΙ	Εὔ[πολις . . .	
...... ο]ς Ι	Κα[λλίστρατος . .	
'Αλκιμέ]νη[ς] Ι	Φρύ[νιχος . .	
.....]ς Ι	'Αμ[ειψίας . .	
Εὐφρόν]ιος Ι	Πλά[των . . .	
'Εκφαν]τίδης ΙΙΙΙ	Φιλ[ωνίδης . .	
Κρατῖ]νος ΓΙ	Λύκ[ις	
Διοπ]είθης ΙΙ	Λεύ[κων	
Κρά]της ΙΙΙ		
Καλλία]ς ΙΙ		

The following new fragment is published by Wilhelm, p. 118.

Πο]σείδιππος ΙΙΙΙ	....	
Σατυρίων Ι	Νίκαρχος Ι	Πο . . .
'Α]πολλόδωρος ΙΙ	Νικόμαχος Ι	'Ο . . .
Φιλ]ήμων ΠΙ	'Αριστοκράτης Ι . . .	
Δαμ]όξενος Ι	Λαίνης ΙΙΙ	
Φοινικ]ίδης ΙΙ	Φιλήμω[ν	

(*b*) At the Lenaea.

This list at present consists of fragments *d–h*, which have been arranged in four columns; one column must have preceded them in the original, and over the head of the lost column and the present first column the title of the list ran, of which only one or two traces remain. It probably (according to Capps) read thus :—οἵδε ἐνίκων τὰ Λήναια ποητῶν κωμικῶν (or τῶν κωμικῶν). The extant portions run as follows (including conjectural restorations ; cf. Wilhelm, op. cit., p. 123). See addendum to p. 27, n. 1. According to Wilhelm the heading was Ληναικαὶ ποητῶν κωμικῶν.

I.	II.	III.	IV.
Τὰ Λήναι]α πο[ητῶν	Πο I	Φίλιπ[πος . .] II	Θ . . . .
κωμι]κῶν	Με[ταγέ]νης II	Χορη[γός . .	Δι . . . . ος I
Ξ]ενόφιλος I	Θεό[πομπ]ος II	'Αναξα[νδρί]δης III.	Κλέα[ρχ]ος . .
Τ]ηλεκλείδης Π	Πολ[ύζηλο]s IIII	Φιλέτα[ιρο]s II	'Αθηνοκλῆς . .
5. 'Αριστομένης II	Νικοφ[ῶν . .	Εὔβουλος III	Πύρ[ων] I
Κρατῖνος III	'Απολ[λοφάν]ης I	Ἔφιππος I	'Αλκ[ήν]ωρ I
Φερεκράτης II	'Αμ[ειψίας	'Α]ντιφάνη[ς ΠIIII	Τιμοκλῆς I
Ἕρμιππος IIII	Νι[κοχάρης . .	Μ]νησίμα[χος] I. II	Προκλείδης I
Φρύνιχος II	Ξεν[οφ]ῶν I	Ναυσ[ικράτ]ης III.	Μ[έν]ανδρος I. .
10 Μυρτίλος I	Φιλύλλιος I	Ευφάνη[ς . .	Φ[ιλ]ήμων III.
Εὔ]πολις III	Φιλόνικος I	Ἄλεξις II. . .	'Απολλόδωρο[ς . .
	. . . . . ς !	'Αρ]ιστο[φῶν . .	Δίφιλος III.
		. . . . .	Φιλιππίδης II
		. . . . .	Νικόστρατος . .
		. . . . .	Καλλιάδης I
		. . . . .	'Αμειν[ία]ς I
		Κηφισόδω]ρος I.	. . . . .
		(Διονυσόδωρος or	
		'Ασκληπιόδωρος,	
		Wilhelm).	

3. Tragic actors.

   (*a*) At the City Dionysia.

      Fragment *e'*.

ὑποκριτῶν τ[ραγικῶν	. . . . . .
'Ηρακλεί[δης . .	. . . . . .
Νικόμαχο[ς . .	. . . . . .
Μυ[ν]ίσκος . .	Ν . . . . . .
Σαώνδας . . .	Θε . . . . . .

Ανδ[ρων ΙΙ   Α]σ . . .
Χ]αι[ρ]έ[σ]τρατος Ι.   'Αθην[όδωρος
Μενεκ]ράτης . .   'Αρι[στόδημος . .
Λεπ]τίν[ης . . .

(*b*) At the Lenaea.

Fragments *o*, *z*, *x* and *b'*, and two fragments published by Wilhelm, who puts all together as follows, op. cit., p. 144.

ὑποκριτῶν τραγικῶν	Χαρίδημος . .	. . . . .	. . . . .
Χαιρέσ[τ]ρατος Ι	Φίλιππος . . .	. . . . .	Ε[
Με]ν[εκρά]της Ι	Φύτιος ΙΙ	. . . . . μ]ος ΙΙ	Βάκχ[. . .
Λεπτίν]ης ΙΙΙ	Εὐπόλεμο[ς	. . . . .]ς ΙΙ	Στεμφ[ύλιος
. . . . .	Θρασύβο[υλος] Ι	'Ε[. . . . . .]ς Ι	Ξένων Ι
Μυννίσκ]ος ΙΙ	'Αριστόδ[ημος] ΙΙ	'Αρ[ιστοφ]ῶν Ι	Χαρίας [
'Ηρακλεί]δης Π	Μίρων ΙΙ	Πο	'Αντιμέ[νης
Νικόστρα]τος ΙΙΙ	Κλ]εο[δάμα]ς Ι	Ν	Τεισίλα[ς
	Θεόδωρος ΙΙΙ	'Αρχίας . . .	Γο[ργ . . .
	"Ιππαρχος Πι	Πραξία[ς . .	Νίκων ΙΙ . .
	'Αμεινίας Ι	'Ιερομν[ήμων] ΙΙΙ	'Αριστόνι[κος
	'Αν]δροσθένης Ι	Φιλ[. . .	Πύρριχος [. .
	Νεο]πτόλεμος Ι	Νικ[. . .	'Αγήτωρ
	Θεττα]λός ΙΙ	'Αρι[. . .	Θηραμέν[ης
	. . . . .]ς ΙΙ	. . . . .	Κλεῖτος
	'Αριστ]ίων Ι		
	. . . . . άδ]ης Ι		

Fragment *l* (previously assigned to the list of poets; but see Wilhelm, op. cit., pp. 161, 253, who dates the fragment before B.C. 375).

Σάτ]υρος Πι
Φι]λήμων ΙΙ
Κα]λλίστρατ[ος . .

4. Comic actors.

Fragments *u*, *v* (probably Lenaean, of the third century B.C.).

'Αρισταγόρας Ι	Πολυ[κλῆς . .
Κάλλιππος ΙΙΙΙ	Λυκίσ[κος
'Α]σκληπιόδωρος Π	Σωσικλ[ῆς .
Π]ολύευκτος Ι	Πολύζηλ[ος
Π]υρραλεύς Ι	Πυθάρατος Ι
Μ]οσχίων ΙΙ	Καλλίας ΙΙΙ
. . μ . . . ν ΙΙ	Μενεκ[λῆ]ς Ι

'Ι]ερώνυμος |||| Δ[ημήτρ]ιος ||
'Α]ριστόμαχος ||| Πιτθεύς |
Δέ]ρκετος | . .   'Ηρακλείδης |[|.]
. . . .
Φιλοκ[λῆς   . . . ρος ||
'Αριστοκράτης | . . . .
'Εμμενίδης | . . . . ||
Αὐτόλυκος | Δ[ημο]κράτης |
Φιλωνίδης | Φιλ[ο]στέφανος |
Σωκράτης | 'Ερμόφαντος |

There are a good many other fragments, containing in some cases
(fragments f', w, p, and possibly d', g') the names of comic actors,
while in other cases the nature of the list and its place in the inscription is uncertain : but the above will serve as specimens.

VIII. The following inscriptions are also of interest :—

1. C. I. A. ii. 1289. (Wilhelm, op. cit., p. 209 ; Capps, Am.
Journ. Arch. iv. p. 76.)

'Ο δῆμος ἐ[χορήγει ἐπὶ 'Αναξι]κράτους ἄρχοντος·   (B. C. 307-6)
ἀγωνοθέ[της Ξενοκλῆς Ξ]είνιδος Σφήττιος·
ποιητὴς τραγῳδοῖς ἐνίκα [Φανόστρατος] 'Ηρακλείδου 'Αλικαρνασσεύς,
ὑποκριτὴς τραγῳδοῖς ἐνίκ[α . . . .]ν Εὐανορίδου Κυδαθηναιεύς,
ποιητὴς κωμῳδοῖς ἐνί[κα Φιλήμω]ν Δάμωνος Διομειεύς,
ὑποκριτὴς κ[ωμῳδοῖς ἐνίκα Κάλλιπ]πος Καλλίου Σουνιεύς.

2. Fragments (found in Rome) of a list of comic poets with their
victories at each festival arranged according to the places they won
(see Wilhelm, pp. 195 ff.).

(a) I. G. xiv. 1097.

ἐ]πὶ 'Αντιοχίδου Κύ[κλωψιν (?) ἐπὶ   (B. C. 434)
. . . . . .]ς κωμῳδίᾳ. ΄δ᾽ ἐν ἄ[στει ἐπὶ
. . . . . . κω]μῳδίᾳ· ἐπὶ Τιμοκλέ[ους . . .   (B. C. 440)
. . . . .] ἐπὶ Θεοδώρου Σατύροις [ἐπὶ . . . . (B. C. 437)
. . . . . 'Υπ]έροις σιδηροῖς· ἐπὶ Πυ[θοδώρου . . . (B. C. 431)
. . . .]οις. ε΄ ἐπὶ 'Αντιοχίδου [. . . .   (B. C. 434)
Λ]ύσιππος ἐνίκα μὲν [ἐν ἄστει ἐπὶ
Γλαυκίπ]που
or Θεοπόμ]που } Καταχήναις [ἐπὶ . . . .   (B. C. 409 or 410)
. . . . .]αις· αὗται μόναι σῶ[αι·

```
. . . . ἐ]πὶ Διοφάντου Διονυ[σ . . . . .          (B. C. 394)
γ′ ἐν ἄσ]τει ἐπὶ Νικοτέλους                        (B. C. 390)
δ′ ἐν ἄστ]ε[ι] ἐπὶ Λυσιμάχου [. . . . . .          (B. C. 435)
ε′ ἐν ἄστε]ι ἐπὶ Μορυχίδου [. . . . ἐπὶ             (B. C. 439)
. . . . . . . ο]υς Κολεοφόροις
```

(*b*) All but the last two lines probably refer to the comic poet
Anaxandrides, as the plays named show. I. G. xiv. 1098.

```
. . . . . ἐπὶ Χιώνος Μαι[νομένῳ (?)                  (B. C. 364)
ἐπὶ Μόλωνος] Διονύσου γονα[ῖς, ἐπὶ                   (B. C. 361)
Νικοφήμου] 'Αμπρακιώτιδι·  γ′ ἐν [ἄστει             (B. C. 360)
ἐπὶ Φανο]στράτου 'Ερεχθεῖ, ἐ[πὶ . . .'.             (B. C. 382)
. . . . . .]λεῖ, ἐπὶ Χαρισάνδρ[ου                    (B. C. 375)
. . . . ἐπὶ ἱπ]ποδάμαντος 'Ιοῖ· ἐ[πὶ Φρασι-    (B. C. 374, 370)
κλείδου] 'Οδυσσεῖ· ἐπὶ Κηφισοδ[ώρου                 (B. C. 365)
. . . . .] ἐπὶ 'Απολλοδώρου 'Αγ[ροίκοις (?)         (B. C. 349)
. . . . . .]ξίππου· Λήναια ἐπ[ὶ
. . . . π]οιῷ, ἐπὶ Ναυσιγένους [. . . .              (B. C. 367)
. . . . . . δ′ ἐ]ν ἄστει· ἐπὶ Χίωνος [               (B. C. 364)
. . . ε′ ἐν ἄστ]ει ἐπὶ 'Αγαθοκλέ[ους                (B. C. 356)
. . . . . . . . ἐ]πὶ Θουδήμου 'Α[. . . .            (B. C. 352)
. . . . . . . . ]ου 'Αντέρωτι [. . . . . .
. . . . . . ἐ]νίκα Λήναι[α . . . .
. . . . β′ ἦν] ἐν ἄστ[ει . . .
```

APPENDIX C

THE ORIGINAL PLACE OF THE LENAEA

THE question where the Lenaean contests took place before the building of the great theatre of Dionysus has been unfortunately complicated with other problems, of which no final solution can be given. For it has been customary to assume that the Lenaeum was identical with the temple of Dionysus ἐν Λίμναις, or at least that the latter was included in the Lenaeum; and thus all the disputes respecting the site of the temple ἐν Λίμναις have been regarded as applying also to the site of the Lenaeum. Hence the discussion of the evidence for the site of the Lenaeum is more difficult than it need be.

I. It is to be noticed in the first place, as Miss Harrison points out (Primitive Athens, pp. 96–7), that, on the one hand, none of those writers who themselves saw the temple ἐν Λίμναις (and indeed hardly any writers, the possible exceptions being considered below) speak of it as the Lenaeum or in connexion with the Lenaeum; while on the other hand, contemporary (and nearly all later) mentions of the dramatic contest at the Lenaea fail to connect it with the Λίμναι. And it is obvious that, as the precinct ἐν Λίμναις was only open once a year, on the 12th of Anthesterion (pseudo-Dem. in Neaer. § 76, see below), the Lenaeum cannot (any more than the temple or precinct of Dionysus Eleuthereus) have been absolutely identical with it, though the possibility is not thereby excluded that the Lenaeum may have been a larger precinct in a part of which the temple ἐν Λίμναις stood.

The passages referring to the ἐν Λίμναις, without reference to the Lenaeum, are Thuc. ii. 15; Aristoph. Ran. 211 sqq.; pseudo-Dem. in Neaer. § 76; and Phanodemus ap. Athen. xi. p. 465 a: there can also be little doubt that Paus. i. 20. 3 refers to the temple ἐν Λίμναις, though he does not name it. I make only such comments on these passages as are necessary for showing that they afford no ground for the identification of the Lenaeum and the ἐν Λίμναις.

(A) Thuc. ii. 15 : τὸ δὲ πρὸ τούτου ἡ ἀκρόπολις ἡ νῦν οὖσα πόλις ἦν καὶ τὸ ὑπ᾽ αὐτὴν πρὸς νότον μάλιστα τετραμμένον· τεκμήριον δέ· τὰ γὰρ ἱερὰ ἐν αὐτῇ τῇ ἀκροπόλει καὶ ἄλλων θεῶν ἐστί, καὶ τὰ ἔξω πρὸς τοῦτο τὸ μέρος τῆς πόλεως μᾶλλον ἵδρυται, τό τε τοῦ Διὸς τοῦ Ὀλυμπίου καὶ τὸ Πύθιον καὶ τὸ τῆς Γῆς καὶ τὸ ἐν Λίμναις Διονύσου, ᾧ τὰ ἀρχαιότερα Διονύσια τῇ δωδεκάτῃ ποιεῖται ἐν μηνὶ Ἀνθεστηριῶνι.

This passage can only be used to prove the ἐν Λίμναις identical with the Lenaeum (or closely connected) if we can identify the ἀρχαιότερα Διονύσια with the Lenaean festival or part of it. Gilbert, Dörpfeld, and others have attempted to do this. (It should be noted that, in the case of Dörpfeld and his followers, this attempt is secondary to an attempt to fix the temple ἐν Λίμναις at a particular spot, where he has discovered the remains of a precinct of Dionysus, containing a wine-press, ληνός.) They argue that the use of the comparative ἀρχαιότερα by Thucydides implies that he knew only of *two* Dionysia, one the older, the other the later. The later must obviously be the Great or City Dionysia; and therefore the earlier, it is argued, must be the Anthesteria, Lenaea and Rural Dionysia, all regarded as one and the same festival; the place of the Anthesteria must therefore be the place of the Lenaea; and as a comparison of Thucydides with the pseudo-Dem. in Neaeram (below) proves that the place of at least one part of the Anthesteria—that which was celebrated on the 12th Anthesterion—was the ἐν Λίμναις, it follows that the Lenaea must also have taken place ἐν Λίμναις, not of course in the actual sanctuary of Dionysus, but close to it.

Now it can be shown (1) that the stress laid on the comparative is unwarranted, (2) that there are other grounds for refusing to identify the Anthesteria and the Lenaea.

(1) There are other passages in classical Greek literature in which the comparative of words denoting age, &c., is used of the oldest, not of two, but of several. Nilsson (Studia de Dionysiis Atticis, p. 54) collects the following, in addition to Homeric instances noted by Kühner-Gerth, Griech. Gramm. § 349, p. 3).

Lys. x. 5 : ὁ γὰρ πρεσβύτερος ἀδελφὸς Πανταλέων ἅπαντα παρέλαβε καὶ ἐπιτροπεύσας ἡμᾶς τῶν πατρῴων ἀπεστέρησεν.

Lys. xiii. 67 : ἦσαν τοίνυν οὗτοι, ὦ ἄνδρες δικασταί, τέτταρες ἀδελφοί. τούτων εἷς μὲν ὁ πρεσβύτερος κτλ.

Xen. Cyr. v. 1. 6 : ὡς δ' ἡμῶν ὁ γεραίτερος εἶπε (where the context shows that a good many people were concerned. The reading γεραίτερος is far better supported than γεραίτατος).

Theocr. xv. 139 : οὔθ' Ἕκτωρ, Ἑκάβας ὁ γεραίτερος εἴκατι παίδων.

Other instances could probably be found, in spite of the tendency of grammarians and editors to force these cases into the supposed orthodox form, by emending the comparative to the superlative (as e.g. they have done in Aelian, Var. H. ii. 41).

All that the comparative really implies is that one individual case is separated off from the rest, and the rest treated as a single combined group. On this view the ἀρχαιότερα Διονύσια will be the older ceremony, the Anthesteria, as contrasted with the group well known to be recent, viz. the great popular festivals, the City Dionysia and the Lenaea. If πρεσβύτερος and γεραίτερος can be used of one brother as opposed to the rest, why not ἀρχαιότερα of one festival as opposed to the rest, these latter being grouped together in thought as recent in comparison with the one?

There is, further, a note by Prof. Capps in the Trans. Amer. Philol. Assoc. vol. xxxii, summarizing a paper in which he claims to distinguish the meaning of ἀρχαιότερα from that of παλαιότερα, to show that previous critics of Thucydides have confused them, and that on the true view of ἀρχαιότερα the view of Gilbert, Dörpfeld, &c., is impossible. But the paper has not been published as a whole.

(2) The Lenaea was celebrated in the month Gamelion, which in other places was called Lenaeon; the Anthesteria in Anthesterion. Gilbert's attempt to prove that the names of the months were changed and the festivals transferred from one month to another breaks down entirely (Nilsson, l. c., pp. 1-37, disproves it completely), nor would the attempt have been made but for the necessity of providing some such explanation, if the two festivals were to be identified. The separation in time of the festivals is sufficient to disprove their identity.

Again, in C. I. A. ii. 834 b (pp. 516 ff.) we have the accounts of certain officials called ἐπιστάται Ἐλευσινόθεν καὶ ταμίαι τοῖν θεοῖν in the year B.C. 329-8. Col. II, containing the accounts ἐπὶ τῆς Πανδιονίδος ἕκτης πρυτανείας, includes in l. 46 ἐπιστάταις Ἐπιλήναια εἰς Διονύσια θῦσαι Δ Δ ⸏, and in l. 68 εἰς Χόας δημοσίοις ἱερεῖον Δ Δ ⊢ ⊢ ⊢. This proves that the Epilenaea (the same form occurs in Ath. Pol. ch. lvii, though it is altered by editors, and probably also in C. I. A. ii. 741) was a distinct festival from the Anthesteria, of which the Choes formed a part. (This was shown by Körte, Rhein. Mus. lii. pp. 168 ff., and Wachsmuth, Abh. der Sächs. Ges. der Wiss. xviii. pp. 40 ff.) A later inscription, C. I. A. iii. 1160, date c. B.C. 193-2, separates equally clearly the Lenaea from the Χύτροι (vide Nilsson, l. c., pp. 42-4): and Nilsson gives other passages quite as conclusive (l. c., p. 143), of which one is worth quoting, a gloss found in Photius, Suidas, &c., s. v. τὰ ἐκ τῶν ἀμαξῶν σκώμματα· ἐπὶ τῶν ἀπαρακαλύπτως σκωπτόντων. Ἀθήνησι γὰρ ἐν τῇ τῶν Χοῶν ἑορτῇ οἱ κωμάζοντες ἐπὶ τῶν ἀμαξῶν τοὺς ἀπαντῶντας ἔσκωπτόν τε καὶ ἐλοιδόρουν. τὸ δ᾽ αὐτὸ καὶ τοῖς Ληναίοις ὕστερον ἐποίουν.

It follows, therefore, that the Anthesteria, the ἀρχαιότερα Διονύσια of

Thucydides, cannot be identified with the Lenaea, and that whatever may be proved from Thucydides as to the site of the temple ἐν Λίμναις, in which the former were partly celebrated, nothing follows in reference to the Lenaeum.

(B) Aristoph. Ran. 211 sqq.:

> λιμναῖα κρηνῶν τέκνα,
> ξύναυλον ὕμνων βοὰν
> φθεγξώμεθ᾽, εὔγηρυν ἐμὰν ἀοιδάν,
> κοὰξ κοάξ,
> ἣν ἀμφὶ Νυσήιον
> Διὸς Διόνυσον ἐν
> Λίμναισιν ἰαχήσαμεν,
> ἡνίχ᾽ ὁ κραιπαλόκωμος
> τοῖς ἱεροῖσι Χύτροισι
> χωρεῖ κατ᾽ ἐμὸν τέμενος λαῶν ὄχλος.

The fact that the play was produced at the Lenaea (B.C. 405) cannot possibly be used to prove that the Lenaea and the Chutroi, at which the 'Frogs' profess to have raised their hymn to Dionysus (in the *past*, it is to be noticed), were the same festival.

(C) Pseudo-Dem. in Neaer. §§ 73 sqq.: καὶ αὕτη ἡ γυνὴ ὑμῖν ἔθυε τὰ ἄρρητα ἱερὰ ὑπὲρ τῆς πόλεως, καὶ εἶδεν ἃ οὐ προσῆκεν αὐτὴν ὁρᾶν ξένην οὖσαν, καὶ τοιαύτη οὖσα εἰσῆλθεν οἶ οὐδεὶς ἄλλος Ἀθηναίων τοσούτων ὄντων εἰσέρχεται ἀλλ᾽ ἢ ἡ τοῦ βασιλέως γυνή, ἐξώρκωσέ τε τὰς γεραρὰς τὰς ὑπηρετούσας τοῖς ἱεροῖς, ἐξεδόθη δὲ τῷ Διονύσῳ γυνή. . . . § 76: καὶ τοῦτον τὸν νόμον γράψαντες ἐν στήλῃ λιθίνῃ ἔστησαν ἐν τῷ ἱερῷ τοῦ Διονύσου παρὰ τὸν βωμὸν ἐν Λίμναις (καὶ αὕτη ἡ στήλη ἔτι καὶ νῦν ἔστηκεν, ἀμυδροῖς γράμμασιν Ἀττικοῖς δηλοῦσα τὰ γεγραμμένα). . . . καὶ διὰ ταῦτα ἐν τῷ ἀρχαιοτάτῳ ἱερῷ τοῦ Διονύσου καὶ ἁγιωτάτῳ ἐν Λίμναις ἔστησαν, ἵνα μὴ πολλοὶ εἰδῶσι τὰ γεγραμμένα· ἅπαξ γὰρ τοῦ ἐνιαυτοῦ ἑκάστου ἀνοίγεται, τῇ δωδεκάτῃ τοῦ Ἀνθεστηριῶνος μηνός. . . . § 78: ὅρκος γεραρῶν. ἁγιστεύω καὶ εἰμὶ καθαρὰ καὶ ἁγνὴ ἀπό τε τῶν ἄλλων τῶν οὐ καθαρευόντων καὶ ἀπ᾽ ἀνδρὸς συνουσίας, καὶ τὰ Θεοίνια καὶ τὰ Ἰοβάκχεια γεραίρω τῷ Διονύσῳ κατὰ τὰ πάτρια καὶ ἐν τοῖς καθήκουσι χρόνοις.

Here there is no hint of the Lenaeum or Lenaea at all.

(D) Paus. i. 20. 3: τοῦ Διονύσου δέ ἐστι πρὸς τῷ θεάτρῳ τὸ ἀρχαιότατον ἱερόν· δύο δέ εἰσιν ἐντὸς τοῦ περιβόλου ναοὶ καὶ Διόνυσοι, ὅ τε Ἐλευθερεὺς καὶ ὃν Ἀλκαμένης ἐποίησεν ἐλέφαντος καὶ χρυσοῦ.

(E) Athen. xi. p. 465 a: Φανόδημος δὲ πρὸς τῷ ἱερῷ φησι τοῦ ἐν Λίμναις Διονύσου τὸ γλεῦκος φέροντας τοὺς Ἀθηναίους ἐκ τῶν πίθων τῷ θεῷ κιρνάναι, εἶτ᾿ αὐτοὺς (v. ll. αὐτοῖς, αὐτοί) προσφέρεσθαι· ὅθεν καὶ Λίμναιον κληθῆναι τὸν Διόνυσον, ὅτι μιχθὲν τὸ γλεῦκος τῷ ὕδατι τότε πρῶτον ἐπόθη κεκραμένον.

Now it is clear that none of the above passages gives us any assistance towards the localization of the Lenaeum. Nor do the references to the Lenaic performances themselves. The festival is called Λήναια (Aristoph. Ach. 1155; Athen. p. 130 d, &c.): ἐπὶ Ληναίῳ ἀγών (Aristoph. Ach. 504): ἐπιλήναια Διονύσια (Ath. Pol. c. 57; C. I. A. ii. 834 b and probably 731), and we have such phrases as ἐπὶ Ληναίῳ νικᾶν, διδάσκειν, &c.: but in none of these cases is there any hint of the Λίμναι (e. g. Plat. Prot. 327 d; Dem. Meid. § 10).

For what reasons, then, drawn from literary evidence, has it been assumed that the Lenaea and the Anthesteria (partly held ἐν Λίμναις) were identical?

(1) The passage of Athenaeus above quoted has been compared with Anon. de Comoed. α΄. l. 6 ff. (Kaibel. Fr. Com. p. 7) τὴν αὐτὴν (sc. τὴν κωμῳδίαν) δὲ καὶ τρυγῳδίαν φασὶ διὰ τὸ τοῖς εὐδοκιμοῦσιν ἐπὶ τῷ Ληναίῳ γλεῦκος δίδοσθαι, ὅπερ ἐκάλουν τρύγα, ἢ ὅτι μήπω προσωπείων ηὑρημένων τρυγὶ διαχρίοντες τὰ πρόσωπα ὑπεκρίνοντο. But the two passages refer to entirely different ceremonies. That of which Athenaeus speaks was part of the Choes, the first drinking of the new wine at the Anthesteria. The second refers to the prize of a bottle of new wine given to successful poets at the Lenaea; it is a conjectural explanation of the name τρ·γῳδία. There is nothing whatever to show that the passages refer to ceremonies in any way connected, except the use of the word γλεῦκος in both.

(2) Hesychius: λίμναι· ἐν ᾿Αθήναις [ἃς] τόπος ἀνειμένος Διονύσῳ, ὅπου τὰ λαῖα ἤγετο. Editors generally, following Musurus, emend to Λήναια, but this is not proof. The true reading may be Λιμναῖα.

(3) The one passage which can be treated seriously is a Schol. on Aristoph. Ach. 961, explaining the origin of the Choes: εἰς τὴν ἑορτὴν τῶν Χοῶν ἐπετελεῖτο δὲ Πυανεψιῶνος ὀγδόῃ· οἱ δὲ ᾿Ανθεστηριῶνος ⟨δω⟩δεκάτῃ. φησὶ δὲ ᾿Απολλόδωρος ᾿Ανθεστήρια καλεῖσθαι κοινῶς τὴν ὅλην ἑορτὴν Διονύσῳ ἀγομένην, κατὰ μέρος δὲ Πιθοιγίαν Χόας Χύτραν. καὶ αὖθις. ὅτι ᾿Ορέστης μετὰ τὸν φόνον εἰς ᾿Αθήνας ἀφικόμενος (ἦν δὲ ἑορτὴ Διονύσου Ληναίου), ὡς μὴ γένοιτο ὁμόσπονδος ἀπεκτονὼς τὴν μητέρα ἐμηχανήσατο τοιόνδε τι Πανδίων . . . καὶ ἀπ᾿ ἐκείνου ᾿Αθηναίοις ἑορτὴ ἐνομίσθη οἱ Χόες. This passage as it stands undoubtedly represents the Choes as instituted to form part of a festival of Dionysus Lenaeus. But our suspicions are aroused when we find that the other versions of the same story make no allusion to Dionysus Lenaeus. The corresponding expression in Schol. ad

Aristoph. Eq. 95 (which Rutherford transfers to Ach. 961) is κατέλαβεν
δὲ αὐτὸν (sc. τὸν Πανδίονα) εὐωχίαν τινα δημοτελῆ ποιοῦντα. (Other versions
are Athen. x. p. 437 b; Plut. Quaest. Symp. p. 613 b and p. 643 a;
Schol. Tzetzae ad Lycophr. 1374; Suidas s. v. Χόες.) It is at least
probable, therefore, that the parenthesis ἦν δὲ ἑορτὴ Διονύσου Ληναίου is
an erroneous gloss by the compiler of the first-quoted scholium, whose
state of mind in regard to the facts concerning the festivals mentioned
is sufficiently indicated by the early part of the scholium. Rutherford
has made plain the unreliability of the scholiasts on Aristophanes, and
this single passage is of no value when compared with the weight of
evidence against the identification of the two festivals. Nilsson (l. c.,
p. 57) may be right in his suggestion that Ληναίου is an error for
Λιμναίου. ΛΗΝΑΙΟΥ and ΛΙΜΝΑΙΟΥ are very much alike, and the latter,
being less familiar, might easily be changed into the former. Athen.
xi. 465 a (quoted above), quoting Phanodemus, mentions Λιμναῖος as
a name of Dionysus, especially connected with the Anthesteria. But
in fact the emendation, though highly probable, is needless so far as
the case against identifying the festivals is concerned. I do not
notice some other passages cited by Gilbert in support of the identification, because so far as I can discover no one does or would now
so use them : in any case Nilsson's reply is sufficient.

II. With regard to the archaeological evidence adduced by Dörpfeld (Ath. Mitth. 1895, Griech. Theat. p. 7) and Miss Harrison, it seems
enough to say that though the precinct discovered by the former, and
identified by them with the precinct ἐν Λίμναις, contains the remains of
a ληνός, this does not itself prove that it was a precinct of Dionysus
Lenaeus, much less that it was the Lenaeum for which we are looking.
If it were the precinct of Dionysus Lenaeus it might contain a ληνός
(though this is not necessary); but to argue the converse is quite
fallacious. Nor does the existence of other ληνοί in the neighbourhood
help the argument. There is some plausibility, indeed, in the idea that
the Lenaeum may have been a place or district in which there were
many ληνοί, but (1) it is certainly not proved that Dörpfeld's precinct
was the temple ἐν Λίμναις, and so, even if it were the Lenaeum, the two
temples would not necessarily be identified, and (2) it is very probable
that the title Λήναιος is not derived from ληνός at all. We will first deal
with these two points before discussing such positive evidence as there
is for the site of the Lenaeum.

(1) As to the temple ἐν Λίμναις, the first important piece of evidence
as to the site is the passage of Thucydides, and next the passages of

pseudo-Dem. in Neaeram and Pausanias, all quoted above. To take Thucydides first. The most natural and obvious interpretation, the one which a reader would assume if not on the look out for difficulties, would take πρὸς τοῦτο τὸ μέρος as = πρὸς τὸ ὑπ' αὐτὴν πρὸς νότον μάλιστα τετραμμένον. It cannot indeed be said that it would be *impossible* for it to mean 'near this original city' (including the acropolis and the land south of it); but, as Prof. E. Gardner points out (Ancient Athens, p. 144), one would expect πρὸς νότῳ (or πρὸς τούτῳ τῷ μέρει) in such a case; and such an interpretation gives us no reason why Thucydides should have mentioned the south at all. On the most natural interpretation then of Thucydides the temple ἐν Λίμναις was to the south of the acropolis (or SW.), not, like Dörpfeld's precinct, on the WNW. Pausanias, moreover, says that the ἀρχαιότατον ἱερόν of Dionysus was πρὸς τῷ θεάτρῳ. (ἱερόν as Carroll points out (Class. Rev. July, 1905) often means the whole precinct, and not merely the shrine or sanctuary; several shrines may be included in one precinct.) Carroll reminds us (l. c.) that 'Fischbach (Wiener Stud. xv. pp. 161–91) has shown conclusively that Pausanias was thoroughly acquainted with Thucydides, and made extensive use of the historian in his description of Athens; so much that he appropriates words, phrases, and terms of expression found in Thucydides. These stylistic resemblances exclude the acceptance of an intermediate channel. Pausanias had also the benefit of a tradition handed down by local guides respecting important sites. Hence when he makes a statement manifestly based on Thucydides, the presumption is that he understood his authority and interpreted him correctly.' Now in the present case it is admitted that Pausanias had Thucydides before him; and when Thucydides speaks of the ἀρχαιότερα Διονύσια as celebrated at the temple ἐν Λίμναις, and when the pseudo-Demosthenes (l. c.), a connecting link, speaks of the ἐν Λίμναις as the ἀρχαιότατον ἱερόν of Dionysus, it is infinitely more natural to suppose that Pausanias also, speaking of the ἀρχαιότατον ἱερόν, refers to the precinct ἐν Λίμναις, and that therefore the temple ἐν Λίμναις was πρὸς τῷ θεάτρῳ, than with Wilamowitz (Hermes, xxi) to construct a theory of clumsy mistakes on Pausanias' part. Of course, for the reasons given by Wilamowitz, the ἐν Λίμναις was not the same as the theatre or temple of Dionysus Eleuthereus, but it may well have been within the same ἱερόν, the same sacred precinct, or quite close to it, on the SW. of the acropolis.

Now Miss Harrison (l. c., p. 83) writes that 'Thucydides himself seems to warn us. He seems to say, "not that precinct which you all

know so well and think so much of, not that theatre where year by
year you all go, but an earlier and more venerable place, and, that
there be no mistake, the place where you go on the 12th day of
Anthesterion, &c."' : and she concludes that Pausanias was wrong in
saying that the oldest sanctuary of Dionysus was πρὸς τῷ θεάτρῳ.
Thucydides, she seems to argue, would not have been at such pains to
distinguish the two ' hiera ' if they had been close to each other. But
(if he is really intending to distinguish them) this may just as well
have been because they *were* close to each other and might be confused. However, so far as this passage goes, the theatre may or may
not have been near the oldest sanctuary ; Thucydides would not
have any reason to think of the theatre *in either case*, for the simple
reason that it was not old enough to add anything to his argument,
and any mention of it would have been irrelevant and confusing.

The most natural conclusion then from the words of Thucydides
and Pausanias is that the temple ἐν Λίμναις was near the theatre, and
not in Dörpfeld's precinct to the WNW. of the acropolis. (In spite
of Miss Harrison it seems that the other temples mentioned by Thucydides can be accommodated with sites at least as well on the view here
taken as on that taken by Dörpfeld, and I should say very much better.
See Bates (Trans. Amer. Phil. Assoc. vol. 30); E. Gardner (l. c.);
Farnell (Class. Rev. 1900, &c.).)

I pass on to the attempt to identify the ἐν Λίμναις with Dörpfeld's
precinct on the evidence of pseudo-Demosthenes. The passage
gives the oath taken by the γεραραί or attendants at the ceremony on
the 12th of Anthesterion. They swear that they celebrate (or will
celebrate, though I cannot find any authority for the reading γεραρῶ)
the Theoinia and Iobaccheia in the customary manner and at the
customary times. Therefore, Miss Harrison seems to wish us to argue,
the Iobaccheia took place like the ceremony on the 12th of Anthesterion in the ἐν Λίμναις, and the Iobacchic inscription discovered in
Dörpfeld's precinct proves this precinct to be the place of the Iobaccheia,
and therefore to be the ἐν Λίμναις. This is simply a case of *non sequitur*.
Suppose a ceremony of the English Church which required of its
attendants a solemn declaration, ' I am (or, I will be) a regular com-
municant,' it could not be inferred that the Communion Service was
part of the ceremony, or took place at the same spot. Even, therefore,
if a Baccheion has been found, guaranteed by the inscription (and of
this there is no doubt), there is nothing to prove either that it, or any
older building beneath it, is the temple ἐν Λίμναις, or that the third-

century inscription on the pillar by the altar is the representative of
the far older στήλη by the altar ἐν Λίμναις mentioned by the pseudo-
Demosthenes. Prof. Ernest Gardner also points out (l. c., p. 113) that
the Iobaccheia mentioned in the oath cannot be the same as the rites
of the Iobacchi of the inscription, for 'the one is a state ceremony, the
other a private one; and, moreover, the Iobaccheia are not among the
festivals which the Iobacchi celebrate, and of which we have a complete
list' (see Roberts and Gardner, Greek Epigraphy, ii. pp. 236 ff.). The
fact that the lower building contains a wine-press and places for an
altar and stelae does not prove that it was the ἐν Λίμναις: it proves at
most that it was an old Βακχεῖον, like the one above it. There is no
proof at all of the crucial point—that the Iobaccheia were celebrated
only, or celebrated at all, in the temple ἐν Λίμναις: Dörpfeld's precinct
is probably only one of the many Βακχεῖα which (as Prof. E. Gardner,
l. c., notes) must have existed in Athens, and the practice of setting up
stelae was too general to allow of any argument being drawn from the
one found. On the whole, the statement 'I celebrate (or, will celebrate) the Iobaccheia at the proper times' suggests that the reference
is to some time *not* the present, and that the Iobaccheia are quite
distinct from the ceremony of the 12th of Anthesterion. The nature
of the enclosure surrounding Dörpfeld's precinct also admits of many
explanations besides the one Miss Harrison offers. Perhaps if it *was*
the ἐν Λίμναις, only open once a year and kept strictly secret, it would
be carefully enclosed, and would have only a small door, and would
contain no votive offerings; but to argue the converse is simply bad
reasoning. Since then Dörpfeld's precinct was probably *not* the temple
ἐν Λίμναις, the place of the Anthesteria, it gives us no ground for
identifying the sites or the ceremonies of the Anthesteria and the
Lenaea; and we have seen that the fact that it contains a ληνός is quite
insufficient to prove that the precinct was the Lenaeum. So that the
discovery of the precinct, interesting as it is in itself, throws no light
whatever on the problem before us—the site of the Lenaeum.

(2) As regards the derivation of the title Λήναιος, the form of the
word suggests derivation from a feminine λήνη, not a masculine ληνός,
and this view finds support on other grounds from Ribbeck (Anfänge
und Entwickelung des Dionysos-Kult in Attika, p. 13); Farnell (Class.
Rev. 1900), and Nilsson (l. c., pp. 111 ff.). Shortly, the reasons for the
derivation from λήνη are as follows. Hesychius gives us λῆναι· βάκχαι·
Ἀρκάδες: and Ribbeck, comparing this with Odyssey xix. 230 ὁ μὲν
(sc. κύων) λᾶε νεβρὸν ἀπάγχων, suggests that the root is λαϝ, 'tear,' and

that the λῆναι were bacchants of the mountains who rent a fawn in their ecstasy. We find also the verb ληναΐζειν. If this is so, the Lenaea probably at first included orgiastic rites, and it is significant in this connexion that there were mysteries connected with Lenaea at Myconos; and it may be added that in C. I. A. 834 b the fact that expenditure for the Lenaea appears in the accounts of the ἐπιστάται Ἐλευσινόθεν has by some been interpreted as pointing in the same direction, and suggesting in connexion with the Lenaea mystic rites having reference to the fertility of the ground. If so, the derivation from ληνός must give way; it is in any case uncertain, though perhaps it was the popular derivation in ancient times. It does not, however, seem to me to follow necessarily (as Dr. Farnell appears to think) that because both the Anthesteria and the Lenaea involved secret rites, they were even probably the same festival. The arguments given by Nilsson and others, and partly reproduced above, are a sufficient reply.

III. Finally, we have to ask, what positive evidence have we for the site of the Lenaeum?

(1) It was in the ἀγορά. This seems to be a legitimate inference from two passages of Photius, viz. ληναῖον· περίβολος μέγας Ἀθήνησιν ἐν ᾧ τοὺς ἀγῶνας ἦγον πρὸ τοῦ τὸ θέατρον οἰκοδομηθῆναι ὀνομάζοντες ἐπὶ Ληναίῳ. ἔστιν δὲ ἐν αὐτῷ καὶ ἱερὸν Διονύσου Ληναίου (so practically Hesych. s. v. ἐπὶ Ληναίῳ ἀγών), and ἴκρια· τὰ ἐν τῇ ἀγορᾷ ἀφ᾽ ὧν ἐθεῶντο τοὺς Διονυσιακοὺς ἀγῶνας πρὶν ἢ κατασκευασθῆναι τὸ ἐν Διονύσου θεάτρον. Again, Schol. ad Dem. de Cor. § 129 describes τὸ κλίσιον τὸ πρὸς τῷ καλαμίτῃ ἥρωϊ as ἐν ἀγορᾷ, while the ἱερόν of the hero is said to be πρὸς τῷ Ληναίῳ. Whatever is to be said about the hero, he at any rate serves to connect the Ληναῖον and the ἀγορά. That there was anciently an orchestra in the market-place at Athens appears also from Photius, ὀρχήστρα· πρῶτον ἐκλήθη ἐν τῇ ἀγορᾷ, and Plato, Laws 817 c, speaks of stages erected in the market-place by tragic poets. Socrates speaks of book-shops in the orchestra (Plato, Apol. 26 E). But the site of the ἀγορά itself is still so much disputed that we are left in uncertainty. The statement of Timaeus, Lex. Plat., ὀρχήστρα τόπος ἐπιφάνης εἰς πανήγυριν ἔνθα Ἁρμοδίου καὶ Ἀριστογείτονος εἰκόνες, does not really help, as the position of these statues is itself disputed. It may have been at the NE. or the NW. corner of the acropolis. We have to be content therefore with the information that the old Lenaic performances took place in a temporary wooden theatre in (or by) the market-place—wherever this was, and that the particular spot in (or by) the market-place was the Lenaeum, a περίβολος μέγας.

(2) The Scholia on Aristophanes twice over state that the Lenaea

took place ἐν ἀγροῖς. Schol. ad Aristoph. Ach. 504 reads οὑπὶ Ληναίῳ τ' ἀγών· ὁ τῶν Διονυσίων ἀγὼν ἐτελεῖτο δὶς τοῦ ἔτους, τὸ μὲν πρῶτον ἔαρος ἐν ἄστει, ὅτε καὶ οἱ φόροι Ἀθήνησιν ἐφέροντο, τὸ δὲ δεύτερον ἐν ἀγροῖς ὁ ἐπὶ Ληναίῳ λεγόμενος, ὅτε ξένοι οὐ παρῆσαν Ἀθήνησι· χειμὼν γὰρ λοιπὸν ἦν: and Schol. id. 202 ἄξω τὰ καὶ ἀγρούς· τὰ Λήναια λεγόμενα. ἔνθεν τὰ Λήναια καὶ ὁ ἐπιλήναιος ἀγὼν τελεῖται τῷ Διονύσῳ· Λήναιον γάρ ἐστιν ἐν ἀγροῖς ἱερὸν τοῦ Διονύσου· διὰ τὸ πλεκτοὺς ἐνταῦθα γεγονέναι, ἢ διὰ τὸ πρῶτον ἐν τούτῳ τῷ τόπῳ ληνὸν τεθῆναι. Μένανδρος· τραγῳδὸς ἦν ἀγών, Διονύσια. So also Steph. Byz. Λήναιος· ἀγὼν Διονύσου ἐν ἀγροῖς ἀπὸ τῆς ληνοῦ· Ἀπολλόδωρος ἐν τρίτῳ χρονικῶν. But the confusion of these remarks is plain (see Nilsson, l. c. 78), and when the Scholia on Aristophanes which comment on the Dionysiac festivals are taken altogether, it is clear that no consistent view is to be found in them and no confidence is to be placed in them. It is enough to note that Schol. ad Ar. Ach. 378 places the Lenaea in autumn. The Scholiasts' ἐν ἀγροῖς is no doubt due to the need of distinguishing the Lenaea from the Dionysia ἐν ἄστει, properly so called in opposition, not to the Lenaea, but to the rural Dionysia. Religious nomenclature is not so consistent that we can assume that *all* the Dionysia except the festival named ἐν ἄστει were once ἐν ἀγροῖς, but it is still possible that the Lenaeum was once outside the walls, and afterwards came to be included in their circuit. Hesychius (s. v. ἐπὶ Ληναίῳ ἀγών) describes it as ἐν τῷ ἄστει.

M. Foucart (Le Culte de Dionysos en Attique, p. 105) thinks that he has found an indication of the site in C. I. A. IV. i. p. 66, in part of an inscription which runs, τὸ δὲ ψήφισμα τόδε . . . ἀναγράψας ὁ γραμματεὺς ὁ τῆς βουλῆς ἐν στήλῃ λιθίνῃ καταθέτω ἐν τῷ Νηλείῳ παρὰ τὰ ἴκρια, and he attempts (l.c., p. 109) to fix the site of this Neleion. But his proof that παρὰ τὰ ἴκρια means 'by the Lenaean theatre' is very weak.

APPENDIX D

THE following extracts are from a series of inscriptions containing the accounts of the priests of Apollo at Delos. These priests had charge of the various public buildings in the island, including the theatre. The part of their accounts which refers to the theatre is of great interest, because of the light which it throws on the theatrical architecture of the time. A collection of the notices concerning the theatre is given by Homolle in Bulletin de Correspondance Hellénique, 1894, pp. 161 ff. The most important passages are given below.

290 B.C.   τοῖς τὴν σκηνὴν ἐργολαβήσασι καὶ τὸ προσκήνιον ΗΗΗΗΔ.

282 B.C.   Ἡρακλείδῃ εἰς τὸ προσκήνιον γράψαντι πίνακας δύο μισθὸς δραχμαὶ ⊢⊢⊢· Ἀντιδότῳ τοῦ προσκηνίου γρά[ψαν]τι πίνακας δύο . . . .

. . . . Θεοδότῳ πίνακα εἰς τὸ προσκήνιον ποιήσαντι μισθὸς δραχμαὶ ΔΔΔ· εἰς τοῦτο κατε[χρήσθη ξύλον] ἐλάτινον τῶν ὑπαρχόντων . . . . . ἀπὸ τούτων ἠλεί[ψα]μεν τὰς θύρας πάσας . . . . . . καὶ ὅσα ἔδει τῆς σκηνῆς τῆς ἐν τῷ θεάτρῳ.

281 B.C.   τοὺς πίνακας εἰς τὸ θέατρον ἀνενέγκασι ||| . . . . χαλκοῦ εἰς τὴν σκηνὴν μνᾶς ||.

279 B.C.   (δραχμὰς) ἃς ἐξέτεισε Ἀρίγνωτος Ἀντιπάτρου ὑπὲρ τῆς ἐγγύης ἧς ἠγγύητο Δίαιτον Ἀπολλοδώρου τῆς τοῦ θεάτρου περιοικοδομίας τὸ καθ' αὑτὸν μέρος . . . . . . τορνίσκον εἰς τὸ θέατρον ἐργασαμένῳ Ἀντιγόνῳ Καΐκου, παρέχοντι αὐτῷ πάντα εἰς τὸ ἔργον πλὴγ ξύλων, μισθὸς . . . . . . τοῦ θεάτρου τὴν ὀρχήστραν καὶ τοὺς ὅλκους ἀνακαθάραντι καὶ τὸν χοῦν ἐξενέγκασι μισθωτοῖς, ἀρχιτέκτονος ἐγδόντος, μισθὸς ⊢⊢⊢ . . . . τῆς σκηνῆς τὸ τέγος καταλείψαντι Ἕρμωνι Δ⊢⊢ . . . . . . εἰς τὸ [λογε]ῖον τῆς σκηνῆς (ξύλον) . . . .

276 B.C.   [ἐργο]λάβαις τοῦ θεάτρου τῶν ὅλκῶν τὴν δευτέραν δόσιν ΧΓᴴ.

274 B.C.   [ἀγαγοῦσι εἰς] τὸ θέατρον ἀπὸ τοῦ νεωκορίου λίθους οὓς εἰργάσατο . . . . . . συστήσαντι τὸ παρασκήνιον . . . . [ἀπενέγκαντι εἰς] τὸ θέατρον λίθους τῶν ἐκ Τήνου δύο καὶ ἐκ τοῦ σταδίου . . . . ἐγλαβόντι τὴν πρισμὴν τῶν στοῶν τῶν εἰς τὰς σκηνάς . . . . . τῷ τοὺς ἥλους ἐγλαβόντι [τοὺς εἰς τὰς σκ]ηνὰς καὶ τὰ παρασκήνια τὴμ μνᾶν ⊢⊢ ἀπεστησάμεθα κατὰ τὴν συγγραφὴν μνᾶς τριάκοντα ἑπτὰ μετὰ τοῦ ἀρχιτέκτονος καὶ τῶν ἐπιμελητῶν . . . . Θεοδήμῳ τῷ ἐγλαβόντι ποιῆσαι τὴν σκηνὴν τὴν μέσην καὶ τὰ παρασκήνια τὰ κάτω δραχμῶν ΗΗΗΗΓᴾΔΔΔΓ⊢⊢⊢ . . . . Ἐπικλύτῃ τῷ ἐγλαβόντι τὰς σκηνὰς τὰς παλαιάς . . . καὶ ἐπισκευάσαι καὶ τὰς ἐπάνω σκηνὰς καινὰς ποιῆσαι δύο καὶ τὰ παρασκήνια τὰ ἄνω καινὰ ποιῆσαι δύο καὶ τοῖς παλαιοῖς πίναξι τῶν παρασκηνίων περι . . . σαι καὶ τὰς ἐξώστρας καὶ τὴν κλίμακα καὶ τοὺς βαθμοὺς

ἐπισκευάσαι ⌐ΔΔΔΓΗ᚜ . . . . τοῖς ἐγλαβοῦσι γράψαι τὰς σκηνὰς
καὶ τὰ παρασκήνια τά τε ἐπάνω καὶ τὰ ὑποκάτω δραχμῶν ΧΧΓ⌐ . . . . .
. . . . . τῷ ἐγλαβόντι . . . . σαι τὸ παρασκήνιον τὸ ἐν τῷ θεάτρῳ δραχμῶν
ΗΗΗΓ⌐ΔΔΔ . . . . Θρασυλέῳ τῷ ἐγλαβόντι ἐργάσασθαι τὸ ἐπι-
στύ[λιον] . . . . \ΙΟΥ . . . . . . 'Αρχέλᾳ . . . καταχρίσαντι τὸ τεῖχος τῆς σκηνῆς
κατὰ τὴν συγγραφὴν ἀπέδομεν τὸ γινόμενον ἀρχιτέκτονος κελεύοιτος καὶ τῶν
ἐπιμελητῶν.

269 B.C.   τὴν σκηνὴν τὴν ἐν τῷ θεάτρῳ ἀνακαθάρασι Η᚜ . . . .
παρὰ Τέλλωνος ἀτράκτους δύο ὥστε κλίμα[κα] εἰς τὸ θέατρον Η᚜Η᚜Η᚜ . . . .
. . . Θεοδήμῳ κλιμακτῆρας παρασχόντι καὶ κατασκευάσαιτι Η᚜Η᚜ΙΙΙ . . . .
Διονυσίῳ ἐγλαβόντι τὴν ὀρχήστραν τοῦ θεάτρου καταχρῖσαι τὴν πρώτην δόσιν
ἔδομεν . . . . Σωσιμένει 'Αιτιγόνου τῶν λίθων τῶν τῆς εἰς τὸν θησαυρὸν (?)
ἔδομεν . . . . . . 'Αντίκῳ τῆς διόδου τῆς ἐν τῷ θεάτρῳ . . . . 'Αντίκῳ
Καΐκου ἐγλαβόντι καθάραι τὸν τόπον τῇ διόδῳ τῇ ἐν τῷ θεάτρῳ πάντα κύκλῳ
ἔδομεν . . . . 'Αριστοκλεῖ καὶ Καλλιμένει τῆς λιθείας τῆς εἰς τὸ παρασκήνιον ἐκ ποδῶν πεντακοσίων ἔδομεν . . . . Φιλανδρίδει Παρίῳ τῆς
[λιθείας] τῆς εἰς τὰς κρηπῖδας [τὰς] ἐν τῷ θεάτρῳ ἐγλαβόντι πόδας χιλίους
ἔδομεν . . . . λίθων τῶν εἰς τὸ θέατρον . . . .

250 B.C.   τὸ θέατρον ἀνακαθάραι·. . . . . κλεῖς καὶ χελώνιον ἐπὶ τὸν
'Ινωπὸν καὶ ἐπὶ τὸ Ἡράκλειον καὶ ἐπὶ τὴν σκηνήν . . . . Παρμένοιτι
ἀνακαθάραντι τὴν ἐπαγωγίδα τὴν ἐν τῷ θεάτρῳ . . . . 'Ωφελίωνι τοὺς κρουνοὺς διακαθάραντι τοὺς ἐν τῇ σκηνῇ . . . . Νεογένει ἐπιγράψαντι ἐπὶ τὸ
προσκήνιον . . . . τῆς λιθείας τῆς εἰς τὸ θέατρον ἐξέδομεν πόδας
διακοσίους, τὸμ πόδα δραχμῶν Γ Η᚜ . . . . τῆς ἐργασίας τοῦ
ἐπιθεάτρου ἐξέδομεν πόδας διακοσίους . . . . Εὐκλείδει ἐργολαβήσαντι τὸν
ὀρθοστάτην καὶ τὸν καταληπτῆρα θεῖναι καὶ ἐργάσασθαι ἐν τῷ ἐπιθεάτρῳ . . . .

180 B.C.   [ξύλον . . . . κατεχρήσθη εἰς] τὴν κατασκευὴν τῶν πινάκων τῶν
ἐπὶ τὸ λογεῖον.

The earliest notices refer to the old wooden structure. The erection
of a stone theatre was apparently begun about 275 B.C, and completed in the course of the third century. A large part of this theatre
still remains. But the stone proscenium of the Vitruvian type, of
which the foundations are preserved, was probably a later work
constructed in the second century B.C. This proscenium is not enclosed
by side-wings (παρασκήνια), but open at both ends (see Fig. 12). But
the inscription for 269 B.C. expressly mentions τῆς λιθείας τῆς εἰς τὸ
παρασκήνιον. Hence it is probable that in the stage-buildings erected
in the middle of the third century the stage was of wood, and was
terminated at each end by stone side-wings. In the second century,

when a regular stone proscenium was erected, these side-wings were removed (see Dörpfeld, Griech. Theater, p. 148).

The word σκηνή is used in the inscriptions in two senses. It denotes (1) the stage-buildings as a whole, e.g. τοὺς κρουνοὺς τοὺς ἐν τῇ σκηνῇ, (2) the wall at the rear of the stage, or the boards by which that wall was covered, e. g. τὴν σκηνὴν τὴν μέσην καὶ τὰ παρασκήνια, τὰς σκηνὰς καὶ τὰ παρασκήνια. This wall or boarding is called ἡ μέση σκηνή as opposed to the παρασκήνια on each side, and αἱ ἐπάνω σκηναί in opposition to the προσκήνιον underneath (so Homolle, l. c., p. 165). Apparently the whole building was only two stories, and the back-scene rose one story above the stage. Bethe, however (Prolegomena, p. 234), suggests that there were three stories; that ἡ μέση σκηνή denoted the middle story, and αἱ ἐπάνω σκηναί the top story, of the back-scene; the bottom story being concealed behind the προσκήνιον. But as only two stories are mentioned in connexion with the side-wings (τὰ παρασκήνια τά τε ἐπάνω καὶ τὰ ὑποκάτω), it seems unlikely that the central part of the building should have had more than two.

Some of the technical terms are new. The lines of seats in the early theatre are called ὁλκοί, as resembling furrows dug in the slope of the auditorium. The horizontal passage dividing the upper belt (διάζωμα) of seats from the lower is the δίοδος. The word περιοικοδομία seems to denote the wall by which the outside of the auditorium was enclosed and supported where necessary. The ἐπιθέατρον must have been the upper belt of seats. The ὀρθοστάτης and καταληπτήρ are explained by Homolle as a sort of balustrade and coping by which the top of the auditorium was finished off. The κλῖμαξ and κλιμακτῆρες may have been the steps leading up from orchestra to stage; but this is not certain. See on these points Homolle, l. c., pp. 163 ff.

GREEK INDEX

A

ἀγκυρίς, 209, 210.
ἀγορά, 377.
ἀγῶνες Χύτρινοι, 31.
αἰγείρου θέα, 83.
αἰῶραι, 209.
αἰώρημα, 209.
ἀναβάδην, 204.
ἀναβαθμοί, 217.
ἀναβαίνειν, 109, 148, 166, 167.
ἀναδιδάσκειν, 71.
ἀνάπαιστοι, 269, 270, 295.
ἀναπίεσμα, 217.
ἀναπλάσματα, 259.
ἀνδρῶν χορός, 9, 10.
Ἀνθεστήρια, 372.
ἀντεπίρρημα, 269.
ἀντιχόρια, 309.
ἀπαγγέλλειν, 68.
ἀπ᾽ αἰγείρου θέα, 83.
ἀπὸ μηχανῆς, 215.
ἀποκρίνεσθαι, 222, 227.
ἀποκριτής, 227.
ἀπολαχεῖν, 32.
ἀριστεροστάτης, 300.
ἅρπαξ, 209.
ἀρχιτέκτων, 334, 379.
ᾆσμα, 56.
αὖθις, 344.
αὐλαία, 219.
αὐληταὶ ἄνδρες, 9.
αὐλητής, 271.
αὐλητῶν χοροί, 9.
ἀψίς, 112, 194.

B

βαθμοί, 379.
βαρύστονος, 275.
βῆμα, 88, 107, 142.
βομβῶν, 275.
βουλευτικόν, 328, 337.
βροντεῖον, 218.
βωμός, 80, 107, 108, 200.
βωμὸς Διονύσου, 142.

Γ

γέρανος, 210.
γεραραί, 375.
γλεῦκος, 371, 372.

γραμμαί, 107.
γραμματεῖον, 33, 34.
γραφαί, 200.

Δ

δεικηλίκτας, 282.
δείξεις, 313.
δεξιοστάτης, 300.
δευτεραγωνιστής, 234.
δευτεροστάτης, 300.
διαζώματα, 98, 381.
διασκευή, 71.
διάλιον, 321.
διδασκαλεῖον, 60.
διδασκαλία, 13, 61.
διδασκαλία ἀστική, 7, 13.
διδασκαλία Ληναϊκή, 13.
διδασκαλία τραγική, 13.
Διδασκαλίαι, 13, 47, 48, 351.
διδασκαλίαν καθιέναι, 13, 32.
διδάσκαλος, 56, 61, 62.
διδάσκειν τραγῳδίαν, 25.
διθύραμβος, 10, 222.
δίοδος, 98, 380, 381.
Διονύσια, 6, 9, 378.
Διονύσια ἀρχαιότερα, 368–70, 374.
Διονύσια τὰ ἀστικά, 7.
Διονύσια τὰ ἐν ἄστει, 7, 9.
Διονύσια τὰ ἐπὶ Ληναίῳ, 6, 372.
Διονύσια τὰ ἐπιλήναια, 6, 370, 372.
Διονύσια τὰ κατ᾽ ἀγρούς, 5, 29, 288.
Διονύσια τὰ κατὰ κώμας, 29.
Διονύσια τὰ κατὰ πόλεις, 29.
Διονύσια τὰ μεγάλα, 7.
Διονυσιακοὶ ἀγῶνες, 377.
Διονυσιακοὶ τεχνῖται, 278.
Διονυσιακὸν θέατρον, 87, 377.
Διόνυσος Ἐλευθερεύς, 6, 7, 371.
Διόνυσος Λήναιος, 24, 372, 373, 377.
Διόνυσος Λιμναῖος, 372, 373.
Διόνυσος ὁ ἐν Λίμναις, 371.
διπλῆ, 317.
διστεγία, 186.
διχορία, 309.
διωβελία, 331.

E

ἐγκύκληθρον, 201.
ἐγκύκλημα, 201, 202, 205.
εἰς ἄστυ καθιέναι, 7.

εἰς ἄστυ καταλέγεσθαι, 31.
εἰσκυκλεῖν, 204.
εἰσκύκλημα, 201.
εἴσοδος, 112.
ἐκβάλλειν, 344.
ἐκκλησία ἐν Διονύσου, 7.
ἐκκυκλεῖν, 201, 204, 205, 211.
ἐκκύκλημα, 201, 211.
ἐκπίπτειν, 344.
ἔκσκευα πρόσωπα, 246.
ἐλεός, 80, 167, 222.
'Ελευθερεύς, 7.
ἐμβάς, 266.
ἐμβάτης, 248.
ἐν ἀγροῖς, 29, 378.
ἐν ἄστει διδάσκειν, 7, 13.
ἐν τοῖν δυοῖν ὀβολοῖν, 330.
ἐξάρχειν, 222.
ἔξοδος, 270, 271, 315.
ἐξώστρα, 209, 379.
ἐπαναβαίνειν, 167.
ἐπεισκυκλεῖν, 211.
ἐπὶ Ληναίῳ, 24, 25, 372, 377, 378.
ἐπιθέατρον, 98, 380, 381.
ἐπιλήναια Διονύσια, 6, 370, 372.
ἐπιμεληταί, 343.
ἐπιμεληταὶ τῆς πομπῆς, 49.
ἐπιμεληταὶ τῶν μυστηρίων, 49.
ἐπιπάροδος, 305.
ἐπίρρημα, 269.
ἐπιστάται 'Ελευσινόθεν, 6, 370, 377.
εὐημερεῖν, 43, 228.
Εὔνους, 261.
εὐφωνία, 273.
ἐφαπτίς, 252.
ἐφηβικόν, 337.
ἐώρημα, 209.

Z

ζυγόν, 299, 301.
ζῶναι, 98.
ζωστῆρες, 209.

H

ἡγεμών, 301.
ἡγεμὼν κορυφαῖος, 301.
ἡμικύκλιον, 101, 218.
ἡμιστρόφιον, 218.
ἡμιχόριον, 304, 307, 309.

Θ

θέα, 324, 341.
θέα παρ' αἰγείρῳ, 81, 83.
θεᾶσθαι, 9.
θεατής, 102, 348.
θεατρίζειν, 107, 142.
θέατρον, 81, 83, 87, 326, 348, 371, 374, 377.

θεατροπώλης, 334.
θεατρώνης, 334.
θεολογεῖον, 126, 213.
θεὸς ἀπὸ μηχανῆς, 211, 215, 216.
θερμαυστρίς, 317.
θεωρικόν, 331.
θίασος, 278.
θυμέλη, 80, 107, 108, 109, 142.
θυμελικοί, 146, 172.

I

ἰαμβεῖον, 267, 269.
ἰαμβύκη, 269.
'Ιάόνιοι νόμοι, 321.
ἴδια ᾄσματα, 310.
ἴκρια, 81, 83, 87, 328, 377.
ἱματιομίσθαι, 64.
ἱματιομισθωταί, 64.
ἱμάτιον, 250, 295.

K

καθάρσιον, 68.
καθέζεσθαι, 32.
καθιέναι, 228.
καθίζειν, 32.
καινὸς ἀγών, 30.
καλαθίσκος, 317.
καλαμίτης ἥρως, 377.
κατὰ ζυγά, 299.
κατὰ στοίχους, 102, 299.
καταβαίνειν, 166.
καταβλήματα, 185, 186, 198.
καταλέγειν, 269.
καταληπτήρ, 380, 381.
καταλογή, 269.
κατατομή, 90.
κέραμος, 186.
κεραυνοσκοπεῖον, 218.
κερκίς, 98, 337.
κίνησις, 278, 314.
κλεψίαμβος, 269.
κλῖμαξ, 129, 148, 379, 381.
κλιμακτῆρες, 380, 381.
κόθορνος, 248.
κόλπωμα, 252.
κόμμος, 268.
κονίστρα, 101, 142.
κόρδαξ, 318.
κορυφαῖος, 300, 301.
κράδη, 210.
κρασπεδίτης, 300.
κρηπίς, 248.
κριτὴν ἐμβάλλειν, 32.
κριτής, 31, 32, 33, 34, 36.
κροῦσις, 269.
κυβίστησις, 317.
κύκλιος χορός, 10.
κῶμος, 9, 20, 352.
κωμῳδοί, 9, 20, 25, 108, 275.

GENERAL INDEX

A

Acoustics, attention paid to, 174.

Acrae, theatre at, 93.

Acting, importance of the voice in, 272 ff. Musical training necessary for, 274. Style of enunciation used in, 275. Gestures used in, 276.

Actors, contests between, 40 ff. Importance of protagonists, 42. Reproduction of old plays by, 43 f. Originally chosen by the poets, afterwards by the state, 57 ff , 229, 230. How assigned to the poets, 58. Paid by the state, 64. Tamper with the text of old plays, 74. The first actor introduced by Thespis, 80. Enter and depart by orchestra, 168, 169, 192 f. Meaning of the term actor, 221. Gradual introduction of, 222 ff. Number of actors in tragedy, comedy, and satyric drama, 223. Effect of small number of, 225. The Greek names for an actor, 226 f. Rise of the actor's profession, 227. Increase in the proportion of, 228, 229. Distribution of parts among, 230 ff. Changes of costume by, 232. Costume of tragic actors, 237 ff.; of satyric actors, 255 ff. ; of comic actors, 257 ff. Importance of the voice in, 272 ff. Musical training of, 274. Style of Greek acting. 275 ff. The Actors' Guild, 278 ff. Privileges of, 278. Social position of, 281. Salaries of, 281. General character of, 282. Celebrated Athenian actors, 282 ff. Comic, lists of, 365.

Aegis, the, worn by Athene, 251.

Aeschines, acted Oenomaus, 29. Hired by Socrates and Simylus, 30. As tritagonist, 33. His accident at Collytus, 249. Taunted by Demosthenes, 281.

Aeschylus, his first appearance as a dramatist, 11, 83. His Oedipodeia, 11, 15. His Oresteia, 12, 14, 15. Trilogies and tetralogies of, 13 ff. His Lycurgeia, 15, 17. His Promethean trilogy, 15. Number of his victories,

34. Records concerning his Oresteia, 48. Exhibits at an early age, 50. Actors of, 57. Trains his choruses, 61. Reproduction of his plays after his death, 73, 76. Text of his plays, 74, 76. Not popular in later times, 76. His stage, 150. His statue in the theatre, 176. Scenery in his plays, 180. Said to have invented scene-painting, 181. Invents stage decorations, 199. Introduces a second actor, 223. Ceases to act in person, 227. His improvements in the tragic costume, 238, 240, 242, 248. His choruses, 285 ff., 289 ff. Designs the dress of the Furies, 291. Improves the tragic dance, 314. His Eumenides, 327. Nearly killed for impiety, 346.

Agathon, his first victory, 28, 70. His treatment of the chorus, 286. Adopts the new style of music, 321.

Agonothetes, the, 54, 55.

Agyrrhius, commissioner of the treasury, 40.

Aixone, comedies at, 30.

Alcamenes, 131.

Alcibiades, admired for his beauty, 9, 327. Corrupts the judges, 35. Assaults Taureas, 66, 343.

Alexander the Great, wishes to make a stage of bronze, 174.

Altar, in the orchestra, 107. On the stage, 200.

Ambassadors, provided with front seats, 324, 336.

Anapaests, given in recitative, 269. Sometimes delivered by the coryphaeus, 308.

Anapiesma, the, 217.

Anaxandrides, never revises his comedies, 71.

Andronicus, victorious in the Epigoni, 43.

Anthesteria, the, distinct from the Lenaea, 6, 369 ff. Where celebrated, 368 ff. Dramatic performances at, 31, 44.

Anti-choregi, 66.

Antisthenes, his success as choregus, 37, 62.

Apaturius, 127.

Himation, the, 250.
Horace, his reference to the Greek stage, 144, 150.
Horses, in the theatre, 201.
Hypodidaskalos, the, 62.
Hypokrites, use of the word, 220. Its derivation, 226.
Hypophrygian Mode, the, 321.
Hyporchemata, 307, 316, 317.
Hyposkenion, the, 123 ff.

I

Iambics, tetrameters, given in recitative, 269.
Iambic trimeters, spoken without musical accompaniment, 267. Rarely sung, 267.
Icaria, dramatic performances at, 29.
Ikria, the, 83, 84, 87.
Inscriptions bearing on the drama, 352 ff.
Iobaccheia, 375.
Ion of Chios, his remark about virtue, 13. His present to the Athenians, 70.
Ionic Mode, the, 321.
Iophon, exhibits plays of his father Sophocles, 51.

J

Judges, in the dramatic contests, their number, 31. Mode of selection, 32 ff. The process of voting, 33. Value of their verdicts, 34 ff. Sometimes corrupted and intimidated, 35. Afraid of the audience, 37. Their seats, 336.

K

Kataloge, 268.
Katatome, the, 90.
Keraunoskopeion, the, 218.
Kerkides, the, 98. Assigned to particular tribes, 337.
Klepsiambos, the, 269.
Knights, chorus of, 296.
Kolpoma, the, 252.
Kommos, the, 268. Accompanied by dances, 316. The kommos in the Persae, 318.
Konistra, the, 101.
Kordax, the, 318.
Kraspeditae, the, 300.
Krepis, the, 248.

L

Laurostatae, the, 170, 300.
Lenaea, the, not part of the Anthesteria, 5, 6, 372 ff. Compared with the City Dionysia, 6, 7, 27. Meaning of the name, 24, 376. Date of, 25. Where

celebrated, 25, 83, 368 ff. General character of, 25, 26. Tragic contests at, 25, 26 ff. Comic contests at, 26, 27. Actors' contests at, 41. Managed by the archon basileus, 49.
Lenaeum, the, 24, 25. Site of, 368 ff. Wooden theatre at, 83, 84.
Lenaeus, title of Dionysus, 24, 372, 376.
Lessee, the, 334.
Licymnius, the actor, victorious in the Propompi, 43. His voice, 273.
Limnaeus, title of Dionysus, 372, 373.
Logeion, the, 117, 163. Not the same as the theologeion, 164.
Lucian, ridicules the tragic actors, 254, 273.
Lycurgus, the orator, his law concerning the Anthesteria, 31. Institutes dithyrambic contests at the Peiraeeus, 39. His law for preserving the text of the great tragic poets, 74. Completes the theatre, 87. Puchstein's theory of, 87, 88, 130 ff.

M

Maeniana, 187.
Magna Graecia, theatres of, 127, 133, 155 ff.
Magnesia, theatre at, its shape, 93. Tunnel in, 109.
Market-place, the, suggested site of the Lenaeon, 25, 377. Dramatic performances at, 83.
Marshes, the, temple in, 24, 368 ff. Site of, 368 ff.
Masks, invention of, 238, 242. Results of the use of, 242, 243. The tragic mask, 244, 245. The mask of Silenus, 256. The masks in the Old Comedy, 259, 260; in the New Comedy, 262 ff. The masks of the tragic chorus, 291; of the satyric chorus, 292; of the comic chorus, 295.
Mechane, the, character of, 209 ff. Instances of the use of, 211 ff. Relation to the theologeion, 213 ff.
Megalopolis, theatre at, chief seats in, 95. Size of, 100. The orchestra in, 105, 106. The gutter, 107. Date of, 119. Stage in, 121, 122, 125. No door in hyposkenion, 124, 154. Date of proscenium, 130. Stage-buildings in, 137. Skanotheka and scaena ductilis in, 160 ff.
Meidias, corrupts the judges, 35. Assaults Demosthenes, 324. Interferes with Demosthenes' chorus, 117, 279.

Tombs, on the stage, 200.

Tragedy, first institution of contests in, 5, 11, 25, 356. At the City Dionysia, 11 ff. Reproduction of old tragedies, 19, 72. At the Lenaea, 25, 26, 356. Number of actors in, 222 ff. Costume of actors in, 237 ff. Decline of the chorus in, 286 ff. Size of the chorus in, 288 ff. Costume of the chorus in, 290. The tragic dance, 316.

Training, of the chorus, 60 ff.

Tralles, theatre at, tunnel in, 110. Steps in, 167.

Tribes, the Attic, dithyrambic contests between, 10. Have no connexion with the dramatic contests, 10. Certain blocks in the theatre appropriated to them, 337.

Tribute, displayed at the City Dionysia, 68.

Trilogies, 13, 14.

Trios, between actors, 268.

Tripods, the prizes in the dithyrambic contests, 39.

Tritagonist, the, 233.

Tritostatae, the, 300.

Trochaic tetrameters, given in recitative, 269.

Tunic, of tragic actors, 250. Of satyric actors, 256.

Tunnels, under the orchestra, 103, 109, 110.

Turban, worn by Darius, 252.

Tyndaris, stage at, 132.

V

Vitruvius, his advice about sites of theatres, 89; about the shape of the auditorium, 93. Description of the Greek and Roman orchestra, 105; of the Greek and Roman stage, 146, 163, 164. Dörpfeld's views about, 145 ff. On scene-painting, 181 ff.

Voice, importance of in the Greek drama, 272. Its strength more regarded than its quality, 273. Training of the voice, 274.

W

Wieseler, his theory of the Greek stage, 140 ff.

Windows, in the back-scene, 188.

Women, admitted to the theatre, 324 ff. Their seats, 337.

X

Xenocles, defeats Euripides, 12.

Z

Zeno, his remark about actors, 273.

ADDENDA ET CORRIGENDA

Page 21, note 1, *for* C.I.G. *read* the Roman inscription I.G.

Page 26, l. 25, *for* It was doubtless . . . But they must *read* It is therefore possible that it was at this festival that comic contests were first regularly organized. If so, they must

Page 27, note 1, *add*: Wilhelm, however (p. 123), does not believe that the first extant column of 977d was preceded by a lost column ; and if he is right, the list of victorious poets at the Lenaea only takes us back at most to about 450 B.C. The question turns partly on the reconstruction of the original heading of this part of the inscription; it must, I think, be regarded as still an open one, and with it, the question of the date of the first comic contests at the Lenaea.

Page 41, note 3, *for* xx. *read* iv.

Page 48, note 4, *add*: According to Wilhelm, p. 257, Körte has proved that the Νῖκαι of Aristotle is the direct source, not of C.I.A. ii. 971, but only of C.I.A. ii. 977. I have not yet been able to obtain Körte's paper : but I see no reason to doubt that 971 also has an Aristotelian basis, even if that basis be not the Νῖκαι.

Page 51, note 2, *add*: Menander also ἐδίδαξε πρῶτον ἔφηβος ὤν (Anon. de Com. : Kaibel, Com. Fr. p. 9).

Page 54, note 5, *add* : [Capps, however, points out (Amer. Journ. Arch. iv. p. 85) that Plutarch does not date precisely Nicanor's acceptance of the office : and that C.I.A. iv. 2. 584b mentions choregi in the year 317-316.]